Jefferson

The Rise and Fall of the Confederate Government

Volume 2

Jefferson Davis

Published in New York
1881

Table of Contents

CHAPTER XV.

Review of 1861.—Summary of Hostile Acts of United States
Government.—Fuller Details of some of them.—Third Session of
Provisional Congress.—Message.—Subjugation of the Southern States
intended.—Obstinacy of the Enemy.—Insensibility of the North as
to the Crisis.—Vast Preparation of the Enemy.—Embargo and
Blockade.—Indiscriminate War waged.—Action of Confederate
Congress.—Confiscation Act of United States Congress.—Declared
Object of the War.—Powers of United States Government.—
Forfeitures inflicted.—Due Process of Law, how interpreted.—"Who
pleads the Constitution?"—Wanton Destruction of Private Property
unlawful—Adams on Terms of the Treaty of Ghent.—Sectional
Hatred.—Order of President Lincoln to Army Officers in Regard to
Slaves.—"Educating the People."—Fremont's Proclamation.—
Proclamation of General T. W. Sherman.—Proclamation of General
Halleck and others.—Letters of Marque.—Our Privateers.—Officers
tried for Piracy.—Retaliatory Orders.—Discussion in the British
House of Lords.—Recognition as a Belligerent of the Confederacy.—
Exchange of Prisoners.—Theory of the United States.—Views of
McClellan.—Revolutionary Conduct of United States Government.—
Extent of the War at the Close of 1861.—Victories of the Year.—
New Branches of Manufactures.—Election of Confederate States
President.—Posterity may ask the Cause of such Hostile Actions.—
Answer.

The inauguration of the permanent government, amid the struggles of war,
was welcomed by our people as a sign of the independence for which all their
sacrifices had been made, and the increased efforts of the enemy for our
subjugation were met by corresponding determination on our part to maintain
the rights our fathers left us at whatever cost. We now enter upon those terrible
scenes of wrong and blood in which the government of the United States, driven
to desperation by our successful resistance, broke through every restraint of the
Constitution, of national law, of justice, and of humanity. But, before
commencing this fearful narration, let us sum up the hostile acts and
usurpations committed during the first year.

Our people had been declared to be combinations of insurrectionists, and
more than one hundred and fifty thousand men had been called to arms to
invade our territory; our ports were blockaded for the destruction of our regular
commerce, and we had been threatened with denunciation as pirates if we
molested a vessel of the United States, and some of our citizens had been
confined in cells to await the punishment of piracy; one of our States was rent
asunder and a new State constructed out of the fragment; every proposition for a
peaceful solution of pending issues had been spurned. An indiscriminate
warfare had been waged upon our peaceful citizens, their dwellings burned and
their crops destroyed; a law had been passed imposing a penalty of forfeiture on
the owner of any faithful slave who gave military or naval service to the
Confederacy, and forbidding military commanders to interfere for the
restoration of fugitives; the United States Government had refused to agree to

4

an exchange of prisoners, and suffered those we had captured to languish in captivity; it had falsely represented us in every court of Europe, to defeat our efforts to obtain a recognition from foreign powers; it had seized a portion of the members of the Legislature of one State and confined them in a distant military prison, because they were thought merely to sympathize with us, though they had not committed an overt act; it had refused all the propositions of another State for a peaceful neutrality, invaded her and seized important positions, where not even a disturbance of the peace had occurred, and perpetrated the most despotic outrages on her people; it rejected the most conciliatory terms offered for the sake of peace by the Governor of another State, claimed for itself an unrestricted right to move and station its troops whenever and wherever its officers might think it to be desirable, and persisted in its aggressions until the people were involved in conflicts, and a provisional government became necessary for their protection. Within the Northern States, which professed to be struggling to maintain the Union, the Constitution, its only bond, and the laws made in pursuance of it, were in peaceful, undisputed existence; yet even there the Government ruled with the tyrant's hand, and the provisions for the freedom of speech, freedom of the press, and the personal liberty of the citizen, were daily violated, and these sacred rights of man suppressed by military force.

But some of these hostile actions require here a more specific consideration. They were the antecedents of oppressive measures which the enemy strove to enforce upon us during the entire war.

The third session of the Provisional Congress commenced at Richmond on July 20, 1861, and ended on August 31st. At the previous session, a resolution had been passed authorizing the President to cause the several executive departments, with the archives thereof, to be removed to Richmond at such time as he might determine prior to July 20th. In my message to the Congress of that date, the cause of removal was stated to be, that the aggressive movements of the enemy required prompt, energetic action; that the accumulation of his forces on the Potomac sufficiently demonstrated that his first efforts were to be directed against Virginia, and from no point could necessary measures for her defense and protection be so effectively provided as from her own capital. My remarks to Congress at this session were confined to such important facts as had occurred during the recess, and to the matters connected with the public defense. "The odious features of the policy and purposes of the Government of the United States stood revealed; the recent grant of a half million of men and four hundred millions of dollars by their Congress, was a confession that their intention was a subjugation of the Southern States."

The fact thus briefly presented in the message was established by the course pursued since the first advent to power of those who had come into possession of the sword and the purse of the Union. Not only by the legislation cited was the intent to make war for the purpose of subjugating the Southern States revealed, but also, and yet more significantly, was the purpose manifested in the evasion and final rejection of every proposition of the Southern States for a peaceful solution of the issues arising from secession.

Such extreme obstinacy was unnatural, unreasonable, and contrary to the general precedents of history, except those which resulted in civil war. This unfavorable indication was also observable in the original party of abolition. Its intolerance had a violence which neither truth nor justice nor religion could restrain, and it was transferred undiluted to their successors. The resistance to the demands of the States and persistence in aggressions upon them were the occasion of constant apprehensions and futile warnings of their suicidal tendency on the part of the statesmen of the period. For thirty years had patriotism and wisdom pointed to dissolution by this perverse uncharitableness. Had the North been contending for a principle only, there would have been a satisfactory settlement, not indeed by compromising the principle, but by adjusting the manner of its operation so that only good results should ensue. But when the contest is for supremacy on one side and self-defense on the other— when the aim of the aggressor is "power, plunder, and extended rule"— there will be no concessions by him, no compromises, no adjustment of results. The alternative is subjugation by the sword, or peace by absolute submission. The latter condition could not be accepted by us. The former was, therefore, to be resisted as best we might.

An amazing insensibility seemed to possess a portion of the Northern people as to the crisis before them. They would not realize that their purpose of supremacy would be so resolutely resisted; that, if persisted in, it must be carried to the extent of bloodshed in sectional war. With them the lust of dominion was stronger than the sense of justice or of the fraternity and the equal rights of the States, which the Union was formed to secure, and so they were blind to palpable results. Otherwise they must have seen, when the remnants of the old Whig party joined hands with abolitionism, that it was like a league with the spirit of evil, in which the conditions of the bond were bestowal of power on one side, and the commission of deeds meet for disunion on the other. The honest masses should have remembered that when scheming leaders abandon principle, and adopt the ideas of dreamers and fanatics, the ladder on which they would mount to power is one on which they can not return, and upon which it would be a fatal delusion to follow.

The reality of armed resistance on our part the North was slow to comprehend. The division of sentiment at the South on the question of the *expediency* of immediate secession, was mistaken for the existence of a submission party, whereas the division was confined to expediency, and wholly disappeared when our territory was invaded. Then was revealed to them the necessity of defending their homes and liberties against the ruthless assault on both, and then extraordinary unanimity prevailed. Then, as Hamilton and Madison had stated, war against the States had effected the deprecated dissolution of the Union.

Adjustment by negotiation the United States Government had rejected, and had chosen to attempt our subjugation. This course, adopted without provocation, was pursued with a ferocity that disregarded all the laws of civilized warfare, and must permanently remain a stain upon the escutcheon of a Government once bright among the nations. The vast provision made by the United States in the material of war, the money appropriated, and the men enrolled, furnished a sufficient refutation to the pretense that they were only engaged in dispersing rioters, and suppressing unlawful combinations too strong for the usual course of judicial proceedings.

Further, they virtually recognized the separate existence of the Confederate States by an interdictive embargo, and blockade of all commerce between them and the United States, not only by sea but by land; not only with those who bore arms, but with the entire population of the Confederate States. They waged an indiscriminate war upon all: private houses in isolated retreats were bombarded and burned; grain-crops in the field were consumed by the torch; and, when the torch was not applied, careful labor was bestowed to render complete the destruction of every article of use or ornament remaining in private dwellings after their female inhabitants had fled from the insults of brutal soldiers; a petty war was made on the sick, including women and children, by carefully devised measures to prevent them from obtaining the necessary medicines. Were these the appropriate means by which to execute the laws, and in suppressing rioters to secure tranquillity and preserve a voluntary union? Was this a government resting on the consent of the governed?

At this session of the Confederate Congress additional forces were provided to repel invasion, by authorizing the President to accept the services of any number of volunteers not exceeding four hundred thousand men. Authority was also given for suitable financial measures hereafter stated, and the levy of a tax. An act of sequestration was also adopted as a countervailing measure against the operations of the confiscation law enacted by the Congress of the United States on August 6, 1861.

This act of the United States Congress, with its complement passed in the ensuing year, will be considered further on in these pages. One of the most indicative of the sections, however, provided that, whenever any person, claimed to be held to labor or service under the laws of any State, shall be permitted, by the person to whom such labor or service is claimed to be due, to take up arms against the United States, or to work, or to be employed in or upon any fort, intrenchment, etc., or in any military or naval service whatever against the Government of the United States, the person to whom such labor is claimed to be due shall forfeit his claim, and, to any attempt to enforce it, a statement of the facts shall be a sufficient answer. The President of the United States, in his message of December 3, 1861, stated that numbers of persons held to service had been liberated and were dependent on the United States, and must be provided for in some way. He recommended that steps be taken for colonizing them at some places in a climate congenial to them.

As the President and the Congress of the United States had declared this to be a war for the preservation of the Constitution, it may not be out of place to see what course they now undertook to pursue under the pretext of preserving the Constitution of the United States. It had been conceded in all time that the Congress of the United States had no power to legislate on slavery in the States, and that this was a subject for State legislation. It was one of the powers not granted in the Constitution, but "reserved to the States respectively." [1] All the powers of the Federal Government were delegated to it by the States, and all which were reserved were withheld from the Federal Government, as well in time of war as in peace. The conditions of peace or war made no change in the powers granted in the Constitution. The attempt, therefore, by Congress, to exercise a power of confiscation, one not granted to it, was a mere usurpation. The argument of forfeiture for treason does not reach the case, because there could be no forfeiture until after conviction, and the Constitution says, "No attainder of treason shall work corruption of blood or forfeiture except during the life of the person attainted." [2] The confiscation act of 1861 undertook to convict and sentence without a trial, and entirely to deprive the owner of slaves of his property by giving final freedom to the slaves. Still further to show how regardless the United States Government was of the limitations imposed upon it by the compact of Union, the reader is referred to the fifth article of the first amendment, being one of those cases in which the people of the several States, in an abundance of caution, threw additional protection around rights which the framers of the Constitution thought already sufficiently guarded. The last two clauses of the article read thus: No person "shall be deprived of life, liberty, or property, without due process of law; nor shall private property be taken for public use, without just compensation."

Here was a political indictment and conviction by the Congress and President, with total forfeitures inflicted in palpable violation of each and of all the cited clauses of the Constitution.

One can scarcely anticipate such effrontery as would argue that "due process of law" meant an act of Congress, that judicial power could thus be conferred upon the President, and private property be confiscated for party success, without violating the Constitution which the actors had sworn to support.

The unconstitutionality of the measure was so palpable that, when the bill was under consideration, Mr. Thaddeus Stevens, a member of Congress from Pennsylvania, said: "I thought the time had come when the laws of war were to govern our action; when constitutions, if they stood in the way of the laws of war in dealing with the enemy, had no right to intervene. Who pleads the Constitution against our proposed action?" [3] This subject is further considered in subsequent chapters on the measures of emancipation adopted by the United States Government.

It is to be remembered in this connection that pillage and the wanton destruction of private property are not permitted by the laws of war among civilized nations. When prosecuting the war with Mexico, we respected private property of the enemy; and when in 1781 Great Britain, attempting to reduce her revolted American colonies, took possession of the country round and about Point Comfort (Fortress Monroe), the homes quietly occupied by the rebellious people were spared by the armies of the self-asserting ruler of the land. At a later date, war existed between Great Britain and the independent States of the Union, during which Great Britain got possession of various points within the States. At the Treaty of Ghent, 1815, by which peace was restored to the two countries, it was stipulated in the first article that all captured places should be restored "without causing any destruction, or carrying away any of the artillery or other public property originally captured in the said forts or places, and which shall remain therein upon the exchange of the ratifications of this treaty; or any slaves or other private property." Persistent efforts were made to avoid the return of deported slaves, and it was attempted to put them in the category of artillery which had been removed before the exchange of ratification. Mr. John Quincy Adams, first as United States Minister to England, and subsequently as United States Secretary of State, conducted with great vigor and earnestness a long correspondence to maintain the true construction of the treaty as recognizing and guarding the right of private property in slaves. In his letter to Viscount Castlereagh, the British Secretary of State for Foreign Affairs, after explaining the distinction between "artillery or other public property" and "slaves or other private property," as used in the treaty, and why it might be impracticable, if they had been removed, to return the former, but that the reasons did not apply to the latter, for, he proceeds to say, "Private property, not having been subject to legitimate capture with the places, was not liable to the reason of limitation." In the same letter, Mr. Adams writes: "Merchant-vessels and effects captured on the high-seas are, by the laws of war between civilized nations, lawful prize, and by the capture become the property of the captors. . . . But, as by the same usages of civilized nations, private property is not the subject of lawful capture in war upon the land, it is perfectly clear that, in every stipulation, private property shall be respected; or that, upon the restoration of places taken during the war, it shall not be carried away." (See "American State Papers," vol. iv, pp. 122, 123.) Sectional hostility and party zeal had not then so far undermined the feeling of fraternity which generated the Union as to make a public officer construe the Constitution as it might favor or injure one section or another, and Great Britain was, from a sense of right, compelled to recognize the wrong done in deporting slaves, the private property of American citizens.

On the 4th of December, 1861, the President of the United States issued an order to the commander-in-chief relative to slaves as above mentioned, in which he said, "Their arrest as fugitives from service or labor should be immediately followed by the military arrest of the parties making the seizure." Had Congress and the President made new laws of war?

Although the Government of the United States did not boldly proclaim the immediate emancipation of all slaves, the tendency of all its actions was directly to that end. To use a favorite expression of its leaders, the Northern people were not at that time "educated up to the point." A revolt from too sudden a revelation of its entire policy was apprehended. Even as late as July 7, 1862, General McClellan wrote to the authorities at Washington from the vicinity of Richmond, "A declaration of radical views, especially upon slavery, will rapidly disintegrate our armies." Nevertheless, when policy indicated it, the declaration came, as will be seen hereafter. Meantime, General Fremont, in command in Missouri, issued a proclamation on August 31, 1861, declaring the property, real and personal, of all persons in arms against the United States, or taking an active part with their enemies, to be confiscated, and their slaves to be free men. This was subsequently modified to conform to the terms of the above-mentioned confiscation act. General Thomas W. Sherman, commanding at Port Royal, in South Carolina, was instructed, on October 14, 1861, to receive all persons, whether slaves or not, and give them employment, "assuring all loyal masters that Congress will provide just compensation to them for the loss of the services of the persons so employed." To others no relief was to be given. This was, by confiscation, to punish a class of citizens, in the emancipation of every slave whose owner rendered support to the Confederate States. Finally, General Halleck, who succeeded Fremont, and General Dix, commanding near Fortress Monroe, issued orders not to permit slaves to come within their lines. They were speedily condemned for this action, because it put a stop to the current of emancipation, which will be hereafter narrated.

Reference has been made to our want of a navy, and the efforts made to supply the deficiency. The usual resort under such circumstances to privateers was, in our case, without the ordinary incentive of gain, as all foreign ports were closed against our prizes, and, our own ports being soon blockaded, our vessels, public or private, had but the alternative of burning or bonding their captures. To those who, nevertheless, desired them, letters of marque were granted by us, and there was soon a small fleet of vessels composed of those which had taken out these letters, and others which had been purchased and fitted out by the Navy Department. They hovered on the coasts of the Northern States, capturing and destroying their vessels, and filling the enemy with consternation. The President of the United States had already declared in his proclamation of April 19th, as above stated, that "any person, who, under the pretended authority of the said (Confederate) States, should molest a vessel of the United States, or the persons or cargo on board," should be held amenable to the laws of the United States for the prevention of piracy. This was another violation of international law, another instance of arrogant disregard for universal opinion. The threat, if meant for intimidation, and to deprive the Confederacy of one of the usual weapons of war, was unbecoming the head of a Government. To have executed it upon a helpless prisoner, would have been a crime intensified by its cowardice. Happily for the United States, the threat was not executed, but the failure to carry out the declared purpose was coupled with humiliation, because it was the result of a notice to retaliate as fully as might need be to stop such a barbarous practice. To yield to the notice thus served, was a practical admission by the United States Government that the Confederacy had become a power among the nations.

On June 3, 1861, the little schooner Savannah, previously a pilot-boat in Charleston Harbor and sailing under a commission issued by authority of the Confederate States, was captured by the United States brig Perry. The crew were placed in irons and sent to New York. It appeared, from statements made without contradiction, that they were not treated as prisoners of war, whereupon a letter was addressed by me to President Lincoln, dated July 6th, stating explicitly that, "painful as will be the necessity, this Government will deal out to the prisoners held by it the same treatment and the same fate as shall be experienced by those captured on the Savannah; and, if driven to the terrible necessity of retaliation by your execution of any of the officers or crew of the Savannah, that retaliation will be extended so far as shall be requisite to secure the abandonment of a practice unknown to the warfare of civilized man, and so barbarous as to disgrace the nation which shall be guilty of inaugurating it." A reply was promised to this letter, but none came. Still later in the year the privateer Jefferson Davis was captured, the captain and crew brought into Philadelphia, and the captain tried and found guilty of piracy and threatened with death. Immediately I instructed General Winder, at Richmond, to select one prisoner of the highest rank, to be confined in a cell appropriated to convicted felons, and treated in all respects as if convicted, and to be held for execution in the same manner as might be adopted for the execution of the prisoner of war in Philadelphia. He was further instructed to select thirteen other prisoners of the highest rank, to be held in the same manner as hostages for the thirteen prisoners held in New York for trial as pirates. By this course the infamous attempt made by the United States Government to commit judicial murder on prisoners of war was arrested.

The attention of the British House of Lords was also attracted to the proclamation of President Lincoln, threatening the officers and crew of privateers with the punishment of piracy. It led to a discussion in which the Earl of Derby said: "He apprehended that, if one thing was clearer than another, it was that privateering was not piracy; and that no law could make that piracy, as regarded the subjects of one nation which was not piracy by the law of nations. Consequently, the United States must not be allowed to entertain this doctrine, and to call upon her Majesty's Government not to interfere." The Lord Chancellor said: "There was no doubt that, if an Englishman engaged in the service of the Southern States, he violated the laws of his country and rendered himself liable to punishment, and that he had no right to trust to the protection of his native country to shield him from the consequences of his act. But, though that individual would be guilty of a breach of the law of his own country, he could not be treated as a pirate, and those who treated him as a pirate would be guilty of murder."

The appearance of this little fleet on the ocean made it necessary for the powers of Europe immediately to define their position relative to the contending powers. Great Britain, adopting a position of neutrality, and recognizing both as belligerents, interdicted the armed ships and privateers of both from carrying prizes into the waters of the United Kingdom or its colonies. All the other powers recognized the Confederate States to be belligerents, but closed their ports against the admission of prizes captured by either belligerent.

It is worthy of notice that the United States Government (though it had previously declined) at this time notified the English and French Governments that it was now willing to adhere to all the conditions of the Paris Congress of 1856, provided the clause abolishing privateers might apply to the Confederate States. The offer, with the proviso, was honorably declined by both France and England.

In the matter of the exchange of prisoners, which became important in consequence of these retaliatory measures, and the number taken by our troops at Manassas, the people of the Northern States were the victims of incessant mortification and distress through the vacillating and cruel conduct of their Government. It based all its immense military movements on the theory that "the laws of the United States have been for some time past and now are opposed and the execution thereof obstructed, . . . by combinations too powerful to be suppressed" by the ordinary methods. Under this theory the United States are assumed to be one nation, and the distinctions among them of States are as little recognized as if they did not exist. This theory was false, and thereby led its originators into constant blunders. When the leaders of a government aspire to the acquisition of absolute, unlimited power, and the sword is drawn to hew the way, it would be more logical and respectable to declare the laws silent than to attempt to justify unlawful acts by unwarranted legislation. If their theory had been true, then their prisoners of war were insurrectionists and rebels, and guilty of treason, and hanging would have been the legitimate punishment. Why were they not hung? Not through pity, but because the facts contradicted the theory. The "combinations" spoken of were great and powerful States, and the danger was that the North would be the greater sufferer by our retaliation. There was no humane course but to exchange prisoners according to the laws of war. With this the Government of the United States refused to comply, lest it might be construed into an acknowledgment of belligerent rights on our part, which would explode their theory of insurrectionary combinations, tend to restore more correct views of the rights and powers of the States, and expose in its true light their efforts to establish the supreme and unlimited sovereignty of the General Government. The reader may observe the tenacity with which the authorities at Washington, and, behind them, the Northern States, clung to this theory. Upon its strict maintenance depended the success of their bloody revolution to secure absolute supremacy over the States. Upon its failure, the dissolution of the Union would have been established; constitutional liberty would have been vindicated; the hopes of mankind in the modern institutions of federation fulfilled; and a new Union might have been formed and held together with a bond of fraternity and not by the sword, as under the above revolutionary theory.

By the exchange of prisoners, nothing was conceded except what was evident to the world—that actual war existed, and that a Christian people should at least conduct it according to the usages of civilized nations. But sectional hate and the vain conceit of newly acquired power led to the idle prophecy of our speedy subjection, and hence the Government of the United States refused to act as required by humanity and the usages of civilized warfare. At length, moved by the clamors of the relatives and friends of the prisoners we held, and by fears of retaliation, it covertly submitted to abandon its declared purpose, and to shut its eyes while the exchanges were made by various commanders under flags of truce. Thus some were exchanged in New York, Washington, Cairo, and Columbus, Kentucky, and by General McClellan in western Virginia and elsewhere. On the whole, the partial exchanges were inconsiderable and inconclusive as to the main question. The condition at the close of the year 1861, summarily stated, was that soldiers captured in battle were not protected by the usage of "exchange," and citizens were arrested without due process of law, deported to distant States, and incarcerated without assigned cause. All this by persons acting under authority of the United States Government, but in disregard of the United States Constitution, which provides that "no person shall be held to answer for a capital or otherwise infamous crime, unless on a presentment or an indictment of a grand jury, nor be deprived of life, liberty, or property without due process of law." [4] "The right of the people to be secure in their persons, houses, papers, and effects, against unreasonable searches and seizures shall not be violated." [5] These provisions were of no avail to protect the citizens from the outrages, because those who derived their authority from the Constitution used that authority to violate its guarantees. It has been stated that the rule upon which the United States Government was conducting affairs was entirely revolutionary. Its efforts to clothe the Government of the Union with absolute power involved the destruction of the rights of the States and the subversion of the Constitution. Hence on every occasion the provisions of the Constitution afforded no protection to the citizens: their rights were spurned; their persons were seized and imprisoned beyond the reach of friends; their houses sacked and burned. If they pleaded the Constitution, the Government of the Constitution was deaf to them, unsheathed its sword, and said the Union was at stake; and the Constitution, which was the compact of union, must stand aside. This was indeed a revolution. A constitutional government of limited powers derived from the people was transformed into a military despotism. The Northern people were docile as sheep under the change, reminding one of the words of the Psalmist: "All we, like sheep, have gone astray."

Posterity may ask with amazement. What cause could there have been for such acts by a government that was ordained "to form a more perfect union, establish justice, insure domestic tranquillity, provide for the common defense, promote the general welfare, and secure the blessings of liberty to ourselves and our posterity"? Posterity may further ask, Where could a government of limited powers, constructed only for certain general purposes—and on the principle that all power proceeds from the people, and that "the powers not delegated by the Constitution, nor prohibited by it to the States, are reserved to the States respectively, or to the people"— find a grant of power, or an authority to perpetrate such injuries upon the States and the people? As to the first question, it may be said: There was no external cause for such acts. All foreign nations were at peace with the United States. No hostile fleets were hovering on her coasts, nor immense foreign armies threatening to invade her territory. The cause, if any plausible one existed, was entirely internal. It lay between it and its citizens. If it had treated them with injustice and oppression, and threatened so to continue, it had departed from the objects of its creation, and they had the resulting right to dissolve it.

Who was to be the umpire in such a case? Not the United States Government, for it was the creature of the States; it possessed no inherent, original sovereignty. The Constitution says, "The powers not delegated to the United States by the Constitution, nor prohibited by it to the States, are reserved to the States respectively, or to the people." [6] The umpireship is, therefore, expressly on the side of the States, or the people. When the State of South Carolina, through a sovereign convention, withdrew from the Union, she exercised the umpireship which rightly belonged to her, and which no other could exercise for her. This involved the dissolution of the Union, and the extinction of the Government of the United States so far as she was concerned; but the officers of that Government, instead of justly acquiescing in that which was constitutionally and legally inevitable, drew the sword, and resolved to maintain by might that which had no longer existence by right. A usurpation thus commenced in wrong was the mother of all the usurpations and wrongs which followed. The unhallowed attempt to establish the absolute sovereignty of the Government of the United States, by the subjugation of States and their people, brought forth its natural fruit. Well might the victim of the guillotine exclaim, "O Liberty, what crimes are committed in thy name!"

As to the other question—Where could a government of limited powers find authority to perpetrate such injuries upon its own constituents?—an answer will be given in succeeding pages.

Up to the close of the year the war enlarged its proportions so as to include new fields, until it then extended from the shores of the Chesapeake to the confines of Missouri and Arizona. Sudden calls from the remotest points for military aid were met with promptness enough not only to avert disaster in the face of superior numbers, but also to roll back the tide of invasion on the border.

At the commencement of the war the enemy were possessed of certain strategic points and strong places within the Confederate States. They greatly exceeded us in numbers, in available resources, and in the supplies necessary for war. Military establishments had been long organized, and were complete; the navy and the army, once common to both, were in their possession. To meet all this we had to create not only an army in the face of war itself, but also military establishments necessary to equip and place it in the field. The spirit of the volunteers and the patriotism of the people enabled us, under Providence, to grapple successfully with these difficulties. A succession of glorious victories at

Bethel, Manassas, Springfield, Lexington, Leesburg, and Belmont, checked the invasion of our soil. After seven months of war the enemy had not only failed to extend their occupancy of the soil, but new States and Territories had been added to our confederacy. Instead of their threatened march of unchecked conquest, the enemy were driven at more than one point to assume the defensive; and, upon a fair comparison between the two belligerents, as to men, military means, and financial condition, the Confederate States were relatively much stronger at the end of the year than when the struggle commenced.

The necessities of the times called into existence new branches of manufactures, and gave a fresh impulse to the activity of those previously in operation, and we were gradually becoming independent of the rest of the world for the supply of such military stores and munitions as were indispensable for war.

At an election on November 6, 1861, the chief executive officers of the provisional Government were unanimously chosen to similar positions in the permanent Government, to be inaugurated on the ensuing 22d of February, 1862.

[Footnote 1: Constitution of the United States, Article X.]
[Footnote 2: Ibid., Article III, section 3.]
[Footnote 3: Congress of the United States, July, 1861.]
[Footnote 4: Constitution of the United States, Article V.]
[Footnote 5: Ibid., Article IV.]
[Footnote 6: Constitution of the United States, Article X.]

CHAPTER XVI.

Military Arrangements of the Enemy.—Marshall and Garfield.—
Fishing Creek.—Crittenden's Report.—Fort Henry; its Surrender.—
Fort Donelson; its Position.—Assaults.—Surrender.—Losses.

Important changes in the military arrangements of the enemy were made about this time. Major-General George B. McClellan was assigned to the chief command of his army, in place of Lieutenant-General Scott, retired. A Department of Ohio was constituted, embracing the States of Ohio, Michigan, Indiana, and Kentucky east of the Cumberland and Tennessee Rivers; and Brigadier-General D. C. Buell was assigned to its command. At the same time. General Henry W. Halleck superseded General John C. Fremont in command of the United States Department of the West. General W. T. Sherman was removed from Kentucky and sent to report to General Halleck. General A. S. Johnston was now confronted by General Halleck in the West and by General Buell in Kentucky. The former, with armies at Cairo and Paducah, under Generals Grant and C. F. Smith, threatened equally Columbus, the key of the lower Mississippi River, and the water-lines of the Cumberland and the Tennessee, with their defenses at Forts Donelson and Henry. The right wing of General Buell also menaced Donelson and Henry, while his center was directed against Bowling Green, and his left was advancing against General Zollicoffer at Mill Spring, on the upper Cumberland. If the last-named position could be forced, the way seemed open to East Tennessee, by either the Jacksboro or the Jamestown routes, on the one hand, and to Nashville on the other. At the northeastern comer of Kentucky there was a force under Colonel Garfield, of Ohio, opposed to the Confederate force under General Humphrey Marshall.

The strength of Marshall's force in effective men was about sixteen hundred. Knowing that a body of the enemy under Colonel Garfield was advancing to meet him, and that a small force was moving to his rear, he fell back some fifteen miles, and took position on Middle Creek, near Prestonsburg. On January 10, 1862, Garfield attacked him. The firing was kept up, with some intervals, about four hours, and was occasionally very sharp and spirited. Marshall says in his report: "The enemy did not move me from any one position I assumed, and at nightfall withdrew from the field, leaving me just where I was in the morning. . . . He came to attack, yet came so cautiously that my left wing never fired a shot, and he never came up sufficiently to engage my center or left wing." Garfield was said to have fallen back fifteen miles to Paintsville, and Marshall seven miles, where he remained two days, then slowly pursued his retreat. He stated his loss at ten killed and fourteen wounded, and that of the enemy to have been severe.

The battle of Fishing Creek has been the subject of harsh criticism, and I think it will be seen by the report herein inserted that great injustice has been done to General George B. Crittenden, who commanded on that occasion.

In July, 1880, I wrote to him requesting a statement of the affair at Fishing Creek, and a short time before his decease he complied with my request by writing as follows:

"In November, 1862, I assumed, by assignment, the command of a portion of East Tennessee and southeastern Kentucky, which embraced the troops stationed at Mill Springs, on the Cumberland River, and under the command of General Zollicoffer, who, as I understood the matter, had been stationed there by General Johnston to prevent the enemy under Schopf, and confronting him on the opposite side of the river, from crossing and penetrating into Tennessee. Schopf's camp was at Somerset, on Fishing Creek, a tributary of the Cumberland, emptying into it a mile above Mill Springs. He was several miles away from the bank of the Cumberland, so that both the river and creek intervened between him and General Zollicoffer. While I was detained in Knoxville, on business connected with my command, I received an official communication from General Zollicoffer, informing me that he had crossed the Cumberland by fording, and was fortifying a camp on the right bank, etc. By the messenger who bore me this communication I ordered him to recross the river and resume his original position on the left bank. Early in January, I reached Mill Springs, and found, to my surprise. General Zollicoffer still on the right bank. He called on me immediately, and informed me that his messenger who bore back my order had lost several days in returning, and that when it was received he supposed that I would arrive almost immediately; and, hoping to be able to convince me that it would be better to remain on the right bank, he had postponed crossing until, by a rise in the river, it had become impossible to do so; that all his artillery and a large portion of his wagons were on the right bank, and his only means of transferring them to the other bank were a small ferry-boat and a very small stem-wheel steamer, entirely inadequate to the purpose. I was dissatisfied, but, as I knew that the General had been actuated by pure motives, I accepted his excuse. Details were promptly placed in the woods, to prepare timber for flat-boats to transport the artillery and wagons to the left bank of the river. The weather was execrable, and the men unskilled, so that the work progressed slowly.

"Such was the posture of affairs, when, on the 18th of January, I was informed that General Thomas was approaching with a large force of all arms, and would encamp that night within a few miles of us. Here was thrust upon me the very contingency which my order to General Zollicoffer was intended to obviate. It rained violently throughout this day until late in the afternoon. It occurred to me that Fishing Creek must so rise as to render it impossible for Schopf to connect with Thomas. Acting upon this idea, I summoned a council of superior officers, and, laying before them the circumstances of the case, asked their advice. There was not one of them who did not concur with me in the opinion that Thomas must be attacked immediately, and, if possible, by surprise; that such attack, if successful merely in repulsing him, would probably give us time to cross the Cumberland with artillery and wagons, by means of our boats, then being built.

"Accordingly, at twelve o'clock in the night, we marched for the position of the enemy, ascertained to be some six miles away. We had scarcely taken up the line of march, when the rain began to fall, the darkness became intense, and the consequent confusion great, so that day dawned before we reached his position. The attack, as a surprise, failed; nevertheless, it was promptly made. It rained violently throughout the action, rendering all the flint-lock guns useless. The men bearing them were allowed to fall back on the reserve.
"The action was progressing successfully, when the fall of General Zollicoffer was announced to me. Apprehending disastrous consequences, I hastened to the front. My apprehensions were well founded. I found the line of battle in confusion and falling back, and, after a vain effort to restore the line, yielded to necessity, and, by the interposition of the reserve, covered the shattered line and effected my retreat to camp without loss.

"I reached camp late in the afternoon. Not long afterward the enemy opened fire at long range; night coming on, he ceased to fire. The few shot and shells that fell in the camp so plainly demonstrated the demoralization of the men, that I doubted, even if I had had rations, which I had not, whether the camp could have been successfully defended for twenty-four hours. There was not, and had not been for some time in the camp, rations beyond the daily need. This state of affairs was due to the exhaustion of the neighboring country, and the impracticability of the roads.

"It became now my sole object to transfer the men with their arms, the cavalry-horses, and teams to the left bank of the river. This was successfully accomplished by dawn of the next day.

"I attributed the loss of the battle, in a great degree, to the inferiority of our arms and the untimely fall of General Zollicoffer, who was known and highly esteemed by the men, who were almost all Tennesseeans. I think I have shown that the battle of Fishing Creek was a necessity, and that I ought not to be held responsible for that necessity. As to how I managed it, I have nothing further to say."

General Crittenden's gallantry had been too often and too conspicuously shown in battle during the war with Mexico and on the Indian frontier to admit of question, and the criticism has been directed solely to the propriety of the attack at Fishing Creek. His explanation is conclusive against any arraignment of him for the presence of the troops on the right bank of the Cumberland, or for his not immediately withdrawing them to the left bank when his position was threatened. Under these circumstances, to attack one portion of the enemy, when a junction with the other part could not be effected, was to act in accordance with one of the best-settled rules of war.

The unforeseen accident of renewed rain, with intense darkness, delayed his march beyond reasonable expectation; and, whereas the whole force should have reached the enemy's encampment before dawn, the advance of two regiments only reached there after broad daylight. To hesitate, would have been to give the enemy time for preparation, and I think it was wisely decided to attack at once and rely upon the rear coming up to support the advance; but the rear, encumbered with their artillery, were so far behind that, though the advance were successful in their first encounter, they did not receive the hoped-for support until they had suffered severely, and then the long-known and trusted commander of the forces there, the gallant and most estimable Zollicoffer, fell; whence confusion resulted. General Crittenden had been but a few days with the troops, a disadvantage which will be readily appreciated. Had the whole force been in position at early dawn, so as to have surprised the enemy, the plan would have been executed, and victory would have been the probable result; after which, Schöpf's force might have been readily disposed of. But, had the attack done no more than to check the advance of Thomas until the boats under construction could have been finished, so as to enable Crittenden to save his artillery and equipments, it would have justified the attempt. I therefore think the strategy not only defensible but commendable, and the affair to be ranked with one of the many brilliant conceptions of the war. The reader will not fail to remark the evidence which General Crittenden's report affords of the

17

fallacy of representing the South as having been prepared by supplying herself with the *materiél* necessary for war. The heart of even a noble enemy must be moved at the spectacle of citizens defending their homes, with muskets of obsolete patterns and shot-guns, against an invader having all the modern improvements in arms. The two regiments constituting the advance were Battle's Twentieth Tennessee and the Fifteenth Mississippi, commanded by Lieutenant-Colonel E. C. Walthall. With dauntless courage they engaged the whole array of the enemy, and drove him from his first position. When at length our forces fell back to their intrenched camp, it was with sullen determination, and the pursuit was so cautious that whenever it ventured too near it was driven back by our rear guard. The valiant advance—the Fifteenth Mississippi and Twentieth Tennessee—bore the burden of the day. The Mississippians lost two hundred and twenty out of four hundred engaged, and the Tennesseeans lost half as many, this being about three fourths the casualties in our force.

That night General Crittenden crossed his troops over the river, with the exception of those too badly wounded to travel. He was compelled to leave his artillery and wagons, not having the means of transporting them across, and moved with the remnant of his army toward Nashville.

Both by General Crittenden and those who have criticised him for making the attack at Fishing Creek, it is assumed that General Zollicoffer made a mistake in crossing to the right bank of the Cumberland, and that thence it resulted as a consequence that General Johnston's right flank of his line through Bowling Green was uncovered. I do not perceive the correctness of the conclusion, for it must be admitted that General Zollicoffer's command was not adequate to resist the combined forces of Thomas and Schopf, or that the Cumberland River was a sufficient obstacle to prevent them from crossing either above or below the position at Mill Springs. General Zollicoffer may well have believed that he could better resist the crossing of the Cumberland by removing to the right bank rather than by remaining on the left. The only difference, it seems to me, would have been that he could have retreated without the discomfiture of his force or the loss of his artillery and equipments, but, in either case, Johnston's right flank would have been alike uncovered.

To Zollicoffer and the other brave patriots who fell with him, let praise, not censure, be given; and to Crittenden, let tardy justice render the meed due to a gallant soldier of the highest professional attainments, and whose fault, if fault it be, was a willingness to dare much in his country's service.

When the State of Tennessee seceded, measures were immediately adopted to occupy and fortify all the strong points on the Mississippi, as Memphis, Randolph, Fort Pillow, and Island No. 10. As it was our purpose not to enter the State of Kentucky and construct defenses for the Cumberland and Tennessee Rivers on her territory, they were located within the borders of Tennessee, and as near to the Kentucky line as suitable sites could be found. On these were commenced the construction of Fort Donelson on the west side of the Cumberland, and Fort Henry on the east side of the Tennessee, and about twelve miles apart. The latter stood on the low lands adjacent to the river about high-water mark, and, being just below a bend in the river and at the head of a straight stretch of two miles, it commanded the river for that distance. It was also commanded by high ground on the opposite bank of the river, which it was intended should be occupied by our troops in case of a land attack. The power of ironclad gunboats against land defenses had not yet been shown, and the low position of the fort brought the battery to the water-level, and secured the advantage of ricochet firing, the most effective against wooden ships.

Fort Donelson was placed on high ground; and, with the plunging fire from its batteries, was thereby more effective against the ironclads brought to attack it on the water side. But on the land side it was not equally strong, and required extensive outworks and a considerable force to resist an attack in that quarter.

In September, 1861, Lieutenant Dixon, of the Engineer Corps, was instructed to make an examination of the works at the two forts. He reported that Fort Henry was nearly completed. It was built, not at the most favorable position, but it was a strong work, and, instead of abandoning it and building at another place, he advised that it should be completed, and other works constructed on the high lands just above the fort on the opposite side of the river. Measures for the accomplishment of this plan were adopted as rapidly as the means at disposal would allow.

In relation to Donelson, it was his opinion that, although a better position might have been chosen for this fortification on the Cumberland, under the circumstances surrounding the command, it would be better to retain and strengthen the position chosen.

General Polk, in a report to General Johnston just previous to the battle of Shiloh, said: "The principal difficulty in the way of a successful defense of the rivers, was the want of an adequate force— a force of infantry and a force of experienced artillerists." This was the unavoidable result of the circumstances heretofore related, but tells only half of the story. To match the vessels of the enemy (floating forts) we required vessels like theirs, or the means of constructing them. We had neither.

The efforts which were put forth to resist the operations on the Western rivers, for which the United States made such vast preparations, were therefore necessarily very limited. There was a lack of skilled labor, of ship-yards, and of materials for constructing ironclads, which could not be readily obtained or prepared in a beset and blockaded country. Proposals were considered both for building gunboats and for converting the ordinary side-wheel, high-pressure steamboats into gunboats. But the engineer department, though anxious to avail itself of this means of defense, decided that it was not feasible. There was not plate-iron with which to armor a single vessel, and even railroad-iron could not be spared from its uses for transportation. Unless a fleet could have been built to match the enemy's, we had to rely on land-batteries, torpedoes, and marching forces. It was thought best to concentrate the resources on what seemed practicable. One ironclad gunboat, however, the Eastport, was undertaken on the Tennessee River, but under so many difficulties that, after the surrender of Fort Henry, while still unfinished, it was destroyed, lest it should fall to the enemy.[7]

The fleet of gunboats prepared by the United States for the Mississippi and its tributaries consisted of twelve, seven of which were iron-clad, and able to resist all except the heaviest solid shot. The boats were built very wide in proportion to their length, so that in the smooth river-waters they might have almost the steadiness of land-batteries when discharging their heavy guns. This flotilla carried one hundred and forty-three guns, some sixty-four pounders, some thirty-two pounders, and some seven-inch rifled guns carrying eighty-pound shells.

On February 2d General Grant started from Cairo with seventeen thousand men on transports. Commodore Foote accompanied him with seven gunboats. On the 4th the landing of the troops commenced three miles or more below Fort Henry. General Grant took command on the east bank with the main column, while General Charles F. Smith, with two brigades of some five to six thousand men, landed on the left bank, with orders to take the earthwork opposite Fort Henry, known as Fort Hindman. On the 5th the landing was completed, and the attack was made on the next day. The force of General Tilghman, who was in command at Fort Henry, was about thirty-four hundred men. It is evident that on the 5th he intended to dispute Grant's advance by land; but on the 6th, before the attack by the gunboats, he changed his purpose, abandoned all hope of a successful defense, and made arrangements for the escape of his main body to Fort Donelson, while the guns of Fort Henry should engage the gunboats. He ordered Colonel Hindman to withdraw the command to Fort Donelson, while he himself would obtain the necessary delay for the movement by use of the battery, and standing a bombardment in Fort Henry. For this purpose he retained his heavy artillery company—seventy-five men—to work the guns, a number unequal to the strain and labor of the defense.[8]

Noon was the time fixed for the attack; but Grant, impeded by the overflow of water, and unwilling to expose his men to the heavy guns of the fort, held them back to await the result of the gunboat attack. In the mean time the Confederate troops were in retreat. Four ironclads, mounting forty-eight heavy guns, approached and took position within six hundred yards of the fort, firing as they advanced. About half a mile behind these came three unarmored gunboats, mounting twenty-seven heavy guns, which took a more distant position, and kept up a bombardment of shells that fell within the works. Some four hundred of the formidable missiles of the ironclad boats were also thrown into the fort. The officers and men inside were not slow to respond, and as many as fifty-nine of their shots were counted as striking the gunboats. On the ironclad Essex a cannon-ball ranged her whole length; another shot, passing through the boiler, caused an explosion that scalded her commander, Porter, and many of the seamen and soldiers on board.

[Map of the Battlefield of Fort Donelson]

Five minutes after the fight began, the twenty-four pounder rifled gun, one of the most formidable in the fort, burst, disabling every man at the piece. Then a shell exploded at the muzzle of one of the thirty-two pounders, ruining the gun, and killing or wounding all the men who served it. About the same moment a premature discharge occurred at one of the forty-two pounder guns, killing three men and seriously injuring others. The ten-inch columbiad, the only gun able to match the artillery of the assailants, was next rendered useless by a priming-wire that was jammed and broken in the vent. An heroic blacksmith labored for a long time to remove it, under the full fire of the enemy, but in vain. The men became exhausted and lost confidence; and Tilghman, seeing this, in person served a thirty-two pounder for some fifteen minutes. Though but four of his guns were disabled, six stood idle for want of artillerists, and but two were replying to the enemy. After an engagement of two hours and ten minutes, he ceased firing and lowered his flag. For this soldierly devotion and self-sacrifice the gallant commander and his brave band must be honored while patriotism has an advocate and self-sacrifice for others has a votary. Our casualties were five killed and sixteen wounded; those of the enemy were sixty-three of all kinds. Twelve officers and sixty-three non-commissioned officers and privates were surrendered with the fort. The Tennessee River was thus open, and a base by short lines was established against Fort Donelson.

The next movement was a combined attack by land and water upon Fort Donelson. This fort was situated on the left bank of the Cumberland, as has been stated, near its great bend, and about forty miles from the mouth of the river. It was about one mile north of the village of Dover, where the commissary and quartermaster's supplies were in depot. The fort consisted of two water-batteries on the hillside, protected by a bastioned earthwork of irregular outline on the summit, inclosing about one hundred acres. The water-batteries were admirably placed to sweep the river approaches, with an armament of thirteen guns; eight thirty-two pounders, three thirty-two pound carronade, one ten-inch columbiad, and one rifled gun of thirty-two pound caliber. The field-work, which was intended for infantry supports, occupied a plateau about one hundred feet above the river, commanding and protecting the water-batteries at close musket range. These works afforded a fair defense against gunboats; but they were not designed or adapted for resistance to a land attack or investment by an enemy.

Generals Pillow and Floyd were ordered with their separate commands to Fort Donelson. General Buckner also was sent with a division from Bowling Green; so that the Confederate effective force at the fort during the siege was between fourteen thousand five hundred and fifteen thousand men.[9] The force of General Grant was not less than thirty to thirty-five thousand men. On February 12th he commenced his movement across from Fort Henry, and the investment of Donelson was made without any serious opposition. On the 13th General Buckner reports that "the fire of the enemy's artillery and riflemen was incessant throughout the day; but was responded to by a well-directed fire from the intrenchments, which inflicted upon the assailant a considerable loss, and almost silenced his fire late in the afternoon." The object of the enemy undoubtedly was to discover the strength and position of our forces. The artillery-fire was continued at intervals during the night. Nearly every Confederate regiment reported a few casualties from the shot and shell which frequently fell inside of the works. Meanwhile, a gunboat of thirteen guns arrived in the morning, and, taking a position behind a headland, fired one hundred and thirty-eight shots, when our one hundred and twenty-eight pound shot crashed through one of her ports, injuring her machinery and crippling her. The enemy's fire did no damage to the fort itself, but a shot disabled a gun and killed Captain Dixon, a valuable engineer, whose loss was greatly deplored.

The weather became cold during the night, and a driving snow-storm prevailed, so that some of the soldiers were frozen, and the wounded between the lines suffered extremely. The fleet of gunboats under Commodore Foote arrived, bringing enforcements to the enemy. These were landed during the night and the next day, which was occupied with placing them in position. Nevertheless, though no assault was made, a rambling and ineffective fire was kept up. About 3 P.M. the commander of the naval force, expecting an easy victory, like that at Fort Henry, brought his four ironclads, followed by two gunboats, up to the attack. Each of the ironclads mounted thirteen guns and the gunboats nine. Any one of them was more than a match for the guns of the fort. Their guns were eight, nine, and ten inch, three in the bow of each. Our columbiad and the rifled gun were the only two pieces effective against the ironclads. The enemy moved directly toward the water-batteries, firing with great weight of metal. It was the intention of Commodore Foote to silence these batteries, pass by, and take a position where he could enfilade the fort with broadsides. The gunboats opened at a mile and a half distance, and advanced until within three or four hundred yards. The shot and shell of the fleet tore up the earthworks, but did no further injury. But the Confederate guns, aimed from an elevation of not less than thirty feet by cool and courageous hands, sent their shot with destructive power, and overcame all the enemy's advantages in number and weight of guns. The bolts of our two heavy guns went crashing through iron and massive timbers with resistless force, scattering slaughter and destruction through the fleet.[10] Hoppin, in his "Life of Commodore Foote," says:

"The Louisville was disabled by a shot, which cut away her rudder-chains, making her totally unmanageable, so that she drifted with the current out of action. Very soon the St. Louis was disabled by a shot through her pilot-house, rendering her steering impossible, so that she also floated down the river. The other two armored vessels were also terribly struck, and a rifled cannon on the Carondelet burst, so that these two could no longer sustain the action; and, after fighting for more than an hour, the little fleet was forced to withdraw. The St. Louis was struck fifty-nine times, the Louisville thirty-six times, the Carondelet twenty-six, the Pittsburg twenty, the four vessels receiving no less than one hundred and forty-one wounds. The fleet, gathering itself together, and rendering mutual help to its disabled members, proceeded to Cairo to repair damages."

The loss of the enemy was fifty-four killed and wounded. The report of Major Gilmer, who laid out these works, says:

> "Our batteries were uninjured, and not a
> man in them killed. The repulse of the
> gunboats closed the operations of the day,
> except a few scattering shots along the land
> defenses."

In consequence of reënforcements to the enemy, the plan of operations for the next day was determined by the Confederate generals about midnight. The whole of the left wing of the army except eight regiments was to move out of the trenches, attack, turn, and drive the enemy's right until the Wynn's Ferry road, which led to Charlotte through a good country, was cleared, and an exit thus secured.

The troops, moving in the small hours of the night over the icy and broken roads, which wound through the obstructed area of defense, made slow progress, and delayed the projected operations. At 4 A.M. on the 15th, Pillow's troops were ready, except one brigade, which came late into action. By six o'clock, Baldwin's brigade was engaged with the enemy, only two or three hundred yards from his lines, and the bloody contest of the day had begun. At one o'clock the enemy's right was doubled back. The Wynn's Ferry road was cleared, and it only remained for the Confederates to do one of two things: The first was, to seize the golden moment and, adhering to the original purpose and plan of the sortie, move off rapidly by the route laid open by such strenuous efforts and so much bloodshed; the other depended on the inspiration of a master-mind, equal to the effort of grasping every element of the combat, and which should complete the partial victory by the utter rout and destruction of the enemy.

"While one or the other alternative seems to have been the only possible safe solution," says the author of "The Life of Gen. Albert Sidney Johnston," "the Confederate commander tried neither. A fatal middle policy was suddenly but dubiously adopted, and not carried out. The spirit of vacillation and divided counsels prevented that unity of action which is essential to success. For seven hours the Confederate battalions had been pushing over rough ground and through thick timber, at each step meeting fresh troops massed, where the discomfited regiments rallied. Hence the vigor of assault slackened, though the wearied troops were still ready and competent to continue their onward movement. Ten fresh regiments, over three thousand men, had not fired a musket. But in the turmoil of battle no one knew the relations of any command to the next, or indeed whether his neighbor was friend or foe.

"General Buckner had halted, according to the preconcerted plan, to allow the army to pass out by the opened road and to cover their retreat. At this point of the fight, Pillow, finding himself at Hindman's position, heard of (or saw) preparations by General C. F. Smith for an assault on the Confederate right; but, whether he understood this to be the purpose or construed the movement as the . . . signs of a flight, was left uncertain by his language at the time. He ordered the regiments which had been engaged to return to the trenches, and instructed Buckner to hasten to defend the imperiled point. Buckner, not recognizing him as a superior authorized to change the plan of battle, or the propriety of such change, refused to obey, and, after receiving reiterated orders, started to find Floyd, who at that moment joined him. He urged upon Floyd the necessity of carrying out the original plan of evacuation. Floyd assented to this view, and told Buckner to stand fast until he could see Pillow. He then rode back and saw Pillow, and, hearing his arguments, yielded to them. Floyd simply says that he found the movement so nearly executed that it was necessary to complete it. Accordingly, Buckner was recalled. In the mean time, Pillow's right brigades were retiring to their places in the trenches, under orders from the commanders."

The conflict on the left soon ended. Three hundred prisoners, five thousand stand of small-arms, six guns, and other spoils of victory, had been won by our forces. But the enemy, cautiously advancing, gradually recovered most of his lost ground. It was about 4 P.M. when the assault on the right was made by General C. F. Smith. The enemy succeeded in carrying the advanced work, which General Buckner considered the key to his position. The loss of the enemy during the siege was four hundred killed, seventeen hundred and eighty-five wounded, and three hundred prisoners. Our losses were about three hundred and twenty-five killed and one thousand and ninety-seven wounded; including missing, it was estimated at fifteen hundred.

After nightfall a consultation of the commanding officers was held, and, after a consideration of the question in all its aspects as to what should be done, it was decided that a surrender was inevitable, and, that to accomplish its objects, it must be made before the assault, which was expected at daylight. General Buckner in his report, says:

"I regarded the position of the army as desperate, and that the attempt to extricate it by another battle, in the suffering and exhausted condition of the troops, was almost hopeless. The troops had been worn down with watching, with labor, with fighting. Many of them were frosted by the cold, all of them were suffering and exhausted by their incessant labors. There had been no regular issue of rations for several days, and scarcely any means of cooking. The ammunition was nearly expended. We were completely invested by a force fully four times the strength of our own."

The decision to surrender having been made, it remained to determine by whom it should be made. Generals Floyd and Pillow declared they would not surrender and become prisoners; the duty was therefore allotted to General Buckner. Floyd said, "General Buckner, if I place you in command, will you allow me to draw out my brigade?" General Buckner replied, "Yes, provided you do so before the enemy act upon my communication." Floyd said, "General Pillow, I turn over the command.". General Pillow, regarding this as a mere technical form by which the command was to be conveyed to Buckner, then said, "I pass it." Buckner assumed the command, sent for a bugler to sound the parley, for pen, ink, and paper, and opened the negotiations for surrender.

There were but two roads by which it was possible for the garrison to retire. If they went by the upper road, they would certainly have to cut through the main body of the enemy; if by the lower road, they would have to wade through water three feet deep. This, the medical director stated, would be death to more than one half the command, on account of the severity of the weather and their physical prostration.

To cut through the enemy, if effected, would, it was supposed, involve the loss of three fourths of the command, a sacrifice which, it was conceded, would not be justifiable.

The enemy had, in the conflict of the preceding day, gained possession of our rifle-pits on the right flank, and General Buckner, an experienced soldier, held that the fort would immediately fall when the enemy attacked in the morning. General Pillow dissented from this conclusion, believing that the fort could be defended until boats could be obtained to convey the garrison across the river, and also advocated an attempt to cut through the investing lines of the enemy. Being overruled on both points, he announced his determination to leave the post by any means available, so as to escape a surrender, and he advised Colonel N. B. Forrest, who was present, to go out with his cavalry regiment, and any others he could take with him through the overflow. General Floyd's brigade consisted of two Virginia regiments and one Mississippi regiment; these, as before mentioned, it was agreed that General Floyd might withdraw before the surrender. Two of the field-officers, Colonel Russell and Major Brown, of the Mississippi regiment, the twentieth, had been officers of the First Mississippi Riflemen in the war with Mexico; and the twentieth, their present regiment, was reputed to be well instructed and under good discipline. This regiment was left to be surrendered with the rest of the garrison, under peculiar circumstances, of which Major Brown, then commanding, gives the following narrative:

"About twelve o'clock of the night previous to the surrender, I received an order to report in person at headquarters. On arriving I met Colonel N. B. Forrest, who remarked: 'I have been looking for you; they are going to surrender this place, and I wanted you with your command to go out with me, but they have other orders for you.' On entering the room. Generals Floyd and Pillow also informed me of the proposed proceedings. General Floyd ordered me to take possession of the steamboat-landing with my command; that he had reserved the right to remove his brigade; that, after having guarded the landing, my command should be taken aboard the boat; the Virginia regiments, first crossing to the other side of the river, could make their way to Clarksville.
"I proceeded at once with my command to the landing; there was no steamboat there, but I placed my regiment in a semicircular line so as to cover the landing-place. About daylight the steamer came down, landed, and was soon loaded with the two Virginia regiments, they passing through my ranks. At the same time the General and staff, or persons claiming to belong to the staff, passed aboard. The boat, being a small one, was considerably crowded. While the staging of the boat was being drawn aboard. General Floyd hallooed to me, from the 'hurricane-roof,' that he would cross the river with the troops aboard and return for my regiment. But, about the time of the departure of the boat, General S. B. Buckner came and asserted that he had turned over the garrison and all the property at sunrise; that, if the boat was not away immediately, he would be charged by the enemy with violating the terms of the surrender. I mention this incident as furnishing, I suppose, the reason why my regiment was left on the bank of the river.
"Sorrowfully I gave the necessary orders to stack arms and surrender. . . .

"Both morally and materially the disaster was a severe blow to us. Many, wise after the event, have shown their skill in telling what all knew afterward, but nobody told before."

[Footnote 7: "The Life of Gen. Albert Sidney Johnston," by his son.]
[Footnote 8: "The Life of Gen. Albert Sidney Johnston," by his son.]
[Footnote 9: "The Life of Gen. Albert Sidney Johnston," by his son.]
[Footnote 10: "The Life of Gen. Albert Sidney Johnston," by his son.]

CHAPTER XVII.

Results of the Surrender of Forts Henry and Donelson.—Retreat from Bowling Green.—Criticism on General A. S. Johnston.—Change of Plan necessary.—Evacuation of Nashville.—Generals Floyd and Pillow.—My Letter to General Johnston.—His Reply.—My Answer.—Defense of General Johnston.—Battle of Elkhorn.—Topography of Shiloh.

The loss of Forts Henry and Donelson opened the river routes to Nashville and north Alabama, and thus turned the positions both at Bowling Green and Columbus. These disasters subjected General Johnston to very severe criticism, of which we shall take notice further on in these pages. A conference was held on February 7th by Generals Johnston, Beauregard (who had been previously ordered to report to Johnston), and Hardee, as to the future plan of campaign. It was determined, as Fort Henry had fallen and Donelson was untenable, that preparations should at once be made for a removal of the army to Nashville, in rear of the Cumberland River, a strong point some miles below that city being fortified forthwith to defend the river from the passage of gunboats and transports. From Nashville, should any further retrograde movement become necessary, it would be made to Stevenson, and thence according to circumstances.

As the possession of the Tennessee river by the enemy separated the array at Bowling Green from the one at Columbus, Kentucky, they must act independently of each other until they could be brought together: the first one having for its object the defense of the State of Tennessee along its line of operation; and the other, of that part of the State lying between the Tennessee River and the Mississippi. But, as the possession of the former river by the enemy rendered the lines of communication of the army at Columbus liable to be cut at any time by a movement from the Tennessee River as a base, and an overpowering force of the enemy was rapidly concentrating from various points on the Ohio, it was necessary, to prevent such a calamity, that the main body of the army should fall back to Humboldt, and thence, if necessary, to Grand Junction, so as to protect Memphis from either point and still have a line of retreat to the latter place, or to Grenada, and, if needful, to Jackson, Mississippi.

Captain Hollins's fleet of improvised gunboats and a sufficient garrison was to be left at Columbus for the defense of the river at that point, with transports near at hand for the removal of the garrison when the position became no longer tenable.

Every preparation for the retreat was silently made. The defenses of Bowling Green, originally slight, had been greatly enlarged by the addition of a cordon of detached forts, mounted with heavy field-guns; yet the garrison was only sufficiently strong to withstand an assault, and it was never proposed to submit to a siege. The ordnance and army supplies were quietly moved southward, and measures were taken to remove from Nashville the immense stores accumulated there. Only five hundred men were in the hospital before the army commenced to retreat, but, when it reached Nashville, five thousand four hundred out of fourteen thousand required the care of the medical officers. On February 11th the troops began to move, and at nightfall on the 16th General Johnston, who had established his headquarters at Edgeville, on the northern bank of the Cumberland, saw the last of his wearied columns defile across and safely establish themselves beyond the river. The evacuation was accomplished by a force so small as to make the feat remarkable, not a pound of ammunition nor a gun being lost, and the provisions were nearly all secured. The first intimation which the enemy had of the intended evacuation, so far as has been ascertained, was when Generals Hindman and Breckinridge, who were in advance near his camp, were seen suddenly to retreat toward Bowling Green. The enemy pursued, and succeeded in shelling the town, while Hindman was still covering the rear. Not a man was lost.[11] At the same time Crittenden's command was brought back within ten miles of Nashville, and thence to Murfreesboro.

Scarcely had the retreat to Nashville been accomplished, when the news of the fall of Donelson was received. The state of feeling which it produced is described by Colonel Munford, an aide-de-camp of General Johnston, in an address delivered in Memphis. "Dissatisfaction was general. Its mutterings, already heard, began to break out in denunciations. The demagogues took up the cry, and hounded on one another and the people in hunting down a victim. The public press was loaded with abuse. The Government was denounced for intrusting the public safety to hands so feeble. The Lower House of Congress appointed a select committee to inquire into the conduct of the war in the Western Department. The Senators and Representatives from Tennessee, with the exception of Judge Swann, waited upon the President." Their spokesman, Senator G. A. Henry, stated that they came for and in behalf of Tennessee to ask for the removal of General A. S. Johnston, and the assignment of a competent officer to the defense of their homes and people. It was further stated that they did not come to recommend any one as the successor; that it was conceded that the President was better able than they were to select a proper officer, and they only asked that he would give them a general.

Painfully impressed by this exhibition of distrust toward an officer whose place, if vacated, I was sure could not be filled by his equal, realizing how necessary public confidence was to success, and wounded by the injustice done to one I had known with close intimacy in peace and in war, and believed to be one of the noblest men with whom I had ever been associated, and one of the ablest soldiers I had ever seen in the field, I paused under conflicting emotions, and after a time merely answered, "If Sidney Johnston is not a general, the Confederacy has none to give you."

On February 17th the rear guard from Bowling Green reached Nashville, and on the 18th General Johnston wrote to the Secretary of War at Richmond, saying:

> "I have ordered the army to encamp to-night midway between Nashville and Murfreesboro. My purpose is to place the force in such a position that the enemy can

not concentrate his superior strength against the command, and to enable me to assemble as rapidly as possible such other troops in addition as it may be in my power to collect. The complete command which their gunboats and transports give them upon the Tennessee and Cumberland renders it necessary for me to retire my line between the rivers. I entertain the hope that this disposition will enable me to hold the enemy for the present in check, and, when my forces are sufficiently increased, to drive him back."

The fall of Fort Donelson made a speedy change of his plans necessary. General Johnston was now compelled to withdraw his forces from the north bank of the Cumberland, and to abandon the defense of Nashville; in a word, to evacuate Nashville or sacrifice the army. Not more than eleven thousand effective men were left to him with which to oppose General Buell with not less than forty thousand men, moving by Bowling Green, while another superior force, under General Thomas, was on the eastern flank; and the armies from Fort Donelson, with the gunboats and transport, had it in their power to ascend the Cumberland, so as to interrupt all communication with the south.

On February 17th and 18th the main body of the command was moved from Nashville to Murfreesboro, while a brigade remained under General Floyd to bring on the stores and property upon the approach of the enemy, all of which would have been saved except for the heavy and general rains. By the junction of the command of General Crittenden and the fugitives from Donelson, who were reorganized, the force of General Johnston was increased to seventeen thousand men. The stores not required for immediate use were ordered to Chattanooga, and those which were necessary on the march were ordered to Huntsville and Decatur. On February 28th the march was commenced for Decatur through Shelbyville and Fayetteville. Halting at those points for the purpose, he saved his provisions and stores, removed his depots and machine-shops, obtained new arms, and finally, at the close of March, joined Beauregard at Corinth with twenty thousand men, making their aggregate force fifty thousand.

Considering the great advantage which the means of transportation upon the Tennessee and Cumberland afforded the enemy, and the peculiar topography of the State, General Johnston found that he could not with the force under his command successfully defend the whole line against the advance of the enemy. He was, therefore, compelled to elect whether the enemy should be permitted to occupy Middle Tennessee, or turn Columbus, take Memphis, and open the valley of the Mississippi. Deciding that the defense of the valley was of paramount importance, he therefore crossed the Tennessee and united with Beauregard.

The evacuation of Nashville and the evident intention of General Johnston to retreat still further, created a panic in the public mind which spread over the whole State. Those who had refused to listen to his warning voice, when it called them to arms, were loudest in their passionate outcry at what they considered a base surrender of them to the mercies of the invader. He was accused of imbecility, cowardice, and treason. An appeal from every class was made to the

President demanding his removal. Congress took the matter in hand, and, though the feeling there resulted merely in a committee of inquiry, it was evident that the case was prejudged. The Confederate House of Representatives created a special committee "to inquire into the military disasters at Fort Henry and Fort Donelson, and the surrender of Nashville to the enemy," and as to the conduct, number, and disposition of the troops under General Johnston. Great feeling was shown in the debates.

Generals Floyd and Pillow, the senior officers at Fort Donelson, after it had been decided to surrender, withdrew, to avoid being made prisoners. The Secretary of War (Mr. Benjamin) wrote, March 11th, to General Johnston as follows:

> "The reports of Brigadier-Generals Floyd and Pillow are unsatisfactory, and the President directs that both these generals be relieved from command until further orders. In the mean time you will request them to add to their reports such statements as they may deem proper on the points submitted. You are further requested to make up a report, from all the sources of information accessible to you, of all the particulars connected with the unfortunate affair, which can contribute to enlighten the judgment of the Executive and of Congress, and to fix the blame, if blame there be, on those who were delinquent in duty."

This state of affairs, under the command of General Johnston, was the occasion of the following correspondence:

Letter from President Davis to General A. S. Johnston.

"RICHMOND, *March 12, 1862.*
"MY DEAR GENERAL: The departure of Captain Wickliffe offers an opportunity, of which I avail myself, to write you an unofficial letter. We have suffered great anxiety because of recent events in Kentucky and Tennessee, and I have been not a little disturbed by the repetitions of reflections upon yourself. I expected you to have made a full report of events precedent and consequent to the fall of Fort Donelson. In the mean time, I made for you such defense as friendship prompted, and many years of acquaintance justified; but I needed facts to rebut the wholesale assertions made against you to cover others and to condemn my administration. The public, as you are aware, have no correct measure for military operations, and the journals are very reckless in their statements.

"Your force has been magnified, and the movements of an army have been measured by the capacity for locomotion of an individual.

"The readiness of the people, among whom you are operating, to aid you in every method, has been constantly asserted; the purpose of your army at Bowling Green wholly misunderstood; and the absence of an effective force at Nashville ignored. You have been held responsible for the fall of Donelson and the capture of Nashville. It is charged that no effort was made to save the stores at Nashville, and that the panic of the people was caused by the army.

"Such representations, with the sad forebodings naturally belonging to them, have been painful to me, and injurious to us both; but, worse than this, they have undermined public confidence and damaged our cause. A full development of the truth is necessary for future success.

"I respect the generosity which has kept you silent, but would impress upon you that the question is not personal but public in its nature; that you and I might be content to suffer, but neither of us can willingly permit detriment to the country. As soon as circumstances will permit, it is my purpose to visit the field of your present operations; not that I shall expect to give you any aid in the discharge of your duties as a commander, but with the hope that my position would enable me to effect something in bringing men to your standard. With a sufficient force, the audacity which the enemy exhibits would no doubt give you the opportunity to cut some of his lines of communication, to break up his plan of campaign, and, defeating some of his columns, to drive him from the soil as well of Kentucky as of Tennessee.

"We are deficient in arms, wanting in discipline, and inferior in numbers. Private arms must supply the first want; time and the presence of an enemy, with diligence on the part of commanders, will remove the second; and public confidence will overcome the third. General Bragg brings you disciplined troops, and you will find in him the highest administrative capacity. General E. K. Smith will soon have in East Tennessee a sufficient force to create a strong diversion in your favor; or, if his strength can not be made available in that way, you will best know how to employ it otherwise. I suppose the Tennessee or the Mississippi River will be the object of the enemy's next campaign, and I trust you will be able to concentrate a force which will defeat either attempt. The fleet which you will soon have on the Mississippi River, if the enemy's gunboats ascend the Tennessee, may enable you to strike an effective blow at Cairo; but, to one so well informed and vigilant, I will not assume to offer suggestions as to when and how the ends you seek may be attained. With the confidence and regard of many years, I am very truly your friend,

"JEFFERSON DAVIS."
Letter of General Johnston in answer to that above.
"DECATUR, ALABAMA, *March 18, 1862.*

"MY DEAR GENERAL: I received the dispatches from Richmond, with your private letter by Captain Wickliffe, three days since; but the pressure of affairs and the necessity of getting my command across the Tennessee prevented me from sending you an earlier reply.

"I anticipated all that you have told me as to the censure which the fall of Fort Donelson drew upon me, and the attacks to which you might be subjected; but it was impossible for me to gather the facts for a detailed report, or to spare time which was required to extricate the remainder of my troops and save the large accumulation of stores and provisions after that disheartening disaster.

"I transmitted the reports of Generals Floyd and Pillow without examining or analyzing the facts, and scarcely with time to read them.

"When about to assume command of this department, the Government charged me with the duty of deciding the question of occupying Bowling Green, Kentucky, which involved not only military but political considerations. At the time of my arrival at Nashville, the action of the Legislature of Kentucky had put an end to the latter by sanctioning the formation of camps menacing Tennessee, by assuming the cause of the Government at Washington, and by abandoning the neutrality it professed; and, in consequence of their action, the occupation of Bowling Green became necessary as an act of self-defense, at least in the first step.

"About the middle of September General Buckner advanced with a small force of about four thousand men, which was increased by the 15th of October to twelve thousand; and, though accessions of force were received, it continued at about the same strength until the end of November—measles and other diseases keeping down the effective force. The enemy's force then was reported to the War Department at fifty thousand, and an advance was impossible. No enthusiasm, as we imagined and hoped, but hostility, was manifested in Kentucky. Believing it to be of the greatest moment to protract the campaign, as the dearth of cotton might bring strength from abroad and discourage the North, and to gain time to strengthen myself by new troops from Tennessee and other States, I magnified my forces to the enemy, but made known my true strength to the department and the Governors of

States. The aid given was small. At length, when General Beauregard came out in February, he expressed his surprise at the smallness of my force, and was impressed with the danger of my position. I admitted what was so manifest, and laid before him my views for the future, in which he entirely concurred, and sent me a memorandum of our conference, a copy of which I send to you. I determined to fight for Nashville at Donelson, and gave the best part of my army to do it, retaining only fourteen thousand men to cover my front, and giving sixteen thousand to defend Donelson. The force at Donelson is stated in General Pillow's report at much less, and I do not doubt the correctness of his statement, for the force at Bowling Green, which I supposed to be fourteen thousand effective men (the medical report showing only a little over five hundred sick in the hospital), was diminished more than five thousand by those who were unable to stand the fatigue of a march, and made my force on reaching Nashville less than ten thousand men. I inclose medical director's report. Had I wholly uncovered my front to defend Donelson, Buell would have known it, and marched directly on Nashville. There were only ten small steamers in the Cumberland, in imperfect condition, only three of which were available at Nashville, while the transportation of the enemy was great.

"The evacuation of Bowling Green was imperatively necessary, and was ordered before, and executed while the battle was being fought at Donelson. I had made every disposition for the defense of the fort my means allowed, and the troops were among the best of my forces. The generals, Floyd, Pillow, and Buckner, were high in the opinion of officers and men for skill and courage, and among the best officers of my command. They were popular with the volunteers, and all had seen much service. No reënforcements were asked. I awaited the event opposite Nashville. The result of the conflict each day was favorable. At midnight on the 15th I received news of a glorious victory; at dawn, of a defeat.

"My column during the day and night was thrown over the river—a battery had been established below the city to secure the passage. Nashville was incapable of defense, from its position, and from the forces advancing from Bowling Green and up the Cumberland. A rear guard was left, under General Floyd, to secure the stores and provisions, but did not completely effect the object. The people were terrified, and some of the troops were disheartened. The discouragement was spreading, and I ordered the command to Murfreesboro, where I managed, by assembling Crittenden's division and the fugitives from Donelson, to collect an army able to offer battle. The weather was inclement, the floods excessive, and the bridges were washed away, but most of the stores and provisions were saved and conveyed to new depots. This having been accomplished, though with serious loss, in conformity with my original design, I marched southward and crossed the Tennessee at this point, so as to coöperate or unite with General Beauregard for the defense of the valley of the Mississippi. The passage is almost completed, and the head of my column is already with General Bragg at Corinth. The movement was deemed too hazardous by the most experienced members of my staff; but the object warranted the risk. The difficulty of effecting a junction is not wholly overcome, but it approaches completion. Day after to-morrow (the 22d), unless the enemy intercepts me, my force will be with Bragg, and my army nearly fifty thousand strong. *This must be destroyed before the enemy can attain his object.*

"I have given this sketch, so that you may appreciate the embarrassment which surrounded me in my attempts to avert or remedy the disaster of Fort Donelson, before alluding to the conduct of the generals.

"When the force was detached, I was in hopes that such disposition would have been made as would have enabled the forces to defend the fort or withdraw without sacrificing the army. On the 14th I ordered General Floyd, by telegraph, 'If he lost the fort, to get his troops to Nashville.' It is possible that might have been done, but justice requires us to look at events as they appeared at the time, and not alone by the light of subsequent information. All the facts in relation to the surrender will be transmitted to the Secretary of War as soon as they can be collected, in obedience to his order. It appears from the information received that General Buckner, being the junior officer, took the lead in advising the surrender, and that General Floyd acquiesced, and that they all concurred in the belief that their force could not maintain the position. All concurred that it would involve a great sacrifice of life to extricate the command.

Subsequent events show that the investment was not so complete as their information from their scouts led them to believe.

"The conference resulted in the surrender. The command was irregularly transferred, and devolved on the junior general; but not apparently to avoid any just responsibility or from any want of personal or moral intrepidity. The blow was most disastrous, and almost without a remedy. I therefore, in my first report, remained silent. This silence you were kind enough to attribute to my generosity. I will not lay claim to the motive to excuse my course. I observed silence, as it seemed to be the best way to serve the cause and the country. The facts were not fully known, discontent prevailed, and criticism and condemnation were more likely to augment than to cure the evil. I refrained, well knowing that heavy censures would fall upon me, but convinced that it was better to endure them for the present, and defer for a more propitious time an investigation of the conduct of the generals; for, in the mean time, their services were required and their influence was useful. For these reasons Generals Floyd and Pillow were assigned to duty, for I still felt confidence in their gallantry, their energy, and their devotion to the Confederacy.

"I have thus recurred to the motives by which I have been governed, from a deep personal sense of the friendship and confidence you have always shown me, and from the conviction that they have not been withdrawn from me in adversity.

"All the reports requisite for a full official investigation have been ordered. Generals Floyd and Pillow have been suspended from command.

"You mention that you intend to visit the field of operations here. I hope soon to see you, for your presence would encourage my troops, inspire the people, and augment the army. To me personally it would give the greatest gratification. Merely a soldier myself, and having no acquaintance with the statesmen or leaders of the South, I can not touch springs familiar to you. Were you to assume command, it would afford me the most unfeigned pleasure, and every energy would be exerted to help you to victory and the country to independence. Were you to decline, still your presence alone would be of inestimable advantage.

"The enemy are now at Nashville, about fifty thousand strong, advancing in this direction by Columbia. He has also forces, according to the report of General Bragg, landing at Pittsburg, from twenty-five to fifty thousand, and moving in the direction of Purdy.

"This army corps, moving to join Bragg, is about twenty thousand strong. Two brigades, Hindman's and Woods's, are, I suppose, at Corinth. One regiment of Hardee's division (Lieutenant-Colonel Patton commanding) is moving by cars to-day (March 20th), and Statham's brigade (Crittenden's division). The brigade will halt at Iuka, the regiment at Burnsville; Cleburne's brigade, Hardee's division, except the regiment, at Burnsville; and Carroll's brigade, Crittenden's division, and Helm's cavalry, at Tuscumbia; Bowen's brigade at Courtland; Breckinridge's brigade here; the regiments of cavalry of Adams and Wharton on the opposite bank of the river; Scott's Louisiana regiment at Pulaski, sending forward supplies; Morgan's cavalry at Shelbyville, ordered on.

"To-morrow Breckinridge's brigade will go to Corinth, then Bowen's. When these pass Tuscumbia and Iuka, transportation will be ready there for the other troops to follow immediately from those points, and, if necessary, from Burnsville. The cavalry will cross and move forward as soon as their trains can be passed over the railroad-bridge. I have troubled you with these details, as I can not properly communicate them by telegram.

"The test of merit in my profession, with the people, is success. It is a hard rule, but I think it right. If I join this corps to the forces of Beauregard (I confess a hazardous experiment), then those who are now declaiming against me will be without an argument.
    "Your friend, A. S. JOHNSTON."
    To this letter the following reply was made:
    "RICHMOND, VIRGINIA, *March 26, 1862.*

"MY DEAR GENERAL: Yours of the 18th instant was this day delivered by your aide, Mr. Jack. I have read it with much satisfaction. So far as the past is concerned, it but confirms the conclusions at which I had already arrived. My confidence in you has never wavered, and I hope the public will soon give me credit for judgment, rather than continue to arraign me for obstinacy.

"You have done wonderfully well, and now I breathe easier in the assurance that you will be able to make a junction of your two armies. If you can meet the division of the enemy moving from the Tennessee before it can make a junction with that advancing from Nashville, the future will be brighter. If this can not be done, our only hope is that the people of the Southwest will rally *en masse* with their private arms, and thus enable you to oppose the vast army which will threaten the destruction of our country.

"I have hoped to be able to leave here for a short time, and would be much gratified to confer with you, and share your responsibilities. I might aid you in obtaining troops; no one could hope to do more unless he underrated your military capacity. I write in great haste, and feel that it would be worse than useless to point out to you how much depends on you.
    "May God bless you, is the sincere prayer of your friend,
    "JEFFERSON DAVIS."
    Let us now review the events which had brought such unmeasured censure on General Johnston for some months preceding this correspondence. We have seen him, with a force numerically much inferior to that of the enemy in his front, holding the position of Bowling Green, and, by active operations of detached commands, keeping up to foe and friend the impression that he had a

large army in position. With self-sacrificing fortitude he remained silent under reproaches for not advancing to attack the enemy. When Forts Donelson and Henry were more immediately threatened, he gave reënforcements from his small command until his own line became more like one of skirmishers than an intrenched line of battle; and when those forts were surrendered, and his position became both untenable and useless, he withdrew in such order and with such skill that his retreat was unmolested by the enemy. Though he continued to be the subject of unreasoning vituperation, he sought not to justify himself by blaming others, or telling what he would have done if his Government had sent him the arms and munitions he asked for, but which his Government he learned did not possess.

There are yet those who, self-assured, demand why Johnston did not go himself to Donelson and Henry, and why his forces were not there concentrated. A slight inspection of the map would suffice to show that, Bowling Green abandoned, the direct road to Nashville would be open to the advance of Buell's army. Then the forts, if held, would cease to answer their purpose, and, being isolated, and also between hostile armies above and below, would be not only valueless but only temporarily tenable; and of his critics it may be asked, Who else than himself could, with the small force retained at Bowling Green, have held the enemy in check so long, and at last have retired without disaster?

To collect the widely separated troops of his command so as to form an army which might offer battle to the invading foe was a problem which must have been impossible, if the organized armies by which he was threatened had been guided by a capacity equal to his own. It was done, and, with the genius of a great soldier, he seized the opportunity, by the rapid combination of new levies and of forces never before united, to attack the armies of the enemy in detail while they were endeavoring to form a junction.

The Southwestern States presented a field peculiarly favorable for the application of a new power in war. Deep rivers, with banks frequently but little elevated above the water, traverse the country. On these rivers iron-plated steamboats with heavy guns may move with a rapidity incomparably greater than that of marching armies. It is as if forts, with armaments, garrison, and stores, were endowed with locomotion more swift and enduring than that of cavalry.

The Ohio, Mississippi, Cumberland, and Tennessee Rivers all were in the field of General Johnston's operations, and at the stage of water most suited to naval purposes. Apart from the heavy guns which could thus be brought to bear at interior places upon an army having only field-artillery, the advantage of rapid transportation for troops and supplies can hardly be over-estimated. It has been seen how these advantages were utilized by the enemy at Henry and Donelson, and not less did they avail him at Shiloh.

As has been elsewhere explained, the condition of the South did not enable the Confederacy to meet the enemy on the water except at great odds.

If it be asked, "Why did not General Johnston wait until the enemy marched from the river instead of attacking him at Shiloh or Pittsburg Landing?" the answer is, "That would have been to delay until the junction of the enemy's armies had been effected." To fight them in detail, it was necessary to attack the first where it lay, backed by its gunboats. That sound judgment and soldierly daring went hand in hand in this attack the sequel demonstrated.

Meantime some active operations had taken place in that part of General Johnston's command west of the Mississippi River. Detached conflicts with the enemy had been fought by the small forces under Generals Price and McCulloch, but no definite result had followed. General Earl Van Dorn had been subsequently assigned to the command, and assumed it on January 29, 1862. General Curtis was then in command of the enemy's forces, numbering about twelve thousand men. He had harassed General Price on his retreat to Fayetteville, Arkansas, and then had fallen back to Sugar Creek, where he proposed to make a stand. Van Dorn, immediately on his arrival at the Confederate camps on Boston Mountain, prepared to attack Curtis. His first movement, however, was to intercept General Sigel, then at Bentonville with sixteen thousand men. The want of coöperation in Van Dorn's forces enabled Sigel to escape. Curtis thus concentrated his forces at Sugar Creek, and, instead of taking him in detail, Van Dorn was obliged to meet his entire army. By a circuitous route, he led Price's army against the enemy's rear, moving McCulloch against the right flank; but his progress was so slow and embarrassed, that the enemy heard of it in season to make his dispositions accordingly.

The battle of Elkhorn, or Pea Ridge, was fought on the morning of March 5th. Van Dorn reported his force to be fourteen thousand men, and Curtis puts his force at about ten thousand. Van Dorn, with Price's division, encountered Carr's division which had already advanced, but was driven back steadily and with heavy loss. Meanwhile, McCulloch's command met a division under Osterhaus, and, after a sharp, quick struggle, swept it away. Pushing forward through the shrub-oak, his wide-extended line met Sigel's, Asboth's, and Davis's divisions. Here on the ragged spurs of the hills ensued a fearful combat. In the crisis of the struggle, McCulloch, dashing forward to reconnoiter, fell a victim to a sharpshooter. Almost at the same moment, McIntosh, his second in command, fell while charging a battery of the enemy with a regiment of Texas cavalry. Without direction or leader, the shattered lines of our forces left the field to rally, after a wide circuit, on Price's division. When Van Dorn heard of this misfortune, he urged his attack, pressing back the enemy until night closed the bloody combat. Van Dorn's headquarters were then at Elkhorn Tavern, where the enemy's headquarters had been in the morning. Each army was now on its opponent's line of communication. Van Dorn found his troops much disorganized and exhausted, short of ammunition, and without food, and made his arrangements to retreat. The wagon-trains and all the men not effective for the coming battle were started by a circuitous route for Van Buren. The effectives remained to cover the retreat. The battle was renewed at 7 A.M., and raged until 10 A.M. The gallant General Henry Little had the covering line with his own and Rives's Missouri brigades; this stout rear-guard holding off the whole army of the enemy. The trains, artillery, and most of the army were by that time well on the road. The order was given to the Missourians to withdraw, and "the gallant fellows faced about with cheers" retired steadily, and encamped ten miles from the battle-field at three o'clock. There was no real pursuit. The attack had failed. Van Dorn put his loss at six hundred killed and wounded, and two hundred prisoners. Curtis reported his loss at two hundred and three killed, nine hundred and seventy-two wounded, and a hundred and seventy-six missing—total, thirteen hundred and fifty-one.[12]

The object of Van Dorn had been to effect a diversion in behalf of General Johnston. This failed; but the enemy was badly crippled, and soon fell back to Missouri, of which he still retained possession.

General Van Dorn was now ordered to join General Johnston by the quickest route. Yet only one of his regiments arrived in time to be present at the battle of Shiloh. As has been already stated, General Beauregard left Nashville on February 14th to take charge in West Tennessee, and made his headquarters at Jackson, Tennessee, on February 17th. He was somewhat prostrated by sickness, which partially disabled him through the campaign. The two grand divisions of his army were commanded by the able Generals Bragg and Polk. On March 26th he permanently removed to Corinth. Under his orders the evacuation of Columbus by General Polk, and the establishment of a new line resting on New Madrid, Island No. 10, and Humboldt, was completed. On March 2d Brigadier-General J. P. McCown, an "old army" officer, was assigned to the command of Island No. 10, forty miles below Columbus, whither he removed his division. A. P. Stewart's brigade was sent to New Madrid. At these points some seven thousand troops were assembled, and the remainder marched under General Cheatham to Union City. General Polk says:

> "In five days we moved the accumulations of six months, taking with us all our commissary and quartermaster's stores—an amount sufficient to supply my whole command for eight months—all our powder and other ammunition and ordnance stores, excepting a few shot, and gun-carriages, and every heavy gun in the fort, except two thirty-two pounders and three carronades in a remote outwork, which had been rendered useless."

The movement of the enemy up the Tennessee River commenced on March 10th. General C. F. Smith led the advance, with a new division under General Sherman. On the 13th Smith assembled four divisions at Savannah, on the west bank of the Tennessee, at the Great Bend. The ultimate design was to mass the forces of Grant and Buell against our army at Corinth. Buell was still in the occupation of Nashville. On the 16th Sherman disembarked at Pittsburg Landing, and made a reconnaissance to Monterey, nearly half-way to Corinth. On the next day General Grant took command. Two more divisions were added, and he assembled his army near Pittsburg Landing, which was the most advantageous base for a movement against Corinth. Here it lay inactive until the battle of Shiloh.

The Tennessee flows northwest for some distance, until, a little west of Hamburg, it takes its final bend to the north. Here two small streams, Owl and Lick Creeks, flowing nearly parallel, somewhat north of east, from three to five miles apart, empty into the Tennessee. Owl Creek forms the northern limit of the ridge, which Lick Creek bounds on the south. These streams, rising some ten or twelve miles back, toward Corinth, were bordered near their mouths by swamps filled with backwater from the Tennessee, and impassable except where the roads crossed them.

[Map used by the Confederate generals at Shiloh]

38

The inclosed space is a rolling table-land, about one hundred feet above the river-level, with its water-shed lying near Lick Creek, and either slope broken by deep and frequent ravines draining into two streams. The acclivities were covered with forests, and often thick set with undergrowth. Pittsburg Landing, containing three or four log-cabins, was situated about midway between the mouths of the creeks, in the narrow morass that borders the Tennessee. It was three or four miles below Hamburg, six or seven above Savannah, the depot of the enemy on the right bank, and twenty-two miles from Corinth. Thus the position of the enemy was naturally strong. With few and difficult approaches, guarded on either flank by impassable streams and morasses, protected by a succession of ravines and acclivities, commanded by eminences to the rear, it seemed safe against attack, and easy to defend. No defensive works were constructed.

[Footnote 11: Colonel R. W. Woolley, In "New Orleans Picayune," March, 1863.]

[Footnote 12: "The Life of Gen. Albert Sidney Johnston," by his son.]

CHAPTER XVIII.

General Buell's March.—Object of General Johnston.—His Force.—Advance from Corinth.-Line of Battle.—Telegram.—The Time of the Battle of Shiloh.—Results of the First Day's Battle.—One Encampment not taken.—Effects.—Reports on this Failure.—Death of General Johnston.—Remarks.

General Buell, who was to make a junction with General Grant, deemed it best that his army should march through by land, as it would facilitate the occupation of the Memphis and Charleston Railroad through north Alabama, where General Mitchell had been assigned. Accordingly, Buell commenced his march from Nashville on March 15th, with a rapid movement of cavalry, followed by a division of infantry, to seize the bridges. The bridge over Duck River being destroyed, it was the 31st before his army crossed. His advance arrived at Savannah on Saturday, April 5th, and our attack on Grant at Pittsburg Landing was made on the next day, the 6th of April. The advance of General Buell anticipated his orders by two days, and likewise the calculations of our commanders.

It had been the object of General Johnston, since falling back from Nashville, to concentrate his army at Corinth, and fight the enemy in detail—Grant first, and Buell afterward. The army of General Polk had been drawn back from Columbus. The War Department ordered General Bragg from Pensacola, with his well-disciplined army, to the aid of Johnston. A brigade was sent by General Lovell from Louisiana, and Chalmers and Walker were already on the line of the Memphis and Charleston road with considerable commands. These forces collected at Corinth, and to them were added such new levies as the Governors had in rendezvous, and a few regiments raised in response to General Beauregard's call. General Bragg, in a sketch of the battle of Shiloh, thus speaks of General Johnston's army:

"In a period of four weeks, fragments of commands from Bowling Green, Kentucky, under Hardee; Columbus, Kentucky, under Polk; and Pensacola, Mobile, and New Orleans, under

Bragg, with such new levies as could be hastily raised, all badly armed and equipped, were united at and near Corinth, and, for the first time, organised as an army. It was a heterogeneous mass, in which there was more enthusiasm than discipline, more capacity than knowledge, and more valor than instruction. Rifles, rifled and smooth-bore muskets—some of them originally percussion, others hastily altered from flint-locks by Yankee contractors, many with the old flint and steel—and shot-guns of all sizes and patterns, held place in the same regiments. The task of organizing such a command in four weeks, and supplying it, especially with ammunition, suitable for action, was simply appalling. It was undertaken, however, with a cool, quiet self-control, calling to his aid the best knowledge and talent at his command, which not only inspired confidence, but soon yielded the natural fruits of system, order, and discipline."

This force, about forty thousand of all arms, was divided into four corps, commanded respectively by Major-Generals Polk, Bragg, and Hardee, and Brigadier-General Breckinridge. General Beauregard was second in command under General Johnston. General Beauregard says, "A want of general officers needful for the proper organization of divisions and brigades of an army brought thus suddenly together, and other difficulties in the way of effective organization, delayed the movements until the night of April 2d."

About one o'clock on the morning of April 3d preliminary orders were issued to hold the troops in readiness to move at a moment's notice, with five days' provisions and a hundred rounds of ammunition. The orders for march and battle were issued in the afternoon. At that time General Hardee led the advance, the Third Corps, from Corinth, by the northernmost route, known as the Ridge road. Bivouacking that night on the way, he arrived next morning at Mickey's, a house about eighteen miles from Corinth and four or five miles from Pittsburg. The Second Corps, under Bragg, marched by the direct road to Pittsburg through Monterey, which it reached about 11 A.M. on the 4th, and bivouacked that night near Mickey's in the rear of Hardee's corps. The First Corps, under General Polk, consisted of two divisions, under Cheatham and Clark. The latter was ordered to follow Hardee on the Ridge road at an interval of half an hour, and to halt near Mickey's, so as to allow Bragg's corps to fall in behind Hardee, at a thousand yards' interval, and form a second line of battle. Polk's corps was to form the left wing of the third line of battle; and Breckinridge's reserve the right wing. The other division of Polk, under Cheatham, was on outpost duty, at and near Bethel, on the Mobile and Ohio Railroad, about as far from Mickey's as Corinth was. He was ordered to assemble his forces at Purdy, and pursue the route to Monterey. He effected his junction on the afternoon of the 5th, and took position on the left wing of Polk's corps. Breckinridge's reserve corps moved from Burnsville early on April 4th, by way of Farmington toward Monterey, distant fourteen miles. It did not effect its junction with the other corps until late on the afternoon of Saturday the 5th, being delayed by the rains on Friday and Saturday. At daylight on the 5th Hardee moved, and by seven o'clock was sufficiently out of the way to allow Bragg to advance. Before ten o'clock Hardee's corps had reached the outposts and developed the lines of the enemy. The corps was immediately deployed into line of battle about a mile and a half west of Shiloh church, where Lick Creek and Owl Creek approach most nearly, and are about three miles apart. Gladden's brigade, of Bragg's corps, was on the right of Hardee's corps, which was not sufficiently strong to occupy the whole front. This line extended from creek to creek. Before seven o'clock Bragg's column was in motion, and the right wing of his line of battle formed about eight hundred yards in the rear of Hardee's line. But the division on the left was nowhere to be seen. Even as late as half-past twelve the missing column had not appeared, nor had any report from it been received. General Johnston, "looking first at his watch, then glancing at the position of the sun, exclaimed: 'This is not *war*! Let us have our horses!' He rode to the rear until he found the missing column standing stock-still, with its head some distance out in an open field. General Polk's reserves were ahead of it, with their wagons and artillery blocking up the road. General Johnston ordered them to clear the road, and the missing column to move forward. There was much chaffering among those implicated as to who should bear the blame. . . . It was about four o'clock when the lines were completely formed—too late, of course, to begin the battle then." [13]

The road was not clear until 2 P.M. General Polk got Clark's division of his corps into line of battle by four o'clock; and Cheatham, who had come up on the left, promptly followed. Breckinridge's line was then formed on Polk's right. Thus was the army arrayed in three lines of battle late Saturday afternoon.[14]

The purpose of General Johnston to attack promptly is evinced in the correspondence already introduced; it is further shown in his telegram of April 3d, as follows:

"To the PRESIDENT, *Richmond.*

"General Buell in motion, thirty thousand strong, rapidly from Colombia by Clifton to Savannah. Mitchell behind him, with ten thousand. Confederate forces forty thousand; ordered forward to offer battle near Pittsburg.

"Division from Bethel, main body from Corinth, reserve from Burnsville, converging to-morrow, near Monterey, on Pittsburg.

"Beauregard second in command, Polk the left, Bragg the center, Hardee the right wing, Breckinridge the reserve.

"Hope engagement before Buell can form junction." [15]

On the 6th of April I sent a telegram as follows:

> "GENERAL A. S. JOHNSTON: Your
> dispatch of yesterday received. I hope you will
> be able to close with the enemy before his two
> columns unite."

[Map: Battle of Shiloh Part II]

Though much inquiry has been made, I have not been able to recover that dispatch "of yesterday" the 4th. It was anxiously sought because, in cipher (private between us), he explained distinctly his plan of battle, as the previous one had his proposed order of march. It was in every respect important to attack at the earliest moment after the advance of Buell's command became known. Every delay diminished the chances of surprising the enemy, and increased the probability of his being reënforced. Had the attack been made a day sooner, not only would Buell's army have been absent, but there would have been no prospect of their timely arrival; and who can measure the moral effect this would have produced? It would be useless to review the controversies as to who was responsible for the confusion and consequent detentions on the march, the evil of which might have been greater if the vigilance of the enemy had been equal to his self-sufficiency.

War has been called a fickle goddess, and its results attributed to chance. The great soldier of our century said, "Fortune favors the heavy battalions"; but is it not rather exact calculation than chance which controls the events of war, and the just determination of the relation of time, space, and motion in the application of force, which decides the effective weight of battalions? Had the battle of Shiloh opened a day sooner, it would have been better; had it been postponed a day, to attack then would have been impracticable. Had the several columns moved on different roads, converging toward the field of battle, the movements of some could not have been obstructed by others, so that the troops would have been in position and the battle have been commenced on Saturday morning. The programme and purpose of General Johnston appear from his dispatch of the 3d, and from the disappointment evinced by him at the failure of a portion of the command to be present on the field on the morning of the 5th (Saturday), as he expected.

General Bragg, in a monograph on the battle of Shiloh, says:

"During the afternoon of the 5th, as the last of our troops were taking position, a casual and partly accidental meeting of general officers occurred just in rear of our second line, near the bivouac of General Bragg. The Commander-in-Chief, General Beauregard, General Polk, General Bragg, and General Breckinridge, are remembered as present. In a discussion of the causes of the delay and its incidents, it was mentioned that some of the troops, now in their third day only, were entirely out of food, though having marched with five days' rations. General Beauregard, confident our movement had been discovered by the enemy, urged its abandonment, a return to our camps for supplies, and a general change of programme. In this opinion no other seemed fully to concur; and when it was suggested that 'the enemy's supplies were much nearer, and could be had for the taking,' General Johnston quietly remarked, 'Gentlemen, we shall attack at daylight to-morrow.' The meeting then dispersed upon an invitation of the commanding general to meet at his tent that evening. At that meeting a further discussion elicited the same views, and the same firm, decided determination. The next morning, about dawn of day, the 6th, as the troops were being put in motion, several generals again met at the camp-fire of the general-in-chief. The discussion was renewed. General Beauregard again expressing his dissent; when, rapid firing in the front indicating that the attack had commenced, General Johnston closed the discussion by remarking: 'The battle has opened, gentlemen; it is too late to change our dispositions.' He prepared to move to the front, and his subordinates promptly joined their respective commands, inspired by his coolness,

42

confidence, and determination. Few men have equaled him in the possession and display, at the proper time, of these great qualities of the soldier."

The results of the first day of the famous battle thus began are very summarily presented in the following brief report of General Beauregard:
"At 5 A.M., on the 6th instant, a reconnoitering party of the enemy having become engaged with our advanced pickets, the commander of the forces gave orders to begin the movement and attack as determined upon, except that Trabue's brigade of Breckinridge's division was detached and advanced to support the left of Bragg's corps and line of battle then menaced by the enemy; and the other two brigades were directed to advance by the road to Hamburg to support Bragg's right; and at the same time Maney's regiment of Polk's corps was advanced by the same road to reënforce the regiment, of cavalry and battery of four pieces, already thrown forward to watch and guard Grier's, Tanner's, and Borland's Fords of Lick Creek.
"Thirty minutes after 5 A.M., our lines and columns were in motion, all animated evidently by a promising spirit. The front line was engaged at once, but advanced steadily, followed in due order, with equal resolution and steadiness, by the other lines, which were brought successively into action with rare skill, judgment, and gallantry by the several corps commanders, as the enemy made a stand with his masses rallied for the struggle for his encampments. Like an Alpine avalanche our troops moved forward, despite the determined resistance of the enemy, until after 6 P.M., when we were in possession of all his encampments between Owl and Lick Creeks but one; nearly all of his field-artillery, about thirty flags, colors, and standards, over three thousand prisoners, including a division commander (General Prentiss), and several brigade commanders, thousands of small-arms, an immense supply of subsistence, forage, and munitions of war, and a large amount of means of transportation, all the substantial fruits of a complete victory—such, indeed, as rarely have followed the most successful battles, for never was an army so well provided as that of our enemy.
"The remnant of his army had been driven in utter disorder to the immediate vicinity of Pittsburg, under the shelter of the heavy guns of his iron-clad gunboats, and we remained undisputed masters of his well-selected, admirably provided cantonments, after our twelve hours of obstinate conflict with his forces, who had been beaten from them and the contiguous covert, but only by the sustained onset of all the men we could bring into action."

There are two words in this report which, if they could have been truthfully omitted, it would have been worth to us the surrender of all "the substantial fruits of a complete victory." It says: "Our troops moved forward, despite the determined resistance of the enemy, until after 6 P.M., when we were in possession of all his encampments between Owl and lick Creeks *but one*." It was that "one" encampment that furnished a foothold for all the subsequent reënforcements sent by Buell, and gave occasion for the final withdrawal of our forces; whereas, if that had been captured, and the "waters of the Tennessee" reached, as General Johnston designed, it was not too much to expect that Grant's army would have surrendered; that Buell's forces would not have crossed the Tennessee; but with a skillful commander, like Johnston, to lead our troops, the enemy would have sought safety on the north bank of the Ohio; that Tennessee, Kentucky, and Missouri would have been recovered, the Northwest disaffected, and our armies filled with the men of the Southwest, and perhaps of the Northwest also.

Let us turn to reports and authorities. The author of "The Life of Gen. Albert Sidney Johnston" says:

"Of the two armies, one was now an advancing, triumphant host, with arm uplifted to give the mortal blow; the other, a broken, mangled, demoralized mob, paralyzed and waiting for the stroke. While the other Confederate brigades, which had shared most actively in Prentiss's capture, were sending back the prisoners and forming again for a final attack, two brigades, under Chalmers and Jackson, on the extreme right, had cleared away all in front of them, and, moving down the river-bank, now came upon the last point where even a show of resistance was made. Being two very bold and active brigadiers, they at once closed with the enemy in their front, crossing a deep ravine and difficult ground to get at him. Here Colonel Webster, of Grant's staff, had gathered all the guns he could find from batteries, whether abandoned or still coherent, and with stout-hearted men, picked up at random, had prepared a resistance. Some infantry, similarly constituted, had been got together; and Ammen's brigade, the van of Nelson's division of Buell's corps, had landed, and was pushing its way through the throng of pallid fugitives at the landing to take up the battle where it had fallen from the hands of Grant and Sherman. It got into position in time to do its part in checking the unsupported assaults of Chalmers and Jackson."

General Chalmers, describing this final attack in his report, says: "It was then about four o'clock in the evening, and, after distributing ammunition, we received orders from General Bragg to drive the enemy into the river. My brigade, together with that of Brigadier-General Jackson, filed to the right and formed facing the river, and endeavored to press forward to the water's edge; but in attempting to mount the last ridge we were met by a fire from a whole line of batteries, protected by infantry and assisted by shells from the gunboats."

In a subsequent memorandum General Chalmers writes: "One more resolute movement forward would have captured Grant and his whole army, and fulfilled to the letter the battle-plan of the great Confederate general, who died in the belief

44

that victory was ours. . . ."—("The Life of Gen. Albert Sidney Johnston," p. 637.)

Brigadier-General Jackson, in his report, says:

My brigade was ordered to change direction again, face toward Pittsburg, where the enemy appeared to have made his last stand, and to advance upon him, General Chalmers's brigade being again on my right, and extending to the swamp of the Tennessee River. Without ammunition, and with only their bayonets to rely on, steadily my men advanced under a heavy fire from light batteries, siege-pieces, and gunboats. Passing through the ravine, they arrived near the crest of the opposite hill, upon which the enemy's batteries were, but could not be urged farther without support. Sheltering themselves against the precipitous sides of the ravine, they remained under this fire for some time. Finding an advance without support impracticable, remaining there under fire useless, and believing that any further forward movement should have been made simultaneously along our whole line, I proceeded to obtain orders from General Withers, but, after seeing him, was ordered by a staff-officer to retire. This order was communicated to me as coming from General Beauregard."

General Hardee, who commanded the first line, says in his report:

"Upon the death of General Johnston, the command having devolved upon General Beauregard, the conflict was continued until near sunset, and the advance divisions were within a few hundred yards of Pittsburg, where the enemy were huddled in confusion, when the order to withdraw was received. The troops were ordered to bivouac on the field of battle."

General Polk's report says:

"We had one hour or more of daylight still left, were within one hundred and fifty to four hundred yards of the enemy's position, and nothing seemed wanting to complete the most brilliant victory of the war but to press forward and make a vigorous assault on the demoralized remnant of his forces."

General Gilmer, the chief engineer of the Confederate States Army, in a letter to Colonel William Preston Johnston, dated September 17, 1872, writes as follows:

"It is my well-considered opinion that if your father had survived the day he would have crushed and captured General Grant's army before the setting of the sun on the 6th. In fact, at the time your father received the mortal wound, advancing with General Breckinridge's command, the day was ours. The enemy having lost all the strong positions on that memorable field, his troops fell back in great disorder on the banks of the Tennessee. To cover the confusion, rapid fires were opened from the gunboats the enemy had placed in the river; but the shots passed entirely over our devoted men, who were exultant and eager to be led forward to the final assault, which must have resulted in a complete victory, owing to the confusion and general disorganization of the Federal troops. I knew the condition of General Grant's army at the moment, as I had reached a high, projecting point on the bank of the river, about a mile above Pittsburg Landing, and could see the hurried movements to get the disordered troops across to the right bank. Several thousand had already passed, and a confused mass of men crowded to the landing to get on the boats that were employed in crossing. I rode rapidly to General Bragg's position to report what I had seen, and suggested that, if he would suspend the fire of his artillery and marshal his infantry for a general advance, the enemy must surrender. General Bragg decided to make the advance, and authorized me and other officers to direct the commanders of the batteries to cease firing.

"In the midst of the preparations, orders reached General Bragg from General Beauregard directing the troops to be withdrawn and placed in camp for the night—the intention being to resume the contest in the morning. This was fatal, as it enabled General Buell and General Wallace to arrive on the scene of action; that is, they came up in the course of the night. Had General Beauregard known the condition of the enemy as your father knew it when he received the fatal shot, the order for withdrawal would certainly not have been given, and, without such order, I know the enemy would have been crushed." [16]

To General Gilmer's opinion as a scientific engineer, a soldier of long experience, and a man of resolute will as well as calm judgment, the greatest respect will be accorded by those who knew him in the United States Army, as well as his associates in the Confederate Army.

General Bragg, in his official report, says:

"As soon as our troops could be again put in motion, the order was given to move forward at all points and sweep the enemy from the field. . . . Our troops, greatly exhausted by twelve hours' incessant fighting without food, mostly responded to the order with alacrity, and the movement commenced with every prospect of success, though a heavy battery in our front and the gunboats on our right seemed determined to dispute every inch of ground. Just at this time an order was received from the commanding General to withdraw the forces beyond the enemy's fire."

In addition to the statements and opinions cited above, I will introduce from a recent publication by Thomas Worthington, late colonel of the Forty-sixth Regiment of Ohio Volunteers, two statements showing the relative condition of the two armies in the afternoon of the day of battle. It may be proper to say that Colonel Worthington was regularly educated as a soldier, and had seen service in Mexico.

He quotes Colonel Geddes, of the Eighth Iowa Volunteers, as follows:

"About 3 P.M. all communications with the river (landing) ceased, and it became evident to me that the enemy was turning the right and left flanks of our army. . . . About 2 P.M. the whole Union right, comprising the Forty-sixth Ohio, which had held that flank two hours or more, was driven back in disorder, and the Confederate flanking force cut the center off from the landing, as stated by Colonel Geddes, soon after General Johnston's fall."

General Beauregard reports as follows:

"It was after 6 P.M. when the enemy's last position was carried, and his force finally broke and sought refuge behind a commanding eminence covering Pittsburg Landing, not more than half a mile distant, and under the guns of the gunboats, which opened on our eager columns a fierce and annoying fire with shot and shell of the heaviest description. Darkness was close at hand. Officers and men were exhausted by a combat of over twelve hours, without food, and jaded by the march of the preceding day through mud and water; it was, therefore, impossible to collect the rich and opportune spoils of war scattered broadcast on the field left in our possession, and impracticable to make any effective dispositions for their removal to the rear.

"I accordingly established my headquarters at the church of Shiloh, in the enemy's encampment, with Major-General Bragg, and directed our troops to sleep on their arms in such positions in advance and rear as corps commanders should determine, hoping, from news received by a special dispatch, that delays had been encountered by General Buell in his march from Columbia, and that his main forces, therefore, could not reach the field of battle in time to save General Grant's shattered fugitives from capture or destruction on the following day."

Such are the representations of those having the best means of information relative to the immediate causes of the failure to drive the enemy from his last foothold, and gain possession of it. Some of the more remote causes of this failure may be noticed. The first was the death of General Johnston, which is thus described by his son:

"General Johnston had passed through the ordeal (the charge upon the enemy) seemingly unhurt. His noble horse was shot in four places; his clothes were pierced by missiles; his boot-sole was cut and torn by a Minie ball; but, if he himself had received any severe wound, he did not know it. At this moment Governor Harris rode up from the right, elated with his own success, and with the vindication of his Tennesseeans. After a few words. General Johnston sent him with an order to Colonel Statham, which, having delivered, he speedily returned. In the mean time knots and groups of Federal soldiers kept up an angry discharge of firearms as they retreated upon their supports, and their last line, now yielding, delivered volley after volley as they retreated. By the chance of war a Minie ball from one of these did its fatal work As General

Johnston, on horseback, sat there, knowing that he had crushed in the arch which had so long resisted the pressure of his forces, and waiting until they could collect sufficiently to give the final stroke, he received a mortal wound. It came in the moment of victory and triumph from a flying foe. It smote him at the very instant when he felt the full conviction that the day was won."

His wound consisted in the cutting of the artery that runs down through the thigh and divides at the knee, and passes along the separate bones of the lower part of the leg. The wound was just above the division or branch of the artery. It was fatal only because the flow of blood was not stopped by a tourniquet. The narrative continues:

"General Beauregard had told General Johnston that morning as he rode off, that if it should be necessary to communicate with him or for him to do anything, he would be found in his ambulance in bed. Governor Harris, knowing this, and how feeble General Beauregard's health was, went first to his headquarters—just in the rear of where the army had deployed into line the evening before. Beauregard and his staff were gone on horseback in the direction of Shiloh Church. He found them there. The Governor told General Beauregard that General Johnston had been killed. Beauregard expressed regret, and then remarked, 'Everything else seems to be going on well on the right.' Governor Harris assented. 'Then,' said Beauregard, 'The battle may as well go on.' The Governor replied that he certainly thought it ought. He offered his services to Beauregard, and they were courteously accepted. General Beauregard then remained where he was, waiting the issue of events." [17]

Sidney Johnston fell in sight of victory; the hour he had waited for, the event he had planned for, had arrived. His fame was vindicated, but far dearer than this to his patriotic spirit was it with his dying eyes to behold his country's flag, so lately drooping in disaster, triumphantly advancing. In his fall the great pillar of the Southern Confederacy was crushed, and beneath its fragments the best hope of the Southwest lay buried. A highly educated and richly endowed soldier, his varied experience embraced also civil affairs, and his intimate knowledge of the country and people of the Southwest so highly qualified him for that special command that it was not possible to fill the place made vacant by his death. Not for the first time did the fate of an army depend upon a single man, and the fortunes of a country hang, as in a balance, on the achievements of a single army. To take an example far from us, in time and place, when Turenne had, after months of successful manoeuvring, finally forced his enemy into a position which gave assurance of victory, and had marshaled his forces for a decisive battle, he was, when making a preliminary reconnaissance, killed by a chance shot; then his successor, instead of attacking, retreated, and all which the one had gained for France, the other lost.

To take another example, not quite so conclusive, it was epigrammatically said by Lieutenant Kingsbury, when writing of the battle of Buena Vista, that if the last shot, fired at the close of the second day's conflict, had killed General

Taylor, the next morning's sun would have risen upon the strange spectacle of two armies in full retreat from each other, the field for which they had fought being in the possession of neither. What material consequences would have flowed from the supposed event—how the Mexican people would have been inspired by the retreat of our army, how far it would have brought out all their resources for war, and to what extent results might have been thereby affected—are speculative inquiries on a subject from which time and circumstance have taken the interest it once possessed.

The extracts which have been given sufficiently prove that, when General Johnston fell, the Confederate army was so fully victorious that, had the attack been vigorously pressed, General Grant and his army would before the setting of the sun have been fugitives or prisoners.

As our troops drew near to the river, the gunboats of the enemy became ineffective, because to fire over the bank required such elevation of the guns that the shot and shell passed high over the heads of our men, falling far away in the rear.

General Polk described the troops in advance for that reason as quite safe from the fire of the gunboats, though it might seem terrible to those far in the rear, and expressed the surprise and regret he felt at the order to retire.

Grant's army being beaten, the next step of General Johnston's programme should have followed, the defeat of Buell's and Mitchell's forces as they successively came up, and a return by our victorious army through Tennessee to Kentucky. The great embarrassment had been the want of good military weapons; these would have been largely supplied by the conquest hoped for, and, in the light of what had occurred, not unreasonably anticipated.

What great consequences would have ensued must be matter of conjecture, but that the people of Kentucky and Missouri generously sympathized with the South was then commonly admitted. Our known want of preparation for war and numerical inferiority may well have caused many to doubt the wisdom of our effort for independence, and to these a signal success would have been the makeweight deciding their course.

I believe that again in the history of war the fate of an army depended on one man; and more, that the fortunes of a country hung by the single thread of the life that was yielded on the field of Shiloh. So great was my confidence in his capacity for organization and administration, that I felt, when he was assigned to the Department of the West, that the undeveloped power of that region would be made sufficient not only for its own safety, but to contribute support if need be to the more seriously threatened East.

There have been various suppositions as to the neglect of the wound which caused General Johnston's death. My own opinion, founded upon the statements of those who were near him, and upon my long acquaintance with him and close observation of him under trying circumstances, is, that his iron nerve and extraordinary concentration of mind made him regardless of his wound, in the fixed purpose to dislodge the enemy from his last position, and, while thus struggling to complete the victory within his grasp, he unheedingly allowed his life-blood to flow away.

It often happens that men do not properly value their richest gifts until taken away. Those who had erroneously and unjustly censured Johnston, convicted of their error by the grandeur of his revealed character, joined in the general lamentation over his loss, and malignity even was silenced by the devoted manner of his death. My estimation of him was based on long and intimate acquaintance; beginning in our youth, it had grown with our growth without check or variation, and, when he first arrived in Richmond, was expressed to some friends yet living, in the wish that I had the power, by resigning, to transfer to him the Presidency of the Confederate States.

[Footnote 13: Colonel Munford's address at Memphis.]
[Footnote 14: "The Life of Gen. Albert Sidney Johnston," by his son.]
[Footnote 15: Original in the possession of Colonel W. P. Johnston.]
[Footnote 16: "The Life of Gen. Albert Sidney Johnston," pp. 635, 636.]
[Footnote 17: "The Life of Gen. Albert Sidney Johnston," p. 616.]

CHAPTER XIX.

Retirement of the Army.—Remnants of Grant's Army.—Its Reënforcements.—Strength of our Army.—Strength of Grant's Army.—Reorganization.—Corinth.—Advance of General Halleck.—Siege of Corinth.—Evacuation.—Retreat to Tupelo.—General Beauregard retires.-General Bragg in Command.—Positions on the Mississippi River occupied by the Enemy.—New Madrid.—Island No. 10.—Fort Pillow.—Memphis.—Attack at Hatteras Inlet.—Expedition of the Enemy to Port Royal.—Expeditions from Port Royal.—System of Coast Defenses adopted by us.—Fort Pulaski.

At the ensuing nightfall our victorious army retired from the front and abandoned its vantage-ground on the bluffs, which had been won at such a cost of blood. The enemy thereby had room and opportunity to come out from their corner, reoccupy the strong positions from which they had been driven, and dispose their troops on much more favorable ground. Called off by staff-officers, who gave no specific instructions, our brigades, according to circumstances, bivouacked on the battle-field, marched to the rear, or made themselves comfortable on the profuse spoils of the enemy's encampments. General Buell says:

> "Of the army of not less than fifty thousand effective men, which Grant had on the west bank of the Tennessee River, not more than five thousand were in ranks and available on the battlefield at nightfall on the 6th, exclusive of Lew Wallace's division, say eight thousand five hundred men that only came up during the night. The rest were either killed, wounded, captured, or scattered in inextricable and hopeless confusion for miles along the banks of the river."

In addition to the arrival of Wallace's division, the entire divisions of Nelson and Crittenden got across the river during the night, and by daylight that of McCook began to arrive; all but the first named belonged to Buell's army. The work of reorganization of fragments of Grant's force also occupied the night. In the morning the arrival of reënforcements to the enemy continued.

On the morning of the 7th the enemy advanced about six o'clock, and opened a heavy fire of musketry and artillery, such as gave assurance that the reënforcements had arrived, to anticipate which the battle of the 6th had been fought. A series of combats ensued, in which the Confederates showed their usual valor; but, after the junction had been effected between Grant and Buell, which Johnston's movement was made to prevent, our force was unequal to resist the combined armies, and retreat was a necessity.

The field return of the Army of Mississippi before and after the battle of Shiloh was as follows: infantry and artillery, effective before the battle, 35,953; cavalry, 4,382; total, 40,335. Infantry and artillery, effective after the battle, 25,555; cavalry, 4,081; total, 29,636. Difference, 10,699. Casualties in battle: killed, 1,728; wounded, 8,012; missing, 959.

The effective force of General Grant's army engaged in the battles of April 6th and 7th at Shiloh was 49,314; reënforcements of General Buell, 21,579; total, 70,893. The casualties in the battle of April 6th in Grant's force were as follows: killed, 1,500; wounded, 6,634; missing, 3,086; total, 11,220; leaving, for duty on the 7th, 59,673.

On April 9th Major-General H. W, Halleck left St. Louis and proceeded to Pittsburg Landing to assume command of the enemy's forces in the field. A reorganization was made, in which General Grant's divisions formed the right wing, those of General Buell the center, and those of General Pope, brought from the west side of the Mississippi, the left wing; and an advance on Corinth was commenced.

Corinth, the position from which our forces had advanced to Shiloh or Pittsburg Landing, and to which they had now retired, was a small village in the northeast corner of the State of Mississippi. It was ninety miles east of Memphis and twenty or twenty-two west of the Tennessee River. The Memphis and Charleston Railroad ran from west to east through it, and the Mobile and Ohio road from south to north. The country between it and the Tennessee River was quite rugged, broken into ridges, and covered with a heavy forest. The position itself was flat, the water poor. Being the point at which two principal railroads crossed, it served admirably for the concentration of our forces.

Corinth was a strategic point of importance, and it was intended to be held as long as circumstances would permit; but it was untenable in the face of a largely superior force, owing to the ease with which the railroad communications in the rear could be cut by the enemy's cavalry. The small streams and contiguous flats in its front formed some obstacles which were not passed by the enemy until after the retreat of our army. The defenses were slight, consisting of rifle-pits and earthworks of little elevation or strength.

The movement of General Halleck against this position commenced from Pittsburg Landing on April 28th with a force exceeding eighty-five thousand effectives. On May 3d he had reached within eight miles of Corinth, and on the 21st his batteries were within three miles. This slow progress was probably the result of a conviction that our force was very large, rather than of the bad state of the roads. So great were his precautions, that every night his army lay in an intrenched camp, and by day it was assailed by skirmishers from our army in more or less force.

General Sherman, in his report of May 30th, says:
"My division has constructed seven distinct intrenched camps since leaving Shiloh, the men working cheerfully and well all the time, night and day. Hardly had we finished one camp

51

before we were called on to move forward and build another. But I have been delighted at this feature in the character of my division, and take this method of making it known. Our intrenchments near Corinth and at Russell's, each built substantially in one night, are stronger works of art than the much-boasted forts of the enemy at Corinth."

The line of railroad on the north and east had been cut by the enemy, and an attempt made on the south. But so well was his apprehension of our strength maintained, that he continued his intrenched approaches until within one thousand yards of our main works.

General Sherman says:

"By 9 A.M. of the 29th our works were substantially done, and our artillery in position, and at 4 P.M. the siege-train was brought forward. . . . So near was the enemy that we could hear the sound of his drums and sometimes of voices in command; and the railroad-cars arriving and departing at Corinth were easily distinguished. For some days and nights cars have been arriving and departing very frequently, especially in the night; but last night (the 29th) more so than usual, and my suspicions were aroused. Before daybreak I instructed the brigade commanders and the field-officer of the day to feel forward as far as possible; but all reported the enemy's pickets still in force in the dense woods to our front. But about 6 A.M. a curious explosion, sounding like a volley of large siege-pieces, followed by others, singly, and in twos and threes, arrested our attention, and soon after a large smoke arose from the direction of Corinth, when I telegraphed to General Halleck to ascertain the cause. He answered that he could not explain it, but ordered me to advance my division and feel the enemy, if still in my front. I immediately put in motion two regiments of each brigade, by different roads, and soon after followed with the whole division—infantry, artillery, and cavalry. General M. L. Smith's brigade moved rapidly down the main road, entering the first redoubt of the enemy at 7 A.M. It was completely evacuated, and by 8 A.M. all my division was at Corinth and beyond."

The force of General Beauregard was less than forty-five thousand effective men. He estimated that of the enemy to be between eighty-five and ninety thousand men. All the troops of the enemy in reserve in Arkansas, Missouri, Kentucky, and Illinois were brought forward, except the force of Curtis, in Arkansas, and placed in front of our position. No definite idea of their number was formed. In the opinion of Beauregard, a general attack was not to be hazarded; but on May 3d an advance was made to attack the corps of General Pope, when only one of his divisions was in position, and that gave way so rapidly it could not be overtaken. Again, on May 9th, an advance was made, hoping to surprise the enemy. But a division, which should have been in position at three o'clock in the morning, or early dawn, was detained until three in the afternoon by the mistakes of the guide. The enemy thus became informed of the movement, and no surprise could be effected. General Beauregard commenced the removal of his sick, preparatory to an evacuation, on May 26th; on the next day arrangements for falling back were made, and the work completed on the 29th. So complete was the evacuation, that not only was the army successfully withdrawn, but also every piece of ordnance, only a quantity of damaged ammunition being left behind. The retreat was continued to Tupelo, without any serious conflict with the enemy; but during the retreat seven locomotives were reported to be lost by the burning of a bridge, and a number of cars, most of which were loaded with stores, were ordered to be burned.

On June 14th orders were sent to General Bragg, from Richmond, to proceed to Jackson, Mississippi, and temporarily to assume command of the department then under command of General Lovell. The order concluded as follows:

> "After General Magruder joins, your
> further services there may be dispensed with.
> The necessity is urgent and absolute.

"J. DAVIS."

On application to General Beauregard for the necessary order, he replied:

> "You can not possibly go. My health does
> not permit me to remain in charge alone here.
> This evening my two physicians were insisting
> that I should go away for one or two weeks,
> furnishing me with another certificate for that
> purpose, and I had concluded to go—
> intending to see you to-morrow on the
> subject, and leave you in command."

The certificate of the physicians was as follows:

"HEADQUARTERS, WESTERN DEPARTMENT,
"TUPELO, *June 14, 1862.*

> "We certify that, after attendance on
> General Beauregard for the past four months,
> and treatment of his case, in our professional
> opinion he is incapacitated physically for the
> arduous duties of his present command, and
> we urgently recommend rest and recreation.

"R. L. Brodie, Surgeon, P. A. C. S.
"Sam Choppin, Surgeon, P. A. C. S."

These facts were telegraphed to me at once by General Bragg. Soon after, I sent a second dispatch to him, renewing the order, and expressing my surprise that he should have hesitated to obey, when the original order stated "the necessity is urgent and absolute." Before this second dispatch was received by General Bragg, General Beauregard had transferred the command to him, and had departed for Bladen Springs. General Bragg thus describes the subsequent proceedings:

> "Prepared to move, I telegraphed back to
> the President that the altered conditions
> induced me to await his further orders. In
> reply to this, I was immediately notified by
> telegraph of my assignment to the 'permanent
> command of the army,' and was directed to

send General Van Dorn to execute my first instructions."

From this statement it appears—1. That General Beauregard was not, as has been alleged, harshly deprived of his command, but that he voluntarily surrendered it, after being furnished with medical certificates of his physical incapacity for its arduous duties. 2. That he did not even notify his Government, still less ask permission to retire. 3. That the order, assigning another to the command he had abandoned, could not be sent through him, when he had departed and gone to a place where there was no telegraph, and rarely a mail. 4. That it is neither customary nor proper to send orders to the commander of an army through a general on sick-leave; and in this case it would have been very objectionable, as a similar order had just been sent and disobeyed.

Meanwhile some other events had occurred in the Western Department which should be mentioned. The movement of the forces of the enemy up the Tennessee River, as has been stated, thus flanking some of our positions on the Mississippi River, was followed by his fitting out a naval fleet to move down that river. This fleet, consisting of seven ironclads and one gun-boat, ten mortar-boats, each carrying a thirteen-inch mortar, a coal-barge, two ordnance-steamers, and two transports with troops, left Cairo on March 14th, and arrived at Hickman that evening. A small force of our cavalry left upon its approach. Columbus, as has been stated, had previously been evacuated by our forces and occupied by the enemy. In the morning the fleet continued down toward Island No. 10. This island is situated in that bend of the river which touches the border of Tennessee, a few miles further up the river than New Madrid, although nearly southeast of that point.

In the latter part of February a large force of the enemy under Major-General Pope left Commerce, Missouri, and moved south about fifty miles to New Madrid, with the object of capturing that place. Aided by the gunboats of Commander Hollins, our small force repulsed the assaults of the enemy three times, but such was the disparity of numbers that it soon became manifest that our forces could not successfully hold the position, and it was evacuated on the night of March 13th. Its defenses consisted of two earthworks, in which about twenty guns were mounted. These were spiked and rendered unfit for use.

The bombardment of Island No. 10, above described, commenced on March 15th, and was continued night and day. Up to April 1st the enemy fired several thousand thirteen-inch and rifle shells. On March 17th a general attack with five gunboats and four mortar-boats was made, and continued nine hours, without any serious result. Finally, the forces of the enemy were greatly increased, and began to occupy both banks of the river, and also the river above and below the island, when a portion of our force retired, and about April 7th the remainder surrendered.

The fleet, on April 12th, proceeded next to Fort Pillow, about a hundred and eighty miles below Island No. 10, and a bombardment was commenced on the next day. This was continued without effect until the night of June 4th, when both Forts Pillow and Randolph, the latter some twelve miles below the former, were evacuated—these positions having become untenable in consequence of the withdrawal of our forces from Corinth and the adjacent portion of Tennessee.

Nothing now remained to oppose the enemy's fleet but our gunboats at Memphis, which were, say, seventy miles farther down the river. The gallantry and efficiency displayed by our improvised river navy at New Madrid and Island No. 10 gave rise to hopes scarcely justified by the number of our vessels or their armament. Our boats had fewer guns than those of the enemy, and they were less substantially constructed, but their officers and crews took counsel of their country's need rather than of their own strength. They manfully engaged the enemy, and disabled one of his rams, but after an hour's conflict were compelled to retire.

The possession of Memphis being no longer disputed, its occupation by the enemy promptly followed.

At an early period of the war the Government of the United States organized some naval and military expeditions, with a view to capture our harbors, to occupy an extensive tract of country in their vicinity, and especially to obtain possession of a portion of our cotton-crop. The first movement of this kind was by a fleet of naval vessels and transports which appeared off Hatteras Inlet on August 27, 1861. This inlet is a gap in the sandy barrier that lines the coast of North Carolina about eighteen miles southwest of Cape Hatteras. It was the principal entrance to Pamlico Sound, a large body of water lying between the sandy beach and the mainland. The channel of the entrance had about seven feet of water, and was protected by two small forts constructed on the sand. Our forces were under the command of Captain Samuel Barron, an officer of distinction, formerly in the United States Navy. After a short bombardment, which developed the strength of the enemy and his own comparative weakness, he capitulated.

A much larger fleet of naval vessels and transports, carrying fifteen thousand men, appeared off the harbor of Port Royal, South Carolina, on November 4, 1861. This harbor is situated midway between the cities of Charleston and Savannah. It is a broad estuary, into which flow some two or three streams, the interlacing of which with creeks forms a group of numerous islands. The parish, of which these are the greater part, constituted the richest agricultural district in the State; its staples being sea-island cotton and rice. The principal defenses were Fort Walker, a strong earthwork on Hilton Head, and Fort Beauregard on Philip's Island. The attack was made by the enemy on the 7th, by a fleet consisting of eight steamers and a sloop-of-war in tow. Some of the steamers were of the first class, as the Wabash and the Susquehanna. The conflict continued for four hours, when the forts, because untenable, were abandoned.

In the early part of 1862 several reconnaissances were sent out from Port Royal, and subsequently an expedition visited Darien and Brunswick in Georgia, and Fernandina, Jacksonville, and St. Augustine in Florida. Its design was to take and keep under control this line of seacoast, especially in Georgia. Some small steamers and other vessels were captured, and some ports were occupied.

The system of coast defenses which was adopted and the preparations which had been at that time made by the Government to resist these aggressions of the enemy should be stated. By reference to the topography of our coast, it will be seen that, in the State of North Carolina, are Albemarle and Pamlico Sounds, penetrating far into the interior; then the Cape Fear River, connecting with the ocean by two channels, the southwest channel being defended by a small inclosed fort and a water-battery. On the coast of South Carolina are

Georgetown and Charleston Harbors. A succession of islands extends along the coast of South Carolina and Georgia, separated from the mainland by a channel which is navigable for vessels of moderate draft from Charleston to Fernandina, Florida. There are fewer assailable points on the Gulf than on the Atlantic. Pensacola, Mobile, and the mouth of the Mississippi were defended by works that had hitherto been regarded as sufficiently strong to repulse any naval attack that might be made upon them. Immediately after the bombardment of Fort Sumter, the work of improving the seacoast defense was begun and carried forward as rapidly as the limited means of the Government would permit.

The work that was now done has been so summarily and satisfactorily described by General A. L. Long, chief of artillery, in a paper contributed to the Southern Historical Society, that I avail myself of a few extracts:[18]

"Roanoke Island and other points on Albemarle and Pamlico Sounds were fortified. Batteries were established on the southeast entrance of Cape Fear River, and the works on the southwest entrance strengthened. Defenses were constructed at Georgetown, and at all assailable points on the northeast coast of South Carolina. The works of Charleston Harbor were greatly strengthened by earthworks and floating batteries. The defenses from Charleston down the coast of South Carolina and Georgia were confined chiefly to the islands and salient points bearing upon the channels leading inland. Defensive works were erected at all important points along the coast. Many of the defenses, being injudiciously located and hastily erected, offered but little resistance to the enemy when attacked. These defeats were not surprising, when we take into consideration the inexperience of the engineers, and the long line of seacoast to be defended. As soon as a sufficient naval force had been collected, an expedition under the command of General E. F. Butler was sent to the coast of North Carolina, and captured several important points. A second expedition, under Admiral Dupont and General Thomas W. Sherman, was sent to make a descent on the coast of South Carolina. On the 7th of November Dupont attacked the batteries that were designed to defend Port Royal harbor, as stated above, and almost without resistance carried them and gained possession of Port Royal. This is the best harbor in South Carolina, and is the strategic key to all the South Atlantic coast. Later, Burnside captured Roanoke Island, and established himself in eastern North Carolina without resistance. The rapid fall of Roanoke Island and Port Royal Harbor struck consternation into the hearts of the inhabitants along the entire coast. The capture of Port Royal gave to the Federals the entire possession of Beaufort Island, which afforded a secure place of rest for the army, while the harbor gave a safe anchorage for the fleet. Beaufort Island almost fills a deep indenture in the main shore, being separated the greater part of its extent by a narrow channel, which is navigable its entire circuit. Its northern extremity extends to within a few miles of the Charleston and Savannah Railroad. The main road from Port Royal to Pocotaligo crosses the channel at this point. The evacuation of Hilton Head, on the southwestern extremity of Beaufort Island, followed the capture of Port Royal. This exposed Savannah, only about twenty-five miles distant, to an attack from that direction. At the same time, the Federals having command of Helena Bay, Charleston was liable to be assailed from North Edisto or Stono Inlet, and the railroad could have been reached without opposition by the route from Port Royal to Pocotaligo.

"Such was the state of affairs when General Lee reached Charleston, about December 1, 1861, to assume the command of the Department of North Carolina, Georgia, and Florida. His vigorous mind at once comprehended the situation, and, with his accustomed energy, he met the difficulties that presented themselves. Directing fortifications to be constructed on the Stono and the Edisto and the Combahee, he fixed his headquarters at Coosawhatchee, the point most threatened, and directed defenses to be erected opposite Hilton Head, and on the Broad and Salkehatchie, to cover Savannah. These were the points requiring immediate attention. He superintended in person the works overlooking the approach to the railroad from Port Royal, and soon infused into his troops a part of his own energy. The works he had planned rose with magical rapidity. A few days after his arrival at Coosawhatchee, Dupont and Sherman sent their first reconnaissance in that direction, which was met and repulsed by shots from the newly erected batteries; and now, whether the Federals advanced toward the railroad or turned in the direction of Charleston or Savannah, they were arrested by our batteries. The people, seeing the Federals repulsed at every point, regained their confidence, and with it their energy.

"The most important points being now secured against immediate attack, the General proceeded to organize a system of seacoast defense different from that which had been previously adopted. He withdrew the troops and material from those works which had been established on the islands and salient points which he could not defend to a strong interior line, where the effect of the Federal naval force would be neutralized. After a careful reconnaissance of the coast, he designated such points as he considered it necessary to fortify. The most important positions on this extensive line were Georgetown, Charleston, Pocotaligo, Coosawhatchee, and Savannah. Coosawhatchee, being central, could communicate with either Charleston or Savannah in two or three hours by railroad, and in case of an attack they could support each other. The positions between Coosawhatchee and Savannah, and those between the former and Charleston, could be reënforced from the positions contiguous to them; there was thus a defensive relation throughout the entire line, extending from Winyaw Bay to the mouth of St. Mary's River, in Georgia, a distance of about two hundred miles. These detached and supporting works covered a most important agricultural country, and sufficed to defend it from the smaller expeditions made against that region.

"About March 1st the gunboats of the enemy entered the Savannah River by way of the channel leading from Hilton Head. Our naval force was too weak to dispute the possession with them, and they thus cut off the communication of Fort Pulaski with the city. Soon after, the enemy landed a force, under General Gillmore, on the opposite side of the fort. By April 1st they had powerful batteries in position, and on that day opened fire on the fort. Having no hope of succor, Fort Pulaski, after striking a blow for honor, surrendered with about five hundred men." [19]

[Footnote 18: "Seacoast Defenses of the Carolinas and Georgia."]
[Footnote 19: General A. L. Long, in Historical Society Papers.]

CHAPTER XX.

Advance of General McClellan toward Centreville; his Report.—Our Forces ordered to the Peninsula.—Situation at Yorktown.—Siege by

General McCellan.—General Johnston assigned to Command; his
Recommendation.—Attack on General Magruder at Yorktown.—Movements
of McClellan.—The Virginia.—General Johnston retires.—Delay at
Norfolk.—Before Williamsburg.—Remark of Hancock.—Retreat up the
Peninsula.—Sub-terra Shells used.-Evacuation of Norfolk.—Its
Occupation by the Enemy.

In a previous chapter the retreat of our army from Centreville has been
described, and reference has been made to the anticipation of the commanding
general, J. E. Johnston, that the enemy would soon advance to attack that
position. Since the close of the war we have gained information not at that time
to us attainable, which shows that, as early as the 31st of January, 1862, the
commanding General of the enemy's forces presented to his President an
argument against that line of operations, setting forth the advantages of a
movement by water-transports down the Chesapeake into the Rappahannock;
and that in the following February, by the direction of President Lincoln,
General McClellan held a council with twelve of the generals of that army, who
decided in favor of the movement by way of Annapolis, and thence to the
Rappahannock, to which their President gave his assent. When General
McClellan, then in the city of Washington, heard that our army had retired, he
ordered a general movement of his troops toward the position we had lately
occupied. A detachment was sent to make reconnaissance as far as the line of
the Rappahannock, by which it was ascertained that our troops had passed
beyond that river. His account of this movement was given in the following
report:

"FAIRFAX COURT-HOUSE, *March 11, 1862,* 8.30 P.M.

"I have just returned from a ride of more than forty miles.
Have examined Centreville, Union Mills, Blackburn's Ford, etc.
The rebels have left all their positions, and, from the
information obtained during our ride to-day, I am satisfied
that they have fallen behind the Rapidan, holding
Fredericksburg and Gordonsville. Their movement from here
was very sudden. They left many wagons, some caissons,
clothing, ammunition, personal baggage, etc. Their winter-
quarters were admirably constructed, many not yet quite
finished. The works at Centreville are formidable; more so than
at Manassas. Except the turnpike, the roads are horrible. The
country entirely stripped of forage and provisions. Having fully
consulted with General McDowell, I propose occupying
Manassas with a portion of Banks's command, and then at
once throwing all forces I can concentrate upon the line agreed
upon last week. The Monitor justifies this course. I telegraphed
this morning to have the transports brought to Washington, to
start from there. I presume you will approve this course.
Circumstances may keep me out here some little time
longer.[20]

"G. B. MCCLELLAN, *Major-General.*

"Hon. E. M. STANTON, *Secretary of War.*"

The reference to the Monitor is to be explained by the condition previously
made in connection with the proposition of going to Fortress Monroe, that the

Merrimac, our Virginia, should first be neutralized. The order to bring the "transports" to Washington was due to the fact that they had not dared to run by our batteries on the Potomac, and intended to avoid them by going to Annapolis for embarkation. The withdrawal of our batteries from the banks of the Potomac had removed the objection to going down that river, and the withdrawal of our forces across the Rappahannock was fatal to the programme of landing on that river, and marching to Richmond before our forces could be in position to resist an attack on the capital. Notwithstanding the assurance given that the destruction of railroads and bridges proved that our army could not intend to advance, apprehension was still entertained of an attack upon Washington.

As soon as we ascertained that the enemy was concentrating his forces at Fortress Monroe, to advance upon our capital by that line of approach, all our disposable force was ordered to the Peninsula, between the James and York Rivers, to the support of General John B. Magruder, who, with a force of seven to eight thousand men, had, by availing himself of the Warwick River, a small stream which runs through a low, marshy country, from near Yorktown to the James River, constructed an intrenched line across the Peninsula, and with equal skill and intrepidity had thus far successfully checked every attempt to break it, though the enemy was vastly superior in numbers to the troops under General Magruder's command. Having a force entirely inadequate to occupy and defend the whole line, over thirteen miles long, he built dams in the Warwick River, so as to form pools, across which the enemy, without bridges, could not pass, and posted detachments at each dam to prevent the use of them by attacking columns of the enemy. To defend the left of his line, where the stream became too small to present a serious obstacle to the passage of troops, redoubts were constructed, with curtains connecting them.

Between Yorktown and Gloucester Point, on the opposite shore, the York River is contracted to less than a mile in width, and General Magruder had constructed batteries at both places, which, by their cross fire, presented a formidable obstacle to the accent of ordinary vessels. The fortifications at Norfolk and the navy-yard, together with batteries at Sewell's Point and Craney Island, in conjunction with the navy, offered means of defense against any attempt to land troops on the south side of James River. After the first trial of strength with our Virginia, there had been an evident disinclination on the part of the enemy's vessels to encounter her, so that, as long as she floated, the deep water of the roads and mouth of James River. was not likely to be invaded by ships of war.

As a second line of defense, a system of detached works had been constructed by General Magruder near to Williamsburg, where the width of the Peninsula, available for the passage of troops, was only three or four miles. The advantage thus secured to his forces, if they should be compelled to retreat, will be readily appreciated. I am not aware that torpedoes had been placed in York River to prevent the entrance of the enemy's vessels; indeed, at that time, but little progress had been made in the development of that means of harbor and river defense. General Rains, as will be seen hereafter, had matured his invention of sensitive fuse-primers for sub-terra shells, and proposed their use for floating torpedoes. Subsequently he did much to advance knowledge in regard to making torpedoes efficient against the enemy's vessels.

Such was the condition of the Virginia Peninsula between the York and James Rivers when General McClellan embarked the mass of the army he commanded in northern Virginia and proceeded to Fortress Monroe; and when the greater part of our army, under the command of General J. E. Johnston, was directed to move for the purpose of counteracting this new plan of the enemy.

Early in April, General McClellan had landed about one hundred thousand men at or near Fortress Monroe.[21] At this time General Magruder occupied the lower Peninsula with his force of seven or eight thousand men. Marshes, creeks, and dense wood gave to that position such advantage that, in his report, made at a subsequent period, he expressed the belief that with twenty or twenty-five thousand men he could have held it against any supposable attack. When McClellan advanced with his immense army, Magruder fell back to the line of Warwick River, which has been imperfectly described, and there checked the enemy; and the vast army of invasion, repulsed in several assaults by the most heroic conduct of our troops, commenced a siege by regular approaches. After the first advance of the enemy, General Magruder was reënforced by some troops from the south side of James River and General Wilcox's brigade, which had been previously detached from the army under General Johnston. On the 9th of April General Magruder's command, thus reënforced, amounted to about twelve thousand. On that day General Early joined with his division from the Army of Northern Virginia. It had gone by rail to Richmond and thence down the York and James Rivers in vessels towed by tugs—except the trains and artillery, which moved by land. This division had about eight thousand officers and men for duty. General Magruder's force was thus increased to about twenty thousand. This was the first detachment from the Army of Northern Virginia which arrived on the Peninsula.

General McClellan, in a cipher dispatch of the 7th of April, two days previous, informed Secretary Stanton that prisoners stated that General J. E. Wharton (no doubt, Johnston) had the day before arrived in Yorktown with strong reënforcements, and adds: "It seems clear that I shall have the whole force of the enemy on my hands, probably not less than one hundred thousand men, and possibly more. . . . When my present command all joins, I shall have about eighty-five thousand men for duty, from which a large force must be taken for guards, escort, etc." After some remarks about the strength of our intrenchments, and his conviction that the great battle which would decide the existing contest would be fought there, he urges as necessary for his success that there should be an attack on the rear of Gloucester Point, and adds: "My present strength will not admit of a detachment for this purpose without materially impairing the efficiency of this column. Commodore Goldsborough thinks the work too strong for his available vessels, unless I can turn Gloucester." [22]

In the cipher dispatch of the 7th of April to President Lincoln, General McClellan acknowledges a telegram of the previous day, and adds, "In reply, I have the honor to state that my entire force for duty only amounts to about eighty-five thousand men." [23] He then mentions the fact that General Wool's command is not under his orders, etc.

Subsequent correspondence clearly shows that General McClellan would not risk making a detachment from his army to turn the position at Gloucester Point, and that the navy would not attempt to operate against the battery at that place. He therefore urgently pressed for reënforcements to act on the north side of York River.

General Magruder had, up to and after the time of receiving the reënforcements before mentioned, worked day and night in constructing and strengthening his defenses. His small force had been assisted in this work by a considerable body of negro laborers, and an active participant and competent judge, General Early, thus wrote of his conduct:

"The assuming and maintaining this line by Magruder, with his small force, in the face of such overwhelming odds, was one of the boldest exploits ever performed by a military commander; and he had so manoeuvred his troops, by displaying them rapidly at different points, as to produce the impression on his opponent that he had a large army."

As soon as it was definitely ascertained that General McClellan, with his main army, was on the Peninsula, General J. E. Johnston was assigned to the command of the Department of the Peninsula and Norfolk, and directed to proceed thither to examine the condition of affairs there. After spending a day on General Magruder's defensive line, he returned to Richmond, and recommended the abandonment of the Peninsula, and that we should take a defensive position nearer to Richmond. The question was postponed, and an appointment made for its discussion, to which I proposed to invite the Secretary of War, General Randolph, and General Lee, then stationed in Richmond, and in general charge of army operations. General Johnston asked that he might invite General Longstreet and General G. W. Smith to be present, to which I assented.

At this meeting. General Johnston announced his plan to be, the withdrawal of General Magruder's troops from the Peninsula, and of General Huger's from Norfolk, to be united with the main body of the Army of Northern Virginia, and the withdrawal of the troops from South Carolina and Georgia, his belief being that General Magruder's line was indefensible with the forces we could concentrate there; that the batteries at Gloucester Point could not be maintained; that the enemy would turn the position at Yorktown by ascending the York River, if the defensive line there should possibly be maintained. To this plan the Secretary of War objected, because the navy-yard at Norfolk offered our best if not our only opportunity to construct in any short time gunboats for coastwise and harbor defense. General Lee, always bold in his views and unusually sagacious in penetrating the designs of the enemy, insisted that the Peninsula offered great advantages to a smaller force in resisting a numerically superior assailant, and, in the comprehensive view which he usually took of the necessities of other places than the one where he chanced to be, objected to withdrawing the troops from South Carolina and Georgia, as involving the probable capture of Charleston and Savannah. By recent service in that section he was well informed as to the condition of those important ports. General G. W. Smith, as well as I remember, was in full accord with General Johnston, and General Longstreet partially so.

After hearing fully the views of the several officers named, I decided to resist the enemy on the Peninsula, and, with the aid of the navy, to hold Norfolk and keep the command of the James River as long as possible. Arrangements were made, with such force as our means permitted, to occupy the country north of Richmond, and the Shenandoah Valley, and, with the rest of General Johnston's command, to make a junction with General Magruder to resist the enemy's forces on the Peninsula. Though General J. E. Johnston did not agree with this decision, he did not ask to be relieved, and I had no wish to separate him from the troops with whom he was so intimately acquainted, and whose confidence I believed he deservedly possessed.

To recur to General Magruder: soon after the landing of the enemy, skirmishes commenced with our forces, and the first vigorous attempt was made to break the line at Lee's Mills, where there were some newly constructed defenses. The enemy was so signally repulsed that he described them as very strong works, and thereafter commenced the construction of parallels and regular approaches, having an exaggerated idea as well of the number of our troops as of the strength of our works at that time. General Magruder, in his report, notices a serious attempt to break his line of the Warwick at Dam No. 1, about the center of the line, and its weakest point. Opening with a heavy bombardment at nine in the morning, which continued until three P.M., heavy masses of infantry then commenced to deploy, and, with musketry-fire, were thrown forward to storm our six-pounder battery, which had been effectively used, and was the only artillery we had there in position. A portion of the column charged across the dam, but Brigadier-General Howell Cobb met the attack with great firmness, the enemy was driven with the bayonet from some of our rifle-pits of which he had gained possession, and the assaulting column recoiled with loss from the steady fire of our troops.

The enemy's skirmishers pressed closely in front of the redoubts on the left of our line, and with their long-range rifles had a decided advantage over our men, armed with smooth-bore muskets. In addition to the rifle-pits they dug, they were covered by a dwelling-house and a large peach-orchard which extended to within a few hundred yards of our works. On the 11th of April General Magruder ordered sorties to be made from all the main points of his line. General Wilcox sent out a detachment from Wynne's Mill which encountered the advance of the enemy in his front and drove it back to the main line. Later in the day General Early sent out from Redoubt No. 5 Colonel Ward's Florida regiment and the Second Mississippi Battalion, under Colonel Taylor. They drove the sharpshooters from their rifle-pits and pursued them to the main road from Warwick Court-House, encountered a battery posted at an earthwork, and compelled it precipitately to retire. On the approach of a large force of the enemy's infantry, Colonel Ward returned to our works, after having set fire to the dwelling-house above mentioned. These affairs developed the fact that the enemy was in strong force, both in front of Wynne's Mill and Redoubts Nos. 4 and 5. On the next night General Early sent out Colonel Terry's Virginia regiment to cut down the peach-orchard and burn the rest of the houses which had afforded shelter to the assailants; and on the succeeding night Colonel McRae, with his North Carolina regiment, went farther to the front and felled the cedars along the main road which partially hid the enemy's movements, and subsequently our men were not annoyed by the sharpshooters. About the middle of April a further reënforcement of two divisions from the Army of Northern Virginia was added to our forces on the Peninsula, which amounted, when General Johnston assumed command, to something over fifty thousand.

The work of strengthening the defenses was still continued. On the 16th of April an assault was made on our line, to the right of Yorktown, which was repulsed with heavy loss to the enemy, and such serious discomfiture that henceforward his plan seemed to be to rely upon bombardment, for which numerous batteries were prepared.

The views of the enemy, as revealed by the testimony before the Committee on the Conduct of the War, were that he could gain possession of Gloucester Point only by reënforcements operating on the north side of York River, or by the previous reduction of Yorktown. In addition to the answer given by General McClellan, I quote from the testimony of General Keyes. He said, "The possession of Gloucester Point by the enemy retarded the taking of Yorktown, and it also enabled the enemy to close the river at that point," and added, "Gloucester must have fallen upon our getting possession of Yorktown, and the York River would then have been open." [24]

With the knowledge possessed by us, General McClellan certainly might have sent a detachment from his army which, after crossing the York River, could have turned the position at Gloucester Point and have overcome our small garrison at that place; but this is but one of the frequent examples of war in which the immunity of one army is derived from the mistakes of the other.

An opinion has existed among some of our best-informed officers that Franklin's division was kept on transports for the purpose of landing on the north side of York River to capture our battery at Gloucester Point, and thus open the way to turn our position by ascending the York River. Upon the authority of Swinton, the fairest and most careful of the Northern writers on the war, it appears that Franklin's division had disembarked before the evacuation of Yorktown; and, upon the authority of the Prince de Joinville, serving on the staff of General McClellan, it appears that his commanding general was not willing to intrust that service to a single division, and plaintively describes the effect produced by the refusal of President Lincoln to send McDowell's corps to reënforce McClellan. He writes thus:

"The news was received by the Federal army with dissatisfaction, although the majority could not then foresee the deplorable consequences of an act performed, it must be supposed, with no evil intention, but with inconceivable recklessness. . . . It was the mainspring removed from a great work already begun. It deranged everything. Among the divisions of the corps of McDowell, there was one—that of Franklin—which was regretted more than all the rest. . . . He [the commander-in-chief] held it in great esteem, and earnestly demanded its restoration. It was sent back to him without any explanation, in the same manner as it had been withheld. This splendid division, eleven thousand strong, arrived, and for a moment the commander thought of intrusting to it alone the storming of Gloucester, but the idea was abandoned."

On the 28th of April General J. E. Johnston wrote to Flag-Officer Tatnall, commanding the naval forces in the James River, requesting him, if practicable, to proceed with the Virginia to York River for the purpose of destroying the enemy's transports, to which Commodore Tatnall replied that it could only be done in daylight, when he would be exposed to the fire of the forts, and have to contend with the squadron of men-of-war stationed below them, and that, if this should be safely done, according to the information derived from the pilots, it would not be possible for the Virginia to reach the enemy's transports at Poquosin, while the withdrawal of the Virginia would be to abandon the defense of Norfolk, and to remove the obstacles she opposed to "the enemy's operations in the James River." [25]

Meanwhile, the brilliant movements of the intrepid Jackson created such apprehension of an attack upon Washington City by the Army of the Shenandoah, that President Lincoln refused the repeated requests of General McClellan to send him McDowell's corps to operate on the north side of the York River against our battery at Gloucester Point.

On the 28th of the following June, Mr. Lincoln, noticing what he regarded as ungenerous complaint, wrote to General McClellan: "If you have had a drawn battle or a repulse, it is the price we pay for the enemy not being in Washington. We protected Washington, and the enemy concentrated on you." [26]

The month of April was cold and rainy, and our men poorly provided with shelter, and with only the plainest rations; yet, under all these discomforts, they steadily labored to perfect the defenses, and, when they were not on the front line, were constantly employed in making traverses and epaulments in the rear. Whether General McClellan, under the pressure from Washington, would have made an early assault,[27] or have adhered to the policy of regular approaches, and, relying on his superiority in artillery, have waited to batter our earthworks in breach, and whether all which had been done, or which it was practicable under the circumstances to do, to strengthen the main line would have made it sufficiently strong to resist the threatened bombardment, is questionable; and how soon that bombardment would have commenced is now indeterminate. A telegram from President Lincoln to General McClellan is suggestive on this point. It reads thus:

"WASHINGTON, *May 1, 1862.*

"Your call for Parrott guns from Washington alarms me—chiefly because it argues indefinite procrastination. Is anything to be done?" [28]

By the following telegram sent by me to General J. E. Johnston, commanding at Yorktown, the contents of that which I had received from him, and of which I am not now possessed, will be readily inferred:

"RICHMOND, VIRGINIA, *May 1, 1862.*

"General J. E. JOHNSTON, *Yorktown, Virginia.*

"Accepting your conclusion that you must soon retire, arrangements are commenced for the abandonment of the navy-yard and removal of public property both from Norfolk and Peninsula. Your announcement to-day that you would withdraw to-morrow night takes us by surprise, and must involve enormous losses, including unfinished gunboats. Will the safety of your army allow more time?

64

"JEFFERSON DAVIS."

My next step was to request the Secretary of War, General Randolph, and the Secretary of the Navy, Mr. Mallory, to proceed to Yorktown and Norfolk to see whether the evacuation could not be postponed, and to make all practicable arrangements to remove the machinery, material, ordnance, and supplies for future use. At the suggestion of the Secretary of War, I agreed that he should first go with the Secretary of the Navy to Norfolk and thence pass over to Yorktown.

On the next morning they left for Norfolk. General Randolph, in his testimony before a joint special committee of the Confederate Congress, said:

"A few hours after we arrived in Norfolk, an officer from General Johnston's army made his appearance, with an order for General Huger to evacuate Norfolk immediately. . . . As that would have involved heavy losses in stores, munitions, and arms, I took the responsibility of giving General Huger a written order to delay the evacuation until he could remove such stores, munitions, and arms as could be carried off. . . . Mr. Mallory was with me and gave similar instructions to the commandant of the navy yard. . . . The evacuation was delayed for about a week. . . . When the council of war met [the conference with the President heretofore referred to], it was supposed that, if the enemy assaulted our army at the Warwick River line, we should defeat them; but that, if instead of assaulting they made regular approaches to either flank of the line and took advantage of their great superiority of heavy artillery, the probability would be that one flank or both of the army would be uncovered, and thus the enemy, ascending the York and James Rivers in transports, could turn the flank of the army and compel it to retreat. . . . They made regular approaches, mounted the largest-sized guns, such as we could not compete with, and made the position of Yorktown untenable. Nearly all of our heavy rifled guns burst during the siege. The remainder of the heavy guns were in the water-batteries," etc.

The permanent occupation of Norfolk after our army withdrew from the lower Peninsula and the enemy possessed it was so obviously impossible as not to require explanation; but, while the enemy was engaged in the pursuit of our retreating columns, it was deemed justifiable to delay the evacuation of Norfolk for the purposes indicated in the above answer of the Secretary of War. The result justified the decision.

The order for the withdrawal of the army from the line of the Warwick River on the night of the 2d of April was delayed until the next night, because, as I have been informed, some of the troops were not ready to move. Heavy cannonading, both on the night of the 2d and 3d, concealed the fact of the purpose to withdraw, and the evacuation was made so successfully, as appears by the testimony before the United States Congressional Committee on the Conduct of the War, that the enemy was surprised the next morning to find the lines unoccupied.

The loss of public property, as was anticipated, was great, the steamboats expected for its transportation not having arrived before the evacuation was made. From a narrative by General Early I make the following extract:

"A very valuable part of the property so lost, and which we stood much in need of, consisted of a very large number of picks and spades, many of them entirely new. All of our heavy guns, including some recently arrived and not mounted, together with a good deal of ammunition piled up on the wharf, had to be left behind."

The land transportation was quite deficient. General Magruder's troops had scarcely any, and others of the more recent organizations were in a like condition; as no supplies had been accumulated at Williamsburg, this want of transportation would necessarily involve want of rations in the event of delays on the retreat.

At Williamsburg, about twelve miles from Yorktown, General Magruder, as has been mentioned, had constructed a line of detached works. The largest of these, Fort Magruder, was constructed at a point a short distance beyond where the Lee's Mill and Yorktown roads united, and where the enemy in his pursuit first encountered our retiring forces, and were promptly repulsed. General Magruder, whose arduous service and long exposure on the Peninsula has been noticed, was compelled by illness to leave his division. His absence at this moment was the more to be regretted, as it appears that the positions of the redoubts he had constructed were not all known to the commanding General, and some of them being unoccupied were seized by the enemy, and held subsequently to our disadvantage. General McClellan, in his official report from "bivouac in front of Williamsburg, May 5, 1862," says, "General Hancock has taken two redoubts and repulsed Early's rebel brigade by a real charge of the bayonet, taking one colonel and one hundred and fifty other prisoners," etc. As this is selected for the brilliant event in the affair before Williamsburg, I will extract fully from General Early's report:

"LYNCHBURG, June 9, 1862.

"In accordance with orders received the evening before, my brigade was in readiness to take up the line of march from its camp west of Williamsburg toward Richmond on the 5th of May. . . . I was directed by Major-General D. H. Hill not to move my infantry, and in a short time I was ordered by him to march back, and report with my regiments to Major-General Longstreet at Williamsburg. . . . Between three and four o'clock, P.M., I was ordered by General Longstreet to move to the support of Brigadier-General Anderson of his division, at or near Fort Magruder. . . . Before my command had proceeded far toward its destination, I received an order from General Longstreet to send him two regiments. . . . With the remainder of my command, being my brigade proper, I proceeded, as near as practicable, to the position designated by General Longstreet on the left and rear of Fort Magruder. . . . In a short time Major-General Hill arrived, and, having ascertained that the enemy had a battery in front of us, he informed me that he wished me to attack and capture the battery with my brigade, but before doing so he must see General Longstreet on the subject. . . . General Hill being on the right and accompanying the brigade, I placed myself on the left with the Twenty-fourth Virginia Regiment for the purpose of directing its movements, as I was satisfied from the sound of the enemy's guns that this regiment would come directly on the battery. . . . In an open field, in view of Fort Magruder, at the end farthest from the fort, the enemy had taken position with a battery of six pieces . . . supported by a brigade of infantry under the command of Brigadier-General Hancock. In this field were two or three redoubts, previously built by our troops, of one, at least, of which the enemy had possession, his artillery being posted in front of it, near some farmhouses, and supported by a body of infantry, the balance of the infantry being in the redoubt, and in the edge of the woods close by. The Twenty-fourth Virginia Regiment, as I had anticipated, came directly upon the battery. . . . This regiment, without pausing or wavering, charged upon the enemy under a heavy fire, and drove back his guns and the infantry supporting them to the cover of the redoubt. ... I sent orders to the other regiments to advance; these orders were anticipated by Colonel McRae of the Fifth North Carolina Regiment, who was on the extreme right of my brigade, and marched down to the support of the Twenty-fourth, traversing the whole front that should have been occupied by the other two regiments."

General Early, having received a severe wound, soon after the Twenty-fourth Virginia Regiment charged the battery, was compelled by exhaustion from loss of blood and intense pain to leave the field just as the Fifth North Carolina Regiment, led by its gallant colonel, charged on the enemy's artillery and infantry. Of that charge General Early writes:

"This North Carolina Regiment, in conjunction with the Twenty-fourth Virginia Regiment, made an attack upon the vastly superior forces of the enemy, which for its gallantry is unsurpassed in the annals of warfare: their conduct was such as to elicit from the enemy himself the highest praise."

This refers to the chivalric remark made by General Hancock to Dr. Cullen, left in charge of our wounded, viz., "The Fifth North Carolina and Twenty-fourth Virginia deserve to have the word immortal inscribed on their banners." Colonel McRae, who succeeded to the command after General Early retired, states in his report that he sent to General Hill for reënforcements in order to advance, and in reply received an order to retire: that his men were holding the enemy to his shelter in such way that they were not at all suffering, but, when he commenced retiring, the enemy rose and fired upon his men, doing the greatest damage that was done. Some of them obliqued too far to the right in going back, and met a regiment of the enemy concealed in the woods, and were thus captured. General Early writes: "The two regiments that united in the assault were not repulsed at all. They drove the enemy to the cover of the redoubt and the shelter of the woods near it, where he was held at bay by my two regiments, which had suffered comparatively little at that time." He confidently expresses the opinion that, had his attack been supported promptly and vigorously, the enemy's force there engaged must have been captured, as it had crossed over to that point on a narrow mill-dam, and had only that way to escape.

The claim of the enemy to have achieved a victory at Williamsburg is refuted by the fact that our troops remained in possession of the field during the night, and retired the next morning to follow up the retreat, which was only interrupted by the necessity of checking the enemy until our trains could proceed far enough to be out of danger. The fact of our wounded being left at Williamsburg was only due to our want of ambulances in which to remove them.

Though General McClellan at this time estimated our force as "probably greater a good deal" than his own, the fact is, it was numerically less than half the number he had for duty. Severe exposure and fatigue must, by sickness, have diminished our force more than it was increased by absentees returning to duty after the middle of April, so that at the end of the month the number was probably less than fifty thousand present for duty. General McClellan's report on the 30th of April, 1862, as shown by the certified statement, gives the aggregate present for duty at one hundred and twelve thousand three hundred and ninety-two.[29]

When the Confederates evacuated Yorktown, General Franklin's division had just been disembarked from the transports. It was reembarked, and started on the morning of the 6th up the York River.[30]

After the battle of Williamsburg our army continued its retreat up the Peninsula. Here, for the first time, sub-terra shells were employed to check a marching column. The event is thus described by General Rains, the inventor:

"On the day we left Williamsburg, after the battle, we worked hard to get our artillery and some we had captured over the sloughs about four miles distant. On account of the tortuous course of the road, we could not bring a single gun to bear upon the enemy who were pursuing us, and shelling the road as they advanced. Fortunately, we found in a mud-hole a broken-down ammunition-wagon containing five loaded shells. Four of these, armed with a sensitive fuse-primer, were planted in our rear, near some trees cut down as obstructions to the road. A body of the enemy's cavalry came upon these sub-terra shells, and they exploded with terrific effect.

"The force behind halted for three days, and finally turned off from the road, doubtless under the apprehension that it was mined throughout. Thus our rear was relieved of the enemy. No soldier will march over mined land, and a corps of sappers, each man having two ten-inch shells, two primers, and a mule to carry them, could stop any army."

Accounts, contemporaneously published at the North, represent the terror inspired by these shells, extravagantly describe the number of them, and speak of the necessity of leaving the road to avoid them.

The next morning after the battle of the 5th, at Williamsburg, Longstreet's and D. H. Hill's divisions, being those there engaged, followed in the line of retreat, Stuart's cavalry moving after them— they marched that day about twelve

68

miles. In the mean time Franklin's division had gone up the York River, and landed a short distance below West Point, on the south side of York River, and moved into a thick wood in the direction of the New Kent road, thus threatening the flank of our line of march. Two brigades of General G. W. Smith's division, Hampton's and Hood's, were detached under the command of General Whiting to dislodge the enemy, which they did after a short conflict, driving him through the wood to the protection of his gunboats in York River.

On the next morning the rear divisions joined those in advance at Barhamsville, and the retreat of the whole army was resumed—Smith's and Magruder's divisions moving by the New Kent Court-House to the Baltimore Cross Roads, and Longstreet's and Hill's to the Long Bridge, where the whole army remained in line facing to the east for five days.

The retreat had been successfully conducted. In the principal action, that at Williamsburg, our forces, after General Hill's division had been brought back to the support of General Longstreet, did not exceed, probably was not equal to, one half that of the enemy. Yet, as has been seen, the position was held as long as was necessary for the removal of our trains, and our troops slept upon the field of battle. The loss of the enemy greatly exceeded our own, which was about twelve hundred; while General Hooker, commanding one division of the Federal army, in his testimony stated the loss in his division to have been seventeen hundred.[31]

Among the gallant and much regretted of those lost by us, was Colonel Ward, of Florida, whose conduct at Yorktown has been previously noticed, and of whom General Early, in his report of the battle of Williamsburg, says:

> "On the list of the killed in the Second Florida Regiment is found the name of its colonel, George T. Ward, as true a gentleman and as gallant a soldier as has drawn a sword in this war, and whose conduct under fire it was my fortune to witness on another occasion. His loss to his regiment, to his State, and to the Confederacy can not be easily compensated."

Colonel Ward, with his regiment, had been detached from General Early's command in the early part of the action. I regret that I have not access to the report of General Longstreet, where, no doubt, may also be found due notice of Colonel Christopher Mott, whom I knew personally. In his youth he served in the regiment commanded by me during the war with Mexico. He was brave, cheerful, prompt, and equal to every trial to which he was subjected, giving early promise of high soldierly capacity. He afterward held various places of honor and trust in civil life, and there were many in Mississippi who, like myself, deeply lamented his death in the height of his usefulness.

General Huger, commanding at Norfolk, and Captain Lee, commanding the navy-yard, by the authority of the Secretaries of War and Navy, delayed the evacuation of both, as stated by General Randolph, Secretary of War, for about a week after General Johnston sent orders to General Huger to leave immediately. While he was employed in removing the valuable stores and machinery, as we learn from the work of the Comte de Paris, President Lincoln and his Secretary of War arrived at Fortress Monroe, and on the 8th of May an expedition against Norfolk by the troops under General Wool was contemplated. He writes:

"Being apprised by the columns of smoke which rose on the horizon that the propitious moment had arrived, Wool proposed to the President to undertake an expedition against Norfolk. Max Weber's brigade was speedily embarked, and, to protect his descent, Commodore Goldsborough's fleet was ordered to escort it. But the Confederate batteries, not yet having been abandoned, fired a few shots in reply, while the Virginia, which, since the wounding of the brave Buchanan, had been commanded by Commodore Tatnall, showed her formidable shell, and the expedition was countermanded. Two more days were consumed in waiting. Finally, on the morning of the 10th, Weber disembarked east of Sewell's Point. This time the enemy's artillery was silent. There was found an intrenched camp mounting a few guns, but absolutely deserted. General Wool reached the city of Norfolk, which had been given up to its peaceful inhabitants the day previous, and hastened to place a military governor there." [32]

Reposing on these cheaply won laurels, the expedition returned to Fortress Monroe, leaving Brigadier-General Viele, with some troops brought from the north side of the river, to hold the place. The navy-yard and workshops had been set on fire before our troops withdrew, so as to leave little to the enemy save the glory of capturing an undefended town. The troops at Fortress Monroe were numerically superior to the command of General Huger, and could have been readily combined, with the forces at and about Roanoke Island, for a forward movement on the south side of the James River. In view of this probability, General Huger, with the main part of his force, was halted for a time at Petersburg, but, as soon as it was ascertained that no preparations were being made by the enemy for that campaign, so palpably advantageous to him, General Huger's troops were moved to the north side of the James River to make a junction with the army of General Johnston.

Previously, detachments had been sent from the force withdrawn from Norfolk to strengthen the command of Brigadier-General J. B. Anderson, who was placed in observation before General McDowell, then at Fredericksburg, threatening to advance with a force four or five times as great as that under General Anderson, and another detachment had been sent to the aid of Brigadier-General Branch, who, with his brigade, had recently been brought up from North Carolina and sent forward to Gordonsville, for the like purpose as that for which General Anderson was placed near Fredericksburg.

[Footnote 20: See "Report on the Conduct of the War," Part I, pp. 10-12, 309-311.]

[Footnote 21: See "Report on the Conduct of the War," p. 319. Letter of President Lincoln to General McClellan, April 6, 1862.]

[Footnote 22: "Report on the Conduct of the War," Part I, p. 320.]

[Footnote 23: Ibid., p. 321.]

[Footnote 24: "Report on the Conduct of the War," Part I, pp. 601, 602.]

[Footnote 25: "Life of Commodore Tatnall," pp. 166, 167.]

[Footnote 26: "Report on the Conduct of the War," p. 340.]

[Footnote 27: On April 6, 1862, President Lincoln wrote to General McClellan as follows: "You now have over one hundred thousand troops with you, independent of General Wool's command. I think you had better break the enemy's line from Yorktown to Warwick River at once. They will probably use time as advantageously as you can."—("Report on the Conduct of the War," pp. 319, 320.)]

[Footnote 28: "Report on the Conduct of the War," p. 324.]

[Footnote 29: "Report on the Conduct of the War," pp. 323, 324.]

[Footnote 30: "Army of the Potomac," Swinton, p. 117.]

[Footnote 31: "Report on the Conduct of the War," p. 579.]

[Footnote 32: "History of the Civil War in America," Comte de Paris, vol. ii, p. 30.]

CHAPTER XXI.

A New Phase to our Military Problem.—General Johnston's Position.—Defenses of James River.—Attack on Fort Drury.—Johnston crosses the Chickahominy.—Position of McClellan.—Position of McDowell.—Strength of Opposing Forces.—Jackson's Expedition down the Shenandoah Valley.—Panic at Washington and the North.—Movements to intercept Jackson.—His Rapid Movements.—Repulses Fremont.—Advance of Shields.—Fall of Ashby.—Port Republic, Battle of.—Results of this Campaign.

The withdrawal of our army to the Chickahominy, the abandonment of Norfolk, the destruction of the Virginia, and opening of the lower James River, together with the fact that McClellan's army, by changing his base to the head of York River, was in a position to cover the approach to Washington, and thus to remove the objections which had been made to sending the large force, retained for the defense of that city, to make a junction with McClellan, all combined to give a new phase to our military problem.

Soon after, General Johnston took position on the north side of the Chickahominy; accompanied by General Lee, I rode out to his headquarters in the field, in order that by conversation with him we might better understand his plans and expectations. He came in after we arrived, saying that he had been riding around his lines to see how his position could be improved. A long conversation followed, which was so inconclusive that it lasted until late in the night, so late that we remained until the next morning. As we rode back to Richmond, reference was naturally made to the conversation of the previous evening and night, when General Lee confessed himself, as I was, unable to draw from it any more definite purpose than that the policy was to improve his position as far as practicable, and wait for the enemy to leave his gunboats, so that an opportunity might be offered to meet him on the land.

In consequence of the opening of the James River to the enemy's fleet, the attempts to utilize this channel for transportation, so as to approach directly to Richmond, soon followed. We had then no defenses on the James River below Drury's Bluff, about seven miles distant from Richmond. There an earthwork had been constructed and provided with an armament of four guns. Rifle-pits had been made in front of the fort, and obstructions had been placed in the river by driving piles, and sinking some vessels. The crew of the Virginia, after her destruction, had been sent to this fort, which was then in charge of Commander Farrand, Confederate States Navy.

On the 15th of April the enemy's fleet of five ships of war, among the number, their much-vaunted Monitor, took position and opened fire upon the fort between seven and eight o'clock. Our small vessel, the Patrick Henry, was lying above the obstruction, and coöperated with the fort in its defense—the Monitor and ironclad Galena steamed up to about six hundred yards' distance; the others, wooden vessels, were kept at long range.

The armor of the flag-ship Galena was badly injured, and many of the crew killed or wounded. The Monitor was struck repeatedly, but the shot only bent her plates. At about eleven o'clock the fleet abandoned the attack, returning discomfited whence they came. The commander of the Monitor, Lieutenant Jeffers, in his report, says that "the action was most gallantly fought against great odds, and with the usual effect against earthworks." . . . He adds, "It was impossible to reduce such works, except with the aid of a land force." The enemy in their reports recognized the efficiency of our fire by both artillery and riflemen, the sincerity of which was made manifest in the failure to renew the attempt.

The small garrison at Fort Drury, only adequate to the service it had performed, that of repelling an attempt by the fleet to pass up James River, was quite insufficient to prevent the enemy from landing below the fort, or to resist an attack by infantry. To guard against its sudden capture by such means, the garrison was increased by the addition of Bryan's regiment of Georgia Rifles.

After the repulse of the enemy's gunboats at Drury's Bluff, I wrote to General Johnston a letter to be handed to him by my aide, Colonel G. W. C. Lee, an officer of the highest intelligence and reputation— referring to him for full information in regard to the affair at Drury's Bluff, as well as to the positions and strength of our forces on the south side of the James River. After some speculations on the probable course of the enemy, and expressions of confidence, I informed the General that my aide would communicate freely to him and bring back to me any information with which he might be intrusted. Not receiving any definite reply, I soon thereafter rode out to visit General Johnston at his headquarters, and was surprised in the suburbs of Richmond, viz., on the other side of Gillis's Creek, to meet a portion of light artillery, and to learn that the whole army had crossed the Chickahominy.

General Johnston's explanation to this (to me) unexpected movement was, that he thought the water of the Chickahominy unhealthy, and had directed the troops to cross and halt at the first good water on the southern side, which he supposed would be found near to the river. He also adverted to the advantage of having the river in front rather than in the rear of him—an advantage certainly obvious enough, if the line was to be near to it on either of its banks.

The considerations which induced General McClellan to make his base on the York River had at least partly ceased to exist. From the corps for which he had so persistently applied, he had received the division which he most valued, and the destruction of the Virginia had left the James River open to his fleet and transports as far up as Drury's Bluff, and the withdrawal of General Johnston across the Chickahominy made it quite practicable for him to transfer his army to the James River, the south side of which had then but weak defenses, and thus by a short march to gain more than all the advantages which, at a later period of the war, General Grant obtained at the sacrifice of a hecatomb of soldiers.

Referring, again, to the work of the Comte de Paris, who may be better authority in regard to what occurred in the army of the enemy than when he writes about Confederate affairs, it appears that this change of base was considered and not adopted because of General McClellan's continued desire to have McDowell's corps with him. The Count states:

"The James River, which had been closed until then by the presence of the Virginia, as York River had been by the cannon of Yorktown, was opened by the destruction of that ship, just as York River had been by the evacuation of the Confederate fortress. But it was only open as far as Drury's Bluff; in order to overcome this last obstacle interposed between Richmond and the Federal gunboats, the support of the land forces was necessary. On the 19th of May Commodore Goldsborough had a conference with General McClellan regarding the means to be employed for removing that obstacle. . . . General McClellan, as we have stated above, might have continued to follow the railway line, and preserved his depots at Whitehouse, on the Pamunkey, . . . but he could also now go to reestablish his base of operations on James River, which the Virginia had hitherto prevented him from doing. By crossing the Chickahominy at Bottom's Bridge, and some other fords situated lower down, . . . could have reached the borders of the James in two or three days. . . . This flank march effected at a sufficient distance from the enemy, and covered by a few demonstrations along the upper Chickahominy, offered him great advantages without involving any risk. . . . If McClellan could have foreseen how deceptive were the promises of reënforcement made to him at the time, he would undoubtedly have declined the uncertain support of McDowell, to carry out the plan of campaign which offered the best chances of success with the troops which were absolutely at his disposal." [33]

Without feeling under any obligations for kind intentions on the part of the Government of the North, it was fortunate for us that it did, as its friend the Comte de Paris represents, deceive General McClellan, and prevent him from moving to the south side of the James River, so as not only to secure the coöperation of his gunboats in an attack upon Richmond, but to make his assault on the side least prepared for resistance, and where it would have been quite possible to cut our line of communication with the more Southern States on which we chiefly depended for supplies and reënforcements.

It is hardly just to treat the failure to fulfill the assurance given by President Lincoln about reënforcements as "deceptive promises," for, as will be seen, the operations in the Valley by General Jackson, who there exhibited a rapidity of movement equal to the unyielding tenacity which had in the first great battle won for him the familiar name "Stonewall," had created such an alarm in Washington, as, if it had been better founded, would have justified the refusal to diminish the force held for the protection of their capital. Indeed, our cavalry, in observation near Fredericksburg, reported that on the 24th McDowell's troops started southward, but General Stuart found that night that they were returning. This indicated that the anticipated junction was not to be made, and of this the Prince of Joinville writes:

"It needed only an effort of the will: the two armies were united, and in the possession of Richmond certain! Alas! this effort was not made. I can not recall those fatal moments without a real sinking of the heart." [34]

General McClellan, in his testimony December 10, 1862, before the court-martial in the case of General McDowell, said:

"I have no doubt, for it has ever been my opinion, that the Army of the Potomac would have taken Richmond had not the corps of General McDowell been separated from it. It is also my opinion that, had the command of General McDowell joined the Army of the Potomac in the month of May, by the way of Hanover Court-House, from Fredericksburg, we would have had Richmond within a week after the junction." [35]

Let us first inquire what was the size of this army so crippled for want of reënforcement, and then what the strength of that to which it was opposed. On the 30th of April, 1862, the official report of McClellan's army gives the aggregate present for duty as 112,392;[36] that of the 20th of June—omitting the army corps of General Dix, then, as previously, stationed at Fortress Monroe, and including General McCall's division, which had recently joined, the strength of which was reported to be 9,514—gives the aggregate present for duty as 105,825, and the total, present and absent, as 156,838.[37]

Two statements of the strength of our army under General J. E. Johnston during the month of May—in which General McClellan testified that he was greatly in need of McDowell's corps—give the following results: First, the official return, 21st May, 1862, total effective of all arms, 53,688; subsequently, five brigades were added, and the effective strength of the army under General Johnston on May 31, 1862, was 62,696.[38]

I now proceed to inquire what caused the panic at Washington.

On May 23d, General Jackson, with whose force that of General Ewell had united, moved with such rapidity as to surprise the enemy, and Ewell, who was in advance, captured most of the troops at Front Royal, and pressed directly on to Winchester, while Jackson, turning across to the road from Strasburg, struck the main column of the enemy in flank and drove it routed back to Strasburg. The pursuit was continued to Winchester, and the enemy, under their commander-in-chief, General Banks, fled across the Potomac into Maryland. Two thousand prisoners were taken in the pursuit. General Banks in his report says, "There never were more grateful hearts in the same number of men, than when, at mid-day on the 26th, we stood on the opposite shore."

When the news of the attack on Front Royal, on May 23d, reached General Geary, charged with the protection of the Manassas Gap Railroad, he immediately moved to Manassas Junction. At the same time, his troops, hearing the most extravagant stories, burned their tents and destroyed a quantity of arms. General Duryea, at Catlett's Station, becoming alarmed on hearing of the withdrawal of Geary, took his three New York regiments, leaving a Pennsylvania one behind, hastened back to Centreville, and telegraphed to Washington for aid. He left behind a large quantity of army stores. The alarm spread to

Washington, and the Secretary of War, Stanton, issued a call to the Governors of the "loyal" States for militia to defend that city.

[Illustration: Lieutenant-General T. J. Jackson.]

The following is the dispatch sent to the Governor of Massachusetts:

"WASHINGTON, *Sunday, May 25, 1862.*

"*To the Governor of Massachusetts.*

"Intelligence from various quarters leaves no doubt that the enemy in great force are marching on Washington. You will please organize and forward immediately all the militia and volunteer force in your State.

"EDWIN M. STANTON, *Secretary of War.*"

This alarm at Washington, and the call for more troops for its defense, produced a most indescribable panic in the cities of the Northern States on Sunday the 25th, and two or three days afterward. The Governor of New York on Sunday night telegraphed to Buffalo, Rochester, Syracuse, and other cities, as follows:

"Orders from Washington render it necessary to send to that city all the available militia force. What can you do?

"E. D. MORGAN."

Governor Curtin, of Pennsylvania, issued the following order:

"(GENERAL ORDER, No. 23.)

"HEADQUARTERS OF PENNSYLVANIA MILITIA,

"Harrisburg, *May 26, 1862.*

"On pressing requisition of the President of the United States in the present emergency, it is ordered that the several major-generals, brigadier-generals, and colonels of regiments throughout the Commonwealth muster without delay all military organizations within their respective divisions or under their control, together with all persons willing to join their commands, and proceed forthwith to the city of Washington, or such other points as may be designated by future orders. By order:

"A. G. CURTIN,

"*Governor and Commander-in-Chief.*"

The Governor of Massachusetts issued the following proclamation:

"*Men of Massachusetts!*

"The wily and barbarous horde of traitors to the people, to the Government, to our country, and to liberty, menace again the national capital. They have attacked and routed Major-General Banks, are advancing on Harper's Ferry, and are marching on Washington. The President calls on Massachusetts to rise once more for its rescue and defense.

"The whole active militia will be summoned by a general order, issued from the office of the adjutant-general, to report on Boston Common to-morrow. They will march to relieve and avenge their brethren and friends, and to oppose, with fierce zeal and courageous patriotism, the progress of the foe. May God encourage their hearts and strengthen their arms, and may he inspire the Government and all the people!

> "Given at headquarters, Boston, eleven o'clock, this (Sunday) evening. May 25, 1862.

"JOHN A. ANDREW."

The Governor of Ohio issued the following proclamation:

"COLUMBUS, Ohio, *May 26, 1862.*

"*To the gallant men of Ohio.*

> "I have the astounding intelligence that the seat of our beloved Government is threatened with invasion, and am called upon by the Secretary of War for troops to repel and overwhelm the ruthless invaders. Rally, then, men of Ohio, and respond to this call, as becomes those who appreciate our glorious Government! . . . The number wanted from each county has been indicated by special dispatches to the several military committees.

"DAVID TOD, *Governor.*"

At the same time the Secretary of War at Washington caused the following order to be issued:

"WASHINGTON, *Sunday, May 25, 1862.*

> "*Ordered:* By virtue of the authority vested by an act of Congress, the President takes military possession of all the railroads in the United States from and after this date, and directs that the respective railroad companies, their officers and servants, shall hold themselves in readiness for the transportation of troops and munitions of war, as may be ordered by the military authorities, to the exclusion of all other business.

"By order of the Secretary of War:

"M. C. MEIGS,

"*Quartermaster-General.*"

At the first moment of the alarm, the President of the United States issued the following order:

"WASHINGTON, *May 24 1862.*

"Major-General MCDOWELL.

"General Fremont has been ordered by telegraph to move to Franklin and Harrisonburg to relieve General Banks and capture or destroy Jackson's and Ewell's forces. You are instructed, laying aside for the present the movement on Richmond, to put twenty thousand men in motion at once for the Shenandoah, moving on the line or in advance of the line of the Manassas Gap Railroad. Your object will be to capture the forces of Jackson and Ewell, either in coöperation with General

Fremont, or, in case want of supplies or transportation has interfered with his movement, it is believed that the force which you move will be sufficient to accomplish the object alone. The information thus far received here makes it probable that, if the enemy operates actively against General Banks, you will not be able to count upon much assistance from him, but may have even to release him. Reports received this morning are that Banks is fighting with Ewell, eight miles from Harper's Ferry.

"ABRAHAM LINCOLN."

When the panic thus indicated in the headquarters of the enemy had disseminated itself through the military and social ramifications of Northern society, the excitement was tumultuous. Meanwhile, General Jackson, little conceiving the alarm his movements had caused in the departments at Washington and in the offices of the Governors of States, in addition to the diversion of McDowell from coöperation in the attack upon Richmond, after driving the enemy out of Winchester, pressed eagerly on, not pausing to accept the congratulations of the overjoyed people at the sight of their own friends again among them, for he learned that the enemy had garrisons at Charlestown and Harper's Ferry, and he was resolved they should not rest on Virginia soil. General Winder's brigade in the advance found the enemy drawn up in line of battle at Charlestown. Without waiting for reënforcements, he engaged them, and after a short conflict drove them in disorder toward the Potomac. The main column then moved on near to Harper's Ferry, where General Jackson received information that Fremont was moving from the west, and the whole or a part of General McDowell's corps from the east, to make a junction in his rear and thus cut off his retreat. At this time General Jackson's effective force was about fifteen thousand men, much less than either of the two armies which were understood to be marching to form a junction against him. We now know that General McDowell had been ordered to send to the relief of General Banks in the Valley twenty to thirty thousand men. The estimated force, of General Fremont when at Harrisonburg was twenty thousand. General Jackson had captured in his campaign down the Valley a very large amount of valuable stores, over nine thousand small-arms, two pieces of artillery, many horses, and, besides the wounded and sick, who had been released on parole, was said to have twenty-three hundred prisoners. To secure these, as well as to save his army, it was necessary to retreat beyond the point where his enemies could readily unite. The amount of captured stores and other property which he was anxious to preserve were said to require a wagon-train twelve miles long. This, under the care of a regiment, was sent forward in advance of the army, which promptly retired up the Valley.

On his retreat, General Jackson received information confirmatory of the report of the movements of the enemy, and of the defeat of a small force he had left at Front Royal in charge of some prisoners and captured stores—the latter, however, the garrison before retreating had destroyed. Strasburg being General Jackson's objective point, he had farther to march to reach that position than either of the columns operating against him. The rapidity of movement which marked General Jackson's operations had given to his command the appellation of "foot cavalry"; and never had they more need to show themselves entitled to the name of Stonewall.

On the night of the 31st of May, by a forced march, General Jackson arrived with the head of his column at Strasburg, and learned that General Fremont's advance was in the immediate vicinity. To gain time for the rest of his army to arrive, General Jackson decided to check Fremont's march by an attack in the morning. This movement was assigned to General Ewell, General Jackson personally giving his attention to preserving his immense trains filled with captured stores. The repulse of Fremont's advance was so easy that General Taylor describes it as offering a temptation to go beyond General Jackson's orders and make a serious attack upon Fremont's army, but recognizes the justice of the restraint imposed by the order, "as we could not waste time chasing Fremont," for it was reported that General Shields was at Front Royal with troops of a different character from those of Fremont's army, who had been encountered near Strasburg, *id est*, the corps "commanded by General O. O. Howard, and called by both sides 'the flying Dutchmen.'" This more formidable command of General Shields therefore required immediate attention.

Leaving Strasburg on the evening of June 1st, always intent to prevent a junction of the two armies of the enemy, Jackson continued his march up the Valley. Fremont followed in pursuit, while Shields moved slowly up the Valley via Luray, for the purpose of reaching New Market in advance of Jackson. On the morning of the 5th Jackson reached Harrisonburg, and, passing beyond that town, turned toward the east in the direction of Port Republic. General Ashby had destroyed all the bridges between Front Royal and Port Republic, to prevent Shields from crossing the Shenandoah to join Fremont. The troops were now permitted to make shorter marches, and were allowed some halts to refresh them after their forced marches and frequent combats. Early on the 6th of June Fremont's reënforced cavalry attacked our cavalry rear-guard under General Ashby. A sharp conflict ensued, which resulted in the repulse of the enemy and the capture of Colonel Percy Wyndham, commanding the brigade, and sixty-three others. General Ashby was in position between Harrisonburg and Port Republic, and, after the cavalry combat just described, there were indications of a more serious attack. Ashby sent a message to Ewell, informing him that cavalry supported by infantry was advancing upon his position. The Fifty-eighth Virginia and the First Maryland Regiments were sent to his support. Ashby led the Fifty-eighth Virginia to attack the enemy, who were under cover of a fence. General Ewell in the mean time had arrived, and, seeing the advantage the enemy had of position, directed Colonel Johnson to move with his regiment so as to approach the flank instead of the front of the enemy, and he was now driven from the field with heavy loss. Our loss was seventeen killed, fifty wounded, and three missing. Here fell the stainless, fearless cavalier, General Turner Ashby, of whom General Jackson in his report thus forcibly speaks:

"As a partisan officer I never knew his superior. His daring was proverbial; his power of endurance almost incredible; his tone of character heroic; and his sagacity almost intuitive in divining the purposes and movements of the enemy."

The main body of General Jackson's command had now reached Port Republic, a village situated in the angle formed by the junction of the North and South Rivers, tributaries of the South Fork of the Shenandoah. Over the North River was a wooden bridge, connecting the town with Harrisonburg. Over the South River there was a ford. Jackson's immediate command was encamped on the high ground north of the village and about a mile from the river. Ewell was some four miles distant, near the road leading from Harrisonburg to Port Republic. General Fremont had arrived with his forces in the vicinity of Harrisonburg, and General Shields was moving up the east side of the Shenandoah, and had reached Conrad's Store. Each was about fifteen miles distant from Jackson's position. To prevent a junction, the bridge over the river, near Shields's position, had been destroyed.

As the advance of General Shields approached on the 8th, the brigades of Taliaferro and Winder were ordered to occupy positions immediately north of the bridge. The enemy's cavalry, accompanied by artillery, then appeared, and, after directing a few shots toward the bridge, crossed South River, and, dashing into the village, planted one of their pieces at the southern entrance of the bridge. Meantime our batteries were placed in position, and, Taliaferro's brigade having approached the bridge, was ordered to dash across, capture the piece, and occupy the town. This was gallantly done, and the enemy's cavalry dispersed and driven back, abandoning another gun. A considerable body of infantry was now seen advancing, when our batteries opened with marked effect, and in a short time the infantry followed the cavalry, falling back three miles. They were pursued about a mile by our batteries on the opposite bank, when they disappeared in a wood.

This attack of Shields had scarcely been repulsed when Ewell became seriously engaged with Fremont, moving on the opposite side of the river. The enemy pushed forward, driving in the pickets, which, by gallant resistance, checked their advance until Ewell had time to select his position on a commanding ridge, with a rivulet and open ground in front, woods on both flanks, and the road to Port Republic intersecting his line. Trimble's brigade was posted on the right, the batteries of Courtney, Lusk, Brockenbrough, and Rains in the center, Stuart's brigade on the left, and Elzey's in rear of the center. Both wings were in the woods. About ten o'clock the enemy posted his artillery opposite our batteries, and a fire was kept up for several hours, with great spirit on both sides. Meantime a brigade of the enemy advanced, under cover, upon General Trimble, who reserved his fire until they reached short range, when he poured forth a deadly volley, under which they fell back; Trimble, supported by two regiments of Elzey's reserve, now advanced, with spirited skirmishing, more than a mile from his original line, driving the opposing force back to its former position. Ewell, finding no attack on his left was designed by the enemy, advanced and drove in their skirmishers, and at night was in position on ground previously occupied by the foe. This engagement has generally been known as the battle of Cross Keys.

As General Shields made no movement to renew the action of the 8th, General Jackson determined to attack him on the 9th. Accordingly, Ewell's forces were moved at an early hour toward Port Republic, and General Trimble was left to hold Fremont in check, or, if hard pressed, to retire across the river and burn the bridge, which subsequently was done, under orders to concentrate against Shields.

Meanwhile the enemy had taken position about two miles from Port Republic, their right on the river-bank, their left on the slope of the mountain which here threw out a spur, between which and the river was a smooth plain of about a thousand yards wide. On an elevated plateau of the mountain was placed a battery of long-range guns to sweep the plain over which our forces must pass to attack. In front of that plateau was a deep gorge, through which flowed a small stream, trending to the southern side of the promontory, so as to leave its northern point in advance of the southern. The mountain-side was covered with dense wood.

Such was the position which Jackson must assail, or lose the opportunity to fight his foe in detail—the object for which his forced marches had been made, and on which his best hopes depended.

General Winder's brigade moved down the river to attack, when the enemy's battery upon the plateau opened, and it was found to rake the plain over which we must approach for a considerable distance in front of Shields's position. Our guns were brought forward, and an attempt made to dislodge the battery of the enemy, but our fire proved unequal to theirs; whereupon General Winder, having been reënforced, attempted by a rapid charge to capture it, but encountered such a heavy fire of artillery and small-arms as to compel his command, composed of his own and another brigade, with a light battery, to fall back in disorder. The enemy advanced steadily, and in such numbers as to drive back our infantry supports and render it necessary to withdraw our guns. Ewell was hurrying his men over the bridge, and there was no fear, if human effort would avail, that he would come too late. But the condition was truly critical. General Taylor describes his chief at that moment thus: "Jackson was on the road, a little in advance of his line, where the fire was hottest, with reins on his horse's neck, seemingly in prayer. Attracted by my approach, he said, in his usual voice, 'Delightful excitement.'" He then briefly gave Taylor instructions to move against the battery on the plateau, and sent a young officer from his staff as a guide. The advance of the enemy was checked by an attack on his flank by two of our regiments, under Colonel Scott; but this was only a temporary relief, for this small command was soon afterward driven back to the woods, with severe loss. Our batteries during the check were all safely withdrawn except one six-pounder gun.

In this critical condition of Winder's command, General Taylor made a successful attack on the left and rear of the enemy, which diverted attention from the front, and led to a concentration of his force upon him. Moving to the right along the mountain acclivity, he was unseen before he emerged from the wood, just as the loud cheers of the enemy proclaimed their success in front. Although opposed by a superior force in front and flank, and with their guns in position, with a rush and shout the gorge was passed, impetuously the charge was made, and the battery of six guns fell into our hands. Three times was this battery lost and won in the desperate and determined efforts to capture and recover it, and the enemy finally succeeded in carrying off one of the guns, leaving both caisson and limber. Thus occupied with Taylor, the enemy halted in his advance, and formed a line facing to the mountain. Winder succeeded in rallying his command, and our batteries were replaced in their former positions.

At the same time reënforcements were brought by General Ewell to Taylor, who pushed forward with them, assisted by the well-directed fire of our artillery.

Of this period in the battle, than which there has seldom been one of greater peril, or where danger was more gallantly met, I copy a description from the work of General Taylor:

"The fighting in and around the battery was hand-to-hand, and many fell from bayonet-wounds. Even the artillerymen used their rammers in a way not laid down in the manual, and died at their guns. I called for Hayes, but he, the promptest of men, and his splendid regiment could not be found. Something unexpected had occurred, but there was no time for speculation. With a desperate rally, in which I believe the drummer-boys shared, we carried the battery for the third time, and held it. Infantry and riflemen had been driven off, and we began to feel a little comfortable, when the enemy, arrested in his advance by our attack, appeared. He had countermarched, and, with left near the river, came into full view of our situation. Wheeling to the right, with colors advanced, like a solid wall he marched straight upon us. There seemed nothing left but to set our back to the mountain and die hard. At the instant, crashing through the underwood, came Ewell, outriding staff and escort. He produced the effect of a reënforcement, and was welcomed with cheers. The line before us halted and threw forward skirmishers. A moment later a shell came shrieking along it, loud Confederate cheers reached our delighted ears, and Jackson, freed from his toils, rushed up like a whirlwind." [39]

The enemy, in his advance, had gone in front of the plateau where his battery was placed, the elevation being sufficient to enable the guns without hazard to be fired over the advancing line; so, when he commenced retreating, he had to pass by the position of this battery, and the captured guns were effectively used against him—that dashing old soldier, "Ewell, serving as a gunner." Mention was made of the inability to find Hayes when his regiment was wanted. It is due to that true patriot, who has been gathered to his fathers, to add Taylor's explanation: "Ere long my lost Seventh Regiment, sadly cut up, rejoined. This regiment was in rear of the column when we left Jackson to gain the path in the woods, and, before it filed out of the road, his thin line was so pressed that Jackson ordered Hayes to stop the enemy's rush. This was done, for the Seventh would have stopped a herd of elephants—but at a fearful cost."

The retreat of the enemy, though it was so precipitate as to cause him to leave his killed and wounded on the field, was never converted into a rout. "Shields's brave 'boys' preserved their organization to the last; and, had Shields himself, with his whole command, been on the field, we should have had tough work indeed."

The pursuit was continued some five miles beyond the battle-field, during which we captured four hundred and fifty prisoners, some wagons, one piece of abandoned artillery, and about eight hundred muskets. Some two hundred and seventy-five wounded were paroled in the hospitals near Port Republic. On the next day Fremont withdrew his forces, and retreated down the Valley. The rapid movements of Jackson, the eagle-like stoop with which he had descended upon each army of the enemy, and the terror which his name had come to inspire, created a great alarm at Washington, where it was believed he must have an immense army, and that he was about to come down like an avalanche upon the capital. Milroy, Banks, Fremont, and Shields were all moved in that direction, and peace again reigned in the patriotic and once happy Valley of the Shenandoah.

The material results of this very remarkable campaign are thus summarily stated by one who had special means of information:

"In three months Jackson had marched six hundred miles, fought four pitched battles, seven minor engagements, and daily skirmishes; had defeated four armies, captured seven pieces of artillery, ten thousand stand of arms, four thousand prisoners, and a very great amount of stores, inflicting upon his adversaries a known loss of two thousand men, with a loss upon his own part comparatively small." [40]

The general effect upon the affairs of the Confederacy was even more important, and the motives which influenced Jackson present him in a grander light than any military success could have done. Thus, on the 20th of March, 1862, he learned that the large force of the enemy before which he had retired was returning down the Valley, and, divining the object to be to send forces to the east side of the mountain to coöperate in the attack upon Richmond, General Jackson, with his small force of about three thousand infantry and two hundred and ninety cavalry, moved with his usual celerity in pursuit. He overtook the rear of the column at Kernstown, attacked a very superior force he found there, and fought with such desperation as to impress the enemy with the idea that he had a large army; therefore, the detachments, which had already started for Manassas, were recalled, and additional forces were also sent into the Valley. Nor was this all. McDowell's corps, under orders to join McClellan, was detained for the defense of the Federal capital.

Jackson's bold strategy had effected the object for which his movement was designed, and he slowly retreated to the south bank of the Shenandoah, where he remained undisturbed by the enemy, and had time to recruit his forces, which, by the 28th of April, amounted to six or seven thousand men. General Banks had advanced and occupied Harrisonburg, about fifteen miles from Jackson's position. Fremont, with a force estimated at fifteen thousand men, was reported to be preparing to join Banks's command.

The alarm at Washington had caused McDowell's corps to be withdrawn from the upper Rappahannock to Fredericksburg. Jackson, anxious to take advantage of the then divided condition of the enemy, sent to Richmond for reënforcements, but our condition there did not enable us to furnish any, except the division of Ewell, which had been left near Gordonsville in observation of McDowell, now by his withdrawal made disposable, and the brigade of Edward Johnson, which confronted Schenck and Milroy near to Staunton. Jackson, who, when he could not get what he wanted, did the best he could with what he had, called Ewell to his aid, left him to hold Banks in check, and marched to unite with Johnson; the combined forces attacked Milroy and Schenck, who, after a severe conflict, retreated in the night to join Fremont. Jackson then returned toward Harrisonburg, having ordered Ewell to join him for an attack on Banks, who in the mean time had retreated toward Winchester, where Jackson attacked and defeated him, inflicting great loss, drove him across the Potomac, and, as has been represented, filled the authorities at Washington with such dread of its capture as to disturb the previously devised plans against Richmond, and led to the operations which have already been described, and brought into full play Jackson's military genius. In all these operations there conspicuously appears the self-abnegation of a devoted patriot. He was not seeking by great victories to acquire fame for himself; but, always alive to the necessities and dangers elsewhere, he heroically strove to do what was possible for the general benefit of the cause he maintained. His whole heart was his country's, and his whole country's heart was his.

[Footnote 33: "History of the Civil War in America," Comte de Paris, vol. ii, pp. 32-34.]

[Footnote 34: "Campaign on the Peninsula," Prince de Joinville, 1862.]

[Footnote 35: Court-Martial of General McDowell, Washington, December 10, 1862.]

[Footnote 36: "Report on the Conduct of the War," Part I, p. 322.]

[Footnote 37: Ibid., p. 337.]

[Footnote 38: "Four Years with General Lee," by Walter H. Taylor, p. 50.]

[Footnote 39: "Destruction and Reconstruction" pp. 75, 76.]

[Footnote 40: "Stonewall Jackson," military biography by John Esten Cooke, p. 194.]

CHAPTER XXII.

Condition of Affairs.—Plan of General Johnston.—The Field of Battle at Seven Pines.—The Battle.—General Johnston wounded.— Advance of General Sumner.—Conflict on the Right.—Delay of General Huger.—Reports of the Enemy.—Losses.—Strength of Forces.—General Lee in Command.

Our army having retreated from the Peninsula, and withdrawn from the north side of the Chickahominy to the immediate vicinity of Richmond, I rode out occasionally to the lines and visited the headquarters of the commanding General. There were no visible preparations for defense, and my brief conversations with the General afforded no satisfactory information as to his plans and purposes. We had, under the supervision of General Lee, perfected as far as we could the detached works before the city, but these were rather designed to protect it against a sudden attack than to resist approaches by a great army. They were, also, so near to the city that it might have been effectually bombarded by guns exterior to them. Anxious for the defense of the ancient capital of Virginia, now the capital of the Confederate States, and remembering a remark of General Johnston, that the Spaniards were the only people who now undertook to hold fortified towns, I had written to him that he knew the defense of Richmond must be made at a distance from it. Seeing no preparation to keep the enemy at a distance, and kept in ignorance of any plan for such purpose, I sent for General B. E. Lee, then at Richmond, in general charge of army operations, and told him why and how I was dissatisfied with the condition of affairs.

He asked me what I thought it was proper to do. Recurring to a conversation held about the time we had together visited General Johnston, I answered that McClellan should be attacked on the other side of the Chickahominy before he matured his preparations for a siege of Richmond. To this he promptly assented, as I anticipated he would, for I knew it had been his own opinion. He then said: "General Johnston should of course advise you of what he expects or proposes to do. Let me go and see him, and defer this discussion until I return."

It may be proper here to say that I had not doubted that General Johnston was fully in accord with me as to the purpose of defending Richmond, but I was not content with his course for that end. It had not occurred to me that he meditated a retreat which would uncover the capital, nor was it ever suspected until, in reading General Hood's book, published in 1880, the evidence was found that General Johnston, when retreating from Yorktown, told his volunteer aide, Mr. McFarland, that "he [Johnston] expected or intended to give up Richmond." [41]

When General Lee came back, he told me that General Johnston proposed, on the next Thursday, to move against the enemy as follows: General. A. P. Hill was to move down on the right flank and rear of the enemy. General G. W. Smith, as soon as Hill's guns opened, was to cross the Chickahominy at the Meadow Bridge, attack the enemy in flank, and by the conjunction of the two it was expected to double him up. Then Longstreet was to cross on the Mechanicsville Bridge and attack him in front. From this plan the best results were hoped by both of us.

On the morning of the day proposed, I hastily dispatched my office business, and rode out toward the Meadow Bridge to see the action commence. On the road I found Smith's division halted, and the men dispersed in the woods. Looking for some one from whom I could get information, I finally saw General Hood, and asked him the meaning of what I saw. He told me he did not know anything more than that they had been halted. I asked him where General Smith was; he said he believed he had gone to a farmhouse in the rear, adding that he thought he was ill. Riding on to the bluff which overlooks the Meadow Bridge, I asked Colonel Anderson, posted there in observation, whether he had seen anything of the enemy in his front. He said that he had seen only two mounted men across the bridge, and a small party of infantry on the other side of the river, some distance below, both of whom, he said, he could show me if I would go with him into the garden back of the house. There, by the use of a powerful glass, were distinctly visible two cavalry videttes at the further end of the bridge, and a squad of infantry lower down the river, who had covered themselves with a screen of green boughs. The Colonel informed me that he had not heard Hill's guns; it was, therefore, supposed he had not advanced. I then rode down the bank of the river, followed by a cavalcade of sight-seers, who, I supposed, had been attracted by the expectation of a battle. The little squad of infantry, about fifteen in number, as we approached, fled over the ridge, and were lost to sight. Near to the Mechanicsville Bridge I found General Howell Cobb, commanding the support of a battery of artillery. He pointed out to me on the opposite side of the river the only enemy he had seen, and which was evidently a light battery.

Riding on to the main road which led to the Mechanicsville Bridge, I found General Longstreet, walking to and fro in an impatient, it might be said fretful, manner. Before speaking to him, he said his division had been under arms all day waiting for orders to advance, and that the day was now so far spent that he did not know what was the matter. I afterward learned from General Smith that he had received information from a citizen that the Beaver-dam Creek presented an impassable barrier, and that he had thus fortunately been saved from a disaster. Thus ended the offensive-defensive programme from which Lee expected much, and of which I was hopeful.

In the mean while the enemy moved up, and, finding the crossing at Bottom's Bridge unobstructed, threw a brigade of the Fourth Corps across the Chickahominy as early as the 20th of May, and on the 23d sent over the rest of the Fourth Corps; on the 25th he sent over another corps, and commenced fortifying a line near to Seven Pines. In the forenoon of the 31st of May, riding out on the New Bridge road, I heard firing in the direction of Seven Pines. As I drew nearer, I saw General Whiting, with part of General Smith's division, file into the road in front of me; at the same time I saw General Johnston ride across the field from a house before which General Lee's horse was standing. I turned down to the house, and asked General Lee what the musketry-firing meant. He replied by asking whether I had heard it, and was answered in the affirmative; he said he had been under that impression himself, but General Johnston had assured him that it could be nothing more than an artillery duel. It is scarcely necessary to add that neither of us had been advised of a design to attack the enemy that day.

We then walked out to the rear of the house to listen, and were satisfied that an action, or at least a severe skirmish, must be going on. General Johnston states in his report that the condition of the air was peculiarly unfavorable to the transmission of sound.

General Lee and myself then rode to the field of battle, which may be briefly described as follows:

The Chickahominy flowing in front is a deep, sluggish, and narrow river, bordered by marshes, and covered with tangled wood. The line of battle extended along the Nine-mile road, across the York River Railroad and Williamsburg stage-road. The enemy had constructed redoubts, with long lines of rifle-pits covered by abatis, from below Bottom's Bridge to within less than two miles of New Bridge, and had constructed bridges to connect his forces on the north and south sides of the Chickahominy. The left of his forces, on the south side, was thrown forward from the river; the right was on its bank, and covered by its slope. Our main force was on the right flank of our position, extending on both sides of the Williamsburg road, near to its intersection with the Nine-mile road. This wing consisted of Hill's, Huger's, and Longstreet's divisions, with light batteries, and a small force of cavalry; the division of General G. W. Smith, less Hood's brigade ordered to the right, formed the left wing, and its position was on the Nine-mile road. There were small tracts of cleared land, but most of the ground was wooded, and much of it so covered with water as to seriously embarrass the movements of troops.

When General Lee and I riding down the Nine-mile road reached the left of our line, we found the troops hotly engaged. Our men had driven the enemy from his advanced encampment, and he had fallen back behind an open field to the bank of the river, where, in a dense wood, was concealed an infantry line, with artillery in position. Soon after our arrival, General Johnston, who had gone farther to the right, where the conflict was expected, and whither reënforcement from the left was marching, was brought back severely wounded, and, as soon as an ambulance could be obtained, was removed from the field.

Our troops on the left made vigorous assaults under most disadvantageous circumstances. They made several gallant attempts to carry the enemy's position, but were each time repulsed with heavy loss.

After a personal reconnaissance on the left of the open in our front, I sent one, then another, and another courier to General Magruder, directing him to send a force down by the wooded path, just under the bluff, to attack the enemy in flank and reverse. Impatient of delay, I had started to see General Magruder, when I met the third courier, who said he had not found General Magruder, but had delivered the message to Brigadier-General Griffith, who was moving by the path designated to make the attack.

On returning to the field, I found that the attack in front had ceased; it was, therefore, too late for a single brigade to effect anything against the large force of the enemy, and messengers were sent through the woods to direct General Griffith to go back.

The heavy rain during the night of the 30th had swollen the Chickahominy; it was rising when the battle of Seven Pines was fought, but had not reached such height as to prevent the enemy from using his bridges; consequently, General Sumner, during the engagement, brought over his corps as a reënforcement. He was on the north side of the river, had built two bridges to connect with the south side, and, though their coverings were loosened by the upward pressure of the rising water, they were not yet quite impassable. With the true instinct of the soldier to march upon fire, when the sound of the battle reached him, he formed his corps and stood under arms waiting for an order to advance. He came too soon for us, and, but for his forethought and promptitude, he would have arrived too late for his friends. It may be granted that his presence saved the left wing of the Federal army from defeat.

As we had permitted the enemy to fortify before our attack, it would have been better to have waited another day, until the bridges should have been rendered impassable by the rise of the river.

General Lee, at nightfall, gave instructions to General Smith, the senior officer on that part of the battle-field, and left with me to return to Richmond.

Thus far I have only attempted to describe events on the extreme left of the battle-field, being that part of which I had personal observation; but the larger force and, consequently, the more serious conflict were upon the right of the line. To these I will now refer. Our force there consisted of the divisions of Major-Generals D. H. Hill, Huger, and Longstreet, the latter in chief command. In his report, first published in the "Southern Historical Society Papers," vol. iii, pp. 277, 278, he writes:

"Agreeably to verbal instructions from the commanding General, the division of Major-General D. H. Hill was, on the morning of the 31st ultimo, formed at an early hour on the Williamsburg road, as the column of attack upon the enemy's front on that road. . . . The division of Major-General Huger was intended to make a strong flank movement around the left

of the enemy's position, and attack him in rear of that flank. . . .
After waiting some six hours for these troops to get into
position, I determined to move forward without regard to
them, and gave orders to that effect to Major-General D. H.
Hill. The forward movement began about two o'clock, and our
skirmishers soon became engaged with those of the enemy.
The entire division of General Hill became engaged about three
o'clock, and drove the enemy steadily back, gaining possession
of his abatis and part of his intrenched camp, General Rodes,
by a movement to the right, driving in the enemy's left. The
only reënforcements on the field in hand were my own
brigades, of which Anderson's, Wilcox's, and Kemper's were
put in by the front on the Williamsburg road, and Colston's and
Pryor's by my right flank. At the same time the decided and
gallant attack made by the other brigades gained entire
possession of the enemy's position, with his artillery, camp-
equipage, etc. Anderson's brigade, under Colonel Jenkins,
pressing forward rapidly, continued to drive the enemy till
nightfall. . . . The conduct of the attack was left entirely to
Major-General Hill. The entire success of the affair is sufficient
evidence of his ability, courage, and skill."

This tribute to General Hill was no more than has been accorded to him by
others who knew of his services on that day, and was in keeping with the
determined courage, vigilance, and daring exhibited by him on other fields.

The reference, made, without qualification, in General Longstreet's report, to
the failure of General Huger to make the attack expected of him, and the
freedom with which others have criticised him, renders it proper that some
explanation should be given of an apparent dilatoriness on the part of that
veteran soldier, who, after long and faithful service, now fills an honored grave.

It will be remembered that General Huger was to move by the Charles City
road, so as to turn the left of the enemy and attack him in flank. The
extraordinary rain of the previous night had swollen every rivulet to the
dimensions of a stream, and the route prescribed to General Huger was one
especially affected by that heavy rain, as it led to the head of the White-Oak
Swamp. The bridge over the stream flowing into that swamp had been carried
away, and the alternatives presented to him was to rebuild the bridge or leave
his artillery. He chose the former, which involved the delay that has subjected
him to criticism. If any should think an excuse necessary to justify this decision,
they are remanded to the accepted military maxim, that the march must never
be so hurried as to arrive unfit for service; and, also, they may be reminded that
Huger's specialty was artillery, he being the officer who commanded the siege-
guns with which General Scott marched from Vera Cruz to the city of Mexico. To
show that the obstacles encountered were not of such slight character as energy
would readily overcome, I refer to the report of an officer commanding a brigade
on that occasion, Brigadier-General R. E. Rodes, whose great merit and dashing
gallantry caused him to be admired throughout the army of the Confederacy. He
said:

"On the morning of the 31st the brigade was stationed on the
Charles City road, three and a half miles from the point on the

Williamsburg road from which it had been determined to start the columns of attack. . . . I received a verbal order from General Hill to conduct my command at once to the point at which the attack was to be made. . . . The progress of the brigade was considerably delayed by the washing away of a bridge near the head of White-Oak Swamp, by reason of which the men had to wade in water waist-deep, and a large number were entirely submerged. At this point the character of the crossing was such that it was absolutely necessary to proceed with great caution to prevent the loss of both ammunition and life. In consequence of this delay, and notwithstanding that the men were carried at double-quick time over very heavy ground for a considerable distance to make up for it, when the signal for attack was given, only my line of skirmishers, the Sixth Alabama and the Twelfth Mississippi Regiments, was in position. . . . The ground over which we were to move being covered with thick undergrowth, and the soil being marshy—so marshy that it was with great difficulty that either horses or men could get over it—and being guided only by the fire in front, I emerged from the woods from the Williamsburg road under a heavy fire of both artillery and musketry, with only five companies of the Fifth Alabama."

General Huger's line of march was farther to the right, therefore nearer to White-Oak Swamp, and the impediments consequently greater than where General Rodes found the route so difficult as to be dangerous even to infantry.

On the next day, the 1st of June, General Longstreet states that a serious attack was made on our position, and that it was repulsed. This refers to the works which Hill's division had captured the day before, and which the enemy endeavored to retake.

From the final report of General Longstreet, already cited, it appears that he was ordered to attack on the morning of the 31st, and he explains why it was postponed for six hours; then he states that it was commenced by the division of General D. H. Hill, which drove the enemy steadily back, pressing forward until nightfall. The movement of Rodes's brigade on the right flank is credited with having contributed much to the dislodgment of the enemy from their abatis and first intrenchments. As just stated. General Longstreet reports a delay of some six hours in making this attack, because he was waiting for General Huger, and then made it successfully with Hill's division and some brigades from his own. These questions must naturally arise in the mind of the reader: Why did not our troops on the left, during this long delay, as well as during the period occupied by Hill's assault, coöperate in the attack? and Why, the battle having been preconceived, were they so far removed as not to hear the first guns? The officers of the Federal army, when called before a committee appointed by their Congress to inquiry into the conduct of the war, have by their testimony made it quite plain that the divided condition of their troops and the length of time required for their concentration after the battle commenced, rendered it practicable for our forces, if united—as, taking the initiative, they well might have been—to have crushed or put to flight first Keyes's and then Heintzelman's corps before Sumner crossed the Chickahominy, between five and six o'clock in the evening.

By the official reports our aggregate loss was, "killed, wounded, and missing," 6,084, of which 4,851 were in Longstreet's command on the right, and 1,233 in Smith's command on the left.

The enemy reported his aggregate loss at 5,739. It may have been less than ours, for we stormed his successive defenses.

Our success upon the right was proved by our possession of the enemy's works, as well as by the capture of ten pieces of artillery, four flags, a large amount of camp-equipage, and more than one thousand prisoners.

Our aggregate of both wings was about 40,500. The force of the enemy confronting us may be approximated by taking his returns for the 20th of June and adding thereto his casualties on the 31st of May and 1st of June, because between the last-named date and the 20th of June no action had occurred to create any material change in the number present. From these data, viz., the strength of Heintzelman's corps, 18,810, and of Keyes's corps, 14,610, on June 20th, by adding their casualties of the 31st of May and 1st of June—4,516—we deduce the strength of these two corps on the 31st of May to have been 37,936 as the aggregate present for duty.

It thus appears that, at the commencement of the action on the 31st of May, we had a numerical superiority of about 2,500. Adopting the same method to calculate the strength of Sumner's corps, we find it to have been 18,724, which would give the enemy in round numbers a force of 16,000 in excess of ours after General Sumner crossed the Chickahominy.

Both combatants claimed the victory. I have presented the evidence in support of our claim. The withdrawal of the Confederate forces on the day after the battle from the ground on which it was fought certainly gives color to the claim of the enemy, though that was really the result of a policy much broader than the occupation of the field of Seven Pines.

On the morning of June 1st I rode out toward the position where General Smith had been left on the previous night, and where I learned from General Lee that he would remain. After turning into the Nine-mile road, and before reaching that position, I was hailed by General Whiting, who saw me at a distance, and ran toward the road to stop me. He told me I was riding into the position of the enemy, who had advanced on the withdrawal of our troops, and there, pointing, he said, "is a battery which I am surprised has not fired on you." I asked where our troops were. He said his was the advance, and the others behind him. He also told me that General Smith was at the house which had been his (Whiting's) headquarters, and I rode there to see him. To relieve both him and General Lee from any embarrassment, I preferred to make the announcement of General Lee's assignment to command previous to his arrival.

After General Lee arrived, I took leave, and, being subsequently joined by him, we rode together to the Williamsburg road, where we found General Longstreet, his command being in front, and then engaged with the enemy on the field of the previous day's combat. The operations of that day were neither extensive nor important, save in the collection of the arms acquired in the previous day's battle.

General R. E. Lee was now in immediate command, and thenceforward directed the movements of the army in front of Richmond. Laborious and exact in details, as he was vigilant and comprehensive in grand strategy, a power, with which the public had not credited him, soon became manifest in all that makes an army a rapid, accurate, compact machine, with responsive motion in all its parts. I extract the following sentence from a letter from the late Colonel R. H. Chilton, adjutant and inspector-general of the army of the Confederacy, because of his special knowledge of the subject:

> "I consider General Lee's exhibition of grand administrative talents and indomitable energy, in bringing up that army in so short a time to that state of discipline which maintained aggregation through those terrible seven days' fights around Richmond, as probably his grandest achievement."

[Footnote 41: For recital and correspondence of 1874, see "Advance and Retreat," by J. B. Hood, Lieutenant-General in the Confederate Army, pp. 153-156.]

CHAPTER XXIII.

The Enemy's Position.—His Intention.—The Plan of Operations.—Movements of General Jackson.—Daring and Fortitude of Lee.—Offensive-Defensive Policy.—General Stuart's Movement.—Order of Attack.—Critical Position of McClellan.—Order of Mr. Lincoln creating the Army of Virginia.—Arrival of Jackson.—Position of the Enemy.—Diversion of General Longstreet.—The Enemy forced back south of the Chickahominy.—Abandonment of the Railroad.

When riding from the field of battle with General Robert E. Lee on the previous day, I informed him that he would be assigned to the command of the army, *vice* General Johnston, wounded, and that he could make his preparations as soon as he reached his quarters, as I should send the order to him as soon as arrived at mine. On the next morning, as above stated, he proceeded to the field and took command of the troops. During the night our forces on the left had fallen back from their position at the close of the previous day's battle, but those on the right remained in the one they had gained, and some combats occurred there between the opposing forces. The enemy proceeded further to fortify his position on the Chickahominy, covering his communication with his base of supplies on York River. His left was on the south side of the Chickahominy, between White-Oak Swamp and New Bridge, and was covered by a strong intrenchment, with heavy guns, and with abatis in front. His right wing was north of the Chickahominy, extending to Mechanicsville, and the approaches defended by strong works.

Our army was in line in front of Richmond, but without intrenchments. General Lee immediately commenced the construction of an earthwork for a battery on our left flank, and a line of intrenchment to the right, necessarily feeble because of our deficiency in tools. It seemed to be the intention of the enemy to assail Richmond by regular approaches, which our numerical inferiority and want of engineer troops, as well as the deficiency of proper utensils, made it improbable that we should be able to resist. The day after General Lee assumed command, I was riding out to the army, when I saw at a house on my left a number of horses, and among them one I recognized as belonging to him. I dismounted and entered the house, where I found him in consultation with a number of his general officers. The tone of the conversation was quite despondent, and one, especially, pointed out the inevitable consequence of the enemy's advance by throwing out *boyaux* and constructing successive parallels. I expressed, in marked terms, my disappointment at hearing such views, and General Lee remarked that he had, before I came in, said very much the same thing. I then withdrew and rode to the front, where, after a short time, General Lee joined me, and entered into conversation as to what, under the circumstances, I thought it most advisable to do. I then said to him, substantially, that I knew of nothing better than the plan he had previously explained to me, which was to have been executed by General Johnston, but which was not carried out; that the change of circumstances would make one modification necessary—that, instead, as then proposed, of bringing General A. P. Hill, with his division, on the rear flank of the enemy, it would, because of the preparation for defense made in the mean time, now be necessary to bring the stronger force of General T. J. Jackson from the Valley of the Shenandoah. So far as we were then informed, General Jackson was hotly engaged with a force superior to his own, and, before he could be withdrawn, it was necessary that the enemy should be driven out of the Valley. For this purpose, as well as to mask the design of bringing Jackson's forces to make a junction with those of Lee, a strong division under General Whiting was detached to go by rail to the Valley to join General Jackson, and, by a vigorous assault, to drive the enemy across the Potomac. As soon as he commenced a retreat which unmistakably showed that his flight would not stop within the limits of Virginia, General Jackson was instructed, with his whole force, to move rapidly on the right flank of the enemy north of the Chickahominy. The manner in which the division was detached to reënforce General Jackson was so open that it was not doubted General McClellan would soon be apprised of it, and would probably attribute it to any other than the real motive, and would confirm him in his exaggerated estimate of our strength.

By the rapidity of movement and skill with which General Jackson handled his troops, he, after several severe engagements, finally routed the enemy before the reënforcement of Whiting arrived; and he then, on the 17th of June, proceeded, with that celerity which gave to his infantry its wonderful fame and efficiency, to execute the orders which General Lee had sent to him.

As evidence of the daring and unfaltering fortitude of General Lee, I will here recite an impressive conversation which occurred between us in regard to this movement. His plan was to throw forward his left across the Meadow Bridge, drive back the enemy's right flank, and then, crossing by the Mechanicsville Bridge with another column, to attack in front, hoping by his combined forces to be victorious on the north side of the Chickahominy; while the small force on the intrenched line south of the Chickahominy should hold the left of the enemy in check. I pointed out to him that our force and intrenched line between that left flank and Richmond was too weak for a protracted resistance, and, if McClellan was the man I took him for when I nominated him for promotion in a new regiment of cavalry, and subsequently selected him for one of the military commission sent to Europe during the War of the Crimea, as soon as he found that the bulk of our army was on the north side of the Chickahominy, he would not stop to try conclusions with it there, but would immediately move upon his objective point, the city of Richmond. If, on the other hand, he should behave like an engineer officer, and deem it his first duty to protect his line of communication, I thought the plan proposed was not only the best, but would be a success. Something of his old *esprit de corps* manifested itself in General Lee's first response, that he did not know engineer officers were more likely than others to make such mistakes, but, immediately passing to the main subject, he added, "If you will hold him as long as you can at the intrenchment, and then fall back on the detached works around the city, I will be upon the enemy's heels before he gets there."

Thus was inaugurated the offensive-defensive campaign which resulted so gloriously to our arms, and turned from the capital of the Confederacy a danger so momentous that, looking at it retrospectively, it is not seen how a policy less daring or less firmly pursued could have saved the capital from capture.

To resume the connected thread of our narrative. Preparatory to this campaign, a light intrenchment for infantry cover, with some works for field-guns, was constructed on the south side of the Chickahominy, and General Whiting, with two brigades, as before stated, was sent to reënforce General Jackson in the Valley, so as to hasten the expulsion of the enemy, after which Jackson was to move rapidly from the Valley so as to arrive in the vicinity of Ashland by the 24th of June, and, by striking the enemy on his right flank, to aid in the proposed attack. The better to insure the success of this movement, General Lawton, who was coming with a brigade from Georgia to join General Lee, was directed to change his line of march and unite with General Jackson in the Valley.

As General Whiting went by railroad, it was expected that the enemy would be cognizant of the fact, but not, probably, assign to it the real motive; and that such was the case is shown by an unsuccessful attack of the 26th, made on the Williamsburg road, with the apparent intention of advancing by that route to Richmond.

To observe the enemy, as well as to prevent him from learning of the approach of General Jackson, General J. E. B. Stuart was sent with a cavalry force on June 8th to cover the route by which the former was to march, and to ascertain whether the enemy had any defensive works or troops in position to interfere with the advance of those forces. He reported favorably on both these points, as well as to the natural features of the country. On the 26th of June General Stuart received confidential instructions from General Lee, the execution of which is so interwoven with the seven days' battles as to be more appropriately noticed in connection with them, of which it is proposed now to give a brief account.

Our order of battle directed General Jackson to march from Ashland on the 25th toward Slash Church, encamping for the night west of the Central Railroad; to advance at 3 A.M. on the 26th, and to turn Beaver-Dam Creek. General A. P. Hill was to cross the Chickahominy at Meadow Bridge when Jackson advanced beyond that point, and to move directly upon Mechanicsville. As soon as the bridge there should be uncovered, Longstreet and D. H. Hill were to cross, the former to proceed to the support of A. P. Hill and the latter to that of Jackson.

The four commands were directed to sweep down the north side of the Chickahominy toward the York River Railroad—Jackson on the left and in advance; Longstreet nearest the river and in the rear. Huger, McLaws, and

Magruder, remaining on the south side of the Chickahominy, were ordered to hold their positions as long as possible against any assault of the enemy; to observe his movements, and to follow him closely if he should retreat. General Stuart, with the cavalry, was thrown out on Jackson's left to guard his flank and give notice of the enemy's movements. Brigadier-General Pendleton was directed to employ the reserve artillery so as to resist any advance toward Richmond, to superintend that portion of it posted to aid in the operations on the north bank, and hold the remainder for use where needed. The whole of Jackson's command did not arrive in time to reach the point designated on the 25th. He had, therefore, more distance to move on the 26th, and he was retarded by the enemy.

Not until 3 P.M. did A. P. Hill begin to move. Then he crossed the river and advanced upon Mechanicsville. After a sharp conflict he drove the enemy from his intrenchments, and forced him to take refuge in his works, on the left bank of Beaver Dam, about a mile distant. This position was naturally strong, the banks of the creek in front being high and almost perpendicular, and the approach to it was over open fields commanded by the fire of artillery and infantry under cover on the opposite side. The difficulty of crossing the stream had been increased by felling the fringe of woods on its banks and destroying the bridges. Jackson was expected to pass Beaver Dam above, and turn the enemy's right, so General Hill made no direct attack. Longstreet and D. H. Hill crossed the Mechanicsville Bridge as soon as it was uncovered and could be repaired, but it was late before they reached the north bank of the Chickahominy. An effort was made by two brigades, one of A. P. Hill and the other Ripley's of D. H. Hill, to turn the enemy's left, but the troops were unable in the growing darkness to overcome the obstructions, and were withdrawn. The engagement ceased about 9 P.M. Our troops retained the ground from which the foe had been driven.

According to the published reports, General McClellan's position was regarded at this time as extremely critical. If he concentrated on the left bank of the Chickahominy, he abandoned the attempt to capture Richmond, and risked a retreat upon the White House and Yorktown, where he had no reserves, or reason to expect further support. If he moved to the right bank of the river, he risked the loss of his communications with the White House, whence his supplies were drawn by railroad. He would then have to attempt the capture of Richmond by assault, or be forced to open new communications by the James River, and move at once in that direction. There he would receive the support of the enemy's navy. This latter movement had, it appears, been thought of previously, and transports had been sent to the James River. During the night, after the close of the contest last mentioned, the whole of Porter's baggage was sent over to the right bank of the river, and united with the train that set out on the evening of the 27th for the James River.

It would almost seem as if the Government of the United States anticipated, at this period, the failure of McClellan's expedition. On June 27th President Lincoln issued an order creating the "Army of Virginia," to consist of the forces of Fremont, in their Mountain Department; of Banks, in their Shenandoah Department; and of McDowell, at Fredericksburg. The command of this army was assigned to

Major-General John Pope. This cut off all reënforcements from McDowell to McClellan.

In expectation of Jackson's arrival on the enemy's right, the battle was renewed at dawn, and continued with animation about two hours, during which the passage of the creek was attempted, and our troops forced their way to its banks, where their progress was arrested by the nature of the stream and the resistance encountered. They maintained their position while preparations were being made to cross at another point nearer the Chickahominy. Before these were completed, Jackson crossed Beaver Dam above, and the enemy abandoned his intrenchments, and retired rapidly down the river, destroying a great deal of property, but leaving much in his deserted camps.

After repairing the bridges over Beaver Dam, the several columns resumed their advance, as nearly as possible, as prescribed in the order. Jackson, with whom D. H. Hill had united, bore to the left, in order to cut off reënforcements to the enemy or intercept his retreat in that direction. Longstreet and A. P. Hill moved nearer the Chickahominy. Many prisoners were taken in their progress; and the conflagration of wagons and stores marked the course of the retreating army. Longstreet and Hill reached the vicinity of New Bridge about noon. It was ascertained that the enemy had taken a position behind Powhite Creek, prepared to dispute our progress. He occupied a range of hills, with his right resting in the vicinity of McGhee's house, and his left near that of Dr. Gaines, on a wooded bluff, which rose abruptly from a deep ravine. The ravine was filled with sharpshooters, to whom its banks gave protection. A second line of infantry was stationed on the side of the hill, overlooking the first, and protected by a breastwork of logs. A third occupied the crest, strengthened with rifle-trenches, and crowned with artillery. The approach to this position was over an open plain, about a quarter of a mile wide, commanded by a triple line of fire, and swept by the heavy batteries south of the Chickahominy. In front of his center and right the ground was generally open, bounded on the side of our approach by a wood, with dense and tangled undergrowth, and traversed by a sluggish stream, which converted the soil into a deep morass. The woods on the further side of the swamp were occupied by sharpshooters, and trees had been felled to increase the difficulty of its passage, and detain our advancing columns under the fire of infantry massed on the slopes of the opposite hills, and of the batteries on their crests.

Pressing on toward the York River Railroad, A. P. Hill, who was in advance, reached the vicinity of New Cold Harbor about 2 P.M., where he encountered the foe. He immediately formed his line nearly parallel to the road leading from that place toward McGhee's house, and soon became hotly engaged. The arrival of Jackson on our left was momentarily expected, and it was supposed that his approach would cause the extension of the opposing line in that direction. Under this impression, Longstreet was held back until this movement should commence. The principal part of the enemy's army was now on the north side of the Chickahominy. Hill's single division met this large force with the impetuous courage for which that officer and his troops were distinguished. They drove it back, and assailed it in its strong position on the ridge. The battle raged fiercely, and with varying fortune, more than two hours. Three regiments pierced the enemy's line, and forced their way to the crest of the hill on his left, but were compelled to fall back before overwhelming numbers. This superior force, assisted by the fire of the batteries south of the Chickahominy, which played incessantly on our columns as they pressed through the difficulties that obstructed their way, caused them to recoil. Though most of the men had never been under fire until the day before, they were rallied, and in turn repelled the advance of our assailant Some brigades were broken, others stubbornly maintained their positions, but it became apparent that the enemy was gradually gaining ground. The attack on our left being delayed by the length of Jackson's march and the obstacles he encountered, Longstreet was ordered to make a diversion in Hill's favor by a feint on the enemy's left. In making this demonstration, the great strength of the position already described was discovered, and General Longstreet perceived that, to render the diversion effectual, the feint must be converted into an attack. He resolved, with his characteristic determination, to carry the heights by assault. His column was quickly formed near the open ground, and, as his preparations were completed, Jackson arrived, and his right division—that of Whiting—took position on the left of Longstreet. At the same time, D. H. Hill formed on our extreme left, and, after a short but bloody conflict, forced his way through the morass and obstructions, and drove the foe from the woods on the opposite side. Ewell advanced on Hill's right, and became hotly engaged. The first and fourth brigades of Jackson's own division filled the interval between Ewell and A. P. Hill. The second and third were sent to the right. The arrival of these fresh troops enabled A. P. Hill to withdraw some of his brigades, wearied and reduced by their long and arduous conflict. The lines being now complete, a general advance from right to left was ordered. On the right, the troops moved forward with steadiness, unchecked by the terrible fire from the triple lines of infantry on the hill, and the cannon on both sides of the river, which burst upon them as they emerged upon the plain. The dead and wounded marked the line of their intrepid advance, the brave Texans leading, closely followed by their no less daring comrades. The enemy were driven from the ravine to the first line of breastworks, over which our impetuous column dashed up to the intrenchments on the crest. These were quickly stormed, fourteen pieces of artillery captured, and the foe driven into the field beyond. Fresh troops came to his support, and he endeavored repeatedly to rally, but in vain. He was forced back with great slaughter until he reached the woods on the banks of the Chickahominy, and night put an end to the pursuit. Long lines of dead and wounded marked each stand made by the enemy in his stubborn resistance, and the field over which he retreated was strewed with the slain. On the left, the attack was no less vigorous and successful. D. H. Hill charged across the open ground in front, one of his regiments having first bravely carried a battery whose fire enfiladed his advance. Gallantly supported by the troops on his right, who pressed forward with unfaltering resolution, he reached the crest of the ridge, and, after a sanguinary struggle, broke the enemy's line, captured several of his batteries, and drove him in confusion toward the Chickahominy, until darkness rendered further pursuit impossible. Our troops remained in undisturbed possession of the field, covered with the dead and wounded of our opponent; and his broken forces fled to the river or wandered through the woods. Owing to the nature of the country, the cavalry was unable to participate in the general engagement. It, however, rendered valuable service in guarding Jackson's flank, and took a large number of prisoners.

On the morning of the 28th it was ascertained that none of the enemy remained in our front north of the Chickahominy. As he might yet intend to give battle to preserve his communications, the Ninth Cavalry, supported by Ewell's division, was ordered to seize the York River Railroad, and General Stuart with his main body to coöperate. When the cavalry reached Dispatch Station, the enemy retreated to the south bank of the Chickahominy, and burned the railroad-bridge. During the forenoon, columns of dust south of the river showed that he was in motion. The abandonment of the railroad and destruction of the bridge proved that no further attempt would be made to hold that line. But, from the position the enemy occupied, the roads which led toward the James River would also enable him to reach the lower bridges over the Chickahominy, and retreat down the Peninsula. In the latter event, it was necessary that our troops should continue on the north bank of the river, and, until the intention of General McClellan was discovered, it was deemed injudicious to change their disposition. Ewell was therefore ordered to proceed to Bottom's Bridge, to guard that point, and the cavalry to watch the bridges below. No certain indications of a retreat to the James River were discovered by our forces on the south side of the Chickahominy, and late in the afternoon the enemy's works were reported to be fully manned. The strength of these fortifications prevented Generals Huger and Magruder from discovering what was passing in their front. Below the enemy's works the country was densely wooded and intersected by swamps, concealing his movements and precluding reconnaissances except by the regular roads, all of which were strongly guarded. The bridges over the Chickahominy in rear of the enemy were destroyed, and their reconstruction by us was impracticable in the presence of his whole army and powerful batteries. We were therefore compelled to wait until his purpose should be developed. Generals Huger and Magruder were again directed to use the utmost vigilance, and to pursue the foe vigorously should they discover that he was retreating. During the afternoon of the 28th the signs were suggestive of a general movement, and, no indications of his approach to the lower bridges of the Chickahominy having been discovered by the pickets in observation at those points, it became inferable that General McClellan was about to retreat to the James River.

CHAPTER XXIV.

Retreat of the Enemy.—Pursuit and Battle.-Night.—Further Retreat of the Enemy.—Progress of General Jackson.—The Enemy at Frazier's Farm.—Position of General Holmes.—Advance of General Longstreet.—Remarkable Features of the Battle.—Malvern Hill.— Our Position.—The Attack.—Expedition of General Stuart.— Destruction of the Enemy's Stores.—Assaults on the Enemy.—Retreat to Westover on the James.—Siege of Richmond raised.—Number of Prisoners taken.—Strength of our Forces.—Strength of our Forces at Seven Pines and after.—Strength of the Enemy.

During the night I visited the several commands along the intrenchment on the south side of the Chickahominy. General Huger's was on the right, General McLaws's in the center, and General Magruder's on the left. The night was quite dark, especially so in the woods in front of our line, and, in expressing my opinion to the officers that the enemy would commence a retreat before morning, I gave special instructions as to the precautions necessary in order certainly to hear when the movement commenced. In the confusion of such a movement, with narrow roads and heavy trains, a favorable opportunity was offered for attack. It fell out, however, that the enemy did move before morning, and that the fact of the works having been evacuated was first learned by an officer on the north side of the river, who, the next morning, the 29th, about sunrise, was examining their works by the aid of a field-glass.

Generals Longstreet and A. P. Hill were promptly ordered to recross the Chickahominy at New Bridge, and move by the Darbytown and Long Bridge roads. General Lee, having sent his engineer. Captain Meade, to examine the condition of the abandoned works, came to the south side of the Chickahominy to unite his command and direct its movements.

Magruder and Huger found the whole line of works deserted, and large quantities of military stores of every description abandoned or destroyed. They were immediately ordered in pursuit, the former by the Charles City road, so as to take the enemy's army in flank; and the latter by the Williamsburg road, to attack his rear. Jackson was directed to cross the "Grapevine" Bridge, and move down the south side of the Chickahominy. Magruder reached the vicinity of Savage Station, where he came upon the rear-guard of the retreating army. Being informed that it was advancing, he halted and sent for reënforcements. Two brigades of Huger's division were ordered to his support, but were subsequently withdrawn, it having been ascertained that the force in Magruder's front was merely covering the retreat of the main body.

Jackson's route led to the flank and rear of Savage Station, but he was delayed by the necessity of reconstructing the "Grapevine" Bridge.

Late in the afternoon Magruder attacked the enemy with one of his divisions and two regiments of another. A severe action ensued, and continued about two hours, when night put an end to the conflict. The troops displayed great gallantry, and inflicted heavy loss; but, owing to the lateness of the hour and the small force engaged, the result was not decisive, and the enemy continued his retreat under cover of night, leaving several hundred prisoners, with his dead and wounded, in our hands. Our loss was small in numbers but great in value. Among others who could ill be spared, here fell the gallant soldier, the useful citizen, the true friend and Christian gentleman, Brigadier-General Richard Griffith. He had served with distinction in foreign war, and, when the South was invaded, was among the first to take up arms in defense of our rights.

At Savage Station were found about twenty-five hundred men in hospital, and a large amount of property. Stores of much value had been destroyed, including the necessary medical supplies for the sick and wounded. The night was so dark that, before the battle ended, it was only by challenging that on several occasions it was determined whether the troops in front were friends or foes. It was therefore deemed unadvisable to attempt immediate pursuit.

Our troops slept upon their arms, and in the morning it was found that the enemy had retreated during the night, and, by the time thus gained, he was enabled to cross the White-Oak Creek, and destroy the bridge.

Early on the 30th Jackson reached Savage Station. He was directed to pursue the enemy on the road he had taken, and Magruder to follow Longstreet by the Darbytown road. As Jackson advanced, he captured so many prisoners and collected so large a number of arms, that two regiments had to be detached for their security. His progress at White-Oak Swamp was checked by the enemy, who occupied the opposite side, and obstinately resisted the rebuilding of the bridge.

Longstreet and A. P. Hill, continuing their advance, on the 30th came upon the foe strongly posted near the intersection of the Long Bridge and Charles City roads, at the place known in the military reports as Frazier's Farm.

Huger's route led to the right of this position, Jackson's to the rear, and the arrival of their commands was awaited, to begin the attack.

On the 29th General Holmes had crossed from the south side of the James River, and, on the 30th, was reënforced by a detachment of General Wise's brigade. He moved down the River road, with a view to gain, near to Malvern Hill, a position which would command the supposed route of the retreating army.

It is an extraordinary fact that, though the capital had been threatened by an attack from the seaboard on the right, though our army had retreated from Yorktown up to the Chickahominy, and, after encamping there for a time, had crossed the river and moved up to Richmond, yet, when at the close of the battles around Richmond McClellan retreated and was pursued toward the James River, we had no maps of the country in which we were operating; our generals were ignorant of the roads, and their guides knew little more than the way from their homes to Richmond. It was this fatal defect in preparation, and the erroneous answers of the guides, that caused General Lee first to post Holmes and Wise, when they came down the River road, at New Market, where, he was told, was the route that McClellan must pursue in his retreat to the James. Subsequently learning that there was another road, by the Willis church, which would better serve the purpose of the retreating foe, Holmes's command was moved up to a position on that road where, at the foot of a hill which concealed from view the enemy's line, he remained under the fire of the enemy's gunboats, the huge, shrieking shells from which dispersed a portion of his cavalry and artillery, though the faithful old soldier remained with the rest of his command, waiting, according to his orders, for the enemy with his trains to pass; but, taking neither of the roads pointed out to General Lee, he retreated by the shorter and better route, which led by Dr. Poindexter's house to Harrison's Landing. It has been alleged that General Holmes was tardy in getting into position, and failed to use his artillery as he had been ordered. Both statements are incorrect. He first took position when and where he was directed, and, soon after, he moved to the last position to which he was assigned. The dust of his advancing column caused a heavy fire from the gunboats to be opened upon him, and, in men who had never before seen the huge shells then fired, they inspired a degree of terror not justified by their effectiveness. The enemy, instead of being a straggling mass moving toward the James River, as had been reported, were found halted between West's house and Malvern Hill on ground commanding Holmes's position, with an open field between them.

General Holmes ordered his chief of artillery to commence firing upon the enemy's infantry, which immediately gave way, but a heavy fire of twenty-five or thirty guns promptly replied to our battery, and formed, with the gunboats, a cross-fire upon General Holmes's command. The numerical superiority of the opposing force, both in infantry and artillery, would have made it worse than useless to attempt an assault unless previously reënforced, and, as no reënforcements arrived, Holmes, about an hour after nightfall, withdrew to a point somewhat in advance of the one he had held in the morning. Though the enemy continued their cannonade until after dark, and most of the troops were new levies, General Holmes reported that they behaved well under the trying circumstances to which they were exposed, except a portion of his artillery and cavalry, which gave way in disorder, probably from the effect of the ten-inch shells, which were to them a novel implement of war; for when I met them, say half a mile from the point they had left, and succeeded in stopping them, another shell fell and exploded near us in the top of a wide-spreading tree, giving a shower of metal and limbs, which soon after caused them to resume their flight in a manner that plainly showed no moral power could stop them within the range of those shells. It was after a personal and hazardous reconnaissance that General Lee assigned General Holmes to his last position; and when I remonstrated with General Lee, whom I met returning from his reconnaissance, on account of the exposure to which he had subjected himself, he said he could not get the required information otherwise, and therefore had gone himself.

After the close of the battle of Malvern Hill, General Holmes found that a deep ravine led up to the rear of the left flank of the enemy's line, and expressed his regret that it had not been known, and that he had not been ordered, when the attack was made in front, to move up that ravine and simultaneously assail in flank and reverse. It was not until after he had explained with regret the lost, because unknown, opportunity, that he was criticised as having failed to do his whole duty at the battle of Malvern Hill.

He has passed beyond the reach of censure or of praise, after serving his country on many fields wisely and well. I, who knew him from our schoolboy days, who served with him in garrison and in the field, and with pride watched him as he gallantly led a storming party up a rocky height at Monterey, and was intimately acquainted with his whole career during our sectional war, bear willing testimony to the purity, self-abnegation, generosity, fidelity, and gallantry which characterized him as a man and a soldier.

General Huger reported that his progress was delayed by trees which his opponent had felled across the Williamsburg road. In the afternoon, after passing the obstructions and driving off the men who were still cutting down trees, they came upon an open field (P. Williams's), where they were assailed by a battery of rifled guns. The artillery was brought up, and replied to the fire. In the mean time a column of infantry was moved to the right, so as to turn the battery, and the combat was ended. The report of this firing was heard at Frazier's Farm, and erroneously supposed to indicate the near approach of Huger's column, and, it has been frequently stated, induced General Longstreet to open fire with some of his batteries as notice to General Huger where our troops were, and that thus the engagement was brought on. General A. P. Hill, who was in front and had made the dispositions of our troops while hopefully waiting for the arrival of Jackson and Huger, states that the fight commenced by fire from the enemy's artillery, which swept down the road, etc. This not only concurs with my recollection of the event, but is more in keeping with the design to wait for the expected reënforcements.

The detention of Huger, as above stated, and the failure of Jackson to force a passage of the White-Oak Swamp, left Longstreet and Hill, without the expected support, to maintain the unequal conflict as best they might. The superiority of numbers and advantage of position were on the side of the enemy. The battle raged furiously until 9 P.M. By that time the enemy had been driven with great slaughter from every position but one, which he maintained until he was enabled to withdraw under cover of darkness. At the close of the struggle nearly the entire field remained in our possession, covered with the enemy's dead and wounded. Many prisoners, including a general of division, were captured, and several batteries with some thousands of small-arms were taken.

After this engagement, Magruder, who had been ordered to go to the support of Holmes, was recalled, to relieve the troops of Longstreet and Hill. He arrived during the night, with the troops of his command much fatigued by the long, hot march.

In the battle of Frazier's Farm the troops of Longstreet and Hill, though disappointed in the expectation of support, and contending against superior numbers advantageously posted, made their attack successful by the most heroic courage and unfaltering determination.

Nothing could surpass the bearing of General Hill on that occasion, and I often recur with admiration to the manner in which Longstreet, when Hill's command seemed about to be overborne, steadily led his reserve to the rescue, as he might have marched on a parade. The mutual confidence between himself and his men was manifested by the calm manner in which they went into the desperate struggle. The skill and courage which made that corps illustrious on former as well as future fields were never more needed or better exemplified than on this.

The current of the battle which was then setting against us was reversed, and the results which have been stated were gained. That more important consequences would have followed had Huger and Jackson, or either of them, arrived in time to take part in the conflict, is unquestionable; and there is little hazard in saying that the army of McClellan would have been riven in twain, beaten in detail, and could never, as an organized body, have reached the James River.

Our troops slept on the battle-field they had that day won, and couriers were sent in the night with instructions to hasten the march of the troops who had been expected during the day.

Valor less true or devotion to their cause less sincere than that which pervaded our army and sustained its commanders would, in this hour of thinned ranks and physical exhaustion, have thought of the expedient of retreat; but, so far as I remember, no such resort was contemplated. To bring up reënforcements and attack again was alike the expectation and the wish.

During the night, humanity, the crowning grace of the knightly soldier, secured for the wounded such care as was possible, not only to those of our own army, but also to those of the enemy who had been left upon the field.

This battle was in many respects one of the most remarkable of the war. Here occurred on several occasions the capture of batteries by the impetuous charge of our infantry, defying the canister and grape which plowed through their ranks, and many hand-to-hand conflicts, where bayonet-wounds were freely given and received, and men fought with clubbed muskets in the life-and-death encounter.

The estimated strength of the enemy was double our own, and he had the advantage of being in position. From both causes it necessarily resulted that our loss was very heavy. To the official reports and the minute accounts of others, the want of space compels me to refer the reader for a detailed statement of the deeds of those who in our day served their country so bravely and so well.

During the night those who fought us at Frazier's Farm fell back to the stronger position of Malvern Hill, and by a night-march the force which had detained Jackson at White-Oak Swamp effected a junction with the other portion of the enemy. Early on the 1st of July Jackson reached the battlefield of the previous day, having forced the passage of White-Oak Swamp, where he captured some artillery and a number of prisoners. He was directed to follow the route of the enemy's retreat, but soon found him in position on a high ridge in front of Malvern Hill. Here, on a line of great natural strength, he had posted his powerful artillery, supported by his large force of infantry, covered by hastily constructed intrenchments. His left rested near Crew's house and his right near Binford's. Immediately in his front the ground was open, varying in width from a quarter to half a mile, and, sloping gradually from the crest, was completely swept by the fire of his infantry and artillery. To reach this open ground our troops had to advance through a broken and thickly wooded country, traversed nearly throughout its whole extent by a swamp passable at only a few places and difficult at these. The whole was within range of the batteries on the heights and the gunboats in the river, under whose incessant fire our movements had to be executed.

Jackson formed his line with Whiting's division on his left and D. H. Hill's on his right, one of Ewell's brigades occupying the interval. The rest of Ewell's and Jackson's own division were held in reserve. Magruder was directed to take position on Jackson's right, but before his arrival two of Huger's brigades came up and were placed next to Hill. Magruder subsequently formed on the right of these brigades, which, with a third of Huger's, were placed under his command. Longstreet and A. P. Hill were held in reserve, and took no part in the engagement. Owing to ignorance of the country, the dense forests impeding necessary communications, and the extreme difficulty of the ground, the whole line was not formed until a late hour in the afternoon. The obstacles presented by the woods and swamp made it impracticable to bring up a sufficient amount of artillery to oppose successfully the extraordinary force of that arm employed by the enemy, while the field itself afforded us few positions favorable for its use, and none for its proper concentration.

General W. N. Pendleton, in whom were happily combined the highest characteristics of the soldier, the patriot, and the Christian, was in chief command of the artillery, and energetically strove to bring his long-range guns and reserve artillery into a position where they might be effectively used against the enemy, but the difficulties before mentioned were found insuperable.

Orders were issued for a general advance at a given signal, but the causes referred to prevented a proper concert of action among the troops. D. H. Hill pressed forward across the open field, and engaged the enemy gallantly, breaking and driving back his first line; but, a simultaneous advance of the other troops not taking place, he found himself unable to maintain the ground he had gained against the overwhelming numbers and numerous batteries opposed to him. Jackson sent to his support his own division and that part of Ewell's which was in reserve; but, owing to the increasing darkness and intricacy of the forest and swamp, they did not arrive in time to render the desired assistance. Hill was therefore compelled to abandon part of the ground he had gained, after suffering severe loss and inflicting heavy damage.

On the right the attack was gallantly made by Huger's and Magruder's commands. Two brigades of the former commenced the action, the other two were subsequently sent to the support of Magruder and Hill. Several determined efforts were made to storm the hill at Crew's house. The brigade advanced bravely across the open field, raked by the fire of a hundred cannon and the musketry of large bodies of infantry. Some were broken and gave way; others approached close to the guns, driving back the infantry, compelling the advance batteries to retire to escape capture, and mingling their dead with those of the enemy. For want of coöperation by the attacking columns, their assaults were too weak to break the enemy's line; and, after struggling gallantly, sustaining and inflicting great loss, they were compelled successively to retire. Night was approaching when the attack began, and it soon became difficult to distinguish friend from foe. The firing continued until after 9 P.M., but no decided result was gained.

Part of our troops were withdrawn to their original positions; others remained in the open field; and some rested within a hundred yards of the batteries that had been so bravely but vainly assailed. The lateness of the hour at which the attack necessarily began gave the foe the full advantage of his superior position, and augmented the natural difficulties of our own.

At the cessation of firing, several fragments of different commands were lying down and holding their ground within a short distance of the enemy's line, and, as soon as the fighting ceased, an informal truce was established by common consent. Numerous parties from both armies, with lanterns and litters, wandered over the field seeking for the wounded, whose groans and calls on all sides could not fail to move with pity the hearts of friend and foe.

The morning dawned with heavy rain, and the enemy's position was seen to have been entirely deserted. The ground was covered with his dead and wounded, and his route exhibited evidence of a precipitate retreat. To the fatigue of hard marches and successive battles, enough to have disqualified our troops for rapid pursuit, was added the discomfort of being thoroughly wet and chilled by rain. I sent out to the neighboring houses to buy, if it could be had, at any price, enough whisky to give to each of the men a single gill, but it could not be found.

The foe had silently withdrawn in the night by a route which had been unknown to us, but which was the most direct road to Harrison's Landing, and he had so many hours the start, that, among the general officers who expressed to me their opinion, there was but one who thought it was possible to pursue effectively. That was General T. J. Jackson, who quietly said, "They have not all got away if we go immediately after them." During the pursuit, which has just been described, the cavalry of our army had been absent, having been detached on a service which was reported as follows: After seizing the York River Railroad, on June 28th, and driving the enemy across the Chickahominy, the force under General Stuart proceeded down the railroad to ascertain if there was any movement of the enemy in that direction. He encountered but little opposition, and reached the vicinity of the White House on the 29th. On his approach the enemy destroyed the greater part of the immense stores accumulated at that depot, and retreated toward Fortress Monroe. With one gun and some dismounted men General Stuart drove off a gunboat, which lay near the White House, and rescued a large amount of property, including more than ten thousand stand of small-arms, partially burned. General Stuart describes his march down the enemy's line of communication with the York River as one in which he was but feebly resisted. He says:

"We advanced until, coming in view of the White House (a former plantation residence of General George Washington), at a distance of a quarter of a mile, a large gunboat was discovered lying at the landing. . . . I was convinced that a few bold sharpshooters could compel the gunboat to leave. I accordingly ordered down about seventy-five, partly of the First and Fourth Virginia Cavalry, and partly of the Jeff Davis Legion, armed with the rifled carbines. They advanced on this monster so terrible to our fancy, and a body of sharpshooters was sent ashore from the boat to meet them. . . . To save time I ordered up the howitzer, a few shells from which, fired with great accuracy, and bursting directly over her decks, caused an instantaneous withdrawal of the sharpshooters, and a precipitous flight under headway of steam down the river. . . . An opportunity was here offered for observing the deceitfulness of the enemy's pretended reverence for everything associated with the name of Washington—for the dwelling-house was burned to the ground, not a vestige left except what told of desolation and vandalism.

"Nine large barges, laden with stores, were on fire as we approached; immense numbers of tents, wagons, and cars in long trains, loaded, and five locomotives; a number of forges; quantities of every species of quartermaster's stores and property, making a total of many millions of dollars—all more or less destroyed. . . . I replied (to a note from the commanding General) that there was no evidence of a retreat of the main body down the Williamsburg road, and I had no doubt that the enemy, since his defeat, was endeavoring to reach the James as a new base, being *compelled* to surrender his connection with the York. If the Federal people can be convinced that this was a part of McClellan's plan, that it was in his original design for Jackson to turn his right flank, and our generals to force him from his strongholds, they certainly never can forgive him for the millions of public treasure that his superb strategy cost."

Leaving one squadron at the White House, he returned to guard the lower bridges of the Chickahominy. On the 30th he was directed to recross and coöperate with Jackson. After a long march, he reached the rear of the enemy at Malvern Hill, on the night of July 1st, at the close of the engagement.

On the 2d of July the pursuit was commenced, the cavalry under General Stuart in advance. The knowledge acquired since the event renders it more than probable that, could our infantry, with a fair amount of artillery, during that day and the following night, have been in position on the ridge which overlooked the plain where the retreating enemy was encamped on the bank of the James River, a large part of his army must have dispersed, and the residue would have been captured. It appears, from the testimony taken before the United States Congressional Committee on the Conduct of the War, that it was not until July 3d that the heights which overlooked the encampment of the retreating army were occupied, and, from the manuscript notes on the war by General J. E. B. Stuart, we learn that he easily gained and took possession of the heights, and with his light howitzer opened fire upon the enemy's camp, producing great commotion. This was described by the veteran soldier, General Casey, of the United States Army, thus:

"The enemy had come down with some artillery upon our army massed together on the river, the heights commanding the position not being in our possession. Had the enemy come down and taken possession of those heights with a force of twenty or thirty thousand men, they would, in my opinion, have taken the whole of our army except that small portion of it that might have got off on the transports."

General Lee was not a man of hesitation, and they have mistaken his character who suppose caution was his vice. He was prone to attack, and not slow to press an advantage when he gained it. Longstreet and Jackson were ordered to advance, but a violent storm which prevailed throughout the day greatly retarded their progress. The enemy, harassed and closely followed by the cavalry, succeeded in gaining Westover, on the James River, and the protection of his gunboats. His position was one of great natural and artificial strength, after the heights were occupied and intrenched. It was flanked on each side by a creek, and the approach in front was commanded by the heavy guns of his shipping, as well as by those mounted in his intrenchments. Under these circumstances it was deemed inexpedient to attack him; and, in view of the condition of our troops, who had been marching and fighting almost incessantly for seven days, under the most trying circumstances, it was determined to withdraw, in order to afford to them the repose of which they stood so much in need.

Several days were spent in collecting arms and other property abandoned by the enemy, and, in the mean time, some artillery and cavalry were sent below Westover to annoy his transports. On July 8th our army returned to the vicinity of Richmond.

Under ordinary circumstances the army of the enemy should have been destroyed. Its escape was due to the causes already stated. Prominent among these was the want of correct and timely information. This fact, together with the character of the country, enabled General McClellan skillfully to conceal his retreat, and to add much to the obstructions with which nature had beset the way of our pursuing columns. We had, however, effected our main purpose. The siege of Richmond was raised, and the object of a campaign which had been prosecuted after months of preparation, at an enormous expenditure of men and money, was completely frustrated.[42]

More than ten thousand prisoners, including officers of rank, fifty-two pieces of artillery, and upward of thirty-five thousand stand of small-arms were captured. The stores and supplies of every description which fell into our hands were great in amount and value, but small in comparison with those destroyed by the enemy. His losses in battle exceeded our own, as attested by the thousands of dead and wounded left on every field, while his subsequent inaction shows in what condition the survivors reached the protection of the gunboats.

In the archive office of the War Department in Washington there are on file some of the field and monthly returns of the strength of the Army of Northern Virginia. These are the original papers which were taken from Richmond. They furnish an accurate statement of the number of men in that army at the periods named. They were not made public at the time, as I did not think it to be judicious to inform the enemy of the numerical weakness of our forces. The following statements have been taken from those papers by Major Walter H. Taylor, of the staff of General Lee, who supervised for several years the preparation of the original returns.

A statement of the strength of the troops under General Johnston shows that on May 21, 1862, he had present for duty as follows:

Smith's division, consisting of the brigades of Whiting, Hood, Hampton, Hatton, and Pettigrew 10,592

Longstreet's division, consisting of the brigades of A. P. Hill, Pickett, R. H. Anderson, Wilson, Colston, and Pryor . . 13,816

Magruder's division, consisting of the brigades of McLaws, Kershaw, Griffith, Cobb, Toombs, and D. R. Jones 15,680

D. H. Hill's division, consisting of the brigades of Early, Rodes, Raines, Featherston, and the commands of Colonels Ward and Crump 11,151

Cavalry brigade 1,289

Reserve artillery 1,160
———
Total effective men 53,688

Statement of the Strength of the Army Commanded by General R. E. Lee on July 20, 1862.

Department of Northern Virginia . . . . Present for Duty

and North Carolina	Officers	Enlisted men
Department of North Carolina	722	11,509
Longstreet's division	557	7,929
D. H. Hill's division	550	8,998
McLaws's division	514	7,188
A. P. Hill's division	519	10,104
Anderson's division	357	5,760
D. R. Jones's division	213	3,500
Whiting's division	252	3,600
Stuart's cavalry	295	3,740
Pendleton's artillery	103	1,716
Rhett's artillery	78	1,355

——— ———

Total, including Department of North Carolina 4,160 . . . 65,399

Army of Northern Virginia, September 22, 1862.

Present for Duty

Officers Enlisted men

Longstreet's command . . . . 1,410 . . . 19,001

Jackson's command:
```
    D. H. Hill's division . . . . . . . . . . 310 . . . . 4,739
    A. P. Hill's division . . . . . . . . . . 318 . . . . 4,435
    Ewell's division . . . . . . . . . . . . 280 . . . . 3,144
    Jackson's division . . . . . . . . . . . 183 . . . . 2,367
                                            ——- ——-
Total . . . . . . . . . . . . . . . . . . 2,501 . . . 33,686
```
        Army of Northern Virginia, September 30, 1862.
                         Present for Duty
                    Officers Enlisted men
```
    Longstreet's command . . . . . . . . . . . 1,927 . . . 26,489
Jackson's command . . . . . . . . . . . . . . 1,629 . . . 21,728
Reserve artillery . . . . . . . . . . . . . 50 . . . 716
                                            ——- ———
Total[43] . . . . . . . . . . . . . . . . . 3,606 . . . 48,933
```
    Major Taylor, in his work,[44] states:

> "In addition to the troops above
> enumerated as the strength of General
> Johnston on May 21, 1862, there were two
> brigades subject to his orders then stationed
> in the vicinity of Hanover Junction, one under
> the command of General Branch; they were
> subsequently incorporated into the division of
> General A. P. Hill, and participated in the
> battles around Richmond."

He has no official data by which to determine their numbers, but, from careful estimates and conference with General Anderson, he estimates the strength of the two at 4,000 effective.

Subsequent to the date of the return of the army around Richmond, heretofore given, but previous to the battle of Seven Pines, General Johnston was reënforced by General Huger's division of three brigades. The total strength of these three brigades, according to the "Reports of the Operations of the Army of Northern Virginia," was 5,008 effectives. Taylor says:

> "If the strength of these five be added to
> the return of May 21st, we shall have sixty-
> two thousand six hundred and ninety-six
> (62,696) as the effective strength of the army
> under General Johnston on May 31, 1862.
>
> "Deduct the losses sustained in the battle
> of Seven Pines as shown by the official reports
> of casualties, say 6,084, and we have 56,612
> as the effective strength of the army when
> General Lee assumed command."

There have been various attempts made to point out the advantage which might have been obtained if General Lee, in succeeding to the command, had renewed on the 1st of June the unfinished battle of the 31st of May; and the representation that he commenced his campaign, known as the "Seven Days' Battles," only after he had collected a great army, instead of moving with a force not greatly superior to that which his predecessor had, has led to the full exposition of all the facts bearing upon the case. In the "Southern Historical Society Papers," June, 1876, is published an extract from an address of Colonel Charles Marshall, secretary and aide-de-camp to General R. E. Lee, before the Virginia Division of the Army of Northern Virginia. In it Colonel Marshall quotes General J. E. Johnston as saying:

"General Lee did not attack the enemy until the 26th of June, because he was employed from the 1st until then in forming a great army by bringing to that which I had commanded 15,000 men from North Carolina under Major-General Holmes, 22,000 men from South Carolina and Georgia, and above 16,000 men from the 'Valley,' in the divisions of Jackson and Ewell," etc.

These numbers added together make 53,000. Colonel Marshall then proceeds, from official reports, to show that all these numbers were exaggerated, and that one brigade, spoken of as seven thousand strong—that of General Drayton—was not known to be in the Army of Virginia until after the "seven days," and that another brigade, of which General Johnston admitted he did not know the strength, Colonel Marshall thought it safer to refer to as the "unknown brigade," which, he suggests, may have been "a small command under General Evans, of South Carolina, who did not join the army until after it moved from Richmond."

General Holmes's report, made July 15, 1862, states that on the 29th of June he brought his command to the north side of the James River, and was joined by General Wise's brigade. With this addition, his force amounted to 6,000 infantry and six batteries of artillery. General Ransom's brigade had been transferred from the division of General Holmes to that of General Huger a short time before General Holmes was ordered to join General Lee. The brigade of General Branch had been detached at an earlier period; it was on duty near to Hanover Junction, and under the command of General J. E. Johnston before the battle of Seven Pines. These facts are mentioned to account for the small size of General Holmes's division, which had been reduced to two brigades. Ripley's brigade on the 26th of June was reported to have an aggregate force of 2,366, including pioneers and the ambulance corps. General Lawton's brigade, when moving up from Georgia to Richmond, was ordered to change direction, and join General Jackson in the Valley. He subsequently came down with General Jackson, and reports the force which he led into the battle of Cold Harbor, on the 27th of June, 1862, as 3,500 men.

General Lee, after the battle of Seven Pines, had sent two large brigades under General Whiting to coöperate with General Jackson in the Valley, and to return with him, according to instructions furnished. These brigades were in the battle of Seven Pines, and were counted in the force of the army when General Lee took command of it. Lawton's Georgia brigade, as has been stated, was diverted from its destination for a like temporary service, and is accounted for as reënforcements brought from the south. These three brigades, though coming with Jackson and Ewell, were not a part of their divisions, and, if their numbers are made to swell the force which Jackson brought, they should be elsewhere subtracted.

General J. A. Early, in the same number of the "Historical Society Papers," in a letter addressed to General J. E. Johnston, February 4, 1875, makes an exhaustive examination from official reports, and applies various methods of computation to the question at issue. Among other facts, he states:

"Drayton's brigade did not come to Virginia until after the battles around Richmond. It was composed of the Fifteenth South Carolina and the Fiftieth and Fifty-first Georgia Regiments and Third South Carolina Battalion. A part, if not all, of it was engaged in the fight at Secessionville, South Carolina, on the 16th of June, 1862. Its first engagement in Virginia was on the Rappahannock, 25th of August, 1862. After Sharpsburg, it was so small that it was distributed among some other brigades in Longstreet's corps."

After minute inquiry, General Early concludes that "the whole command that came from the Valley, including the artillery, the regiment of cavalry, and the Maryland regiment and a battery, then known as 'The Maryland Line,' could not have exceeded 8,000 men." In this, General Early does not include either Lawton's brigade or the two brigades with Whiting, and reaches the conclusion that "the whole force received by General Lee was about 23,000—about 30,000 less than your estimate."

Taking the number given by General Early as the entire reënforcement received by General Lee after the battle of Seven Pines and before the commencement of the seven days' battles—which those who know his extreme accuracy and minuteness of inquiry will be quite ready to do—and deducting from the 23,000 the casualties in the battle of Seven Pines (6,084), we have 16,916; if to this be added whatever number of absentees may have joined the army in anticipation of active operations, a number which I have no means of ascertaining, the result will be the whole increment to the army with which General Lee took the offensive against McClellan.

It appears from the official returns of the Army of the Potomac that on June 20th General McClellan had present for duty 115,102 men. It is stated that McClellan reached the James River with "between 85,000 and 90,000 men," and that his loss in the seven days' battles was 15,249; this would make the army 105,000 strong at the commencement of the battles.[45] Probably General Dix's corps of 9,277 men, stationed at Fortress Monroe, is not included in this last statement.

[Footnote 42: Reports of Generals Robert E. Lee, Pendleton, A. P. Hill, Huger, Alexander, and Major W. H. Taylor, in his "Four Years with Lee," have been drawn upon for the foregoing.]

[Footnote 43: No report of cavalry]

[Footnote 44: "Four Years with General Lee."]

[Footnote 45: Swinton's "History of the Army of the Potomac."]

CHAPTER XXV.

Forced Emancipation.—Purposes of the United States Government at the Commencement of 1862.—Subjugation or Extermination.—The Willing Aid of United States Congress.—Attempt to legislate the Subversion of our Social Institutions.—Could adopt any Measure Self-Defense would justify.—Slavery the Cause of all Troubles, therefore must be removed.—Statements of President Lincoln's

Inaugural.—Declaration of Sumner.—Abolition Legislation.—The Power based on Necessity.—Its Formula.—The System of Legislation devised.—Confiscation.—How permitted by the Law of Nations.—Views of Wheaton; of J. Q. Adams; of Secretary Marcy; of Chief-Justice Marshall.—Nature of Confiscation and Proceedings.—Compared with the Acts of the United States Congress.—Provisions of the Acts.—Five Thousand Millions of Property involved.—Another Feature of the Act.—Confiscates Property within Reach.—Procedure against Persons.—Held us as Enemies and Traitors.—Attacked us with the Instruments of War and Penalties of Municipal Law.—Emancipation to be secured.—Remarks of President Lincoln on signing the Bill.—Remarks of Mr. Adams compared.—Another Alarming Usurpation of Congress.—Argument for it.—No Limit to the War-Power of Congress; how maintained.—The Act to emancipate Slaves in the District of Columbia.—Compensation promised.—Remarks of President Lincoln.—The Right of Property violated.—Words of the Constitution.—The Act to prohibit Slavery in the Territories.-The Act making an Additional Article of War.—All Officers forbidden to return Fugitives.—Words of the Constitution.—The Powers of the Constitution unchanged in Peace or War.—The Discharge of Fugitives commanded in the Confiscation Act.—Words of the Constitution.

At the commencement of the year 1862 it was the purpose of the United States Government to assail us in every manner and at every point and with every engine of destruction which could be devised. The usual methods of civilized warfare consist in the destruction of an enemy's military power and the capture of his capital. These, however, formed only a small portion of the purposes of our enemy. If peace with fraternity and equality in the Union, under the Constitution as interpreted by its framers, had been his aim, this was attainable without war; but, seeking supremacy at the cost of a revolution in the entire political structure, involving a subversion of the Constitution, the subjection of the States, the submission of the people, and the establishment of a union under the sword, his efforts were all directed to subjugation or extermination. Thus, while the Executive was preparing immense armies, iron-clad fleets, and huge instruments of war, with which to invade our territory and destroy our citizens, the willing aid of an impatient, enraged Congress was invoked to usurp new powers, to legislate the subversion of our social institutions, and to give the form of legality to the plunder of a frenzied soldiery.

That body had no sooner assembled than it brought forward the doctrine that the Government of the United States was engaged in a struggle for its existence, and could therefore resort to any measure which a case of self-defense would justify. It pretended not to know that the only self-defense authorized in the Constitution for the Government created by it, was by the peaceful method of the ballot-box; and that, so long as the Government fulfilled the objects of its creation (see preamble of the Constitution), and exercised its delegated powers within their prescribed limits, its surest and strongest defense was to be found in that ballot-box.

The Congress next declared that our institution of slavery was the cause of all the troubles of the country, and therefore the whole power of the Government must be so directed as to remove it. If this had really been the cause of the troubles, how easily wise and patriotic statesmen might have furnished a relief. Nearly all the slaveholding States had withdrawn from the Union, therefore those who had been suffering vicariously might have welcomed their departure, as the removal of the cause which disturbed the Union, and have tried the experiment of separation. Should the trial have brought more wisdom and a spirit of conciliation to either or both, there might have arisen, as a result of the experiment, a reconstructed fraternal Union such as our fathers designed.

The people of the seceded States had loved the Union. Shoulder to shoulder with the people of the other States, they had bled for its liberties and its honor. Their sacrifices in peace had not been less than those in war, and their attachment had not diminished by what they had given, nor were they less ready to give in the future. The concessions they had made for many years and the propositions which followed secession proved their desire to preserve the peace.

The authors of the aggressions which had disturbed the harmony of the Union had lately acquired power on a sectional basis, and were eager for the spoil of their sectional victory. To conceal their real motive, and artfully to appeal to the prejudice of foreigners, they declared that slavery was the cause of the troubles of the country, and of the "rebellion" which they were engaged in suppressing. In his inaugural address in March, 1861, President Lincoln said: "I have no purpose, directly or indirectly, to interfere with the institution of slavery in the States where it exists. I believe I have no lawful right to do so, and I have no inclination to do so." The leader (Sumner) of the Abolition party in Congress, on February 25, 1861, said in the Senate, "I take this occasion to declare most explicitly that I do not think that Congress has any right to interfere with slavery in a State." The principle thus announced had regulated all the legislation of Congress from the beginning of its first session in 1789 down to the first session of the Thirty-seventh Congress, commencing July 4, 1861.

A few months after the inaugural address above cited and the announcement of the fact above quoted were made, Congress commenced to legislate for the abolition of slavery. If it had the power now to do what it before had not, whence was it derived? There had been no addition in the interval to the grants in the Constitution; not a word or letter of that instrument had been changed since the possession of the power was disclaimed; yet after July 4, 1861, it was asserted by the majority in Congress that the Government had power to interfere with slavery in the States. Whence came the change? The answer is, It was wrought by the same process and on the same plea that tyranny has ever employed against liberty and justice—the time-worn excuse of usurpers—necessity; an excuse which is ever assumed as valid, because the usurper claims to be the sole judge of his necessity.

The formula under which it was asserted was as follows:
"Whereas the laws of the United States
have been for some time past and now are
opposed, and the execution thereof
obstructed, etc., by combinations too
powerful to be suppressed by the ordinary
course of judicial proceedings," etc.

Therefore, says the plea of necessity, a new power is this day found under the Constitution of the United States. This means that certain circumstances had transpired in a distant portion of the Union, and the powers of the Constitution had thereby become enlarged. The inference follows with equal reason that, when the circumstances cease to exist, the powers of the Constitution will be contracted again to their normal state; that is, the powers of the Constitution of the United States are enlarged or contracted according to circumstances. Mankind can not be surprised at seeing a Government, administered on such an interpretation of powers, blunder into a civil war, and approach the throes of dissolution.

Nevertheless, these views were adopted by the Thirty-seventh Congress of the United States, and a system of legislation was devised which embraced the following usurpations: universal emancipation in the Confederate States through confiscation of private property of all kinds; prohibition of the extension of slavery to the Territories; emancipation of slavery in all places under the exclusive control of the Government of the United States; emancipation with compensation in the border States and in the District of Columbia; practical emancipation to follow the progress of the armies; all restraints to be removed from the slaves, so that they could go free wherever they pleased, and be fed and clothed, when destitute, at the expense of the United States, literally to become a "ward of the Government."

The emancipation of slaves through confiscation in States where the United States Government had, under the Constitution, no authority to interfere with slavery, was a problem which the usurpers found it difficult legally or logically to solve, but these obstacles were less regarded than the practical difficulty in States where the Government had no physical power to enforce its edicts. The limited powers granted in the Constitution to the Government of the United States were not at all applicable to such designs, or commensurate with their execution. Now, let us see the little possibility there was for constitutional liberties and rights to survive, when intrusted to such unscrupulous hands.

In Article I, section 8, the Constitution says:

"The Congress shall have power to declare war, grant letters of marque and reprisal, and make rules concerning captures on land and water; to raise and support armies; to provide and maintain a navy; to make rules for the government and regulation of the land and naval forces," etc.

This is the grant of power under which the Government of the United States makes war upon a foreign nation. If it had not been given in the Constitution, there would not have been any power under which to conduct a foreign war, such as that of 1812 against Great Britain or that of 1846 against Mexico. In such conflicts the nations engaged recognize each other as separate sovereignties and as public enemies, and use against each other all the powers granted by the law of nations. One of these powers is the confiscation of the property of the enemy. Under the law of nations of modern days this confiscation is limited in extent, made under a certain form, and for a defined object.

For the modern laws of war one must look to the usages of civilized states and to the publicists who have explained and enforced them. These usages constitute themselves the laws of war.

In relation to the capture and confiscation of private property on land, in addition to what has been said in previous pages, it may be added that the whole matter has never been better stated than by our great American publicist, Mr. Wheaton, in these words:

> "By the modern usages of nations, which have now acquired the force of law, temples of religion, public edifices devoted to civil purposes only, monuments of art, and repositories of science, are exempted from the general operations of war. Private property on land is also exempt from confiscation, with the exception of such as may become booty in special cases, when taken from enemies in the field or in besieged towns, and of military contributions levied upon the inhabitants of the hostile territory. This exemption extends even to the case of an absolute and unqualified conquest of the enemy's country,"—("Elements of International Law," p. 421.)

Mr. John Quincy Adams, in a letter to the Secretary of State, dated August 22, 1815, says:

"Our object is the restoration of all the property, including slaves, which, by the usages of war among civilized nations, ought not to have been taken. All private property on shore was of that description. It was entitled by the laws of war to exemption from capture."—(4 "American State Papers," 116, etc.)

Again, Mr. William L. Marcy, Secretary of State, in a letter to the Count de Sartiges, dated July 28, 1856, says:

> "The prevalence of Christianity and the progress of civilization have greatly mitigated the severity of the ancient mode of prosecuting hostilities. . . . It is a generally received rule of modern warfare, so far at least as operations upon land are concerned, that the persons and effects of non-combatants are to be respected. The wanton pillage or uncompensated appropriation of individual, property by an army even in possession of an enemy's country is against the usage of modern times. Such a proceeding at this day would be condemned by the enlightened judgment of the world, unless warranted by particular circumstances."

The words of the late Chief-Justice Marshall on the capture and confiscation of private property should not be omitted:

> "It may not be unworthy of remark that it is very unusual, even in cases of conquest, for the conqueror to do more than displace the sovereign, and assume dominion over the country. The modern usage of nations, which

has become law, would be violated; that sense of justice and of right which is acknowledged and felt by the whole civilized world would be outraged, if private property should be generally confiscated and private rights annulled. The people change their allegiance; their relation to their ancient sovereign is dissolved; but their relations to each other and their rights of property remain undisturbed."—("United States vs. Percheman," 7 Peters, 51.)

The Government of the United States recognized us as under the law of nations by attempting to use against us one of the powers of that law. Yet, if we were subject to this power, we were most certainly entitled to its protection. This was refused. That Government exercised against us all the severities of the law, and outraged that sense of justice and of right which is acknowledged and felt by the whole civilized world by rejecting the observance of its ameliorations. The act of confiscation is a power exercised under the laws of war for the purpose of indemnifying the captor for his expense and losses; and it is upon this basis that it is recognized. At the same time there is a mode of procedure attached to its exercise by which it is reserved from the domain of plunder and devastation. As has been already shown, there are, under the law, exemptions of certain classes of property. It is further required that the property subject to confiscation shall be actually captured and taken possession of. It shall then be adjudicated as prize by a proper authority, then sold, and the money received must be deposited in the public Treasury. Such are the conditions attached by the law of nations to legal confiscation.

Now, compare these conditions with the act of Congress, that in its true light the usurpations of that body may be seen. The act of Congress allowed no exemptions of private property, but confiscated all the property of every kind belonging to persons residing in the Confederate States who were engaged in hostilities against the United States or who were aiding or abetting those engaged in hostilities. This includes slaves as well as other property. The act provided that the slaves should go free; that is, they were exempted from capture, from being adjudicated and sold, and no proceeds of sale were to be put into the public Treasury. The following sections are from the act of the United States Congress, passed on August 6, 1861:

"Section 1. That if, during the present or any future insurrection against the Government of the United States after the President of the United States shall have declared by proclamation that the laws of the United States are opposed and the execution thereof obstructed by combinations too powerful to be suppressed by the ordinary course of judicial proceedings or by the power vested in the marshals by law, any person, or persons, his, her, or their agent, attorney, or employee shall purchase or acquire, sell or give, any property, of whatsoever kind or description, with intent to use or employ the same, or suffer the same to be used or employed in aiding, abetting, or promoting such insurrection or resistance to the laws, or any person or persons engaged therein, or if any person or persons, being the owner or owners of any such property, shall knowingly use or employ or consent to the use or employment of the same as aforesaid, all such property is hereby declared to be lawful subject of prize and capture wherever found; and it shall be the duty of the President of the United States to cause the same to be seized, confiscated, and condemned.

"Section 3. The proceedings in court shall be for the benefit of the United States and the informer equally.

"Section 4. That whenever hereafter, during the present insurrection against the Government of the United States, any person claimed to be held to labor or service under the law of any State shall be required or permitted by the person to whom such labor or service is claimed to be due, or by the lawful agent of such person, to take up arms against the United States, or shall be required or permitted by the person to whom such labor or service is claimed to be due, or his lawful agent, to work or to be employed in or upon any fort, navy-yard, dock, armory, ship, intrenchment, or in any military or naval service whatsoever against the Government and lawful authority of the United States, then, and in every such case, the person to whom such labor or service is claimed to be due shall forfeit his claim to such labor, any law of the State or of the United States to the contrary notwithstanding. And, whenever thereafter the person claiming such labor or service shall seek to enforce his claim, it shall be a full and sufficient answer to such claim that the person whose service or labor is claimed had been employed in hostile service against the Government of the United States contrary to the provisions of this act."

The following sections are from the act of Congress passed on July 17, 1862:

"Section 6. That if any person, within any State or Territory of the United States other than those named aforesaid" (Confederate officers, etc.), "after the passage of this act, being engaged in armed rebellion against the Government of the United States or aiding or abetting such rebellion, shall not within sixty days after public warning and proclamation duly given and made by the President of the United States, cease to aid, countenance, and abet such rebellion and return to his allegiance to the United States, all the estate and property, moneys, stocks, and credits of such person shall be liable to seizure as aforesaid, and it shall be the duty of the President to seize and use them as aforesaid, or the proceeds thereof. And all sales, transfers, or conveyances of any such property, after the expiration of the said sixty days from the date of such warning and proclamation, shall be null and void; and it shall be a sufficient bar to any suit brought by such person for the possession or use of such property, or any of it, to allege and prove that he is one of the persons described in this section.

"Section 7. That to secure the condemnation and sale of any such property, after the same shall have been seized, so that it may be made available for the purpose aforesaid, proceedings *in rem* shall be instituted in the name of the United States in any district court thereof, or in any territorial court, or in the United States District Court for the District of Columbia, within which the property above described, or any part thereof, may be found, or into which the same, if movable, may first be brought, which proceedings shall conform as nearly as may be to proceedings in admiralty or revenue cases; and if said property, whether real or personal, shall be found to have belonged to a person engaged in rebellion, or who has given aid or comfort thereto, the same shall be condemned as enemy's property and become the property of the United States, and may be disposed of as the court shall decree, and the proceeds thereof paid into the Treasury of the United States for the purposes aforesaid.

"Section 9. That all slaves of persons who shall hereafter be engaged in rebellion against the Government of the United States, or who shall in any way give aid or comfort thereto, escaping from such persons and taking refuge within the lines of the army; and all slaves captured from such persons or deserted by them and coming under the control of the Government of the United States; and all slaves of such persons found or being within any place occupied by rebel forces and afterward occupied by the forces of the United States, shall be deemed captives of war, and shall be for ever free of their servitude, and not again held as slaves.

"Section 10. That no slave escaping into any State, Territory, or the District of Columbia from any other State, shall be delivered up, or in any way impeded or hindered of his liberty, except for crime or some offense against the laws, unless the person claiming said fugitive shall first make oath that the person, to whom the labor or service of such fugitive is alleged to be due, is his lawful owner, and has not borne arms against the United States in the present rebellion, nor in any way given aid and comfort thereto; and no person engaged in the military and naval service of the United States shall, under any pretense whatever, assume to decide on the validity of the claim of any person to the service or labor of any other person, or surrender up any such person to the claimant, on pain of being dismissed from the service."

These above-mentioned proceedings violated all the principles of the law of nations, without a shadow of authority for it under the Constitution of the United States. The armies of the United States were literally authorized to invade the Confederate States, to seize all property as plunder, and to let the negroes go free. Our posterity, reading that history, will blush that such facts are on record. It was estimated on the floor of the House of Representatives that the aggregate amount of property within our limits subject to be acted upon by the provisions of this act would affect upward of six million people, and would deprive them of property of the value of nearly five thousand million dollars.

Said Mr. Garrett Davis, of Kentucky:

"Was there ever, in any country that God's sun ever beamed upon, a legislative measure involving such an amount of property and such numbers of property-holders?"

But this is only one feature of the confiscation act which was applied to persons who were within the Confederate States, in such a position that the ordinary process of the United States courts could not be served upon them. They could be reached only by the armies. There was another feature equally flagrant and criminal. It was extended to all that class of persons giving aid and comfort, who could be found within the United States, or in such position that the ordinary process of law could be served on them. It was derived from Article III, section 3, of the Constitution, which says:

"The Congress shall have the power to declare the punishment of treason, but no attainder of treason shall work corruption of blood, or forfeiture, except during the life of the person attainted."

The mode of procedure against persons under this power was determined by other clauses of the Constitution. Article III, section 2, declared that—

"The trial of all crimes, except in cases of impeachment, shall be by jury; and such trial shall be held in the State where the said crimes shall have been committed."

In section 3, of the same article, it was provided that—

"No person shall be convicted of treason unless on the testimony of two witnesses to the same overt act, or on confession in open court."

This feature of the confiscation act, passed by the Congress of the United States, provided for the punishment of the owner of property, on the proof of the crime, but excluded the trial by jury, and made the forfeiture of the property absolute instead of a forfeiture for life. Heavy fines were imposed, and property was sold in fee. The property to which the act applied was not a prize under the law of nations, nor booty, nor contraband of war, nor enforced military contributions, nor used or employed in the war or in resistance to the laws. It was private property, outside of the conflict of arms, and forfeited, not because it was the instrument of offense, but as a penalty for the assertion of his rights by the owner, which was imputed to him as a crime. Such proceeding was, in effect, punishment by the forfeiture of a man's entire estate, real and personal, without trial by jury, and in utter disregard of the provisions of the Constitution. It was an attempt to get a man's property, real and personal, "silver spoons" included, into a prize court, to be tried by the laws of war.

It will be seen that we were treated by the Congress of the United States as holding the twofold relation of enemies and traitors, and that they used against us all the instruments of war, and all the penalties of municipal law which made the punishment of treason to be death. The practical operation, therefore, of these laws was that, under a Constitution which defined treason to consist in levying war against the United States, which would not suffer the traitor to be condemned except by the judgment of his peers, and, when condemned, would not forfeit his estate except during his life, the Government of the United States did proceed against six million people, without indictment, without trial by jury, without the proof of two witnesses, did adjudge our six millions of people guilty of treason in levying war, and decree to deprive us of all our estate, real and personal, for life, and in fee, being nearly five thousand million dollars. And, after we had been thus punished, without trial by jury, and by the loss in fee of our whole estate, the Government of the United States assumed the power, on the same charge of levying war, to try us and to hang us.

The first object to be secured by this act of confiscation was the emancipation of all our slaves. Upon his approval of the bill, President Lincoln sent a message to Congress, in which he said:

"It is startling to say that Congress can free a slave within a State, and yet, if it were said the ownership of the slave had first been transferred to the nation, and Congress had then liberated him, the difficulty would at once vanish. And this is the real case. The traitor against the General Government forfeits his slave at least as justly as he does any other property; and he forfeits both to the Government against which he offends. The Government, so far as there can be ownership, thus owns the forfeited slaves, and the question for Congress in regard to them is, 'Shall they be made free or sold to new masters?'"

It is amazing to see the utter forgetfulness of all constitutional obligations and the entire disregard of the conditions of the laws of nations manifested in these words of the President of the United States. Was he ignorant of their existence, or did he seek to cover up his violation of them by a deceptive use of language. It may not be unseasonable to repeat here the words of John Quincy Adams, in his letter of August 22, 1815, as above stated:

"Our object is the restoration of all the property, including slaves, which, by the usages of war among civilized nations, ought not to have been taken."

Let posterity answer the questions: Who were the revolutionists? Who were really destroying the Constitution of the United States?

The agitation of this subject brought out another still more alarming usurpation in Congress, and showed that the majority were ready to throw aside the last fragments of the Constitution in order to secure our subjugation. The argument for this usurpation was thus framed: Assuming that the state of the "nation" was one of general hostility, and that, being so involved, it possessed the power of self-defense, it was asserted that the supreme power of making and conducting war was expressly placed in Congress by the Constitution. "The whole powers of war are vested in Congress."—("United States Supreme Court, Brown vs. United States," 1 Cranch.) There is no such power in the judiciary, and the Executive is simply "commander-in-chief of the army and navy"; all other powers not necessarily implied in the command of the military and naval forces are expressly given to Congress.

The theory was that the contingency of actual hostilities suspended the Constitution and gave to Congress the sovereign power of a nation creating new relations and conferring new rights, imposing extraordinary obligations on the citizens, and subjecting them to extraordinary penalties. There is, under that view, therefore, no limit on the power of Congress; it is invested with the absolute powers of war—the civil functions of the Government are, for the time being, in abeyance when in conflict, and all State and "national" authority subordinated to the extreme authority of Congress, as the supreme power, in the peril of external or internal hostilities. The ordinary provisions of the Constitution peculiar to a state of peace, and all laws and municipal regulations, were to yield to the force of martial law, as resolved by Congress. This was designated as the "war power" of the United States Government.

I should deem an apology to be due to my readers, in offering for their perusal such insane extravagances, under a constitutional Government of limited powers, had not this doctrine been adopted by the United States Government, and subsequently made the basis of some most revolutionary measures for the emancipation of the African slaves and the enslavement of the free citizens of the South. One must allow that the Chamber of Deputies of the French National Assembly of 1798 had some claims to a respectable degree of political virtue when compared with the Thirty-seventh Congress and the Executive of the United States.

The specious argument for this tremendous and sweeping usurpation, designated as the "war power," as presented by its adherents, may be stated in a few words, thus: The Constitution confers on Congress all the specific powers incident to war, and then further authorizes it "to make all laws which shall be necessary and proper for carrying into execution the foregoing powers." The words are these:

"Congress shall have power to declare war; to grant letters of marque and reprisal; to make rules concerning captures on land and water; to raise and support armies; to provide and maintain a navy; to make rules for the government and regulation of the land and naval forces; to provide for calling forth the militia to execute the laws of the Union, suppress insurrections, and repel invasion; and to make all laws which shall be necessary and proper for carrying into execution the foregoing powers and all other powers vested by this Constitution in the Government of the United States, or in any department or officer thereof." [46]

It will be seen that this unlimited, despotic power was claimed for Congress in the conduct of the war under the last clause above, viz., "to make all laws which," etc; whereas no one familiar with the rules of legal interpretation will seriously contend that the powers of Congress are one atom greater by the insertion of this provision than they would have been if it had not appeared in the Constitution. The delegation of a power gives the incidental means *necessary* for its execution.

Another step in the usurpations begun for the destruction of slavery was the passage by Congress of an act for the emancipation of slaves in the District of Columbia. The act emancipated all persons of African descent held to service within the District, immediately upon its passage. Those owners of slaves who had not sympathized with us were allowed ninety days to prepare and present to commissioners, appointed for that purpose, the names, ages, and personal description of their slaves, who were to be valued by commissioners. No single slave could be estimated to be worth more than three hundred dollars. One million dollars was appropriated to carry the act into effect. All claims were to be presented within ninety days after the passage of the act, and not thereafter; but there was no saving clause for minors, *femmes covert*, insane or absent persons. On his approval of the act, the Executive of the United States sent a message to Congress, in which he said:

> "I have never doubted the constitutional authority of Congress to abolish slavery in the District, and I have ever desired to see the national capital freed from the institution in some satisfactory way. Hence there never has been in my mind any questions upon the subject, except those of expediency, arising in view of all the circumstances."

For the previous twenty-five or thirty years the subject had again and again been presented in Congress, and was always rejected. One of the incidents that led to our withdrawal from the Union was the apprehension that it was the intention of the United States Government to violate the constitutional right of each State to adopt and maintain, to reject or abolish slavery, as it pleased. This step showed the justness of our apprehensions.

Among the rights guaranteed to every citizen of the United States, including the District of Columbia, was the right of property. No one could be deprived of his property by the Government, except in the manner prescribed and authorized by the Constitution. Its words are these:

> "No person shall be deprived of life, liberty, or property without due process of law; nor shall private property be taken for public use without just compensation." [47]

Whenever it was necessary in the administration of affairs that the Government should take private property for public use, it had the right to take that private property on the condition of making compensation for it, and on no other condition. Also, it could not be taken except for public use, even by making just compensation for it; nor could it be taken to be destroyed. The simple and sole condition on which the inviolability of private property could be broken by the Government itself was, that it was necessary for public use. Otherwise, there was no constitutional right on the part of the Government to take the property at all.

Again, this property, thus necessary, must be taken by due process of law. The Government had not the right to declare the mode, and arbitrarily fix the limit of price which should be paid. The negro could be taken only as other property, even admitting that he could be taken for emancipation. The due process of law required that the citizen's property should be appraised judicially. A court must proceed judicially in every case, summon a jury, appoint commissioners, and, under the supervision and sanction of the court, the valuation of the slave by them must proceed as it does in relation to any other property of the citizen that might be taken by the lawful exercise of the power of Congress or of the United States Government. Thus it will be seen that by this usurpation of power the Constitution was violated, not only by taking private property for other purposes than for public use, but in the neglect to observe the due process of law which the Constitution required.

The next step in the usurpation of power for the destruction of the right of citizens to hold property in slaves was the passage by Congress of an act which declared that, after its passage—

"There shall be neither slavery nor
involuntary servitude in any of the Territories
of the United States now existing, or which
may at any time hereafter be formed or
acquired by the United States, otherwise than
in the punishment of crimes," etc.

The subject had been brought forward at every session of Congress for a number of years, and was uniformly resisted by the advocates of equality among the States. We claimed an equal right with the other States to the occupation and settlement of the Territories which were the common property of the Union; and that any infringement of this right was not only a violation of the spirit of the Constitution, but destructive of that equality of the States so necessary for the maintenance of their Union. We further claimed our right under this express provision of the Constitution:

"The Congress shall have power to dispose
of and make all needful rules and regulations
respecting the Territory or other property
belonging to the United States; and nothing in
this Constitution shall be so construed as to
prejudice any claims of the United States or of
any particular States." [48]

The obstinate resistance of the consolidation school to our views was an evidence of their aggressive purposes, and justified still further our apprehensions of their intention to violate our constitutional rights.

Another step taken to accomplish the emancipation of our slaves was the passage by Congress of an act making an additional article of war for the government of the army of the United States. It was in these words:

"All officers or persons in the military or
naval service of the United States are
prohibited from employing any of the forces
under their respective commands for the
purpose of returning fugitives from service or
labor, who may have escaped from any
persons to whom such service or labor is
claimed to be due; and any officer who shall
be found guilty by a court-martial of violating
this article shall be dismissed from the
service."

The Constitution of the United States expressly declares that all such persons "Shall be delivered up on claim of the party to whom such service or labor may be due." [49]

In this instance Congress passed an act declaring that they shall not be delivered up on such claim; and, as a penalty for disobedience, any officer of the army or navy should be dismissed from the service. Thus an act of Congress directly forbade that which the Constitution commanded. A more flagrant outrage upon the constitutional obligation could not be committed.

But, it may be said, a state of war existed. That does not diminish the crime of the Congress. The commands of the Constitution are positive, direct, unchanged, and unrelaxed by circumstances. They are equally in force in a state of war and in a state of peace. The powers are delegated, and can not be amended or changed by war or peace. Its words are these:

"This Constitution, and the laws of the
United States, which shall be made in
pursuance thereof, shall be the supreme law,
and the judges in every State shall be bound
thereby, anything in the Constitution or laws
of any State to the contrary notwithstanding.
The Senators and Representatives before
mentioned, and the members of the several
State Legislatures, and all executive and
judicial officers, both of the United States and
of the several States, shall be bound by oath
or affirmation to support this Constitution."
[50]

It declares itself to be, within its province, the supreme law of the United States, not merely during the condition of peace, but continuing through all times and events supreme throughout the Union, until it should be altered or amended in the manner prescribed.

Another instance of the like flagrant violation of the Constitution is to be found in the ninth and tenth sections of the confiscation act previously referred to. The Constitution of the United States in Article IV, section 3, says:

"No person held to service or labor in one
State, under the laws thereof, escaping into
another, shall, in consequence of any law or
regulation therein, be discharged from such
service or labor."

It will be seen, by reference to the Constitution, that the first part of the clause here referred to forbids the discharge of the fugitive, and the second part commands his delivery to the claimant. It has just been stated in what manner Congress commanded the claim for delivery to be repudiated. The "discharge from such service and labor," in consequence of any State law or regulation, is forbidden. This is a part of the Constitution, and it is thereby made the duty of the executive, legislative, and judicial departments of the United States Government to enforce the prohibition, to make sure that the fugitive is not discharged by any action of a State.

Will the friends of constitutional liberty believe our assertion that these acts, the execution of which it was so expressly made the duty of the United States Government to prevent, that Government itself did do in the most explicit and effective manner? The Constitution forbids the discharge; Congress and the Executive, each, not only commanded the discharge, but, to make it sure and thorough, forbade the incipiency of an apprehension—not even permitting the shadow of an occasion for a discharge. Could human ingenuity devise a method for a more perfect subversion of a constitutional duty? The provisions of the act are in these words:

"All slaves of persons who shall hereafter be engaged in rebellion against the Government of the United States, or who shall in any way give aid or comfort thereto, escaping from such persons and taking refuge within the lines of the army; and all slaves captured from such persons or deserted by them and coming under the control of the Government of the United States; and all slaves of such persons found or being within any place occupied by rebel forces and afterward occupied by the forces of the United States, shall be deemed captives of war, and shall be for ever free of their servitude, and not again held as slaves."

Again, the next section of the same act says:

"No slave escaping into any State, Territory, or the District of Colombia from any other State, shall be delivered up, or in any way impeded or hindered of his liberty, except for crime or some offense against the laws, unless the person claiming said fugitive shall first make oath that the person, to whom the labor or service of such fugitive is alleged to be due, is his lawful owner, and has not borne arms against the United States in the present rebellion, nor in any way given aid and comfort thereto." [51]

In this connection it is worth while to read again the words of the Constitution:

"No person held to service or labor in one State, under the laws thereof, escaping into another, shall, in consequence of any law or regulation therein, be discharged from such service or labor, but shall be delivered up on claim of the party to whom such service or labor may be due."

Let it be observed that there is no limitation, no qualification, no condition whatever attached to this clause of the Constitution. The words "no person held to service" included every slave in the United States. In Article I, section 9, and in Article V, are exceptions suspending the operation of the general provision. But in this provision there are none, because it was intended there should be none. The provision was designed to include every slave, and to be in force under all circumstances.

Perhaps it may be urged as an objection to this assertion, that the Confederate States were out of the Union and beyond the protection of the provisions of the Constitution. This objection can not be admitted in extenuation of this crime of Congress and the Executive; for there was, thus far, no act of Congress, nor proclamation of the President in existence, showing that either of them regarded the Confederate States in any other position than as States within the Union, whose citizens were subject to all the penalties contained in the Constitution, and therefore entitled to the benefit of all its provisions for their protection. Unhesitatingly it may be said, and as will be still more apparent farther on in these pages, that all the conduct of the Confederate States, pertaining to the war, consisted in just efforts to preserve to themselves and their posterity rights and protections guaranteed to them in the Constitution of the United States; and that the actions of the Federal Government consisted in efforts to subvert those rights, destroy those protections, and subjugate us to compliance with its arbitrary will; and that this conduct on their part involved the subversion of the Constitution and the destruction of the fundamental principles of liberty. Who is the criminal? Let posterity answer.

[Footnote 46: Constitution of the United States, Article I, section 8.]

[Footnote 47: Constitution of the United States, Article V.]

[Footnote 48: Constitution of the United States, Article IV, section 3, clause 2.]

[Footnote 49: Constitution of the United States, Article IV, section 2.]

[Footnote 50: Ibid., Article VI.]

[Footnote 51: Laws of the United States, 1862.]

CHAPTER XXVI.

Forced Emancipation concluded.—Emancipation Acts of President Lincoln.—Emancipation with Compensation proposed to Border States.—Reasons urged for it.—Its Unconstitutionality.—Order of General Hunter.—Revoked by President Lincoln.—Reasons.—"The Pressure" on him.—One Cause of our Secession.—The Time to throw off the Mask at Hand.—The Necessity that justified the President and Congress also justified Secession.—Men united in Defense of Liberty called Traitors.—Conference of President Lincoln with Senators and Representatives of Border States.—Remarks of Mr. Lincoln.—Reply of Senators and Representatives.—Failure of the Proposition.—Three Hundred Thousand more Men called for.— Declarations of the Antislavery Press.—Truth of our Apprehensions.—Reply of President Lincoln.—Another Call for Men.—Further Declarations of the Antislavery Press.—The Watchword adopted.—Memorial of So-called Christians to the President.—Reply of President Lincoln.—Issue of the Preliminary Proclamation of Emancipation.—Issue of the Final Proclamation.—The Military Necessity asserted.—The Consummation verbally reached.—Words of the Declaration of Independence.—Declarations by the United States Government of what it intended to do.—True Nature of the Party unveiled.—Declarations of President Lincoln.—Vindication of the Sagacity of the Southern People.—His Declarations to European Cabinets.—Object of these Declarations.—Trick of the Fugitive Thief.—The Boast of Mr. Lincoln calmly considered.

The attention of the reader is now invited to a series of usurpations in which the President of the United States was the principal actor. On March 6, 1862, he began a direct and unconstitutional interference with slavery by sending a message to Congress recommending the adoption of a resolution which should declare that the United States ought to coöperate with any State which might adopt the gradual abolition of slavery, giving to such State pecuniary aid, to be used by such State in its discretion, to compensate for the inconvenience, public and private, produced by such change of system. The reason given for the recommendation of the adoption of the resolution was that the United States Government would find its highest interest in such a measure as one of the most important means of self-preservation. He said, in explanation, that "the leaders of the existing rebellion entertain the hope that this Government will ultimately be forced to acknowledge the independence of some part of the disaffected region, and that all the slave States north of such part will then say, 'The Union for which we have struggled being already gone, we now choose to go with the Southern section.' To deprive them of this hope substantially ends the rebellion, and the initiation of emancipation deprives them of it and of all the States initiating it."

When it was asked where the power was found in the Constitution to appropriate the money of the people to carry out the purposes of the resolution, it was replied that the legislative department of the Government was competent, under these words in the preamble of the Constitution, "to provide for the general welfare," to do anything and everything which could be considered as promoting the general welfare. It was further said that this measure was to be consummated under the war power; that whatever was necessary to carry on the war to a successful conclusion might be done without restraint under the authority, not of the Constitution, but as a military necessity. It was further said that the President of the United States had thus far failed to meet the just expectations of the party which elected him to the office he held; and that his friends were to be comforted by the resolution and the message, while the people of the border slave States could not fail to observe that with the comfort to the North there was mingled an awful warning to them. It was denied by the President that it was an interference with slavery in the States. It was an artful scheme to awaken a controversy in the slave States, and to commence the work of emancipation by holding out pecuniary aid as an inducement. In every previous declaration the President had said that he did not contemplate any interference with domestic slavery within the States. The resolution was passed by large majorities in each House.

This proposition of President Lincoln was wholly unconstitutional, because it attempted to do what was expressly forbidden by the Constitution. It proposed a contract between the State of Missouri and the Government of the United States which, in the language of the act, shall be "irrepealable without the consent of the United States." The words of the Constitution are as follows:

"No State shall enter into any treaty, alliance, or confederation, grant letters of marque and reprisal, coin money, etc." [52]

This is a prohibition not only upon the power of one State to enter into a compact, alliance, confederation, or agreement with another State, but also with the Government of the United States.

Again, if the State of Missouri could enter into an irrepealable agreement or compact with the United States, that slavery should not therein exist after the acceptance on the part of Missouri of the act, then it would be an agreement on the part of that State to surrender its sovereignty and make the State unequal in its rights of sovereignty with the other States of the Union. The other States would have the complete right of sovereignty over their domestic institutions while the State of Missouri would cease to have such right. The whole system of the United States Government would be abrogated by such legislation. Again, it is a cardinal principle of the system that the people in their sovereign capacity may, from time to time, change and alter their organic law; and a provision incorporated in the Constitution of Missouri that slavery should never thereafter exist in that State could not prevent a future sovereign convention of its people from reestablishing slavery within its limits.

It will be observed, from what has been said in the preceding pages, that the usurpations by the Government of the United States, both by the legislative and executive departments, had not only been tolerated but approved. Feeling itself, therefore, fortified in its unlimited power from "necessity," the wheels of the revolution were now to move with accelerated velocity in their destructive work. Accordingly, a manifesto soon comes from the Executive on universal emancipation. On April 25, 1862, the United States Major-General Hunter, occupying a position at Hilton Head, South Carolina, issued an order declaring the States of Georgia, Florida, and South Carolina under martial law. On May 9th the same officer issued another order, declaring "the persons held as slaves in those States to be for ever free." The Executive of the United States, on May 19th, issued a proclamation declaring the order to be void, and said:

"I further make known that, whether it be competent for me as commander-in-chief of the army and navy to declare the slaves of any State or States free, and whether at any time or in any case it shall have become a necessity indispensable to the maintenance of the Government to examine such supposed power, are questions which, under my responsibility, I reserve to myself, and which I can not feel justified in leaving to the decision of commanders in the field."

Speaking of this order of Major-General Hunter soon afterward, President Lincoln, in remarks on July 12, 1862, to the border States Representatives, said:

"In repudiating it, I gave dissatisfaction, if not offense, to many whose support the country can not afford to lose. And this is not the end of it. The pressure in this direction is still upon me, and is increasing."

This pressure consisted in the demand of his extreme partisans that the whole authority of the Government should be exerted for the immediate and universal emancipation of the slaves.

By a reference to the statement of the causes of our withdrawal from the Union of the United States, it will be seen that one of them consisted in the conviction that the newly elected officers of the Government would wield its powers for the destruction of the institutions of the Southern States. The facts already related in these pages furnish ample proofs of the justice and accuracy of this conviction.

The time was now close at hand when the mask was to be thrown off, and, at a single dash of the pen, four hundred millions of our property was to be annihilated, the whole social fabric of the Southern States disrupted, all branches of industry to be disarranged, good order to be destroyed, and a flood of evils many times greater than the loss of property to be inflicted upon the people of the South, thus consummating the series of aggressions which had been inflicted for more than thirty years. All constitutional protections were to be withdrawn, and the powers of a common government, created for common and equal protection to the interests of all, were to be arrayed for the destruction of our institutions. The President of the United States says: "This is not the end. The pressure in this direction is still upon me, and is increasing." How easy it would have been for the Northern people, by a simple, honest obedience to the provisions of the Constitution, to have avoided the commission of all these crimes and horrors! For the law which demands obedience to itself guarantees in return life and safety. It is not necessary to ask again where the President of the United States or the Congress found authority for their usurpations. But it should be remembered that, if the necessity which they pleaded was an argument to justify their violations of all the provisions of the Constitution, the existence of such a necessity on their part was a sufficient argument to justify our withdrawal from union with them. If necessity on their part justified a violation of the Constitution, necessity on our part justified secession from them. If the preservation of the existence of the Union by coercion of the States was an argument to justify these violent usurpations by the United States Government, it was still more forcibly an argument to justify our separation and resistance to invasion; for we were struggling for our natural rights, but the Government of the United States has no natural rights.

How can a people who glory in a Declaration of Independence which broke the slumbers of a world declare that men united in defense of liberty, property, and the pursuit of happiness are "traitors"? Is it henceforth to be a dictum of humanity that man may no more take up arms in defense of rights, liberty, and property? Shall it never again in the course of human events become lawful "for one people to dissolve the political bands which have connected them with another, and to assume among the powers of the earth the separate and equal station to which the laws of nature and of nature's God entitle them"? Is the highwayman, henceforth, to be the lord of the highway, and the poor, plundered traveler to have no property which he may defend at the risk of the life of the highwayman?

On July 12, 1862, the President of the United States, persistent in his determination to destroy the institution of slavery, invited the Senators and Representatives of the border slaveholding States to the Executive Mansion, and addressed them on emancipation in their respective States. He said:

"I intend no reproach or complaint when I assure you that, in my opinion, if you all had voted for the resolution in the gradual emancipation message of last March, the war would now be substantially ended. And the plan therein proposed is yet one of the most potent and swift means of ending it. Let the States which are in rebellion see definitely and certainly that in no event will the States you represent ever join their proposed confederacy, and they can not much longer maintain the contest. But you can not divest them of their hope to ultimately have you with them so long as you show a determination to perpetuate the institution within your own States. Beat them at elections as you have overwhelmingly done, and, nothing daunted, they still claim you as their own. You and I know what the lever of their power is. Break that lever before their faces, and they can shake you no more for ever."

He further said that the incidents of the war might extinguish the institution in their States, and added:

"How much better for you as seller and the nation as buyer to sell out and buy out that without which the war could never have been, than to sink both the thing to be sold and the price of it in cutting one another's throats!"

The reply of the majority, consisting of twenty of the twenty-nine Senators and Representatives, subsequently made to the President, is worthy of notice. They said that they were not of the belief that funds would be provided for the object, or that their constituents would reap the fruits of the promise held out, and added:

"The right to hold slaves is a right appertaining to all the States of the Union. They have the right to cherish or abolish the institution, as their tastes or their interests may prompt, and no one is authorized to question the right, or limit its enjoyment. And no one has more clearly affirmed that right than you have. Your inaugural address does you great honor in this respect, and inspired the country with confidence in your fairness and respect for law."

After asserting that a large portion of our people were fighting because they believed the Administration was hostile to their rights, and was making war on their domestic institutions, they further said:

"Remove their apprehensions; satisfy them that no harm is intended to them and their institutions; that this Government is not making war on their rights of property, but is simply defending its legitimate authority, and they will gladly return to their allegiance."

This measure of emancipation with compensation soon proved a failure. A proposition to appropriate five hundred thousand dollars to the object was voted down in the United States Senate with great unanimity. The Government was, step by step, "educating the people" up to a proclamation of emancipation, so as to make entire abolition one of the positive and declared issues of the contest.

The so-called pressure upon the President was now organized for a final onset. The Governors of fifteen States united in a request that three hundred thousand more men should be called out to fill up the reduced ranks, and it was done. The anti-slavery press then entered the arena. Charges were made against the President, in the name of

"Twenty millions of people, that a groat proportion of those who triumphed in his election were sorely disappointed and deeply pained by the policy he seemed to be pursuing with regard to the slaves of the rebels."

This is a simple statement of the progress of events, and it shows to the world how well founded were our apprehensions, at the hour of its election, that the Administration intended the destruction of our property and community independence. They further said:

"You are strangely and disastrously remiss in the discharge of your official and imperative duty with regard to the emancipation provisions of the new confiscation act."

They further boldly added:

"We complain that the Union cause has suffered, and is now suffering, immensely from mistaken deference to rebel slavery.

Had you, sir, in your inaugural address, unmistakably given notice that, in case the rebellion already commenced was persisted in, and your efforts to preserve the Union and enforce the laws should be resisted by armed force, you would recognize no loyal person as rightfully held in slavery by a traitor, we believe the rebellion would therein have received a staggering if not fatal blow."

The President replied at length, saying:

"I shall do less whenever I shall believe what I am doing hurts the cause, and I shall do more whenever I shall believe doing more will help the cause. I shall try to correct errors when shown to be errors; and I shall adopt new views so fast as they shall appear to be true views. I have here stated my purpose according to my view of official duty; and I intend no modification of my oft-expressed personal wish that all men everywhere could be free."

The education of the conservative portion of the Northern people up to emancipation was becoming more complete every day, notwithstanding the professed reluctance of the President. Another call for three hundred thousand men was made, but enlistments were slow, so that threats of a draft and most liberal bounties were required. The champions of emancipation sought to derive an advantage from this circumstance. They asserted that the reluctance of the people to enter the army was caused by the policy of the Government in not adopting bold emancipation measures. If such were adopted, the streets and by-ways would be crowded with volunteers to fight for the freedom of the "loyal blacks," and thrice three hundred thousand could be easily obtained. They said that slavery in the seceded States should be treated as a military question; it contributed nearly all the subsistence which supported the Southern men in arms, dug their trenches, and built their fortifications. The watchword which they now adopted was, "The abolition of slavery by the force of arms for the sake of the Union."

Meantime, on September 13th, a delegation from the so-called "Christians" in Chicago, Illinois, presented to President Lincoln a memorial, requesting him to issue a proclamation of emancipation, and urged in its favor such reasons as occurred to their minds. President Lincoln replied:

"What good would a proclamation of emancipation from me do, especially as we are now situated? I do not want to issue a document that the whole world would see must necessarily be inoperative, like the Pope's bull against the comet. Would my word free the slaves, when I can not even enforce the Constitution in the rebel States? Is there a single court, or magistrate, or individual that would be influenced by it there? And what reason is there to think it would have any greater effect upon the slaves than the late law of Congress which I approved, and which offers protection and freedom to the slaves of rebel masters who come within our lines? Yet I can not learn that that law has caused a single slave to come over to us. And suppose they could be induced by a proclamation of freedom from me to throw themselves upon us, what should we do with them? How can we feed and care for such a multitude? . . .

"If, now, the pressure of the war should call off our forces from New Orleans to defend some other point, what is to prevent the masters from reducing the blacks to slavery again? . . . Now, then, tell me, if you please, what possible result of good would follow the issuing of such a proclamation as you desire? I have not decided against a proclamation of liberty to the slaves, but hold the matter under advisement."

Nine days after these remarks were made—on September 22, 1862—the preliminary proclamation of emancipation was issued by the President of the United States. It declared that at the next session of Congress the proposition for emancipation in the border slaveholding States would be again recommended, and that on January 1, 1863—

"All persons held as slaves within any State or designated part of a State, the people whereof shall then be in rebellion against the United States, shall be then, thenceforward, and for ever free; and the Executive Government of the United States, including the military and naval authority thereof, will recognize and maintain the freedom of such persons, and will do no act or acts to repress such persons, or any of them, in any efforts they may make for their actual freedom."

Also, all persons engaged in the military and naval service were ordered to obey and enforce the article of war and the sections of the confiscation act before mentioned. On January 1, 1863, another proclamation was issued by the President of the United States declaring the emancipation to be absolute within the Confederate States, with the exception of a few districts. The closing words of the proclamation were these:

"And upon this act, sincerely believed to
be an act of justice, warranted by the
Constitution upon military necessity, I invoke
the considerate judgment of mankind and the
gracious favor of Almighty God."

Let us test the existence of the military necessity here spoken of by a few facts. The white male population of the Northern States was then 13,690,364. The white male population of the Confederate States was 5,449,463. The number of troops which the United States had called into the field exceeded one million men. The number of troops which the Confederate Government had then in the field was less than four hundred thousand men. The United States Government had a navy which was only third in rank in the world. The Confederate Government had a navy which at that time consisted of a single small ship on the ocean. The people of the United States had a commerce afloat all over the world. The people of the Confederate States had not a single port open to commerce. The people of the United States were the rivals of the greatest nations in all kinds of manufactures. The people of the Confederate States had few manufactures, and those were of articles of inferior importance. The Government of the United States possessed the Treasury of a Union of eighty years with its vast resources. The Confederate States had to create a Treasury by the development of financial resources. The ambassadors and representatives of the former were welcomed at every court in the world. The representatives of the latter were not recognized anywhere.

Thus the consummation of the original antislavery purposes was verbally reached; but even that achievement was attended with disunion, bloodshed, and war. In the words of the Declaration of Independence:

"We hold these truths to be self-evident, that, whenever any form of government becomes destructive of these ends" (life, liberty, and the pursuit of happiness), "it is the right of the people to alter or to abolish it, and to institute a new government, laying its foundation on such principles, and organizing its powers in such form, as to them shall seem most likely to effect their safety and happiness. . . . When a long train of abuses and usurpations, pursuing invariably the same object, evinces a design to reduce them under absolute despotism, it is their right, it is their duty, to throw off such government, and to provide new guards for their future security."

It is thus seen what the United States Government did, and our view of this subject would not be complete if we should omit to present their solemn declarations of that which they intended to do. In his proclamation of April 15, 1861, calling for seventy-five thousand men, the President of the United States Government said:

"In any event, the utmost care will be observed, consistently with the objects aforesaid, to avoid any devastation, any destruction of or interference with property, or any disturbance of peaceful citizens in any part of the country."

On the 22d of July, 1861, Congress passed a resolution relative to the war, from which the following is an extract:

"That this war is not waged on our part in any spirit of oppression, or for any purpose of conquest or subjugation, or purpose of overthrowing or interfering with the rights or established institutions of those [Confederate] States; but to defend and maintain the supremacy of the Constitution, and to preserve the Union with all the dignity, equality, and rights of the several States unimpaired; and that, as soon as these objects are accomplished, the war ought to cease."

The vote in favor of the resolution was: in the Senate, yeas 30, nays 4; in the House of Representatives, yeas 117, nays 2.

It may further be observed that these proclamations cited above afforded to our whole people the complete and crowning proof of the true nature of the designs of the party which elevated to power the person then occupying the Presidential chair at Washington, and which sought to conceal its purposes by every variety of artful device and by the perfidious use of the most solemn and repeated pledges on every possible occasion. A single example may be cited from the declaration made by President Lincoln, under the solemnity of his oath as Chief Magistrate of the United States, on March 4, 1861:

"Apprehension seems to exist among the people of the Southern States that, by the accession of a Republican Administration, their property and their peace and personal security are to be endangered. There has never been any reasonable cause for such apprehensions. Indeed, the most ample evidence to the contrary has all the while existed and been open to their inspection. It is found in nearly all the public speeches of him who now addresses you. I do but quote from one of those speeches when I declare that I have no purpose, directly or indirectly, to interfere with the institution of slavery in the States where it exists. I believe I have no lawful right to do so, and I have no inclination to do so. Those who nominated and elected me did so with full knowledge that I had made this and many similar declarations, and had never recanted them. And more than this, they placed in the platform for my acceptance, and as a law to themselves and to me, the clear and emphatic resolution which I now read:

"*Resolved*, That the maintenance inviolate of the rights of the States, and especially the right of each State to order and control its own domestic institutions according to its own judgment exclusively, is essential to that balance of power on which the perfection and endurance of our political fabric depend, and we denounce the lawless invasion by armed force of the soil of any State or Territory, no matter under what pretext, as among the gravest crimes."

Nor was this declaration of the want of power or disposition to interfere with our social system confined to a state of peace. Both before and after the actual commencement of hostilities, the Executive of the United States repeated in formal official communications to the Cabinets of Great Britain and France, that it was utterly without constitutional power to do the act which it subsequently committed, and that in no possible event, whether the secession of these States resulted in the establishment of a separate Confederacy or in the restoration of the Union, was there any authority by virtue of which it could either restore a disaffected State to the Union by force of arms, or make any change in any of its institutions. I refer especially for the verification of this assertion to the dispatches addressed by the Secretary of State of the United States, under direction of the President, to the Ministers of the United States at London and Paris, under date of the 10th and 22d of April, 1861.

This proclamation was therefore received by the people of the Confederate States as the fullest vindication of their own sagacity in foreseeing the uses to which the dominant party in the United States intended from the beginning to apply their power.

For what honest purpose were these declarations made? They could deceive no one who was familiar with the powers and duties of the Federal Government; they were uttered in the season of invasion of the Southern States, to coerce them to obedience to the agent established by the compact between the States, for the purpose of securing domestic tranquillity and the blessings of liberty. The power to coerce States was not given, and the proposition to make that grant received no favor in the Convention which formed the Constitution; and it is seen by the proceedings in the States, when the Constitution was submitted to each of them for their ratification or rejection as they might choose, that a proposition which would have enabled the General Government, by force of arms, to control the will of a State, would have been fatal to any effort to make a more perfect Union. Such declarations as those cited from the diplomatic correspondence, though devoid of credibility at home, might avail in foreign countries to conceal from their governments the real purpose of the action of the majority. Meanwhile, the people of the Confederacy plainly saw that the ideas and interests of the Administration were to gain by war the empire that would enable it to trample on the Constitution which it professed to defend and maintain.

It was by the slow and barely visible approaches of the serpent seeking its prey that the aggressions and usurpations of the United States Government moved on to the crimes against the law of the Union, the usages of war among civilized nations, the dictates of humanity and the requirements of justice, which have been recited. The performance of this task has been painful, but persistent and widespread misrepresentation of the cause and conduct of the South required the exposure of her slanderer. To unmask the hypocrisy of claiming devotion to the Constitution, while violating its letter and spirit for a purpose palpably hostile to it, was needful for the defense of the South. In the future progress of this work it will be seen how often we have been charged with the very offenses committed by our enemy—offenses of which the South was entirely innocent, and of which a chivalrous people would be incapable. There was in this the old trick of the fugitive thief who cries "Stop thief!" as he runs.

In his message to Congress one year later, on December 8, 1863, the President of the United States thus boasts of his proclamation:

"The preliminary emancipation proclamation, issued in September, was running its assigned period to the beginning of the new year. A month later the final proclamation came, including the announcement that colored men of suitable condition would be received into the war service. The policy of emancipation and of employing black soldiers gave to the future a new aspect, about which hope and fear and doubt contended in uncertain conflict. According to our political system, as a matter of civil administration, the General Government had no lawful power to effect emancipation in any State, and for a long time it had been hoped that the rebellion could be suppressed without resorting to it as a military measure. . . . Of those who were slaves at the beginning of the rebellion, full one hundred thousand are now in the United States military service, about one half of which number actually bear arms in the ranks, thus giving the double advantage of taking so much labor from the insurgent cause, and supplying the places which otherwise must be filled with so many white men. So far as tested, it is difficult to say they are not as good soldiers as any."

Let the reader pause for a moment and look calmly at the facts presented in this statement. The forefathers of these negro soldiers were gathered from the torrid plains and malarial swamps of inhospitable Africa. Generally they were born the slaves of barbarian masters, untaught in all the useful arts and occupations, reared in heathen darkness, and, sold by heathen masters, they were transferred to shores enlightened by the rays of Christianity. There, put to servitude, they were trained in the gentle arts of peace and order and civilization; they increased from a few unprofitable savages to millions of efficient Christian laborers. Their servile instincts rendered them contented with their lot, and their patient toil blessed the land of their abode with unmeasured riches. Their strong local and personal attachment secured faithful service to those to whom their service or labor was due. A strong mutual affection was the natural result of this life-long relation, a feeling best if not only understood by those who have grown from childhood under its influence. Never was there happier dependence of labor and capital on each other. The tempter came, like the serpent in Eden, and decoyed them with the magic word of "freedom." Too many were allured by the uncomprehended and unfulfilled promises, until the highways of these wanderers were marked by corpses of infants and the aged. He put arms in their hands, and trained their humble but emotional natures to deeds of violence and bloodshed, and sent them out to devastate their benefactors. What does he boastingly announce?—"It is difficult to say they are not as good soldiers as any." Ask the bereaved mother, the desolate widow, the sonless aged sire, to whom the bitter cup was presented by those once of their own household. With double anguish they speak of its bitterness. What does the President of the United States further say?—"According to our political system, as a matter of civil administration, the General Government had no lawful power to effect emancipation in any State." And further on, as if with a triumphant gladness, he adds, "Thus giving the double advantage of taking so much labor from the insurgent cause, and supplying the places which otherwise must be filled with so many white men." A rare mixture of malfeasance with traffic in human life! It is submitted to the judgment of a Christian people how well such a boast befits the President of the United States, a federation of sovereigns under a voluntary compact for specific purposes.

[Footnote 52: Article I, section 10.]

CHAPTER XXVII.

Naval Affairs.—Organization of the Navy Department.—Two Classes of Vessels.—Experiments for Floating Batteries and Rams.—The Norfolk Navy-Yard.—Abandonment by the Enemy.—The Merrimac Frigate made an Ironclad.—Officers.—Trial-Trip.—Fleet of the Enemy.—Captain Buchanan.—Resolves to attack the Enemy.—Sinks the Cumberland.—Burns the Congress.—Wounded.—Executive Officer Jones takes Command.—Retires for the Night.—Appearance of the Monitor.—The Virginia attacks her.—She retires to Shoal Water.— Refuses to come out.—Cheers of English Man-of-war.—Importance of the Navy-Yard.—Order of General Johnston to evacuate.—Stores saved.—The Virginia burned.—Harbor Defenses at Wilmington.— Harbor Defenses at Charleston.—Fights in the Harbor.—Defenses of Savannah.—Mobile Harbor and Capture of its Defenses.—The System of Torpedoes adopted.—Statement of the Enemy.—Sub-terra Shells placed in James River.—How made.—Used in Charleston Harbor; in Roanoke River; in Mobile Harbor.—The Tecumseh, how destroyed.

The organization of the Navy Department comprised under its general supervision a bureau of orders and details, one of ordnance and hydrography, one of provisions and clothing, and one of medicine and surgery. The grades of officers consisted of admirals, captains, commanders, surgeons, lieutenants, and midshipmen. Of the officers at the close of the first year there were one admiral, twelve captains, thirty commanders, and one hundred and twelve first and second lieutenants. All of the principal officers had belonged to the United States Navy. Owing to the limited number of vessels afloat, many of these officers were employed on shore-duties.

The vessels of the navy may be reduced to two classes: those intended for river and harbor defense, as ironclads, rams, floating batteries, or river-steamboats transformed into gunboats; and sea-going steamers of moderate size, some of them of great speed, but, not having been designed for war purposes, were all unsuited for a powerful armament, and could not be expected to contend successfully with ships of war.

Early in 1861 discussions and experiments were instituted by the Navy Department to determine how floating batteries and naval rams could be best constructed and protected by iron plates. Many persons had submitted plans, according to which cotton-bales might be effectively used as a shield against shot. Our deficiency in iron, and also in rolling-mills to prepare it into plates, caused cotton to be sometimes so employed; though the experiments had satisfied the Navy Department that, instead of cotton being rendered impenetrable by compression, it was really less so than in looser condition, and that iron must needs be of great thickness to resist the direct impact of heavy shot at short ranges. An officer of the navy, as skillful in ordnance as he was in seamanship, and endowed with high capacity for the investigation of new problems—Lieutenant Catesby Ap R. Jones— had conducted many of these experiments, and, as will be seen hereafter, made efficient use of his knowledge both in construction and in battle.

After Virginia had seceded from the United States, but before she had acceded to the Confederate States—viz., on the 19th of April, 1861—General Taliaferro, in command of Virginia forces, arrived at Norfolk. Commodore McCauley, United States Navy, and commandant of the navy-yard, held a conference with General Taliaferro, the result of which was "that none of the vessels should be removed, nor a shot fired except in self-defense." The excitement which had existed in the town was quieted by the announcement of this arrangement; but it was soon ascertained that the Germantown and Merrimac, frigates in the port, had been scuttled, and the former otherwise injured. About midnight, as elsewhere stated, a fire was started in the navy-yard, which continued to increase, involving the destruction of the ship-houses, a ship of the line, and the unfinished frame of another; several frigates, in addition to those mentioned, had been scuttled and sunk; and other property destroyed, to an amount estimated at several million dollars. The Pawnee, which arrived on the 19th, had been kept under steam, and, taking the Cumberland in tow, retired down the harbor, freighted with a great portion of valuable munitions and the commodore and other officers of the yard.[53] In the haste and secrecy of the conflagration, a large amount of material remained uninjured. The Merrimac, a beautiful frigate, in the yard for repairs, was raised by the Virginians, and the work immediately commenced, on a plan devised by Lieutenant Brooke, Confederate States Navy, to convert her hull, with such means as were available, into an iron-clad vessel. Two-inch plates were prepared, and she was covered with a double-inclined roof of four inches thickness. This armor, though not sufficiently thick to resist direct shot, sufficed to protect against a glancing ball, and was as heavy as was consistent with the handling of the ship. The shield was defective in not covering the sides sufficiently below the water-line, and the prow was unfortunately made of cast-iron; but, when all the difficulties by which we were surrounded are remembered, and the service rendered by this floating battery considered, the only wonder must be that so much was so well done under the circumstances.

Her armament consisted of ten guns, four single-banded Brooke rifles, and six nine-inch Dahlgren shell-guns. Two of the rifles, bow and stern pivots, were seven inch; the other two were six and four tenths inch, one on each broadside. The nine-inch gun on each side, nearest the furnaces, was fitted for firing hot shot. The work of construction was prosecuted with all haste, the armament and crew were put on board, and the vessel started on her trial-trip as soon as the workmen were discharged. She was our first ironclad; her model was an experiment, and many doubted its success. Her commander, Captain (afterward Admiral) Franklin Buchanan, with the wisdom of age and the experience of sea-service from his boyhood, combined the daring and enterprise of youth, and with him was Lieutenant Catesby Ap R. Jones, who had been specially in charge of the battery, and otherwise thoroughly acquainted with the ship. His high qualifications as an ordnance officer were well known in the "old navy," and he was soon to exhibit a like ability as a seaman in battle.

Now the first Confederate ironclad was afloat, the Stars and Bars were given to the breeze, and she was new-christened "the Virginia." She was joined by the Patrick Henry, six guns, Commander John R. Tucker; the Jamestown, two guns. Lieutenant-commanding John N. Barney; the Beaufort, one gun, Lieutenant-commanding W. H. Parker; the Raleigh, one gun, Lieutenant-commanding J. W. Alexander; the Teaser, one gun, Lieutenant-commanding W. A. Webb.

The enemy's fleet in Hampton Roads consisted of the Cumberland, twenty-four guns; Congress, fifty guns; St. Lawrence, fifty guns; steam-frigates Minnesota and Roanoke, forty guns each. The relative force was as twenty-one guns to two hundred and four, not counting the small steamers of the enemy, though they had heavier armament than the small vessels of our fleet, which have been enumerated. The Cumberland and the Congress lay off Newport News; the other vessels were anchored about nine miles eastward, near to Fortress Monroe. Strong shore-batteries and several small steamers, armed with heavy rifled guns, protected the frigates Cumberland and Congress.

Buchanan no doubt felt the inspiration of a sailor when his vessel bears him from the land, and the excitement of a hero at the prospect of battle, and thus we may understand why the trial-trip was at once converted into a determined attack upon the enemy. After the plan of the Virginia had been decided upon, the work of her construction was pushed with all possible haste. Her armament was on board, and she was taken out of the dock while the workmen were still employed upon her—indeed, the last of them were put ashore after she was started on her first experimental trip. Few men, conscious as Flag-officer Buchanan was of the defects of his vessel, would have dared such unequal conflict. Slowly—about five knots an hour—he steamed down to the roads. The Cumberland and Congress, seeing the Virginia approach, prepared for action, and, from the flag-ship Roanoke, signals were given to the Minnesota and St. Lawrence to advance. The Cumberland had swung so as to give her full broadside to the Virginia, which silently and without any exhibition of her crew, moved steadily forward. The shot from the Cumberland fell thick upon her plated roof, but rebounded harmless as hailstones. At last the prow of the Virginia struck the Cumberland just forward of her starboard fore-chains. A dull, heavy thud was heard, but so little force was given to the Virginia that the engineer hesitated about backing her. It was soon seen, however, that a gaping breach had been made in the Cumberland, and that the sea was rushing madly in. She reeled, and, while the waves ingulfed her, her crew gallantly stood to their guns and vainly continued their fire. She went down in nine fathoms of water, and with at least one hundred of her gallant crew, her pennant still flying from her mast-head.

The Virginia then ran up stream a short distance, in order to turn and have sufficient space to get headway, and come down on the Congress. The enemy, supposing that she had retired at the sight of the vessels approaching to attack her, cheered loudly, both ashore and afloat. But, when she turned to descend upon the Congress, as she had on the Cumberland, the Congress slipped her cables and ran ashore, bows on. The Virginia took position as near as the depth of water would permit, and opened upon her a raking fire. The Minnesota was fast aground about one mile and a half below. The Roanoke and St. Lawrence retired toward the fort. The shore-batteries kept up their fire on the Virginia, as did also the Minnesota at long range, and quite ineffectually. The Congress, being aground, could but feebly reply. Several of our small vessels came up and joined the Virginia, and the combined fire was fearfully destructive to the Congress. Her commander was killed, and soon her colors were struck, and the white flag appeared both at the main and spanker gaff. The Beaufort, Lieutenant-commanding W. H. Parker, and the Raleigh, Lieutenant-commanding J. W. Alexander, tugs which had accompanied the Virginia, were ordered to the Congress to receive the surrender. The flag of the ship and the sword of its then commander were delivered to Lieutenant Parker, by whom they were subsequently sent to the Navy Department at Richmond. Other officers delivered their swords in token of surrender, and entreated that they might return to assist in getting their wounded out of the ship. The permission was granted to the officers, and they then took advantage of the clemency shown them to make their escape. In the mean time the shore-batteries fired upon the tugs, and compelled them to retire. By this fire five of their own men, our prisoners, were wounded. Flag-officer Buchanan had stopped the firing upon the Congress when she struck her flag, and ran up the white flag, as heretofore described. Lieutenant Jones in his official report, referring to the Congress, writes: "But she fired upon us with the white flag flying, wounding Lieutenant Minor and several of our men. We again opened fire upon her, and she is now in flames." The crew of the Congress escaped, as did that of the Cumberland, by boats, or by swimming, and generously our men abstained from firing on them while so exposed. Flag-officer Buchanan was wounded by a rifle-ball, and had to be carried below. His intrepid conduct won the admiration of all. The executive and ordnance officer, Lieutenant Catesby Ap R. Jones, succeeded to the command. It was now so near night and the change of the tide that nothing further could be attempted on that day. The Virginia, with the smaller vessels attending her, withdrew and anchored off Sewell's Point. She had sunk the Cumberland, left the Congress on fire, had blown up a transport-steamer, sunk one schooner, and had captured another. Casualties, reported by Lieutenant Jones, were two killed and eight wounded. The prow of the Virginia was somewhat damaged, her anchor and all her flag-staffs were shot away, and her smoke-stack and steam-pipe were riddled; otherwise, the vessel was uninjured, and, as will be seen, was ready for action on the next morning. The prisoners and wounded were immediately sent up to the hospital at Norfolk.

During the night the Monitor, an iron-clad turret-steamer, of an entirely new model, came in, and anchored near the Minnesota. Like our Virginia she was an invention, and her merits and demerits were to be tested in the crucible of war. She was of light draught, and very little save the revolving turret was visible above the water, was readily handled, and had good speed; but, also, like the Virginia, was not supposed by nautical men to be capable of braving rough weather at sea.

The Virginia was the hull of a frigate, modified into an ironclad vessel. She was only suited to smooth water, and it had not been practicable to obtain for her such engines as would have given her the requisite speed. Her draught, twenty-two feet, was too great for the shoal water in the roads, and the apprehension which was excited lest she should go up to Washington might have been allayed by a knowledge of the deep water necessary to float her. Her great length, depth, and want of power, caused difficulty in handling to be anticipated. In many respects she was an experiment, and, had we possessed the means to build a new vessel, no doubt a better model could have been devised. Commander Brooke, who united much science to great ingenuity, was not entirely free in the exercise of either. Our means restricted us to making the best of that which chance had given us.

In the morning the Virginia, with the Patrick Henry, the Jamestown, and the three little tugs, jestingly called the "mosquito fleet," returned to the scene of the previous day's combat, and to the completion of the work, the destruction of the Minnesota, which had, the evening before, been interrupted by the change of tide and the coming of night. The Monitor, which had come in during the previous night, and had been seen by the light of the burning Congress, opened fire on the Virginia when about the third of a mile distant. The Virginia sought to close with her, but the greater speed of the Monitor and the celerity with which she was handled made this impracticable. The ships passed and repassed very near each other, and frequently the Virginia delivered her broadside at close quarters, but with no perceptible effect. The Monitor fired rapidly from her revolving turret, but not with such aim as to strike successively in the same place, and the armor of the Virginia, therefore, remained unbroken. Lieutenant-commanding Catesby Jones, to whom Buchanan had intrusted the ship when he was removed to the hospital, soon discovered that the Monitor was invulnerable to his shells. He had a few solid shot, which were intended only to be fired from the nine-inch guns as hot shot, and therefore had necessarily so much windage that they would be ineffective against the shield of the Monitor. He, therefore, determined to run her down, and got all the headway he could obtain for that purpose, but the speed was so small that it merely pushed her out of her way. It was then decided to board her, and all hands were piped for that object. Then the Monitor slipped away on to shoal water where the Virginia could not approach her, and Commander Jones, after waiting a due time, and giving the usual signals of invitation to combat, without receiving any manifestation on the part of the Monitor of an intention to return to deep water, withdrew to the navy-yard.

In the two days of conflict our only casualties were from the Cumberland as she went down valiantly fighting to the last, from the men on shore when the tugs went to the Congress to receive her surrender, or from the perfidious fire from the Congress while her white flags were flying. None were killed or wounded in the fight with the Monitor.

As this was the first combat between two iron-clad vessels, it attracted great attention and provoked much speculation. Some assumed that wooden ships were henceforth to be of no use, and much has been done by the addition of armor to protect seagoing vessels; but certainly neither of the two which provoked the speculation could be regarded as seaworthy, or suited to other than harbor defense.

A new prow was put on the Virginia, she was furnished with bolts and solid shot, and the slight repairs needed were promptly made. The distinguished veteran. Commodore Josiah Tatnall, was assigned to the command of the Virginia, vice Admiral Buchanan, temporarily disabled. The Virginia, as far as possible, was prepared for battle and cruise in the Roads, and, on the 11th of April, Commodore Tatnall moved down to invite the Monitor to combat. But her officers kept the Monitor close to the shore, with her steam up, and under the guns of Fortress Monroe. To provoke her to come out, the little Jamestown was sent in and pluckily captured many prizes, but the Monitor lay safe in the shoal water under the guns of the formidable fortress. An English man-of-war, which was lying in the channel, witnessed this effort to draw the Monitor out into deep water in defense of her weaker countrymen, and, as Barney on the Jamestown passed with his prizes, cut out in full view of the enemy's fleet, the Englishmen, with their national admiration of genuine "game," as a spectator described it, "unable to restrain their generous impulses, from the captain to the side-boy, cheered our gunboat to the very echo." I quote further from the same witness: "Early in May, a magnificent Federal fleet, the Virginia being concealed behind the land, had ventured across the channel, and some of them, expressly fitted to destroy our ship, were furiously bombarding our batteries at Sewell's Point. Dashing down comes old Tatnall on the instant, as light stepping and blithe as a boy. . . . But the Virginia no sooner draws into range than the whole fleet, like a flushed covey of birds, flatters off into shoal water and under the guns of the forts"—where they remained. After some delay, and there being no prospect of active service, the Commodore ordered the executive officer to fire a gun to windward and take the ship back to her buoy. Here, ready for service, waiting for an enemy to engage her, but never having the opportunity, she remained until the 10th of the ensuing month.

The Norfolk Navy-Yard, notwithstanding the injury done to it by conflagration, was yet the most available and equipped yard in the Confederacy. A land-force under General Huger had been placed there for its protection, and defensive works had also been constructed with a view to hold it as well for naval construction and repair as for its strategic importance in connection with the defense of the capital, Richmond. On the opposite side of the lower James, on the Peninsula between the James and York Rivers, we occupied an intrenched position of much natural strength. The two positions, Norfolk and the Peninsula, were necessary to each other, and the command of the channel between them essential to both. As long as the Virginia closed the entrance to the James River, and the intrenchment on the Peninsula was held, it was deemed possible to keep possession of Norfolk.

On the 1st of May General Johnston, commanding on the Peninsula, having decided to retreat, sent an order to General Huger to evacuate Norfolk. The Secretary of War, General Randolph, having arrived just at that time in Norfolk, assumed the authority of postponing the execution of the order "until he [General Huger] could remove such stores, munitions, and arms as could be carried off." The Secretary of the Navy, Mr. Mallory, was there also, and gave like instructions to the commandant of the yard. To the system and energy with which General Huger conducted the removal of heavy guns, machinery, stores, and munitions, we were greatly indebted in our future operations, both of construction and defense. A week was thus employed in the removal of machinery, etc, and the enemy, occupied with the retreating army on the Peninsula, did not cross the James River above, either to interrupt the transportation or to obstruct the retreat of the garrisons of the forts at Norfolk and its surroundings. When our army had been withdrawn from the Peninsula, and Norfolk had been evacuated, and the James River did not furnish depth of channel which would suffice for the Virginia to ascend it more than a few miles, her mission was ended. It is not surprising that her brilliant career created a great desire to preserve her, and that it was contemplated to lighten her and thus try to take her up the river, but the pilots declared this to be impracticable, and the court which subsequently investigated the matter sustained their opinion that "the only alternative was then and there to abandon and burn the ship." The statement of Commodore Tatnall shows that the Virginia could not have been taken seaward, and that such was the opinion of her first commander. He said: "I consulted Commodore Buchanan on the character and power of the ship. He expressed the distinct opinion that she was unseaworthy, that she was not sufficiently buoyant, and that in a common sea she would founder." She could not, it therefore appears, ascend the river, was unseaworthy, and was uncovered by the retreat of the troops with whom she had coöperated. So, on the 10th of May, the Virginia was taken to Craney Island, one mile above, and there her crew were landed; they fell in and formed on the beach, and, in the language of the eye-witness heretofore quoted, "then and there, on the very field of her fame, within sight of the Cumberland's top-gallant-masts, all awash, within sight of that magnificent fleet still cowering on the shoal, with her laurels all fresh and green, we hauled down her drooping colors, and, with mingled pride and grief, we gave her to the flames." [54]

At Wilmington, North Carolina, the Southwest bar was defended by Fort Caswell, and New Inlet bar by Fort Fisher. The naval defenses consisted of two ironclads, the North Carolina and the Raleigh. The former could not cross any of the bars in consequence of her draught of water. Her steam-power hardly gave propulsion. She sank during the war off Smithville. The Raleigh's services were almost valueless in consequence of her deep draught and her feeble steam-power. She made one futile trip out of New Inlet, and after a few hours attempted to return, but was wrecked upon the bar.

The brave and invincible defense of Fort Sumter gave to the city of Charleston, South Carolina, additional luster. For four years that fort, located in its harbor, defied the army and navy of the United States. When the city was about to be abandoned to the army of General Sherman, the forts defending the harbor were embraced in General Hardee's plan of evacuation. The gallant commander of Fort Sumter, Colonel Stephen Elliott, Jr., with unyielding fortitude, refused to be relieved, after being under incessant bombardment day and night for weeks. It was supposed he must be exhausted, and he was invited to withdraw for rest, but, on receiving the general order of retreat, he assembled his brave force on the rugged and shell-crushed parade-ground, read his instructions, and, in a voice that trembled with emotion, addressed his men in the glowing language of patriotism and unswerving devotion to the Confederate cause. The cheers, which responded to the utterances of their colonel, came from manly and chivalric throats. Yielding to the inevitable, they claimed for the Stars and Bars a salute of one hundred guns. As it was fired from Sumter, it was reëchoed by all the Confederate batteries, and startled the outside blockaders with the idea that a great victory had been won by the Confederacy.

The naval force of the Confederacy in Charleston Harbor consisted of three ironclads. Their steam-power was totally inadequate for the effective use of the vessels. In fact, when the wind and tide were moving in the same direction, it was impossible for the vessels to advance against them, light though the wind might be. Under such circumstances it was necessary to come to an anchor. On one occasion the ironclads Palmetto State and Chicora ran out of Charleston Harbor under favorable circumstances. The Palmetto State assaulted the Mercideta, commanded by Captain Stellwagen, who unconditionally surrendered. But the ironclad being under orders to follow her consort in chase of the enemy, and having no boats to which to transfer her prisoners, the parole of the officers and men was accepted, with their promise to observe the same until its return. The surrender was accepted, and an honest parole was the consideration for not being sunk on the spot. Captain Stellwagen abided but a short time, when, getting up steam, he broke his plighted word, and ran off with the captured vessel. The deficiency of speed on the part of the Confederate ironclads frustrated their efforts to relieve the city of Charleston from continued blockade.

The harbor defenses of Savannah were intrusted to Commodore Tatnall, who defended the approach to the city with a small steamer of one gun, an inefficient floating battery and ironclad, which had been constructed from a blockade-runner. Several attempts were made to attack the enemy's vessels with the ironclad, but these were frustrated by the delay in opening a passage through the obstructions in the river when tide and opportunity were offered. Her draught was too great for the depth of water, except at high tides, and these were at long intervals. The ironclad was armed with a battery of four guns, two seven-inch and two six-inch. Her force consisted of some twenty-one officers and twenty-four men, when she was fully furnished. Another vessel was under construction and nearly completed, and Commodore Tatnall, notwithstanding his well-known combative instincts, was understood to be unwilling to send the Atlanta alone against the enemy's blockading vessels. Lieutenant Webb, who had been lately placed in command of the Atlanta, took her to Warsaw Sound to deliver battle singly to the two ironclads Weehawken and Nahant, which awaited her approach. The Atlanta got twice aground—the second time, inextricably so. In this situation she was attacked, and, though hopelessly, was bravely defended, but was finally forced to surrender.

Mobile Harbor was thought to be adequately provided for, as torpedoes obstructed the approach, and Forts Morgan and Gaines commanded the entrance, aided by the improvised fleet of Admiral Buchanan, which consisted of the wooden gunboats Morgan and Gaines, each carrying six guns, and Selma four guns, with the ram Tennessee of six guns—in all, twenty-two guns and four hundred and seventy men. On August 4, 1864, Fort Gaines was assaulted by the United States force from the sea-side of the beach. The resistance made was feeble, and the fort soon surrendered. On the next day Admiral Farragut stood into the bay with a force consisting of four monitors, or ironclads, and fourteen steamers, carrying one hundred and ninety-nine guns and twenty-seven hundred men. One ironclad was sunk by a torpedo. Admiral Buchanan advanced to meet this force, and sought to run into the larger vessels with the Tennessee, but they avoided him by their superior speed. Meanwhile the gunboats became closely engaged with the enemy, but were soon dispersed by his overwhelming force. The Tennessee again stood for the enemy and renewed the attack with the hope of sinking some of them with her prow, but she was again foiled by their superior speed in avoiding her. The engagement with the whole fleet soon became general, and lasted an hour. Frequently the Tennessee was surrounded by the enemy, and all her guns were in action almost at the same moment. Four of their heaviest vessels ran into her under full steam with the view of sinking her. While surrounded by six of these heavy vessels which were suffering fearfully from her heavy battery, the steering-gear of the Tennessee was shot away, and her ability to manoeuvre was completely destroyed, leaving the formidable Confederate entirely at the disposal of the enemy. This misfortune, it was believed, saved the greater part of Farragut's fleet. Further resistance becoming unavailable, the wounded Admiral was under the painful necessity of ordering a surrender. His little fleet became a prey to the enemy, except the Morgan, which made good her escape to Mobile.

This unequal contest was decidedly creditable to the Confederacy. The entire loss of the enemy, most of which is ascribed to the Tennessee, amounted to quite three hundred in killed and wounded, exclusive of one hundred lost on the sunken ironclad, making a number almost as large as the entire Confederate force. On August 22d, Fort Morgan was bombarded from the land, also by ironclads at sea, and by the fleet inside. Thus Forts Powel, Morgan, and Gaines shared the fate of the Confederate fleet, and the enemy became masters of the bay. On this as on other occasions, the want of engines of sufficient power constituted a main obstacle to the success which the gallantry and skill of the seamen so richly deserved.

The system of torpedoes adopted by us was probably more effective than any other means of naval defense. The destructiveness of these little weapons had long been known, but no successful modes for their application to the destruction of the most powerful vessels of war and ironclads had been devised. It remained for the skill and ingenuity of our officers to bring the use of this terrible instrument to perfection. The success of their efforts is very frankly stated by one of the most distinguished of the enemy's commanders—Admiral Porter.[55] He says:

"Most of the Southern seaports fell into our possession with comparative facility; and the difficulty of capturing Charleston, Savannah, Wilmington, and Mobile was in a measure owing to the fact that the approaches to these places were filled with various kinds of torpedoes, laid in groups, and fired by electricity. The introduction of this means of defense on the side of the Confederates was for a time a severe check to our naval forces, for the commanders of squadrons felt it their duty to be careful when dealing with an element of warfare of which they knew so little, and the character and disposition of which it was so difficult to discover. In this system of defense, therefore, the enemy found their greatest security; and, notwithstanding all the efforts of Du Pont and Dahlgren, Charleston, Wilmington, and Savannah remained closed to our forces until near the close of the war."

In 1862, while General McClellan was in command of the enemy's forces below Richmond, it was observed that they had more than a hundred vessels in the James River, as if they were about to make an advance by that way upon the city. This led to an order placing General G. J. Rains in charge of the submarine defenses; and, on the James River opposite Drewry's Bluff, the first submarine torpedo was made. The secret of all his future success consisted in the sensitive primer, which is unrivaled by any other means to explode torpedoes or sub-terra shells.

The torpedoes were made of the most ordinary material generally, as, beer-barrels fixed with conical heads, coated within and without with rosin dissolved in coal-tar; some were made of cast-iron, copper, or tin; and glass demijohns were used. There were three essentials to success, viz., the sensitive fuse-primer, a charge of sixty pounds of gunpowder, and actual contact between the torpedo and the bottom of the vessel.

There were one hundred and twenty-three of these torpedoes placed in Charleston Harbor and Stono River. It was blockaded by thirteen large ships and ironclads, with six or seven storeships, and some twenty other vessels. The position of each one was known, and they could be approached within a half-mile, which made it easy to attack, destroy, or disperse them at night by floating torpedoes, connected together by twos by a rope one hundred and thirty yards long, buoyed up and stretched across the current by two boats, which were to be dropped in ebbing tide, to float down among the vessels. This plan, says General Rains, was opposed by General Gilmer, of the engineer corps, on the ground that "they might float back and destroy our own boat." One was sent down to go in the midst of the fleet, and made its mark. An act of devoted daring was here performed by Commander W. T. Glassell, Confederate States Navy, which claims more than a passing notice. While the enemy was slowly contracting his lines around Charleston, his numerous ships of war kept watch-and-ward outside of the harbor. Our few vessels, almost helpless by their defective engines, could effect little against their powerful opponents. The New Ironsides, the pride of their fleet, lay off Morris's Island. This Glassell resolved to attack with a steam-launch carrying a torpedo spar at the bow. With an engineer, pilot, and fireman, he steered for the Ironsides under cover of a hazy night. As he approached, he was hailed by the lookout, and the next moment struck the Ironsides, exploding the torpedo about fifteen feet from the keel. An immense volume of water was thrown up, covering the little boat, and, pieces of timber falling in the engine, it was rendered entirely unmanageable, so as to deprive

Commander Glassell of the means of escape on which he had relied. A rapid fire was concentrated upon him from the deck of the ship, and there remained no chance except to attempt an escape by swimming ashore. To secure liberty to his country, he risked and lost his own, and found, for the indignity to which he was subjected, compensation, inasmuch as the famous New Ironsides was long rendered useless to the enemy.

One hundred and one torpedoes were planted in Roanoke River, North Carolina, after a flotilla of twelve vessels had started up to capture Fort Branch. The torpedoes destroyed six of the vessels and frustrated the attack.

Every avenue to the outworks or to the city of Mobile was guarded by submarine torpedoes, so that it was impossible for any vessel drawing three feet of water to get within effective cannon-range of the defenses. Two ironclads attempted to get near enough to Spanish Fort to take part in the bombardment. They both struck torpedoes, and went to the bottom on Apalachie bar; thenceforward the fleet made no further attempt to encounter the almost certain destruction which they saw awaited any vessel which might attempt to enter the torpedo-guarded waters. But many were sunk when least expecting it. Some went down long after the Confederate forces had evacuated Mobile. The Tecumseh was probably sunk, says Major-General D. H. Maury,[56] on her own torpedo. While steaming in lead of Farragut's fleet she carried a torpedo affixed to a spar, which projected some twenty feet from her bows; she proposed to use this torpedo against the Tennessee, our only formidable ship; but, while passing Fort Morgan, a shot from that fort cut away the stays by which the torpedo was secured; it then doubled under her, and, exploding fairly under the bottom of the ill-fated ship, she careened and sank instantly in ten fathoms of water. Only six or eight of her crew of a hundred or more were saved. The total number of vessels sunk by torpedoes in Mobile Bay was twelve, viz., three ironclads, two tinclads, and seven transports. Fifty-eight vessels were destroyed in Southern waters by torpedoes during the war; these included ironclads and others of no mean celebrity.

[Footnote 53: See "Annual Cyclopaedia," 1861, p. 536.]

[Footnote 54: "The Story of the Confederate Ship Virginia," by William Norris, Colonel Signal Corps, Confederate Army.]

[Footnote 55: See "Torpedo Warfare," "North American Review," September-October, 1878.]

[Footnote 56: Southern Historical Society Papers, January, 1877.]

CHAPTER XXVIII.

Naval Affairs (continued).—Importance of New Orleans.—Attack feared from up the River.—Preparations for Defense.—Strength of the Forts.—Other Defenses.-The General Plan.—Ironclads.— Raft-Fleet of the Enemy.—Bombardment of the Forts commenced.— Advance of the Fleet.—Its Passage of the Forts.—Batteries below the City.—Darkness of the Night.—Evacuation of the City by General Lovell on Appearance of the Enemy.—Address of General Duncan to Soldiers in the Forts.—Refusal to surrender.—Meeting of the Garrison of Fort Jackson.—The Forts surrendered.—Ironclad Louisiana destroyed.—The Tugs and Steamers.—The Governor Moore.— The Enemy's Ship Varuna sunk.—The McRae.—The State of the City

and its Defenses considered.—Public Indignation.—Its Victims.—
Efforts made for its Defense by the Navy Department.—The
Construction of the Mississippi.

New Orleans was the most important commercial port in the Confederacy, being the natural outlet of the Mississippi Valley, as well to the ports of Europe as to those of Central and Southern America. It was the depot which, at an early period, had led to controversies with Spain, and its importance to the interior had been a main inducement to the purchase of Louisiana. It had become before 1861 the chief cotton-mart of the United States, and its defense attracted the early attention of the Confederate Government. The approaches for an attacking party were numerous. They could through several channels enter Lake Pontchartrain, to approach the city in rear for land-attack, could ascend the Mississippi from the Gulf, or descend it from the Northwest, where it was known that the enemy was preparing a formidable fleet of iron-clad gunboats. In the early part of 1862, so general an opinion prevailed that the greatest danger to New Orleans was by an attack from above, that General Lovell sent to General Beauregard a large part of the troops then in the city.

At the mouth of the Mississippi there is a bar, the greatest depth of water on which seldom exceeded eighteen feet, and it was supposed that heavy vessels of war, with their armament and supplies, would not be able to cross it. Such proved to be the fact, and the vessels of that class had to be lightened to enable them to enter the river. In that condition of affairs, an inferior fleet might have engaged them with a prospect of success. Captain Hollins, who was in command of the squadron at New Orleans, and who had on a former occasion shown his fitness for such service, had been sent with the greater part of his fleet up the river to join the defense there being made. Two powerful vessels were under construction, the Louisiana and the Mississippi, but neither of them was finished. A volunteer fleet of transport-vessels had been fitted up by some river-men, but it was in the unfortunate condition of not being placed under the orders of the naval commander. A number of fire-rafts had been also provided, which were to serve the double purpose of lighting up the river in the event of the hostile fleet attempting to pass the forts under cover of the night, and of setting fire to any vessel with which they might become entangled.

After passing the bar, there was nothing to prevent the ascent of the river until Forts Jackson and St. Philip were reached. These works, constructed many years before, were on opposite banks of the river. Their armament, as reported by General Lovell, December 5, 1861, consisted of—Fort Jackson: six forty-two-ponders, twenty-six twenty-four-pounders, two thirty-two-pounder rifles, sixteen thirty-two-pounders, three eight-inch columbiads, one ten-inch columbiad, two eight-inch mortars, one ten-inch mortar, two forty-pounder howitzers, and ten twenty-four-pounder howitzers. Fort St. Philip: six forty-two-ponders, nine thirty-two-pounders, twenty-two twenty-four-pounders, four eight-inch columbiads, one eight-inch mortar, one ten-inch mortar, and three field-guns.

General Duncan reported that, on the 27th of March, he was informed by Lieutenant-Colonel Higgins, commanding Forts Jackson and St. Philip, of the coast-defenses, which were under his (General Duncan's) command, that the enemy's fleet was crossing the bars, and entering the Mississippi River in force; whereupon he repaired to Fort Jackson. After describing the condition of the forts from the excess of water and sinking of the entire site, as well as the deficiency of guns of heavy caliber in the forts, he proceeds:

"It became necessary in their present condition to bring in and mount, and to build the platforms for, the three ten-inch and three eight-inch columbiads, the rifled forty-two-pounder, and the five ten-inch seacoast mortars recently obtained from Pensacola on the evacuation of that place, together with the two rifled seven-inch guns temporarily borrowed from the naval authorities in New Orleans. It was also found necessary to repair the old water-battery to the rear of and below Fort Jackson, which had never been completed, for the reception of a portion of these guns, as well as to construct mortar-proof magazines, and shell-rooms within the same."

One of the seven-inch rifled guns borrowed from the navy was subsequently returned, so that, when the forts were attacked, the armament was one hundred and twenty-eight guns and mortars.

The garrisons of Forts Jackson and St. Philip were about one thousand men on December 5, 1861; afterward, so far as I know, the number was not materially changed.

The prevailing belief that vessels of war, in a straight, smooth channel, could pass batteries, led to the construction of a raft between the two forts which, it was supposed, would detain the ships under fire of the forts long enough for the guns to sink them, or at least to compel them to retire. The power of the river when in flood, and the drift-wood it bore upon it, broke the raft; another was constructed, which, when the drift-wood accumulated upon it, met a like fate. Whether obstructions differently arranged—such as booms secured to the shores, with apparatus by which they could be swung across the channel when needful, or logs such as were used, except that, being unconnected together, but each separately secured by chain and anchor, they might severally yield to the pressure of the driftwood, sinking, so as to allow it to pass over them, and, when relieved of the weight, rising again—or whether other expedient could have been made permanent and efficient, is a problem which need not be discussed, as the time for its application has passed from us.

The general plan for the defense of New Orleans consisted of two lines of works: an exterior one, passing through the forts near the mouth of the river, and the positions taken to defend the various water approaches; nearer to the city was the interior line, embracing New Orleans and Algiers, which was intended principally to repel an attack by land, but also, by its batteries on the river-bank, to resist approach by water. The total length of the intrenchments on this interior line was more than eight miles. When completed, it formed, in connection with impassable swamps, a very strong line of defense. At the then high stage of the river, all the land between it and the swamps was so saturated with water, that regular approaches could not have been made. The city, therefore, was at the time supposed to be doubly secure from a land-attack.

In the winter of 1861-'62 I sent one of my aides-de-camp to New Orleans to make a general inspection, and hold free conference with the commanding General. Upon his return, he reported to me that General Lovell was quite satisfied with the condition of the land-defenses—so much so as to say that his only fear was that the enemy would not make a land-attack.

Considered since the event, it may seem strange that, after the fall of Donelson and Henry, and the employment of the enemy's gunboats in the Tennessee and Cumberland, it was still generally argued that the danger to New Orleans was that the gunboats would descend the Mississippi, and applications were made to have the ship Louisiana sent up the river as soon as she was completed.

The interior lines of defense mounted more than sixty guns of various caliber, and were surrounded by wide and deep ditches. On the various water approaches, including bays and bayous on the west and east sides of the river, there were sixteen different forts, and these, together with those on the river and the batteries of the interior line, had in position about three hundred guns.

One ironclad, the Louisiana, mounting sixteen guns of heavy caliber, though she was not quite completed, was sent down to coöperate with the forts. Her defective steam-power and imperfect steering apparatus prevented her from rendering active coöperation. The steamship Mississippi, then under construction at New Orleans, was in such an unfinished condition as to be wholly unavailable when the enemy arrived. In the opinion of naval officers she would have been, if completed, the most powerful ironclad then in the world, and could have driven the enemy's fleet out of the river and raised the blockade at Mobile. There were also several small river-steamers which were lightly armed, and their bows were protected so that they could act as rams and otherwise aid in the defense of the river; but, from the reports received, they seem, with a few honorable exceptions, to have rendered little valuable service.

The means of defense, therefore, mainly relied on were the two heavy-armed forts, Jackson and St. Philip, with the obstruction placed between them: this was a raft consisting of cypress-trees, forty feet long, and averaging four or five feet at the larger end. They were placed longitudinally in the river, about three feet apart, and held together by gunwales on top, and strung upon two two-and-a-half-inch chain cables fastened to their lower sides. This raft was anchored in the river, abreast of the forts.

The fleet of the enemy below the forts consisted of seven steam sloops of war, twelve gunboats, and several armed steamers, under Commodore Farragut; also, a mortar-fleet consisting of twenty sloops and some steam-vessels. The whole force was forty-odd vessels of different kinds, with an armament of three hundred guns of heavy caliber, of improved models.

The bombardment of the forts by the mortar-fleet commenced on April 18th, and, after six days of vigorous and constant shelling, the resisting power of the forts was not diminished in any perceptible degree. On the 23d there were manifest preparations by the enemy to attempt the passage of the forts. This, as subsequently developed, was to be done in the following manner. The sloops of war and the gunboats were each formed in two divisions, and, selecting the darkest hour of the night, between 3 and 4 A.M. of the 24th, moved up the river in two columns. The commanders of the forts had vainly endeavored to have the river lighted up in anticipation of an attack by the fleet.

In the mean time, while the fleet moved up the river, there was kept up from the mortars a steady bombardment on the forts, and these opened a fire on the columns of ships and gunboats, which, from the failure to send down the fire-rafts to light up the river, was less effective than it otherwise would have been. The straight, deep channel enabled the vessels to move at their greatest speed, and thus the forts were passed.

Brigadier-General J. K. Duncan, commanding the coast defenses, says, in his report of the passing of Forts Jackson and St. Philip by the enemy's fleet:

"The enemy evidently anticipated a strong demonstration to be made against him with fire-barges. Finding, upon his approach, however, that no such demonstration was made, and that the only resistance offered to his passage was the anticipated fire of the forts—the broken and scattered raft being no obstacle—I am satisfied that he was suddenly inspired, for the first time, to run the gantlet at all hazards, although not a part of his original design. Be that as it may, a rapid rush was made by him in columns of twos in echelon, so as not to interfere with each other's broadsides. The mortar-fire was furiously increased upon Fort Jackson, and, in dashing by, each of the vessels delivered broadside after broadside, of shot, shell, grape, canister, and spherical case, to drive the men from our guns.

"Both the officers and men stood up manfully under this galling and fearful hail, and the batteries of both forts were promptly opened at their longest range, with shot, shell, hot shot, and a little grape, and most gallantly and rapidly fought, until the enemy succeeded in getting above and beyond our range. The absence of light on the river, together with the smoke of the guns, made the obscurity so dense that scarcely a vessel was visible, and, in consequence, the gunners were obliged to govern their firing entirely by the flashes of the enemy's guns. I am fully satisfied that the enemy's dash was successful mainly owing to the cover of darkness, as a frigate and several gunboats were forced to retire as day was breaking. Similar results had attended every previous attempt made by the enemy to pass or to reconnoiter when we had sufficient light to fire with accuracy and effect."

The vessels which passed the fort anchored at the quarantine station about six miles above, and in the forenoon proceeded up the river. Batteries had been constructed where the interior line of defense touched both the right and the left bank of the river. The high stage of the river gave to its surface an elevation above that of the natural bank; but a continuous levee to protect the land from inundation existed on both sides of the river. When the ascending fleet approached these batteries, a cross-fire, which drove two of the vessels back, was opened upon it, and continued until all the ammunition was exhausted. The garrison was then withdrawn-casualties, one killed and one wounded. The regret which would naturally arise from the fact of these batteries not having a sufficient supply of ammunition is modified, if not removed, by the statement of the highly accomplished and gallant officer, Major-General M. L. Smith, who was then in command of them. He reported:

> "Had the fall of New Orleans depended
> upon the enemy's first taking Forts Jackson
> and Philip, I think the city would have been
> safe from an attack from the Gulf. The forts,
> in my judgment, were impregnable as long as
> they were in free and open communication
> with the city. This communication was not
> endangered while the obstruction existed. The
> conclusion, then, is briefly this: While the
> obstruction existed, the city was safe; when it
> was swept away, as the defenses then existed,
> it was within the enemy's power."

On the other hand, General Duncan, whose protracted, skillful, and gallant defense of the forts is above all praise, closes his official report with the following sentence: "Except for the cover afforded by the obscurity of the darkness, I shall always remain satisfied that the enemy would never have succeeded in passing Forts Jackson and St. Philip." The darkness to which he referred was not only that of night, but also the absence of the use of the means prepared to light up the river. As further proof of the intensity of the darkness, and the absence of that intelligent design and execution which had been claimed, I will quote a sentence from the report of Commodore Farragut: "At length the fire slackened, the smoke cleared off, and we saw to our surprise that we were above the forts."

On the 25th of April the enemy's gunboats and ships of war anchored in front of the city and demanded its surrender. Major-General M. Lovell, then in command, refused to comply with the summons, but, believing himself unable to make a successful defense, and in order to avoid a bombardment, agreed to withdraw his forces, and turn it over to the civil authorities. Accordingly, the city was evacuated on the same day. The forts still continued defiantly to hold their position. By assiduous exertion the damage done to the works was repaired, and the garrisons valiantly responded to the resolute determination of General Duncan and Colonel Higgins to defend the forts against the fleet still below, as well as against that which had passed and was now above. On the 26th Commodore Porter, commanding the mortar-fleet below, sent a flag-of-truce boat to demand the surrender of the forts, saying that the city of New Orleans had surrendered. To this Colonel Higgins replied, April 27th, that he had no official information that New Orleans had been evacuated, and until such notice was received he would not entertain for a moment a proposition to surrender the forts. On the same day General Duncan, commanding the coast-defenses, issued the following address:

"SOLDIERS OF FORTS JACKSON AND ST. PHILIP: You have nobly, gallantly, and heroically sustained with courage and fortitude the terrible ordeals of fire, water, and a hail of shot and shell wholly unsurpassed during the present war. But more remains to be done. The safety of New Orleans and the cause of the Southern Confederacy—our homes, families, and everything dear to man—yet depend upon our exertions. We are just as capable of repelling the enemy to-day as we were before the bombardment. Twice has the enemy demanded your surrender, and twice has he been refused.

"Your officers have every confidence in your courage and patriotism, and feel every assurance that you will cheerfully and with alacrity obey all orders, and do your whole duty as men and as becomes the well-tried garrisons of Forts Jackson and St. Philip. Be vigilant, therefore, stand by your guns, and all will yet be well.

"J. K. DUNCAN,
"*Brigadier-General, commanding coast-defenses.*"

Not less lofty and devoted was the spirit evinced by Colonel Higgins. His naval experience had been energetically applied in the attempts to preserve and repair the raft. As immediate commander of Fort St. Philip he had done all which skill and gallantry could achieve, and, though for forty-eight hours during the bombardment he never left the rampart, yet, with commendable care for his men, he kept them so under cover that, notwithstanding the long and furious assault to which the fort was subjected, the total of casualties in it was two killed and four wounded. Their conduct was such as was to be anticipated, for, had these officers been actuated by a lower motive than patriotism, had they been seeking the rewards which power confers, they would not have taken service with the weaker party. Their meed was the consciousness of duty well done in a righteous cause, and the enduring admiration and esteem of a people who had only these to confer.

During the 25th, 26th, and 27th, there had been an abatement of fire on the forts, and with it had subsided the excitement which imminent danger creates in the brave. A rumor became current that the city had surrendered, and no reply had been received to inquiries sent on the 24th and 25th. About midnight on the 27th the garrison of Fort Jackson revolted *en masse*, seized upon the guard, and commenced to spike the guns. Captain S. O. Comay's company, the Louisiana Cannoneers of St. Mary's Parish, and a few others remained true to their cause and country. The mutiny was so general that the officers were powerless to control it, and therefore decided to let those go who wished to leave, and after daybreak to communicate with the fleet below and negotiate for the terms which had been previously offered and declined.

Under the incessant fire to which the forts had been exposed, and the rise of the water in the casemates and lower part of the works, the men had been not only deprived of sleep, but of the opportunity to prepare their food. Heroically they had braved alike dangers and discomfort; had labored constantly to repair damages; to extinguish fires caused by exploding shells; to preserve their ammunition by bailing out the water which threatened to submerge the magazine: yet, in a period of comparative repose, these men, who had been cheerful and obedient, as suddenly as unexpectedly, broke out into open mutiny. Under the circumstances which surrounded him, General Duncan had no alternative. It only remained for him to accept the proposition which had been made for a surrender of the forts. As this mutiny became known about midnight of the 27th, soon after daylight of the 28th a small boat was procured, and notice of the event was sent to Captain Mitchell, on the Louisiana, and also to Fort St. Philip. The officers of that fort concurred in the propriety of the surrender, though none of their men had openly revolted.

A flag of truce was sent to Commodore Porter to notify him of a willingness to negotiate for the surrender of the forts. The gallantry with which the defense had been conducted was recognized by the enemy, and the terms were as liberal as had been offered on former occasions.

The garrisons were paroled, the officers were to retain their side-arms, and the Confederate flags were left flying over the forts until after our forces had withdrawn. If this was done as a generous recognition of the gallantry with which the forts had been defended, it claims acknowledgment as an instance of martial courtesy—the flower that blooms fairest amid the desolations of war.

Captain Mitchell, commanding the Confederate States naval forces, had been notified by General Duncan of the mutiny in the forts and of the fact that the enemy had passed through a channel in rear of Fort St. Philip and had landed a force at the quarantine, some six miles above, and that, under the circumstances, it was deemed necessary to surrender the forts. As the naval forces were not under the orders of the general commanding the coast-defenses, it was optional with the naval commander to do likewise or not as to his fleet. After consultation with his officers. Captain Mitchell decided to destroy his flagship, the Louisiana, the only formidable vessel he had, rather than allow her to fall into the hands of the enemy. The crew was accordingly withdrawn, and the vessel set on fire.

Commodore Porter, commanding the fleet below, came up under a flag of truce to Fort Jackson, and, while negotiations were progressing for the surrender, the Louisiana, in flames, drifted down the river, and, when close under Fort St. Philip, exploded and sank.

The defenses afloat, except the Louisiana, consisted of tugs and river-steamers, which had been converted to war purposes by protecting their bows with iron so as to make them rams, and putting on them such armament as boats of that class would bear; and these were again divided into such as were subject to control as naval vessels, and others which, in compliance with the wish of the Governor of Louisiana and many influential citizens, were fitted out to a great extent by State and private sources, with the condition that they should be commanded by river-steamboat captains, and should not be under the control of the naval commander. This, of course, impaired the unity requisite in battle. For many other purposes they might have been used without experiencing the inconvenience felt when they were brought together to act as one force against the enemy. The courts of inquiry and the investigation by a committee of Congress have brought out all the facts of the case, but with such conflicting opinions as render it very difficult, in reviewing the matter, to reach a definite and satisfactory conclusion. This much it may be proper to say, that expectations, founded upon the supposition that these improvised means could do all which might fairly be expected from war-vessels, were unreasonable, and a judgment based upon them is unjust to the parties involved. The machinery of the Louisiana was so incomplete as to deprive her of locomotion, but she had been so well constructed as to possess very satisfactory resisting powers, as was shown by the fact that the broadsides of the enemy's vessels, fired at very close quarters, had little or no effect upon her shield. Without power of locomotion, her usefulness was limited to employment as a floating battery. The question as to whether she was in the right position, or whether, in her unfinished condition, she should have been sent from the city, is one, for an answer to which I must refer the inquirer to the testimony of naval men, who were certainly most competent to decide the issue.

One of the little river-boats, the Governor Moore, commanded by lieutenant Beverly Kennon, like the others, imperfectly protected at the bow, struck and sunk the Varuna, in close proximity to other vessels of the enemy's fleet. Such daring resulted in his losing, in killed and wounded, seventy-four out of a crew of ninety-three. Then finding that he must destroy his ship to prevent her from falling into the hands of the enemy, he set her on fire, and testified as follows:

"I ordered the wounded to be placed in a boat, and all the men who could to save themselves by swimming to the shore and hiding themselves in the marshes. I remained to set the ship on fire. After doing so, I went on deck with the intention of leaving her, but found the wounded had been left with no one to take care of them. I remained and lowered them into a boat, and got through just in time to be made a prisoner. The wounded were afterward attended by the surgeons of the Oneida and Eureka."

This, he says, was the only foundation for the accusation of having burned his wounded with his ship. Another, the Manassas, lieutenant-commanding Warley, though merely an altered "tug-boat," stoutly fought the large ships; but, being wholly unprotected, except at her bow, was perforated in many places, as soon as the guns were brought to bear upon her sides, and floated down the river a burning wreck. Another of the same class is thus referred to by Colonel Higgins:

"At daylight, I observed the McRae, gallantly fighting at terrible odds, contending at close quarters with two of the enemy's powerful ships. Her gallant commander, Lieutenant Thomas B. Huger, fell during the conflict, severely, but I trust not mortally, wounded."

This little vessel, after her unequal conflict, was still afloat, and, with permission of the enemy, went up to New Orleans to convey the wounded as well from our forts as from the fleet.

On the 23d of April, 1862, General Lovell, commanding the military department, had gone down to Fort Jackson, where General Duncan, commanding the coast-defenses, then made his headquarters. The presence of the department commander did not avail to secure the full coöperation between the defenses afloat and the land-defenses, which was then of most pressing and immediate necessity.

When the enemy's fleet passed the forts, he hastened back to New Orleans, his headquarters. The confusion which prevailed in the city, when the news arrived that the forts had been passed by the enemy's fleet, shows how little it was expected. There was nothing to obstruct the ascent of the river between Forts Jackson and St. Philip and the batteries on the river where the interior line of defense rested on its right and left banks, about four miles below the city. The guns were not sufficiently numerous in these batteries to inspire much confidence; they were nevertheless well served until the ammunition was exhausted, after which the garrisons withdrew, and made their way by different routes to join the forces withdrawn from New Orleans.

Under the supposition entertained by the generals nearest to the operations, the greatest danger to New Orleans was from above, not from below, the city; therefore, most of the troops had been sent from the city to Tennessee, and Captain Hollins, with the greater part of the river-fleet, had gone up to check the descent of the enemy's gunboats.

Batteries like those immediately below the city had been constructed where the interior line touched the river above, and armed to resist an attack from that direction. Doubtful as to the direction from which, and the manner in which, an attempt might be made to capture the city, such preparations as circumstances suggested were made against many supposable dangers by the many possible routes of approach. To defend the city from the land, against a bombardment by a powerful fleet in the river before it, had not been contemplated. All the defensive preparations were properly, I think, directed to the prevention of a near approach by the enemy. To have subjected the city to bombardment by a direct or plunging fire, as the surface of the river was then higher than the land, would have been exceptionally destructive. Had the city been filled with soldiers whose families had been sent to a place of safety, instead of being filled with women and children whose natural protectors were generally in the army and far away, the attempt might have been justified to line the levee with all the effective guns and open fire on the fleet, at the expense of whatever property might be destroyed before the enemy should be driven away. The case was the reverse of the hypothesis, and nothing could have been more unjust than to censure the commanding General for withdrawing a force large enough to induce a bombardment, but insufficient to repel it. His answer to the demand for the surrender showed clearly enough the motives by which he was influenced. His refusal enabled him to withdraw the troops and most of the public property, and to use them, with the ordnance and ordnance stores thus saved, in providing for the defense of Vicksburg, but especially it deprived the enemy of any pretext for bombarding the town and sacrificing the lives of the women and children. It appears that General Lovell called for ten thousand volunteers from the citizens, but failed to get them. There were many river-steamboats at the landing, and, if the volunteers called for were intended to man these boats and board the enemy's fleet before their land-forces could arrive, it can not be regarded as utterly impracticable. The report of General Butler shows that he worked his way through one of the bayous in rear of Fort St. Philip to the Mississippi River above the forts so as to put himself in communication with the fleet at the city, and to furnish Commodore Farragut with ammunition. From this it is to be inferred that the fleet was deficient in ammunition, and the fact would have rendered boarding from river-boats the more likely to succeed. In this connection it may be remembered that, during the war, John Taylor Wood, Colonel and A. D. C. to the President, who had been an officer of high repute in the "old Navy," did in open boats attack armed vessels, board and capture them, though found with nettings up, having been warned of the probability of such an attack.[57]

Many causes have been assigned for the fall of New Orleans. Two of them are of undeniable force: First, the failure to light up the channel; second, the want of an obstruction which would detain the fleet under fire of the forts. General Duncan's report and testimony justify the conclusion that to the thick veil of darkness the enemy was indebted for his ability to run past the forts.

The argument that the guns were not of sufficiently large caliber to stop the fleet is not convincing. If all the guns had been of the largest size, that would not have increased the accuracy but would have diminished the rapidity of the fire, and therefore in the same degree would have lessened the chances of hitting objects in the dark. Further, it appears that the forts always crippled or repulsed any vessels which came up in daylight.

The forts would have been better able to resist bombardment if they had been heavily plated with iron; but that would not have prevented the fleet from passing them as they did. Torpedoes might have been placed on the bar at the mouth of the river before the enemy got possession of it, and subsequently, if attached to buoys, they might have been used in the deep channel above. Many other things which were omitted might and probably would have been done had attention been earlier concentrated on the danger which at last proved fatal. If the volunteer river-defense fleet was ineffective, as alleged, because it was not subject to the orders of the naval commander, that was an evil without a remedy. The Governor of Louisiana had arranged with the projectors that they should not be subject to the naval commander, and the alternative of not accepting them with that condition was that they would not agree to convert their steamers into war-vessels. Unless, therefore, it can be shown that they were worse than none, their presence can not be properly enumerated among the causes of the failure.

The fall of New Orleans was a great disaster, over which there was general lamentation, mingled with no little indignation. The excited feeling demanded a victim, and conflicting testimony of many witnesses most nearly concerned made it convenient to select for censure those most removed and least active in their own justification. Thus the naval constructors of the Mississippi and the Secretary of the Navy became the special objects of attack. The selection of these had little of justice in it, and could not serve to relieve others of their responsibility, as did the old-time doom of the scapegoat. New Orleans had never been a ship-building port, and when the Messrs. Tift, the agents to build the iron-dad steamer Mississippi, arrived there, they had to prepare a ship-yard, procure lumber from a distance, have the foundries and rolling-mills adapted to such iron-work as could be done in the city, and contract elsewhere for the balance. They were ingenious, well informed in matters of ship-building, and were held in high esteem in Georgia and Florida, where they had long resided. They submitted a proposition to the Secretary of the Navy to build a vessel on a new model. The proposition was accepted after full examination of the plan proposed, the novelty of which made it necessary that they should have full control of the work of construction. To the embarrassments above mentioned were added interruptions by calling off the workmen occasionally for exercise and instruction as militiamen, the city being threatened by the enemy. From these causes, unexpected delay in the completion of the ship resulted, regret for which increased as her most formidable character was realized.

These constructors—the brothers Tift—hoped to gain much reputation by the ship which they designed, and, from this motive, agreed to give their full service and unremitted attention in its construction without compensation or other allowance than their current expenses. It would, therefore, on the face of it, seem to have been a most absurd suspicion that they willingly delayed the completion of the vessel, and at last wantonly destroyed it.

Mr. E. C. Murray, who was the contractor for building the Louisiana, in his testimony before a committee of the Confederate Congress, testified that he had been a practical ship-builder for twenty years and a contractor for the preceding eighteen years, having built about a hundred and twenty boats, steamers, and sailing-vessels. There was only a fence between his shipyard and that where the Mississippi was constructed. Of this latter vessel he said:

"I think the vessel was built in less time than any vessel of her tonnage, character, and requiring the same amount of work and materials, on this continent. That vessel required no less than two million feet of lumber, and, I suppose, about one thousand tons of iron, including the false works, blockways, etc. I do not think that amount of materials was ever put together on this continent within the time occupied in her construction. I know many of our naval vessels, requiring much less materials than were employed in the Mississippi, that took about six or twelve months in their construction. She was built with rapidity, and had at all times as many men at work upon her as could work to advantage—she had, in fact, many times more men at work upon her than could conveniently work. They worked on nights and Sundays upon her, as I did upon the Louisiana, at least for a large portion of the time."

The Secretary of the Navy knew both of the Tifts, but had no near personal relations or family connection with either, as was recklessly alleged.

He, in accepting their proposition, connected with it the detail of officers of the navy to supervise expenditures and aid in procuring materials. Assisted by the chief engineer and constructor of the navy, minute instructions were given as to the manner in which the work was to be conducted. As early as the 19th of September he sent twenty ship-carpenters from Richmond to New Orleans to aid in the construction of the Mississippi. On the 7th of October authority was given to have guns of heaviest caliber made in New Orleans for the ship. Frequent telegrams were sent in November, December, and January, showing great earnestness about the work on the ship. In February and March notice was given of the forwarding from Richmond of capstan and main-shaft, which could not be made in New Orleans. On March 22d the Secretary, by telegraph, directed the constructors to "strain every nerve to finish the ship," and added, "work day and night." April 5th he again wrote: "Spare neither men nor money to complete her at the earliest moment. Can not you hire night-gangs for triple wages?" April 10th the Secretary again says: "Enemy's boats have passed Island 10. Work day and night with all the force you can command to get the Mississippi ready. Spare neither men nor money." April 11th he asks, "When will you launch, and when will she be ready for action?" These inquiries indicate the prevalent opinion, at that time, that the danger to New Orleans was from the ironclad fleet above, and not the vessels at the mouth of the river; but the anxiety of the Secretary of the Navy and the efforts made by him were of a character applicable to either or both the sources of danger. Thus we find as early as the 24th of February, 1862, that he instructed Commander Mitchell to make all proper exertions to have guns and carriages ready for both the iron-clad vessels the Mississippi and the Louisiana. Reports having reached him that the work on the latter vessel was not pushed with sufficient energy, on the 15th of March he authorized Commander Mitchell to consult with General Lovell, and, if the contractors were not doing everything practicable to complete her at the earliest moment, that he should take her out of their hands, and, with the aid of General Lovell, go on to complete her himself. On the 5th of April, 1862, Secretary Mallory instructed Commander Sinclair, who had been assigned to the command of the Mississippi, to urge on by night and day the completion of the ship. In March, 1861, the Navy Department sent from Montgomery officers to New Orleans, with instructions to purchase steamers and fit them for war purposes. Officers were also sent to the North to purchase vessels suited to such uses, and in the ensuing May an agent was dispatched to Canada and another to Europe for like objects; and in April, 1861, contracts were made with foundries at Richmond and New Orleans to make guns for the defense of New Orleans. On the 8th of May, 1861, the Secretary of the Navy communicated at some length to the Committee on Naval Affairs of the Confederate Congress his views in favor of iron-clad vessels, arguing as sell for their efficiency as the economy in building them, believing that one such vessel could successfully engage a fleet of the wooden vessels which constituted the enemy's navy. His further view was that we could not hope to build wooden fleets equal to those with which the enemy were supplied. The committee, if it should be deemed expedient to construct an iron-clad ship, was urged to prompt action by the forcible declaration, "Not a moment should be lost."

Commander George Minor, Confederate States Navy, Chief of the Bureau of Ordnance, reported the number of guns sent by the Navy Department to New Orleans, between July 1, 1861, and the fall of the city, to have been one hundred and ninety-seven, and that before July twenty-three guns had been sent there from Norfolk, being a total of two hundred and twenty guns, of which forty-five were of large caliber, supplied by the Navy Department for the defense of New Orleans.

Very soon after the Government was removed to Richmond, the Secretary of the Navy, with the aid of Commander Brooke, designed a plan for converting the sunken frigate Merrimac into an iron-clad vessel. She became the famous Virginia, the brilliant career of which silenced all the criticisms which had been made upon the plan adopted. On May 20, 1861, the Secretary of the Navy instructed Captain Ingraham, Confederate States Navy, to ascertain the practicability of obtaining wrought-iron plates suited for ships' armor. After some disappointment and delay, the owners of the mills at Atlanta were induced to make the necessary changes in the machinery, and undertake the work. Efforts at other places in the West had been unsuccessful, and this was one of the difficulties which an inefficient department would not have overcome. The iron-clad gunboats Arkansas and Tennessee were commenced at Memphis, but the difficulty in obtaining mechanics so interfered with their construction, that the Secretary of the Navy was compelled, December 24, 1861, to write to General Polk, who was commanding at Columbus, Kentucky, asking that mechanics might be detached from his forces, so as to insure the early completion of the vessels. So promptly had the iron-clad boats been put under contract, that the arrangements had all been made in anticipation of the appropriation, and the contract was signed "on the very day the law was passed."

On December 25, 1861, Lieutenant Isaac N. Brown, Confederate States Navy, a gallant and competent officer, well and favorably known in his subsequent service as commander of the ram Arkansas, was sent to Nashville. Information had been received that four river-boats were there, and for sale, which were suited for river defense. Lieutenant Brown was instructed to purchase such as should be adaptable to the required service, "and to proceed forthwith with the necessary alteration and armament."

In the latter part of 1861, it having been found impossible with the means in Richmond and Norfolk to answer the requisitions for ordnance and ordnance stores required for the naval defenses of the Mississippi, a laboratory was established in New Orleans, and authority given for the casting of heavy cannon, construction of gun-carriages, and the manufacture of projectiles and ordnance equipments of all kinds. On December 12, 1861, the Secretary of the Navy submitted an estimate for an appropriation to meet the expenses incurred "for ordnance and ordnance stores for the defense of the Mississippi River."

Secretary Mallory, in answer to inquiries of a joint committee of Congress, in 1863, replied that he had sent a telegram to Captain Whittle, April 17, 1862, as follows:

"Is the boom, or raft, below the forts in order to resist the enemy, or has any part of it given way? State condition."

On the next day the following answer was sent:

"I hear the raft below the forts is not in best condition; they are strengthening it by additional lines. I have furnished anchors."

To further inquiry about the raft by the Committee, the Secretary answered:

"The commanding General at New Orleans had exclusive charge of the construction of the raft, or obstruction, in question, and his correspondence with the War Department induced confidence in the security of New Orleans from the enemy. I was aware that this raft had been injured, but did not doubt that the commanding General would renew it, and place an effectual barrier across the river, and I was anxious that the navy should afford all possible aid. . . . A large number of anchors were sent to New Orleans from Norfolk for the raft."

Though much more might be added, it is hoped that what has been given above will sufficiently attest the zeal and capacity of the Secretary of the Navy, and his anxiety, in particular, to protect the city of New Orleans, whether assailed by fleets descending or ascending the river.

Having thus reviewed at length the events, immediate and remote, which were connected with the great catastrophe, the fall of our chief commercial city, and the destruction of the naval vessels on which our hopes most rested for the protection of the lower Mississippi and the harbors of the Gulf, the narrative is resumed of affairs at the city of New Orleans.

[Footnote 57: Captain Wood had a number of light row-boats built, holding each about twenty men. They were fitted with cradles to wagons, and could be quickly moved to any point by road or rail. He writes: "In August, 1863, I left Richmond with four boats and sixty men for the Rappahannock, to look after one or two gunboats that had been operating in that river. Finding always two cruising together, I determined to attempt the capture of both at once. About midnight, with muffled oars, we pulled for them at anchor near the mouth of the river. They discovered us two hundred yards off. We dashed alongside, cut our way through and over the boarder nettings with the old navy cutlass, gained the deck, and, after a sharp, short fight, drove the enemy below. The prizes proved to be the gunboats Satellite and Reliance, two guns each. Landing the prisoners, we cruised for two days in the Chesapeake Bay. A number of vessels were captured and destroyed."]

CHAPTER XXIX.

Naval Affairs (continued).—Farragut demands the Surrender of New Orleans.—Reply of the Mayor.—United States Flag hoisted.—Advent of General Butler.—Barbarities.—Antecedents of the People.— Galveston.—Its Surrender demanded.—The Reply.—Another visit of the Enemy's Fleet.—The Port occupied.—Appointment of General Magruder.—Recapture of the Port.—Capture of the Harriet Lane.— Report of General Magruder.—Position and Importance of Sabine Pass.—Fleet of the Enemy.—Repulse by Forty-four Irishmen.— Vessels captured.—Naval Destitution of the Confederacy at first.— Terror of Gunboats on the Western Rivers.—Their Capture.—The most Illustrious Example.—The Indianola.—Her Capture.—The Ram Arkansas.—Descent of the Yazoo River.—Report of her Commander.— Runs through the Enemy's Fleet.—Description of the Vessel.—Attack on Baton Rouge.—Address of General Breckinridge.—Burning of the Arkansas.

Sad though the memory of the fall of New Orleans must be, the heroism, the fortitude, and the patriotic self-sacrifice exhibited in the eventful struggle at the forts must ever remain the source of pride and of such consolation as misfortune gathers from the remembrance of duties well performed.

After the troops had been withdrawn and the city restored to the administration of the civil authorities, Commodore Farragut, on April 26, 1862, addressed the Mayor, repeating his demand for the surrender of the city. In his letter he said: "It is not within the province of a naval officer to assume the duties of a military commandant," and added, "The rights of persons and property shall be secured." He proceeded then to demand "that the emblem of sovereignty of the United States be hoisted over the City Hall, Mint, and Custom-House by meridian this day. All flags and other emblems of sovereignty other than those of the United States must be removed from all the public buildings by that hour." To this the Mayor replied, and the following extracts convey the general purport of his letter:

"The city is without the means of defense, and is utterly destitute of the force and material that might enable it to resist an overpowering armament displayed in sight of it. . . . To surrender such a place were an idle and unmeaning ceremony. . . . As to hoisting any flag other than the flag of our own adoption and allegiance, let me say to you that the man lives not in our midst whose hand and heart would not be paralyzed at the mere thought of such an act; nor could I find in my entire constituency so wretched and desperate a renegade as would dare to profane with his hand the sacred emblem of our aspirations. . . . Peace and order may be preserved without resort to measures which I could not at this moment prevent. Your occupying the city does not transfer allegiance from the government of their choice to one which they have deliberately repudiated, and they yield the obedience which the conqueror is entitled to extort from the conquered.

"Respectfully,

"JOHN T. MONROE, *Mayor.*"

On the 29th of April Admiral Farragut adopted the alternative presented by the answer of the Mayor, and sent a detachment of marines to hoist the United States flag over the Custom-House, and to pull down the Confederate flag from the staff on the City Hall. An officer and some marines remained at the Custom-House to guard the United States flag hoisted over it until the land-forces under General Butler arrived. On the 1st of May General Butler took possession of the defenseless City; then followed the reign of terror, pillage, and a long train of infamies, too disgraceful to be remembered without a sense of shame by any one who is proud of the name American.

Had the population of New Orleans been vagrant and riotous, the harsh measures adopted might have been excused, though nothing could have justified the barbarities which were practiced; but, notable as the city had always been for freedom from tumult, and occupied as it then was mainly by women and children, nothing can extenuate the wanton insults and outrages heaped upon them. That those not informed of the character of the citizens may the better comprehend it, a brief reference is made to its history.

When Canada, then a French colony, was conquered by Great Britain, many of the inhabitants of greatest influence and highest cultivation, in a spirit of loyalty to their flag, migrated to the wilds of Louisiana. Some of them established themselves in and about New Orleans, and their numerous descendants formed, down to a late period, the controlling element in the body-politic. Even after they had ceased, because of large immigration, to control in the commercial and political affairs of the city, their social standard was still the rule. No people were more characterized by refinement, courtesy, and chivalry. Of their keen susceptibility the Mayor informed Commodore Farragut in his correspondence with that officer.

When the needy barbarians of the upper plains of Asia descended upon the classic fields of Italy, their atrocities were such as shocked the common-sense of humanity; but, if any one shall inquire minutely into the conduct of Butler and his followers at New Orleans, he will find there a history yet more revolting.

Soon thereafter, on May 17, 1862, Captain Eagle, United States Navy, commanding the naval forces before Galveston, summoned it to surrender, "to prevent the effusion of blood and the destruction of property which would result from the bombardment of the town," adding that the land and naval forces would appear in a few days. The reply was that, "when the land and naval forces made their appearance, the demand would be answered." The harbor and town of Galveston were not prepared to resist a bombardment, and, under the advice of General Herbert, the citizens remained quiet, resolved, when the enemy should attempt to penetrate the interior, to resist his march at every point. This condition remained without any material change until the 8th of the following October, when Commander Renshaw with a fleet of gunboats, consisting of the Westfield, Harriet Lane, Owasco, Clifton, and some transports, approached so near the city as to command it with his guns. Upon a signal, the Mayor *pro tem*, came off to the flag-ship and informed Commander Renshaw that the military and civil authorities had withdrawn from the town, and that he had been appointed by a meeting of citizens to act as mayor, and had come for the purpose of learning the intentions of the naval commander. In reply he was informed that there was no purpose to interfere with the municipal affairs of the city; that he did not intend to occupy it before the arrival of a military commander, but that he intended to hoist the United States flag upon the public buildings, and claim that it should be respected. The acting Mayor informed him that persons over whom he had no control might take down the flag, and he could not guarantee that it should be respected. Commander Renshaw replied that, to avoid any difficulty like that which occurred in New Orleans, he would send with the flag a sufficient force to protect it, and would not keep the flag flying for more than a quarter or half an hour.

The vessels of the fleet were assigned to positions commanding the town and the bridge which connected the island with the mainland, and a battalion of Massachusetts volunteers was posted on one of the wharves.

Late in 1862 General John B. Magruder, a skillful and knightly soldier, who had at an earlier period of the year rendered distinguished service by his defense of the peninsula between the James and York Rivers, Virginia, was assigned to the command of the Department of Texas. On his arrival, he found the enemy in possession of the principal port, Galveston, and other points upon the coast. He promptly collected the scattered arms and field artillery, had a couple of ordinary high-pressure steamboats used in the transportation of cotton on Buffalo Bayou protected with cotton-bales piled from the main deck to and above the hurricane-roof, and these, under the command of Captain Leon Smith, of the Texas Navy, in coöperation with the volunteers, were relied upon to recapture the harbor and island of Galveston. Between night and morning on the 1st of January, 1863, the land-forces entered the town, and the steamboats came into the bay, manned by Texas cavalry and volunteer artillery. The field artillery was ran down to the shore, and opened fire upon the boats. The battalion of the enemy having torn up the plank of the wharf, our infantry could only approach them by wading through the water, and climbing upon the wharf. The two steamboats attacked the Harriet Lane, the gunboat lying farthest up the bay. They were both so frail in their construction that their only chance was to close and board. One of them was soon disabled by collision with the strong vessel, and in a sinking condition ran into shoal water. The other closed with the Harriet Lane, boarded and captured the vessel. The flag-ship Westfield got aground and could not be got off, though assisted by one of the fleet for that purpose. General Magruder then sent a demand that the enemy's vessels should surrender, except one, on which the crews of all should leave the harbor, giving until ten o'clock for compliance with his demand, to enforce which he put a crew on the Harriet Lane, then the most efficient vessel afloat of the enemy's fleet, and, while waiting for an answer, ceased firing. This demand was communicated by a boat from the Harriet Lane to the commander on the Clifton, who said that he was not the commander of the fleet, and would communicate the proposal to the flag-officer on the Westfield. Flags of truce were then flying on the enemy's vessels, as well as on shore. Commander Renshaw refused to accede to the proposition, directing the commander of the Clifton to get all the vessels, including the Corypheus and Sachem, which had recently joined, out of port as soon as possible, and that he would blow up the Westfield, and leave on the transports lying near him with his officers and crew. In attempting to execute this purpose, Commander Renshaw and ten or fifteen others perished soon after leaving the ship, in consequence of the explosion being premature. The General commanding made the following preliminary report:

"HEADQUARTERS, GALVESTON, TEXAS.

"This morning, the 1st January, at three o'clock, I attacked the enemy's fleet and garrison at this place, captured the latter and the steamer Harriet Lane, two barges, and a schooner. The rest, some four or five, escaped ignominiously under cover of a flag of truce. I have about six hundred prisoners and a large quantity of valuable stores, arms, etc. The Harriet Lane is very little injured. She was carried by boarders from two high-pressure cotton-steamers, manned by Texas cavalry and artillery. The line troops were gallantly commanded by Colonel Green, of Sibley's brigade, and the ships and artillery by Major Leon Smith, to whose indomitable energy and heroic daring the country is indebted for the successful execution of a plan which I had considered for the destruction of the enemy's fleet. Colonel Bagby, of Sibley's brigade, also commanded the volunteers from his regiment for the naval expedition, in which every officer and every man won for himself imperishable renown.

"J. BANKHEAD MAGRUDER,
"*Major General.*"

The conduct of Commander Renshaw toward the inhabitants of Galveston had been marked by moderation and propriety, and the closing act of his life was one of manly courage and fidelity to the flag he bore.

Commander Wainright and Lieutenant-commanding Lea, who fell valiantly defending their ship, were buried in the cemetery with the honors of war: thus was evinced that instinctive respect which true warriors always feel for their peers. The surviving officers were paroled.

It would be a pleasing task, if space allowed, to notice the many instances of gallantry in this affair, as daring as they were novel, but want of space compels me to refer the reader to the full accounts which have been published of the "cavalry charge upon a naval fleet."

The capture of the enemy's fleet in Galveston Harbor, by means so novel as to excite surprise as well as grateful admiration, was followed by another victory on the coast of Texas, under circumstances so remarkable as properly to be considered marvelous. To those familiar with the events of that time and section, it is hardly necessary to say that I refer to the battle of Sabine Pass.

The strategic importance to the enemy of the possession of Sabine River caused the organization of a large expedition of land and naval forces to enter and ascend the river. If successful, it gave the enemy short lines for operation against the interior of Texas, and relieved them of the discomfiture resulting from their expulsion from Galveston Harbor.

The fleet of the enemy numbered twenty-three vessels. The forces were estimated to be ten thousand men. No adequate provision had been made to resist such a force, and, under the circumstances, none might have been promptly made on which reliance could have been reasonably placed. A few miles above the entrance into the Sabine River, a small earthwork had been constructed, garrisoned at the time of the action by forty-two men and two lieutenants, with an armament of six guns. The officers and men were all Irishmen, and the company was called the "Davis Guards." The captain, F. H. Odlum, was temporarily absent, so that the command devolved upon Lieutenant E. W. Dowling. Wishing to perpetuate the history of an affair, in which I believe the brave garrison did more than an equal force had ever elsewhere performed, I asked General Magruder, when I met him after the war, to write out a full account of the event; he agreed to do so, but died not long after I saw him, and before complying with my request. From the publications of the day I have obtained the main facts, as they were then printed in the Texas newspapers, and, being unwilling to summarize the reports, give them at length.

Captain F. H. Odlum's Official Report.

"HEADQUARTERS, SABINE PASS,

"*September 9, 1863.*

"Captain A. N. MILLS, *Assistant Adjutant-General.*

"SIR: I have the honor to report that we had an engagement with the enemy yesterday and gained a handsome victory. We captured two of their gunboats, crippled a third, and drove the rest out of the Pass. We took eighteen fine guns, a quantity of smaller arms, ammunition and stores, killed about fifty, wounded several, and took one hundred and fifty prisoners, without the loss or injury of any one on our side or serious damage to the fort.

"Your most obedient servant,

"F. H. ODLUM, *Captain, commanding Sabine Pass.*"

Commodore Leon Smith's Official Report.

"Captain E. P. TURNER, *Assistant Adjutant-General.*

"SIR: After telegraphing the Major-General before leaving Beaumont, I took a horse and proceeded with all haste to Sabine Pass, from which direction I could distinctly hear a heavy firing. Arriving at the Pass at 3 P.M., I found the enemy off and inside the bar, with nineteen gunboats and steamships and other ships of war, carrying, as well as I could judge, fifteen thousand men. I proceeded with Captain Odlum to the fort, and found Lieutenant Dowling and Lieutenant N. H. Smith, of the engineer corps, with forty-two men, defending the fort. Until 3 P.M. our men did not open on the enemy, as the range was too distant. The officers of the fort coolly held their fire until the enemy had approached near enough to reach them. But, when the enemy arrived within good range, our batteries were opened, and gallantly replied to a galling and most terrific fire from the enemy. As I entered the fort, the gunboats Clifton, Arizona, Sachem, and Granite State, with several others, came boldly up to within one thousand yards, and opened their batteries, which were gallantly and effectively replied to by the Davis Guards. For one hour and thirty minutes a most terrific bombardment of grape, canister, and shell was directed against our heroic and devoted little band within the fort. The shot struck in every direction, but, thanks be to God! not one of the noble Davis Guards was hurt. Too much credit can not be awarded Lieutenant Dowling, who displayed the utmost heroism in the discharge of the duty assigned him and the defenders of the fort. God bless the Davis Guards, one and all! The honor of the country was in their hands, and nobly they sustained it. Every man stood at his post, regardless of the murderous fire that was poured upon them from every direction. The result of the battle, which lasted from 3.30 to 5 P.M., was the capturing of the Clifton and Sachem, eighteen heavy guns, one hundred and fifty prisoners, and the killing and wounding of fifty men, and driving outside the bar the enemy's fleet, comprising twenty-three vessels in all. I have the honor to be your obedient servant,

"LEON SMITH,

"*Commanding Marine Department of Texas.*"

"HEADQUARTERS DISTRICT OF TEXAS, NEW MEXICO, AND ARIZONA, HOUSTON,

TEXAS, *September 9, 1863.*

"(SPECIAL ORDER.)

"Another glorious victory has been won by the heroism of Texans. The enemy, confident of overpowering the little garrison at Sabine Pass, boldly advanced to the work of capture. After a sharp contest he was entirely defeated, one gunboat hurrying off in a crippled condition, while two others, the Clifton and Sachem, with their armaments and crews, including the commander of the fleet, surrendered to the gallant defenders of the fort. The loss of the enemy has been heavy, while not a man on our side has been killed or wounded. Though the enemy has been repulsed in his naval attacks, his land-forces, reported as ten thousand strong, are still off the coast waiting an opportunity to land.

"The Major-General calls on every man able to bear arms to bring his guns or arms, no matter of what kind, and be prepared to make a sturdy resistance to the foe.

"Major-General J. B. MAGRUDER.

"EDMUND P. TURNER, *Assistant Adjutant-General.*"

The "Daily Post," Houston, Texas, of August 22, 1880, has the following:

"A few days after the battle each man that participated in the fight was presented with a silver medal inscribed as follows: On one side 'D. G.,' for the Davis Guards, and on the reverse Side, 'Sabine Pass, September 8, 1863.'

"Captain Odlum and Lieutenant R. W. Dowling have gone to that bourn whence no traveler returns, and but few members of the heroic band are in the land of the living, and those few reside in the city of Houston, and often meet together, and talk about the battle in which they participated on the memorable 8th of September, 1863.

"The following are the names of the company who manned the guns in Fort Grigsby, and to whom the credit is due for the glorious victory:

"Lieutenants R. W. Dowling and N. H. Smith; Privates Timothy McDonough, Thomas Dougherty, David Fitzgerald, Michael Monahan, John Hassett, John McKeefer, Jack W. White, Patrick McDonnell, William Gleason, Michael Carr, Thomas Hagerty, Timothy Huggins, Alexander McCabe, James Flemming, Patrick Fitzgerald, Thomas McKernon, Edward Pritchard, Charles Rheins, Timothy Hurley, John McGrath, Matthew Walshe, Patrick Sullivan, Michael Sullivan, Thomas Sullivan, Patrick Clare, John Hennessey, Hugh Deagan, Maurice Powers, Abner Carter, Daniel McMurray, Patrick Malone, James Corcoran, Patrick Abbott, John McNealis, Michael Egan, Daniel Donovan, John Wesley, John Anderson, John Flood, Peter O'Hare, Michael Delaney, Terence Mulhern."

The inquiry may naturally arise how this small, number of men could take charge of so large a body of prisoners. This required that to their valor they should add stratagem. A few men were placed on the parapet as sentinels, the rest were marched out as a guard to receive the prisoners and their arms. Thus was concealed the fact that the fort was empty. The report of the guns bombarding the fort had been heard, and soon after the close of the battle reinforcements arrived, which relieved the little garrison from its embarrassment.

Official reports of officers in the assaulting column, as published in the "Rebellion Record," vol. vii, page 425, *et seq.*, refer to another fort, and steamers in the river, coöperating in the defense of Fort Grigsby. The success of the single company which garrisoned the earthwork is without parallel in ancient or modern war. It was marvelous; but it is incredible—more than marvelous—that another garrison in another fort, with cruising steamers, aided in checking the advance of the enemy, yet silently permitted the forty-two men and two officers of Fort Grigsby to receive all the credit for the victory which was won. If this be supposable, how is it possible that Captain Odlum, Commander Smith, General

Magruder, and Lieutenant Dowling, who had been advised to abandon the work, and had consulted their men as to their willingness to defend it, should nowhere have mentioned the putative fort and coöperating steamers?

The names of the forty-four must go down to posterity, unshorn of the honor which their contemporaries admiringly accorded.

At the commencement of the war the Confederacy was not only without a navy, all the naval vessels possessed by the States having been, as explained elsewhere, left in the hands of our enemies; but worse than this was the fact that ship-building had been almost exclusively done in the Northern States, so that we had no means of acquiring equality in naval power. The numerous deep and wide rivers traversing the Southern States gave a favorable field for the operation of gunboats suited to such circumstances. The enemy rapidly increased their supply of these by building on the Western waters, as well as elsewhere, and converting existing vessels into iron-dad gunboats. The intrepidity and devotion of our people met the necessity by new expedients and extraordinary daring. This was especially seen in the operations of western Louisiana, where numerous bayous and rivers, with difficult land-routes, gave an advantage to the enemy which might well have paralyzed anything less than the most resolute will.

In the earlier period of the war, the gunboats had inspired a terror which their performances never justified. There was a prevailing opinion that they could not be stopped by land-batteries, or resisted on water by anything else than vessels of their own class. Against the first opinion General Richard Taylor, commanding in Louisiana, south of Red River, stoutly contended, and maintained his opinion by the repulse and capture of some of the enemy's vessels by land-batteries having guns of rather light caliber.

One by one successful conflicts between river-boats and gunboats impaired the estimate which had been put upon the latter. The most illustrious example of this was the attack and capture of the Indianola, a heavy ironclad, with two eleven-inch guns forward, and two nine-inch aft, all in iron casemates. She had passed the batteries at Vicksburg, and was in the section of the river between Vicksburg and Port Hudson, which, in February, 1863, was the only gate of communication which the Confederacy had between the east and west sides of the Mississippi. The importance of keeping open this communication, always great, became vital from the necessity of drawing commissary's stores from the trans-Mississippi.

Major Brent, of General Taylor's staff, proposed, with the tow-boat Webb, which had been furnished as a ram, and the Queen of the West, which had been four or five days before captured by the land-battery at Fort De Russy, to go to the Mississippi and attack the Indianola. On the 19th of February the expedition started, though mechanics were still working upon the needed repairs of the Queen of the West. The service was so hazardous that volunteers only formed the crews, but of these more offered than were wanted. On the 24th, while ascending the Mississippi, Major Brent learned, when about sixty miles below Vicksburg, that the Indianola was a short distance ahead, with a coal-barge lashed on either side. He determined to attack in the night, being assured that, if struck by a shell from one of the eleven- or nine-inch guns, either of his boats would be destroyed. At 10 P.M. the Queen, followed by the Webb, was driven at full speed directly upon the Indianola. The momentum of the Queen was so great as to cut through the coal-barge, and indent the iron plates of the Indianola. As the Queen backed out, the Webb dashed in at full speed, and tore away the remaining coal-barge. Both the forward guns fired at the Webb, but missed her. Again the Queen struck the Indianola, abaft the paddle-box, crushing her frame and loosening some plates of armor, but received the fire of the guns from the rear casemates. One shot carried away a dozen bales of cotton on the right side; the other, a shell, entered the forward port-hole and exploded, killing six men and disabling two field-pieces. Again the Webb followed the Queen, struck near the same spot, pushing aside the iron plates and crushing timbers. Voices from the Indianola announced the surrender, and that she was sinking. The river here sweeps the western shore, and there was deep water up to the bank. General Grant's army was on the west side of the river, and, for either or both of these reasons. Major Brent towed the Indianola to the opposite side, where she sank on a bar, her gun-deck above water. Both boats were much shattered in the conflict, and Major Brent returned to the Red River to repair them. A tender accompanied the Queen and the Webb, and a frail river-boat without protection for her boilers, which was met on the river, turned back and followed them, but, like the tender, could be of no service in the battle. For these particulars I am indebted to General Richard Taylor's book, "Destruction and Reconstruction," pages 123-125.

The ram Arkansas, which has been previously noticed as being under construction at Memphis, was removed before she was finished to the Yazoo River, events on the river above having rendered this necessary for her security. After she was supposed to be ready for service, Commander Brown, then as previously in charge of her, went down the Yazoo to enter the Mississippi and proceed to Vicksburg. The enemy's fleet of some twelve or thirteen rams, gunboats, and sloops of war, were in the river above Vicksburg, and below the point where the Yazoo enters the Mississippi. Anticipating the descent of the Arkansas, a detachment had been made from this fleet to prevent her exit. The annexed letter of Commander Brown describes what occurred in the Yazoo River:

"STEAMER ARKANSAS, *July 15, 1862.*

"GENERAL: The Benton, or whatever ironclad we disabled, was left with colors down, evidently aground to prevent sinking, about one mile and a half above the mouth of the Yazoo (in Old River), on the right-hand bank, or bank across from Vicksburg.

"I wish it to be remembered that we whipped this vessel, made it run out of the fight and haul down colors, with two less guns than they had; and at the same time fought two rams, which were firing at us with great guns and small-arms; this, too, with our miscellaneous crew, who had never, for the most part, been on board a ship, or at big guns.

"I am, General, very respectfully, your obedient servant,

"J. N. BROWN,

"*Lieutenant commanding.*

"To Brigadier-General M. L. SMITH, *commanding defenses at Vicksburg.*"

When entering the Mississippi the fleet of the enemy was found disposed as a phalanx, but the heroic commander of the Arkansas moved directly against it; and, though in passing through this formidable array he was exposed to the broadsides of the whole fleet, the vessel received no other injury than from one eleven-inch shot which entered the gun-room, and the perforation in many places of her smoke-stack. The casualties to the crew were five killed, four wounded—among the latter was the gallant commander. General Van Dorn, commanding the department, in a dispatch from Vicksburg, July 15th, states the number of the enemy's vessels above Vicksburg, pays a high compliment to the officers and men, and adds:

"All the enemy's transports and all the vessels of war of the lower fleet (i. e., the fleet just below Vicksburg), except a sloop of war, have got up steam, and are off to escape from the Arkansas."

A vessel inspiring such dread is entitled to a special description. She was an iron-clad steamer, one hundred feet in her length, her armament ten Parrott guns, and her crew one hundred men, who had volunteered from the land-forces for the desperate service proposed. Her commander had been from his youth in the navy of the United States, and his capacity was such as could well supplement whatever was wanted of naval knowledge in his crew. The care and skill with which the vessel had been constructed were tested and proved under fire. Had her engines been equal to the hull and armor of the vessel, it is difficult to estimate the value of the service she might have performed. At this period the enemy occupied Baton Rouge, with gunboats lying in front of it to coöperate with the troops in the town. The importance of holding a section of the Mississippi, so as to keep free communication between the eastern and western portions of the Confederacy, has been heretofore noticed. To this end it was deemed needful to recover the possession of Baton Rouge, and it was decided to make a land-attack in coöperation with the Arkansas, to be sent down against the enemy's fleet.

Major-General J. C. Breckinridge was assigned to the command of the land-forces. This distinguished citizen and alike distinguished soldier, surmounting difficulties which would have discouraged a less resolute spirit, approached Baton Rouge, and moved to the attack at the time indicated for the arrival of the Arkansas. In his address to the officers and soldiers of his command, after the battle, viz., on August 6, 1862, he compliments the troops on the fortitude with which they had borne a severe march, on the manner in which they attacked the enemy, superior in numbers and admirably posted, drove him from his positions, taking his camps, and forcing him to seek protection under cover of the guns of his fleet. Major-General Breckinridge attributes his failure to achieve entire success to the inability of the Arkansas to coöperate with his forces, and adds:

"You have given the enemy a severe and salutary lesson, and now those who so lately were ravaging and plundering this region do not care to extend their pickets beyond the sight of their fleet."

The Arkansas in descending the river moved leisurely, having ample time to meet her appointment; but, when about fifteen miles above Baton Rouge, her starboard engine broke down. Repairs were immediately commenced, and, by 8 A.M. on the 5th of August, were partially completed. General Breckinridge had commenced the attack at four o'clock, and the Arkansas, though not in condition to engage the enemy, moved on, and, when in sight of Baton Rouge, her starboard engine again broke down, and the vessel was run ashore. The work of repair was resumed, and next morning the Federal fleet was seen coming up. The Arkansas was moored head down-stream and cleared for action. The Essex approached and opened fire; at that moment the engineers reported the engines able to work half a day. The lines were cut, and the Arkansas started for the Essex, when the other— the larboard—engine suddenly stopped, and the vessel was again secured to the shore stern-down. The Essex now valiantly approached, pouring a hot fire into her disabled antagonist. Lieutenant Stevens, then commanding the Arkansas, ordered the crew ashore, fired the vessel, and, with her flag flying, turned her adrift—a sacrificial offering to the cause she had served so valiantly in her brief but brilliant career. Lieutenant Reed, of the ram Arkansas, in his published account of the affair, states, "After all hands were ashore, the Essex fired upon the disabled vessel most furiously."

CHAPTER XXX.

Naval Affairs (continued).—Necessity of a Navy.—Raphael Semmes.— The Sumter.—Difficulties in creating a Navy.—The Sumter at Sea.— Alarm.—Her Captures.—James D. Bullock.—Laird's Speech in the House of Commons.—The Alabama.—Semmes takes Command.—The Vessel and Crew.—Goes to Sea.—Banks's Expedition.—Magruder at Galveston.—The Steamer Hattaras Sunk.—The Alabama not a Pirate.— An Aspinwall Steamer ransomed.—Other Captures.—Prizes burned.— At Cherbourg.—Fight with the Kearsarge.—Rescue of the Men.— Demand of the United States Government for the Surrender of the Drowning Men.—Reply of the British Government.—Sailing of the Oreto.—Detained at Nassau.—Captain Maffit.—The Ship Half Equipped.—Arrives at Mobile.—Runs the Blockade.—Her Cruise.— Capture and Cruise of the Clarence.—The Captures of the Florida.— Captain C. M. Morris.—The Florida at Bahia.—Seized by the Wachusett.—Brought to Virginia and sunk.—Correspondence.—The Georgia.—Cruises and Captures.—The Shenandoah.—Cruises and Captures.—The Atlanta.—The Tallahassee.—The Edith.

To maintain the position assumed by the Confederate States as a separate power among the nations, it was obviously necessary to have a navy, not only for the defense of their coast, but also for the protection of their commerce. These States, after their secession from the Union, were in that regard in a destitute condition, similar to that of the United States after their Declaration of Independence.

It has been shown that among the first acts of the Confederate Administration was the effort to buy ships which could be used for naval purposes. The policy of the United States Government being to shut up our commerce rather than protect their own, induced the wholesale purchase of the vessels found in the Northern ports—not only such as could be made fit for cruisers, but also any which would serve even for blockading purposes. There was little shipping of any kind in the Southern ports, and to that scanty supply we were, for the time, restricted.

A previous reference has been made to the Sumter, Commander Raphael Semmes, but a more extended notice is considered due. Educated in the naval service of the United States, Raphael Semmes had attained the rank of commander, and was distinguished for his studious habits and varied acquirements. When Alabama passed her ordinance of secession, he was on duty at Washington as a member of the Lighthouse Board; he promptly tendered his resignation, and, at the organization of the Confederate Government, repaired to Montgomery and tendered his services to it. The efforts which had been made to obtain steamers suited to cruising against the enemy's commerce had been quite unsuccessful, none being found which the naval officers charged with their selection regarded fit for the service. One of the reports described a small propeller-steamer of five hundred tons burden, sea-going, low-pressure engine, sound, and capable of being so strengthened as to carry an ordinary battery of four or five guns; speed between nine and ten knots, but the board condemned her because she could carry but five days' fuel, and had no accommodations for the crew.

The Secretary of the Navy showed this to Commander Semmes, who said: "Give me that ship; I think I can make her answer the purpose." She was to be christened the Sumter, in commemoration of our first victory, and had the honor of being the first ship of war commissioned by the Confederate States, and the first to display the Stars and Bars of the Confederacy on the high-seas. The Sumter was at New Orleans, to which place Commander Semmes repaired; and, as forcibly presenting the difficulties under which we labored in all attempts to create a navy, I will quote from his memoirs the account of his effort to get the Sumter ready for sea:

"I now took my ship actively in hand and set gangs of mechanics at work to remove her upper cabins and other top hamper, preparatory to making the necessary alterations. These latter were considerable, and I soon found that I had a tedious job on my hands. It was no longer the case, as it had been in former years, when I had had occasion to fit out a ship, that I could go into a navy-yard, with well-provided workshops and skilled workmen, ready with all the requisite materials at hand to execute my orders. Everything had to be improvised, from the manufacture of a water-tank to the kids and cans of the berth-deck messes, and from a gun-carriage to a friction-primer. . . . Two long, tedious months were consumed in making alterations and additions. My battery was to consist of an eight-inch-shell gun, to be pivoted amidships, and of four light thirty-two-pounders of thirteen hundred weight each, in broadside."

On the 3d of June, 1861, the Sumter was formally put in commission, and a muster-roll of the officers and men transmitted to the Navy Department. On the 18th of June she left New Orleans and steamed down and anchored near the mouth of the river. While lying at the head of the passes, the commander reported a blockading squadron outside, of three ships at Passe a l'Outre, and one at the Southwest Pass. The Brooklyn, at Passe a l'Outre, was not only a powerful vessel, but she had greater speed than the Sumter. The Powhatan's heavy armament made it very hazardous to pass her in daylight, and the absence of buoys and lights made it next to impossible to keep the channel in darkness. The Sumter, therefore, had been compelled to lie at the head of the passes and watch for some opportunity in the absence of either the Brooklyn or the Powhatan to get to sea. Fortunately, neither of these vessels came up to the head of the passes, where, there being but a single channel, it would have been easy to prevent the exit of the Sumter.

On the 30th of June, one bright morning, a boatman reported that the Brooklyn had gone off in chase of a sail. Immediately the Sumter was got under way, when it was soon discovered that the Brooklyn was returning, and that the two vessels were about equally distant from the bar. By steady courage and rare seamanship the Sumter escaped from her more swift pursuer, and entered on her career of cutting the enemy's sinews of war by destroying his commerce.

Numerous armed vessels of the enemy were hovering on our coast, yet this one little cruiser created a general alarm, and, though a regularly commissioned vessel of the Confederacy, was habitually denounced as a "pirate," and the many threats to destroy her served only to verify the adage that the threatened live long.

During her cruise up to January 17, 1862, she captured three ships, five brigs, six barks, and three schooners, but the property destroyed formed a very small part of the damage done to the enemy's commerce. Her appearance on the seas created such alarm that Northern ships were, to a large extent, put under foreign flags, and the carrying-trade, in which the United States stood second only to Great Britain, passed rapidly into other hands. The Sumter, while doing all this mischief, was nearly self-sustaining, her running expenses to the Confederate Government being but twenty-eight thousand dollars when, at the close of 1861, she arrived at Gibraltar. Not being able to obtain coal, she remained there until sold.

Captain James D. Bullock, an officer of the old navy, of high ability as a seaman, and of an integrity which stood the test under which a less stern character might have given way, was our naval agent at Liverpool. In his office he disbursed millions, and, when there was no one to whom he could be required to render an account, paid out the last shilling in his hands, and confronted poverty without prospect of other reward than that which he might find id a clear conscience. He contracted with the Messrs. Laird, of Birkenhead, to build a strong steam merchant-ship—the same which was afterward christened "The Alabama" when, in a foreign port, she had received her armament and crew. So much of puerile denunciation has been directed against the builder and the ship, which, in the virulent language of the day, our enemies denominated a "pirate," that the case claims at my hands a somewhat extended notice.

The senior Mr. Laird was a member of the British Parliament, and, because of the complaints made by the United States Government, and the abuse heaped upon him by the Northern newspapers, he made a speech in the House of Commons, in which he stated that, in 1861, he was applied to to build vessels for the Northern Government, first, by personal application, and subsequently by a letter from Washington, asking him, on the part of the United States Navy

Department, to give the terms on which he would build an iron-plated ship, "to be finished complete, with guns and everything appertaining." Mr. Laird continued: "On the 14th of August I received another letter from the same gentleman, from which the following is an extract: 'I have this morning a note from the Assistant-Secretary of the Navy, in which he says, "I hope your friends will tender for the two iron-plated steamers."'" Mr. Laird then said that, while he would not give the name of his correspondent, who was a gentleman of the highest respectability, he was willing, in confidence, to submit the original letters to the Speaker of the House or the first Minister of the Crown; that, as "the American Government is making so much work about other parties whom they charge with violating or evading the law, when in reality they have not done so, I think it only right to state these facts."

Those who have listened with credulity to the abuse of the Confederate Government, as well as that of Great Britain, the one for contracting for the building of the Alabama and the other for permitting her to leave a British port, will thus see how little of sincerity there was in the complaints of the United States Government. For more than a generation the British people have been the great ship-builders of the world, and it is a matter of surprise that they should have given respectful consideration to charges of a breach of neutrality because they allowed a merchantman to be built in one of their ports and to leave it without any armament or crew, which could have enabled it, in that condition, to make war upon a country with which Great Britain was at peace.

Referring to the Alabama, as she was when she left the Mersey, Mr. Laird said:

"If a ship without guns and without arms is a dangerous article, surely rifled guns and ammunition of all sorts are equally and even more dangerous. I have referred to the bills of entry in the custom-houses of London and Liverpool, and I find that there have been vast shipments of implements of war to the Northern States through the celebrated houses of Baring & Co.; Brown, Shipley & Co.; and a variety of other names. . . . I have obtained from the official custom-house returns some details of the sundries exported from the United Kingdom to the Northern States of America from the 1st of May, 1861, to the 31st of December, 1862. There were—muskets, 41,500; rifles, 341,000; gun-flints, 26,500; percussion-caps, 49,982,000; and swords, 2,250. The best information I could obtain leads me to believe that one third to a half may be added to these numbers for items which have been shipped to the Northern States as hardware . . . so that, if the Southern States have got two ships unarmed, unfit for any purpose of warfare— for they procured their armament somewhere else—the Northern States have been well supplied from this country, through the agency of some most influential persons."

The speech of Mr. Laird, exposing the hypocrisy of the representations which had been made, as well by commercial bodies as by the highest officers of the United States, called forth repeated cheers from the Parliament.

There had been no secrecy about the building of the Alabama. The same authority above quoted states that she was frequently visited while under construction, and it is known that the British Government was applied to to prevent her from leaving port. It was feared that she might be delayed; but it was not considered possible that British authorities would prevent an unarmed merchant-ship from leaving her coast, lest she might elsewhere procure an armament, and, in the service of a recognized belligerent, revive the terror in the other belligerent which the little Sumter had recently inspired.

When the Alabama was launched and ready for sea, Captain Bullock summoned Captain Semmes, lately commander of the Sumter, to Liverpool, where he spent a few days in financial arrangements, and in collecting the old officers of the Sumter. The Alabama, then known as the 290, had proceeded a few days before to her rendezvous, the Portuguese Island of Terceira, one of the group of the Azores. The story that the name 290 belonged to the fact that she had been built by two hundred and ninety Englishmen, sympathizers in our struggle, was a mere fiction. She was built under a contract with the Confederate States, and paid for with Confederate money. She happened to be the two hundred and ninetieth ship built by the Lairds, and, not having been christened, was called 290. Captain Semmes followed her, accompanied by Captain Bullock on the steamer Bahama, and found her at the place of rendezvous, also a sailing-ship which had been dispatched before the Alabama with her battery and stores. Captain Semmes, with a sailor's enthusiasm, describes his first impression on seeing the ship which was to be his future home. The defects of the Sumter had been avoided, so that he found his new ship "a perfect steamer and a perfect sailing-ship, at the same time neither of her two modes of locomotion being at all dependent upon the other. . . . She was about nine hundred tons burden, two hundred and thirty feet in length, thirty-two feet in breadth, twenty feet in depth, and drew, when provisioned and coaled for a cruise, fifteen feet of water. Her model was of the most perfect symmetry, and she sat upon the water with the lightness and grace of a swan." She was yet only a merchant-ship, and the men on board of her, as well as those who came out with the Captain on the Bahama, were only under articles for the voyage. She therefore had no crew for future service. When her armament and stores had been put on board, she steamed from the harbor out to the open sea, where she was to be christened and put in commission. Captain Bullock went out on her and stood sponsor at the ceremony. He had just cause to be proud of the ship, and we to be thankful to him for the skill and care with which he had designed her and supervised her construction. The scantling of the vessel was comparatively light, having been intended for a scourge to the enemy's commerce rather than for battle, and merely to defend herself if it became necessary. Her masts were proportioned so as to carry large canvas, and her engine was of three hundred horse-power, with an apparatus for condensing vapor to supply the crew with all the fresh water requisite. The coal, stores, and armament having been received from the supply-ships, she steamed out to sea on Sunday morning, August 24, 1862. There, more than a marine league from the shore, on the blue water over which man holds no empire, Captain Semmes read the commission of the President of the Confederacy appointing him a captain, and the order of the Secretary of the Navy assigning him to the command of the Alabama. There, where no government held jurisdiction, where the commission of the Confederacy was as valid as that of any power, the Alabama was christened, and was henceforth a ship of war in the navy of the Confederate States. The men who had come thus far under articles no longer binding were left to their option whether to be paid off with a free passage to Liverpool, or to enlist in the crew of the Alabama. Eighty of the men who had come out in the several vessels enrolled themselves in the usual manner. Captain Semmes had a full complement of officers, and with this, though less than the authorized crew, he commenced his long and brilliant cruise. The ship's armament consisted of six thirty-two-pounders in broadsides and two pivot-guns amidships, one of them a smooth-bore eight-inch, the other a hundred-pounder rifled Blakely.

Captain Semmes, from his varied knowledge of affairs both on sea and land, did not sail by chance in quest of adventure, but directed his course to places where the greatest number of the enemy's merchantmen were likely to be found, and to this the large number of captures he made is in no small degree attributable. On board one of the ships captured they got New York papers, from which he learned that General Banks, with a large fleet of transports, was to sail on a certain day for Galveston. On this he decided to go to the rendezvous appointed for his coal-ship, and make all due preparation for a dash into the fleet when they should arrive at the harbor of Galveston, and therefore directed his course into the Gulf of Mexico.

In the mean time General Magruder had recaptured Galveston, so that on his arrival the lookout informed him that, instead of a fleet, there were five ships of war blockading the harbor and throwing shells into the town, from which his keen perception drew the proper conclusion that we had possession of the town, and that he was confronted by ships of war, not transports laden with troops. As each of the five ships observed by the lookout were supposed to be larger than his own, he had of course no disposition to run into that fleet. It therefore only remained to tempt one of the ships to follow him beyond supporting distance. The hope was soon realized, as a vessel was seen to come out from the fleet. The Alabama was under sail, and Captain Semmes says: "To carry out my design of decoying the enemy, I now wore ship as though I were fleeing from his pursuit, and lowered the propeller into the water. When about twenty miles from the fleet, the Alabama was prepared for action, and wheeled to meet her pursuer. To the first hail made, the answer from the Alabama was, 'This is her Britannic Majesty's steamer Petrel,' and the answer was, 'This is the United States ship, — ——' name not heard." Captain Semmes then directed the first lieutenant to call out through his trumpet, "This is the Confederate States steamer Alabama." A broadside was instantly returned by the enemy. Captain Semmes describes the state of the atmosphere as highly favorable to the conduct of sound, and the wind blowing in the direction of the enemy's fleet. The Federal Admiral, as afterward learned, immediately got under way with the Brooklyn and two others of his steamers to go to the rescue. The crews of both ships must have been standing at their guns, as the broadsides so instantly followed each other. In thirteen minutes after firing the first gun the enemy hoisted a light and fired an off-gun as a signal that he had been beaten. Captain Semmes steamed quite close to the Hatteras and asked if he had surrendered; then, if he was in want of assistance. An affirmative answer was given to both questions. The boats of the Alabama were lowered with such promptitude and handled with such care that, though the Hatteras was sunk at night, none of her crew were drowned. When her captain came on board, Captain Semmes learned that he had been engaged with the United States steamer Hatteras, "a larger ship than the Alabama by one hundred tons," with an equal number of guns, and a crew numbering two less than that of the Alabama. There was a "considerable disparity between the two ships in the weight of their pivot-guns, and the Alabama ought to have won the fight, which she did in thirteen minutes." The Alabama had received no appreciable injury, and, continuing her cruise to the Island of Jamaica, entered the harbor of Port Royal, where, by the permission of the authorities. Captain Semmes landed his prisoners, putting them on parole.

As an answer to the stereotyped charges against Captain Semmes as a "pirate" and robber, I will select from the many unarmed ships captured by him one case. He had gone to the track of the California steamers between Aspinwall and New York, in the hope of capturing a vessel homeward bound with Government treasure. On the morning before such a vessel was expected, a large steamer, the Ariel, was seen, but unfortunately not going in the right direction. An exciting chase occurred, when she was finally brought to, but, instead of the million of dollars in her safe, she was outward bound, with a large number of women and children on board. A boarding officer was sent on her, and returned, giving an account of great alarm, especially among the ladies. Captain Semmes sent a lieutenant on board to assure them that they had "fallen into the hands of Southern gentlemen, under whose protection the were entirely safe." Among the passengers were a battalion of marines and some army and navy officers. These were all paroled, rank and file numbering one hundred and forty, and the vessel was released on ransom-bond. Captain Semmes states that there were five hundred passengers on board. It is fair to presume that each passenger had with him a purse of from three to five hundred dollars. Under the laws of war all this money would have been good prize, but not one dollar of it was touched, or indeed so much as a passenger's baggage examined.

The Alabama now proceeded to run down the Spanish Main, thence bore eastward into the Indian Ocean, and, after a cruise into every sea where a blow at American commerce could be struck, came around the Cape of Good Hope, and, sailing north, ran up to the thirtieth parallel, where so many captures had been made at a former time. Of the ship at this date Captain Semmes wrote: "The poor old Alabama was not now what she had been then. She was like the wearied fox-hound, limping back after a long chase, foot-sore, and longing for quiet repose."

She had, in her mission to cripple the enemy's commerce and cut his sinews of war, captured sixty-three vessels, among them one of the enemy's gunboats, the Hatteras, sunk in battle, had released nine under ransom-bond, and had paroled all prisoners taken.

All neutral ports being closed against her prizes, the rest of the vessels were, of necessity, burned at sea. Much complaint was made on account of the burning of these merchantmen, though very little reflection would have taught the complainants that the interests of the captor would have induced him to save the vessels, and send them into the nearest port for condemnation as prizes; and, therefore, whatever grievance existed was the result of the blockade and of the rule which prevented the captures from being sent into a neutral port to await the decision of a prize court.

On the morning of the 11th of June, 1864, the Alabama entered the harbor of Cherbourg. "An officer was sent to call on the port admiral, and ask leave to land the prisoners from the last two ships captured; this was readily granted." The next day Captain Semmes went on shore to consult the port admiral "in relation to docking and repairing" the Alabama. As there were only government docks at Cherbourg, the application had to be referred to the Emperor. Before an answer was received, the Kearsarge steamed into the harbor, sent a boat ashore, and then ran out and took her station off the breakwater. Captain Semmes learned that the boat from the Kearsarge sent on shore had borne a request that the prisoners discharged from the Alabama might be delivered to the Kearsarge. It will be remembered that the Government of the United States, in many harsh and unjust phrases, had refused to recognize the Alabama as a ship of war, and held that the paroles given to her were void. This request was therefore regarded by Captain Semmes as an attempt to recruit for the Kearsarge from the prisoners lately landed by the Alabama, and he so presented the facts to the port admiral, who rejected the application from the Kearsarge.

Captain Semmes sent notice to Captain Winslow, of the Kearsarge, whose presence in the offing was regarded as a challenge, that, if he would wait until the Alabama could receive some coal on board, she would come out and give him battle.

As has been shown by extracts previously made, Captain Semmes knew that, after his long cruise, the Alabama needed to go into dock for repairs. It had not been possible for him, on account of the rigid enforcement of "neutrality," to replenish his ammunition. Unless the niter is more thoroughly purified than is usually, if ever, done by those who manufacture for an open market, it is sure to retain nitrate of soda, and the powder, of which it is the important ingredient, to deteriorate by long exposure to a moist atmosphere. The Kearsarge was superior to the Alabama in size, and, having in stanchness of construction, her armament was also greater, the latter being measured, not by the number of guns, but by the amount of metal she could throw at a broadside. The crew of the Kearsarge, all told, was one hundred and sixty-two; that of the Alabama, one hundred and forty-nine. Captain Semmes says: "Still the disparity was not so great but that I might hope to beat my enemy in a fair fight. But he did not show me a fair fight, for, as it afterward turned out, his ship was iron-clad." This expression "iron-clad" refers to the fact that the Kearsarge had chains on her sides, which Captain Semmes describes as concealed by planking, the forward and after ends of which so accorded with the lines of the ship as not to be detected by telescopic observation. Many of that class of critics whose wisdom is only revealed after the event have blamed Captain Semmes for going out under the circumstances. Like most other questions, there are two sides to this. If he had gone into dock for repairs, the time required would have resulted in the dispersion of his crew, and, from the known improvidence of sailors, it would have been more than doubtful whether they could have been reassembled. It was, moreover, probable that other vessels would have been sent to aid the Kearsarge in effectually blockading the port, so that, if his crew had returned, the only chance would have been to escape through the guarding fleet. Proud of his ship, and justly confiding in his crew, surely something will be conceded to the Confederate spirit so often exhibited and so often triumphant over disparity of force.

On the 19th of June, 1864, the Alabama left the harbor of Cherbourg to engage the Kearsarge, which had been lying off and on the port for several days previously. Captain Semmes in his report of the engagement writes:

"After the lapse of about one hour and ten minutes, our ship was ascertained to be in a sinking condition . . . to reach the French coast, I gave the ship all steam, and set such of the fore and aft sails as were available. The ship filled so rapidly, however, that, before we had made much progress, the fires were extinguished. I now hauled down my colors, and dispatched a boat to inform the enemy of our condition. Although we were now but four hundred yards from each other, the enemy fired upon me five times after my colors had been struck. It is charitable to suppose that a ship of war, of a Christian nation, could not have done this intentionally."

Captain Semmes states that, his waist-boats having been torn to pieces, he sent the wounded, and such of the boys of the ship as could not swim, in his quarter-boats, off to the enemy's ship, and, as there was no appearance of any boat coming from the enemy, the crew, as previously instructed, jumped overboard, each to save himself if he could. All the wounded—twenty-one—were saved; ten of the crew were ascertained to have been drowned. Captain Semmes stood on the quarter-deck until his ship was settling to go down, then threw his sword into the sea, there to lie buried with the ship he loved so well, and leaped from the deck just in time to avoid being drawn down into the vortex created by her sinking. He and many of his crew were picked up by a humane English gentleman in the boats of his yacht, the Deerhound. Others were saved by two French pilot-boats which were near the scene. The remainder, it is hoped, were picked up by the enemy. Captain Semmes states in his official report, two days after the battle, that about the time of his rescue by the Deerhound the "Kearsarge sent one and then tardily another boat." The reader is invited to compare this with the conduct of Captain Semmes when he sank the Hatteras, and, when, though it was in the night, by ranging up close to her, and promptly using all his boats, he saved her entire crew.

Mention has been made of the defective ammunition of the Alabama, and in that connection I quote the following passage from Captain Semmes's book, on which I have so frequently and largely drawn for facts in regard to the Sumter and the Alabama (pages 761, 762):

"I lodged a rifle percussion shell near to her [the Kearsarge's] sternpost—where there were no chains—which failed to explode because of the defect of the cap. If the cap had performed its duty, and exploded the shell, I should have been called upon to save Captain Winslow's crew from drowning, instead of his being called upon to save mine."

As it appears by the same authority that the Kearsarge had greater speed than the Alabama, it followed that, though the Captain of the Kearsarge might have closed with and boarded the Alabama, the Captain of the Alabama could not board the Kearsarge, unless by consent.

The Alabama, built like a merchant-ship, sailed in peaceful garb from British waters, on a far-distant sea received her crew and armament, fitted for operations against the enemy's commerce. On "blue-water" she was christened, and in the same she was buried. She lived the pride of her friends and the terror of her enemies. She went out to fight a wooden vessel and was sunk by one clad in secret armor. Those rescued by the Deerhound from the water were landed at Southampton, England.

The United States Government then, through its minister, Mr. Charles Francis Adams, made the absurd demand of the English Government that they should be delivered up to her as escaped prisoners. To this demand Lord John Russell replied as follows:

"With regard to the demand made by you, by instructions from your Government, that those officers and men should now be delivered up to the Government of the United States, as being escaped prisoners of war, her Majesty's Government would beg to observe that there is no obligation by international law which can bind the government of a neutral state to deliver up to a belligerent prisoners of war who may have escaped from the power of such belligerent, and may have taken refuge within the territory of such neutral. Therefore, even if her Majesty's Government had any power, by law, to comply with the above-mentioned demand, her Majesty's Government could not do so without being guilty of a violation of the duties of hospitality. In point of fact, however, her Majesty's Government have no lawful power to arrest and deliver up the persons in question. They have been guilty of no offense against the laws of England, and they have committed no act which would bring them within the provisions of a treaty between Great Britain and the United States for the surrender of the offenders; and her Majesty's Government are, therefore, entirely without any legal means by which, even if they wished to do so, they could comply with your above-mentioned demand."

It will be observed that her Majesty's Minister mercifully forbore to expose the pretensions that "the persons in question" had been prisoners, and confined his answer to the case as it would have been had that allegation been true. There are other points in this transaction which will be elsewhere presented.

The Oreto, which sailed from Liverpool about the 23d of March, 1862, was, while under construction at Liverpool, the subject of diplomatic correspondence and close scrutiny by the customs officers. After her arrival off Nassau, upon representations by the United States consul at that port, she was detained and again examined, and, it being found that she had none of the character of a vessel of war, she was released. Captain Maffitt, who had gone out with a cargo of cotton, here received a letter which authorized him to take charge of the Oreto and get her promptly to sea. She was a steamer of two hundred and fifty horse-power, tonnage five hundred and sixty, bark-rigged; speed, under steam, eight to nine knots; with sail, in a fresh breeze, fourteen knots; crew twenty-two, all told. The United States Minister, Mr. Adams, had made a report to the British Government, which, it was apprehended, would cause her seizure at once. This was soon done, and with great difficulty the vessel was saved to the Confederacy by her commander. She arrived at Nassau on the 28th of April, and was detained until the session of the Admiralty Court in August. As soon as discharged by the proceedings therein, she sailed for the uninhabited island "Green Kay," ninety miles to the southward of Providence Island, with a tender in tow having equipments provided by a Confederate merchant, where she anchored the next day, and proceeded to take on board her military armament sent out on the tender. She now became a ship of the Confederate Navy, and was christened Florida. Her long detention in Nassau had caused the ship to be infected with yellow fever, and, as she had no surgeon on board, the vessel was directed to the Island of Cuba, and ran into the harbor of Cardenas for aid. The crew was reduced to one fireman and two seamen, and eventually the Captain was prostrated by the fever. The Governor of Cardenas, under his view of the neutrality proclaimed by his Government, refused to send a physician aboard, and warned the steamer that she must leave in twenty-four hours. Lieutenant Stribling, executive officer of the ship, had been sent to Havana to report her condition to the Captain-General, Marshal Serrano. That chivalrous gentleman, soldier, and statesman, at once invited the ship to the hospitalities of the harbor of Havana, whither she repaired and received the kindness which her forlorn situation required.

On the 1st of September, 1862, the vessel left Havana to obtain a crew; and, to complete her equipment, which was so imperfect that her guns could not all be used, the vessel was directed to the harbor of Mobile. On approaching that harbor she found several blockading vessels on the station, and boldly ran through them, escaping, with considerable injury to her masts and rigging, to the friendly shelter of Fort Morgan, where, while in quarantine, Lieutenant Stribling was attacked with fever and died. He was an officer of great merit, and his loss was much regretted, not only by his many personal friends, but by all who foresaw the useful service he could render to his country if his life were prolonged. Under the disadvantages of being an infected ship and remote from the workshops, repairs were commenced, and the equipment of the ship completed.

In the mean time the blockading squadron had been increased, with the boastful announcement that the cruiser should be "hermetically sealed" in the harbor of Mobile. Some impatience was manifested after the vessel was ready for sea that she did not immediately go out, but Captain Maffitt, with sound judgment and nautical skill, decided to wait for a winter storm and a dark night before attempting to pass through the close investment. When the opportunity offered, he steamed out into a rough sea and a fierce north wind. As he passed the blockading squadron he was for the first time discovered, when a number of vessels gave chase, and continued the pursuit throughout the night and the next day. In the next evening all except the two fastest had hauled off, and, as night again closed in, the smoke and canvas of the Florida furnished their only guide. Captain Maffitt thus describes the ruse by which he finally escaped: "The canvas was secured in long, neat bunts to the yards, and the engines were stopped. Between high, toppling seas, clear daylight was necessary to enable them to distinguish our low hull. In eager pursuit the Federals swiftly passed us, and we jubilantly bade the enemy good night, and steered to the northward." She was now fairly on the high-seas, and after long and vexatious delays entered on her mission to cruise against the enemy's commerce. She commenced her captures in the Gulf of Mexico, then progressed through the Gulf of Florida to the latitude of New York, and thence to the equator, continuing to 12 deg. south, and returned again within thirty miles of New York. When near Cape St. Roque, Captain Maffitt captured a Baltimore brig, the Clarence, and fitted her out as a tender. He placed on her Lieutenant C. W. Read, commander, fourteen men, armed with muskets, pistols, and a twelve-pound howitzer. The instructions were to proceed to the coast of America, to cruise against the enemy's commerce. Under these orders he destroyed many Federal vessels. Of him Captain Maffitt wrote: "Daring, even beyond the point of martial prudence, he entered the harbor of Portland at midnight, and captured the revenue cutter Caleb Cushing; but, instead of instantly burning her, ran her out of the harbor; being thus delayed, he was soon captured by a Federal expedition sent out against him." While under the command of Captain Maffitt, the Florida, with her tenders, captured some fifty-five vessels, many of which were of great value. The Florida being built of light timbers, her very active cruising had so deranged her machinery, that it was necessary to go into some friendly harbor for repairs. Captain Maffitt says: "I selected Brest, and, the Government courteously consenting to the Florida having the facilities of the navy-yard, she was promptly docked." The effects of the yellow fever from which he had suffered and the fatigue attending his subsequent service had so exhausted his strength that he asked to be relieved from command of the ship. In compliance with this request, Captain C. M. Morris was ordered to relieve him.

After completing all needful repairs, Captain Morris proceeded to sea and sighted the coast of Virginia, where he made a number of important captures. Turning from that locality he crossed the equator, destroying the commerce of the Northern States on his route to Bahia. Here he obtained coal, and also had some repairs done to the engines, when the United States steamship Wachusett entered the harbor. Not knowing what act of treachery might be attempted by her commander on the first night after his arrival, the Florida was kept in a watchful condition for battle.

This belligerent demonstration in the peaceful harbor of a neutral power alarmed both the governor and the admiral, who demanded assurances that the sovereignty of Brazil and its neutrality should be strictly observed by both parties. The pledge was given. In the evening, with a chivalric belief in the honor of the United States commander, Captain Morris unfortunately permitted a majority of his officers to accompany him to the opera, and also allowed two thirds of the crew to visit the shore on leave. About one o'clock in the morning the Wachusett was surreptitiously got under way, and her commander, with utter abnegation of his word of honor, ran into the Florida, discharging his battery and boarding her. The few officers on board and small number of men were unable to resist this unexpected attack, and the Florida fell an easy prey to this covert and dishonorable assault. She was towed to sea amid the execrations of the Brazilian forces, army and navy, who, completely taken by surprise, fired a few ineffectual shots at the infringer upon the neutrality of the hospitable port of Bahia. The Confederate was taken to Hampton Roads.

Brazil instantly demanded her restoration intact to her late anchorage in Bahia. Mr. Lincoln was confronted by a protest from the different representatives of the courts of Europe, denouncing this extraordinary breach of national neutrality, which placed the Government of the United States in a most unenviable position. Mr. Seward, with his usual diplomatic insincerity and Machiavellianism, characteristically prevaricated, while he plotted with a distinguished admiral as to the most adroit method of disposing of the "elephant." The result of these plottings was that an engineer was placed in charge of the stolen steamer, with positive orders to "open her sea-cock at midnight, and not to leave the engine-room until the water was up to his chin, as at sunrise *the Florida must be at the bottom*." The following note was sent to the Brazilian *chargé d'affaires* by Mr. Seward:

"While awaiting the representations of the Brazilian Government, on the 28th of November she [the Florida] sank, owing to a leak, which could not be seasonably stopped. The leak was at first represented to have been caused, or at least increased, by collision with a war-transport. Orders were immediately given to ascertain the manner and circumstances of the occurrence. It seemed to affect the army and navy. A naval court of inquiry and also a military court of inquiry were charged with the investigation. The naval court has submitted its report, and a copy thereof is herewith communicated. The military court is yet engaged. So soon as its labors shall have ended, the result will be made known to your Government. In the mean time it is assumed that the loss of the Florida was in consequence of some unforeseen accident, which casts no responsibility on the Government of the United States."

The restitution of the ship having thus become impossible, the President expressed his regret that "the sovereignty of Brazil had been violated; dismissed the consul at Bahia, who had advised the offense; and sent the commander of the Wachusett before a court-martial." [58]

The commander of the Wachusett experienced no annoyance, and was soon made an admiral.

The Georgia was the next Confederate cruiser that Captain Bullock succeeded in sending forth. She was of five hundred and sixty tons, and fitted out on the coast of France. Her commander, W. L. Maury, Confederate States Navy, cruised in the North and South Atlantic with partial success. The capacity of the vessel in speed and other essentials was entirely inadequate to the service for which she was designed. She proceeded as far as the Cape of Good Hope, and returned, after having captured seven ships and two barks. Then she was laid up and sold.

The Shenandoah, once the Sea King, was purchased by Captain Bullock, and placed under the command of Lieutenant-commanding J. J. Waddell, who fitted her for service under many difficulties at the barren island of Porto Santo, near Madeira. After experiencing great annoyances, through the activity of the American consul at Melbourne, Australia, Captain Waddell finally departed, and commenced an active and effective cruise against American shipping in the Okhotak Sea and Arctic Ocean. In August, 1865, hearing of the close of the war, he ceased his pursuit of United States commerce, sailed for Liverpool, England, and surrendered his ship to the English Government, which transferred it to the Government of the United States. The Shenandoah was a full-rigged ship of eight hundred tons, very fast under canvass. Her steam-power was merely auxiliary.

This was the last but not the first appearance of the Confederate flag in Great Britain; the first vessel of the Confederate Government which unfurled it there was the swift, light steamer Nashville, E. B. Pegram, commander. Having been constructed as a passenger-vessel, and mainly with reference to speed and the light draught suited to the navigation of the Southern harbors, she was quite too frail for war purposes and too slightly armed for combat.

On her passage to Europe and back, she, nevertheless, destroyed two merchantmen. Nearing the harbor on her return voyage, she found it blockaded, and a heavy vessel lying close on her track. Her daring commander headed directly for the vessel, and ran so close under her guns that she was not suspected in her approach, and had passed so far before the guns could be depressed to bear upon her that none of the shots took effect. Being little more than a shell, a single shot would have sunk her; and she was indebted to the address of her commander and the speed of his vessel for her escape. Wholly unsuited for naval warfare, this voyage terminated her career.

A different class of vessels than those adapted to the open sea was employed for coastwise cruising. In the month of July, 1864, a swift twin-screw propeller called the Atlanta, of six hundred tons burden, was purchased by the Secretary of the Navy, and fitted out in the harbor of Wilmington, North Carolina, for a cruise against the commerce of the Northern States. Commander J. Taylor Wood, an officer of extraordinary ability and enterprise, was ordered to command her, and her name was changed to "The Tallahassee." This extemporaneous man-of-war ran safely through the blockade, and soon lit up the New England coast with her captures, which consisted of two ships, four brigs, four barks, and twenty schooners. Great was the consternation among Northern merchants. The construction of the Tallahassee exclusively for steam made her dependent on coal; her cruise was of course brief, but brilliant while it lasted.

About the same time another fast double-screw propeller of five hundred and eighty-five tons, called the Edith, ran into Wilmington, North Carolina, and the Navy Department requiring her services, bought her and gave to her the name of "Chickamauga." A suitable battery was placed on board, with officers and crew, and Commander John Wilkinson, a gentleman of consummate naval ability, was ordered to command her. When ready for sea, he ran the blockade under the bright rays of a full moon. Strange to say, the usually alert sentinels neither hailed nor halted her. Like the Tallahassee, though partially rigged for sailing, she was exclusively dependent upon steam in the chase, escape, and in all important evolutions. She captured seven vessels, despite the above-noticed defects.

[Footnote 58: M. Bernard's "Neutrality of Great Britain during the American Civil War."]

CHAPTER XXXI.

Naval Affairs (concluded).—Excitement in the Northern States on the Appearance of our Cruisers.—Failure of the Enemy to protect their Commerce.—Appeal to Europe not to help the So-called "Pirates."— Seeks Iron-plated Vessels in England.—Statement of Lord Russell.— What is the Duty of Neutrals?—Position taken by President Washington.—Letter of Mr. Jefferson.—Contracts sought by United States Government.—Our Cruisers went to Sea unarmed.—Mr. Adams asserts that British Neutrality was violated.—Reply of Lord Russell.—Rejoinder of Mr. Seward.—Duty of Neutrals relative to Warlike Stores.—Views of Wheaton; of Kent.—Charge of the Lord

The excitement produced in the Northern States by the effective operations of our cruisers upon their commerce was such as to receive the attention of the United States Government. Reasonably, it might have been expected that they would send their ships of war out on the high-seas to protect their commerce by capturing or driving off our light cruisers, but, instead of this, their fleets were employed in blockading the Confederate ports, or watching those in the West Indies, from which blockade-runners were expected to sail, and, by capturing which, either on the high-seas or at the entrance of a Confederate port, a harvest of prizes might be secured. For this dereliction of duty, in the failure to protect commerce, no better reason offers itself than greed and malignity. There was, however, in this connection, a more humiliating feature in the conduct of the United States Government.

While, from its State Department, the Confederacy was denounced as an insurrection soon to be suppressed, and the cruisers, regularly commissioned by the Confederate States, were called "pirates," diplomatic demands were made upon Great Britain to prevent the so-called "pirates" from violating international law, as if it applied to pirates. Appeals to that Government were also made to prevent the sale of the materials of war to the Confederacy, and thus indirectly to aid the United States in performing what, according to the representation, was a police duty, to suppress a combination of some evil-disposed persons—gallantly claiming that they, armed *cap-a-pie*, should meet their adversary in the list, he to be without helmet, shield, or lance.

To one who from youth to age had seen, with exultant pride, the flag of his country as it unfolded, disclosing to view the stripes recordant of the original size of the family of States, and the Constellation, which told of that family's growth, it could but be deeply mortifying to witness such paltry exhibition of deception and unmanliness in the representatives of a Government around which fond memories still linger, despite the perversion of which it was the subject.

If this attempt, on the part of the United States, to deny the existence of war after having, by proclamation of blockade, compelled all nations to take notice that war did exist, and to claim that munitions should not be sold to a country because there were some disorderly people in it, had been all, the attempt would have been ludicrously absurd, and the contradiction too bald to require refutation; but this would have been but half of the story. Subsequently the United States Government claimed reclamation from Great Britain for damage inflicted by vessels which had been built in her ports, and which had elsewhere been armed and equipped for purposes of war. International law recognizes the right of a neutral to sell an unarmed vessel, without reference to the use to which the purchaser might subsequently apply it. The United States Government had certainly not practiced under a different rule, but had gone even further than this—so much further as to transgress the prohibition against armed vessels.

It has already been stated that the Government of the United States, at the commencement of the war, sought to contract for the construction of iron-plated vessels in the ports of England, which were to be delivered fully armed and equipped to her. To this it may be added that her armies were recruited from almost all the countries of Europe, down almost to the last month of the war; a portion of their arms were of foreign manufacture, as well as the munitions of war; a large number of the sailors of her fleets came from the seaports of Great Britain and Germany; in a word, whatever could be of service to her in the conflict was unhesitatingly sought among neutrals, regardless of the law of nations. At the same time an effort was made on her part to make Great Britain responsible for the damage done by our cruisers, and for the warlike stores sold to our Government.

Some statements of Lord Russell on this point, in a letter to Minister Adams, dated December 19, 1862, deserve notice. He says:

"It is right, however, to observe that the party which has profited by far the most by these unjustifiable practices, has been the Government of the United States, because that Government, having a superiority of force by sea, and having blockaded most of the Confederate ports, has been able, on the one hand, safely to receive all the warlike supplies which it has induced British manufacturers and merchants to send to the United States ports in violation of the Queen's proclamation; and, on the other hand, to intercept and capture a great part of the supplies of the same kind which were destined from this country to the Confederate States.

"If it be sought to make her Majesty's Government responsible to that of the United States because arms and munitions of war have left this country on account of the Confederate Government, the Confederate Government, as the other belligerent, may very well maintain that it has a just cause of complaint against the British Government because the United States arsenals have been replenished from British sources. Nor would it be possible to deny that, in defiance of the Queen's proclamation, many subjects of her Majesty, owing allegiance to her crown, have enlisted in the armies of the United States. Of this fact you can not be ignorant. Her Majesty's Government, therefore, has just ground for complaint against both of the belligerent parties, but most especially against the Government of the United States, for having systemically, and in disregard of the comity of nations which it was their duty to observe, induced subjects of her Majesty to violate those orders which, in conformity with her neutral position, she has enjoined all her subjects to obey."

Perhaps it may be well to inquire what is, under international law, the duty of neutral nations with regard to the construction and equipment of cruisers for either belligerent, and the supply of warlike stores. Thus the groundlessness of the claims put forth by the Government of the United States for damages to be paid by Great Britain will be more manifest, and the lawfulness of the acts of the Confederate Government demonstrated.

After the outbreak of the French Revolution in 1789, the Government of France, owing to the temporary inferiority of her naval force, openly and deliberately equipped privateers in our ports. These privateers captured British vessels in United States waters, and brought them as prizes into United States ports. These facts formed the basis of demands made upon the United States by the British plenipotentiary. The demands had reference, not to the accidental evasion of a municipal law of the United States by a particular ship, but to a systematic disregard of international law upon some of the most important points of neutral obligation.

To these demands Mr. Jefferson, then Secretary of State under President Washington, thus replied on September 3, 1793:

"We are bound by our treaties with three of the belligerent nations, by all the means in our power, to protect and defend their vessels and effects in our ports or waters, or on the seas near our shores, and to recover and restore the same to the right owners when taken from them. If all the means in our power are used, and fail in this effort, we are not bound by our treaties with those nations to make compensation. Though we have no similar treaty with Great Britain, it was the opinion of the President that we should use toward that nation the same rule which, under this Article, was to govern us with other nations, and even to extend it to the captures made on the high-seas and brought into our ports, if done by vessels which had been armed within them."

It will be observed that the justice of restitution, or compensation, for captures made on the high-seas and brought into our ports, is only admitted by President Washington upon one condition, which is expressed in these words: "If done by vessels which had been armed within them." The terms of the contract, which the Government of the United States endeavored to make at the ship-yards of England, were for the delivery of the ship or ships of war, "to be finished complete, with guns and everything appertaining." The contract was not taken, as too little time was allowed for its execution. But, if entered into and executed, it would have been a direct violation of international law.

In the instance of our cruisers built in the ports of England, it will be observed that they went to sea without arms or warlike stores, and, at other ports than those of Great Britain, they were converted into ships of war and put into commission by the authority of the Confederate Government. The Government of the United States asserted that they were built in the ports of Great Britain, and thereby her duty of neutrality was violated, and the Government made responsible for the damages sustained by private citizens of the United States in consequence of her captures on the seas. To this declaration of Mr. Adams, Earl Russell (he had been made an earl) replied on September 14, 1863, thus:

"When the United States Government assumes to hold the Government of Great Britain responsible for the captures made by vessels which may be fitted out as vessels of war in a foreign port, because such vessels were originally built in a British port, I have to observe that such pretensions are entirely at variance with the principles of international law, and with the decisions of American courts of the highest authority; and I have only, in conclusion, to express my hope that you may not be instructed again to put forward claims which her Majesty's Government can not admit to be founded on any grounds of law or justice."

On October 6, 1863, Mr. Seward, the Secretary of State of the United States Government, replied to this declaration of Earl Russell, saying:

"The United States do insist, and must continue to insist, that the British Government is justly responsible for the damages which the peaceful, law-abiding citizens of the United States [!] sustain by the depredations of the Alabama."

Earl Russell answered on October 26, 1863, thus:

"I must request you to believe that the principle contended for by her Majesty's Government is not that of commissioning, equipping, and manning vessels in our ports to cruise against either of the belligerent parties—a principle which was so justly and unequivocally condemned by the President of the United States in 1793. . . . But the British Government must decline to be responsible for the acts of parties who fit out a seeming merchant-ship, send her to a port or to waters far from the jurisdiction of British courts, and there commission, equip, and man her as a vessel of war."

The duty of neutral nations relative to the supply of warlike stores is expressed in these words:

"It is not the practice of nations to undertake to prohibit their own subjects by previous laws from trafficking in articles contraband of war. Such trade is carried on at the risk of those engaged in it, under the liabilities and penalties prescribed by the law of nations or particular treaties." [59]

We now quote from the great American commentator on the Constitution of the United States and on the law of nations:

"It is a general understanding that the powers at war may seize and confiscate all contraband goods, without any complaint on the part of the neutral merchant, and without any imputation of a breach of neutrality in the neutral sovereign himself. It was contended on the part of the French nation, in 1796, that neutral governments were bound to restrain their subjects from selling or exporting articles contraband of war to the belligerent powers. But it was successfully shown, on the part of the United States, that neutrals may lawfully sell at home to a belligerent power, or carry themselves to the belligerent powers, contraband articles, subject to the right of seizure *in transitu*. This right has been explicitly declared by the judicial authorities of this country [United States]. The right of the neutral to transport, and of the hostile power to seize, are conflicting rights, and neither party can charge the other with a criminal act." [60]

In accordance with these principles, President Pierce's message of December 31, 1855, contains the following passage:

"In pursuance of this policy, the laws of the United States do not forbid their citizens to sell to either of the belligerent powers articles contraband of war, to take munitions of war or soldiers on board their private ships for transportation; and, although in so doing the individual citizen exposes his property or person to some of the hazards of war, his acts do not involve any breach of international neutrality, nor of themselves implicate the Government."

Perhaps it may not be out of place here to notice the charge of the Lord Chief Baron of the Exchequer to the jury in the case of the Alexandra, a vessel of one hundred and twenty tons, under construction at Liverpool for our Government. The case came on for trial on June 22, 1863, in the Court of Exchequer, sitting at *nisi prius*, before the Lord Chief Baron and a special jury. After it had been summed up, the Lord Chief Baron said:

"This is an information on the part of the Crown for the seizure and confiscation of a vessel that was in the course of preparation but had not been completed. It is admitted that it was not armed, and the question is, whether the preparation of the vessel in its then condition was a violation of the Foreign Enlistment Act. The main question you will have to decide is this: Whether, under the seventh section of the act of Parliament, the vessel, as then prepared at the time of seizure, was liable to seizure? The statute was passed in 1819, and upon it no question has ever arisen in our courts of justice; but there have been expositions of a similar statute which exists in the United States. I will now read to you the opinions of some American lawyers who have contributed so greatly to make law a science. [His lordship then read a passage from Story and others.] These gentlemen are authorities which show that, when two belligerents are carrying on a war, a neutral power may supply, without any breach of international law and without a breach of the Foreign Enlistment Act, munitions of war—gunpowder, every description of arms, in fact, that can be used for the destruction of human beings.

"Why should ships be an exception? I am of opinion, in point of law, they are not. The Foreign Enlistment Act was an act to prevent the enlistment or engagement of his Majesty's subjects to serve in foreign armies, and to prevent the fitting out and equipping in his Majesty's dominions vessels for warlike purposes without his Majesty's license. The title of an act is not at all times an exact indication or explanation of the act, because it is generally attached after the act is passed. But, in adverting to the preamble of the act, I find that provision is made against the equipping, fitting out, furnishing, and arming of vessels, because it may be prejudicial to the peace of his Majesty's dominions.

"The question I shall put to you is, Whether you think that vessel was merely in a course of building to be delivered in pursuance of a contract that was perfectly lawful, or whether there was any intention in the port of Liverpool, or any other English port, that the vessel should be fitted out, equipped, furnished, and armed for purposes of aggression. Now, surely, if Birmingham, or any other town, may supply any quantity of munitions of war of various kinds for the destruction of life, why object to ships? Why should ships alone be in themselves contraband? I asked the Attorney-General if a man could not make a vessel intending to sell it to either of the belligerent powers that required it, and which would give the largest price for it, would not that be lawful? To my surprise, the learned Attorney-General declined to give an answer to the question, which I think a grave and pertinent one. But you, gentlemen, I think, are lawyers enough to know that a man may make a vessel and offer it for sale. If a man may build a vessel for the purpose of offering it for sale to either belligerent party, may he not execute an order for it? That appears to be a matter of course. The statute is not made to provide means of protection for belligerent powers, otherwise it would have said, 'You shall not sell powder or guns, and you shall not sell arms'; and, if it had done so, all Birmingham would have been in arms against it. The object of the statute was this: that we should not have our ports in this country made the ground of hostile movements between the vessels of two belligerent powers, which might be fitted out, furnished, and armed in these ports. The Alexandra was clearly nothing more than in the course of building.

"It appears to me that, if true that the Alabama sailed from Liverpool without any arms at all, as a mere ship in ballast, and that her armament was put on board at Terceira, which is not in her Majesty's dominions, then the Foreign Enlistment Act was not violated at all."

After reading some of the evidence, his lordship said:

"If you think that the object was to furnish, fit out, equip, and arm that vessel at Liverpool, that is a different matter; but if you think the object really was to build a ship in obedience to an order, in compliance with a contract, leaving those who bought it to make what use they thought fit of it, then it appears

186

to me that the Foreign Enlistment Act has not
been broken."

The jury immediately returned a verdict for the defendants. An appeal was made, but the full bench decided that there was no jurisdiction. Against this decision an appeal was taken to the House of Lords, and there dismissed on some technical ground.

Sufficient has been said to show that the action of the Confederate Government relative to these cruisers is sustained and justified by international law. The complaints made by the Government of the United States against the Government of Great Britain for acts involving a breach of neutrality find no support in the letter of the law or in its principles, and were conclusively answered by the interpretations of *American jurists*. At the same time they are condemned by the antecedent acts of the United States Government. Some of these will be presented.

In the War of the American Revolution, Dr. Franklin and Silas Deane were sent to France as commissioners to look after the interests of the colonies. In the years 1776 and 1777 they became extensively connected with naval movements. They built, and purchased, and equipped, and commissioned ships, all in neutral territory; even filling up blank commissions sent out to them by the Congress for the purpose. Among expeditions fitted out by them was one under Captain Wickes to intercept a convoy of linen-ships from Ireland. He went first into the Bay of Biscay, and afterward entirely around Ireland, sweeping the sea before him of everything that was not of force to render the attack hopeless. Mr. Deane observes to Robert Morris that it "effectually alarmed England, prevented the great fair at Chester, occasioned insurance to rise, and even deterred the English merchants from shipping in English bottoms at any rate, so that, in a few weeks, forty sail of French ships were loading in the Thames, on freight, an instance never before known."

In the spring of 1777 the Commissioners sent an agent to Dover, who purchased a fine, fast-sailing English-built cutter, which was taken across to Dunkirk. There she was privately equipped as a cruiser, and put in command of Captain Gustavus Conyngham, who was appointed by filling up a blank commission from John Hancock, the President of Congress. This commission bore date March 1, 1777, and fully entitled Mr. Conyngham to the rank of captain in the navy. His vessel, although built in England, like many of our cruisers, was not armed or equipped there, nor was his crew enlisted there, but in the port of a neutral. This vessel was finally seized under some treaty obligations between France and England. The Commissioners immediately fitted out another cruiser, and still another. It was also affirmed that the money advanced to Mr. John Adams for traveling expenses, when he arrived in Spain a year or two later, was derived from the prizes of these vessels, which had been sent into the ports of Spain.

Captain Conyngham was a very successful commander, but he was made a prisoner in 1779. The matter was brought before Congress in July of the same year, and a committee reported that this "late commander of an armed vessel in the service of the States, and taken on board of a private armed cutter, had been treated in a manner contrary to the dictates of humanity, and the practice of Christian civilized nations." Whereupon it was resolved to demand of the British Admiral in New York that good and sufficient reason be given for this conduct, or that he be immediately released from his rigorous and ignominious confinement. If a satisfactory answer was not received by August 1st, so many persons as were deemed proper were ordered to be confined in safe and close custody, to abide the fate of the said Gustavus Conyngham. No answer having been received, one Christopher Hale was thus confined. In December he petitioned Congress for an exchange, and that he might procure a person in his room. Congress replied that his petition could not be granted until Captain Conyngham was released, "as it had been determined that he must abide the fate of that officer." Conyngham was subsequently released.

The whole number of captures made by the United States in this contest is not known, but six hundred and fifty prizes are said to have been brought into port. Many others were ransomed, and some were burned at sea.

Prescribed limits will not permit me to follow out in detail the past history of the United States as a neutral power. It must suffice to recall the memory of readers to a few significant facts in our more recent history:

The recognition of the independence of Greece in her struggle with Turkey, and the voluntary contributions of money and men sent to her; the recognition of the independence of the Spanish provinces of South America, and the war-vessels equipped and sent from the ports of the United States to Brazil during the struggle with Spain for independence; the ships sold to Russia during her war with England, France, and Turkey; the arms and munitions of war manufactured at New Haven, Connecticut, and Providence, Rhode Island, sold and shipped to Turkey to aid her in her late struggle with Russia.

The reader will observe the promptitude with which the Government of the United States not only accorded belligerent rights, but, even more, recognized the independence of nations struggling for deliverance from oppressive rulers. The instances of Greece and the South American republics are well known, and that of Texas must be familiar to every one. One could scarcely believe, therefore, that the chief act of hostility, or, rather, the great crime of the Government of Great Britain in the eyes of the Government of the United States, was the recognition by the latter of the Confederate States as a belligerent power, and that a state of war existed between them and the United States. This was the constantly repeated charge against the British Government in the dispatches of the United States Government from the commencement of the war down nearly to the session of the Geneva Conference in 1872. In the correspondence of the Secretary, in 1867, he says:

> "What is alleged on the part of the United
> States is, that the Queen's proclamation,
> which, by conceding belligerent rights to the
> insurgents, lifted them up for the purpose of
> insurrection to an equality with the nation
> which they were attempting to overthrow, was
> premature because it was unnecessary, and
> that it was, in its operation, unfriendly
> because it was premature."

Again he says, and, if sincerely, shows himself to be utterly ignorant of the real condition of our affairs:

"Before the Queen's proclamation of
neutrality, the disturbance in the United
States was merely a local insurrection. It
wanted the name of war to enable it to be a
civil war and to live, endowed as such, with
maritime and other belligerent rights.
Without the authorized name, it might die,
and was expected not to live and be a flagrant
civil war, but to perish a mere insurrection."

The first extract in itself contains a fiction. If the Queen's proclamation possessed such force as to raise the Confederate States to an equality with the United States as a belligerent, perhaps another proclamation of the Queen might have possessed such force, if it had been issued, as to have lifted the Confederate States from the state of equality to one of independence. This is a novel virtue to be ascribed to a Queen's proclamation. This idea must have been borrowed from our neighbors of Mexico, where a *pronunciamiento* dissolves one and establishes a rival administration. How much more rational it would have been, to say that the resources and the military power of the Confederate States placed them, at the outset, on the footing of a belligerent, and the Queen's proclamation only declared a fact which the announcement of a blockade of the Southern ports by the Government of the United States had made manifest!— blockade being a means only applicable as against a foreign foe.

Nevertheless, the Government of the United States, although refusing to concede belligerent rights to the Confederate States, was very ready to take advantage of such concession by other nations, whenever an opportunity offered. The voluminous correspondence of the Secretary of State of the United States Government, relative to the Confederate cruisers and their so-called "depredations," was filled with charges of violations of international law, which could be committed only by a belligerent, and which, it was alleged, had been allowed to be done in the ports of Great Britain. On this foundation was based the subsequent claim for damages, advanced by the Government of the United States against that of Great Britain; and, for the pretended lack of "due diligence" in watching the actions of this Confederate belligerent in her ports, she was mulcted in a heavy sum by the Geneva Conference, and paid it to the Government of the United States.

It is a remarkable fact that the Government of the United States, in no one instance, from the opening to the close of the war, formally spoke of the Confederate Government or States as belligerents. Although on many occasions it acted with the latter as a belligerent, yet no official designations were ever given to them or their citizens but those of "insurgents," or "insurrectionists." Perhaps there may be something in the signification of the words which, combined with existing circumstances, would express a state of affairs that the authorities of the Government of the United States were in no degree willing to admit, and vainly sought to prevent from becoming manifest to the world.

The party or individuality against which the Government of the United States was conducting hostilities consisted of the people within the limits of the Confederate States. Was it against them as individuals in an unorganized condition, or as organized political communities? In the former condition they might be a mob; in the latter condition they formed a State. By the actions of unorganized masses may arise insurrections, and by the actions of organized people or states, arise wars.

The Government of the United States adopted a fiction when it declared that the execution of the laws in certain States was impeded by "insurrection." The persons whom it designated as insurrectionists were the organized people of the States. The ballot-boxes used at the elections were State boxes. The judges who presided at the elections were State functionaries. The returns of the elections were made to the State officers. The oaths of office of those elected were administered by State authority. They assembled in the legislative chambers of the States. The results of their deliberations were directory to the State, judicial, and executive officers, and by them put in operation. Is it not evident that, only by a fiction of speech, such proceedings can be called an insurrection?

Why, then, did an intelligent and powerful Government, like that of the United States, so outrage the understanding of mankind as to adopt a fiction on which to base the authority and justification of its hostile action? The United States Government is the result of a compact between the States—a written Constitution. It owes its existence simply to a delegation of certain powers by the respective States, which it is authorized to exercise for their common welfare. One of these powers is to "suppress insurrections"; but there is no power delegated to subjugate States, the authors of its existence, or to make war on any of the States. If, then, without any delegated power or lawful authority for its proceedings, the Government of the United States commenced a war upon some of the States of the Union, how could it expect to be justified before the world? It became the aggressor—the Attila of the American Continent. Its action inflicted a wound on the principles of constitutional liberty, a crashing blow to the hopes that men had begun to repose in this latest effort for self-government, which its friends should never forgive nor ever forget. To palliate the enormity of such an offense, its authors resorted to a vehement denial that their hostile action was a war upon the States, and persistently asserted the fiction that their immense armies and fleets were merely a police authority to put down insurrection. They hoped to conceal from the observation of the American people that the contest, on the part of the central Government, was for empire, for its absolute supremacy over the State governments; that the Constitution was roiled up and laid away among the old archives; and that the conditions of their liberty, in the future, were to be decided by the sword or by "national" control of the ballot-box.

With like disregard for truth, our cruisers were denounced as "*pirates*" by the Government of the United States. A pirate, or armed piratical vessel, is by the law of nations the enemy of mankind, and can be destroyed by the ships of any nation. The distinction between a lawful cruiser and a pirate is that the former has behind it a government which is recognized by civilized nations as entitled to the rights of war, and from which the commander of the cruiser receives his commission or authority, but the pirate recognizes no government, and is not recognized by any one. As the Attorney-General of Great Britain said in the Alexandra case:

"Although a recognition of the Confederates as an independent power was out of the question, yet it was right they should be admitted by other nations within the circle of lawful belligerents—that is to say, that their forces should not be treated as pirates, nor their flag as a piratical flag.

Therefore, as far as the two belligerents were concerned, on the part of this and other governments, they were so far put on a level that each was to be considered as entitled to the right of belligerents—the Southern States as much as the other."

The Government of the United States well knew that, after the issue of the Queen's proclamation recognizing our Government, the application of the word pirate to our cruisers was simply an exhibition of vindictive passion on its part. A *de facto* Government by its commission legalizes among nations a cruiser. That there was such a Government even its own courts also decided. In a prize case (2 Black, 635), Justice Greer delivered the opinion of the Supreme Court, saying:

"It [the war] is not less a civil war, with belligerent parties in hostile array, because it may be called an 'insurrection' by one side, and the insurgents be considered as rebels and traitors. It is not necessary that the independence of the revolted province or State be acknowledged in order to constitute it a party belligerent in a war, according to the laws of nations. Foreign nations acknowledge it a war by a declaration of neutrality. The condition of neutrality can not exist unless there be two belligerent parties."

In the case of the Santissima Trinidad (7 Wheaton, 337), the United States Supreme Court says:

> "The Government of the United States has
> recognized the existence of a civil war
> between Spain and her colonies, and has
> avowed her determination to remain neutral
> between the parties. Each party is therefore
> deemed by us a belligerent, having, so far as
> concerns us, the sovereign rights of war."

The belligerent character of the Confederate States was thus fully acknowledged by the highest judicial tribunal of the United States. This involved an acknowledgment of the Confederate Government as a Government *de facto* having "the sovereign rights of war," yet the Executive Department of the United States Government, with reckless malignity, denounced our cruisers as "pirates," our citizens as "insurgents" and "traitors," and the action of our Government as an "insurrection."

It has been stated that during the war of the colonies with Great Britain many of the prizes of the colonial cruisers were destroyed. This was done by Paul Jones and other commanders, although during the entire period of the war some of the colonial ports were open, into which prizes could be taken. In that war Great Britain did not attempt to blockade all the ports of the colonies. Sailing-vessels only were then known, and with these a stringent blockade at all seasons could not have been maintained. But, at the later day of our war, the powerful steamship had appeared, and revolutionized the commerce and the navies of the world. During the first months of the war all the principal ports of the Confederacy were blockaded, and finally every inlet was either in possession of the enemy or had one or more vessels watching it. The steamers were independent of wind and weather, and could hold their positions before a port day and night. At the same time the ports of neutrals had been closed against the prizes of our cruisers by proclamations and orders in council. Says Admiral Semmes:

"During my whole career upon the sea, I
had not so much as a single port open to me,
into which I could send a prize."

Our prizes had been sent into ports of Cuba and Venezuela under the hope that they might gain admittance, but they were either handed over to the enemy under some fraudulent pretext, or expelled. Thus, by the action of the different nations and by the blockade with steamers, no course was left to us but to destroy the prizes, as was done in many instances under the Government of the United States Confederation.

The laws of maritime war are well known. The enemy's vessel when captured becomes the property of the captor, which he may immediately destroy; or he may take the vessel into port, have it adjudicated by an admiralty court as a lawful prize, and sold. That adjudication is the basis of title to the purchaser against all former owners. In these cases the captor sends his prizes to a port of his own country or to a friendly port for adjudication. But, if the ports of his own country are under blockade by his enemy, and the recapture of the prizes, if sent there, most probable, and if, at the same time, all friendly ports are closed against the entrance of his prizes, then there remains no alternative but to destroy the prizes by sinking or burning. Courts of admiralty are established for neutrals; not for the enemy, who has no right of appearance before them. If, therefore, any neutrals suffered during our war for want of adjudication, the fault is with their own Government, and not with our cruisers.

Many other objections were advanced by the United States Government as evidence that we committed a breach of international law with our cruisers, but their principles are embraced in the preceding remarks, or they were too frivolous to deserve notice. Suffice it to say that, if the Confederate Government had been successful in taking to sea every vessel which it built, it would have swept from the oceans the commerce of the United States, would have raised the blockade of at least some of our ports, and, if by such aid our independence had been secured, there is little probability that such complaints as have been noticed would have received attention, if, indeed, they would have been uttered.

In January, 1871, the British Government proposed to the Government of the United States that a joint commission should be convened to adjust certain differences between the two nations relative to the fisheries, the Canadian boundary, etc. To this proposition the latter acceded, on condition that the so-called Alabama claims should also be considered. To this condition Great Britain assented. In the Convention the American Commissioners proposed an arbitration of these claims. The British Commissioners replied that her Majesty's Government could not admit that Great Britain had failed to discharge toward the United States the duties imposed on her by the rules of international law, or that she was justly liable to make good to the United States the losses occasioned by the acts of the cruisers to which the American Commissioners referred.

Without following the details, it may be summarily stated that the Geneva Conference ensued. That decided that "England should have fulfilled her duties as a neutral by the exercise of a diligence equal to the gravity of the danger," and that "the circumstances were of a nature to call for the exercise, on the part of her Britannic Majesty's Government, of all possible solicitude for the observance of the rights and duties involved in the proclamation of neutrality issued by her Majesty on May 18, 1861." The Conference also added: "It can not be denied that there were moments when its watchfulness seemed to fail, and when feebleness in certain branches of the public service resulted in great detriment to the United States."

The claims presented to the Conference for damages done by our several cruisers were as follows: The Alabama, $7,050,293.76; the Boston, $400; the Chickamauga, $183,070.73; the Florida, $4,057,934.69; the Clarence, tender of the Florida, $66,736.10; the Tacony, tender of the Florida, $169,198.81; the Georgia, $431,160.72; the Jefferson Davis, $7,752; the Nashville, $108,433.95; the Retribution, $29,018.53; the Sallie, $5,540; the Shenandoah, $6,656,838.81; the Sumter, $179,697.67; the Tallahassee, $836,841.83. Total, $19,782,917.60. Miscellaneous, $479,033; increased insurance, $6,146,19.71. Aggregate, $26,408,170.31.

The Conference rejected the claims against the Boston, the Jefferson Davis, and the Sallie, and awarded to the United States Government $15,500,000 in gold.

But the indirect damages upon the commerce of the United States produced by these cruisers were far beyond the amount of the claims presented to the Geneva Conference. The number of ships owned in the United States at the commencement of the war, which were subsequently transferred to foreign owners by a British register, was 715, and the amount of their tonnage was 480,882 tons. Such are the laws of the United States that not one of them has been allowed to resume an American register.

In the year 1860 nearly seventy per cent. of the foreign commerce of the country was carried on in American ships. But, in consequence of the danger of capture by our cruisers to which these ships were exposed, the amount of this commerce carried by them had dwindled down in 1864 to forty-six per cent. It continued to decline after the war, and in 1872 it had fallen to twenty-eight and a half per cent.

Before the war the amount of American tonnage was second only to that of Great Britain, and we were competing with her for the first place. At that time the tonnage of the coasting trade, which had grown from insignificance, was 1,735,863 tons. Three years later, in 1864, it had declined to about 867,931 tons.

The damage to the articles of export is illustrated by the decline in breadstuffs exported from the Northern States. In the last four months of each of the following years the value of this export was as follows: 1861, $42,500,000; 1862, $27,842,090; 1863, $8,909,043; 1864, $1,850,819. Some of this decline resulted from good crops in England; but, in other respects, it was a consequence of causes growing out of the war.

The increase in the rates of marine insurance, in consequence of the danger of capture by the cruisers, was variable. But the gross amount so paid was presented as a claim to the Conference, as given above.

[Footnote 59: Wheaton's "International Law" sixth edition, p. 571, 1855.]
[Footnote 60: Ken's "Commentaries," vol i, p. 145, 1854.]

CHAPTER XXXII.

Attempts of the United States Government to overthrow States.—
Military Governor of Tennessee appointed.—Object.—Arrests and
Imprisonments.—Measures attempted.—Oath required of Voters.—A
Convention to amend the State Constitution.—Results.—Attempt in
Louisiana.—Martial Law.—Barbarities inflicted.—Invitation of
Plantations.—Order of General Butler, No. 28.—Execution of
Mumford.—Judicial System set up.—Civil Affairs to be administered
by Military Authority.—Order of President Lincoln for a Provisional
Court.—A Military Court sustained by the Army.—Words of the
Constitution.—"Necessity," the reason given for the Power to create
the Court.—This Doctrine fatal to the Constitution; involves its
Subversion.—Cause of our Withdrawal from the Union.—Fundamental
Principles unchanged by Force.—The Contest is not over; the Strife
not ended.—When the War closed, who were the Victors?—Let the
Verdict of Mankind decide.

On the capture of Nashville, on February 25, 1862, Andrew Johnson was
made military Governor of Tennessee, with the rank of brigadier-general, and
immediately entered on the duties of his office. This step was taken by the
President of the United States under the pretense of executing that provision of
the Constitution which is in these words:

"The United States shall guarantee to
every State in this Union a republican form of
government."

The administration was conducted according to the will and pleasure of the
Governor, which was the supreme law. Public officers were required to take an
oath of allegiance to the United States Government, and upon refusal were
expelled from office. Newspaper-offices were closed, and their publication
suppressed. Subsequently the offices were sold out under the provisions of the
confiscation act. All persons using "treasonable and seditious" language were
arrested and required to take the oath of allegiance to the Government of the
United States, and give bonds for the future, or to go into exile. Clergymen, upon
their refusal to take the oath, were confined in the prisons until they could be
sent away. School-teachers and editors and finally large numbers of private
citizens were arrested and held until they took the oath. Conflicts became
frequent in the adjacent country. Murders and the violent destruction of
property ensued.

On October 21, 1862, an order for an election of members of the United
States Congress in the ninth and tenth State districts was issued. Every voter
was required to give satisfactory evidence of "loyalty" to the Northern
Government. Two persons were chosen and admitted to seats in that body.

That portion of the State in the possession of the forces of the United States
continued without change, under the authority of the military Governor, until
the beginning of 1864. Measures were then commenced by the Governor for an
organization of a State government in sympathy with the Government of the
United States. These measures were subsequently known as the "process for
State reconstruction." The Governor issued his proclamation for an election of
county officers on March 5th, to be held in the various counties of the State
whenever it was practicable. "It is not expected," says the Governor, "that the

enemies of the United States will propose to vote, nor is it intended that they be permitted to vote or hold office." In addition to the possession of the usual qualifications, the voter was required to take the following oath:

"I solemnly swear that I will henceforth
support the Constitution of the United States,
and defend it against the assaults of all its
enemies; that I will hereafter be, and conduct
myself as, a true and faithful citizen of the
United States, freely and voluntarily claiming
to be subject to all the duties and obligations,
and entitled to all the rights and privileges, of
such citizenship; that I ardently desire the
suppression of the present insurrection and
rebellion against the Government of the
United States, the success of its armies, and
the defeat of all those who oppose them; and
that the Constitution of the United States, and
all laws and proclamations made in
pursuance thereof, may be speedily and
permanently established and enforced over all
the people, States, and Territories thereof;
and, further, that I will hereafter aid and
assist all loyal people in the accomplishment
of these results."

Thus to invoke the Constitution was like Satan quoting Scripture. The election was a failure, and all further efforts at reconstruction were for a time suspended. An attempt was made at the end of 1864 to obtain a so-called convention to amend the State Constitution, and a body was assembled which, without any regular authority, adopted amendments. These were submitted to the voters on February 22, 1865, and declared to be ratified by a vote of twenty-five thousand, in a State where the vote, in 1860, was one hundred and forty-five thousand. Slavery was abolished, other changes made, so-called State officers elected, and this body of voters was proclaimed as the reconstructed State of Tennessee, and one of the United States. Such was the method adopted in Tennessee to execute the provision of the Constitution which says:

"The United States shall guarantee to
every State in this Union a republican form of
government."

The next attempt to guarantee "a republican form of government" to a State was commenced in Louisiana by the military occupation of New Orleans, on May 1, 1862. The United States forces were under the command of Major-General Benjamin F. Butler. Martial law was declared, and Brigadier-General George F. Shepley was appointed military Governor of the State. It is unnecessary to relate in detail the hostile actions which were committed, as they had no resemblance to such warfare as is alone permissible by the rules of international law or the usages of civilization. Some examples taken from contemporaneous publications of temperate tone, will suffice.

Peaceful and aged citizens, unresisting captives, and noncombatants, were confined at hard labor with chains attached to their limbs, and held in dungeons and fortresses; others were subjected to a like degrading punishment for selling medicine to the sick soldiers of the Confederacy. The soldiers of the invading force were incited and encouraged by general orders to insult and outrage the wives and mothers and sisters of the citizens; and helpless women were torn from their homes and subjected to solitary confinement, some in fortresses and prisons-and one, especially, on an island of barren sand, under a tropical sun— and were fed with loathsome rations and exposed to vile insults. Prisoners of war, who surrendered to the naval forces of the United States on the agreement that they should be released on parole, were seized and kept in close confinement. Repeated pretexts were sought or invented for plundering the inhabitants of the captured city, by fines levied and collected under threat of imprisonment at hard labor with ball and chain. The entire population were forced to elect between starvation by the confiscation of all their property and taking an oath against their conscience to bear allegiance to the invader. Egress from the city was refused to those whose fortitude stood the test, and even to lone and aged women and to helpless children; and, after being ejected from their houses and robbed of their property, they were left to starve in the streets or subsist on charity. The slaves were driven from the plantations in the neighborhood of New Orleans, until their owners consented to share their crops with the commanding General, his brother, and other officers. When such consent had been extorted, the slaves were restored to the plantations and compelled to work under the bayonets of a guard of United States soldiers. Where that partnership was refused, armed expeditions were sent to the plantations to rob them of everything that could be removed; and even slaves too aged and infirm for work were, in spite of their entreaties, forced from the homes provided by their owners, and driven to wander helpless on the highway. By an order (No. 91), the entire property in that part of Louisiana west of the Mississippi River was sequestrated for confiscation, and officers were assigned to the duty, with orders to gather up and collect the personal property, and turn over to the proper officers, upon their receipts, such of it as might be required for the use of the United States army; and to bring the remainder to New Orleans, and cause it to be sold at public auction to the highest bidders. This was an order which, if it had been executed, would have condemned to punishment, by starvation, at least a quarter of a million of persons, of all ages, sexes, and conditions. The African slaves, also, were not only incited to insurrection by every license and encouragement, but numbers of them were armed for a servile war, which in its nature, as exemplified in other lands, far exceeds the horrors and merciless atrocities of savages. In many instances the officers were active and zealous agents in the commission of these crimes, and no instance was known of the refusal of any one of them to participate in the outrages.

The order of Major-General Butler, to which reference is made above, was as follows:

"HEADQUARTERS, DEPARTMENT OF THE GULF, NEW ORLEANS.
        "As officers and soldiers of the United
        States have been subject to repeated insults
        from women, calling themselves ladies, of
        New Orleans, in return for the most
        scrupulous non-interference and courtesy on
        our part, it is ordered hereafter, when any

female shall, by mere gesture or movement, insult, or show contempt for any officers or soldiers of the United States, she shall be regarded and held liable to be treated as a woman about town plying her vocation.

"By command of Major-General BUTLER."

This order was issued on May 15, 1862, and known as General Order No. 28.

Another example was the cold-blooded execution of William B. Mumford on June 7th. He was an unresisting and noncombatant captive, and there was no offense ever alleged to have been committed by him subsequent to the date of the capture of the city. He was charged with aiding and abetting certain persons in hauling down a United States flag hoisted on the mint, which was left there by a boat's crew on the morning of April 26th, and five days before the military occupation of the city. He was tried before a military commission, sentenced, and afterward hanged.

On December 15, 1862, Major-General N. P. Banks took command of the military forces, and Major-General Butler retired. The military Governor, early in August, had attempted to set on foot a judicial system for the city and State. For this purpose he appointed judges to two of the district courts, of which the judges were absent, and authorized a third, who held a commission dated anterior to 1861, to resume the sessions. This was an establishment of three new courts, with the jurisdiction and powers pertaining to the courts that previously bore their names, by a military officer representing the Executive of the United States. These were the only courts within the territory of the State held by the United States forces which claimed to have civil jurisdiction. But this jurisdiction was limited to citizens of the parish of Orleans as against defendants residing in the State. As to other residents of the State, outside the parish of Orleans, there was no court in which they could be sued. In this condition several parishes were held by the United States forces.

It was therefore necessary to take another step in order to enable the military power to administer civil affairs. This involved, as every reader must perceive, a complete subversion of the fundamental principles of social organization. According to this advanced step, the military power, instituted by an organization of its own, creates for itself a new nature, fixes at will its rules and modes of action, and determines the limits of its power. It absorbs by force the civil functions, with absolute disregard of the fundamental principle that the military shall be subject to the civil authority.

This attempt to administer civil affairs on the basis of military authority involved, as has been said, the subversion of fundamental principles. The military power may remove obstacles to the exercise of the civil authority; but, when these are removed, it can not enter the forum, put on the toga, and sit in judgment upon civil affairs, any more than the hawk becomes the dove by assuming her plumage.

However, the next step was taken. It consisted in the publication of the following order by the President of the United States:

"EXECUTIVE MANSION, WASHINGTON, *October 20, 1862.*

"The insurrection which has for some time prevailed in several of the States of this Union, including Louisiana, having temporarily subverted and swept away the civil institutions of that State, including the judiciary and the judicial authorities of the Union, so that it has become necessary to hold the State in military occupation; and it being indispensably necessary that there shall be some judicial tribunal existing there capable of administering justice, I have therefore thought it proper to appoint, and I do hereby constitute a provisional court, which shall be a court of record for the State of Louisiana; and I do hereby appoint Charles A. Peabody, of New York, to be a provisional judge to hold said court, with authority to hear, try, and determine all causes civil and criminal, including causes in law, equity, revenue, and admiralty, and particularly with all such powers and jurisdiction as belong to the District and Circuit Courts of the United States, conforming his proceedings, so far as possible, to the course of proceedings and practice which has been customary in the courts of the United States and Louisiana—his judgment to be final and conclusive. And I do hereby authorize and empower the said judge to make and establish such rules and regulations as may be necessary for the exercise of his jurisdiction, and to appoint a prosecuting attorney, marshal, and clerk of the said court, who shall perform the functions of attorney, marshal, and clerk according to such proceedings and practice as before mentioned, and such rules and regulations as may be made and established by said judge. These appointments are to continue during the pleasure of the President, not extending beyond the military occupation of the city of New Orleans, or the restoration of the civil authority in that city and in the State of Louisiana. These officers shall be paid out of the contingent fund of the War Department, and compensation shall be as follows.

"By the President: ABRAHAM LINCOLN.

"W. H. SEWARD, *Secretary of State.*"

This so-called court, as its judge said, "was always governed by the rules and principles of law, adhering to all the rules and forms of civil tribunals, and avoiding everything like a military administration of justice. In criminal matters it summoned a grand jury, and submitted to it all charges for examination." Yet, when its judgments and mandates were to be executed, that execution could come only from the same power by which the court was constituted, and that was the military power of the United States holding the country in military occupation. Therefore, to this end the military and naval forces were pledged. Hence it was the military power, as has been said, administering civil affairs.

The Constitution of the United States says:

"The judicial power of the United States shall be vested in one Supreme Court, and in such inferior courts as the Congress may from time to time ordain and establish," [61]

This provisional court was neither ordained nor established by Congress; it had not, therefore, vested in it any of the judicial power of the United States. Neither does the Constitution give to Congress any power by which it can constitute an independent State court within the limits of any State in the Union, as Louisiana was said to be.

This provisional court, therefore, was a mere instrument of martial law, constituted by the Commander-in-Chief of the United States forces, not for the usual purposes which justify the establishment of such courts, but to enter the domain of civil affairs and administer justice between man and man in the ordinary transactions of peaceful life. The ministers of martial law are only the representatives of the conqueror, and they sit in his seat of authority to relieve him from the burden of excessive duties, and to administer justice to offenders against his authority and the social welfare, during his presence. On such grounds the existence of such courts is justified; but, for the establishment of a court like this provisional one, no legitimate authority is to be found either in the Constitution of the United States or outside of it, "*Inter arma silent leges*" is a maxim nearly two thousand years old; it means that, under the exercise of military power, the civil administration ceases.

When called upon to state any just grounds for such a measure, the invader has usually replied that he had, *ex necessitate rei*, the right to establish such a tribunal. Thus said the Commander-in-Chief of the United States, and Congress acquiesced—indeed, leading the way, it had urged the same plea to justify the passage of its confiscation act. The judiciary has observed the silence of acquiescence. Thus the doctrine of necessity—the rule that, in the administration of affairs, both military and civil, the necessity of the case may and does afford ample authority and power to subvert or to suspend the provisions of the Constitution, and to exercise powers and do acts unwarranted by the grants of that instrument—has apparently become incorporated as an unwritten clause of the Constitution of the United States.

What, then, is this necessity? Its definition would require an explanation, from the persons who act under it, of the objects for which, in every instance, they act. Suffice it to say that the political wisdom of mankind has consecrated this truth as a fundamental maxim, that no man can be trusted with the exercise of power and be, at the same time, the final judge of the limits within which that power may be exercised. It has fortified this with other maxims, such as, "Necessity is the plea of despotism"; "Necessity knows no law." The fathers of the Constitution of the United States sought to limit every grant of power so exactly that it should observe its bounds as invariably as a planetary body does its orbit. Yet within the first hundred years of its existence all these limits have been disregarded, and the people have silently accepted the plea of necessity.

It must be manifest to every one that there has been a fatal subversion of the Constitution of the United States. In estimating the results of the war, this is one of the most deplorable; because it is self-evident that, when a constitutional Government once oversteps the limits fixed for the exercise of its powers, there is nothing beyond to check its further aggression, no place where it will voluntarily halt until it reaches the subjugation of all who resist the usurpation. This was the sole issue involved in the conflict of the United States Government with the Confederate States; and every other issue, whether pretended or real, partook of its nature, and was subordinate to this one. Let us repeat an illustration: In strict observance of their inalienable rights, in abundant caution reserved, when they formed the compact or Constitution—whichever the reader pleases to call it—of the United States, the Confederate States sought to withdraw from the Union they had assisted to create, and to form a new and independent one among themselves. Then the Government of the United States broke through all the limits fixed for the exercise of the powers with which it had been endowed, and, to accomplish its own will, assumed, under the plea of necessity, powers unwritten and unknown in the Constitution, that it might thereby proceed to the extremity of subjugation. Thus it will be perceived that the question still lives. Although the Confederate armies may have left the field, although the citizen soldiers may have retired to the pursuits of peaceful life, although the Confederate States may have renounced their new Union, they have proved their indestructibility by resuming their former places in the old one, where, by the organic law, they could only be admitted as republican, equal, and sovereign States of the Union. And, although the Confederacy as an organization may have ceased to exist as unquestionably as though it had never been formed, the fundamental principles, the eternal truths, uttered when our colonies in 1776 declared their independence, on which the Confederation of 1781 and the Union of 1788 were formed, and which animated and guided in the organization of the Confederacy of 1861, yet live, and will survive, however crushed they may be by despotic force, however deep they may be buried under the debris of crumbling States, however they may be disavowed by the time-serving and the fainthearted; yet I believe they have the eternity of truth, and that in God's appointed time and place they will prevail.

The contest is not over, the strife is not ended. It has only entered on a new and enlarged arena. The champions of constitutional liberty must spring to the struggle, like the armed men from the seminated dragon's teeth, until the Government of the United States is brought back to its constitutional limits, and the tyrant's plea of "necessity" is bound in chains strong as adamant:

"For Freedom's battle once begun,
Bequeathed by bleeding sire to son,
Though baffled oft, it ever won."

When the war closed, who were the victors? Perhaps it is too soon to answer that question. Nevertheless, every day, as time rolls on, we look with increasing pride upon the struggle our people made for constitutional liberty. The war was one in which fundamental principles were involved; and, as force decides no truth, hence the issue is still undetermined, as has been already shown. We have laid aside our swords; we have ceased our hostility; we have conceded the physical strength of the Northern States. But the question still lives, and all nations and peoples that adopt a confederated agent of government will become champions of our cause. While contemplating the Northern States—with their Federal Constitution gone, ruthlessly destroyed under the tyrant's plea of "necessity," their State sovereignty made a byword, and their people absorbed in an aggregated mass, no longer, as their fathers left them, protected by reserved rights against usurpation—the question naturally arises: On which side was the victory? Let the verdict of mankind decide.

[Footnote 61: Constitution of the United States, Article III, section 1.]

CHAPTER XXXIII.

Further Attempts of the United States Government to overthrow States.—Election of Members of Congress under the Military Governor of Louisiana.—The Voters required to take an Oath to support the United States Government.—The State Law violated.—Proposition to hold a State Convention; postponed.—The President's Plan for making a Union State out of a Fragment of a Confederate State.—His Proclamation.—The Oath required.—Message.—"The War-Power our Main Reliance."—Not a Feature of the Republican Government in the Plan.—What are the True Principles?—The Declaration of Independence asserts them.—Who had a Right to institute a Government for Louisiana?—Its People only.—Under what Principles could the Government of the United States do it?—As an Invader to subjugate.—Effrontery and Wickedness of the Administration.—It enforces a Fiction.—Attempt to make Falsehood as good as Truth.—Proclamation for an Election of State Officers.—Proclamation for a State Convention.—The Monster Crime against the Liberties of Mankind.—Proceedings in Arkansas.—Novel Method adopted to amend the State Constitution.—Perversion of Republican Principles in Virginia.—Proceedings to create the State of West Virginia.—A Falsehood by Act of Congress.—Proceedings considered under Fundamental Principles.—These Acts sustained by the United States Government.—Assertion of Thaddeus Stevens.—East Virginia Government.—Such Acts caused Entire Subversion of States.—Mere Fictions thus constituted.

But to resume our narration. On December 3d, in compliance with an order of the military Governor Shepley, a so-called election was held for members of the United States Congress in the first and second State districts, each composed of about half the city of New Orleans and portions of the surrounding parishes. Those who had taken the oath of allegiance were allowed to vote. In the first district, Benjamin F. Flanders received 2,370 votes, and all others 273. In the second district, Michael Hahn received 2,799 votes, and all others 2,318. These persons presented themselves at Washington, and resolutions to admit them to seats were reported by the Committee on Elections in the House of Representatives. It was urged that the military Governor had conformed in every particular to the Constitution and laws of Louisiana, so that the election had every essential of a regular election in a time of most profound peace, with the exception of the fact that the proclamation for the election was issued by the military instead of the civil Governor of the State. The law required the proclamation to be issued by the civil Governor; so that, if these persons were admitted to seats after an election called by a military Governor, Congress thereby recognized as valid a military order of a so-called Executive that unceremoniously set aside a provision of the State civil law, and was anti-republican and a positive usurpation. Again, all the departments of the United States Government had acted on the theory that the Confederate States were in a state of insurrection, and that the Union was unbroken; under this theory, they could come back to the Union only with all the laws unimpaired which they themselves had made for their own government. Congress was as much bound to uphold the laws of Louisiana, in all their extent and in all their parts, as it was to uphold the laws of New York, or any other State, whose civil policy had not been disturbed. Both those persons, however, were admitted to seats—yeas, 92; nays, 44.

The work of constituting the State of Louisiana out of the small portion of her population and of her territory held by the forces of the United States still went on. The proposition now was to hold a so-called State Convention and frame a new Constitution, but its advocates were so few that nothing was accomplished during the year 1863. The object of the military power was to secure such civil authority as to enforce the abolition of slavery; and, until the way was clear to that result, every method of organization was held in abeyance.

Meanwhile, on December 8, 1863, the President of the United States issued a proclamation which contained his plan for making a Union State out of a fragment of a Confederate State, and also granting an amnesty to the general mass of the people on taking an oath of allegiance. His plan was in these words:

"And I do further proclaim, declare, and make known that, whenever, in any of the States of Arkansas, Texas, Louisiana, Mississippi, Tennessee, Alabama, Georgia, Florida, South Carolina, and North Carolina, a number of persons, not less than one tenth in number of the votes cast in such State at the Presidential election of 1860, each having taken the following oath and not having since violated it, and being a qualified voter by the election laws of the State existing immediately before the so-called act of secession, and excluding all others, shall reestablish a State government which shall be republican, and in nowise contravening said oath, such shall be recognized as the true government of the State, and the State shall receive thereunder the benefits of the constitutional provision which declares that The United States shall guarantee to every State in this Union a republican form of government, and shall protect each of them against invasion; and, on application of the Legislature or the Executive (when the Legislature can not be convened), against domestic violence."

The oath required to be taken was as follows:

"I, ——- ——-, do solemnly swear, in presence of Almighty God, that I will henceforth support, protect, and defend the Constitution of the United States and the Union of the States thereunder; and that I will in like manner abide by and faithfully support all acts of Congress, passed during the existing rebellion, with reference to slaves, so long and so far as not repealed, modified, or held void by Congress, or by decision of the Supreme Court, and that I will, in like manner, abide by and faithfully support all proclamations of the President, made during the existing rebellion, having reference to slaves, so long and so far as not modified or declared void by decision of the Supreme Court. So help me God!"

In a message to Congress, of the same date with the preceding proclamation, the President of the United States, after explaining the objects of the proclamation, says:

"In the midst of other cares, however important, we must not lose sight of the fact that the war-power is still our main reliance. To that power alone can we look, for a time, to give confidence to the people in the contested regions that the insurgent power will not again overrun them."

The intelligent reader will observe that this plan of the President of the United States to restore States to the Union, to occupy the places of those which he had been attempting to destroy, does not contain a single feature to secure a republican form of government, nor a single provision authorized by the Constitution of the United States. With his usurped war-power to sustain him in the work of destruction, he found it easy to destroy; but he was powerless to create or to restore. In the former case, he had gone imperiously forward, trampling under foot every American political principle, and breaking through every constitutional limitation. In the latter case, he could not advance one step without recognizing sound political principles and complying with their dictates. On each foundation he must construct, or his work would be like the house founded on the sand.

It will now be shown what the true principles are, and then that the President of the United States perverted them, misstated them, and sought to reach his ends by groundless fabrications—as if he would enforce a fiction or establish a fallacy to be as good as truth. It might be still farther shown, if it had not already become self-evident, that this method was pursued with such a perversity and wickedness as to render it a characteristic feature of that war administration on whose skirts is the blood of more than a million of human beings.

The whole science of a republican government is to be found in this sentence of the Declaration of Independence, made by the representatives of the United States of America, in Congress assembled, on July 4, 1776. It says:

"That, to secure these rights [certain unalienable rights], governments are instituted among men—deriving their just powers from the consent of the governed; that, whenever any form of government becomes destructive of these ends, it is the right of the people to alter or abolish it, and to institute a new government, laying its foundation on such principles, and organizing its powers in such form, as to them shall seem most likely to effect their safety and happiness."

Thus it will be seen that civil and political sovereignty was held to be implanted by our Creator in the individual, and no human government has any original, inherent, just sovereignty whatever, and no acquired sovereignty either, beyond that which may be granted to it by the individuals as "most likely to effect their safety and happiness." "Deriving their just powers from the consent of the governed," says the Declaration of Independence. All other powers than those thus derived are not "just powers." Any government exercising powers "not just" has no right to survive. "It is the right of the people to alter or abolish it," says the Declaration of Independence, "and to institute a new government."

Who, then, had a right to "institute" a republican government for Louisiana? No human beings whatever but the people of Louisiana; not the strangers, not the slaves, but the manhood that knew its rights and dared to maintain them. Under what principles, then, could a citizen of Massachusetts, whether clothed in regimentals or a civilian's dress, come into Louisiana and attempt to set up a State government? Under no principles, but only by the power of the invader and the usurper. If the true principles of a republican government had prevailed and could have been enforced when Major-General Butler appeared at New Orleans, he would have been hanged on the first lamp-post, and his successor, Major-General Banks, would have been hanged on the second.

Under what principles, then, could the Government of the United States appear in Louisiana and attempt to institute a State government? As has been said above, it was the act of an invader and a usurper. Yet it proposed to "institute" a republican State government. The absurdity of such intention is too manifest to need argument. How could an invader attempt to "institute" a republican State government? an act which can be done only by the free and unconstrained action of the people themselves. It has been charged that this and every similar act of the President of the United States was in violation of his duty to maintain and observe the requirements and restrictions of the Constitution, and to uphold in each State a republican form of government. To specify, the following is offered as an example. He did "proclaim, declare, and make known—

> that, whenever any number of persons, not
> less than one tenth of the number of voters at
> the last Presidential election, shall reestablish
> a State government, which shall be republican
> [!] and in no wise contravening said oath,
> such shall be recognized as the true
> government of the State."

One tenth of the voters can not establish a republican State government, which requires the consent of the people of the State to make its powers just, as has been shown above. Therefore, such a government had not one element of republicanism in it. But what is astonishingly remarkable is the stultification of requiring the one tenth of the people to "reestablish a State government, which shall be republican and in no wise contravening said oath." Either he did not know how a republican State government was "instituted," or, if he knew, then he was a participant in that perversity and wickedness, which was above charged to be the characteristic of his war Administration.

It will now be shown how he sought "to enforce a fiction or establish a fallacy to be as good as truth." Of the government thus established by one tenth of the voters, he says:

> "Such shall be recognized as the true
> government of the State, and the State shall
> receive thereunder the benefits of the
> constitutional provision which declares that
> 'the United States shall guarantee to every
> State in this Union a republican form of
> government.'"

It is proper here to inquire who and what was the tenth to whom this power to rule the State was to be given. It will be seen, by reference to the proclamation, that each voter of the one tenth, in order to be qualified, is required to take an oath with certain promises in it, which are prescribed by an outside or foreign authority. This condition of itself is fatal to a republican State government, that "derives its just powers from the consent of the governed." Free consent—not cheerful consent, but unconstrained and unconditioned consent—is required that "just powers" may be derived from it. In this instance, the invader prescribes the requisite qualifications of the voter, and makes it a condition that the government established shall "in no wise contravene" certain stipulations expressed in the oath taken to give the qualification. A State government thus formed derives its powers from the consent of the invader, and not "from the consent of the governed." It has no "just powers" whatever. It is a groundless fabrication. Yet the President of the United States declared, "The State shall receive thereunder the benefits of the constitutional provision which declares that 'the United States shall guarantee to every State in this Union a republican form of government.'" Is not this an attempt, while pretending to establish, to destroy true republicanism?

Now, let the reader bear in mind that these remarks relate to Louisiana alone, of which more remains to be told; and that there were eleven States that withdrew from the Union, whose restoration was to be effected on this rotten system, in addition to several constitutional amendments, the adoption of which was to be effected and secured by the votes of these groundless fabrications, in which a fiction was to be considered as good as the truth. Having attained all these facts which are yet to be stated, he may begin to form some estimate of the remnants of the Constitution, and of the probable existence of any true union of the States.

To proceed with the narration. Under the above-mentioned proclamation of the President of the United States, Major-General Banks issued at New Orleans, on January 11, 1864, a proclamation for an election of State officers, and for members of a State Constitutional Convention. The State officers, when elected, were to constitute, as the proclamation said, "the civil government of the State under the Constitution and laws of Louisiana, except so much of the said Constitution and laws as recognize, regulate, or relate to slavery, which, being inconsistent with the present condition of public affairs, and plainly inapplicable to any class of persons now existing within its limits, must be suspended." The number of votes given for State officers was 10,270. The population of the State in 1860 was 708,902. The so-called Government was inaugurated on March 4th, and on March 11th he was invested with the powers hitherto exercised by the military Governor for the President of the United States. On the same day Major-General Banks issued an order relative to the election of delegates to a so-called State Convention. The most important provisions of it defined the qualifications of voters. The delegates were elected entirely within the army lines of the forces of the United States. The so-called Convention assembled and adopted a so-called Constitution, declaring "instantaneous, universal, uncompensated, unconditional emancipation of slaves." The meager vote on the Constitution was, for its adoption, 6,836; for its rejection, 1,566. The vote of New Orleans was, yeas 4,664, nays 789. This state of affairs continued after the close of the war. Violent disputes arose as to the validity of the so-called

Constitution. The so-called Legislature elected under it adopted Article XIII as an amendment to the Constitution of the United States, prohibiting the existence of slavery in the United States.

It will be seen from these facts that the State of Louisiana was not a republican State instituted by the consent of the governed; that its Legislature was an unconstitutional body, without any "just powers," and that the vote which it gave for the amendment of the Constitution of the United States was no vote at all; for it was given by a body that had no authority to give it, because it had no "just powers" whatever. Yet this vote was counted among those necessary to secure the passage of the constitutional amendment. Was this an attempt to enforce a fiction or to establish the truth? Such are the deeds which go to make up the record of crime against the liberties of mankind.

The proceedings in Arkansas to "institute" a republican State government were inaugurated by an order from the President of the United States to Major-General Steele, commanding the United States forces in Arkansas. At this time the regular government of the State, established by the consent of the people, was in fall operation outside the lines of the United States army. The military order of the President, dated January 20, 1864, said:

> "Sundry citizens of the State of Arkansas petitioned me that an election may be held in that State, in which to elect a Governor; that it be assumed at that election, and thenceforward, that the Constitution and laws of the State, as before the rebellion, are in full force, except that the Constitution is so modified as to declare that there shall be neither slavery nor involuntary servitude," etc.

The order then directs the election to be held for State officers, prescribes the qualifications of voters and the oath to be taken, and directs the General to administer to the officers thus chosen an oath to support the Constitution of the United States, and the "modified Constitution of the State of Arkansas," when they shall be declared qualified and empowered immediately to enter upon the duties of their offices.

The reader can scarcely fail to notice the novel method here adopted to modify or amend the State Constitution. It should be called the process by "assumption"—that is, assume it to be modified, and it is so modified. Then the President orders the officers-elect to be required to swear, on their oath, to support "the modified Constitution of the State of Arkansas." Now, unless the Constitution was thus modified by assuming it to be modified, these State officers were required by oath to support that which did not exist. But it was not so modified. No Constitution or other instrument in the world containing a grant of powers can be modified by assumption, unless it be the Constitution of the United States, as shown by recent experience. Yet the chief object for which these officers were elected and qualified was to carry out these so-called modifications of the State Constitution. This adds another to the deeds of darkness done in the name of republicanism.

Meantime some persons in the northern part of Arkansas, acting under the proclamation of December 8, 1863, got together a so-called State Convention on

January 8, 1864, and adopted a revised Constitution, containing the slavery prohibition, etc. This was ordered to be submitted to a popular vote, and at the same time State officers were to be elected. President Lincoln acceded to these proceedings after they had been placed under the direction of the military commander, General Steele. The election was held, the Constitution received twelve thousand votes, and the State officers were declared to be elected. Then Arkansas came forth a so-called republican State, "instituted" by military authority, and, of course, received the benefit of the constitutional provision, which declares that "the United States shall guarantee to every State in this Union a republican form of government." It should be added that Arkansas, thus "instituted" a State, was regarded by the Government of the United States as competent to give as valid a vote as New York, Massachusetts, or any other Northern State, for the ratification of Article XIII, as an amendment to the Constitution of the United States, prohibiting the existence of slavery in the United States. The vote was thus given; it was counted, and served to make up the exact number deemed by the managers to be necessary. Thus was fraud and falsehood triumphant over popular rights and fundamental law.

The perversion of true republican principles was greater in Virginia than in any other State, through the coöperation of the Government of the United States. In the winter of 1860-'61 a special session of the Legislature of the State convened at Richmond and passed an act directing the people to elect delegates to a State Convention to be held on February 14, 1861. The Convention assembled, and was occupied with the subject of Federal relations and the adjustment of difficulties until the call for troops by President Lincoln was made, when an ordinance of secession was passed. The contiguity of the northwestern counties of the State to Ohio and Pennsylvania led to the manifestation of much opposition to the withdrawal of the State from the Union, and the determination to reorganize that portion into a separate State. This resulted in the assembling of a so-called convention of delegates at Wheeling on June 11th. One of its first acts was to provide for a reorganization of the State government of Virginia by declaring its offices vacant, and the appointment of new officers throughout. This new organization assumed to be the true representative of the State of Virginia, and, after various fortunes, was recognized as such by President Lincoln, as will be presently seen. The next act of the Convention was "to provide for the formation of a new State out of a portion of the territory of this State." Under this act delegates were elected to a so-called Constitutional Convention which framed a so-called Constitution for the new State of West Virginia, which was submitted to a vote of the people in April, 1862, and carried by a large majority of that section. Meantime the Governor of the reorganized government of Virginia, above mentioned, issued his proclamation calling for an election of members, and the assembling of an extra session of the so-called Legislature. This body assembled on May 6, 1862, and, adopting the new Federal process of assumption, it assumed to be the Legislature of the State of Virginia. This body, or Legislature, so called, immediately passed an act giving its consent to the formation of a new State out of the territory of Virginia. The formal act of consent and the draft of the new Constitution of West Virginia above mentioned were ordered by this so-called Legislature to be sent to the Congress of the United States, then in session, with the request that "the said new State be admitted into the Union." On December

31, 1862, the President of the United States approved an act of Congress entitled "An act for the admission of the State of West Virginia into the Union," etc. The act recited as follows:

> "*Whereas*, The Legislature of Virginia, by an act passed May 13, 1862, did give its consent to the formation of a new State within the jurisdiction of the said State of Virginia, to be known by the name of West Virginia," etc.

Again it recites:

> "And whereas both the Convention and the Legislature aforesaid have requested that the new State should be admitted into the Union, and the Constitution aforesaid being republican in form, Congress doth hereby consent that the said forty-eight counties may be formed into a separate and independent State."

It were well to pause for a moment and consider these proceedings in the light of fundamental republican principles. The State of Virginia was not a confederation, but a republic, or nation. Its government was instituted with the consent of the governed, and its powers, therefore, were "just powers." When the State Convention at Richmond passed an ordinance of secession, which was subsequently ratified by sixty thousand majority, it was as valid an act for the people of Virginia as was ever passed by a representative body. The legally expressed decision of the majority was the true voice of the State. When, therefore, disorderly persons in the northwestern counties of the State assembled and declared the ordinance of secession "to be null and void," they rose up against the authority of the State. When they proceeded to elect delegates to a convention to resist the act of the State, and that Convention assembled and organized and proceeded to action, an insurrection against the government of Virginia was begun. When the Convention next declared the State offices to be vacant, and proceeded to fill them by the choice of Francis H. Pierpont for Governor, and other State officers, assuming itself to be the true State Convention of Virginia, it not only declared what notoriously did not exist, but it committed an act of revolution. And, when the so-called State officers elected by it entered upon their duties, they inaugurated a revolution. The subsequent organization of the State of West Virginia and its separation from the State of Virginia were acts of secession. Thus we have, in these movements, insurrection, revolution, and secession.

The reader, in his simplicity, may naturally expect to find the Government of the United States arrayed, with all its military forces, against these illegitimate proceedings. Oh, no! It made all the difference in the world, with the ministers of that Government, "whose ox it was that was gored by the bull." She was the nursing-mother to the whole thing, and to insure its vitality fed it, not, like the fabled bird, with her own blood, but by the butchery of the mother of States. The words of the Constitution of the United States applicable to this case are these:

> "No new State shall be formed or erected within the jurisdiction of any other State; nor any State be formed by the junction of two or

more States, or parts of States, without the
consent of the Legislatures of the States
concerned, as well as of the Congress." [61]

Will any intelligent person assert that the consent of the State of Virginia was given to the formation of this new State, or that the government of Francis H. Pierpont held the true and lawful jurisdiction of the State of Virginia? Yet the Congress of the United States asserted in the act above quoted that "the Legislature of Virginia did give its consent to the formation of a new State within the jurisdiction of the State of Virginia." This was not true, but was an attempt, by an act of Congress, to aid a fraud and perpetuate a monstrous usurpation. For there is no grant of power to Congress in the Constitution nor in the American theory of government to justify it. If it is said that the government of Francis H. Pierpont was the only one recognized by Congress as the government of the State of Virginia, that does not alter the fact. The recognition of Congress can not make a State of an organization which is not a State. There is no grant of power to Congress in the Constitution for that purpose. If it is said that the government of Francis H. Pierpont was established by the only qualified voters in the State of Virginia, that is as equally unfounded as the other assertions. Neither the Congress of the United States nor the Government of the United States can determine the qualifications of voters at an election for delegates to a State Constitutional Convention, or for the choice of State officers. There was no grant of power either to the President or to Congress for that purpose. All these efforts were usurpations, by which it was sought, through groundless fabrications, to reach certain ends, and they add to the multitude of deeds which constitute the crime committed against States and the liberties of the people.

When the question of the admission of West Virginia was before the House of Representatives of the United States Congress, Mr. Thaddeus Stevens, of Pennsylvania, declared, with expiatory frankness, that he would not stultify himself by claiming the act to be constitutional. He said, "We know that it is not constitutional, but it is necessity."

It now became necessary for the Government of Virginia, represented by Francis H. Pierpont, to emigrate; for the new State of West Virginia embraced the territory in which he was located. He therefore departed, with his carpet-bag, and located at Alexandria, on the Potomac, which became the seat of government of so-called East Virginia. On February 13, 1864, a convention, consisting of a representative from each of the ten counties in part or wholly under the control of the United States forces, assembled at Alexandria to amend the Constitution of the State of Virginia. Some sections providing for the abolition of slavery were declared to be added to the Constitution, and the so-called Convention adjourned. Nothing of importance occurred until after the occupation of Richmond by the United States forces. On May 9, 1865, President Johnson issued an "Executive order to reestablish the authority of the United States, and execute the laws within the geographical limits known as the State of Virginia." The order closed in these words:

"That, to carry into effect the guarantee of
the Federal Constitution of a republican form
of State government, and afford the
advantage of the security of domestic laws, as
well as to complete the reestablishment of the

> authority of the laws of the United States and
> the full and complete restoration of peace
> within the limits aforesaid, Francis H.
> Pierpont, Governor of the State of Virginia,
> will be aided by the Federal Government, so
> far as may be necessary, in the lawful
> measures which he may take for the extension
> and administration of the State government
> throughout the geographical limits of said
> State."

This order recognized the factitious organization, which was begun in West Virginia and then transplanted to Alexandria, as the true government of the State of Virginia, and, by the aid of the United States Government, was now removed to Richmond and set up there. No person was allowed to take any part in this government or to vote under it unless he had previously taken the purgatorial oath above mentioned, and had not held office under the Confederate or any State government. Thus, the taking of this oath, which was prescribed by the President of the United States, became the most important of the qualifications of a voter. Here was a condition prescribed by a foreign authority as necessary to be fulfilled before the first act could be done by a citizen relative to his State government. Such a government was not republican, for its powers were not derived from the consent of the governed. Its powers were derived from voters who had, under oath, said:

> "I will abide by and faithfully support all
> acts of Congress, passed during the existing
> rebellion with reference to slaves, so long and
> so far as not repealed, modified, or held void
> by Congress or by decision of the Supreme
> Court; and that I will in like manner abide by
> and faithfully support all proclamations of the
> President, made during the existing rebellion
> having reference to slaves, so long and so far
> as not modified or declared void by decision
> of the Supreme Court."

Such a State government was not in the interest of the people, but in the interest of the United States Government. The true republican organization, which had been "instituted" by the free "consent of the governed to effect their safety and happiness," had been repudiated by the Government of the United States as in rebellion to it; and this fiction had been set up, not by the free consent of the people, which alone could give to it any "just powers," not "to effect their safety and happiness," for which alone a republican State government can be instituted, but solely to secure the safety and supremacy of the Government of the United States. The qualification of the voter was prescribed by the United States Government, and the oath required him to recognize allegiance to the Union as supreme over that to the State of which he was a citizen. Thus the voters under the State government of Virginia were required first to protect the Government of the United States, and then they were at liberty to look after their own interests through the State government.

Now, it is charged that such acts on the part of the United States Government were not only entirely unconstitutional, but they caused the complete subversion of the States. The Constitution of the United States knows States in the Union only as they are republican States. The Government of the United States was conscious of this fact, and publicly recognized it when it promised to guarantee a republican form of government to each one that it sought to reconstruct. But it violated the Constitution when it sought to place in the Union mere fictions which had' not the first element of a republic, which were groundless fabrications of its own minions that could not have existed a day without the military support which they received. Further, it is to be remembered that it does not come within the grants of the Constitution, consequently not within the powers of the Government of the United States, to institute a republican form of government at any time or in any place. Such an act is neither contemplated nor known in the Constitution, as such a government can be instituted only by the free consent of those who are to be governed by it. Any interference on the part of the United States to limit, modify, or control this consent goes directly to the nature and objects of the State government, and it ceases to be republican. To admit a State under such a government is entirely unauthorized, revolutionary, subversive of the Constitution, and destructive of the Union of States.

[Footnote 61: Constitution of the United States, Article IV, section 3.]

CHAPTER XXXIV.

Address to the Army of Eastern Virginia by the President.—Army of General Pope.—Position of McClellan.—Advance of General Jackson.—Atrocious Orders of General Pope.—Letter of McClellan on the Conduct of the War.—Letter of the President to General Lee.—Battle of Cedar Run.—Results of the Engagement.—Reënforcements to the Enemy.—Second Battle of Manassas.—Capture of Manassas Junction.—Captured Stores.—The Old Battle-Field.—Advance of General Longstreet.—Attack on him.—Attack on General Jackson.—Darkness of the Night.—Battle at Ox Hill.—Losses of the Enemy.

This defeat of McClellan's army led me to issue the following address:

"RICHMOND, July 5, 1862.

"*To the Army of Eastern Virginia.*

"SOLDIERS: I congratulate you on the series of brilliant victories which, under the favor of Divine Providence, you have lately won, and, as the President of the Confederate States, do heartily tender to you the thanks of the country, whose just cause you have so skillfully and heroically served. Ten days ago an invading army, vastly superior to you in numbers and the materials of war, closely beleaguered your capital and vauntingly proclaimed its speedy conquest; you marched to attack the enemy in his intrenchments; with well-directed movements and death-defying valor you charged upon him in his strong positions, drove him from field to field over a distance of more than thirty-five miles, and despite his reënforcements compelled him to seek safety under the cover of his gunboats, where he now lies cowering before the army so lately derided and threatened with entire subjugation. The fortitude with which you have borne toil and privation, the gallantry with which you have entered into each successive battle, must have been witnessed to be fully appreciated; but a grateful people will not fail to recognize you, and to bear you in loved remembrance. Well may it be said of you that you have 'done enough for glory'; but duty to a suffering country and to the cause of constitutional liberty claims from you yet further effort. Let it be your pride to relax in nothing which can promote your future efficiency; your one great object being to drive the invader from your soil, and, carrying your standards beyond the outer boundaries of the Confederacy, to wring from an unscrupulous foe the recognition of your birthright, community independence.

"JEFFERSON DAVIS."

After the retreat of General McClellan to Westover, his army remained inactive about a month. His front was closely watched by a brigade of cavalry, and preparations made to resist a renewal of his attempt upon Richmond from his new base. The main body of our army awaited the development of his intentions, and no important event took place.

Meantime, another army of the enemy, under Major-General Pope, advanced southward from Washington, and crossed the Rappahannock as if to seize Gordonsville, and move thence upon Richmond. Contemporaneously the enemy appeared in force at Fredericksburg, and threatened the railroad from Gordonsville to Richmond, apparently for the purpose of coöperating with the movements of General Pope. To meet the advance of the latter, and restrain, as far as possible, the atrocities which he threatened to perpetrate upon our defenseless citizens, General Jackson, with his own and Ewell's division, was ordered to proceed on July 13th toward Gordonsville.

The nature of the atrocities here alluded to may be inferred from the orders of Major-General Pope, which were as follows:

"HEADQUARTERS OF THE ARMY OF VIRGINIA, WASHINGTON, *July 18, 1862.*

"(GENERAL ORDERS, No 5.)

"Hereafter, as far as practicable, the troops of this command will subsist upon the country in which their operations are carried on. In all cases supplies for this purpose will be taken by the officers to whose department they properly belong, under the orders of the commanding officer of the troops for whose use they are intended. Vouchers will be given to the owners, stating on their face that they will be payable at the close of the war upon sufficient testimony being furnished that such owners have been loyal citizens of the United States since the date of the vouchers. . . .

"By command of Major-General Pope:

"GEORGE D. RUGGLES,

"*Colonel, A. A.-General, and Chief of Staff.*"

"HEADQUARTERS OF THE ARMY OF VIRGINIA, *July 18, 1862.*

"(GENERAL ORDERS, No. 6.)

"Hereafter, in any operations of the cavalry forces in this command, no supply or baggage trains of any description will be used, unless so stated especially in the order for the movement. Two days' cooked rations will be carried on the persons of the men, and all villages and neighborhoods through which they pass will be laid under contribution in the manner specified by General Orders, No. 5, current series, from these headquarters, for the subsistence of men and horses. . . .

"By command of Major-General Pope:
"GEORGE D. RUGGLES,
"*Colonel, A. A.-General, and Chief of Staff.*"
"HEADQUARTERS ARMY OF VIRGINIA, WASHINGTON, *July 18, 1862.*
"(GENERAL ORDERS, No. 7.)

"The people of the Valley of the Shenandoah and throughout the region of operations of this army, living along the lines of railroad and telegraph, and along routes of travel in the rear of United States forces, are notified that they will be held responsible for any injury done the track, line, or road, or for any attacks upon the trains or straggling soldiers, by bands of guerrillas in their neighborhood. . . . Evil-disposed persons in the rear of our armies, who do not themselves engage directly in these lawless acts, encourage by refusing to interfere, or give any information by which such acts can be prevented or the perpetrators punished. Safety of the life and property of all persons living in the rear of our advancing army depends upon the maintenance of peace and quiet among themselves, and upon the unmolested movements through their midst of all pertaining to the military service. They are to understand distinctly that the security of travel is their only warrant of personal safety. . . . If a soldier or legitimate follower of the army be fired upon from any house, the house shall be razed to the ground and the inhabitants sent prisoners to the headquarters of this army. If such an outrage occur at any place distant from settlements, the people within five miles around shall be held accountable, and made to pay an indemnity sufficient for the case; and any person detected in such outrages, either during the act or at any time afterward, shall be shot, without waiting civil process. . . .

"By command of Major-General Pope:
"GEORGE D. RUGGLES, *Colonel.*"
"HEADQUARTERS ARMY OF VIRGINIA, WASHINGTON, *July 23, 1862.*
"(GENERAL ORDERS, No. 11.)

"Commanders of army corps, divisions, brigades, and detached commands will proceed immediately to arrest all disloyal male citizens within their lines, or within their reach in the rear of their respective stations.

"Such as are willing to take the oath of allegiance to the United States, and will furnish sufficient security for its observance, shall be permitted to remain at their homes, and pursue in good faith their accustomed avocations. Those who refuse shall be conducted south beyond the extreme pickets of the army, and be notified that, if found again anywhere within our lines or at any point in the rear, they will be considered spies, and subjected to the extreme rigor of the military law. . . .

"By command of Major-General Pope:

"GEORGE D. RUGGLES,

"*Colonel, A. A.-General, and Chief of Staff.*"

Thus was announced a policy of pillage, outrage upon unarmed, peaceable people, arson, and ruthless insult to the defenseless. Had the vigor of the campaign been equal to the bombastic manifesto of this disgrace to the profession of arms, the injuries inflicted would have been more permanent; the conduct could scarcely have been more brutal.

In recurring to the letter of General George B. McClellan, written at "Camp near Harrison's Landing, Virginia, July 7, 1862," to the President of the United States, one must be struck with the strong contrast between the suggestions of General McClellan and the orders of General Pope. The inquiry naturally arises, Was it because of this difference that Pope had been assigned to the command of the Army of Virginia? McClellan wrote:

"This rebellion has assumed the character of a war; as such it should be regarded, and it should be conducted upon the highest principles known to Christian civilization. It should not be a war looking to the subjugation of the people of any State, in any event. It should not be at all a war upon population, but against armed forces and political organizations. Neither confiscation of property, political executions of persons, territorial organizations of States, or forcible abolition of slavery, should be contemplated for a moment.

"In prosecuting the war, all private property and unarmed persons should be strictly protected, subject only to the necessity of military operations; all private property taken for military use should be paid or receipted for; pillage and waste should be treated as high crimes; all unnecessary trespass sternly prohibited, and offensive demeanor by the military toward citizens promptly rebuked. Military arrests should not be tolerated, except in places where active hostilities exist; and oaths, not required by enactments constitutionally, should be neither demanded nor received."

Had these views been accepted, and the conduct of the Government of the United States been in accordance with them, the most shameful chapters in American history could not have been written, and some of the more respectable newspapers of the North would not have had the apprehensions they expressed of the evils which would befall the country when an army habituated to thieving should be disbanded.

On the reception of copies of the orders issued by General Pope, inserted above, I addressed to General Lee, commanding our army in Virginia, the following letter:

"RICHMOND, VIRGINIA, *July 31, 1862.*

214

"SIR: On the 23d of this month a cartel for a general exchange of prisoners of war was signed between Major-General D. H. Hill, in behalf of the Confederate States, and Major-General John A. Dix, in behalf of the United States.

"By the terms of that cartel, it is stipulated that all prisoners of war hereafter taken shall be discharged on parole until exchanged.

"Scarcely had that cartel been signed, when the military authorities of the United States commenced a practice changing the character of the war, from such as becomes civilized nations, into a campaign of indiscriminate robbery and murder.

"The general order issued by the Secretary of War of the United States, in the city of Washington, on the very day that the cartel was signed in Virginia, directs the military commanders of the United States to take the private property of our people for the convenience and use of their armies, without compensation.

"The general order issued by Major-General Pope, on the 23d of July, the day after the signing of the cartel, directs the murder of our peaceful inhabitants as spies, if found quietly tilling their farms in his rear, *even outside of his lines*; and one of his brigadier-generals, Steinwehr, has seized upon innocent and peaceful inhabitants, to be held as hostages, to the end that they may be murdered in cold blood if any of his soldiers are killed by some unknown persons, whom he designates as 'bushwhackers.'

"Under this state of facts, this Government has issued the inclosed general order, recognizing General Pope and his commissioned officers to be in the position which they have chosen for themselves, that of robbers and murderers, and not that of public enemies, entitled, if captured, to be considered as prisoners of war.

"We find ourselves driven by our enemies in their steady progress toward a practice which we abhor, and which we are vainly struggling to avoid. Some of the military authorities of the United States seem to suppose that better success will attend a savage war in which no quarter is to be given and no sex to be spared than has hitherto been secured by such hostilities as are alone recognized to be lawful by civilized men in modern times.

"For the present, we renounce our right of retaliation on the innocent, and shall continue to treat the private enlisted soldiers of General Pope's army as prisoners of war; but if, after notice to the Government at Washington of our confining repressive measures to the punishment only of commissioned officers, who are willing participants in these crimes, these savage practices are continued, we shall reluctantly be forced to the last resort of accepting the war on the terms chosen by our foes, until the outraged voice of a common humanity forces a respect for the recognized rules of war.

"While these facts would justify our refusal to execute the generous cartel, by which we have consented to liberate an excess of thousands of prisoners held by us beyond the number held by the enemy, a sacred regard to plighted faith, shrinking from the mere semblance of breaking a promise, prevents our resort to this extremity. Nor do we desire to extend to any other forces of the enemy the punishment merited alone by General Pope and such commissioned officers as choose to participate in the execution of his infamous orders.

"You are therefore instructed to communicate to the commander-in-chief of the armies of the United States the contents of this letter and a copy of the inclosed general order, to the end that he may be notified of our intention not to consider any officers hereafter captured from General Pope's army as prisoners of war. Very respectfully, yours, etc.,

"JEFFERSON DAVIS."

When General Jackson arrived near Gordonsville on July 19, 1862, he was at his request reënforced by Major-General A. P. Hill. Receiving information that only a part of General Pope's army was at Culpeper Court-House, General Jackson, hoping to defeat it before reënforcements should arrive, moved in that direction the divisions of Ewell, Hill, and Jackson, on August 7th, from their encampments near Gordonsville. As the enemy's cavalry displayed unusual activity and the train of Jackson's division was seriously endangered, General Lawton with his brigade was ordered to guard it. On August 9th Jackson arrived within eight miles of Culpeper Court-House and found the foe in his front near Cedar Run and a short distance west and north of Slaughter Mountain. When first seen, the cavalry in large force occupied a ridge to the right of the road. A battery opened upon it and soon forced it to retire. Our fire was responded to by some guns beyond the ridge from which the advance had just been driven. Soon after, the cavalry returned to the position where it was first seen, and General Early was ordered forward, keeping near the Culpeper road, while General Ewell with his two remaining brigades diverged from the road to the right, advancing along the western slope of Slaughter Mountain. General Early, forming his brigade in line of battle, moved into the open field, and, passing a short distance to the right of the road but parallel to it, pushed forward, driving the opposing cavalry before him to the crest of a hill which overlooked the ground between his troops and the opposite hill, along which the enemy's batteries were posted, and opened upon him as soon as he reached the eminence. Early retired his troops under the protection of the hill, and a small battery of ours, in advance of his right, opened. Meantime General Winder with Jackson's brigade was placed on the left of the road, Campbell's brigade, Lieutenant-Colonel Garnett commanding, being on the left, Taliaferro's parallel to the road, supporting the batteries, and Winder's own brigade under Colonel Roland in reserve. The battle opened with a fierce fire of artillery, which continued about two hours, during which Brigadier-General Charles S. Winder, while directing the positions of his batteries, received a wound, from the effects of which he expired in a few hours. General Jackson thus spoke of him in his report:

"It is difficult, within the proper reserve of an official report, to do justice to the merits of this accomplished officer. Urged by the medical director to take no part in the movements of the day, because of the then enfeebled state of his health, his ardent patriotism and military pride could bear no restraint. Richly endowed with those qualities of mind and person which fit an officer for command, and which attract the admiration and excite the enthusiasm of troops, he was rapidly rising to the front rank of his profession. His loss has been severely felt."

Charles Winder had attracted my special notice, when I was Secretary of War of the United States, by an act of heroism and devotion to duty which it gives me pleasure to record. A regiment of artillery, in which he was a second-lieutenant, being under orders for California, embarked on the steamer San Francisco, and in a storm became disabled; drifting helplessly at sea, she was approached by a bark which, to give succor, hove to. Not being able to receive all the passengers, the commissioned officers left, as the Colonel naively reported, in the order of their rank. Winder alone remained with the troops; in great discomfort and by strenuous exertion the wreck was kept afloat until a vessel bound for Liverpool came to the relief of the sufferers.

Arriving at Liverpool, Winder left the soldiers there, went to the American consul in London, got means to provide for their needs, and returned with them. Soon afterward, four regiments were added to the army, and, for his good conduct so full of promise, he was nominated to be a captain of infantry, and, notwithstanding his youth, was confirmed and commissioned accordingly. He died manifesting the same spirit as on the wreck—that which holds life light when weighed against honor.

The enemy's infantry advanced about 5 P.M., and attacked General Early in front, while another body, concealed by the inequality of the ground, moved upon his right. Thomas's brigade, of A. P. Hill's division, which had now arrived, was sent to his support, and the contest soon became animated. In the mean time the main body of the opposing army, under cover of a wood and the undulations of the field, gained the left of Jackson's division, now commanded by Brigadier-General Taliaferro, and poured a destructive fire into its flank and rear. Campbell's brigade fell back in confusion, exposing the flank of Taliaferro's, which also gave way, as did the left of Early's. The rest of his brigade, however, firmly held its ground.

Winder's brigade, with Branch's, of A. P. Hill's division, on its right, advanced promptly to the support of Jackson's division, and after a sanguinary struggle the assailants were repulsed with loss. Pender's and Archer's brigades, also of Hill's division, came up on the left of Winder's, and by a general charge the foe was driven back in confusion, leaving the ground covered with his dead and wounded. General Ewell, with the two brigades on the extreme right, had been prevented from advancing by the fire of our own artillery, which swept his approach to the enemy's left. The obstacle being now removed, he pressed forward under a hot fire, and came gallantly into action. Repulsed and vigorously followed on our left and center, and now hotly pressed on our right, the whole line of the enemy gave way, and was soon in full retreat. Night had now set in, but General Jackson, desiring to enter Culpeper Court-House before morning, determined to pursue. Hill's division led the advance; but, owing to the darkness, it was compelled to move slowly and with caution.

The enemy was found about a mile and a half in the rear of the field of battle, and information was received that reënforcements had arrived. General Jackson thereupon halted for the night, and the next day, becoming satisfied that the enemy's force had been so largely increased as to render a further advance on his part imprudent, he sent his wounded to the rear, and proceeded to bury the dead and collect the arms from the battlefield. On the 11th the enemy asked and received permission to bury those of his dead not already interred. General Jackson remained in position during the day, and at night returned to the vicinity of Gordonsville. In this engagement 400 prisoners, including a brigadier-general were captured, and 5,300 stand of small-arms, one piece of artillery, several caissons, and three colors, fell into our hands. Our killed were 229, wounded 1,047, total 1,276. The loss on the other side exceeded 1,500, of whom nearly 300 were taken prisoners.

The victory of Cedar Run effectually checked the invader for the time; but it soon became apparent that his army was receiving a large increase. The corps of Major-General Burnside, from North Carolina, which had reached Fredericksburg, was reported to have moved up the Rappahannock, a few days after the battle, to unite with General Pope, and a part of General McClellan's army had left Westover for the same purpose. It therefore seemed that active operations on the James were no longer contemplated, and that the most effectual way to relieve Richmond from any danger of an attack would be to reënforce General Jackson and advance upon General Pope.

Accordingly, on August 13th, Longstreet, Anderson, and Stuart were ordered to proceed to Gordonsville. On the 16th the troops began to move from the vicinity of Gordonsville toward the Rapidan, on the north side of which, extending along the Orange and Alexandria Railroad in the direction of Culpeper Court-House, the army of invasion lay in great force. It was determined, with the cavalry, to destroy the railroad-bridge over the Rappahannock in rear of the enemy, while Jackson and Longstreet crossed the Rapidan and attacked his left flank. But, the enemy becoming apprised of our design, hastily retreated beyond the Rappahannock. On the 21st our forces moved toward that river, and some sharp skirmishing ensued with our cavalry that had crossed at Beverly's Ford. As it had been determined in the mean time not to attempt the passage of the river at that point with the army, the cavalry withdrew to the south side. Soon afterward the enemy appeared in great strength on the opposite bank, and an active fire was kept up during the rest of the day between his artillery and the batteries attached to Jackson's leading division, under Brigadier-General Taliaferro.

But, as our positions on the south bank of the Rappahannock were commanded by those on the north bank, and which served to guard all the fords, General Lee determined to seek a more favorable place to cross higher up the river, and thus gain his adversary's right. Accordingly, General Longstreet was directed to leave Kelly's Ford on the 21st, and take the position in the vicinity of Beverly's Ford and the Orange and Alexandria Railroad bridge, then held by Jackson, in order to mask the movement of the latter, who was instructed to ascend the river. On the 22d Jackson proceeded up the Rappahannock, leaving Trimble's brigade near Freeman's Ford to protect his train. In the afternoon

Longstreet sent General Hood with his own and Whiting's brigade to relieve Trimble. Hood had just reached the position, when he and Trimble were attacked by a considerable force which had crossed at Freeman's Ford. After a short but spirited engagement, the enemy was driven precipitately over the river with heavy loss. General Jackson attempted to cross at Warrenton Springs Ford, but was interrupted by a heavy rain, which caused the river to rise so rapidly as to be impassable for infantry and artillery, and he withdrew the troops that had reached the opposite side. General Stuart, who had been directed to cut the railroad in rear of General Pope's army, crossed the Rappahannock on the morning of the 22d, about six miles above the Springs, with parts of Lee's and Robertson's brigades. He reached Catlet's Station that night, but was prevented destroying the railroad-bridge there by the same storm that arrested Jackson's movements. He captured more than three hundred prisoners, including a number of officers. Apprehensive of the effect of the rain upon the streams, he recrossed the Rappahannock at Warrenton Springs. The rise of the river, rendering the lower fords impassable, enabled the enemy to concentrate his main body opposite General Jackson, and on the 24th Longstreet was ordered by General Lee to proceed to his support. Although retarded by the swollen condition of Hazel River and other tributaries of the Rappahannock, he reached Jeffersonton in the afternoon. General Jackson's command lay between that place and the Spring's Ford, and a warm cannonade was progressing between the batteries of General A. P. Hill's division and those in his front. The enemy was massed between Warrenton and the Springs, and guarded the fords of the Rappahannock as far above as Waterloo.

The army of General McClellan had left Westover, and a part had marched to join General Pope. It was reported that the rest would soon follow. The greater part of the army of General Cox had also been withdrawn from the Kanawha Valley for the same purpose. Two brigades of D. H. Hill's division, under General Ripley, had already been ordered from Richmond, and the remainder were to follow; also, McLaws's division, two brigades under General Walker, and Hampton's cavalry brigade. In pursuance of the plan of operations now determined upon, Jackson was directed, on the 25th, to cross above Waterloo and move around the enemy's right, so as to strike the Orange and Alexandria Railroad in his rear. Longstreet, in the mean time, was to divert his attention by threatening him in front, and to follow Jackson as soon as the latter should be sufficiently advanced.

General Jackson crossed the Rappahannock on the 25th, about four miles above Waterloo, and, after sunset on the 26th, reached the railroad at Bristoe Station. At Gainesville he was joined by General Stuart, with the brigades of Robertson and Fitzhugh Lee, who continued with him during his operations, and effectually guarded both his flanks.

General Jackson was now between the large army of General Pope and Washington City, without having encountered any considerable force. At Bristoe two trains of cars were captured and a few prisoners taken. Determining, notwithstanding the darkness of the night and the long and arduous march of the day, to capture the depot of the enemy at Manassas Junction, about seven miles distant, General Trimble volunteered to proceed at once to that place with the Twenty-first North Carolina and the Twenty-first Georgia Regiments. The offer was accepted, and, to render success more certain, General Stuart was directed to accompany the expedition with part of his cavalry. About midnight the place was taken with little difficulty. Eight pieces of artillery, with their horses, ammunition, and equipments were captured; more than three hundred prisoners, one hundred and seventy-five horses, besides those belonging to the artillery, two hundred new tents, and immense quantities of commissary and quartermaster's stores, fell into our hands.

Ewell's division, with the Fifth Virginia Cavalry under Colonel Bosser, were left at Bristoe Station, and the rest of the command arrived at the Junction early on the 27th. Soon a considerable force of the enemy, under Brigadier-General Taylor, of New Jersey, approached from the direction of Alexandria, and pushed forward boldly to recover the stores. After a sharp engagement he was routed and driven back, leaving his killed and wounded on the field. The troops remained at Manassas Junction during the day, and supplied themselves with everything they required. In the afternoon, two brigades advanced against General Ewell, at Bristoe, from the direction of Warrenton Junction, but were broken and repulsed. Their place was soon supplied with fresh troops, but it was apparent that the commander had now become aware of the situation of affairs, and had turned upon General Jackson with his whole force. General Ewell, perceiving the strength of the column, withdrew and rejoined General Jackson, having first destroyed the railroad-bridge over Broad Run. The enemy halted at Bristoe. General Jackson, having a much inferior force to General Pope, retired from Manassas Junction and took a position west of the turnpike-road from Warrenton to Alexandria, where he could more readily unite with the approaching column of Longstreet. Having supplied the wants of his troops, he was compelled, through lack of transportation, to destroy the rest of the captured property. Many thousand pounds of bacon, a thousand barrels of corned beef, two thousand barrels of salt pork, and two thousand barrels of floor, besides other property of great value, were burned.

During the night of the 27th of August Taliaferro's division crossed the turnpike near Groveton and halted on the west side, near the battle-field of July 21, 1861, where it was joined on the 28th by the divisions of Hill and Ewell. During the afternoon the enemy, approaching from the direction of Warrenton down the turnpike toward Alexandria, exposed his left flank, and General Jackson determined to attack him. A fierce and sanguinary conflict ensued which continued until about 9 P.M., when he slowly fell back and left us in possession of the field, the loss on both sides was heavy. On the next morning (the 29th) the enemy had taken a position to interpose his army between General Jackson and Alexandria, and about 10 A.M. opened with artillery upon the right of Jackson's line. The troops of the latter were disposed in rear of Groveton, along the line of the unfinished branch of the Manassas Gap Railroad, and extending from a point a short distance west of the turnpike toward Sudley Mill, Jackson's division under Brigadier-General Starke being on the right, Swell's under General Lawton in the center, and A. P. Hill on the left. The attacking columns were evidently concentrating on Jackson with the design of overwhelming him before the arrival of Longstreet. This latter officer left his position opposite Warrenton Springs on the 26th and marched to join Jackson. On the 28th, arriving at Thoroughfare Gap, he found the enemy prepared to dispute his progress. Holding the eastern extremity of the pass with a large force, the enemy directed a heavy fire of artillery upon the road leading to it and upon the sides of the mountain. An attempt was made to turn his right, but, before our troops reached their destination, he advanced to the attack, and, being vigorously repulsed, withdrew to his position at the eastern end of the Gap, keeping up an active fire of artillery until dark. He then retreated. On the morning of the 29th Longstreet's command resumed its march, the sound of cannon at Manassas announcing that Jackson was already engaged. The head of the column came upon the field in rear of the enemy's left, which had already opened with artillery upon Jackson's right, as above stated. Longstreet immediately placed some of his batteries in position, but, before he could complete his dispositions to attack the force before him, it withdrew to another part of the field. He then took position on the right of Jackson, Hood's two brigades, supported by Evans, being deployed across the turnpike and at right angles to it. These troops were supported on the left by three brigades under General Wilcox, and by a like force on the right under General Kemper. D. B. Jones's division formed the extreme right of the line, resting on the Manassas Gap Railroad. The cavalry guarded our right and left flanks, that on the right being under General Stuart in person. After the arrival of Longstreet the enemy changed his position and began to concentrate opposite Jackson's left, opening a brisk artillery-fire, which was responded to by some of A. P. Hill's batteries.

Soon afterward General Stuart reported the approach of a large force from the direction of Bristoe Station, threatening Longstreet's right. But no serious attack was made, and, after firing a few shots, that force withdrew. Meanwhile a large column advanced to assail the left of Jackson's position, occupied by the division of General A. P. Hill. The attack was received by his troops with their accustomed steadiness, and the battle raged with great fury. The enemy was repeatedly repulsed, but again pressed on the attack with fresh troops. Once he succeeded in penetrating an interval between General Gregg's brigade on the extreme left and that of General Thomas, but was quickly driven back with great slaughter by the Fourteenth South Carolina Regiment, then in reserve, and the Forty-ninth Georgia of Thomas's brigade. The contest was close and obstinate; the combatants sometimes delivered their fire at a few paces. General Gregg, who was most exposed, was reënforced by Hays's brigade under Colonel Forno. Gregg had successfully and most gallantly resisted the attack until the ammunition of his brigade was exhausted and all his field-officers but two killed or wounded. The reënforcement was of like high-tempered steel, and together in hand-to-hand fight they held their post until they were relieved, after several hours of severe fighting, by Early's brigade and the Eighth Louisiana Regiment. General Early drove the enemy back with heavy loss, and pursued about two hundred yards beyond the line of battle, when he was recalled to the position on the railroad, where Thomas, Pender, and Archer had firmly held their ground against every attack. While the battle was raging on Jackson's left, Hood and Evans were ordered by Longstreet to advance, but, before the order could be obeyed, Hood was himself attacked, and his command became at once warmly engaged. The enemy was repulsed by Hood after a severe contest, and fell back, closely followed by our troops.

The battle continued until 9 P.M., the foe retreating until he reached a strong position, which he held with a large force. Our troops remained in their advanced position until early next morning, when they were withdrawn to their first line. One piece of artillery, several stands of colors, and a number of prisoners were captured. Our loss was severe. On the morning of the 30th the enemy again advanced, and skirmishing began along the line. The troops of Jackson and Longstreet maintained their position of the previous day. At noon the firing of the batteries ceased, and all was quiet for some hours.

About 3 P.M. the enemy, having massed his troops in front of General Jackson, advanced against his position in strong force. His front line pushed forward until it was engaged at close quarters by Jackson's troops, when its progress was cheeked, and a fierce and bloody struggle ensued. A second and third line of great strength moved up to support the first, but in doing so came within easy range of a position a little in advance of Longstreet's left. He immediately ordered up two batteries, and, two others being thrown forward about the same time by Colonel S. D. Lee, the supporting lines were broken, and fell back in confusion under their well-directed and destructive fire. Their repeated efforts to rally were unavailing, and Jackson's troops, being thus relieved from the pressure of overwhelming numbers, began to press steadily forward, driving everything before them. The enemy retreated in confusion, suffering severely from our artillery, which advanced as he retired. General Longstreet, anticipating the order for a general advance, now threw his whole command against the center and left. The whole line swept steadily on, driving the opponents with great carnage from each successive position, until 10 P.M., when darkness put an end to the battle and the pursuit.

The obscurity of the night and the uncertainty of the fords of Bull Run rendered it necessary to suspend operations until morning, when the cavalry, being pushed forward, discovered that the retreat had continued to the strong position of Centreville, about four miles beyond Bull Run. The prevalence of a heavy rain, which began during the night, threatened to render Bull Bun impassable, and to impede our movements. Longstreet remained on the battle-field to engage attention and to protect parties for the burial of the dead and the removal of the wounded, while Jackson proceeded by Sudley's Ford to the Little River turnpike to turn the enemy's right, and intercept his retreat to Washington. Jackson's progress was retarded by the inclemency of the weather and the fatigue of his troops. He reached the turnpike in the evening, and the next day (September 1st) advanced by that road toward Fairfax Court-House. The enemy in the mean time was falling back rapidly toward Washington, and had thrown a strong force to Germantown, on the Little River turnpike, to cover his line of retreat from Centreville. The advance of Jackson encountered him at Ox Hill, near Germantown, about 5 P.M. Line of battle was at once formed, and two brigades were thrown forward to attack and ascertain the strength of the position. A cold and drenching rain-storm drove in the faces of our troops as they advanced and gallantly engaged. They were subsequently supported, and the conflict was obstinately maintained until dark, when the enemy retreated, having lost two general officers, one of whom— Major-General Kearney—was left dead on the field. Longstreet's command arrived after the action was over, and the next morning it was found that the retreat had been so rapid that the attempt to intercept was abandoned. The proximity of the fortifications around Alexandria and Washington was enough to prevent further pursuit. Our army rested during the 2d near Chantilly, the retreating foe being followed only by our cavalry, who continued to harass him until he reached the shelter of his intrenchments.

In the series of engagements on the plains of Manassas more than seven thousand prisoners were taken, in addition to about two thousand wounded left in our hands. Thirty pieces of artillery, upward of twenty thousand stand of small-arms, numerous colors, and a large amount of stores, besides those taken by General Jackson at Manassas Junction, were captured.

Major-General Pope in his report says:

"The whole force that I had at Centreville, as reported to me by the corps commanders, on the morning of the 1st of September, was as follows: McDowell's corps, 10,000 men; Sigel's corps, about 7,000; Heintzelman's corps, about 6,000; Reno's, 6,000; Banks's, 5,000; Sumner's, 11,000; Porter's, 10,000; Franklin's, 8,000—in all, 63,000 men. . . . The small fraction of 20,500 men was all of the 91,000 veteran troops from Harrison's landing which ever drew trigger under my command."

Our losses in the engagement at Manassas Plains were considerable. The number killed was 1,090; wounded, 6,154—total, 7,244. The loss of the enemy in killed, wounded, and missing was estimated between 15,000 and 20,000. The strength of our army in July and September is stated on a preceding page.

CHAPTER XXXV.

Return of the Enemy to Washington.—War transferred to the Frontier.—Condition of Maryland.—Crossing the Potomac.— Evacuation of Martinsburg.—Advance into Maryland.—Large Force of the Enemy.—Resistance at Boonesboro.—Surrender of Harper's Ferry.—Our Forces reach Sharpsburg.—Letter of the President to General Lee.—Address of General Lee to the People.—Position of our Forces at Sharpsburg.—Battle of Sharpsburg.—Our Strength.— Forces withdrawn.—Casualties.

The enemy having retired to the protection of the fortifications around Washington and Alexandria, Lee's army marched, on September 3d, toward Leesburg. The armies of Generals McClellan and Pope had now been brought back to the point from which they set out on the campaign of the spring and summer. The objects of those campaigns had been frustrated, and the hostile designs against the coast of North Carolina and in western Virginia, thwarted by the withdrawal of the main body of the forces from those regions.

Northeastern Virginia was freed from the presence of the invader. His forces had withdrawn to the intrenchments of Washington. Soon after the arrival of our army at Leesburg, information was received that the hostile troops which had occupied Winchester had retired to Harper's Ferry. The war was thus transferred from the interior to the frontier, and the supplies of rich and productive districts were made accessible to our army. To prolong a state of affairs, in every way desirable, and not to permit the season for active operations to pass without endeavoring to impose further check on our assailant, the best course appeared to be the transfer of our army into Maryland. Although not properly equipped for invasion, lacking much of the material of war, and deficient in transportation, the troops poorly provided with clothing, and thousands of them without shoes, it was yet believed to be strong enough to detain the opposing army upon the northern frontier until the approach of winter should render its advance into Virginia difficult, if not impracticable.

The condition of Maryland encouraged the belief that the presence of our army, though numerically inferior to that of the North, would induce the Washington Government to retain all its available force to provide against contingencies which its conduct toward the people of that State gave reason to apprehend. At the same time it was hoped that military success might afford us an opportunity to aid the citizens of Maryland in any efforts they should be disposed to make to recover their liberty. The difficulties that surrounded them were fully appreciated, and we expected to derive more assistance in the attainment of our object from the just fears of the Washington Government than from any active demonstration on the part of the people of Maryland, unless success should enable us to give them assurance of continued protection. Influenced by these considerations, the army was put in motion.

It was decided to cross the Potomac east of the Blue Ridge, in order, by threatening Washington and Baltimore, to cause the enemy to withdraw from the south bank, where his presence endangered our communications and the safety of those engaged in the removal of our wounded and the captured property from the late battle-field. Having accomplished this result, it was proposed to move the army into western Maryland, establish our communication with Richmond through the Valley of the Shenandoah, and, by threatening Pennsylvania, induce the enemy to withdraw from our territory for the protection of his own.

General D. H. Hill's division, being in advance, crossed the Potomac, between September 4th and 7th, at the ford near Leesburg, and encamped in the vicinity of Frederick. It had been supposed that this advance would lead to the evacuation of Martinsburg and Harper's Ferry, thus opening the line of communication through the Shenandoah Valley. This not having occurred, it became necessary to dislodge the garrisons from those positions before concentrating the army west of the mountains. For this purpose General Jackson marched very rapidly, crossed the Potomac near Williamsport on the 11th, sent Hill's division directly to Martinsburg, and disposed of the rest of the command so as to cut off retreat to the westward. The enemy evacuated Martinsburg and retired to Harper's Ferry on the night of the 11th, and Jackson entered the former on the 12th. Meanwhile General McLaws had been ordered to seize Maryland Heights on the north side of the Potomac, opposite Harper's Ferry, and General Walker took possession of Loudon Heights, on the east side of the Shenandoah, where it unites with the Potomac, and was in readiness to open fire upon Harper's Ferry. But McLaws found the heights in possession of the foe, with infantry and artillery, protected by intrenchments. On the 13th he assailed the works, and after a spirited contest they were carried; the troops made good their retreat to Harper's Ferry, and on the next day its investment was complete.

At the same time that the march of these troops upon Harper's Ferry began, the remainder of General Longstreet's command and the division of D. H. Hill crossed the South Mountain and moved toward Boonsboro. General Stuart with the cavalry remained east of the mountains to observe the enemy and retard his advance. Longstreet continued his march to Hagerstown, and Hill halted near Boonsboro to support the cavalry and to prevent the force invested at Harper's

Ferry from escaping through Pleasant Valley. The advance of the hostile army was then so slow as to justify the belief that the reduction of Harper's Ferry would be accomplished and our troops concentrated before they would be called upon to meet the foe. In that event it had not been intended to oppose his passage through South Mountain, as it was desired to engage him as far as possible from his base. But a copy of Lee's order, directing the movement of the army from Frederick, happening to fall into the hands of McClellan, disclosed to him the disposition of our forces. He immediately began to push forward rapidly, and on the afternoon of the 13th was reported as approaching the pass in South Mountain on the Boonsboro and Frederick road. General Stuart's cavalry impeded his progress, and time was thus gained for preparations to oppose his advance.

In Taylor's "Four Years with General Lee" some facts relative to this lost order are stated. An order of battle was issued, stating in detail the position and duly assigned to each command of the army:

"It was the custom to send copies of such orders, marked 'confidential,' to the commanders of separate corps or divisions only, and to place the address of such separate commander in the bottom left-hand corner of the sheet containing the order. General D. H. Hill was in command of a division which had not been attached to nor incorporated with either of the two wings of the Army of Northern Virginia. A copy of the order was, therefore, in the usual course, sent to him. After the evacuation of Frederick City by our forces, a copy of General Lee's order was found in a deserted camp by a soldier, and was soon in the hands of General McClellan. The copy of the order, it was stated at the time, was addressed to 'General D. H Hill, commanding division.' General Hill has assured me that it could not have been his copy, because he still has the original order received by him in his possession." [62]

General D. H. Hill guarded the Boonsboro Gap, and Longstreet was ordered to support him, in order to prevent a force from penetrating the mountains at this point, in the rear of McLaws, so as to relieve the garrison at Harper's Ferry. Early on the 14th a large body of the enemy attempted to force its way to the rear of the position held by Hill, by a road south of the Boonsboro and Frederick turnpike. The small command of Hill, with Garland's brigade, repelled the repeated assaults of the army, and held it in check for five hours. Longstreet, leaving a brigade at Hagerstown, hurried to the assistance of Hill, and reached the scene of action between 3 and 4 P.M. The battle continued with great animation until night. On the south of the turnpike the assailant was driven back some distance, and his attack on the center repulsed with loss. Darkness put an end to the contest.

The effort to force the pass of the mountain had failed, but it was manifest that without reënforcements Lee could not hazard a renewal of the engagement; for McClellan, by his great superiority of numbers, could easily turn either flank. Information was also received that another large body of his troops had, during the afternoon, forced its way through Crampton Gap, only five miles in rear of McLaws. Under these circumstances it was determined to retire to Sharpsburg, where we would be on the flank and rear of the enemy should he move against

McLaws, and where we could more readily unite with the rest of our army. This movement, skillfully and efficiently covered by the cavalry brigade of General Fitzhugh Lee, was accomplished without interruption. The advance of McClellan's army did not appear on the west side of the pass at Boonsboro until about 8 A.M. on the following morning.

The resistance that our troops had offered there secured sufficient time to enable General Jackson to complete the reduction of Harper's Ferry. The attack on the garrison began at dawn on the 15th. A rapid and vigorous fire was opened by the batteries of General Jackson, in conjunction with those on Maryland and Loudon Heights. In about two hours, the garrison, consisting of more than eleven thousand men, surrendered. Seventy-three pieces of artillery, about thirteen thousand small-arms, and a large quantity of military stores fell into our hands. General A. P. Hill remained formally to receive the surrender of the troops and to secure the captured property.

The commands of Longstreet and D. H. Hill reached Sharpsburg on the morning of the 15th. General Jackson arrived early on the 16th, and General J. G. Walker came up in the afternoon. The movements of General McLaws were embarrassed by the presence of the enemy in Crampton Gap. He retained his position until the 14th, when, finding that he was not to be attacked, he gradually withdrew his command toward the Potomac, then crossed at Harper's Ferry, and marched by way of Shepardstown. His progress was slow, and he did not reach the battle-field at Sharpsburg until some time after the engagement of the 17th began.

At this time the letter, from which the following extract is made, was addressed by me to General R. E. Lee, commanding our forces in Maryland:

"SIR: It is deemed proper that you should, in accordance with established usage, announce, by proclamation, to the people of Maryland, the motives and purposes of your presence among them at the head of an invading army; and you are instructed in such proclamation to make known," etc.

In obedience to instructions, General Lee issued the following address:

"HEADQUARTERS, ARMY OF NORTHERN VIRGINIA, NEAR FREDERICK,
September 8, 1862.

"TO THE PEOPLE OF MARYLAND: It is right that you should know the purpose that has brought the army under my command within the limits of your State, so far as that purpose concerns yourselves.

"The people of the Confederate States have long watched, with the deepest sympathy, the wrongs and outrages that have been inflicted upon the citizens of a Commonwealth allied to the States of the South by the strongest social, political, and commercial ties, and reduced to the condition of a conquered province.

"Under the pretense of supporting the Constitution, but in violation of its most valuable provisions, your citizens have been arrested and imprisoned upon no charge, and contrary to the forms of law.

"A faithful and manly protest against this outrage, made by a venerable and illustrious Marylander, to whom in his better days no citizen appealed for right in vain, was treated with scorn and contempt.

"The government of your chief city has been usurped by armed strangers; your Legislature has been dissolved by the unlawful arrest of its members; freedom of the press and of speech has been suppressed; words have been declared offenses by an arbitrary decree of the Federal Executive; and citizens ordered to be tried by military commissions for what they may dare to speak.

"Believing that the people of Maryland possess a spirit too lofty to submit to such a Government, the people of the South have long wished to aid yon in throwing off this foreign yoke, to enable you again to enjoy the inalienable rights of freemen, and restore the independence and sovereignty of your State.

"In obedience to this wish, our army has come among you, and is prepared to assist yon with the power of its arms in regaining the rights of which you have been so unjustly despoiled.

"This, citizens of Maryland, is our mission, so far as yon are concerned. No restraint upon your free-will is intended; no intimidation will be allowed within the limits of this army at least. Marylanders shall once more enjoy their ancient freedom of thought and speech. We know no enemies among you, and will protect all of you in every opinion.

"It is for you to decide your destiny freely and without constraint. This army will respect your choice, whatever it may be; and while the Southern people will rejoice to welcome you to your natural position among them, they will only welcome you when you come of your own free will.

"R. E. LEE, *General commanding.*"

The commands of Longstreet and D. H. Hill, on their arrival at Sharpsburg, were placed in position along the range of hills between the town and the Antietam, nearly parallel to the course of that stream, Longstreet on the right of the road to Boonsboro and Hill on the left. The advance of the enemy was delayed by the determined opposition he encountered from Fitzhugh Lee's cavalry, and he did not appear on the opposite side of the Antietam until about 2 P.M. During the afternoon the batteries on each side were partially engaged. On the 16th the artillery-fire became warm, and continued throughout the day. A column crossed the Antietam beyond the reach of our batteries and menaced our left. In anticipation of this movement Hood's two brigades had been transferred from the right and posted between D. H. Hill and the Hagerstown road. General Jackson was now directed to take position on Hood's left, and formed his line with his right resting on the Hagerstown road and his left extending toward the Potomac, protected by General Stuart with the cavalry and horse-artillery. General Walker with his two brigades was stationed on Longstreet's right. As evening approached, the enemy fired more vigorously with his artillery and bore down heavily with his infantry upon Hood, but the attack was gallantly repulsed. At 10 P.M. Hood's troops were relieved by the brigades of Lawton and Trimble, of Ewell's division, commanded by General Lawton.

Jackson's own division, under General J. K. Jones, was on Lawton's left, supported by the remaining brigades of Ewell.

At early dawn on the 17th his artillery opened vigorously from both sides of the Antietam, the heaviest fire being directed against our left. Under cover of this fire a large force of infantry attacked General Jackson's division. They were met by his troops with the utmost resolution, and for several hours the conflict raged with intense fury and alternate success. Our troops advanced with great spirit; the enemy's lines were repeatedly broken and forced to retire. Fresh troops, however, soon replaced those that were beaten, and Jackson's men were in turn compelled to fall back. Nearly all the field officers, with a large proportion of the men, were killed or wounded. Our troops slowly yielded to overwhelming numbers, and fell back, obstinately disputing every point. General Early, in command of Ewell's division, was ordered with his brigade to take the place of Jackson's division, most of which was withdrawn, its ammunition being nearly exhausted and its numbers much reduced. The battle now raged with great violence, the small commands under Hood and Early holding their ground against many times their own infantry force and under a tremendous fire of artillery. Hood was reënforced; then the enemy's lines were broken and driven back, but fresh numbers advanced to their support, and they began to gain ground. The desperate resistance they encountered, however, delayed their progress until the troops of McLaws arrived, and those of General J. G. Walker could be brought from the right. Hood's brigade, though it had suffered extraordinary loss, only withdrew to replenish their ammunition, their supply being entirely exhausted. They were relieved by Walker's command, who immediately attacked vigorously, driving his combatant back with much slaughter. Upon the arrival of the reënforcements under McLaws, General Early attacked resolutely the large force opposed to him. McLaws advanced at the same time, and the forces before them were driven back in confusion, closely followed by our troops beyond the position occupied at the beginning of the engagement.

The attack on our left was speedily followed by one in heavy force on the center. This was met by part of Walker's division and the brigades of G. B. Anderson and Rodes, of D. H. Hill's command, assisted by a few pieces of artillery. General R, H. Anderson's division came to Hill's support, and formed in rear of his line. At this time, by a mistake of orders, Rodes's brigade was withdrawn from its position; during the absence of that command a column pressed through the gap thus created, and G. B. Anderson's brigade was broken and retired. The heavy masses moved forward, being opposed only by four pieces of artillery, supported by a few hundred of our men belonging to different brigades rallied by Hill and other officers, and parts of Walker's and B. H. Anderson's commands. Colonel Cooke, with the Twenty-seventh North Carolina Regiment, stood boldly in line without a cartridge. The firm front presented by this small force and the well-directed fire of the artillery checked the progress of the enemy, and in about an hour and a half he retired. Another attack was made soon afterward a little farther to the right, but was repulsed by Miller's guns, of the Washington Artillery, which continued to hold the ground until the close of the engagement, supported by a part of R. H. Anderson's troops. The corps designated the Washington Artillery was composed of Louisiana batteries, organized at New Orleans in the beginning of the war, under Colonel I. B.

Walton. It was distinguished by its services in the first great battle of Manassas, and in nearly every important conflict, as well of the army of Virginia as that of Tennessee, to the close of the war. In the official reports and in the traditions of both armies the names of the batteries of the Washington Artillery have frequent and honorable mention.

While the attack on the center and left was in progress, repeated efforts were made to force the passage of the bridge over the Antietam, opposite the right wing of Longstreet, commanded by Brigadier-General D. R. Jones. The bridge was defended by General Toombs with two regiments of his brigade and the batteries of General Jones. This small command repulsed five different assaults, made by a greatly superior force. In the afternoon the enemy, in large numbers, having passed the stream, advanced against General Jones, who held the ridge with less than two thousand men. After a determined and brave resistance, he was forced to give way, and the summit was gained. General A. P. Hill, having arrived from Harper's Ferry, was now ordered to reënforce General Jones. He moved to his support and attacked the force now flushed with success. Hill's batteries were thrown forward and united their fire with those of Jones, and one of D. H. Hill's also opened with good effect from the left of the Boonsboro road. The progress of the enemy was immediately arrested, and his line began to waver. At this moment General Jones ordered Toombs to charge the flank, while Archer, supported by Branch and Gregg, moved on the front of the enemy's line. After a brief resistance, he broke and retreated in confusion toward the Antietam, pursued by the troops of Hill and Jones, until he reached the protection of the batteries on the opposite side of the river.

It was now nearly dark, and McClellan had massed a number of batteries to sweep the approach to the Antietam, on the opposite side of which the corps of General Porter, which had not been engaged, now appeared to dispute our advance. Our troops were much exhausted, and greatly reduced in numbers by fatigue and the casualties of battle. Under these circumstances it was deemed injudicious to push our advantage further in the face of these fresh troops added to an army previously much exceeding the number of our own. Ours were accordingly recalled, and formed on the line originally held by General Jones. The repulse on the right ended the engagement, a protracted and sanguinary conflict in which every effort to dislodge us from our position had been defeated with severe loss.

This great battle was fought by less than forty thousand men on our side, all of whom had undergone the greatest labors and hardships in the field and on the march. Nothing could surpass the determined valor with which they met the large army of the enemy, fully supplied and equipped, and the result reflected the highest credit on the officers and men engaged.[63]

On the 18th our forces occupied the position of the preceding day, except in the center, where our line was drawn in about two hundred yards, our ranks were increased by the arrival of a number of troops, who had not been engaged the day before, and, though still too weak to assume the offensive, Lee waited without apprehension a renewal of the attack. The day passed without any hostile demonstration. During the night of the 18th our army was withdrawn to the south side of the Potomac, crossing near Shepardstown, without loss or molestation. The enemy advanced on the next morning, but was held in check by General Fitzhugh Lee with his cavalry. The condition of our troops now demanded repose, and the army marched to the Opequan, near Martinsburg, where it remained several days, and then moved to the vicinity of Bunker Hill and Winchester. General McClellan seemed to be concentrating in and near Harper's Ferry, but made no forward movement.

The contest on our left in this battle was the most violent. This and the deprivation of our men are very forcibly shown in the following account of Major-General Hood:[64]

"On the morning of the 15th my forces were again in motion. My troops at this period were sorely in need of shoes, clothing, and food. We had had issued to us no meat for several days, and little or no bread; the men had been forced to subsist principally on green corn and green apples. Nevertheless, they were in high spirits and defiant as we contended with the advanced guard of McClellan on the 15th and forenoon of the 16th. During the afternoon of this day I was ordered, after great fatigue and hunger endured by my soldiers, to take position near the Hagerstown turnpike, in open field in front of the Dunkard church. General Hooker's corps crossed the Antietam, swung round with its front on the pike, and about an hour before sunset encountered my division. I had stationed one or two batteries on a hillock in a meadow, near the edge of a corn-field, and just by the pike. The Texas Brigade had been disposed on the left, and that of Law on the right. We opened fire, and a spirited action ensued, which lasted till a late hour in the night. When the firing had in a great measure ceased, we were so close to the enemy that we could distinctly hear him massing his heavy bodies in our immediate front.

"The extreme suffering of my troops for want of food induced me to ride back to General Lee, and request him to send two or more brigades to our relief, at least for the night, in order that the soldiers might have a chance to cook their meager rations. He said that he would cheerfully do so, but he knew of no command that could be spared for the purpose; he, however, suggested that I should see General Jackson, and endeavor to obtain assistance from him. After riding a long time in search of the latter, I finally discovered him alone, lying upon the ground asleep by the root of a tree. I aroused him, and made known the half-starved condition of my troops; he immediately ordered Lawton's, Trimble's, and Hays's brigades to our relief. He exacted of me, however, a promise that I would come to the support of these forces the moment I was called upon. I quickly rode off in search of my wagons that the men might prepare and cook their flour, as we were still without meat; unfortunately, the night was then far advanced, and, although every effort was made in the darkness to get the wagons forward, dawn of the morning of the 17th broke upon us before many of the men had time to do more than prepare the dough. Soon, thereafter, an officer of Lawton's staff dashed up to me, saying, 'General Lawton sends his compliments, with the request that you come at once to his support.' 'To arms!' was instantly sounded, and quite a large number of my brave soldiers were again obliged to march to the front, leaving their uncooked rations in camp.

"Not far distant in our front were drawn up, in close array, heavy columns of Federal infantry; not leas than two corps were in sight to oppose my small command, numbering approximately two thousand effectives. However, with the trusty Law on my right, in the edge of the wood, and the gallant Colonel Wafford in command of the Texas Brigade on the left, near the pike, we moved forward to the assault. Notwithstanding the overwhelming odds of over ten to one against us, we drove the enemy from the wood and corn-field back upon his reserves, and forced him to abandon his guns on our left. This most deadly combat raged till our last round of ammunition was expended. The First Texas Regiment had lost in the corn-field fully two thirds of its number; and whole ranks of brave men, whose deeds were unrecorded save in the hearts of loved ones at home, were mowed down in heaps to the right and left. Never before was I so continually troubled with fear that my horse would further injure some wounded fellow-soldier lying helpless upon the ground. Our right flank, during this short but seemingly long space of time, was toward the main line of the Federals, and, after several ineffectual efforts to procure reënforcements and our last shot had been fired, I ordered my troops back to Dunkard church for the same reason which had previously compelled Lawton, Hays, and Trimble to retire (a want of cartridges). Upon the arrival of McLaws's division we marched to the rear, renewed our supply of ammunition, and returned to our position in the wood near the church, which ground we held till a late hour in the afternoon, when we moved somewhat farther to the right and bivouacked for the night. With the close of this bloody day ceased the hardest-fought battle of the war."

The following account of Colonel Taylor, in his "Four Years with General Lee," is more comprehensive, embracing the other forces besides Hood's brigade:

"On the afternoon of the 16th, General McClellan directed an attack by Hooker's corps on the Confederate left—Hood's two brigades—and during the whole of the 17th the battle was waged, with varying intensity, along the entire line. When the issue was first joined, on the afternoon of the 16th, General Lee had with him less than eighteen thousand men, consisting of the commands of Longstreet and D. H. Hill, the two divisions of Jackson, and two brigades under Walker. Couriers were sent to the rear to hurry up the divisions of A. P. Hill, Anderson, and McLaws, hastening from Harper's Ferry, and these several commands, as they reached the front at intervals during the day, on the 17th, were immediately deployed and put to work. Every man was engaged. We had no reserve.

"The fighting was heaviest and most continuous on the Confederate left. It is established by Federal evidence that the three corps of Hooker, Mansfield, and Sumner were completely shattered in the repeated but fruitless efforts to turn this flank, and two of these corps were rendered useless for further aggressive movements. The aggregate strength of the attacking column at this point reached forty thousand men, not counting the two divisions of Franklin's corps, sent at a late hour in the day to rescue the Federal right from the impending danger of being itself destroyed; while the Confederates, from first to last, had less than fourteen thousand men on this flank, consisting of Jackson's two divisions, McLaws's division, and the two small divisions, of two brigades each, under Hood and Walker, with which to resist their fierce and oft-repeated assaults. The disproportion in the center and on our right was as great as, or even more decided than, on our left."

In the "Report of Committee on the Conduct of the War," Part I, p. 368, General Sumner testifies as follows:

"General Hooker's corps was dispersed; there is no question about that. I sent one of my staff-officers to find where they were, and General Rickets, the only officer he could find, said that he could not raise three hundred men of the corps. There were troops lying down on the left, which I took to belong to Mansfield's command. In the mean time General Mansfield had been killed, and a portion of his corps had also been thrown into confusion."

The testimony of General McClellan, in the same report, Part I, p. 441, is to the same effect:

"The next morning (the 18th) I found that our loss had been so great, and there was so much disorganization in name of the commands, that I did not consider it proper to renew the attack that day, especially as I was sure of the arrival that day of two fresh divisions, amounting to about fifteen thousand men. As an instance of the condition of some of the troops that morning, I happen to recollect the returns of the First Corps. General Hooker's, made on the morning of the 18th, by which there were thirty-five hundred men reported present for duty. Four days after that, the returns of the same corps showed thirteen thousand five hundred."

On the night of the 19th our forces crossed the Potomac, and some brigades of the enemy followed. In the morning General A. P. Hill, who commanded the rear-guard, was ordered to drive them back. Having disposed his forces, an attack was made, and, as the foe massed in front of General Pender's brigade and endeavored to turn his flank, General Hill says, in his report:

"A simultaneous daring charge was made, and the enemy driven pell-mell into the river. Then commenced the most terrible slaughter that this war has yet witnessed. The broad surface of the Potomac was blue with the floating bodies of our foe. But few escaped to tell the tale. By their own account, they lost three thousand men killed and drowned from one brigade alone. Some two hundred prisoners were taken."

General McClellan states, in his official report, that he had in this battle, in action, 87,164 men of all arms.

The official reports of the commanding officers of our forces, made at the time, show our total effective infantry to have been 27,255. The estimate made for the cavalry and artillery, which is rather excessive, is 8,000. This would make General Lee's entire strength 35,255.

The official return of the Army of Northern Virginia, on September 22, 1862, after its return to Virginia, and when the stragglers had rejoined their commands, shows present for duty, 36,187 infantry and artillery; the cavalry, of which there is no report, would perhaps increase these figures to 40,000 of all arms.[65]

The return of the United States Army of the Potomac on September 20, 1862, shows present for duty, at that date, of the commands that participated in the battle of Sharpsburg, 85,930 of all arms.[66]

The loss of the enemy at Boonsboro and Sharpsburg was 14,794.[67]

[Footnote 62: To these remarks Colonel W. H. Taylor adds the following note: "Colonel Venable, one of my associates on the staff of General Lee, says in regard to this matter: 'This is very easily explained. One copy was sent directly to Hill from headquarters. General Jackson sent him a copy, as he regarded Hill in his command. It is Jackson's copy, in his own handwriting, which General Hill has. The other was undoubtedly left carelessly by some one at Hill's quarters." says General McClellan, "Upon learning the contents of this order, I at once gave orders for a vigorous pursuit."—(General McClellan's testimony, "Report on the Conduct of the War," Part I, p. 440.)]

[Footnote 63: Report of General R. E. Lee.]

[Footnote 64: "Advance and Retreat," by J. B. Hood, p. 41.]

[Footnote 65: Taylor's "Four Years with General Lee."]

[Footnote 66: Official return from Adjutant-General's office, United States Army. "Report of Committee on Conduct of the War," Part I, p. 492.]

[Footnote 67: Ibid., p. 42.]

CHAPTER XXXVI.

Efforts of the Enemy to obtain our Cotton.—Demands of European Manufacturers.—Thousands of Operatives resorting to the Poor-Rates.—Complaint of her Majesty's Secretary of State.—Letter of Mr. Seward.—Promise to open all the Channels of Commerce.— Series of measures adopted by the United States.—Act of Congress.— Its Provisions.—Its Operation.—Unconstitutional Measures.— President Lincoln an Accomplice.—Not authorized by a State of War.—Case before Chief-Justice Taney.—His Decision.—Expeditions sent by the United States Government to seize Localities.—An Act providing for the Appointment of Special Agents to seize Abandoned or Captured Property.—The Views of General Grant.—Weakening his Strength One Third.—Our Country divided into Districts, and Federal Agents Appointed.—Continued to the Close of the War.

A class of measures was adopted by the Government of the United States, the object of which was practically and effectually to plunder us of a large portion of our crop of cotton, and secure its transportation, to the manufacturers of Europe. The foreign necessity for our cotton is represented in these words of her Majesty's Secretary of State for Foreign Affairs, on May 6, 1862, when speaking of the blockade of our ports:

"Thousands are now obliged to resort to the poor-rates for subsistence, owing to this blockade, yet her Majesty's Government have not sought to take advantage of the obvious imperfections of this blockade, in order to declare it ineffective. They have, to the loss and detriment of the British nation, scrupulously observed the duties of Great Britain to a friendly state."

The severity of the distress thus alluded to was such, both in Great Britain and France, as to produce an intervention of the Governments of those countries to alleviate it. Instead, however, of adopting those measures required in the exercise of justice to the Confederacy, and which would have been sustained by the law of nations, by declaring the blockade "ineffective," as it really was, they sought, through informal applications to Mr. Seward, the Secretary of State for the United States, to obtain opportunities for an increased exportation of cotton from the Confederacy. This is explained by Mr. Seward in a letter to Mr. Adams, the Minister at London, dated July 28, 1862, in which he writes as follows:

"The President has given respectful consideration to the desire informally expressed to me by the Governments of Great Britain and France for some farther relaxation of the blockade in favor of that trade. They are not rejected, but are yet held under consideration, with a view to ascertain more satisfactorily whether they are really necessary, and whether they can be adopted without such serious detriment to our military operations as would render them injurious rather than beneficial to the interests of all concerned."

In the same letter Mr. Seward had previously said:

"We shall speedily open all the channels of commerce, and free them from military embarrassments; and cotton, so much desired by all nations, will flow forth as freely as heretofore. We have ascertained that there are three and a half millions of bales yet remaining in the region where it was produced, though large quantities of it are yet unginned and otherwise unprepared for market. We have instructed the military authorities to favor, so far as they can consistently with the public safety, its preparation for and dispatch to the markets where it is so much wanted."

It has been stated elsewhere in these pages that "it became apparent that by some understanding, express or tacit, Europe had decided to leave the initiative in all actions touching the contest on this continent to the two powers just named (Great Britain and France), who were recognized to have the largest interest involved." By the preceding extracts the demands of the Governments of Great Britain and France for increased facilities, by which to obtain a greater supply of cotton, are evident; at the same time the determination of the

Government of the United States to fulfill those demands is apparent, although it placed itself under the necessity of fitting out some military expeditions against those portions of our territory where it was supposed the foraging for cotton would be likely to meet with the greatest success.

By reference to the series of measures adopted by the Government of the United States to secure possession of our cotton, it will be seen that it was inaugurated as early as July 13, 1861. This was within ten days after the commencement of the first and extra session of Congress, under the Administration of President Lincoln. It is scarcely credible that that Government, at so early a day, foresaw the pressing demand from Europe for cotton which would ensue a year later. Yet it would seem that we must suppose such to have been its foresight, or else conclude that the first of these measures was the inauguration of a grand scheme for the plunder of our cotton-crop, to enrich whomsoever it might concern.

The act of the United States Congress of July 13, 1861, above mentioned, was entitled "An act to provide for the collection of duties on imports, and for other purposes." Under the "other purposes" the important features of the act are contained. Section 5 provides that—

"when said insurgents claim to act under the authority of any State or States, and such claim is not disclaimed or repudiated by the persons exercising the functions of government in such State or States, or in the part or parts thereof in which said combination exists, or such insurrection suppressed by said State or States, then and in such case it may and shall be lawful for the President, by proclamation, to declare that the inhabitants of such State, or any section or part thereof, where such insurrection exists, are in a state of insurrection against the United States, and thereupon all commercial intercourse by and between the same and the citizens thereof and the citizens of the rest of the United States shall cease, and be unlawful, so long as such condition of hostility shall continue; and all goods and chattels, wares and merchandise, coming from said State or section into the other parts of the United States, and all proceeding to such State or section, by land or water, shall, together with the vessel or vehicle conveying the same, or conveying persons to or from such State or section, be forfeited to the United States: *Provided, however*, That the President may, in his discretion, license and permit commercial intercourse with any such part of said State or section, the inhabitants of which are so declared in a state of insurrection, in such articles, and for such time, and by such persons, as he, in his discretion, may think most conducive to the public interest; and such intercourse, so far as by him licensed, shall be conducted and carried on only in pursuance of rules and regulations prescribed by the Secretary of the Treasury. And the Secretary of the Treasury may appoint such officers at places where officers of the customs are not now authorized by law, as may be needed to carry into effect such licenses, rules, and regulations."

It was provided in Section 9 as follows:

"Proceedings on seizures for forfeitures, under this act, may be pursued in the courts of the United States in any district into which the property so seized may be taken, and proceedings instituted."

It will be seen, by reference to the provisions of this section, that the President of the United States was authorized to issue his proclamation, declaring the inhabitants of any of our States, or of a portion of any one of them, to be in insurrection, and thereupon all commercial intercourse became unlawful, and was required to cease, and all goods and chattels, wares and merchandise, on the way to, or from, the State or part of a State, were forfeited to the United States, together with the vessel, or vehicle, in which they were conveyed. Two effects follow this proclamation: first, the cessation of all commercial intercourse with the citizens of the United States; second, the forfeiture of all goods *in transitu*. When this condition has been reached, the act then authorizes the President, in his discretion, by license, to reopen the trade in such articles, and for such time, and by such persons, as he may think most conducive to the public interest. The articles of trade were to be chiefly cotton and tobacco; the time during which it might be continued was evidently so long as it could be used for the purpose in view; the persons were those who would most skillfully advance the end to be accomplished; and the public interest was the collection and transportation of the cotton to the European manufacturers.

One may search the Constitution of the United States in vain to find any grant of power to Congress, by which it could be authorized to pass this act; much less to find any authority conferred upon the President to approve the act, or to justify him in a violation of the oath he had taken to support and maintain the provisions of the Constitution. Congress was guilty of a most flagrant usurpation by the passage of the act, and the President, instead of being a check upon their unconstitutional measures, for which object the veto power was granted to him, became, by his approval, an accomplice in their usurpation. For nothing is more evident than that it is one of the powers reserved to the States to regulate the commercial intercourse between their citizens, to the extent even of the establishment of inspection and quarantine regulations. The former of these is a benefit to commerce, and the latter, in some special cases, only retards it temporarily, to secure the health of a community.

Neither did a state of war authorize the Government of the United States to interfere with the commercial intercourse between the citizens of the States, although under the law of nations it might be so justified with regard to foreign enemies. But this relation it persistently refused to concede to the Confederate States or to their citizens. It constantly asserted that they were its subjects, in a state of insurrection; and, if so, they were equally entitled to the provisions of the Constitution for their protection as well as to its penalties. Still less could the Government make an absolute forfeiture of the goods seized, as has already been shown when treating of the Confiscation Act.

But that a state of war did not enlarge the powers of the Government, as was assumed by this act, was expressly decided by Chief-Justice Taney, in a case that arose under this act. The Secretary of the Treasury issued the regulations for trade, as the act assumed the power to authorize him to do, in the section presented on a previous page. One Carpenter neglected or refused to obtain the permit required, and his goods were seized. He contested the right of seizure, and the Chief-Justice gave a decision at Baltimore, in May, 1863. He said:

"If these regulations had been made directly by Congress, they could not be sustained by a court of justice, whose duty it is to administer the law according to the Constitution of the United States. For from the commencement of the Government to this day it has been admitted on all hands, and repeatedly decided by the Supreme Court, that the United States have no right to interfere with the internal and domestic trade of a State. They have no right to compel it to pass through their custom-houses, nor to tax it. This is so plainly set forth in the Constitution, that it has never been supposed to be open to controversy or question. Undoubtedly, the United States authorities may take proper measures to prevent trade or intercourse with the enemy. But it does not by any means follow that they disregard the limits of all their own powers as prescribed by the Constitution, or the rights and powers reserved to the States and the people.

"A civil war, or any other, does not enlarge the powers of the Federal Government over the States or the people beyond what the compact has given to it in time of war. A state of war does not annul the tenth article of the amendment to the Constitution, which declares that 'the powers not delegated to the United States by the Constitution, nor prohibited by it to the States, are reserved to the States respectively, or to the people.' Nor does a civil war, or any other war, absolve the judicial department from the duty of maintaining with an even and firm hand the rights and powers of the Federal Government, and of the States, and of the citizens, as they are written in the Constitution, which every judge is sworn to support. Upon the whole the Court is of opinion that the regulations in question are illegal and void, and that the seizure of the goods of Carpenter, because he refused to comply with them, can not be sustained. The judgment of the District Court must, therefore, be reversed, and the goods delivered to the claimant, his agent, or proctor."

The proclamation of the President required by the act was issued on August 16, 1861, declaring certain States and parts of States to be in insurrection, etc. Under it some licenses were issued to places in Kentucky and Missouri where the United States forces were located, without any fruitful results. Some strong military and naval expeditions were fitted out to invade us and occupy the ports where cotton and other valuable products were usually shipped. An advance was made up the Cumberland and Tennessee Rivers and down the Mississippi, as has been stated elsewhere. The ports of Beaufort, North Carolina, Port Royal, South Carolina, and New Orleans, Louisiana, were declared by proclamation of the President of the United States to be open for trade under the new system.

Licenses were granted to foreign vessels by United States consuls and to coasting vessels by the Treasury Department, and the blockade was relaxed so far as related to those ports, except as "to persons, property, and information contraband of war." Collectors were appointed at the above-mentioned ports, and a circular was addressed to the foreign Ministers at Washington announcing the reopening of communication with conquered Southern localities.

Again, on March 3, 1863, an act was passed which authorized the Secretary of the Treasury to appoint special agents to receive and collect all abandoned or captured property in any State or portion of a State designated as in insurrection. Under this act a paper division of the whole of our territory was made into five special districts, and to each a special agent was appointed with numerous assistants. Abandoned property was defined to be that which had been deserted by the owners, or that which had been voluntarily abandoned by them to the civil or military authorities of the United States. Property which had been seized or taken from hostile possession by the military or naval forces was also to be turned over to the special agents to be sold. All property not transported in accordance with the Treasury regulations was forfeitable. All expenses incurred in relation to the property were charged upon it.

The views of General Grant on the operation of this system of measures, as tending to retard the success of subjugation, which was the object of the war, were presented to the Secretary of the United States Treasury in a letter dated at Vicksburg on July 21, 1863. He writes:

"My experience in West Tennessee has convinced me that any trade whatever with the rebellious States is weakening to us at least thirty-three per cent. of our force. No matter what restrictions are thrown around trade, if any whatever is allowed, it will be made the means of supplying to the enemy what they want. Restrictions, if lived up to, make trade unprofitable, and hence none but dishonest men go into it. I will venture to say that no honest man has made money in West Tennessee in the last year, while many fortunes have been made there during the time. The people in the Mississippi Valley are now nearly subjugated. Keep trade out for a few months, and I doubt not but that the work of subjugation will be so complete that trade can be opened freely with the States of Arkansas, Louisiana, and Mississippi."

On September 11, 1863, revised regulations were issued by the Secretary which divided the country into thirteen districts, from Wheeling, West Virginia, to Natchez, on the Mississippi, and a complete system of trade and transportation was organized. In December, 1864, new regulations were issued, which authorized the purchase of our products at certain points from any person with bonds furnished by the Treasury. The products were sold, transportation was allowed, and the proceeds were made to constitute a fund for further purchases. A vigorous traffic sprang up under these regulations, which were suspended by an order of General Grant, issued on March 10, 1865, and revoked on April 11th by himself. On April 29, 1865, all restrictions upon internal, domestic, and coastwise commercial intercourse with all the country east of the Mississippi River were discontinued.

CHAPTER XXXVII.

The Enemy crosses the Potomac and concentrates at Warrenton.—Advances upon Fredericksburg.—Its Position.—Our Forces.—The Enemy crosses the Rappahannock.—Attack on General Jackson.—The Main Attack.—Repulse of the Enemy on the Right.—Assaults on the Left.—The Enemy's Columns broke and fled.—Recross the River.—Casualties.—Position during the Winter.—The Enemy again crosses the Rappahannock.—Also crosses at Kelly's Ford.—Converging toward Chancellorsville, to the Rear of our Position.—Inactivity on our Front.—Our Forces concentrate near Chancellorsville and encounter the Enemy.—Position of the Enemy.—Attempt to turn his Right.—The Enemy surprised and driven in the Darkness.—Jackson fired upon and wounded.—Stuart in Command.—Battle renewed.—Fredericksburg reoccupied.—Attack on the Heights.—Repulse of the Enemy.—The Enemy withdraws in the Night.—Our Strength.—Losses.—Death of General Jackson.—Another Account.

About the middle of October, 1862, General McClellan crossed the Potomac east of the Blue Ridge and advanced southward, seizing the passes of the mountains as he progressed. In the latter part of the month he began to incline eastwardly from the mountains, moving in the direction of Warrenton, about which he finally concentrated, his cavalry being thrown forward beyond the Rappahannock in the direction of Culpeper Court-House.

On November 15th the enemy was in motion. The indications were that Fredericksburg was again to be occupied. Sumner's corps had marched in the direction of Falmouth, and gunboats and transports had entered Acquia Creek.

McLaws's and Ransom's divisions were ordered to proceed to that city; and on the 21st it became apparent that the whole army—under General Burnside, who had succeeded General McClellan—was concentrating on the north side of the Rappahannock.

About November 26th Jackson was directed to advance toward Fredericksburg, and, as some of the enemy's gunboats had appeared in the river at Port Royal, and it was possible that an attempt might be made to cross in that vicinity, D. H. Hill's division was stationed near that place, and the rest of Jackson's corps so disposed as to support Hill or Longstreet, as occasion might require. The fords of the Rappahannock above Fredericksburg were closely guarded by our cavalry, and the brigade of General W. H. F. Lee was stationed near Port Royal to watch the river above and below. The interval before the advance of the foe was employed in strengthening our lines, extending from the river about a mile and a half above Fredericksburg along the range of hills in the rear of the city to the Richmond Railroad, As these hills were commanded by the opposite heights, in possession of General Burnside's force, earthworks were constructed on their crest at the most eligible positions for artillery. To prevent gunboats ascending the river, a battery, protected by epaulements, was placed on the bank four miles below the city. The plain of Fredericksburg is so completely commanded by the Stafford Heights, that no effectual opposition could be made to the passage of the river without exposing our troops to the destructive fire of the numerous batteries on the opposite heights. At the same time, the narrowness of the Rappahannock and its winding course presented opportunities for laying down pontoon-bridges at points secure from the fire of our artillery. Our position was therefore selected with a view to resist an advance after crossing, and the river was guarded by detachments of sharpshooters to impede the laying of pontoons until our army could be prepared for action.

Before dawn, on December 11th, General Burnside was in motion. About 2 A.M. he commenced preparations to throw two bridges over the Rappahannock opposite Fredericksburg, and one about a mile and a quarter below, near the mouth of Deep Run. From daybreak until 4 P.M., the troops, sheltered behind the houses on the river-bank, repelled his repeated efforts to lay bridges opposite the town, driving back his working parties and their supports with great slaughter. At the lower point, where there was no such protection, he was successfully resisted until nearly noon, when, being exposed to the severe fire of the batteries on the opposite heights and a superior force of infantry on the river-banks, our troops were withdrawn, and about 1 P.M. the bridge was completed. Soon afterward, one hundred and fifty pieces of artillery opened a furious fire upon the city, causing our troops to retire from the river-bank about 4 P.M. The enemy then crossed in boats, and proceeded rapidly to lay down the bridges. His advance into the town was bravely contested until dark, when our troops were recalled, the necessary time for concentration having been gained.

Brigadier-General William Barksdale, who commanded the force placed in Fredericksburg to resist the crossing, performed that service with his well-known gallantry. The enemy was prevented from constructing bridges, and his attempts to cross in boats, under the cover of artillery and musketry fire, were repelled until late in the afternoon, when General Barksdale was ordered to retire; he had directed Lieutenant-Colonel Fizer, commanding the Seventeenth Mississippi Regiment, of Barksdale's brigade, to select some skillful marksmen, and proceed to check the operations of the pioneers, who had commenced to lay pontoons above the city. Colonel Fizer described to me the novel and bold expedient to which he successfully resorted. He said his sharpshooters were placed in rifle-pits, on the bank opposite to that from which the bridge was started; that his men were instructed to aim only at the bridge-builders. At dawn the workmen came forward to lay the cover on the bridge; fire was opened, some were killed, and the rest of the party driven ashore. Then the enemy's batteries and riflemen opened a heavy fire on his position, when his men would sit down in the rifle-pits and remain quiet until the cannonade ceased. Probably under the supposition that our sharpshooters had been driven off, the workmen would return; our sharpshooters would arise and repeat the lesson lately given. This, he said, with intervals of about an hour, during which a continuous and heavy fire of artillery was kept up, occurred nine times, with the same result—a repulse with severe loss; and that, for twelve hours, every attempt to construct a bridge at that point was defeated. Then, under orders, they withdrew.

During the night and the succeeding day the enemy crossed in large numbers at and below the town, secured from material interruption by a dense fog.

Longstreet's corps constituted our left, with Anderson's division resting on the river, and those of McLaws, Pickett, and Hood extending to the right. A. P. Hill, of Jackson's corps, was posted between Hood's right and Hamilton's Crossing, on the railroad. His front line occupied the edge of a wood. Early and Taliaferro's divisions constituted Jackson's second line, D. H. Hill's division his reserve. His artillery was distributed along his line in the most eligible positions, so as to command the open ground in front.

Shortly after 9 A.M., the partial rising of the mist disclosed a large force moving in line of battle against Jackson. Dense masses appeared in front of A. P. Hill, stretching far up the river in the direction of Fredericksburg. As they advanced, Major Pelham, of Stuart's horse-artillery, opened a rapid and well-directed enfilade fire, which arrested their progress. Four batteries immediately turned upon him, and, upon his withdrawal, the enemy extended his left down the Port Royal road, and his numerous batteries opened with vigor upon Jackson's line. Eliciting no response, his infantry moved forward to seize the position occupied by Lieutenant-Colonel Walker. The latter, reserving the fire of his fourteen pieces until their line had approached within less than eight hundred yards, opened upon it with such destructive effect as to cause it to waver and soon retreat in confusion.

About 1 P.M., the main attack on the right began by a furious cannonade, under cover of which three compact lines of infantry advanced against Hill's front. They were received as before and momentarily checked, but, soon recovering, they pressed forward, until, coming within range of our infantry, the contest became fierce and bloody. Archer and Lane, who occupied the edge of a wood, repulsed those portions of the line immediately in front of them; but, before the interval between these commands could be closed, the assailants pressed through in overwhelming numbers and turned the left of Archer and the right of Lane. Attacked in front and flank, two regiments of the former and a brigade of the latter, after a brave resistance, gave way. Archer held his line until the arrival of reënforcements. Thomas came to the relief of Lane and repulsed the column that had broken his line, and drove it back to the railroad. In the mean time a large force had penetrated the wood as far as Hill's reserve, where it was met by a fire for which it was not unprepared. General Hill says:[68] "The advancing columns of the enemy encountered an obstacle at the military road which they little expected. Gregg's brigade of South Carolinians stood in the way." The advancing Federals were allowed to approach quite near, when that brigade poured a withering fire into the faces of Meade's men, and Early's division from the second line swept forward, and the contest in the woods was short and decisive. The enemy was quickly routed and driven out with very heavy loss, and, though largely reënforced, was pressed back and pursued to the shelter of the railroad embankment. Here he was gallantly charged by the brigades of Hoke and Atkinson, and driven across the plain to his batteries. The attack on Hill's left was repulsed by the artillery on that part of the line, against which a hot fire from twenty-four guns was directed. The repulse of the foe on our right was decisive and the attack was not renewed, but his batteries kept up an active fire at intervals, and sharpshooters skirmished along the front during the afternoon.

While these events were transpiring on our right, the enemy, in formidable numbers, made repeated and desperate assaults upon the left of our line. About

11 A.M., having massed his troops under cover of the houses of Fredericksburg, he moved forward in strong columns to seize Marye's and Willis's Hills. All his batteries on the Stafford Heights directed their fire upon the positions occupied by our artillery, with a view to silence it, and cover the movement of the infantry. Without replying to this furious cannonade, our batteries poured a rapid and destructive fire into the dense lines of the infantry as they advanced to the attack, frequently breaking their ranks, and forcing them to retreat to the shelter of the houses. Six times did he, notwithstanding the havoc inflicted by our batteries, press on with great determination to within one hundred yards of the foot of the hill; but here, encountering the deadly fire of our infantry, his columns were broken, and fled in confusion to the town. The last assault was made shortly before dark. This effort met the fate of those that preceded it, and, when night closed in, his shattered masses had disappeared in the town, leaving the field covered with his dead and wounded.

During the night our lines were strengthened by the construction of earthworks at exposed points, and preparations made to receive the enemy on the next day. The 14th passed, however, without a renewal of the attack. The hostile batteries on both sides of the river played upon our lines at intervals, our own firing but little. On the 15th General Burnside still retained his position, apparently ready for battle, but the day passed as the preceding. But, on the morning of the 16th, it was discovered that he had availed himself of the darkness of the night and the prevalence of a violent storm of wind and rain to recross the river. The town was immediately reoccupied, and our positions on the river-bank resumed.

In the engagement we captured more than 900 prisoners and 9,000 stand of arms. A large quantity of ammunition was found in Fredericksburg, On our side 458 were killed and 3,743 wounded; total, 4,201. The loss of the enemy was 1,152 killed, 9,101 wounded, and 3,234 missing; total, 13,771.

General Burnside testified before the Committee on the Conduct of the War that he "had about 100,000 men on the south side of the river, and every single man of them was under artillery-fire, and about half of them were at different times formed in columns of attack." [69]

Lee's then 20,000 Confederate troops were actively engaged. This number composed about one fourth of the army under General Lee, The returns of the Army of Northern Virginia show that on the 10th of December, 1862, General Lee had present for duty 78,228, and, on December 20th, 75,524 of all arms.[70]

Upon being asked what causes he assigned for the failure of his attack, General Burnside replied to the Committee on the Conduct of the War: "It was found impossible to get the men up to the works. The enemy's fire was too hot for them." [71]

After the battle of Fredericksburg the Army of Northern Virginia remained encamped on the south side of the Rappahannock until the latter part of April, 1863. The Federal army occupied the north side of the river opposite Fredericksburg, extending to the Potomac. Two brigades of Anderson's division—those of Mahone and Posey—were stationed near United States Mine or Bank Mill Ford. The cavalry was distributed on both flanks—Fitzhugh Lee's brigade picketing the Rappahannock above the mouth of the Rapidan and W. H. F. Lee's near Port Royal. General Longstreet, with two divisions of his corps, was detached for service south of James River in February, and did not rejoin the army until after the battle of Chancellorsville. Excepting a cavalry engagement near Kelly's Ford, on March 17th, nothing of interest transpired during this period of inactivity. On April 14, 1863, the enemy's cavalry was concentrating on the upper Rappahannock, but his efforts to establish himself on the south side of the river were successfully resisted. About the 21st, small bodies of infantry appeared at Kelly's Ford and the Rappahannock Bridge; at the same time a demonstration was made opposite Port Royal. These, movements indicated that the army, now commanded by Major-General Hooker, was about to resume active operations. On the 28th, early in the morning, the enemy crossed the river in boats near Fredericksburg, laid a pontoon-bridge, and built another about a mile below. A considerable force crossed on these bridges during the day, and was massed under the high banks of the river, which afforded protection from our artillery, while the batteries on the opposite heights completely commanded the wide plain between our lines and the narrow river. As in the first battle at Fredericksburg, our dispositions were made with a view to resist a direct advance against us. But the indications were that the principal effort would be made in some other quarter. On the 29th it was reported that he had crossed in force near Kelly's Ford, and that a heavy column was moving from Kelly's toward Germania Ford on the Rapidan, and another toward Ely's Ford. The routes they were pursuing, after crossing the Rapidan, converged near Chancellorsville, whence several roads led to the rear of our position at Fredericksburg. General Anderson proceeded to cover these roads on the 29th, but, learning that the enemy had crossed the Rapidan and was approaching in strong force, he retired early on the next morning to the intersection of the Mine and plank roads near Tabernacle Church, and began to intrench himself. His rear-guard, as he left Chancellorsville, was attacked by cavalry, but, being vigorously repulsed, offered no further opposition to his march.

The enemy on our front near Fredericksburg continued inactive, and it was now apparent that the main attack would be made upon our flank and rear. It was therefore determined to leave sufficient troops to hold our lines, and with the main body of the army to give battle to the approaching column. Early's division of Jackson's corps and Barksdale's brigade of McLaws's division, with part of the reserve artillery under General Pendleton, were intrusted with the defense of our position at Fredericksburg, and at midnight on the 30th General McLaws marched with the rest of his command toward Chancellorsville. General Jackson followed at dawn next morning with the remaining divisions of his corps. He reached the position occupied by General Anderson at 8 A.M., and immediately began to make preparations to advance. At 11 A.M. the troops moved forward on the plank and old turnpike roads. The enemy was soon encountered on both roads, and heavy skirmishing with infantry and artillery ensued, our troops pressing steadily forward. A strong attack upon McLaws was repulsed with spirit by Semmes's brigade; and General Wright, by direction of General Anderson, diverging to the left of the plank-road, marched by way of the unfinished railroad from Fredericksburg to Gordonsville and turned the Federal right. His whole line thereupon retreated rapidly, vigorously pursued by our troops until they arrived within about one mile of Chancellorsville. Here the enemy had assumed a position of great natural strength, surrounded on all sides by a dense forest filled with a tangled undergrowth, in the midst of which breastworks of logs had been constructed with trees felled in front so as to form an almost impenetrable abatis. His artillery swept the few narrow roads by which his position could be approached from the front, and commanded the adjacent woods. The left of his line extended from Chancellorsville toward the Rappahannock, covering the Bank Mill Ford, where he communicated with the north bank of the river by a pontoon-bridge. His right stretched westward along the Germania Ford road more than two miles. Darkness was approaching before the strength and extent of his line could be ascertained; and, as the nature of the country rendered it hazardous to attack by night, our troops were halted and formed in line of battle in front of Chancellorsville at right angles to the plank-road, extending on the right to the Mine road, and to the left in the direction of the "Furnace."

It was evident that a direct attack by us would be attended with great difficulty and loss, in view of the strength of his position and his superiority of numbers. It was therefore resolved to endeavor to turn his right flank and gain his rear, leaving a force in front to hold him in check and conceal the movement. The execution of this plan was intrusted to Lieutenant-General Jackson with his three divisions. The commands of Generals McLaws and Anderson, with the exception of Wilcox's brigade which during the night had been ordered hack to Banks's Ford, remained in front of the enemy. Early on the morning of the 2d General Jackson marched by the Furnace and Brock roads, his movement being effectually covered by Fitzhugh Lee's cavalry under General Stuart in person. As the rear of his train was passing the furnace a large force of the enemy advanced from Chancellorsville and attempted its capture, but this advance was arrested. After a long and fatiguing march General Jackson's leading division under General Rodes reached the old turnpike about three miles in rear of Chancellorsville at 4 P.M. As the different divisions arrived, they were formed at right angles to the road— Rodes's in front, Trimble's, under Brigadier-General Colston, in the second, and A. P, Hill's in the third line. At 6 P.M. the advance was ordered. The enemy was taken by surprise, and fled after a brief resistance. General Rodes's men pushed forward with great vigor and enthusiasm, followed closely by the second and third lines. Position after position was carried, the guns captured, and every effort of the foe to rally defeated by the impetuous rush of our troops. In the ardor of pursuit through the thick and tangled woods, the first and second lines at last became mingled and moved on together as one. The fugitives made a stand at a line of breastworks across the road, but the troops of Rodes and Colston dashed over the intrenchments together, and the flight and pursuit were resumed and continued until our advance was arrested by the abatis in front of the line of works near the central position at Chancellorsville. It was now dark, and General Jackson ordered the third line under General Hill to advance to the front and relieve the troops of Rodes and Colston, who were completely blended and in such disorder from their advance through intricate woods and over broken ground that it was necessary to reform them. As Hill's men moved forward, General Jackson, with his staff and escort, returning from the extreme front, met the skirmishers advancing, and in the obscurity of the night were mistaken for the enemy and fired upon. Captain Boswell, chief engineer of the corps, and several others, were killed and a number wounded, among whom was General Jackson, who was borne from the field. The command devolved upon Major-General Hill, whose division under General Heath was advanced to the line of intrenchments which had been reached by Rodes and Colston. A furious fire of artillery was opened upon them, under cover of which infantry advanced to the attack, but were handsomely repulsed. General Hill was soon afterward disabled, and the command was turned over to General Stuart. He immediately proceeded to reconnoiter the ground and make himself acquainted with the disposition of the troops. The darkness of the night and the difficulty of moving through the woods and undergrowth rendered it advisable to defer further operations until morning, and the troops rested on their arms in line of battle.

As soon as the sound of cannon gave notice of Jackson's attack on the enemy's right, the troops in front began to press strongly on the left to prevent reënforcements being sent to the point assailed. They advanced up to the intrenchments, while several batteries played with good effect until prevented by the increasing darkness.

Early on the morning of May 3d General Stuart renewed the attack upon General Hooker, who had strengthened his right wing during the night with additional breastworks, while a large number of guns, protected by intrenchments, were posted so as to sweep the woods through which our troops had to advance. Hill's division was in front, with Colston in the second line, and Rodes in the third. The second and third lines soon advanced to the support of the first, and the whole became hotly engaged. The breastworks at which the attack was suspended on the preceding evening were carried by assault, under a terrible fire of musketry and artillery. In rear of these breastworks was a barricade, from which the enemy was quickly driven. The troops on the left of the plank-road, pressing through the woods, attacked and broke the next line, while those on the right bravely assailed the extensive earthworks behind which General Hooker's artillery was posted. Three times were these works carried, and as often were the brave assailants compelled to abandon them—twice by the retirement of the troops on their left, who fell back after a gallant struggle with superior numbers, and once by a movement of the enemy on their right caused by the advance of General Anderson. The left, being reënforced, finally succeeded in driving back the enemy, and the artillery under Lieutenant-Colonels Carter and Jones, being thrown forward to occupy favorable positions secured by the advance of the infantry, began to play with great precision and effect. Anderson, in the mean time, pressed gallantly forward directly upon Chancellorsville, his right resting upon the plank-road and his left extending around the furnace, while McLaws made a strong demonstration to the right of the road. As the troops advancing upon the enemy's front and right converged upon his central position, Anderson effected a junction with Jackson's corps, and the whole line pressed irresistibly. General Hooker's army was driven from all its fortified positions with heavy loss in killed, wounded, and prisoners, and retreated toward the Rappahannock. By 10 A.M. we were in full possession of the field. The troops, having become somewhat scattered by the difficulties of the ground and the ardor of the contest, were immediately reformed, preparatory to renewing the attack. The enemy had withdrawn to a strong position nearer to the Rappahannock, which he had fortified. His superiority of numbers, the unfavorable nature of the ground, which was densely wooded, and the condition of our troops, after the arduous and sanguinary conflict in which they had been engaged, rendered great caution necessary. Our operations were just completed, when further movements were arrested by intelligence received from Fredericksburg.

Before dawn, on the morning of the 3d, it was known that the enemy had occupied Fredericksburg in large force, and laid down a bridge at the town. He made a demonstration against the extreme right of the force left to hold our lines, which was easily repulsed by General Early. Soon afterward a column moved from Fredericksburg along the river-banks, as if to gain the heights on the extreme left which commanded those immediately in rear of the town. This attempt was foiled. Very soon the enemy advanced in large force against Marye's, and the hills to the right and left of it. Two assaults were gallantly repulsed. After the second, a flag of truce was sent from the town to obtain permission to provide for the wounded. Three heavy lines advanced immediately upon the return of the flag and renewed the attack. They were bravely repulsed on the right and left, but the small force at the foot of Marye's Hill, overpowered by more than ten times their numbers, was captured after an heroic resistance and the hill carried. The success of the enemy enabled him to threaten our communications by moving down the Telegraph road, or to come upon our rear at Chancellorsville by the plank-road. He began to advance on the plank-road, his progress being gallantly disputed by the brigade of General Wilcox, who fell back slowly until he reached Salem Church on the plank-road, about five miles from Fredericksburg.

In this state of affairs in our rear, General Lee led General McLaws with his three brigades to reënforce General Wilcox. He arrived at Salem Church early in the afternoon, where he found General Wilcox in line of battle, with a large force of the enemy—consisting, as was reported, of one army corps and part of another—in his front. The enemy's artillery played vigorously upon our position for some time, when his infantry advanced in three strong lines, the attack being directed mainly against General Wilcox, but partially involving the brigades on his left. The assault was met with the utmost firmness, and after a fierce struggle the first line was repulsed with great slaughter. The second then came forward, but immediately broke under the close and deadly fire which it encountered, and the whole mass fled in confusion to the rear. They were pursued by the brigades of Wilcox and Semmes, which advanced nearly a mile, when they were halted to reform in the presence of the hostile reserve, which now appeared in large force. It being quite dark, General Wilcox deemed it imprudent to push the attack with his small numbers, and retired to his original position, the enemy making no attempt to follow. The next morning General Early advanced along the Telegraph road, and recaptured Marye's and the adjacent hills without difficulty, thus gaining the rear of the enemy's left. In the mean time General Hooker had so strengthened his position near Chancellorsville, that it was deemed inexpedient to assail it with less than our whole force, which had been reduced by the detachment led to Fredericksburg to relieve us from the danger that menaced our rear.

It has been heretofore stated that General Longstreet had been sent with two divisions of Lee's array to coöperate with General French on the south side of the James River, in the capture of Suffolk, the occupation of which by the enemy interrupted our collection of supplies in the eastern counties of North Carolina and Virginia. When the advance of Hooker threatened General Lee's front, instructions were sent to General Longstreet to hasten his return to the army with the large force detached with him. These instructions were repeated with urgent insistence, yet his movements were so delayed that, though the battle of Chancellorsville did not occur until many days after he was expected to join, his force was absent when it occurred. Had he rejoined his command in due time, Lee need not have diminished his force in front of Hooker, so as to delay the renewal of the attack and force him to a precipitate retreat, involving the loss of his artillery and trains. It was accordingly resolved still further to reënforce the troops in front, in order, if possible, to drive Hooker across the Rappahannock. Some delay occurred in getting the troops into position, owing to the broken and irregular nature of the ground, and the difficulty of ascertaining the disposition of the opposing forces. The attack did not begin until 6 P.M., when the enemy's troops were rapidly driven across the plank-road in the direction of the Rappahannock. The speedy approach of darkness prevented General McLaws from perceiving the success of the attack, until the foe began to recross the river a short distance below Banks's Ford, where he had laid one of his pontoon-bridges. His right brigades advanced through the woods in the direction of the firing, but the retreat was so rapid that they could only join in the pursuit. A dense fog settled over the field, increasing the obscurity and rendering great caution necessary to avoid collision between our own troops. Their movements were consequently slow. The next morning it was found that the enemy had made good his escape and removed his bridges. Fredericksburg was evacuated, and our rear no longer threatened. But, as General Hooker had it in his power to recross, it was deemed best to leave a force to hold our lines as before. McLaws and Anderson being directed to return to Chancellorsville, they reached their destination during the afternoon, in the midst of a violent storm, which continued throughout the night and most of the following day. Preparations were made to assail the enemy's works at daylight on the 6th, but, on advancing our skirmishers, it was found that, under cover of the storm and darkness of the night, he had retreated over the river. A detachment was left to guard the battle-field, while the wounded were removed and the captured property collected. The rest of the army returned to its former position.

The loss of the enemy, according to his own statement, was 1,512 killed and 9,518 wounded; total, 11,030. His dead and a large number of wounded were left on the field. About 5,000 prisoners, exclusive of the wounded, were taken, and 13 pieces of artillery, 19,500 stand of arms, 17 colors, and a large quantity of ammunition fell into our hands.

Our loss was much less in killed and wounded than that of the enemy, but of the number was one, a host in himself, Lieutenant-General Jackson, who was wounded, and died on May 10th. Of this great captain, General Lee, in his anguish at his death, justly said, "I have lost my right arm." As an executive officer he had no superior, and war has seldom shown an equal. Too devoted to the cause he served to have any personal motive, he shared the toils, privations, and dangers of his troops when in chief command; and in subordinate position his aim was to understand the purpose of his commander and faithfully to promote its success. He was the complement of Lee; united, they had achieved such results that the public felt secure under their shield. To us his place was never filled.

The official return of the Army of Northern Virginia, on March 31, 1863, shows as present for duty 57,112, of which 6,509 were cavalry and 1,621 reserve artillery. On May 20th, two weeks after the battle, and when Pickett's and Hood's divisions had rejoined the army, the total infantry force numbered but 55,261 effective men, from which, if the strength of Hood's and Pickett's divisions is deducted, there would remain 41,358 as the strength of the commands that participated in the battles of Chancellorsville.[72]

The Army of the Potomac numbered 120,000 men, infantry and artillery, with a body of 12,000 well-equipped cavalry, and an artillery force of four hundred guns.[73]

A brief and forcible account of this battle is given by Taylor:[74]

"A formidable force under General Sedgwick was thrown across the river below Fredericksburg, and made demonstrations of an intention to assail the Confederate front. Meanwhile, with great celerity and secrecy, General Hooker, with the bulk of his array, crossed at the upper fords, and, in an able manner and wonderfully short time, had concentrated four of his seven army corps, numbering fifty-six thousand men, at Chancellorsville, about ten miles west of Fredericksburg. His purpose was now fully developed to General Lee, who, instead of awaiting its further prosecution, immediately determined on the movement the least expected by his opponent. He neither proceeded to make strong his left against an attack from the direction of Chancellorsville nor did he move southward so as to put his army between that of General Hooker and the Confederate capital, but, leaving General Early, with about nine thousand men, to take care of General Sedgwick, he moved with the remainder of his army, numbering forty-eight thousand men, toward Chancellorsville. As soon as the advance of the enemy was encountered, it was attacked with vigor, and very soon the Federal army was on the defensive in its apparently impregnable position. It was not the part of wisdom to attempt to storm this stronghold; but Sedgwick would certainly soon be at work in the rear, and Early, with his inadequate force, could not do more than delay and harass him. It was, therefore, imperatively necessary to strike—to strike boldly, effectively, and at once. There could be no delay. Meanwhile, two more army corps had joined General Hooker, who now had about Chancellorsville ninety-one thousand men—six corps except one division of the Second Corps (Conch's), which had been left with Sedgwick at Fredericksburg. It was a critical position for the Confederate commander, but his confidence in his trusted lieutenant and brave men was such that he did not long hesitate. Encouraged by the counsel and confidence of General Jackson, he determined to still further divide his army; and, while he, with the divisions of Anderson and McLaws, less than fourteen thousand men, should hold the enemy in his front, he would hurl Jackson upon his flank and rear, and crush and crumble him as between the upper and nether millstone. The very boldness of the movement contributed much to insure its success.

"The flank movement of Jackson's wing was attended with extraordinary success. On the afternoon of the 2d of May, he struck such a blow to the enemy on their extreme right as to cause dismay and demoralization to their entire army; this advantage was promptly and vigorously followed up the next day, when Generals Lee and Stuart (the latter then in command of Jackson's wing) joined elbows; and, after most heroic and determined effort, their now united forces finally succeeded in storming and capturing the works of the enemy.

"Meantime Sedgwick had forced Early out of the heights at Fredericksburg, and had advanced toward Chancellorsville, thus threatening the Confederate rear. General Lee, having defeated the greater force and driven it from its stronghold, now gathered up a few of the most available of his victorious brigades and turned upon the lesser. On May 3d Sedgwick's force was encountered near Salem Church, and its further progress checked by General McLaws, with the five brigades detached by General Lee for this service, including Wilcox's, which had been stationed at Banks's Ford. On the next day. General Anderson was sent to reënforce McLaws with three additional brigades. Meanwhile, General Early had connected with these troops, and in the afternoon, so soon as dispositions could be made for attack, Sedgwick's lines were promptly assailed and broken, the main assault being made on the enemy's left by Early's troops. The situation was now a critical one for the Federal lieutenant. Darkness came to his rescue, and on the night of the 4th be crossed to the north side of the river.

"On the 5th General Lee concentrated for another assault on the new line taken up by General Hooker; but on the morning of the 6th it was ascertained that the enemy, in General Lee's language, 'had sought safety beyond the Rappahannock,' and the river flowed again between the hostile hosts."

[Footnote 68: "Reports of the Army of Northern Virginia," vol. ii, p. 463.]

[Footnote 69: "Report of Committee on the Conduct of the War," Part I, p. 656.]

[Footnote 70: Taylor's "Four year with General Lee."]

[Footnote 71: "Report of Committee on the Conduct of the War," Part I, p. 656.]

[Footnote 72: Taylor's "Four Years with General Lee."]

[Footnote 73: Swinton's "Army of the Potomac," p. 269.]

[Footnote 74: "Four Years with General Lee."]

CHAPTER XXXVIII.

Relations with Foreign Nations.—The Public Questions.—Ministers abroad.—Usages of Intercourse between Nations.—Our Action.—

Mistake of European Nations; they follow the Example of England and France.—Different Conditions of the Belligerents.—Injury to the Confederacy with a Single Exception.—These Agreements remained inoperative.—Extent of the Pretended Blockade.—Remonstrances against its Recognition.—Sinking Vessels to block up Harbors.— Every Proscription of Maritime Law violated by the United States Government.—Protest.—Addition made to the Law by Great Britain.— Policy pursued favorable to our Enemies.—Instances.—Mediation proposed by France to Great Britain, and Russian Letter of French Minister.—Reply of Great Britain.—Reply of Russia.—Letter to French Minister at Washington.—Various Offensive Actions of the British Government.—Encouraging to the United States.—Hollow Profession of Neutrality.

The public questions arising out of our foreign relations were too important to be overlooked. At the end of the first year of the war the Confederate States had been recognized by the leading governments of Europe as a belligerent power. This continued unchanged to the close. Mr. Mason became our representative in London, Mr. Slidell in Paris, Mr. Rost in Spain, and Mr. Mann in Belgium. They performed with energy and skill the positions, but were unsuccessful in obtaining our recognition as an independent power.

The usages of intercourse between nations require that official communication be made to friendly powers of all organic changes in the constitution of states. To those who are familiar with the principles upon which the States known as the United States were originally constituted, as well as those upon which the Union was formed, the organic changes made by the secession and confederation of the Southern States are very apparent. But to others an explanation may be necessary. Each of the States was originally declared to be sovereign and independent. In this condition, at a former period, all of those then existing were severally recognized by name by the only one of the powers which had denied their right to independence. This gave to each a recognized national sovereignty. Subsequently they formed a compact of voluntary union, whereby a new organization was constituted, which was made the representative of the individual States in all general intercourse with other nations. So long as the compact continued in force, this agent represented merely the sovereignty of the States. But, when a portion of the States withdrew from the compact and formed a new one under the name of the Confederate States, they had made such organic changes in their Constitution as to require official notice in compliance with the usages of nations.

For this purpose the Provisional Government took early measures for sending to Europe Commissioners charged with the duty of visiting the capitals of the different powers and making arrangements for the opening of more formal diplomatic intercourse. Prior, however, to the arrival abroad of these Commissioners, the Government of the United States had addressed communications to the different Cabinets of Europe, in which it assumed the attitude of being sovereign over the Confederate States, and alleged that these independent States were in rebellion against the remaining States of the Union, and threatened Europe with manifestations of its displeasure if it should treat the Confederate States as having an independent existence. It soon became known that these pretensions were not considered abroad to be as absurd as they were known to be at home; nor had Europe yet learned what reliance was to be placed in the official statements of the Cabinet at Washington. The delegation of power granted by the States to the General Government to represent them in foreign intercourse had led European nations into the grave error of supposing that their separate sovereignty and independence had been merged into one common sovereignty, and had ceased to have a distinct existence. Under the influence of this error, which all appeals to reason and historical fact were vainly used to dispel, our Commissioners were met by the declaration that foreign Governments could not assume to judge between the conflicting representations of the two parties as to the true nature of their previous relations. The Governments of Great Britain and France accordingly signified their determination to confine themselves to recognizing the self-evident fact of the existence of a war, and to maintain a strict neutrality during its progress. Some of the other powers of Europe pursued the same course of policy, and it became apparent that by some understanding, express or tacit, Europe had decided to leave the initiative in all action touching the contest on this continent to the two powers just named, who were recognized to have the largest interests involved, both by reason of proximity to and of the extent of intimacy of their commercial relations with the States engaged in war.

It was manifest that the course of action adopted by Europe, while based on an apparent refusal to determine the question or to side with either party, was, in point of fact, an actual decision against our rights and in favor of the groundless pretensions of the United States. It was a refusal to treat us as an independent government. If we were independent States, the refusal to entertain with us the same international intercourse which was maintained with our enemy was unjust, and was injurious in its effects, whatever might have been the motive which prompted it. Neither was it in accordance with the high moral obligations of that international code, whose chief sanction is the conscience of sovereigns and the public opinion of mankind, that those eminent powers should have declined the performance of a duty peculiarly incumbent on them, from any apprehension of the consequences to themselves. One immediate and necessary result of their declining the responsibility of a decision, which must have been adverse to the extravagant pretensions of the United States, was the prolongation of hostilities to which our enemies were thereby encouraged, and which resulted in scenes of carnage and devastation on this continent and of misery and suffering on the other such as have scarcely a parallel in history. Had those powers promptly admitted our right to be treated as all other independent nations, none can doubt that the moral effect of such action would have been to dispel the pretension under which the United States persisted in their efforts to accomplish our subjugation.

There were other matters in which less than justice was rendered to the Confederacy by "neutral" Europe, and undue advantage conferred on the aggressors in a wicked war. At the inception of hostilities, the inhabitants of the Confederate States were almost exclusively agriculturists; those of the United States were also to a large extent mechanics, merchants, and navigators. We had no commercial marine, while their merchant-vessels covered the ocean. We were without a navy, while they had powerful fleets built by the money we had in full share contributed. The power which they possessed for inflicting injury on our coasts and harbors was thus counterbalanced in some measure by the exposure of their commerce to attack by private armed vessels. It was known to Europe that within a very few years past the United States had peremptorily refused to accede to proposals for the abolition of privateering, on the ground, as alleged by them, that nations owning powerful fleets would thereby obtain undue advantage over those possessing inferior naval force. Yet no sooner was war flagrant between the Confederacy and the United States than the maritime powers of Europe issued orders prohibiting either party from bringing prizes into their ports. This prohibition, directed with apparent impartiality against both belligerents, was in reality effective against, the Confederate States only, for they alone could find a hostile commerce on the ocean. Merely nominal against the United States, the prohibition operated with intense severity on the Confederacy by depriving it of the only means of maintaining its struggle on the ocean against the crashing superiority of naval force possessed by its enemies. The value and efficiency of the weapon which was thus wrested from our grasp by the combined action of "neutral" European powers, in favor of a power which professes openly its intention of ravaging their commerce by privateers in any future war, is strikingly illustrated by the terror inspired among commercial classes of the United States by a single cruiser of the Confederacy. One small steamer, commanded by officers and manned by a crew who were debarred by the closure of neutral ports from the opportunity of causing captured vessels to be condemned in their favor as prizes, sufficed to double the rates of marine insurance in Northern ports, and consign to forced inaction numbers of Northern vessels, in addition to the direct damage inflicted by captures at sea.

But it was especially in relation to the so-called blockade that the policy of European powers was so shaped as to cause the greatest injury to the Confederacy, and to confer signal advantages on the United States. A few words in explanation may here be necessary.

Prior to the year 1856 the principles regulating this subject were to be gathered from the writings of eminent publicists, the decisions of admiralty courts, international treaties, and the usages of nations. The uncertainty and doubt which prevailed in reference to the true rules of maritime law, in time of war, resulting from the discordant and often conflicting principles announced from such varied and independent sources, had become a grievous evil to mankind. Whether a blockade was allowable against a port not invested by land as well as by sea, whether a blockade was valid by sea if the investing fleet was merely sufficient to render ingress to the blockaded port evidently dangerous, or whether it was further required for its legality that it should be sufficient "really to prevent access," and numerous other similar questions, had remained doubtful and undecided.

Animated by the highly honorable desire to put an end "to differences of opinion between neutrals and belligerents, which may occasion serious difficulties and even conflicts" (such was the official language), the five great powers of Europe, together with Sardinia and Turkey, adopted in 1856 the following declaration of principles:

"1. Privateering is and remains abolished.

"2. The neutral flag covers enemy's goods, with the exception of contraband of war.

"3. Neutral goods, with the exception of contraband of war, are not liable to capture under enemy's flag.

"4. Blockades, in order to be binding must be effective, that is to say, maintained by a force sufficient really to prevent access to the coast of the enemy."

Not only did this solemn declaration announce to the world the principles to which the signing powers agreed to conform in future wars, but it contained a clause to which these powers gave immediate effect, and which provided that the states, not parties to the Congress of Paris, should be invited to accede to the declaration. Under this invitation every independent state in Europe yielded its assent—at least, no instance is known to me of a refusal; and the United States, while declining to assent to the proposition which prohibited privateering, declared that the three remaining principles were in entire accordance with their own views of international law.

No instance is known in history of the adoption of rules of public law under circumstances of like solemnity, with like unanimity, and pledging the faith of nations with a sanctity so peculiar.

When, therefore, this Confederacy was formed, and when neutral powers, while deferring action on its demand for admission into the family of nations, recognized it as a belligerent power, Great Britain and France made informal proposals, about the same time, that their own rights as neutrals should be guaranteed by our acceding, as belligerents, to the declaration of principles made by the Congress of Paris. The request was addressed to our sense of justice, and therefore met immediate and favorable response in the resolutions of the Provisional Congress of the 13th of August, 1861, by which all the principles announced by the Congress of Paris were adopted as the guide of our conduct during the war, with the sole exception of that relative to privateering. As the right to make use of privateers was one in which neutral nations had, as to the then existing war, no interest; as it was a right which the United States had refused to abandon, and which they remained at liberty to employ against us; as it was a right of which we were already in actual enjoyment, and which we could not be expected to renounce *flagrante bello* against an adversary possessing an overwhelming superiority of naval forces— it was reserved with entire confidence that neutral nations could not fail to perceive that just reason existed for the reservation. Nor was this confidence misplaced; for the official documents published by the British Government contained the expression of the satisfaction of that Government with the conduct of officials who conducted successfully the delicate transaction confided to their charge.

These solemn declarations of principle, this implied agreement between the Confederacy and the two powers just named, were suffered to remain inoperative against the menaces and outrages on neutral rights committed by the United States with unceasing and progressing arrogance during the whole period of the war. Neutral Europe remained passive when the United States, with a naval force insufficient to blockade effectively the coast of a single State, proclaimed a paper blockade of thousands of miles of coast, extending from the Capes of the Chesapeake to those of Florida, and encircling the Gulf of Mexico from Key West to the mouth of the Rio Grande. Compared with this monstrous pretension of the United States, the blockades known in history under the names of the Berlin and Milan Decrees, and the British Orders in Council, in the years 1806 and 1807, sink into insignificance. Those blockades were justified by the powers that declared them, on the sole ground that they were retaliatory; yet they have since been condemned by the publicists of those very powers as violations of international law. It will be remembered that those blockades evoked angry remonstrances from neutral powers, among which the United States were the most conspicuous, and were in their consequences the chief cause of the war between Great Britain and the United States in 1812; also, that they formed one of the principal motives that led to the declaration of the Congress of Paris in 1856, in the fond hope of imposing an enduring check on the very abuse of maritime power which was renewed by the United States in 1861 and 1862, under circumstances and with features of aggravated wrong without precedent in history.

Repeated and formal remonstrances were made by the Confederate Government to neutral powers against the recognition of that blockade. It was shown by evidence not capable of contradiction, and which was furnished in part by the officials of neutral nations, that the few ports of the Confederacy, before which any naval forces at all were stationed, were invested so inefficiently that hundreds of entries were effected into them after the declaration of the blockade; that our enemies admitted the inefficiency of their blockade in the most forcible manner, by repeated official complaints of the sale to us of goods contraband of war—a sale which could not possibly have affected their interests if their pretended blockade had been sufficient "really to prevent access to our coasts"; that they alleged their inability to render their paper blockade effective as the excuse for the odious barbarity of destroying the entrance to one of the harbors by sinking vessels loaded with stone in the channel; that our commerce with foreign nations was interrupted, not by the effective investment of our ports, but by watching the ports of the West Indies; not only by the seizure of ships in the attempt to enter the Confederate ports, but by the capture on the high-seas of neutral vessels by the cruisers of our enemies, whenever supposed to be bound to any point on our extensive coast, without inquiry whether a single blockading vessel was to be found at such point; that blockading vessels had left the ports at which they were stationed for distant expeditions, were absent for many days, and returned without notice either of the cessation or renewal of the blockade; in a word, that every prescription of maritime law and every right of neutral nations to trade with a belligerent under the sanction of principles heretofore universally respected were systematically and persistently violated by the United States. Neutral Europe received our remonstrances, and submitted in almost unbroken silence to all the wrongs that the United States chose to inflict on its commerce. The Cabinet of Great Britain, however, did not confine itself to such implied acquiescence in these breaches of international law which resulted from simple inaction, but, in a published dispatch of the Minister for Foreign Affairs, assumed to make a change in the principle enunciated by the Congress of Paris, to which the faith of the British Government was considered to be pledged. The change was so important and so prejudicial to the interests of the Confederacy that, after a vain attempt to obtain satisfactory explanations from that Government, I directed a solemn protest to be made.

[Illustration: Members of the Confederate Cabinet]

In a published dispatch from her Majesty's Foreign Office to her Minister at Washington, under date of February 11th, 1862, occurred the following passage:

"Her Majesty's Government, however, are of opinion that, assuming that the blockade was duly notified, and also that a number of ships is stationed and remains at the entrance of a port sufficient really to prevent access to it, *or to create an evident danger of entering it or leaving it*, and that these ships do not voluntarily permit ingress or egress, the fact that various ships may have successfully escaped through it (as in the particular instance here referred to), will not of itself prevent the blockade from being an effectual one by international law."

The words which I have italicized were an addition made by the British Government of its own authority to a principle, the exact terms of which were settled with deliberation by the common consent of civilized nations, and by implied convention with our Government, as already explained, and their effect was clearly to reopen to the prejudice of the Confederacy one of the very disputed questions on the law of blockade which the Congress of Paris proposed to settle. The importance of this change was readily illustrated by taking one of our ports as an example. There was "evident danger," in entering the port of Wilmington, from the presence of a blockading force, and by this test the blockade was effective. "Access is not really prevented" by the blockading fleet to the same port; for steamers were continually arriving and departing, so that, tried by this test, the blockade was ineffective and invalid. Thus, while every energy of our country was evoked in the struggle for maintaining its existence, the neutral nations of Europe pursued a policy which, nominally impartial, was practically most favorable to our enemies and most detrimental to us.

The exercise of the neutral right of refusing entry into their ports to prizes taken by both belligerents was especially hurtful to the Confederacy. It was sternly adhered to and enforced.

The assertion of the neutral right of commerce with a belligerent, whose ports are not blockaded by fleets sufficient really to prevent access to them, would have been eminently beneficial to the Confederate States, and only thus hurtful to the United States. It was complaisantly abandoned.

The duty of neutral states to receive with cordiality and recognize with respect any new confederation that independent states may think proper to form, was too clear to admit of denial, but its postponement was equally beneficial to the United States and detrimental to the Confederacy. It was postponed.

In this statement of our relations with the nations of Europe, it has been my purpose to point out distinctly that the Confederacy had no complaint to make that those nations declared their neutrality. It could neither expect nor desire more. The complaint was, that the declared neutrality was delusive, not real; that recognized neutral rights were alternately asserted and waived in such manner as to bear with great severity on us, while conferring signal advantages on our enemy.

Perhaps it may not be out of place here to notice a correspondence between the Cabinets of France, Great Britain, and Russia, relative to a mediation between the Confederacy and the United States. On October 30, 1862, the French Minister of Foreign Affairs, Drouyn de l'Huys, addressed a note to the ambassadors of France at London and St. Petersburg. In this dispatch he stated that the Emperor had followed with painful interest the struggle which had then been going on for more than a year on this continent. He observed that the proofs of energy, perseverance, and courage, on both sides, had been given at the expense of innumerable calamities and immense bloodshed; to the accompaniments of civil conflict was to be added the apprehension of servile war, which would be the climax of so many irreparable misfortunes.

If these calamities affected America only, these sufferings of a friendly nation would be enough to excite the anxiety and sympathy of the Emperor; but Europe also had suffered in one of the principal branches of her industry, and her artisans had been subjected to most cruel trials. France and the maritime powers had, during the struggle, maintained the strictest neutrality, but the sentiments by which they were animated, far from imposing on them anything like indifference, seem, on the contrary, to require that they should assist the two belligerent parties in an endeavor to escape from a position which appeared to have no issue. The forces of the two sides had hitherto fought with balanced success, and the latest accounts did not show any prospect of a speedy termination of the war.

These circumstances, taken together, seemed to favor the adoption of measures which might bring about a truce. The Emperor of the French, therefore, was of the opinion that there was now an opportunity of offering to the belligerents the good offices of the maritime powers. He, therefore, proposed to her Majesty, as well as to the Emperor of Russia, that the three courts should endeavor, both at Washington and in communication with the Confederate States, to bring about a suspension of arms for six months, during which time every act of hostility, direct or indirect, should cease, at sea as well as on land. This armistice might, if necessary, be renewed for a further period.

This proposal, he proceeded to say, would not imply, on the part of the three powers, any judgment on the origin of the war, or any pressure on the negotiations for peace, which it was hoped would take place during the armistice. The three powers would only interfere to smooth the obstacles, and only within the limits which the two interested parties would prescribe. The French Government was of the opinion that, even in the event of a failure of immediate success, those overtures might have proved useful in leading the minds of men heated by passion to consider the advantages of conciliation and peace.

The reply of Great Britain, through Lord John Russell, on November 13, 1862, is really contained in this extract:

"After weighing all the information which has been received from America, her Majesty's Government are led to the conclusion that there is no ground at the present moment to hope that the Federal Government would accept the proposal suggested, and a refusal from Washington at the present time would prevent any speedy renewal of the offer."

The Russian Government, in reply, said:

"According to the information we have hitherto received, we are inclined to believe that a combined step between France, England, and Russia, no matter bow conciliatory, and how cautiously made, if it were taken with an official and collective character, would run the risk of causing precisely the very opposite of the object of pacification, which is the aim of the wishes of the three courts."

The unfavorable reception of the proposal was communicated by the French Minister of Foreign Affairs to the representative of France at Washington. In this communication he said:

"Convinced as we were that an understanding between the three powers in the sense presented by us would answer as much the interests of the American people as our own; that even that understanding was, in the existing circumstances, a duty of humanity, you will easily form an idea of our regret at seeing the initiative we have taken after mature reflection remain without results. Being also desirous of informing Mr. Dayton, the United States Minister, of our project, I confidently communicated it to him, and even read in his presence the dispatch sent to London and St. Petersburg. I could not but be surprised that the Minister of the United States should oppose his objections to the project I communicated to him, and to hear him express personally some doubts as to the reception which would be given by the Cabinet at Washington to the joint offers of the good offices of France, Russia, and Great Britain."

It has already been stated that, by common understanding, the initiative in all action touching the contest on this continent had been left by foreign powers to the two great maritime nations of Western Europe, and that the Governments of these two nations had agreed to take no measures without previous concert. The result of these arrangements, therefore, placed it in the power of either France or England to obstruct at pleasure the recognition to which the Confederacy was justly entitled, or even to prolong the continuance of hostilities on this side of the Atlantic, if the policy of either could be promoted by the postponement of peace. Each, too, thus became possessed of great influence in so shaping the general exercise of neutral rights in Europe as to render them subservient to the purpose of aiding one of the belligerents, to the detriment of the other. Perhaps it may not be out of place to present a few examples by which to show the true nature of the neutrality professed in this war.

In May, 1861, the Government of her Britannic Majesty assured our enemies that "the sympathies of this country [Great Britain] were rather with the North than with the South."

On June 1, 1861, the British Government interdicted the use of its ports to "armed ships and privateers, both of the United States and the so-called Confederate States," with their prizes. The Secretary of State of the United States fully appreciated the character and motive of this interdiction, when he observed to Lord Lyons, who communicated it, that "this measure and that of the same character which had been adopted by France would probably prove a death-blow to Southern privateering"—a means, it will be remembered, which the United States had refused to abandon for themselves.

On the 12th of June, 1861, the United States Minister in London informed her Majesty's Minister for Foreign Affairs that the fact of his having held interviews with the Commissioners of our Government had given "great dissatisfaction, and that a protraction of this would be viewed by the United States as hostile in spirit, and to require some corresponding action accordingly." In response to this intimation her Majesty's Minister gave assurance that "he had no expectation of seeing them any more."

Further extracts will show the marked encouragement to the United States to persevere in its paper blockade, and unmistakable intimations that her Majesty's Government would not contest its validity.

On May 21, 1801, Earl Russell pointed out to the United States Minister in London that "the blockade might, no doubt, be made effective, considering the small number of harbors on the Southern coast, even though the extent of three thousand miles were comprehended in the terms of that blockade."

On January 14, 1862, her Majesty's Minister in Washington communicated to his Government that, in extenuation of the barbarous attempt to destroy the port of Charleston by sinking a stone fleet in the harbor, Mr. Seward had explained that "the Government of the United States had, last spring, with a navy very little prepared for so extensive an operation, undertaken to blockade upward of three thousand miles of coast. The Secretary of the Navy had reported that he could stop up the 'large holes' by means of his ships, but that he could not stop up the 'small ones.' It has been found necessary, therefore, to close some of the numerous small inlets by sinking vessels in the channel."

On May 6, 1862, so far from claiming the right of British subjects as neutrals to trade with us as belligerents, and to disregard the blockade on the ground of this explicit confession by our enemy of his inability to render it effective, her Majesty's Minister for Foreign Affairs claimed credit with the United States for friendly action in respecting it. His lordship stated that—

"The United States Government, on the allegation of a rebellion pervading from nine to eleven States of the Union, have now, for more than twelve months, endeavored to maintain a blockade of three thousand miles of coast. This blockade, kept up irregularly, but, when enforced, enforced severely, has seriously injured the trade and manufactures of the United Kingdom.

"Thousands are now obliged to resort to the poor-rates for subsistence owing to this blockade. Yet her Majesty's Government have never sought to take advantage of the obvious imperfections of this blockade, in order to declare it ineffective. They have, to the loss and detriment of the British nation, scrupulously observed the duties of Great Britain toward a friendly state."

It is not necessary to pursue this subject further. Suffice it to say that the British Government, when called upon to redeem its pledge made at Paris in 1856, and renewed to the Confederacy in 1861, replied that it could not regard the blockade of Southern ports as having been otherwise than "practically effective in February, 1862," and that "the manner in which it has since been enforced gives to neutral governments no excuse for asserting that the blockade had not been effectively maintained."

The partiality of her Majesty's Government in favor of our enemies was further evinced in the marked difference of its conduct on the subject of the purchase of supplies by the two belligerents. This difference was conspicuous from the very commencement of the war. As early as May 1, 1861, the British Minister in Washington was informed by the Secretary of State of the United States that he had sent agents to England, and that others would go to France, to purchase arms; and this fact was communicated to the British Foreign Office, which interposed no objection. Yet, in October of the same year, Earl Russell entertained the complaint of the United States Minister in London, that the Confederate States were importing contraband of war from the Island of Nassau, directed inquiry into the matter, and obtained a report from the authorities of the island denying the allegations, which report was inclosed to Mr. Adams, and received by him as satisfactory evidence to dissipate "the suspicion thrown upon the authorities by that unwarrantable act." So, too, when the Confederate Government purchased in Great Britain, as a neutral country (with strict observance both of the law of nations and the municipal law of Great Britain), vessels which were subsequently armed and commissioned as vessels of war after they had been far removed from English waters, the British Government, in violation of its own laws, and in deference to the importunate demands of the United States, made an ineffectual attempt to seize one vessel, and did actually seize and detain another which touched at the Island of Nassau, on her way to a Confederate port, and subjected her to all unfounded prosecution, at the very time when cargoes of munitions of war were openly shipped from British ports to New York, to be used in warfare against us. Further instances need not be adduced to show how detrimental to us, and advantageous to our enemy, was the manner in which the leading European power observed its hollow profession of neutrality toward the belligerents.

CHAPTER XXXIX.

Advance of General E. K. Smith.—Advance of General Bragg.—Retreat of General Buell to Louisville.—Battle at Perryville, Kentucky.— General Morgan at Hartsville.—Advance of General Rosecrans.— Battle of Murfreesboro.—General Van Dorn and General Price.— Battle at Iuka.—General Van Dorn.—Battle of Corinth.—General Little.—Captures at Holly Springs.—Retreat of Grant to Memphis.— Operations against Vicksburg.—The Canal.—Concentration.—Raid of Grierson.—Attack near Port Gibson.—Orders of General Johnston.— Reply of General Pemberton.—Baker's Creek.—Big Black Bridge.— Retreat to Vicksburg.—Siege.—Surrender.—Losses.—Surrender of Port Hudson.—Some Movements for its Relief.

Operations in the West now claim attention. General Bragg, soon after taking command, as has been previously stated, advanced from Tupelo and occupied Chattanooga. Meantime General E. K. Smith with his force held Knoxville, in East Tennessee. Subsequently, in August, he moved toward Kentucky, and entered that State through Big Creek Gap, some twenty miles south of Cumberland Gap. After several small and successful affairs, he reached Richmond in the afternoon of August 30th. Here a force of the enemy had been collected to check his progress, but it was speedily routed, with the loss of some hundred killed and several thousand made prisoners, and a large number of small-arms, artillery, and wagons were captured. Lexington was next occupied; thence he advanced to Frankfort; and, moving forward toward the Ohio River, a great alarm was created in Cincinnati, then so little prepared for defense that, had his campaign been an independent one, he probably could and would have crossed the Ohio and captured that city. His division was but the advance of General Bragg's, and his duty to coöperate with it was a sufficient reason for not attempting so important a movement.

General Bragg marched from Chattanooga on September 5th, and, without serious opposition, entered Kentucky by the eastern route, thus passing to the rear of General Buell in Middle Tennessee, who, becoming concerned for his line of communication with Nashville and Louisville, and especially for the safety of the latter city, collected all his force and retreated rapidly to Louisville. This was a brilliant piece of strategy on the part of General Bragg, by which he manoeuvered the foe out of a large and to us important territory. By it north Alabama and Middle Tennessee were relieved from the presence of the enemy, without necessitating a single engagement.

General Buell in his retreat followed the line of the railroad from Nashville to Louisville. General Bragg moved more to the eastward, so as to unite with the forces under General E. K. Smith, which was subsequently effected when the army was withdrawing from Kentucky.

On September 18th General Bragg issued an address to the citizens of Kentucky. Some recruits joined him, and an immense amount of supplies was obtained, which he continued to send to the rear until he withdrew from the State. The enemy, having received reënforcements, as soon as our army began to retire, moved out and pressed so heavily on its rear, under Major-General Hardee, that he halted and checked them near Perryville. General Bragg then determined there to give battle.

Concentrating three of the divisions of his old command, then under Major-General Polk, he directed him to attack on the morning of October 8th. The two armies were formed on opposite sides of the town. The action opened at 12.30 P.M., between the skirmishers and artillery on both sides. Finding the enemy indisposed to advance, General Bragg ordered him to be assailed vigorously. The engagement became general soon after, and was continued furiously until dark. Although greatly outnumbered, our troops did not hesitate to engage at any odds, and, though the battle raged with varying fortune, our men eventually carried every position, and drove the Federals about two miles. The intervention of night terminated the action. Our force captured fifteen pieces of artillery, killed one and wounded two brigadier-generals and a very large number of inferior officers and men, estimated at no lees than four thousand, and captured four hundred prisoners. Our loss was twenty-five hundred killed, wounded, and missing.

Ascertaining that the enemy was heavily reënforced during the night, General Bragg on the next morning withdrew his troops to Harrodsburg. General Smith arrived the next day with most of his forces, and the whole were then withdrawn to Bryantsville, the foe following slowly but not closely. General Bragg finally took position at Murfreesboro, and the hostile forces concentrated at Nashville, General Buell having been superseded by General Rosecrans.

Meantime, on November 30th, General Morgan with thirteen hundred men made an attack on a brigade of the enemy at Hartsville. It was found strongly posted on a hill in line of battle. Our line was formed under fire, and the advance was made with great steadiness. The enemy was driven from his position, through his camps, losing a battery of Parrott guns, and finally hemmed in on the river-bank, where he surrendered. The contest was severe, and lasted an hour and a half. The prisoners numbered twenty-one hundred.

Late in the month of December General Rosecrans commenced his advance from Nashville upon the position of General Bragg at Murfreesboro. His movement began on December 26th by various routes, but such was the activity of our cavalry as to delay him four days in reaching the battle-field, a distance of twenty-six miles. On the 29th General Wheeler with his cavalry brigade gained the rear of Rosecrans's army, and destroyed several hundreds of wagons loaded with supplies and baggage. After clearing the road, he made the circuit of the enemy and joined our left. Their strength, as we have ascertained, was 65,000 men. The number of fighting men we had on the field on December 31st was 35,000, of which 30,000 were infantry and artillery.

Our line was formed about two miles from Murfreesboro, and stretched transversely across Stone River, which was fordable from the Lebanon pike on the right to the Franklin road on the left. As General Rosecrans made no demonstration on the 30th, General Bragg determined to begin the conflict early on the morning of the 31st by the advance of his left. The enemy was taken completely by surprise, and his right was steadily driven until his line was thrown entirely back at a right angle to his first position and near to the railroad, along which he had massed reserves. Their resistance after the first surprise was most gallant and obstinate. At night he had been forced from every position except the one on his extreme left, which rested on Stone River, and was strengthened by a concentration of artillery, and now seemed too formidable for assault.

On the next day (January 1st) the cannonading opened on the right center about 8 A.M., and after a short time subsided. The enemy had withdrawn from the advanced position occupied by his left flank; one or two short contests occurred on the 3d, but his line was unchanged. Our forces had now been in line of battle five days and nights, with little rest, as there were no reserves. Their tents had been packed in the wagons, which were four miles to the rear. The rain was continuous, and the cold severe. Intelligence was received that heavy reënforcements were coming to Rosecrans by a rapid transfer of all the troops from Kentucky, and for this and the reasons before stated General Bragg decided to fall back to Tullahoma, and the army was withdrawn in good order.

In the series of engagements near Murfreesboro we captured over 6,000 prisoners, 30 pieces of artillery, 6,000 small-arms, a number of ambulances, horses, and mules, and a large amount of other property. Our losses exceeded 10,000, and that of the enemy was estimated at over 25,000.

After the battle of Shiloh, West Tennessee and north Mississippi were occupied by a force under General Grant. Subsequently this force was increased, and General Rosecrans assigned to its command. Many positions were held in West Tennessee and north Mississippi, extending from Memphis to the northeastern part of the State of Mississippi, with garrisons aggregating about 42,000 men. The most important of these positions was that of the fortified town of Corinth. As part of the plan to subjugate the Southwestern States, extensive preparations were made for an advance through Mississippi and an attack on Vicksburg by combined land and naval forces. A large number of troops occupied Middle Tennessee and north Alabama. To defeat their general plan, and to relieve the last-mentioned places of the presence of the enemy, General Bragg moved his army into Kentucky, which, by this time, the Federal Government thought it needless to overawe by the presence of garrisons. General Van Dorn and General Price commanded the Confederate troops then in north Mississippi. General Bragg, when he advanced into Kentucky, had left them with instructions to operate against the Federals in that region, and especially to guard against their junction with Buell in Middle Tennessee. Though Van Dorn was superior in rank, he had no power to command General Price, unless they should happen to join in the field and do duty together. General Price on this as on other occasions manifested his entire willingness to make a junction with his superior officer, and about the last of August proposed to General Van Dorn to join him, but at that time Van Dorn's available force for the field had been sent with General Breckinridge in his campaign against Baton Rouge. After that force had rejoined General Van Dorn, he wrote to Price, inviting him to unite with him, that, with their two divisions, they might make an attack upon Corinth, by the capture of which main position of the enemy in that section of the country he hoped to be subsequently able to drive him from north Mississippi and West Tennessee. Price felt constrained by his instructions to observe and if possible to prevent Rosecrans's forces in Mississippi from effecting a junction with Buell's in Tennessee; therefore the invitation was unfortunately postponed to a future time.

Subsequently General Price learned that Rosecrans was moving to cross the Tennessee and join Buell; he therefore marched from Tupelo and reached Iuka on the 19th of September. His cavalry advance found the place occupied by a force, which retreated toward Corinth, abandoning a considerable amount of stores. On the 24th Van Dorn renewed in urgent terms his request for Price to come with all his forces to unite with him and make an attack upon Corinth. On the same day Price received a letter from General Ord, informing him that "Lee's army had been destroyed at Antietam; that, therefore, the rebellion must soon terminate, and that, in order to spare the further effusion of blood, he gave him this opportunity to lay down his arms." Price replied, correcting the rumor about Lee's army, thanked Ord for his kind feeling, and promised to "lay down his arms whenever Mr. Lincoln should acknowledge the independence of the Southern Confederacy, and not sooner." On that night General Price held a council of war, at which it was agreed on the next morning to fall back and make a junction with Van Dorn, it being now satisfactorily shown that the enemy was holding the line on our left instead of moving to reënforce Buell. The cavalry pickets had reported that a heavy force was moving from the south toward Iuka on the Jacinto road, to meet which General Little had advanced with his Missouri brigade, an Arkansas battalion, the Third Louisiana Infantry, and the Texas Legion. It proved to be a force commanded by General Rosecrans in person. A bloody contest ensued, and the latter was driven back, with the loss of nine guns. Our own loss was very serious. General Maury states that the Third Louisiana regiment lost half its men, that Whitfield's legion suffered heavily, and adds that these two regiments and the Arkansas battalion of about a hundred men had charged and captured the enemy's guns. In this action General Henry Little fell, an officer of extraordinary merit, distinguished on many fields, and than whom there was none whose loss could have been more deeply felt by his Missouri brigade, as well as by the whole army, whose admiration he had so often attracted by gallantry and good conduct. It was afterward ascertained that this movement of Rosecrans was intended to be made in concert with one by Grant moving from the west, but the former had been beaten before the latter arrived. Before dawn Price moved to make the proposed junction with Van Dorn, which was effected at Ripley on the 28th of September, at which time Van Dorn in his report says: "Field returns showed my strength to be about 22,000. Rosecrans at Corinth had about 15,000, with about 8,000 additional men at outposts from twelve to fifteen miles distant." In addition to this force, the enemy had at Memphis, under Sherman, about 6,000 men; at Bolivar, under Ord, about 8,000; at Jackson, Tennessee, under Grant, about 3,000; at bridges and less important points, 2,000 or 3,000—making an aggregate of 42,000 in West Tennessee and north Mississippi.

Corinth, though the strongest, was from its salient position the point it was most feasible to attack, and, under the circumstances, the most important to gain. Van Dorn, therefore, decided to move so rapidly upon it as to take it by surprise, and endeavor to capture it before reënforcements could arrive. In a previous chapter notice has been taken of the character and conduct of General Price; here it is proposed in like manner to say something of General Van Dorn, rendered the more appropriate because of the criticism to which his attack upon Corinth has been subjected. He was an educated soldier, had served with marked distinction in the war with Mexico; indeed, had been quite as often noticed in official reports for gallantry and good conduct as any officer who served in that war. After its close he had served on the Western frontier, and in Indian warfare exhibited a like activity and daring as that shown in the greater battles with Mexico. Immediately on the secession of his native State, Mississippi, he resigned from the United States Army, and, together with his veteran commander in Texas, General Twiggs, commenced recruiting men for the anticipated war. He was among the first to leave the service of the United States, and came to offer his sword to Mississippi. In the military organization there authorized, he was appointed a brigadier-general, and, when the State troops were transferred to the Confederacy, he entered its service. Gentle as he was brave, and generous, freely sharing all the dangers and privations to which his troops were subjected, he possessed, like his associate Price, both the confidence and affection of his men. Without entering into details of the disposition of his troops in the attack on the works at Corinth, the result shows that they were skillfully made, and, though final success did not crown the effort, the failure was due to other causes than the defect of plan or want of energy and personal effort on the part of Van Dorn. His opponent, Rosecrans, was an engineer of high ability, and proved himself one of the best generals in the United States Army. He had materially strengthened the works around Corinth, and had interposed every possible obstacle to an assault. Our army had moved rapidly from Ripley, its point of junction, had cut the railroad between Corinth and Jackson, Tennessee, and at daybreak on the 3d of March was deployed for attack. By ten o'clock our force confronted the enemy inside his intrenchments. In half an hour the whole line of outer works was carried, the obstructions passed, and the battle opened in earnest; the foe, obstinately disputing every point, was finally driven from his second line of detached works, and at sunset had retreated to the innermost lines.

The battle had been mainly fought by Price's division on our left. The troops had made a quick march of ten miles over dusty roads without water; the line of battle had been formed in forests with undergrowth; the combats of the day had been so severe that General Price thought his troops unequal to further exertion on that day, and it was decided to wait until morning. Of this, General Van Dorn says:

"I saw with regret the sun sink behind the horizon as the last shot of our sharpshooters followed the retreating foe into their innermost lines. One hour more of daylight, and victory would have soothed our grief for the loss of the gallant dead who sleep on that lost but not dishonored field."

During the night batteries were put in position to open on the town at 4 A.M. At daybreak the action was to begin on the left, to be immediately followed by an advance on the extreme right. The order was not executed, the commander of the wing which was to make the attack failed to do so, and another officer was sent to take his place. In the mean time the center became engaged, and the action extended to the left. The plan had been disarranged; nevertheless, the center and left pushed forward and planted their colors on the last stronghold of the enemy; his "heavy guns were silenced, and all seemed about to be ended, when a heavy fire from fresh troops that had succeeded in reaching Corinth was poured into our thin ranks," and, with this combined assault on Price's exhausted corps, which had sustained the whole conflict, those gallant troops were driven back. The day was lost. The enemy, reënforced, was concentrated against our left, and Lovell's division, which was at this time advancing, pursuant to orders, and was on the point of assaulting the works, was ordered to move to the left to prevent a sortie, and cover their retreat. Our army retired during the day to Chewalla without pursuit, and rested for the night free from molestation.

Our loss was very heavy of gallant men and officers. In the fierce conflicts the officers displayed not only daring, but high military skill, their impetuous charges being marked by judicious selection of time and place. Colonel William S. Barry, who, as commander of the burial party, visited General Rosecrans, was courteously received by that officer, who, while declining to admit the command within his lines, sent assurance to General Van Dorn that "every becoming respect should be shown to his dead and wounded. . . . He had the grave of Colonel Rodgers, who led the Second Texas sharpshooters, inclosed and marked with a slab, in respect to the gallantry of his charge. Rodgers fell before Gates called on me to reënforce him on the edge of the ditch of Battery Robbinet." [75] This officer, W. P. Rodgers, was a captain in the First Regiment of Mississippi Rifles in the war with Mexico, and the gallantry which attracted the admiration of the enemy at Corinth was in keeping with the character he acquired in the former service referred to. Of this retreat, that able soldier and military critic, General Dabney H. Maury, in a contribution to the "Annals of the War," wrote:

"Few commanders have ever been so beset as Van Dorn was in the forks of the Hatchie, and very few would have extricated a beaten army as he did then. One, with a force stated at ten thousand men, headed him at the Hatchie Bridge; while Rosecrans, with twenty thousand men, was attacking his rear at the Tuscumbia Bridge, only five miles off. The whole road between was occupied by a train of nearly four hundred wagons, and a defeated army of about eleven thousand muskets. But Van Dorn was never for a moment dismayed. He repulsed Ord, and punished him severely; while he checked Rosecrans at the Tuscumbia, until he could turn his train and army short to the left, and cross the Hatchie by the Boneyard road, without the loss of a wagon."

He then moved near Holly Springs, Mississippi, to await farther developments. In the mean time General Grant massed a heavy force, estimated at eighty thousand men, at various points on the Memphis and Charleston Railroad. Thence he moved south, through the interior of Mississippi, until he encamped near Water Valley. The country was teeming with great quantities of breadstuffs and forage, and he accumulated an immense depot of supplies at Holly Springs, and hastened every preparation necessary to continue his advance southward. Unless his progress was arrested, the interior of the State, its capital, Jackson, Vicksburg, and its railroads, would fall into his possession. As we had no force in front sufficient to offer battle, our only alternative was to attack his communications. For this purpose. General Van Dorn, on the night of December 15th, quietly withdrew our cavalry, amounting to less than twenty-five hundred men, from the enemy's front, and marched for Holly Springs. That place was occupied by a brigade of infantry and a portion of the Seventh Illinois Cavalry. The movement of Van Dorn was so rapid that early on the morning of the 19th he surprised and captured the garrison, and before eight o'clock was in quiet possession of the town. The captured property, amounting to millions of dollars, was burned before sunset, with the exception of the small quantity used in arming and equipping his command. General Grant was thus forced to abandon his campaign and to retreat hastily from the State.

After the battle of Murfreesboro, which closed in the first days of 1863, there was a cessation of active operations in that portion of Tennessee, and attention was concentrated upon the extensive preparations which were in progress for a campaign into Mississippi, with Vicksburg as the objective point. The plan, as it was developed, was for a combined movement by land and river, the former passing through the interior of Mississippi to approach Vicksburg in rear, the latter to descend the Mississippi River and attack the city in front. General Pemberton, with the main body of his command, held the position on the Tallahatchie and Yazoo Rivers, and among the various devices to turn that position was one more ingenious than ingenuous. It was an offer to furnish, at prices lower than ruled in our markets, provisions of which we stood in need, to be sent through the Yazoo Pass and transported in boats through to the Yazoo River if we should desire. I had, some time before, directed that cypress rafts, as far as practicable, of sinking timber, should be thrown into the main channel leading down from the Yazoo Pass; and saw that, if it was not the purpose of the proposer, the effect of accepting the proposition would be to open a water line of approach from the Mississippi, below Memphis, then in the hands of the enemy, to the interior in rear of Vicksburg: for that reason, I resisted much importunity in favor of allowing the supplies to be brought in that manner.

In the latter part of December General Sherman, having descended the Mississippi River, entered the Yazoo with four divisions of land troops and five gunboats, the object being to reduce our work at Haines's Bluff and turn Vicksburg so as to attack it in rear. The first point at which the range of hills extending from Vicksburg up the Yazoo approaches near to the river is at Haines's Bluff, some twenty miles by the course of the Yazoo from the Mississippi River. Here the troops were landed the 26th of December to attack the redoubts which had been built upon the bluff.

On the 27th little progress was made. On the 28th the attempt, by one division, to approach the causeway north of the Chickasaw Bayou, was repulsed with heavy loss. The troops were withdrawn and moved down the river to a point below the bayou, there to unite with the rest of the command. At daylight on the 29th the attack was resumed and continued throughout the most of the day; the enemy were again repulsed with heavy loss. On the next day there was firing on both sides without conclusive results. On the 31st General Sherman sent in a flag of trace to bury the dead.

[Illustration: Map of action of December 26-31]

Thereafter nothing important occurred until the latter part of January, when the troops under General Grant embarked at Memphis and moved down the Mississippi River to Young's Point, on the Louisiana shore, a few miles above Vicksburg. The expected coöperation by his forces with those of Sherman had been prevented by the brilliant cavalry expedition under Van Dorn, which captured and destroyed the vast supplies collected at Holly Springs for the use of Grant's forces in the land movement referred to. This compelled Grant to retreat to Memphis, and frustrated the combined movement which had been projected, in connection with the river campaign, by Sherman, and a new plan of operations resulted therefrom, in which, however, still prominently appears the purpose of turning Vicksburg on the north. After General Grant, descending the Mississippi from Memphis, arrived (2d of February, 1863) in the neighborhood of Vicksburg and assumed command of the enemy's forces, an attempt was made, by removing obstructions to the navigation of the Yazoo Pass and Cold Water, small streams which flow from the Mississippi into the Tallahatchie River, to pass to the rear of Fort Pemberton at the mouth of the latter. The never-to-be-realized hope was to reduce that work, and thus open the way down the Yazoo River to the right flank of the defenses of Vicksburg.

[Illustration: Map of action north of Vicksburg]

At the same time another attempt was made, by means of the network of creeks and bayous on the north side of the Yazoo, to pass around and enter the Yazoo above Haines's Bluff; but our sharpshooters, availing themselves of every advantageous position, picked off the men upon the boats, and Colonel (afterward General) Ferguson, with a few men and a section of field-pieces, so harassed and beset them that they were driven back utterly discomfited.

Admiral Porter had, with his fleet, gone some distance up Deer Creek, and, but for the land-forces sent to sustain him, would probably never have returned, an adventurous party having passed in below him with axes to fell trees so as to prevent his egress. He is described as follows:[76]

"I soon found Admiral Porter, who was on the deck of one of his ironclads, with a shield made of the section of a smoke-stack, and I doubt if he was ever more glad to meet a friend than he was to see me. He explained that he had almost reached the Rolling Fork, when the woods became full of sharpshooters, who, taking advantage of trees, stumps, and the levee, would shoot down every man that poked his nose outside the protection of their armor. . . . He informed me at one time things looked so critical that he had made up his mind to blow up the gunboats, and to escape with his men through the swamp to the Mississippi River."

This attempt to get through to Yazoo, above Haines's Bluff, had so signally failed, that the expedition was ordered back to the Louisiana shore above Vicksburg, where they arrived on the 27th of March, 1863. General Grant was now in command of a large army, holding various positions on the Mississippi River opposite to Vicksburg, extending from Milliken's Bend above to New Carthage below, with a fleet of gunboats in the river above Vicksburg, and another some eight miles below. Lieutenant-General Pemberton's military district included Vicksburg, and Major-General Gardner was in command at Port Hudson. These posts, as long as they could be maintained, gave us some control over the intermediate space of the river, about two hundred and sixty miles in length, and to that extent secured our communication with the trans-Mississippi. The enemy, after his repeated and disastrous attempts to turn the right flank of Vicksburg, applied his attention to the opposite direction. General Grant first endeavored to divert the Mississippi from its channel, by cutting a canal across the peninsula opposite to Vicksburg, so as to make a practicable passage for transport-vessels from a point above to one below the city. His attempt was quite unsuccessful, and, whatever credit may be awarded to his enterprise, none can be given to his engineering skill, as the direction given to his ditch was such that, instead of being washed out by the current of the river, it was filled up by its sediment.

[Illustration: Map of area north of Vicksburg]

Another attempt to get into the Mississippi, without passing the batteries at Vicksburg, was by digging a canal to connect the river with the bayou in rear of Milliken's Bend, so as to have water communication by way of Richmond to New Carthage. These indications of a purpose to get below Vicksburg caused General Pemberton, early in February, 1863, to detach Brigadier-General John S. Bowen, with his Missouri Brigade, to Grand Gulf, near the mouth of the Big Black, and establish batteries there to command the mouth of that small river, which might be used to pass to the rear of Vicksburg, and also by their fire to obstruct the navigation of the Mississippi.

On the 19th of March the flag-ship of Admiral Farragut, with one gunboat from the fleet at New Orleans, passed up the river in defiance of our batteries; but, on the 25th, four gunboats from the upper fleet attempted to pass down and were repulsed, two of them completely disabled.

On the 16th of April a fleet of ironclads with barges in tow, Admiral Porter commanding, under cover of the night ran the Vicksburg batteries. One of the vessels was destroyed, and another one crippled, but towed out of range. Subsequently, on the night of the 26th, a fleet of transports with loaded barges was floated past Vicksburg. One or more of them was sunk, but enough escaped to give the enemy abundant supplies below Vicksburg and boats enough for ferriage uses. On the 20th of April the movement of the enemy commenced through the country on the west side of the river to their selected point of crossing below Grand Gulf.

On the 29th the enemy's gunboats came down and took their stations in front of our batteries and rifle-pits at Grand Gulf. A furious cannonade was continued for many hours, and the fleet withdrew, having one gunboat disabled, and otherwise receiving and inflicting but little damage. Among the casualties on our side was that of Colonel William Wade, the chief of artillery, an officer of great merit, alike respected and beloved, whose death was universally regretted.

In a short time the fleet reappeared from behind a point which had concealed them from view. The gunboats now had transports lashed to their farther side, and, protected by their iron shields, ran by our batteries at full speed, losing but one transport on the way.

On the evening of the 29th of April the enemy commenced ferrying over troops from the Louisiana to the Mississippi shore to a landing just below the mouth of Bayou Pierre. General Green with his brigade moved thither, and, when the enemy on the night of the 30th commenced his advance, General Green attacked him with such impressive vigor as to render their march both cautious and slow. As additional forces came up, Green retired, skirmishing. In the mean time Generals Tracy and Baldwin, with their brigades, had by forced marches joined General Green, and about daylight a more serious conflict occurred, lasting some two hours and a half, during which General Tracy, a distinguished citizen of Alabama, of whom patriotism made a soldier, fell while gallantly leading his brigade in the unequal combat in which it was engaged. Step by step, disputing the ground, Green retired to the range of hills three miles southwest of Port Gibson, where General Bowen joined him and arranged a new line of battle. The enemy's forces were steadily augmented by the arrival of reënforcements from the rear. Our troops continued most valiantly to resist until, between nine and ten o'clock, outflanked both on our right and left, their condition seemed almost hopeless, when, by a movement to which desperation gave a power quite disproportionate to the numbers, the right wing of the enemy was driven back, and our forces made good their retreat across the bridge over Bayou Pierre. General Cockerell, commanding our left wing, led this forlorn hope in person, and to the fortune which favors the brave must be attributed the few casualties which occurred in a service so hazardous. General Bowen promptly intrenched his camp on the east side of Bayou Pierre and waited for future developments. The relative forces engaged in the battle of the 1st of May were, as nearly as I have been able to learn, fifty-five hundred Confederates and twenty thousand Federals. Fresh troops were reported to be joining Grant's army, and one of his corps had been sent to cross by a ford above so as to get in rear of our position. The reënforcements which were *en route* to Bowen had not yet approached so near as to give him assurance of coöperation.

To divert notice from this movement to get in the rear of Bowen, on the morning of the 2d, Grant ordered artillery-fire to be opened on our intrenchments across Bayou Pierre. It was quite ineffectual, and probably was not expected to do more than occupy attention. During the forenoon Bowen sent a flag of truce to ask suspension of hostilities for the purpose of burying the dead. This was refused, and a demand made for surrender. That was as promptly as decidedly rejected, and, as the day wore away without the arrival of reënforcement, Bowen, under cover of night, commenced a retreat, his march being directed toward Grand Gulf. General Loring with his division soon joined him. Directions were sent to the garrison at Grand Gulf to dismantle the fortifications and evacuate the place. On the morning of the 3d General Grant commenced a pursuit of the retreating force, which, however, was attended with only unimportant skirmishes; Bowen, with the reënforcements which were marching to his support, recrossed the Big Black at Hankinson's Ferry, and all, under the orders of General Pemberton, were assigned to their respective positions in the army he commanded.

While the events which have just been narrated were transpiring, Colonel Grierson with three regiments of cavalry made a raid from the northern border of Mississippi through the interior of the State, and joined General Banks at Baton Rouge in Louisiana. Among the expeditions for pillage and arson this stands prominent for savage outrages against defenseless women and children, constituting a record alike unworthy a soldier and a gentleman.

Grant with his large army was now marching into the interior of Mississippi, his route being such as might either be intended to strike the capital (Jackson) or Vicksburg. The country through which he had to pass was for some distance composed of abrupt hills, and all of it poorly provided with roads. There was reasonable ground to hope that, with such difficult communications with his base of supplies, and the physical obstacles to his progress, he might be advantageously encountered at many points and be finally defeated. In such warfare as was possible, that portion of the population who were exempt or incapable of full service in the army could be very effective as an auxiliary force. I therefore wrote to the Governor, Pettus, a man worthy of all confidence, as well for his patriotism as his manhood, requesting him to use all practicable means to get every man and boy, capable of aiding their country in its need, to turn out, mounted or on foot, with whatever weapons they had, to aid the soldiers in driving the invader from our soil. The facilities the enemy possessed in river transportation and the aid which their iron-clad gunboats gave to all operations where land and naval forces could be combined were lost to Grant in this interior march which he was making. Success gives credit to military enterprises; had this failed, as I think it should, it surely would have been pronounced an egregious blunder. Other efforts made to repel the invader will be noticed in the course of the narrative.

After the retreat of Bowen which has been described. General Pemberton, anticipating an attack on Vicksburg from the rear, concentrated all the troops of his command for its defense. All previous demonstrations indicated the special purpose of the enemy to be its capture. Its strategic importance justified the belief that he would concentrate his efforts upon that object, and this opinion was enforced by the difficulty of supplying his army in the region into which he was marching, and the special advantages of Vicksburg as his base. The better mode of counteracting his views, whatever they might be, it would be more easy now to determine than it was when General Pemberton had to decide that question. The superior force of the enemy enabled him at the same time, while moving the main body of his troops through Louisiana to a point below Vicksburg, to send a corps to renew the demonstration against Haines's Bluff. Finding due preparation made to resist an attack there, this demonstration was merely a feint, but, had Pemberton withdrawn his troops, that feint could have been converted into a real attack, and the effort so often foiled to gain the heights above Vicksburg would have become a success. When that corps retired, and proceeded to join the rest of Grant's army which had gone toward Grand Gulf, Pemberton commenced energetically to prepare for what was now the manifest object of the enemy. From his headquarters at Jackson, Mississippi, he, on the 23d of April, directed Major-General Stevenson, commanding at Vicksburg, "that communications, at least for infantry, should be made by the shortest practicable route to Grand Gulf. The indications now are that the attack will not be made on your front or right, and all troops not absolutely necessary to hold the works at Vicksburg should be held as a movable force for either Warrenton or Grand Gulf." On the 28th Brigadier-General Bowen, commanding at Grand Gulf, reported that "transports and barges loaded down with troops are landing at Hard-Times on the west bank." Pemberton replied by asking: "Have you force enough to hold your position? If not, give me the smallest additional number with which you can." At this time the small cavalry force remaining in Pemberton's command compelled him to keep infantry detachments at many points liable to be attacked by raiding parties of the enemy's mounted troops, a circumstance seriously interfering with the concentration of the forces of his command. Instructions were sent to all the commanders of his cavalry detachments to move toward Grand Gulf, to harass the enemy in flank and rear, obstructing, as far as might be, communications with his base. A dispatch was sent to Major-General Buckner, commanding at Mobile, asking him to protect the Mobile and Ohio Railroad, as Pemberton required all the troops he could spare to strengthen General Bowen. A dispatch was also sent to General J. E. Johnston, at Tullahoma, saying that the Army of Tennessee must be relied on to guard the approaches through north Mississippi. To Major-General Stevenson, at Vicksburg, he sent a dispatch: "Hold five thousand men in readiness to move to Grand Gulf, and, on the requisition of Brigadier-General Bowen, move them; with your batteries and rifle-pits manned, the city front is impregnable." At the same time the following was sent to General Bowen: "I have directed General Stevenson to have five thousand men ready to move on your requisition, but do not make requisition unless absolutely necessary for your position. I am also making arrangements for sending you two or three thousand men from this direction in case of necessity."

The policy was here manifested of meeting the enemy in the hills east of the point of his debarkation, yet all unfriendly criticism has treated General Pemberton's course on that occasion as having been voluntarily to withdraw his troops to within the intrenchments of Vicksburg. His published reports show what early and consistent efforts he made to avoid that result.

After General J. E. Johnston had recovered from the wound received at Seven Pines, he was on the 24th of November, 1862, by special order No. 275, assigned to the command of a geographical department including the States of Tennessee, Mississippi, Alabama, and parts of Louisiana, Georgia, and North Carolina. The order gives authority to establish his headquarters wherever, in his judgment, will best secure facilities for ready communication with the troops of his command; and provides that he "will repair to any part of said command whenever his presence may for the time be necessary or desirable." While the events which have been described were occurring in Pemberton's command, he felt seriously the want of cavalry, and was much embarrassed by the necessity for substituting portions of his infantry to supply the deficiency of cavalry.

These embarrassments and the injurious consequences attendant upon them were frequently represented. In his report he states, after several other applications for cavalry, that on March 25th he wrote to General Johnston, commanding department, "urgently requesting that the division of cavalry under Major-General Van Dorn, which had been sent to the Army of Tennessee for special and temporary purposes, might be returned." He gives the following extract from General Johnston's reply of April 3d to his request:

"In the present aspect of affairs, General Van Dorn's cavalry is much more needed in this department than in that of Mississippi and East Louisiana, and can not be sent back as long as this state of things exists. You have now in your department five brigades of the troops you most require, viz., infantry, belonging to the Army of Tennessee. This is more than a compensation for the absence of General Van Dorn's cavalry command."

To this Pemberton rejoined that cavalry was dispensable, stating the positions where the enemy was operating on his communications, and the impossibility of defending the railroads by infantry. Referring to the advance of the enemy from Bruinsburg, Pemberton, in his report, makes the following statement:

"With a moderate cavalry force at my disposal, I am firmly convinced that the Federal army under General Grant would have been unable to maintain its communication with the Mississippi River, and that the attempt to reach Jackson and Vicksburg would have been as signally defeated in May, 1863, as a like attempt from another base had, by the employment of cavalry, been defeated in December, 1862."

Pemberton commenced, after the retreat of Bowen, to concentrate all his forces for the great effort of checking the invading army, and on the 6th of May telegraphed to the Secretary of War that the reënforcements sent to him were very insufficient, adding: "The stake is a great one; I can see nothing so important." On the 12th of May he sent a telegram to General J. E. Johnston, and a duplicate to the President, announcing his purpose to meet the enemy then moving with heavy force toward Edwards's Depot, and indicated that as the battle-field; he urgently asked for more reënforcements: "Also, that three thousand cavalry be at once sent to operate on this line. I urge this as a positive necessity. The enemy largely outnumbers me, and I am obliged to hold back a large force at the ferries on Big Black." This was done to prevent the foe passing to his rear.

Large bodies of troops continued to descend the river, land above Vicksburg, and, to avoid our batteries at that place, to move on the west side of the river to reënforce General Grant. This seemed to justify the conclusion that the main effort in the West was to be made by that army, and, supposing that General Johnston would be convinced of the fact if he repaired to that field in person, as well as to avail ourselves of the public confidence felt in his military capacity, he was ordered, on the 9th of May, 1863, to "proceed at once to Mississippi and take chief command of the forces, giving to those in the field, as far as practicable, the encouragement and benefit of your personal direction. Arrange to take, for temporary service, with you, or to be followed without delay, three thousand good troops," etc.

On the 12th, the same day General Pemberton had applied for reënforcements, he instructed Major-General Stevenson as follows:

"From information received, it is evident
that the enemy is advancing in force on
Edwards's Depot and Big Black Bridge; hot
skirmishing has been going on all the
morning, and the enemy are at Fourteen-Mile
Creek. You must move with your whole
division to the support of Loring and Bowen
at the bridge, leaving Baldwin's and Moore's
brigades to protect your right."

In consequence of that information, Brigadier-General Gregg, who was near Raymond, received cautionary instruction; notwithstanding which, he was attacked by a large body of the enemy's forces, and his single brigade, with great gallantry and steadiness, held them in check for several hours, and then retired in such good order as to attract general admiration. Meantime, bodies of the enemy's troops were sent into the interior villages, and much damage was done in them, and to the defenseless, isolated homes in the country.

General Johnston arrived at Jackson on the 13th of May, 1863, and telegraphed to J. A. Seddon, Secretary of War, as follows:

"I arrived this evening, finding the enemy
in force between this place and General
Pemberton, cutting off the communication. I
am too late."

In the order assigning General Johnston to the geographical Department of the West, he was directed to repair in person to any part of his command, whenever his presence might be for the time necessary or desirable. On the 9th of May, 1863, he was ordered to proceed at once to Mississippi and take chief command of the forces in the field.

When he reached Jackson, learning that the enemy was between that place and the position occupied by General Pemberton's forces, about thirty miles distant, he halted there and opened correspondence with Pemberton, from which a confusion with consequent disaster resulted, which might have been avoided had he, with or without his reënforcements, proceeded to Pemberton's headquarters in the field. What that confusion or want of co-intelligence was, will best appear from citing the important part of the dispatches which passed between them. On May 13th General Johnston, then at Jackson, sent the following dispatch to General Pemberton, which was received on the 14th:

"I have lately arrived, and learn that Major-General
Sherman is between us, with four divisions at Clinton. It is
important to reestablish communications, that you may be
reënforced. If practicable, come up in his rear at once—to beat
such a detachment would be of immense value. Troops here
could coöperate. All the troops you can quickly assemble
should be brought. Time is all-important."

On the same day, the 14th, General Pemberton, then at Bovina, replied:

"I have the honor to acknowledge receipt of your communication. I moved at once with whole available force, about sixteen thousand, leaving Vaughan's brigade, about fifteen hundred, at Big Black Bridge; Tilghman's brigade, fifteen hundred, now at Baldwin's Ferry, I have ordered to bring up the rear of my column; he will be, however, from fifteen to twenty miles behind it. Baldwin's Ferry will be left, necessarily, unprotected. To hold Vicksburg are Smith's and Forney's divisions, extending from Snyder's Mills to Warrenton, numbering effectives seven thousand eight hundred men. . . . I do not think that you fully comprehend the position that Vicksburg will be left in; but I comply at once with your order."

On the same day, General Pemberton, after his arrival at Edwards's Depot, called a council of war of all the general officers present. He placed General Johnston's dispatch before them, and stated his own views against the propriety of an advance, but expressed the opinion that the only possibility of success would be by a movement on the enemy's communications. A majority of the officers present expressed themselves favorable to the plan indicated by General Johnston. The others, including Major-Generals Loring and Stevenson, "preferred a movement by which the army might attempt to cut off the enemy's supplies from the Mississippi River." General Pemberton then sent the following dispatch to General Johnston:

EDWARDS'S DEPOT, *May 14, 1863.*

"I shall move as early to-morrow morning as practicable, with a column of seventeen thousand men, to Dillon's, situated on the main road leading from Raymond to Port Gibson, seven and a half miles below Raymond, and nine and a half miles from Edwards's Depot. The object is to cut the enemy's communication and to force him to attack me, as I do not consider my force sufficient to justify an attack on the enemy in position, or to attempt to cut my way to Jackson. At this point your nearest communication would be through Raymond."

The movement commenced about 1 P.M. on the 15th, General Pemberton states that the force at Clinton was an army corps, numerically greater than his whole available force in the field; that—

"The enemy had at least an equal force to the south, on my right flank, which would be nearer Vicksburg than myself, in case I should make the movement proposed. I had, moreover, positive information that he was daily increasing his strength. I also learned, on reaching Edwards's Depot, that one division of the enemy (A. J. Smith's) was at or near Dillon's."

On the morning of the 16th, about 6.30 o'clock, Colonel Wirt Adams, commanding the cavalry, reported to General Pemberton that his pickets were skirmishing with the enemy on the Raymond road in our front. At the same moment a courier arrived and delivered the following dispatch from General Johnston:

"CANTON ROAD, TEN MILES FROM JACKSON,

"*May 15, 1863,* 8.30 o'clock A.M.

"Our being compelled to leave Jackson makes your plan impracticable. The only mode by which we can unite is by your moving directly to Clinton and informing me, that we may move to that point with about six thousand."

Pemberton reversed his column to return to Edwards's Depot and take the Brownsville road, so as to proceed toward Clinton on the north side of the railroad, and sent a reply to General Johnston to notify him of the retrograde movement and the route to be followed. Just as the reverse movement commenced, the enemy drove in the cavalry pickets and opened fire with artillery.

The continuance of the movement was ordered, when, the demonstrations of the enemy becoming more serious, orders were issued to form a line of battle, with Loring on the right, Bowen in the center, and Stevenson on the left. Major-General Stevenson was ordered to make the necessary dispositions for protecting the trains on the Clinton road and the crossing of Baker's Creek. The line of battle was quickly formed in a position naturally strong, and the approaches from the front well covered. The enemy made his first demonstration on the right, but, after a lively artillery duel for an hour or more, this attack was relinquished, and a large force was thrown against the left, where skirmishing became heavy. About ten o'clock the battle began in earnest along Stevenson's entire front. About noon Loring was ordered to move forward and crush the enemy in his front, and Bowen to coöperate. No movement was made by Loring; he said the force was too strongly posted to be attacked, but that he would seize the first opportunity to assault if one should offer. Stevenson soon found that unless reënforced he would be unable to resist the heavy and repeated attacks along his line. Aid was sent to him from Bowen, and for a time the tide of battle turned in our favor. The enemy still continued to move troops from his left to his right, thus increasing on that flank his vastly superior forces. General Pemberton, feeling assured that there was no important force in front of Loring, again ordered him to move to the left as rapidly as possible. To this order, the answer was given that the enemy was in strong force and endeavoring to turn his flank. As there was no firing on the right, the order was repeated. Much time was lost in exchanging these messages. At 4 P.M. a part of Stevenson's division broke badly and fell back. Some assistance finally came from Loring, but it was too late to save the day, and the retreat was ordered. Had the left been promptly supported when it was first so ordered, it is not improbable that the position might have been maintained and the enemy possibly driven back, although his increasing numbers would have rendered it necessary to withdraw during the night to save our communications with Vicksburg unless promptly reënforced. The dispatch of the 15th from General Johnston, in obedience to which Pemberton reversed his order of march, gave him the first intelligence that Johnston had left Jackson; but, while making the retrograde movement, a previous dispatch from Johnston, dated "May 14, 1863, camp seven miles from Jackson," informed Pemberton that the body of Federal troops, mentioned in his dispatch of the 13th, had compelled the evacuation of Jackson, and that he was moving by the Canton road; he refers to the troops east of Jackson as perhaps able to prevent the enemy there from drawing provisions from that direction, and that his command might effect the same thing in regard to the country toward Panola, and then asks these significant questions:

"Can he supply himself from the
Mississippi? Can you not cut him off from it?
Above all, should he be compelled to fall back
for want of supplies, beat him? As soon as the
reënforcements are all up, they must be
united to the rest of the army. . . . If prisoners
tell the truth, the force at Jackson must be
half of Grant's array. It would decide the
campaign to beat it, which can only be done
by concentrating, especially when the
remainder of the eastern troops arrive. They
are to be twelve or thirteen thousand."

From Pemberton's communication it is seen that he did not feel his army
strong enough to attack the corps in position at Clinton, and that he hoped by
the course adopted to compel the enemy to attack our force in position. Whether
the movement toward Dillon's was well or ill advised, it was certainly a
misfortune to reverse the order of march in the presence of the enemy, as it
involved the disadvantage of being attacked in rear. As has been described, the
dispositions for battle were promptly made, and many of the troops fought with
a gallantry worthy of all praise. Though defeated, they were not routed.

Stevenson's single division for a long time resisted a force estimated by him
at "more than four times" his own. In the afternoon he was reënforced by the
unfaltering troops of Bowen's division. Cockerell, commanding the First
Missouri Brigade, fought with like fortitude under like disadvantage. When
Pemberton saw that the masses assailing his left and left center by their
immense numbers were pressing our forces back into old fields, where the
advantages of position would be in his adversary's favor, he directed his troops
to retire, and sent to Brigadier-General Lloyd Tilghman instructions to hold the
Raymond road to protect the retreat. General Pemberton says of him:

"It was in the execution of this important
duty, which could not have been confided to a
fitter man, that the lamented General bravely
lost his life."

He was the officer whose devoted gallantry and self-sacrificing generosity
were noticed in connection with the fall of Fort Henry. This severe battle was
signalized by so many feats of individual intrepidity that its roll of honor is too
long for the limits of these pages.

Though some gave way in confusion, and others failed to respond when
called on, the heroism of the rest shed luster on the field, and "the main body of
the troops retired in good order." The gallant brigades of Green and Cockerell
covered the rear.

The topographical features of the position at the railroad-bridge across the
Big Black were such as, with the artificial strength given to it, made it quite
feasible to defend it against a direct approach even of an army as much superior
in numbers to that of Pemberton as was that of Grant; but the attack need not be
made by a direct approach. The position could be turned by moving either above
or below by fords and ferries, and thus advancing upon Vicksburg by other and
equally eligible routes. From what has already been quoted, it will be
understood that General Pemberton considered the occupation of Vicksburg

vitally important in connection with the command of the Mississippi River, and the maintenance of communication with the country beyond it. It was therefore that he had been so reluctant to endanger his connection with that point as his base. Pressed as he was by the enemy, whose object, it had been unmistakably shown, was to get possession of Vicksburg and its defenses, the circumstances made it imperative that he should abandon a position, the holding of which would not effect his object, and that he should withdraw his forces from the field to unite them with those within the defenses of Vicksburg, and endeavor, as speedily as possible, to reorganize the depressed and discomfited troops.

One of the immediate results of the retreat from Big Black was the necessity of abandoning our defenses on the Yazoo, at Snyder's Mills; this position and the line of Chickasaw Bayou were no longer tenable. All stores that could be transported were ordered to be sent into Vicksburg as rapidly as possible, the rest, including heavy guns, to be destroyed. During the night of the 17th nothing of importance occurred. On the morning of the 18th the troops were disposed from right to left on the defenses. On the entire line, one hundred and two pieces of artillery of different caliber, principally field-guns, were placed in position at such points as were deemed most suitable to the character of the gun. Instructions had been given from Bovina that all the cattle, sheep, and hogs, belonging to private parties, and likely to fall into the hands of the enemy, should be driven within our lines. Grant's army appeared on the 18th.

The development of the intrenched line from our extreme right was about eight miles, the shortest defensible line of which the topography of the country admitted. It consisted of a system of detached works, redans, lunettes, and redoubts, on the prominent and commanding points, with the usual profile of raised field-works, connected in most cases by rifle pits. To hold the entire line there were about eighteen thousand five hundred infantry, but these could not all be put in the trenches, as it was necessary to keep a reserve always ready to reënforce any point heavily threatened.

The campaign against Vicksburg had commenced as early as November, 1862, and reference has been made to the various attempts to capture the position both before and after General Grant arrived and took command in person. He had now by a circuitous march reached the rear of the city, established a base on the Mississippi River a few miles below, had a fleet of gunboats in the river, and controlled the navigation of the Yazoo up to Haines's Bluff, and was relieved from all danger in regard to supplying his army. We had lost the opportunity to cut his communications while he was making his long march over the rugged country between Bruinsburg and the vicinity of Vicksburg. Pemberton had by wise prevision endeavored to secure supplies sufficient for the duration of an ordinary siege, and, on the importance which he knew the Administration attached to the holding of Vicksburg, he relied for the coöperation of a relieving army to break any investment which might be made. Disappointed in the hope which I had entertained that the invading army would be unable to draw its supplies from Bruinsburg or Grand Gulf, and be driven back before crossing the Big Black, it now only remained to increase as far as possible the relieving army, and depend upon it to break the investment. The ability of the Federals to send reënforcements was so much greater than ours, that the necessity for prompt action was fully realized; therefore, when General Johnston on May 9th was ordered to proceed to Mississippi, he was directed to take from the Army of Tennessee three thousand good troops, and informed that he would find reënforcements from General Beauregard. On May 12th a dispatch was sent to him at Jackson, stating, "In addition to the five thousand men originally ordered from Charleston [Beauregard], about four thousand more will follow. I fear more can not be spared to you." On May 22d I sent the following dispatch to General Bragg, at Tullahoma, Tennessee:

"The vital issue of holding the Mississippi at Vicksburg is dependent on the success of General Johnston in an attack on the investing force. The intelligence from there is discouraging. Can you aid him?"

To this he replied on the 23d of May, 1863:

"Sent thirty-five hundred with the General, three batteries of artillery and two thousand cavalry since; will dispatch six thousand more immediately."

In my telegram to General Bragg, after stating the necessity, I submitted the whole question to his judgment, having full reliance in the large-hearted and comprehensive view which his self-denying nature would take of the case, and I responded to him:

"Your answer is in the spirit of patriotism heretofore manifested by you. The need is sore, but you must not forget your own necessities."

On the 1st of June General Johnston telegraphed to me that the troops at his disposal available against Grant amounted to twenty-four thousand one hundred, not including Jackson's cavalry command and a few hundred irregular cavalry. Mr. Seddon, Secretary of War, replied to him stating the force to be thirty-two thousand. In another dispatch, of June 5th, the Secretary says his statement rested on official reports of numbers sent, regrets his inability to promise more, as we had drained our resources even to the danger of several points, and urged speedy action. "With the facilities and resources of the enemy time works against us." Again, on the 16th, Secretary Seddon says:

"If better resources do not offer, you must hazard attack."

On the 18th, while Pemberton was inspecting the intrenchments along which his command had been placed, he received by courier a communication from General Johnston, dated "May 17, 1863, camp between Livingston and Brownsville," in answer to Pemberton's report of the result of the battles of Baker's Creek and Big Black, and the consequent evacuation of Snyder's Mills. General Johnston wrote:

"If Haines's Bluff is untenable, Vicksburg is of no value and can not be held. If, therefore, you are invested in Vicksburg, you must ultimately surrender. Under such circumstances, instead of losing both troops and place, we must, if possible, save the troops. If it is not too late, evacuate Vicksburg and its dependencies, and march to the northeast."

Pemberton, in his report, remarks:

"This meant the fall of Port Hudson, the surrender of the Mississippi River, and the severance of the Confederacy."

He recurs to a former correspondence with myself in which he had suggested the possibility of the investment of Vicksburg by land and water, and the necessity for ample supplies to stand a siege, and says his application met my favorable consideration, and that additional ammunition was ordered. Confident in his ability, with the preparations which had been made, to stand a siege, and firmly relying on the desire of the President and of General Johnston to raise it, he "felt that every effort would be made, and believed it would be successful." He, however, summoned a council of war, composed of all his general officers, laid before them General Johnston's communication, and desired their opinion on "the question of practicability," and on the 18th replied to General Johnston that he had placed his instructions before the general officers of the command, and that "the opinion was unanimously expressed that it was impossible to withdraw the army from this position with such morale and material as to be of further service to the Confederacy." He then announces his decision to hold Vicksburg as long as possible, and expresses the hope that he may be assisted in keeping this obstruction to the enemy's free navigation of the Mississippi River. He closes his letter thus:

"I still conceive it to be the most important point in the Confederacy."

While the council of war was assembled, the guns of the enemy opened on the works, and the siege proper commenced.

Making meager allowance for a reserve, it required the whole force to be constantly in the trenches, and, when they were all on duty, it did not furnish one man to the yard of the *developed line*. On the 19th two assaults were made at the center and left. Both were repulsed and heavy loss inflicted; our loss was small. At the game time the mortar-fleet of Admiral Porter from the west side of the peninsula kept up a bombardment of the city.

Vicksburg is built upon hills rising successively from the river. The intrenchments were upon ridges beyond the town, only approaching the river on the right and left flanks, so that the fire of Porter's mortar-fleet was mainly effective upon the private dwellings, and the women, the children, and other noncombatants.

The hills on which the city is built are of a tenacious calcareous clay, and caves were dug in these to shelter the women and children, many of whom resided in them during the entire siege. From these places of refuge, heroically facing the danger of shells incessantly bursting over the streets, gentlewomen hourly went forth on the mission of humanity to nurse the sick, the wounded, and to soothe the dying of their defenders who were collected in numerous hospitals. Without departing from the softer character of their sex, it was often remarked that, in the discharge of the pious duties assumed, they seemed as indifferent to danger as any of the soldiers who lined the trenches.

During the 20th, 21st, and the forenoon of the 22d, a heavy fire of artillery and musketry was kept up by the besiegers, as well as by the mortar- and gun-boats in the river. On the afternoon of the 22d preparation was made for a general assault. The attacking columns were allowed to approach to within good musket-range, when every available gun was opened with grape and canister, and our infantry, "rising in the trenches, poured into their ranks volley after volley with so deadly an effect that, leaving the ground literally covered in some places with their dead and wounded, they [the enemy] precipitately retreated." One of our redoubts had been breached by their artillery previous to the assault, and a lodgment made in the ditch at the foot of the redoubt, on which two colors were planted. General Stevenson says in his report:

"The work was constructed in such a manner that the ditch was commanded by no part of the line, and the only means by which they could be dislodged was to retake the angle by a desperate charge, and either kill or compel the surrender of the whole party by the use of hand-grenades. A call for volunteers for this purpose was made, and promptly responded to by Lieutenant-Colonel E. W. Pettus, Twentieth Alabama Regiment, and about forty men of Waul's Texas Legion. A more gallant feat than this charge has not illustrated our arms during the war. The preparations were quietly and quickly made, but the enemy seemed at once to divine our intentions, and opened upon the angle a terrible fire of shot, shell, and musketry. Undaunted, this little band, its chivalrous commander at its head, rushed upon the work, and, in less time than it required to describe it, the flags were in our possession. Preparations were then quickly made for the use of hand-grenades, when the enemy in the ditch, being informed of our purpose, immediately surrendered.

"From this time forward, although on several occasions their demonstrations seemed to indicate other intentions, the enemy relinquished all idea of assaulting us, and confined himself to the more cautious policy of a system of gradual approaches and mining."

His force was not less than sixty thousand men. Thus affairs continued until July 1st, when General Pemberton thus describes the causes which made capitulation necessary:

"It must be remembered that, for forty-seven days and nights, those heroic men had been exposed to burning suns, drenching rains, damp fogs, and heavy dews, and that during all this period they never had, by day or by night, the slightest relief. The extent of our works required every available man in the trenches, and even then they were in many places insufficiently manned. It was not in my power to relieve any portion of the line for a single hour. Confined to the narrow limits of trench, with their limbs cramped and swollen, without exercise, constantly exposed to a murderous storm of shot and shell. . . . Is it strange that the men grew weak and attenuated? . . . They had held the place against an enemy five times their number, admirably clothed and fed, and abundantly supplied with all the appliances of war. Whenever the foe attempted an assault, they drove him back discomfited, covering the ground with his killed and wounded, and already had they torn from his grasp five stands of colors as trophies of their prowess, none of which were allowed to fall again into his hands."

Under these circumstances, he says, he became satisfied that the time had arrived when it was necessary either to evacuate the city by cutting his way out or to capitulate. Inquiries were made of the division commanders respecting the ability of the troops to make the marches and undergo the fatigues necessary to accomplish a successful sortie and force their way through the enemy; all of whom reported their several commands quite unequal to the performance of such all effort. Therefore, it was resolved to seek terms of capitulation. These were obtained, and the city was surrendered on July 4th.

The report of General Pemberton contains this statement:

"Knowing the anxious desire of the Government to relieve Vicksburg, I felt assured that, if within the compass of its power, the siege would be raised; but, when forty-seven days and nights had passed, with the knowledge I then possessed that no adequate relief was to be expected, I felt that I ought not longer to place in jeopardy the brave men whose lives had been intrusted to my care. Hence, after the suggestion of the alternative of cutting my way out, I determined to make terms, not because my men were starved out, not because I could not hold out yet a little longer, but because they were overpowered by numbers, worn down with fatigue, and each day saw our defenses crumbling beneath their feet. . . . With an unlimited supply of provisions, the garrison could, for the reasons already given, have held out much longer."

At the close of General Pemberton's report he notices two officers, whose gallant services have been repeatedly mentioned in the foregoing pages, as follows:

"I can not close this report without brief tribute to the memory of two of the best soldiers in the Confederate service. I refer to Major-General John S. Bowen and Brigadier-General Martin E. Green. Always faithful, zealous, and brave, they fell, as became them, in the discharge of their duty. General Green died upon the lines he had so long and so gallantly defended. General Bowen, having passed scathless through the bloody scenes of Shiloh, Iuka, Corinth, Grand Gulf, Port Gibson, Baker's Creek, and Vicksburg, perished by disease after the capitulation."

With an unlimited supply of provisions the garrison could not, for the reasons already given, have held out much longer. Our loss in killed, wounded, and missing, from the landing of the enemy on the east to the capitulation, was 5,632; that of the enemy, according to his own statement, was 8,875. The number of prisoners surrendered, as near as I can tell, did not exceed 28,000.

In addition to the efforts made to relieve Vicksburg by an attack on Grant's army in the rear, instructions were sent to General Kirby Smith, commanding on the west side of the river, to employ a part of his forces in coöperation with our troops on the east side. From General Richard Taylor's work, "Destruction and Reconstruction," I learn that—

"the Federal army withdrew from
Alexandria [a town on Red River, Louisiana]
on the 13th of May, and on the 23d crossed
the Mississippi and proceeded to invest Port
Hudson. . . . A communication from General
Kirby Smith informed me that Major-General
Walker, with a division of infantry and three
batteries, four thousand strong, was on the
march from Arkansas, and would reach me
within the next few days; and I was directed
to employ Walker's force to relieve Vicksburg,
now invested by General Grant, who had
crossed the Mississippi on the 1st of May."

General Taylor states that his view was that this force might be best
employed for the relief of Vicksburg by a movement to raise the siege of Port
Hudson, which he regarded as feasible, while a direct movement toward
Vicksburg he considered would be unavailing, because the peninsula opposite to
that city was partially occupied by the enemy and commanded by the gunboats
in the river; he states, however, that he was overruled, and proceeded with
Walker's division to cross the Tensas and attack two Federal camps on the bank
of the Mississippi, the one ten and the other fourteen miles above Vicksburg, but
that, after driving the troops over the levee, the gunboats in the river protected
them from any further assault. Then, being convinced that nothing useful could
be effected in that quarter, he, in conformity with his original idea, ordered
General Walker to retire to Alexandria, intending to go thence to the Têche. He
says this order was countermanded and the division kept in the region between
the Tensas and the Mississippi until the fall of Vicksburg. Taylor had left
Mouton's and Green's brigades in the country west of the Têche, and thither he
went in person. At Alexandria he found three regiments of Texan mounted men,
about six hundred and fifty aggregate, under the command of Colonel
(afterward Brigadier-General) Major, and these were ordered to Morgan's Ferry
on the Atchafalaya. Taylor then proceeded to the camps of Mouton and Green,
on the lower Têche. After giving instructions preparatory to an attack on a work
which the Federals had constructed at Berwick's Bay, Taylor returned to join
Colonel Major's command on the Atchafalaya, and with it moved down the
Fardoche and Grossetete to Fausse Rivière, opposite to Port Hudson. Here the
noise of the bombardment then in progress could be distinctly heard, and here
he learned that the Federal force left in New Orleans did not exceed one
thousand men.

It was now the 10th of June. He was about one hundred miles from the
Federal force at Berwick's Bay. He furnished Colonel Major with guides,
informed him that he must be at Berwick's Bay on the morning of the 23d, as
Mouton and Green would attack at dawn on that day. Taylor then hastened to
the camp of Mouton and Green. The country through which Major was to march
was in possession of the enemy, therefore secrecy and celerity were alike
required for success. The men carried their rations, and the wagons were sent
back across the Atchafalaya. In his rapid march. Major captured seventy
prisoners and burned two steamers, and the combined movements of Mouton,
Green, and Major, all reached their goal at the appointed time, of which General

Taylor says: "Although every precaution had been taken to exclude mistakes and insure coöperation, such complete success is not often attained in combined military movement; and I felt that sacrifices were due to fortune."

At Berwick's Bay the Federals had constructed works to strengthen a position occupied as a depot of supplies. The effective garrison was small, the principal number of those present being sick and convalescents. The works mounted twelve guns, thirty-twos and twenty-fours, and a gunboat was anchored in the bay. Our object was to capture Berwick's Bay, and thence proceed to the execution of the plan above indicated. For this purpose, having arrived on the Têche, a short distance above Berwick's Bay, some small boats (skiffs) and a number of sugar-coolers were collected, in which the men were embarked. Major Hunter, of the Texas regiment, and Major Blair, of the Second Louisiana, were placed in command, and detachments were drawn from the forces. They embarked at night, and paddled down the Têche to the Atchafalaya and Grand Lake. They had about twelve miles to go, and were expected to reach the northeast end of the island, a mile from Berwick's, before daylight, where they were to remain until they heard the guns of our force on the west side of the bay. At dawn on June 23d our guns opened on the gunboat and speedily drove it away. Fire was then directed on the earthworks, and the enemy attempted to reply, when a shout was heard in the rear, and Hunter with his party came rushing on. Resistance ceased at once. The spoils of Berwick's were of vast importance. Twelve thirty-two- and twenty-four-pounder guns, many small arms and accouterments, great quantities of quartermaster's and commissary's, ordnance, and medical stores, and seventeen hundred prisoners were taken. Then, as promptly as circumstances would permit, Taylor, with three thousand men of all arms, proceeded, with the guns and munitions he had acquired, to the execution of the object of his campaign—to raise the siege of Port Hudson, by cutting Banks's communication with New Orleans and making a demonstration which would arouse that city. "Its population of two hundred thousand was bitterly hostile to Federal rule, and the appearance of a Confederate force on the opposite bank of the river would raise such a storm as to bring Banks from Port Hudson, the garrison of which could then unite with General Joseph Johnston in the rear of General Grant."

In the first week in July, twelve guns were placed on the river below Donaldsonville. Fire was opened and one transport destroyed and several turned back. Gunboats attempted to dislodge our batteries, but were driven away by dismounted men, protected by the levee. For three days the river was closed to transports, and mounted scouts were pushed down to a point opposite Kenner, sixteen miles above New Orleans. A few hours more, and there would have been great excitement in the city. But, by the surrender of Port Hudson on July 9th, the enemy were in sufficient force, not only to arrest Taylor's movements, but to require a withdrawal from the exposed position which this little command had assumed for the great object of relieving that place, and thus giving of its garrison, perhaps about five thousand men, as a reënforcement to break the investment of Vicksburg.

Port Hudson, which thus capitulated, was situated on a bend of the Mississippi, about twenty-two miles above Baton Rouge, Louisiana, and one hundred and forty-seven above New Orleans. The defenses in front, or on the water-side, consisted of three series of batteries situated on a bluff and extending along the river above the place. Farther up was an impassable marsh forming a natural defense, and in the rear the works were strong, consisting of several lines of intrenchments and rifle-pits, with heavy trees felled in every direction. General Banks with a large force landed on May 21, 1863, and on the 27th an assault was made on the works, and repulsed. A bombardment from the river was then kept up for several days, and on June 14th another unsuccessful assault was made. This was their last assault, but the enemy, resorting to mines and regular approaches, was slowly progressing with these when the news of the surrender of Vicksburg was received. Major-General Gardner, who was in command, then made a proposal to General Banks to capitulate, which was accepted by the latter, and the position was yielded to him on the next day. The surrender included about six thousand persons all told, fifty-one pieces of artillery, and a quantity of ordnance stores. Our loss in killed and wounded in the assaults was small compared to that of the enemy, and by the fall of Vicksburg the position of Port Hudson had ceased to have much importance.

[Illustration: Map of Port Hudson]

More than six weeks the garrison, which had resisted a vastly superior force attacking by both land and water, had cheerfully encountered danger and fatigue without a murmur, had borne famine and had repulsed every assault, and yielded Port Hudson only when the fall of Vicksburg had deprived the position of its importance. A chivalric foe would have recognized the gallantry of the defense in the terms usually given under like circumstances; such, for instance, as were granted to Major Anderson at Fort Sumter, or, at the least, have paroled the garrison.

I had regarded it of vast importance to hold the two positions of Vicksburg and Port Hudson. Though gunboats had passed the batteries of both, they had found it hazardous, and transport-vessels could not prudently risk it. The garrisons of both places had maintained them with extraordinary gallantry, inspired no doubt as well by consciousness of the importance of their posts as by the soldierly character common to Confederate troops. Taylor on the 10th received intelligence of the fall of Port Hudson, and some hours later learned that Vicksburg had surrendered. His batteries and outposts were ordered in to the Lafourche, and Mouton was sent to Berwick's to cross the stores to the west side of the bay. On the 13th a force of six thousand men followed his retreat down the Lafourche; but Green, with fourteen hundred dismounted men and a battery, attacked the Federals so vigorously as to drive them into Donaldsonville, capturing two hundred prisoners, many small-arms, and two guns. Undisturbed thereafter, Taylor continued his march, removed all the stores from the fortification at Berwick's, and on the 21st of July moved up the Têche. The pickets left at Berwick's reported that the enemy's scouts only reached the bay twenty-four hours after Taylor's troops had withdrawn.

In the recital of those events connected with the sieges of Port Hudson and Vicksburg, enough has been given to show the great anxiety of the Administration to retain those two positions as necessary to continued communication between the Confederate States on the east and west sides of the Mississippi River. The reader will not have failed to observe that General Johnston, commanding the department, and General Pemberton, the district commander, entertained quite different views. The former considered the safety of the garrisons of such paramount importance, that the position should be evacuated rather than the loss of the troops hazarded; the latter regarded the holding of Vicksburg as of such vital consequence that an army should be hazarded to maintain its possession. When General Pemberton and his forces were besieged in Vicksburg, every effort was made to supply General Johnston with an army which might raise the siege. While General Johnston was at Jackson, preparing to advance against the army investing Vicksburg, the knowledge that the enemy was receiving large reënforcements made it evident that the most prompt action was necessary for success; of this General Johnston manifested a dear perception, for on the 25th of May he sent Pemberton the following message:

"Bragg is sending a division; when it comes, I will move to you."

After all the troops which could be drawn from other points had been sent to him, it was suggested that he might defeat the force investing Port Hudson, and unite the garrison with his troops at Jackson, but he replied:

"We can not relieve Port Hudson without giving up Jackson, by which we should lose Mississippi."

On June 29th General Johnston reports that—

"Field transportation and other supplies having been obtained, the army marched toward the Big Black, and on the evening of July 1st encamped between Brownsville and the river."

The 2d and 3d of July were spent in reconnaissance, from which the conclusion was reached that an attack on the north side of the railroad was impracticable, and examinations were commenced on the south side of the railroad. On the 3d a messenger was sent to General Pemberton that an attempt would be made about the 7th, by an attack on the enemy, to create a diversion which might enable Pemberton to cut his way out. The message was not received, and Pemberton, despairing of aid from the exterior, capitulated on the 4th.

General Grant, in expectation that an attack in his rear would be made by General J. E. Johnston, formed a provisional corps by taking brigades from several corps, and assigned General Sherman to command it. He was sent in the direction of Big Black. Colonel Wilson, then commanding the Fifteenth Illinois Cavalry, was sent to the Big Black River to watch for the expected advance of Johnston, when Sherman was to be notified, so that he might meet and hold Johnston in check until additional reënforcements should arrive. Wilson never sent the notice. An officer of Grant's army, whose rank and position gave opportunity for accurate information, writes:

"It was always a matter of surprise to Grant and his commanders that Johnston failed to make the attempt to break up the siege of Vicksburg, of which from the long line and consequent weakness of the army of the North there seemed a fair chance of accomplishment."

General Johnston, being informed on the 5th of the surrender of Vicksburg, fell back to Jackson, where his army arrived on the 7th.

"On the morning of the 9th the enemy appeared in heavy force in front of the works thrown up for the defense of the place; these,

consisting of a line of rifle-pits prepared at
intervals for artillery, . . . were badly located
and constructed, presenting but a slight
obstacle to a vigorous assault." [77]

The weather was hot, deep dust covered the country roads, and for about ten miles there was no water to supply the troops who were advancing in heavy order of battle from Clinton; and the circumstances above mentioned caused General Johnston, as he states, to expect that the enemy "would be compelled to make an immediate assault." Sherman, in command of the attacking column, did not, however, elect to assault the intrenchments, but moved the left of his line around so as to rest upon Pearl River above, and then, extending his right so as to reach the river below, commenced intrenching a line of investment. As early as May 27th Brigadier-General J. G. Rains had been directed to report to General Johnston in connection with torpedoes and sub-terra shells, and a request had been made for "all reasonable facilities and aid in the supply of men or material for the fair trial of his torpedoes and shells." There could scarcely have been presented a better opportunity for their use than that offered by the heavy column marching against Jackson, and the enemy would have been taken at great disadvantage if our troops had met them midway between Jackson and Clinton. As the defenses of Jackson had not been so corrected in location and increased in strength as to avail against anything other than a mere assault, it is greatly to be regretted that the railroad-bridge across Pearl River was not so repaired that the large equipments of the Central road might have been removed for use elsewhere and at other times. One of the serious embarrassments suffered in the last two years of the war was from the want of rolling-stock, with which to operate our railroads, as required for the transportation of troops and supplies. On the 12th of July a heavy cannonade was opened, and the missiles reached all parts of the town. An assault was also made on Major-General Breckinridge's position on our extreme left. His division, with the aid of Cobb's and Slocum's batteries, repulsed it, inflicting severe loss, and capturing two hundred prisoners, besides the wounded, and taking three regimental colors. On the 15th General Johnston was assured that the remainder of Grant's army was moving from Vicksburg to Jackson, and on the night of the 16th he, having previously sent forward his sick and wounded, successfully withdrew his army across the Pearl River, and moved toward Brandon, and continued the march as far as Morton, about thirty-five miles from Jackson. The enemy followed no farther than Brandon, which was reached on the 19th, and manifested no higher purpose than that of arson, which was exhibited on a still larger scale at Jackson.

Thus, within the first half of July, our disasters had followed close upon the heels of one another. Though not defeated at Gettysburg, we had suffered a check, and an army, to which nothing was considered impossible, had been compelled to retire, leaving its opponent in possession of the field of battle. The loss of Vicksburg and Port Hudson was the surrender of the Mississippi to the enemy. It was true that gunboats had run by our batteries, but not with impunity, and some of them had been sunk in the attempt. Transports for troops, supplies, and merchandise could not, except at great risk, use the river while our batteries at those two points remained effective, and gunboats cruising between them would have but a barren field. Moreover, they needed to be very numerous to prevent intercourse between the two sides of the river, which, thus far, they had never been able to effect.

[Footnote 75: General D. H. Maury.]

[Footnote 76: "Memoirs of General W. T. Sherman," vol i, pp. 310, 311.]

[Footnote 77: General Johnston's "Report of Operations in Mississippi and East Louisiana," pp. 12, 13.]

CHAPTER XL.

Inactivity in Tennessee.—Capture of Colburn's Expedition.—Capture of Streight's Expedition.—Advance of Rosecrans to Bridgeport.—Burnside in East Tennessee.—Our Force at Chattanooga.—Movement against Burnside.—The Enemy moves on our Rear near Ringgold.—Battle at Chickamauga.—Strength and Distribution of our Forces.—The enemy withdraws.—Captures.—Losses.—The Enemy evacuates Passes of Lookout Mountain.—His Trains captured.—Failure of General Bragg to pursue.—Reënforcements to the Enemy, and Grant to command.—His Description of the Situation.—Movements of the Enemy.—Conflict at Chattanooga.

After the battle at Murfreesboro, in Tennessee, a period of inactivity ensued between the large armed forces, which was disturbed only by occasional expeditions by small bodies on each side. On March 5, 1863, an expedition of the enemy, under Colonel Colburn, was captured at Spring Hill, ten miles south of Franklin, by Generals Van Dorn and Forrest. Thirteen hundred prisoners were taken. In April another expedition, under Colonel Streight, into northern Georgia, was captured near Rome by our vigilant, daring cavalry leader, Forrest. This was one of the most remarkable, and, to the enemy, disastrous raids of the war. Seventeen hundred prisoners were taken. In June some movements were made by General Rosecrans, which were followed by the withdrawal of our forces from Middle Tennessee, and a return to the occupation of Chattanooga. At this time General Buckner held Knoxville and commanded the district of East Tennessee; General Samuel Jones commanded the district of southwest Virginia, his headquarters at Arlington, Virginia. Between the two was Cumberland Gap, the well-known pass by which the first pioneer, Daniel Boone, went into Kentucky, and the only one in that region through which it was supposed an army, with the usual artillery and wagon-train, could march from the north into East Tennessee or southwest Virginia. It was, therefore, occupied and partially fortified, which, with the precipitous heights flanking it on the right and left, would, it was hoped, suffice against an attack in front, and prove an adequate barrier to an advance on our important line of communication in its rear, which Buckner and Jones were relied on to defend.

On the 20th of August Brigadier-General I. W. Frazier, an educated soldier in whom I had much confidence, assumed, by assignment, the command of this position, and energetically commenced to perfect the defenses, and ingeniously though unsuccessfully endeavored to bring a supply of water into the fortifications. He reported his force to amount to seventeen hundred effective infantry and artillery, and about six hundred cavalry; the supply of ammunition was deficient, and some of it damaged by a badly constructed magazine.

About August 20th it was ascertained that the army under General Rosecrans had crossed the mountains to Stevenson and Bridgeport. His force of infantry and artillery amounted to seventy thousand men, divided into four corps. About the same time General Burnside advanced from Kentucky, crossed, by using pack-mules, the rugged mountains west of Cumberland Gap, and, about the 1st of September, approached Knoxville, East Tennessee, with a force estimated at over twenty-five thousand men. General Buckner, therefore, evacuated Knoxville, and took position at Loudon, with a force of about five thousand infantry, artillery, and cavalry; this rendered the occupation of Cumberland Gap hazardous to the garrison, and comparatively of little value to us, but, when its surrender was demanded by a force which might be resisted, General Frazier promptly refused to comply with the demand. Subsequently, General Burnside advanced with a large body of troops, and, approaching from the south, renewed the demand, when General Frazier, recognizing the inutility as well as futility of resistance, surrendered on the 9th of September, 1863.[78] The main body of our army was encamped near Chattanooga, while the cavalry force was recruiting from fatigue and exhaustion near Rome, Georgia. The enemy first attempted to strike Buckner in the rear, but failing, commenced a movement against our left and rear. On the last of August he had crossed his main force over the Tennessee River at Carpenter's Ferry, near Stevenson. Our effective force of infantry and artillery was about thirty-five thousand. By active reconnaissance of our cavalry, which had been brought forward, it was ascertained that Rosecrans's general movement was toward our left and rear, in the direction of Dalton and Rome, keeping Lookout Mountain between us. The want of supplies in the country and the force under Burnside on our right rendered hazardous a movement on the rear of the former with our force. General Lee, with commendable zeal for the public welfare and characteristic self-denial, had consented to remain for a time on the defensive for the purpose of reenforcing Bragg's army, and General Longstreet had been detached with his corps for that purpose. These troops were to come by rail from Atlanta, and might soon be expected to arrive. It was, therefore, determined to retire toward our expected reënforcements, as well as to meet the foe in front when he should emerge from the mountain-gorges.

As we could not thus hold Chattanooga, our army, on September 7th and 8th, took position from Lee and Gordon's Mill to Lafayette, on the road leading south from Chattanooga and fronting the east slope of Lookout Mountain. The forces on the Hiawassee and at Chickamauga Station took the route by Ringgold. A small cavalry force was left in observation at Chattanooga, and a brigade of infantry at Ringgold to cover the railroad.

The enemy immediately moved the corps that threatened Buckner into Chattanooga, and, shortly after, it commenced to move on our rear by the roads to Lafayette and Ringgold. Another corps was nearly opposite the head of McLemore Cove, in Will's Valley, and one at Colonel Winston's opposite Alpine. During the 9th it was ascertained that a column, between four and five thousand, had crossed Lookout Mountain by Stevens's and Cooper's Gaps into McLemore's Cove. An effort was made by General Bragg to capture this column, with intent then to turn upon the others, and beat each in succession. But, some delay having occurred in the advance of our forces through the gap, the enemy took advantage of it and retreated to the mountain-passes. He then withdrew his corps from the route toward Alpine to unite with the one near McLemore's Cove, which was gradually extended toward Lee and Gordon's Mills. It was now determined to turn upon the Third Corps of the enemy, approaching us from the direction of Chattanooga. The forces sent toward the Cove were accordingly withdrawn to Lafayette, and Polk's and Walker's corps were moved immediately in the direction of Lee and Gordon's Mills, Lieutenant-General Polk commanding. He was ordered to attack early the next morning, as the enemy's corps was known to be divided, and it was hoped by successive attacks to crush his army in detail; but the expectation was not realized, as his forces withdrew and formed a junction. Our trains and supplies were then put in a safe position, and all our forces were concentrated along the Chickamauga, threatening the opposing force in front. Major-General Wheeler, with two divisions of cavalry, occupied the extreme left, vacated by Hill's corps, and was directed to press the enemy in McLemore's Cove; to divert his attention from the real movement, General Forrest covered the movement on our front and right; General B. R. Johnson was moved from Ringgold to the extreme right of the line; Walker's corps formed on his left opposite Alexander's Bridge, Buckner's next, near Tedford Ford, Polk opposite Lee and Gordon's Mills, and Hill on the extreme left. Orders were issued to cross the Chickamauga at 6 A.M., commencing by the extreme right.

The movements were unexpectedly delayed by the difficulty of the roads and the resistance of the enemy's cavalry. The right column did not effect its crossing until late in the afternoon of the 18th; at this time, Major-General Hood, from the Army of Northern Virginia, arrived and assumed command of the column. General W. H. T, Walker had a severe skirmish at Alexander's Bridge, from which he finally drove the enemy, but not before he had destroyed it; General Walker, however, found a ford, crossed, and Hood united with him after night. The advance was resumed at daylight on the 19th, when Buckner's corps with Cheatham's division of Polk's corps crossed the Chickamauga, and our line of battle was thus formed: Buckner's left rested on the bank of the stream about one mile below Lee and Gordon's Mills; on his right came Hood with his own and Johnson's divisions, and Walker's formed the extreme right; Forrest with his cavalry was in advance to the right. He soon became engaged with such a large force that two brigades were sent from Walker's division to his support. Forrest, here fighting with his usual tenacity, desperately held in check the comparatively immense force which he was resisting. General Walker, being ordered to commence the attack on the right, boldly advanced, and soon developed opposing forces greatly superior to his own; he, however, drove them handsomely, capturing several batteries of artillery, by dashing charges. As he pressed back the force in his front, it rested upon such heavy masses in the rear, that he was in turn repulsed. Cheatham's division was ordered to his support; it came too late. Before it could reach him, assailed on both flanks, he had been forced back to his first position, but the two commands united, though yet greatly outnumbered, and, by a spirited attack, recovered our advantage. These movements on our right were in such direction as to create an opening between the left of Cheatham's division and the right of Hood's. To fill this, Stewart's division, the reserve of Buckner's corps, was ordered up, and soon became engaged, as now did Hood's whole front. The enemy had transferred forces from his extreme right so as to concentrate his main body on his left, acutely perceiving the probability of an effort on our part to gain his rear, and cut off his communication with his base at Chattanooga. The main part of the battle, therefore, was fought on the opposite flank from that where both armies had probably expected it. Lieutenant-General Polk was now directed to move the remainder of his corps across the stream, and to assume command in person; Hill's corps was also directed to move to our right. Stewart, by a gallant assault, broke the enemy's center, and pushed forward until he became exposed to an enfilading fire. Hood steadily advanced, driving the force in his front until night. Cleburne, of Hill's corps, immediately on reaching the right, closed so impetuously with the enemy as to create surprise, and drove him in great disorder. From prisoners and otherwise, the commanding General became satisfied that his antagonist had by marching night and day succeeded in concentrating his whole force, and that it had that day been fought on the field of Chickamauga. A part of the forces on our extreme left had not reached the field of actual conflict in time to participate in the engagement of that day; they, together with the remainder of Longstreet's corps, were brought up and put in position to renew the battle in the morning. Our troops slept upon the field they had so bravely contested. The Confederate troops engaged on the right were as follows:

General W. H. T. Walker's division 5,500
Cheatham's division 7,000
A. P. Stewart's division 4,040
Cleburne's division 5,115
Hood's, B. R. Johnson's, and Trigg's troops 8,428
Forrest's and Pegram's cavalry 3,500
———
Total 33,583

General Wheeler with his cavalry had been in observation on the left, and for a fortnight, daily skirmishing with the enemy. On the 17th he was ordered to move into McLemore's Cove to make a demonstration in that direction, where, after a severe engagement, he developed a force too large to be dislodged. On the 18th he was directed to hold the gap in Pigeon Mountain, so as to prevent the enemy from moving on our left. As appeared subsequently, General Rosecrans, by forced marches, had made a *détour*, and formed a junction of his forces in front of ours, so that it was no longer needful to hold the passes of the Pigeon Mountain, and Wheeler with his cavalry was called to take position on the left of our line.

On the night of the 19th, the whole force having been assembled, including the five thousand effective infantry sent for temporary service from Virginia, the command was organized as two corps, the one on the right to be commanded by Lieutenant-General Polk; the other, on the left, to be commanded by Lieutenant-General Longstreet. These corps consisted respectively as follows: Polk's right wing, of Breckenridge's, Cleburne's, Cheatham's, and Walker's divisions, and Forrest's cavalry—aggregate, 22,471; Longstreet's left wing, of Preston's, Hindman's, Johnson's (Hood's), Law's, Kershaw's, Stewart's divisions, and Wheeler's cavalry—aggregate, 24,850: grand aggregate of both wings, 47,321, The forces under Rosecrans, as has been subsequently learned, consisted of McCook's corps, 14,345; Thomas's, 24,072; Crittenden's, 13,975; Granger's, about 5,000; cavalry, 7,000: whole number, 64,392. On the night of the 19th General Bragg gave his instructions orally, to the general officers whom he had summoned to his camp-fire, as to the position of the different commands; and the order of battle was that the attack should commence on the right at daybreak, and be taken up successively to the left. From a combination of mishaps, it resulted that the attack was not commenced until nine or ten o'clock in the day, and, what was much more important, the troops from right to left did not in rapid succession engage, so as to have that effectiveness which would have resulted from concert of action. Prodigies of valor were performed, many partial successes were gained in the beginning of the battle, but in the first operations the troops so frequently moved to the assault without the necessary cohesion in a charging line, that nearly all early assaults by our right wing were successively repulsed with loss. Though at first invariably successful, our troops were subsequently compelled to retire before the heavy reënforcements constantly brought.

Wheeler with his cavalry struck boldly at the enemy's extreme right and center, and with such effect that, in the Federal battle reports, it appears the attack was mistaken for a flank movement by General Longstreet.

Rosecrans having transferred his main strength to our right, the attack of the left met with less resistance, and was successfully and vigorously followed up. About 4 P.M. a general assault was made by the right, and the attack was pressed from right to left until the enemy gave way at different points, and, finally, about dark, yielded along the whole line. Our army bivouacked on the ground it had so gallantly won. The foe, though driven from his lines, continued to confront us when the action closed. But it was found the next morning that he had availed himself of the night to withdraw from our front, and that his main body was soon in position within his lines at Chattanooga. We captured over eight thousand prisoners, fifty-one pieces of artillery, fifteen thousand stand of small arms, and quantities of ammunition, with wagons, ambulances, teams, and medicines with hospital stores in large quantities. From the appearance of the field the enemy's losses must have largely exceeded ours, and the victory was complete; but these results could not console us for the lives they cost. Pride in the gallantry of our heroes, rejoicing at the repulse of the invader, was subdued by the memory of our fallen brave.

After General Rosecrans's retreat to Chattanooga, he withdrew his forces from the passes of Lookout Mountain, which covered his line of supplies from Bridgeport. These commanding positions were immediately occupied by our troops, and a cavalry force was sent across the Tennessee, which destroyed a large wagon-train in the Sequatchie Valley, captured McMinnsville and other points on the railroad, and thus temporarily cut off the source of supplies for the army at Chattanooga.

The reasons why General Bragg did not promptly pursue are stated in his report thus:

"Our supplies of all kinds were greatly reduced, the railroad having been constantly occupied in transporting troops, prisoners, and our wounded, and the bridges having been destroyed to a point two miles south of Ringgold. These supplies were ordered to be replenished, and, as soon as it was seen that we could be subsisted, the army was moved forward to seize and hold the only communication the enemy had with his supplies in the rear. His important road, and the shortcut by half to his depot at Bridgeport, lay along the south bank of the Tennessee. The holding of this all-important route was confided to Lieutenant-General Longstreet's command, and its possession forced the enemy to a road double the length, over two ranges of mountains, by wagon transportation. At the same time, our cavalry, in large force, was thrown across the river to operate on this long and difficult route. These dispositions, faithfully sustained, insured the enemy's speedy evacuation of Chattanooga for want of food and forage."

These reverses caused the enemy to send forward reënforcements from the army at Vicksburg, and also to assign General Grant to the command in Tennessee. As early as September 23d the Eleventh and Twelfth Corps of the Army of the Potomac were detached, and sent under General Hooker to Tennessee, and assigned to protect Rosecrans's line of communication from Bridgeport to Nashville. It was on October 23d that General Grant arrived at Chattanooga, and only in time to save their army from starvation or evacuation. The investment by General Bragg had been so close and their communications had been so destroyed that Bragg was on the point of realizing the evacuation of Chattanooga, which he had anticipated. The report of Grant thus describes the situation on his arrival:

"Up to this period our forces in Chattanooga were practically invested, the enemy's lines extending from the Tennessee River, above Chattanooga, to the river at and below the point of Lookout Mountain, below Chattanooga, with the south bank of the river picketed nearly to Bridgeport, his main force being fortified in Chattanooga Valley, at the foot of and on Missionary Ridge and Lookout Mountain, and a brigade in Lookout Valley. True, we held possession of the country north of the river, but it was from sixty to seventy miles over the most impracticable roads to army supplies.

"The artillery horses and mules had become so reduced by starvation that they could not have been relied upon for moving anything. An attempt at retreat must have been with men alone, and with only such supplies as they could carry. A retreat would have been almost certain annihilation, for the enemy, occupying positions within gunshot of and overlooking our very fortifications, would unquestionably have pursued retreating forces. Already more than ten thousand animals had perished in supplying half rations to the troops by the long and tedious route from Stevenson and Bridgeport to Chattanooga over Waldron's Ridge. They could not have been supplied another week."

The first movement under Grant was, therefore, to establish a new and shorter line of supplies. For this purpose a night expedition was sent down the river from Chattanooga, which seized the range of hills at the mouth of Lookout Valley, and covered the Brown's Ferry road. By 10 A.M. a bridge was laid across the river at the ferry, which secured the end of the road nearest to our forces and the shorter line over which the enemy could move troops. General Hooker also entered Lookout Valley at Wauhatchie, and took up positions for the defense of the road from Whiteside's, over which he had marched, and also the road leading from Brown's Ferry to Kelly's Ferry. General Palmer crossed from the north side of the river opposite Whiteside's, and held the road passed over by Hooker. An unsuccessful attack was made on a portion of Hooker's troops the first night after he entered the valley. Subsequently, we lost the remaining heights held by us west of Lookout Creek.

Further operations of the enemy were delayed until the arrival of Sherman's force from Memphis. After his arrival, on November 23d, an attempt was made to feel our lines. This was done with so much force as to obtain possession of Indian Hill and the low range of hills south of it. That night Sherman began to move to obtain a position just below the mouth of the South Chickamauga, and by daylight on the 24th he had eight thousand men on the south side of the Tennessee, and fortified in rifle-trenches. By noon pontoon-bridges were laid across the Tennessee and the Chickamauga, and the remainder of his forces crossed. During the afternoon he took possession of the whole northern extremity of Missionary Ridge nearly to the railroad-tunnel, and fortified the position equally with that held by us. A raid was also made on our line of communication, cutting the railroad at Cleveland. On the same day Hooker sealed the western slope of Lookout Mountain. On the 26th he took possession of the mountain-top with a part of his force, and with the remainder crossed Chattanooga Valley to Rossville. Our most northern point was assailed by Sherman, and the attack kept up all day. He was reënforced by a part of Howard's corps. In the afternoon the whole force of the enemy's center, consisting of four divisions, was moved to the attack. They got possession of the rifle-pits at the foot of Missionary Ridge, and commenced the ascent of the mountain from right to left, and continued it until the summit was reached, notwithstanding the volleys of grape and canister discharged at them. Our forces retreated from the ridge as the multitudinous assailants neared the thin line on the crest, and during the night withdrew from the positions on the plain below. General Grant, after advancing a short distance from Chattanooga, dispatched a portion of his forces to the relief of Burnside in East Tennessee, where he was closely besieged by General Longstreet in Knoxville. Longstreet moved east into Virginia, and ultimately joined General Lee. He had left the army of General Lee, and moved to the West with his force, on the condition that he should return when summoned. This summons had been sent to him. The loss of the enemy in the conflicts at Chattanooga was 757 killed, 4,529 wounded, and 337 missing; total, 5,616. Our loss in killed and wounded was much less than theirs.

[Footnote 78: Some of the garrison of Cumberland Gap escaped, and stated to General Jones that the surrender had been made without resistance, on the demands of the smaller detachments which had preceded General Burnside, and I was not advised of the fact that Buckner had previously retreated toward Chattanooga, and that Burnside was in possession of Knoxville. In my message of December 12, 1863, I referred to the event, as reported to the War Department, as follows:

"The country was painfully surprised by the intelligence that the officer in command of Cumberland Gap had surrendered that important and easily defensible pass, without firing a shot, upon the summons of a force still believed to have been inadequate to its reduction, and when reënforcements were in supporting distance and had been ordered to his aid.

The entire garrison, including its commander, being still held prisoners by the enemy, I am unable to suggest any explanation of this disaster which laid open Eastern Tennessee and Southwestern Virginia to hostile operations."

So far as censure of General Frazier was implied in these remarks, I am now fully satisfied it was unjust, and I can only regret that the authentic information recently furnished to me had not been received at an earlier date, so that I might have relieved General Frazier from the reflection while I held executive authority. It gives me pleasure now to say that full and exact information justifies the high estimate I placed upon him when he was assigned to the separate command of that important post. Full justice can be done to General Frazier only when his report and those of his subordinate officers shall have been published.]

CHAPTER XLI.

Movement to draw forth the Enemy.—Advance to Culpeper Court-House.—Cavalry Engagement at Beverly's and Kelly's Fords.—Movement against Winchester.—Milroy's Force captured.—Prisoners.—The Enemy retires along the Potomac.—Maryland entered.—Advance into Pennsylvania.—The Enemy driven back toward Gettysburg.—Position of the Respective Forces.—Battle at Gettysburg.—The Army Retires.—Prisoners.—The Potomac swollen.—No Interruption by the Enemy.—Strength of our Force.—Strength of the Enemy.—The Campaign closed.—Observations.—Kelly's Ford.—Attempt to surprise our Army.—System of Breastworks.—Prisoners.

In the spring of 1863 the enemy occupied his former position before Fredericksburg. He was in great strength, and, so far as we could learn, was preparing on the grandest scale for another advance against Richmond, which in political if not military circles was regarded as the objective point of the war. The consolidated report of the Army of the Potomac, then under the command of Major-General Hooker, states the force present on May 10, 1863, to be 136,704.

General Lee's forces had been reorganized into three army corps, designated the First, Second, and Third Corps. In the order named, they were commanded by Lieutenant-Generals Longstreet, Ewell, and A. P. Hill.

The zeal of our people in the defense of their country's cause had brought nearly all of the population fit for military service to the various armies then in the field, so that but little increase could be hoped for by the Army of Northern Virginia. Under these circumstances, to wait until the enemy should choose to advance was to take the desperate hazard of the great inequality of numbers, as well as ability to reënforce, which he possessed. In addition to the army under General Hooker, a considerable force occupied the lower part of the Valley of the Shenandoah.

It was decided by a bold movement to attempt to transfer hostilities to the north side of the Potomac, by crossing the river and marching into Maryland and Pennsylvania, simultaneously driving the foe out of the Shenandoah Valley. Thus, it was hoped, General Hooker's army would be called from Virginia to meet our advance toward the heart of the enemy's country. In that event, the vast preparations which had been made for an advance upon Richmond would be foiled, the plan for his summer's campaign deranged, and much of the season for active operations be consumed in the new combinations and dispositions which would be required. If, beyond the Potomac, some opportunity should be offered so as to enable us to defeat the army on which our foe most relied, the measure of our success would be full; but, if the movement only resulted in freeing Virginia from the presence of the hostile army, it was more than could fairly be expected from awaiting the attack which was clearly indicated.

Actuated by these and other considerations, the campaign was commenced on June 3, 1863. Our forces advanced to Culpeper Court-House, leaving A. P. Hill to occupy the lines in front of Fredericksburg. On the 5th Hooker, having discovered our movement, crossed an army corps to the south side of the Rappahannock, but, as this was apparently for observation, it was not thought necessary to oppose it.

On the 9th a large force of the enemy's cavalry crossed at Beverly's and Kelly's Fords and attacked General Stuart. A severe engagement ensued, continuing from early in the morning until late in the afternoon, when Stuart forced his assailant to recross the river with heavy loss, leaving four hundred prisoners, three pieces of artillery, and several stands of colors in our hands.

Meantime, General Jenkins with a cavalry brigade had been ordered to advance toward Winchester, to coöperate with an infantry expedition into the lower Valley, and General Imboden made a demonstration toward Romney to cover the movement against Winchester, and prevent reënforcements from the line of the Baltimore and Ohio Railroad. Both these officers were in position when Ewell left Culpeper Court-House on the 6th. Crossing the Shenandoah near Front Royal, Rodes's division went to Berryville to dislodge the force stationed there, and cut off the communication between Winchester and the Potomac. General Ewell, on the 13th of June, advanced directly upon Winchester, driving the enemy into his works around the town. On the next day he stormed the works, and the whole army of General Milroy was captured or put to flight. Most of those who attempted to escape were intercepted and made prisoners. Unfortunately, among the exceptions, was their commander, who had been guilty of most unpardonable outrages upon defenseless non-combatants.

General Rodes marched from Berryville to Martinsburg, entering the latter place on the 14th, and capturing seven hundred prisoners, five pieces of artillery, and a considerable quantity of stores. These operations cleared the Valley of the enemy. More than four thousand prisoners, twenty-nine pieces of artillery, two hundred and seventy wagons and ambulances, with four hundred horses, were captured, besides a large amount of military stores. Our loss was small. On the night that Ewell appeared at Winchester, the enemy at Fredericksburg recrossed the Rappahannock, and on the next day disappeared behind the hills of Stafford.

The whole army of General Hooker, in retiring, pursued the roads near the Potomac, offering no favorable opportunity for attack. His purpose seemed to be to take a position which would enable him to cover the approaches to Washington City. To draw him farther from his base, and to cover the march of A. P. Hill, who had left for the Valley, Longstreet moved from Culpeper Court-House on the 15th, and occupied Ashby's and Snicker's Gaps. The cavalry under General Stuart was in front of Longstreet to watch the enemy, and encountered his cavalry on the 17th near Aldie, and drove it back. The engagement was renewed on the next day, but the cavalry of the latter being now strongly supported by infantry, Stuart was compelled to retire. He had, however, taken in these engagements about four hundred prisoners and a considerable number of horses and arms.

Meantime, General Ewell, with the advance of his corps, had entered Maryland. Jenkins, with his cavalry, penetrated as far as Chambersburg, Pennsylvania. As these demonstrations did not cause the hostile army to leave Virginia, nor did it seem disposed to advance upon Longstreet's position, he was withdrawn to the west side of the Shenandoah. General Hill had already reached the Valley. General Stuart was left to guard the passes of the mountains and observe the movements of the enemy, whom he was instructed to harass and impede as much as possible should he attempt to cross the Potomac, In that event General Stuart was directed to move into Maryland, crossing the Potomac east or west of the Blue Ridge, as in his judgment should seem best, and take position on the right of our column as it advanced. General Longstreet says:

"General Stuart held the gap for a while, and then hurried around beyond Hooker's army, and we saw nothing more of him until the evening of July 2d, when he came down from York and joined us, having made a complete circuit of the Federal army."

Longstreet and Hill crossed the Potomac, to be within supporting distance of Ewell, and advanced into Pennsylvania, encamping near Chambersburg on the 27th of June. The cavalry, under Colonel White, advanced to the Susquehanna.

On the night of the 27th information was received that General Hooker had crossed the Potomac, and was advancing northward, and that the head of the column had reached South Mountain. This menaced our communications, and it was resolved to prevent his further progress by concentrating our army on the east side of the mountain. Accordingly, the different commands were ordered to proceed to Gettysburg. This march was conducted more slowly than it would have been had the movements of Hooker been known. Heth's, the leading division of Hill's corps, met the enemy in front of Gettysburg on the morning of July 1st, driving him back to within a short distance of the town; the advance there encountered a larger force, with which two of Hill's divisions became engaged. Ewell, coming up with two of his divisions, joined in the engagement; and the opposing force was driven through Gettysburg with heavy loss, including about five thousand prisoners and several pieces of artillery.

Under the instructions given to them not to bring on a general engagement, these corps bivouacked on the ground they had won.

In an address delivered at Lexington, Virginia, on January 17, 1873, General W. N. Pendleton, chief of artillery, makes the following statement:

"The ground southwest of the town was carefully examined by me after the engagement on July 1st. Being found much less difficult than the steep ascent fronting the troops already up, its practicable character was reported to our commanding General. He informed me that he had ordered Longstreet to attack on that front at sunrise the next morning. And he added to myself, 'I want you to be out long before sunrise so as to reexamine and save time.' He also desired me to communicate with General Longstreet as well as with himself. The reconnaissance was accordingly made, as soon as it was light enough on the 2d, and made through a long distance—in fact, very close to what there was of the enemy's line. No insuperable difficulty appearing, and the marching up—far off, the enemy's reenforcing columns being seen—the extreme desirableness of immediate attack there, was at once reported to the commanding General; and, according to his wish, message was also sent to the intrepid but deliberate corps commander whose sunrise attack there had been ordered. There was, however, unaccountable delay. My own messages went repeatedly to General Lee, and his, I know, was urgently pressed on General Longstreet, until, as I afterward learned from officers who saw General Lee, as I could not at the time, he manifested extreme displeasure with the tardy corps commander. That hard-fighting soldier, to whom it had been committed there to attack early in the day, did not, in person, reach the commanding General, and with him ride to a position whence to view the ground and see the enemy's arriving masses, until twelve o'clock; and his column was not up and ready for the assault until 4 P.M. All this, as it occurred under my personal observation, it is nothing short of imperative duty that I should thus fairly state."

For the reasons set forth by General Pendleton, whose statement, in regard to a fact coming under his personal observation, none who know him will question, preparations for a general engagement were unfortunately delayed until the afternoon, instead of being made at sunrise; then troops had been concentrated, and "Round-Top," the commanding position, unoccupied in the morning, had received the force which inflicted such disaster on our assaulting columns. The question as to the responsibility for this delay has been so fully discussed in the Southern Historical Society papers as to relieve me from the necessity of entering into it.

The position at Gettysburg was not the choice of either side. South from the town an irregular, interrupted line of hills runs, which is sometimes called the "Gettysburg Ridge." This ridge, at the town, turns eastward and then southward. At the turn eastward is Cemetery Hill and at the turn southward Culps's Hill. From Cemetery Hill the line runs southward about three miles in a well-defined ridge, since the battle called Cemetery Ridge, and terminates in a high, rocky, and wooded peak named Round-Top, which was the key of the enemy's position, as it flanked their line. The less elevated portion, near where the crest rises into Round-Top, is termed "Little Round-Top," a rough and bold spur of the former. Thus, while Cemetery and Culps's Hills require the formation of a line of battle to face northward, the direction of Cemetery Ridge requires the line to face westward. The crest has a good slope to the rear, while to the west it falls off in a cultivated and undulating valley, which it commands. About a mile distant is a parallel crest, known as Seminary Ridge, and which our forces occupied during the battle. Longstreet, with the divisions of Hood and McLaws, faced Round-Top and a good part of Cemetery Ridge; Hill's three divisions continued the line from the left of Longstreet, fronting the remainder of Cemetery Ridge; while Ewell, with his three divisions, held a line through the town, and, sweeping round the base of Cemetery Hill, terminated the left in front of Culps's Hill.

These were the positions of the three corps after the arrival of General Longstreet's troops.

The main purpose of the movement across the Potomac was to free Virginia from the presence of the enemy. If this could be done by manoeuvering merely, a most important result would be cheaply obtained. The contingency of a battle was of course deemed probable, and, with any fair opportunity, the Army of Northern Virginia was considered sure to win a victory.

[Illustration: Lieutenant-General James Longstreet]

It had not been intended to fight a general battle at such a distance as Gettysburg from our base, unless attacked; but, being unexpectedly confronted by the opposing army, it became a matter of difficulty to withdraw through the mountains with our large trains. At the same time the country was unfavorable for collecting supplies while in the presence of the main army of the enemy, as he was enabled to restrain our foraging parties by occupying the passes of the mountains with both regular and local troops. Encouraged by the successful issue of the engagement of the first day, and in view of the valuable results that would ensue from the defeat of the army of General Meade (who had succeeded General Hooker), General Lee thought it preferable to renew the attack.

General Meade held the high ridge above described, along which he had massed a large amount of artillery. General Ewell occupied the left of our line, General Hill the center, and General Longstreet the right. In front of General Longstreet the enemy held a position, from which, if he could be driven, it was thought that our army could gain the more elevated ground (Round-Top) beyond, and thus enable our guns to rake the crest of the ridge. That officer was directed to endeavor to carry this position, while General Ewell attacked directly the high ground on the enemy's right, which had already been partially fortified. General Hill was instructed to threaten the center of the line, in order to prevent reënforcements to either wing, and to avail himself of any opportunity that might present itself to attack. After a severe struggle Longstreet succeeded in getting possession of and holding the ground in his immediate front. Ewell also carried some of the strong positions which he assailed, and the result was such as to lead to the belief that he would ultimately be able to dislodge the force in his front. The battle ceased at dark. These partial successes determined Lee to continue the assault on the next day. Pickett, with three of his brigades, joined Longstreet on the following morning, and our batteries were moved forward to the position gained by him on the day before. The general plan of attack was unchanged, except that one division and two brigades of Hill's corps were ordered to support Longstreet.

General Meade, in the mean time, had strengthened his line with earthworks. The morning was occupied in necessary preparations, and the battle recommenced in the afternoon of the 3d, and raged with great violence until sunset. Our troops succeeded in entering the advanced works of the enemy, and getting possession of some of his batteries; but, our artillery having nearly expended its ammunition, the attacking columns became exposed to the heavy fire of the numerous batteries near the summit of the ridge, and, after a most determined and gallant struggle, were compelled to relinquish their advantage and fall back to their original positions with severe loss.

Owing to the strength of the enemy's position and the exhaustion of our ammunition, a renewal of the engagement could not be hazarded, and the difficulty of procuring supplies rendered it impossible to continue longer where we were. Such of the wounded as could be removed and a part of the arms collected on the field were ordered to Williamsport. The army remained at Gettysburg during the 4th, and at night began to retire by the road to Fairfield, carrying with it about four thousand prisoners. Nearly two thousand had been previously paroled; but the numerous wounded that had fallen into our hands after the first and second day's engagements were left behind. Little progress was made that night, owing to a severe storm, which greatly embarrassed our movements. The rear of the column did not leave its position near Gettysburg until after daylight on the 5th. The march was continued during that day without interruption by the enemy, except an unimportant demonstration upon our rear in the afternoon, when near Fairfield, which was easily checked. The army, after a tedious march, rendered more difficult by the rains, reached Hagerstown on the afternoon of the 6th and morning of the 7th of July.

The Potomac was so much swollen by the rains, that had fallen almost incessantly since our army entered Maryland, as to be unfordable. A pontoon-train had been sent from Richmond, but the rise in the river gave to it a width greater than was expected, so that additional boats had to be made by the army on its retreat. Our communication with the south side was thus interrupted, and it was found difficult to procure either ammunition or subsistence, the latter difficulty being enhanced by the high water impeding the working of the mills. The trains with the wounded and prisoners were compelled to wait at Williamsport for the subsiding of the river or the construction of additional pontoon-boats. The enemy had not yet made his appearance, but, as he was in a condition to obtain large reënforcements and our want of supplies was daily becoming more embarrassing, it was deemed advisable to recross the river. By the 13th a good bridge was thrown over at Falling Waters. On the 12th Meade's army approached. A position had been previously selected to cover the Potomac from Williamsport to Falling Waters, and an attack was awaited during that and the succeeding day. This did not take place, though the two armies were in close proximity, the enemy being occupied in fortifying his own lines.

General Meade, in his testimony before the Committee on the Conduct of the War, said that he ordered an attack on our forces on the morning of the 14th, and, if it had been made, it was his opinion that "it would have resulted disastrously." When asked the reasons for that opinion, he replied:

"If I had attacked the enemy in the position which he then occupied—he having the advantage of position, and being on the defensive, his artillery in position, and his infantry behind parapets and rifle-pits—the very same reasons and causes which produced my success at Gettysburg would have operated in his favor there, and be likely to produce success on his part."

Our preparations being completed, and the Potomac, though still deep, being pronounced fordable, the army commenced to withdraw to the south side on the night of the 13th. Ewell's corps forded the river at Williamsport, those of Longstreet and Hill crossed upon the bridge. Owing to the condition of the roads the troops did not reach the bridge until after daylight on the 14th, and the crossing was not completed until 1 P.M., when the bridge was removed. General Lee said that the enemy offered no serious interruption, and the movement was attended with no loss of material except a few disabled wagons and two pieces of artillery, which the horses were unable to move through the deep mud. During the slow and tedious march to the bridge, in the midst of a violent storm of rain, some of the men lay down by the way to rest. Officers sent back for them failed to find many in the obscurity of the night, and these, with some stragglers, a few of Heth's division most remote from the bridge, were captured. On the following day the army marched to Bunker Hill, in the vicinity of which it encamped for several days. Owing to the swollen condition of the Shenandoah River, the campaign which was contemplated when the Potomac was recrossed, could not be immediately commenced. Before the waters had subsided, the movements of the enemy required us to cross the Blue Ridge and take position south of the Rappahannock.

The strength of our army at Gettysburg is stated at 62,000 of all arms.[79] The report of the Army of the Potomac under General Meade, on June 30, 1863, states the force present at 112,988 men. Before the Committee on the Conduct of the War, General Meade, in reference to his force at Gettysburg, said, "Including all arms of the service, my strength was a little under 100,000 men—about 95,000."

If the strength of General Lee's forces, according to the last accessible report before the movement northward, be compared with that made after his return into Virginia, there is a decrease of nineteen thousand of the brave men who had set the seal of invincibility upon the Army of Northern Virginia.

General Lee, in his report, noticing the large loss of men and officers, says:

"I can not speak of these brave men as their merits and exploits deserve. Some of them are appropriately mentioned in the accompanying reports, and the memory of all will be gratefully and affectionately cherished by the people in whose defense they fell.

"The loss of Major-General Pender is severely felt by the army and the country. . . . Brigadier-Generals Armistead, Barksdale, Garnet, and Semmes, died as they had lived, discharging the highest duty of patriots with devotion that never faltered, and courage that shrank from no danger."

The testimony of General Meade, above mentioned, contains this statement respecting his losses:

"On the evening of the 2d of July, after the battle of that day had ceased, and darkness had set in, being aware of the very heavy losses of the First and Eleventh Corps on the 1st of July, and knowing how severely the Third Corps, the Fifth Corps, and other portions of the army, had suffered in the battle of the 2d of July—in fact, as subsequently ascertained, out of the twenty-four thousand men killed, wounded, and missing, which was the amount of my losses and casualties at Gettysburg—over twenty thousand of them had been put *hors de combat* before the night of the 2d of July."

Thus closed the campaign in Pennsylvania. The wisdom of the strategy was justified by the result. The battle of Gettysburg was unfortunate. Though the loss sustained by the enemy was greater than our own, theirs could be repaired, ours could not.

Had General Lee been able to compel the enemy to attack him in position, I think we should have had a complete victory, and the testimony of General Meade quoted above shows that he was not at all inclined to make the experiment. If General Lee, by moving to the right, would only have led General Meade to fall back on his preferred position of Pipe Creek, his ability to wait and the impossibility under such circumstances for General Lee to supply his army for any length of time seem to me an answer to that point in the criticism to which our great Captain has been subjected. To compel Meade to retire would have availed but little to us, unless his army had first been routed. To beat that army was probably to secure our independence. The position of Gettysburg would have been worth nothing to us if our army had found it unoccupied. The fierce battle that Lee fought there must not be considered as for the position; to beat the great army of the North was the object, and that it was of possible attainment is to be inferred from the various successes of our arms. Had there been a concentrated attack at sunrise on the second day, with the same gallantry and skill which were exhibited in the partial assaults, it may reasonably be assumed that the enemy would have been routed. This, from the best evidence we have, was the plan and the expectation of General Lee. These having failed, from whatever cause, and Meade having occupied in force the commanding position of Round-Top, it must be conceded that it would have been better to withdraw than to renew the attack on the third day. The high morale and discipline of our army, together with the unqualified confidence of the men in their commanding General, excluded the supposition that they would be demoralized by retreat. Subsequent events proved how little cause there was to fear it. It is not admitted that our army was defeated, and the enemy's claim to a victory is refuted by the fact that, when Lee halted on the banks of the Potomac, Meade, instead of attacking as a pursuing general would a defeated foe, halted also, and commenced intrenching.

The Battle of Gettysburg has been the subject of an unusual amount of discussion, and the enemy has made it a matter of extraordinary exultation. As an affair of arms it was marked by mighty feats of valor to which both combatants may point with military pride. It was a graceful thing in President Lincoln if, as reported, when he was shown the steeps which the Northern men persistently held, he answered, "I am proud to be the countryman of the men who assailed those heights."

The consequences of the battle have justified the amount of attention it has received. It may be regarded as the most eventful struggle of the war. By it the drooping spirit of the North was revived. Had their army been there defeated, those having better opportunities to judge than I or any one who was not among them, have believed it would have ended the war. On the other hand, a drawn battle, where the Army of Northern Virginia made an attack, impaired the confidence of the Southern people so far as to give the malcontents a power to represent the Government as neglecting for Virginia the safety of the more southern States.

In all free governments, the ability of its executive branch to prosecute a war must largely depend upon public opinion; in an infant republic, this, for every reason, is peculiarly the case. The volume given to the voice of disaffection was therefore most seriously felt by us.

Shattered, it is true, but not disheartened, the Army of Northern Virginia after recrossing the Potomac rose like the son of Terra, with renewed vigor, and entered on the brilliant campaign hereafter to be generally described.

Early in October General Lee, with two corps (Ewell's and Hill's), the First Corps of his army having been temporarily detached for service in Tennessee, crossed the Rapidan to attack the flank of the enemy, or to compel him to retreat. It resulted in the capture of fifteen hundred prisoners, and forced Meade's army back to Alexandria and Centreville. The campaign was an unbroken success, with the exception of a rash and ill-conducted affair at Bristoe Station, where our advance engaged a corps, and was repulsed, losing a number of men and five guns. Thus, without a general battle, a large portion of the State was for the time liberated.

On November 7th the enemy advanced upon our force at Kelly's Ford, of the Rappahannock River, effected a crossing, and, rushing upon two brigades who were at Rappahannock Station defending the bridges, overwhelmed and captured most of them, taking between twelve and fifteen hundred men, and four pieces of artillery. The movements of the enemy were concealed by the darkness, and his attack was a surprise.

On November 26th the army under General Meade crossed the Rapidan, with the intention of interposing between the widely separated wings of his adversary. Instead of being successful, this movement resulted in an entire failure. General Meade found Lee's army posted behind Mine Run, and ready to receive an attack whenever he was disposed to make it. "Meade declared, it is related, that he could carry the position with a loss of thirty thousand men; but, as that idea was frightful, there seemed nothing to do but retreat." [80] Lee had inaugurated that system of breastworks which did him good service in his long campaign with General Grant. When the troops were halted in a wood, the men felled the large trees, heavy logs were dragged without loss of time to the prescribed line, where they were piled upon one another in double walls, which were filled in rapidly with earth; so that, in a short space of time, defenses which would turn a cannon-shot were often constructed. In front, for some distance, the felled timber made a kind of abatis. As General Meade did not attack, General Lee, on the night of December 1st, determined to assail his adversary on the next morning; but, when the dawn broke over the hills, his camps were seen to be deserted. General Meade had abandoned the campaign, and was in full retreat toward the Rapidan. Pursuit was immediately made, but he had too much the start, and reached the north side of the Rapidan before he could be overtaken. Both armies then retired to their original positions. We captured about seven hundred prisoners, four hundred mules and horses, and destroyed or secured one hundred and twenty wagons.

[Footnote 79: "Four Years with General Lee."]

CHAPTER XLII.

Subjugation of the States of Tennessee, Louisiana, Arkansas, and Virginia.—Object of a State Government; its Powers are "Just Powers"; how exercised; its Duty; necessarily sovereign; its Entire Order; how founded; how destroyed.—The Crime against Constitutional Liberty.—What is the Government of the United States?—It partakes of the Nature of a Limited Partnership; its Peaceful Objects.—Distinction between the Governments of the States and that of the United States.—Secession.—The Government of the United States invades the State; refuses to recognize its Government; thus denies the Fundamental Principle of Popular Liberty.—Founded a New State Government based on the Sovereignty of the United States Government.—Annihilation of Unalienable Rights.—Qualification of Voters fixed by Military Power.—Condition of the Voter's Oath.—Who was the Sovereign in Tennessee?—Case of Louisiana.—Registration of Voters.—None allowed to register who could not or would not take a Certain Oath; its Conditions.—Election of State Officers.—Part of the State Constitution declared void.—All done under the Military Force of the United States Government.

The most painful pages of this work are those which now present the subjugation of the State governments by the Government of the United States. The patriot, the lover of his country and of the liberties of mankind, can not contemplate these facts without a feeling of grief which will not be comforted. That the work of the fathers of the republic, that the most magnificent system of constitutional government which the wisdom of man has devised, should be turned from its object, changed from its order, rendered powerless to protect the unalienable rights and sovereignty of the people, and made the instrument by which to establish and maintain imperialism, is a revolution unlike any other that may be found in the history of mankind. The result established the truthfulness of the assertion, so often made during the progress of the war, that the Northern people, by their unconstitutional warfare to gain the freedom of certain negro slaves, would lose their own liberties.

It has been shown that the governments of the States were instituted to secure certain unalienable rights of the citizens with which they were endowed by their Creator, and that among these rights were life, liberty, and the pursuit of happiness; that they derived their just powers from the consent of the governed; and that these powers were organized by the citizens in such form as seemed to them most likely to effect their safety and happiness. Where must the American citizen look for the security of the rights with which he has been endowed by his Creator? To his State government. Where shall he look to find security and protection for his life, security and protection for his personal liberty, security and protection for his property, security and protection for his safety and happiness? Only to his State government.

The powers which the State government possesses for the security of his life, his liberty, his property, his safety, and his happiness, are "just powers." They have been derived from the unconstrained consent of the governed, and they have been organized in such form as seems most likely to effect these objects.

Is the citizen's life in danger from violence? The State guarantees his protection, and it is its duty to rescue him from danger and obtain redress from the offender, whether an individual or a foreign nation. Are the freedom and personal liberty of the citizen in danger from unlawful arrest and imprisonment? The State guarantees both, and it is its duty to secure and preserve his freedom. Is the property of the citizen in danger of a violent and unjust seizure and unlawful detention or destruction? The State government guarantees his title, restores the property, or obtains damages. Is the personal property of the citizen in danger of robbery or abduction? The State government throws over it the shield of its protection, and regards the burglar and the robber as the enemies of society. It is unnecessary to proceed further with this enumeration.

The duty of the State government is to give to its citizens perfect and complete security. It is necessarily sovereign within its own domain, for it is the representative and the constituted agent of the inherent sovereignty of the individuals. For the performance of its duty of protection it may unite with other sovereignties; and also, for better safety and security to its citizens, it may withdraw or secede from such Union.

It will be seen that the entire order of the State government is founded on the free consent of the governed. From this it springs; from this it receives its force and life. It is this consent alone from which "just powers" are derived. They can come from no other source, and their exercise sources a true republican government. All else are usurpations, their exercise is a tyranny, and their end is the safety and security of the usurper, to obtain which the unalienable rights of the people are sacrificed. The "just powers," thus derived, are organized in such form as shall seem to the governed to be most likely to secure their safety and happiness. It is the governed who determine the form of the government, and not the ruler nor his military force, unless he comes as a conqueror to make the subjugated do his will. The object, or end, for which these "just powers" are derived from the consent of the governed and organized in such form as seems most likely to effect that object, is solely to secure the unalienable rights of men—such as life, liberty, property, justice, peace and order, and the pursuit of happiness.

It will now be seen by the reader that, whenever any one of the features of this order is perverted in its origin or progress, or thwarted, or caused to deviate from its natural operation by any internal or external interference, the order is destroyed, and the State government, which represents it, is subverted, turned from its object, changed from its natural purpose, rendered powerless to protect the unalienable rights of its citizens, and made an instrument to strengthen the hands of despotism. The commission of such a subversion of the peaceful and fraternal States of this once happy republic is fearlessly charged upon the Government of the United States, as in itself constituting a monstrous crime against constitutional liberty; and it is asserted that, when the circumstances attending the deed are considered—the rage against a whole people, the pillage, the arson, the inciting of servile war, the slaughter of defenseless non-combatants, the devastation of whole peaceful regions, the indiscriminate destruction of property—no parallel can be found in the annals of mankind.

What, then, is the Government of the United States? It is an organization of a few years' duration. It might cease to exist, and yet the States and the people continue prosperous, peaceful, and happy. Unlike the governments of the States, which find their origin deep in the nature of man, it sprang from certain circumstances which existed in the course of human affairs. Unlike the governments of the States and of separate nations, which have a divine sanction, it has no warrant for its authority but the ratification of the sovereign States. Unlike the governments of the States, which were instituted to secure generally the unalienable rights of man, it has only the enumerated objects, and is restrained from passing beyond them by the express reservation of all delegated functions. It keeps no records of property, and guarantees to no one the possession of his estate. Marriage, from which springs the family and the State, it can neither confirm nor annul. It partakes of the nature of an incorporation for certain purposes, beyond which it has neither influence nor authority. It is an anomaly among governments, and arose out of the articles of agreement made by certain friendly States, which proposed to form a society of States and invest a common agent with specified functions of sovereignty. Its duration was intended to be permanent, as it was hoped thus to promote the peaceful ends for which it was established; but, to have declared it *perpetual*, would have been to deny the right of a people to alter or abolish their government when it should cease to answer the ends for which it was instituted.

The objects which its creation was designed to secure to the States and their people were of a truly peaceful nature, and commended themselves to the approbation of men. They were stated by its authors in a form called "the preamble" of their work, which is in these words:

> "We, the people of the United States, in order to form a more perfect union, establish justice, insure domestic tranquillity, provide for the common defense, promote the general welfare, and secure the blessings of liberty to ourselves and our posterity, do ordain and establish this Constitution of the United States."

Mankind must contemplate with horror the fact that an organization established for such peaceful and benign ends did, within the first century of its existence, lead the assault in a civil war that brought nearly four millions of soldiers into the field, destroyed thousands and thousands of millions of treasure, trampled the unalienable rights of the people under foot, subverted and subjugated the governments of the States, and ended by establishing itself as supreme and sovereign over all. Some Christian writer has suggested the thought that there may not be a spot of the earth's surface in the Old World but has witnessed the commission of some human crime or been wet with human gore. How nearly true this may be of the New World's once-vaunted asylum for the victims of despotism, misrule, and oppression, these pages can bear some testimony. After all, it is the civil disorders, the violations of rights, and the perversions of wise and useful institutions, that are the most disastrous in their consequences. They last for ages; and often, too often, the lapse of time brings no remedy to the suffering people. In their despair, they say the past is gone for ever—a new era has opened; but what horrors may be developed in its revolving years no mortal can foresee, so they hug the chains they feel powerless to break.

How distinct in its nature and objects was the Government of the United States from the governments of the States, may be seen from that which has already been said. The former was established by common consent to look after the common interests. It was to make peace or war with foreign nations, protect the frontiers, extend the boundaries, decide disputes between citizens of different States, and administer general affairs in a manner to promote the peace, the order, and the happiness of all. But, to the fostering care of the State government, the man, the citizen, the head of the family, the parent, the child, the woman, the scholar, and the Christian all looked with full confidence as to their natural and divinely sanctioned protector against all foes within or without; and relied upon its ever-present arm for the safety and security of their persons, their homes, their property, and their institutions. How wofully the confiding people were betrayed when the usurper came, let some of the Northern States answer!

Now let us proceed to notice the acts of the Government of the United States, which subjugated the State governments. The details in the case of Tennessee have been already stated. In that instance, the government of the State, which derived its powers from the consent of the governed, so that they were "just powers," found, in the discharge of its duty to protect the institutions of its people, that there were no means by which it could fulfill that duty but by a withdrawal from the Union, so as to be rid of the Government of the United States, and thus escape the threatened dangers of usurpation and sectional hostility. It therefore resolved to withdraw from the Union, and the people gave their assent to this resolution; so that the State no longer considered itself a member of the Union, nor recognized the laws and authority of its Government. The Government of the United States, then, with a powerful military force, planted itself at Nashville, the State capital. It refused to recognize the State government, or any organization under it, as having any existence, or to recognize the people otherwise than as a hostile community. It said to them, in effect: "I am the sovereign and you are the subjects. If you are stronger than I am, then drive me out of the State; if I am stronger than you are, then I demand an unconditional surrender to my sovereignty." It is evident that the Government of the United States was not there by the consent of those who were to be governed. It had not, therefore, any "just powers" of government within the State of Tennessee. For, says the Declaration of Independence of our fathers, governments "derive their 'just powers' from the consent of the governed." It is further evident that, by this action, the Government of the United States denied the fundamental principle of popular liberty—that the people are the source of all political power. In this instance, it not only subverted the State government, but carried that subversion to the extent of annihilation. It, therefore, proceeded to establish a new order of affairs, founded, not on the principle of the sovereignty of the people, which was wholly rejected, but on the assumption of sovereignty in the United States Government. It appointed its military Governor to be the head of the new order, and recognized no civil or political existence in any man, except some of its notorious adherents, until, betraying the State, he had taken an oath of allegiance to the sovereignty of the Government of the United States. Now commenced a system of denial of unalienable rights, for the methods of the usurper are the same everywhere. Freedom of speech was suppressed by the imposition of fines on those using "seditious" language, and the demand of security for their future humility. The freedom of the press was suppressed by suspension of publications and the confiscation of the offices. Personal liberty was destroyed by arrests, imprisonment, and exile.

In process of time, an effort was made to erect a form of State government which should be subservient and subject to the United States Government. For this purpose, no one could be a voter until he had bound himself by an oath to support and defend the Government of the United States. Under the State governments, manhood, which came by nature, and residence, which came by one's own will, were sufficient qualifications for the voter.

It will be apparent from this statement that the voter's right to cast his ballot came not to him as an unalienable right, but rested upon the permission of the Government of the United States, as his sovereign, to whom his allegiance was due, and to whom he was required, in the first instance, to bind himself by an oath of allegiance without any mention whatever of a State government. Indeed, a little later, the same oath was required with additional conditions before a man was permitted to vote for a State constitutional convention, or for delegates to such a convention. These conditions were, that he would faithfully support all acts of Congress and all proclamations of the President of the United States, passed or made during the rebellion, having reference to slaves. Thus, the voter's right was made to rest, not only upon his binding himself in allegiance to the United States as his sovereign, but in the binding by oath his consent to certain unconstitutional acts and proclamations expressly designed to destroy one of the most important institutions of the State. This, sustained by a military force, was exacted by the United States Government as the lord paramount—the sovereign within the State. At the same time, the action of the voter, which should be perfectly free and unconstrained (for, under American political principles, he is the sovereign over all), is limited and bound down by an oath faithfully to support certain acts to which it was presumable he had ever been conscientiously opposed.

Under these circumstances, who was the sovereign in Tennessee? The Government of the United States. Where was the government of the State of Tennessee and the sovereign people? The former was subverted and overthrown, and the latter subjugated. The approval by Tennessee, under such circumstances, of Article XIII, as an amendment to the Constitution of the United States prohibiting the existence of slavery, was of no force; for consent given by a party under constraint has neither legal nor moral validity. The State Constitution was so amended as to contain certain new provisions prescribed by the Government of the United States by a so-called convention of delegates elected by the voters above specified, and then submitted to these voters, and said to be ratified by them. They were little more in numbers than a handful of the people of Tennessee. Was this a Constitution amended and approved by the consent of the people of Tennessee, the only sovereigns known under our institutions, or was it a Constitution amended and voted for by a small fraction of its population acting under the authority of the Government of the United Stales, as the only sovereign in the State? Admitting, even, that those who voted for the amended Constitution were the only legal voters in the State, the Government of the United States was no less an unlawful intruder and usurper when it prescribed the amendments of the Constitution and designated the voters. Nevertheless, this work was recognized by it, as constituting a republican State government under the Constitution.

Let us next notice some points in the subversion of the State government of Louisiana. One of the earliest steps taken for a civil organization, after the occupation of New Orleans, was to make a registration of voters. The United States Government was in possession by military force, and the object was to secure its permanent supremacy. Therefore, the oath which was administered to the person applying for registration contained this condition:

"I now register myself as a voter, freely and voluntarily, for the purpose of organizing a State government in Louisiana, loyal to the Government of the United States."

It was also announced, with the approval of the military Governor, that any person swearing falsely to any material part of the oath would be deemed to be guilty of perjury, and be liable to prosecution and punishment. The effect of this measure was to secure a registration only of persons who would maintain the supremacy of the Government of the United States. A proclamation was next issued by the commander of the United States forces for an election of State officers under the laws and Constitution of the State. It was declared that these officers, when thus elected, would constitute the so-called civil government of the State, under the Constitution and laws of Louisiana, "except so much of the said Constitution and laws as recognize, regulate, or relate to slavery," which were also declared to be inoperative and void. It was further provided, in the same proclamation, as follows:

"In order that the organic law of the State may be made to conform to the will of the people and harmonize with the spirit of the age, as well as to maintain and preserve the ancient landmarks of civil and religions liberty, an election of delegates to a convention for the revision of the Constitution will be held," etc.

The effect of these acts was to establish a number of persons, pledged to support the Government of the United States, as the only qualified voters in the State, and to elect so-called State officers and delegates to a so-called Constitutional Convention by their ballots. But this was a work that could be done only by the sovereign people acting through their lawful State government. It was not so done, because the Government of the United States, with a powerful military force, had taken possession of New Orleans, refused to recognize the officers of the State government, and sought to capture and imprison them, although it recognized the validity of the State Constitution in part, and commanded these things to be done as if it was the ultimate sovereign over all.

Thus the government of the State was subverted, the Constitution of the State in part set aside, and the sovereignty of the people trampled down by a power that had no rightful authority for such acts. Subsequently, a so-called convention was held, a so-called new Constitution adopted, complying with the views of the Government of the United States, the amendment to the Constitution of the United States as above mentioned was adopted, the State

Representatives were admitted to seats in Congress, and the people acquiesced in the fraud which they had not the power to correct.

The proceedings in the States of Arkansas and Virginia, which resulted in an entire subversion of the State Governments, the destruction of the sovereignty of the people, and the establishment of the supremacy of the Government of the United States, have been stated on a preceding page.

CHAPTER XLIII.

Subjugation of the Border States, Maryland, Kentucky, and Missouri.— A Military Force invades Maryland and occupies Baltimore.—Martial Law declared.—A Military Order.—Banishment from the State.— Civil Government of the State suspended.—Unalienable Rights of the Citizens invaded.—Arrests of Citizens commenced.—Number.—Case of John Merryman.—Opinion of Chief-Justice Taney.—Newspapers seized.—Houses searched for Arms.—Order of Commanding General to Marshals to put Test to Voters.—The Governor appeals to the President.—His Reply.—Voters imprisoned.—Statement of the Governor.—Result of the Election.—State Constitutional Convention.—Emancipation hardly carried.—First Open Measures in Kentucky.—Interference at the State Election by the United States Government.—Voters excluded.—Martial Law declared.—Soldiers keeping the Polls.—The Vote.—Statement of the Governor.—Attempt to enroll Able-bodied Negroes.—The Governor visits Washington.— The Result.—Arrests, Imprisonment, and Exile of Citizens.— Suspension of the Writ of *Habeas Corpus* by President Lincoln.— Interference with the State Election.—Order to the Sheriffs.— Proclamation of the Governor.—Enlistment of Slaves.—Emancipation by Constitutional Amendment.—Violent *Measures* in Missouri.—The Governor calls out the Militia.—His Words.—The Plea of the Invader.—"The Authority of the United States is Paramount," said President Lincoln.—Bravery of the Governor.—Words of the Commanding General.—Troops poured into the State.—Proceedings of the State Convention.—Numberless Usurpations.—Provisional Governor.—Emancipation Ordinance passed.

If the State government is instituted with certain powers which become "just powers" by the formal consent of the governed, for the purpose of enforcing security to the unalienable rights of man, it must be evident that any interference with those rights by which their enjoyments diminished, endangered, or destroyed, is not only an obstruction to the operation of the "just powers" of the State government, but is subversive of the purpose which it was instituted to effect.

In this manner the State government of Maryland was subjugated. A military force, under the authority of the Government of the United States, occupied the city of Baltimore at a time when no invasion of the State was threatened, and when there had been no application of the Legislature, or of the Executive, for protection against domestic violence, which circumstances alone could give a constitutional authority for this organized military force to occupy the State. The commanding General, Schenck, soon issued an order, of which the following is an extract:

308

"Martial law is declared and hereby established in the city and county of Baltimore, and in all the counties of the Western Shore of Maryland. The commanding General gives assurance that this suspension of civil government within the limits defined shall not extend beyond the necessities of the occasion. All the civil courts, tribunals, and political functionaries of State, county, or city authority, are to continue in the discharge of their duties as in times of peace, only in no way interfering with the exercise of the predominant power assumed and asserted by the military authority."

It will be noticed that this military force of the Government of the United States had no constitutional permission to come into Maryland and exercise authority; that the commanding General says that the civil government of the State is suspended within certain limits; that this suspension will be continued according to the necessities of the occasion; that the courts and political functionaries may discharge their duties, only in no way interfering with the exercise of the predominant military power. Now, where were the "just powers" of the State government at this time? They were suspended in a part of the State, says the commanding General, and for so long a time as the military authority may judge the necessities of the occasion to require, and that the courts and political functionaries may discharge their duties while recognizing the supremacy of the military power. Thus was the State government subjugated.

A further subversion of the State government was now commenced by an invasion and denial of some of the unalienable rights of the citizens, for the security of which that government was instituted. The Constitution of the United States says:

"No person shall be deprived of life, liberty, or property, without due process of law." [81]

"The right of the people to be secure in their persons, houses, papers, and effects, against unreasonable searches and seizures, shall not be violated." [82]

"Excessive bail shall not be required, nor excessive fines imposed, nor cruel and unusual punishments inflicted." [83]

"Congress shall make no law abridging the freedom of speech, or of the press." [84]

The Declaration of Independence says:

"That they are endowed by their Creator with certain unalienable rights; that among these are life, liberty, and the pursuit of happiness; that, to secure these rights, governments are instituted among men."

Immediately upon the issue of the order of the commanding General, the arrests of citizens commenced by provost-marshals. The family residence of a lady was forced open; she was seized, put on board of a steamer, and sent to the Confederate States. A man was arrested for being "disloyal" to the United States Government, and held for examination. Another was charged with interfering with the enrollment; he was held for further examination. Another, charged with being "disloyal" to the United States Government, took the oath of allegiance, and was released. A woman charged with the attempt to resist the enrollment was arrested, and subsequently released. A man, on a charge of "disloyalty," took the oath, and was released. Another, charged with having given improper information to enrolling officers, was released on furnishing the information. Another, charged with having powder in his possession, was released on taking the oath of allegiance. Two others, charged with abuse of the negroes laboring on the fortifications, were held for examination. Another, charged with rendering assistance to wounded Confederate soldiers, and expressing treasonable sentiments, took the oath of allegiance and was released. Another, charged with being a soldier in the Confederate army and paroled, was ordered to be sent across the lines. A man, charged with treasonable language, was ordered to be sent across the lines. Two others, charged with aiding Confederate soldiers, took the oath of allegiance and were discharged. Another, charged with receiving letters from Confederates for the purpose of delivery, took the oath of allegiance, and was discharged. Another, charged with expressing treasonable sentiments, was held for examination. Two, charged with cheering for Jefferson Davis, took the oath and were released.

One case more most be stated. On May 25, 1861, John Merryman, a most respectable citizen of the State, residing in Baltimore County, was seized in his bed by an armed force, and imprisoned in Fort McHenry. He petitioned the Chief-Justice of the United States that a writ of *habeas corpus* might be issued, which was granted. The officer upon whom it was served declined to obey the writ. An attachment was issued against the officer. The marshal was refused admittance to the fort to serve it. Upon such return being made, the Chief-Justice said:

"I ordered the attachment yesterday, because upon the face of the return the detention of the prisoner was unlawful upon two grounds:

"1. The President, under the Constitution and laws of the United States, can not suspend the privilege of the writ of *habeas corpus*, nor authorize any military officer to do so.

"2. A military officer has no right to arrest and detain a person not subject to the rules and articles of war for an offense against the laws of the United States, except in aid of the judicial authority and subject to its control; and, if the party is arrested by the military, it is the duty of the officer to deliver him over immediately to the civil authority, to be dealt with according to law.

"Under the Constitution of the United States, these principles are the fundamental law of the Union. In relation to the present return, I propose to say that the marshal has legally the power to summon out the *posse comitatus* to seize and bring into court the party named in the attachment; but it is apparent he will be resisted in the discharge of that duty by a force notoriously superior to the *posse comitatus* and, such being the case, the Court has no power under the law to order the necessary force to compel the appearance of the party.

"I shall reduce to writing the reasons under which I have acted, and which have led me to the conclusions expressed in my opinion, and shall report them, with these proceedings, to the President of the United States, and call upon him to perform his constitutional duty to enforce the laws; in other words, to enforce the process of this court."

During the month of July arrests were made of 361 persons, on charges like the above mentioned, by the military authority. Of this number, 317 took the oath of allegiance to the Government of the United States, and were released; 5 were sent to Fort McHenry, 3 to Washington for the action of the authorities there, 11 to the North, 6 across the lines, and 19 were held for further examination.

On September 11, 1863, one of the city newspapers published the poem entitled "The Southern Cross." The publishers and editor were immediately arrested, not allowed communication with any person whatever, and on the same day sent across the lines, with the understanding that they should not return during the war. On July 2d an order was issued which forbade the citizens of Baltimore City and County to keep arms unless they were enrolled as volunteer companies. The Fifty-first Regiment of Massachusetts Volunteers was placed at the disposal of General E. B. Tyler, assisted by the provost-marshal and the chief of police. The soldiers, in concert with the police, formed into parties of three or four, and were soon diligently engaged in searching houses. Large wagons were provided, and muskets, carbines, rifles, revolvers of all kinds, sabers, bayonets, swords, and bird and ducking guns in considerable quantities were gathered. The Constitution of the United States says:

"The right of the people to keep and bear arms shall not be infringed." [85]

A further subversion of the State government of Maryland was next made by a direct interference with the elections. An election was to be held in the State for members of the Legislature and members of Congress on November 3, 1863. The commanding General, on October 27th, issued an order to all marshals and military officers to cause their direct interference with the voters. The Governor (Bradford) applied to the President of the United States to have the order revoked, and protested against any person who offered to vote being put to any test not found in the laws of Maryland. President Lincoln declined to interfere with the order, except in one less important point. The Governor issued a proclamation on the day preceding the election, which the military commander endeavored to suppress, and issued an order charging that the tendency of the proclamation was to invite and suggest disturbance. One or more regiments of soldiers were sent out and distributed among several of the counties to attend the places of election, in defiance of the known laws of the State prohibiting their presence. Military officers and provost-marshals were ordered to arrest voters, guilty, in their opinion, of certain offenses, and to menace judges of election with the power of the army in case this order was not respected.

But, perhaps, the forcible language of the Governor to the Legislature will furnish the most undeniable statement of the facts. He says:

"On Monday evening preceding the election I issued a proclamation giving the judges of election the assurance of the protection of the

State to the extent of its ability. Before the following morning, orders were sent to the Eastern Shore, directing its circulation to be suppressed; the public papers were forbidden to publish it, and an embargo laid on all steamers in port trading with that part of the State, lest they might carry it.

"The abuses commenced even before the opening of the polls. On the day preceding the election, the officer in command of the regiment which had been distributed among the counties of the Eastern Shore, and who had himself landed in Kent County, commenced his operations by arresting and sending across the bay some ten or more of the most estimable and distinguished of its citizens, including several of the most steadfast and most uncompromising loyalists of the Shore. The jail of the county was entered, the jailer seized, imprisoned, and afterward sent to Baltimore, and prisoners confined therein under indictment set at liberty. The commanding officer gave the first clew to the kind of disloyalty against which he considered himself as particularly commissioned, by printing and publishing a proclamation in which, referring to the election to take place on the next day, he invited all the truly *loyal* to avail themselves of that opportunity and establish their *loyalty*, 'by giving a full and ardent support to the whole Government ticket, upon the platform adopted by the Union League Convention,' declaring that 'none other is recognized by the Federal authorities as loyal or worthy of the support of any one who desires the peace and restoration of the Union.'

"This Government ticket was in several, if not all, of those counties designated by its color. It was a yellow ticket, and, armed with that, a voter could safely run the gantlet of the sabers and carbines that guarded the entrance to the polls, and known sympathizers with the rebellion were allowed to vote unquestioned if they would vote that ticket, while loyal and respected citizens, ready to take the oath, were turned back by the officer in charge without even allowing them to approach the polls. In one district the military officer took his stand at the polls before they were opened, declaring that none but the 'yellow ticket should be voted,' and excluded all others throughout the day. In another district a similar officer caused every ballot offered to be examined, and, unless it was the favored one, the voter was required to take the oath, and not otherwise. In another district, after one vote only had been given, the polls wore closed, the judges were all arrested and sent out of the county, and military occupation taken of the town. Other statements might be made.

"These abuses present a humiliating record, such as I had never supposed we should be called upon to read in any State, still less in a loyal one like this. Unless it be, indeed, a fallacy to suppose that any rights whatever remain to such a State, or that any line whatever marks the limit of Federal power, a bolder stride across that line that power never made, even in a rebel State, than it did in Maryland on the 3d of last November. A part of the army, which a generous people had supplied for a very different purpose, was on that day engaged in stifling the freedom of election in a faithful State, intimidating its sworn officers, violating the constitutional rights of its loyal citizens, and obstructing the usual channels of communication between them and their Executive."

The result was the election of a majority of members of the Legislature in favor of a State Constitutional Convention. The acts necessary for this object were passed. At the election of delegates, the military authority again interfered in order to secure a majority in favor of immediate and unconditional emancipation. The so-called Convention assembled and drafted a so-called Constitution, in which the twenty-third article of the Bill of Rights prohibited the existence of slavery in the State, and said, "All persons held to service or labor as slaves are hereby declared free."

It was urged, in objection to the adoption of the so-called Constitution by the Convention, that "the election by which the Convention was called and its members elected was not free for the legal voters of the State, but was held and conducted in clear violation of the rights of voters, in consequence of which a majority of the legal voters of the State were excluded from the polls." A rigid article on the qualifications of voters at the State elections was embodied in the Constitution, with the shameless provision that it should be in force at the election for ratification or rejection of the so-called Constitution which was to create the disabilities. The instrument also authorized a poll to be opened in each company of every Maryland regiment in the service of the United States at the quarters of the commanding officer, and that the commissioned officers of such company should act as the judges of election. The aid of the President of the United States was also obtained to help on the ratification of the new Constitution, and he concludes a letter on the subject by saying, "I shall be gratified exceedingly if the good people of the State shall, by their votes, ratify the new Constitution."

Notwithstanding the aid of the President, of the soldiers' votes, and a most stringent oath, and the exclusion of every person who had in any manner, by word or act, aided the cause of the Confederacy, the majority for the so-called Constitution was only 375. The total vote was 59,973. In 1860 the vote of the State was 92,502. Thus was the State government subjugated and made an instrument of destruction to the people; thus were their rights ruthlessly violated, and property millions of dollars in value annihilated.

The reader must have noticed, in all these proceedings which resulted in the subjugation of the State governments, the cautious and stealthy manner in which the Government of the United States proceeded at the outset in each instance until it got a strong foothold, that then the mask was thrown off, and both Governor and people were made the unresisting victims of its unscrupulous and lawless outrages.

In the State of Kentucky, the first open and direct measures taken by the Government of the United States for the subjugation of the State government and people, thereby to effect the emancipation of the slaves, consisted in an interference with the voters at the State election in August, 1863. This interference was by means of a military force stationed at the polls to sustain and enforce the action of some of the servants of the Government of the United States, the object being to overawe the judges of election, secure the administration of a rigid oath of allegiance, and thereby the rejection of as many antagonistic votes as possible. Indeed, it was intended that none but so-called "Union" men should vote—that is, men who were willing to approve of every measure which the Government of the United States might adopt to carry on the war and revolutionize the State. At the same time, no man was allowed to be a candidate or to receive any votes unless he was a well-known advocate of the Government of the United States. It will be seen that these measures excluded the largest portion of the former Democratic party, although they might be practically "Union" men, and placed everything in the hands of the Administration party, where, by the use of similar machinery, it remained a great many years after the war closed.

Meantime, on July 31, 1863, the commanding General of the Department of the Ohio issued an order declaring the State under martial law, and said, "It is for the purpose, only, of protecting, if necessary, the rights of loyal citizens and the freedom of elections." He would have more correctly said, "It is for the purpose of enforcing and securing a majority for the candidates of my views." The General in command in the western part of the State issued an order to regulate the election in that quarter, and the colonels at every post did likewise. In Louisville, on the day of election, there were ten soldiers with muskets at each voting-place who, with crossed bayonets, stood in the doors, preventing all access of voters to the polls but by their permission, and who arrested and carried to the military prison all whom they were told to arrest. Out of some eight thousand voters in the city, less than five thousand votes were taken. How many of the missing three thousand were deterred from attempting to vote could not be ascertained, nor was it necessary, for the intimidation of three thousand voters is no greater outrage than the intimidation of only three hundred. The interpretation generally put on the order of the commanding officer by the opposition party was, that no man was to have the privilege of having his right to vote tested by the judges of election if he was pointed out to the guard by any one of the detectives as a proper person to be arrested. As the commanding officer had not the semblance of legal or rightful power to interfere with the election, the most sinister suspicions were naturally aroused, and very many were said to have been deterred from going to the polls through fear that they would be made the victims to personal or party malice. Similar intimidation was practiced in other parts of the State. The result was, that there was not only direct military interference with the election, but it was conducted in most of the State under the intimidation of the bayonets of the Government of the United States. The total vote was 85,695. In 1860 the vote of the State was 146,216. The Governor-elect in his message spoke, of such an unjust election, as follows:

> "The recent elections clearly and
> unmistakably define the popular will and
> public judgment of Kentucky. It is settled that
> Kentucky will, with unwavering faith and
> unswerving purpose, stand by and support

the Government in every effort to suppress
the rebellion and maintain the Union."

The true sense of this language is, that the Government of the United States had so far subverted the State government and destroyed the sovereignty of the people that they could not withstand its further aggressions.

The Government of the United States was now ready to move forward in its design to destroy one of the most valuable institutions of the State. Steps were taken by its officers to enroll all able-bodied male negroes in the State between the ages of twenty and forty-five years, that they might form a part of its forces. The effect of this measure was to break up the labor system of the State, and meanwhile the pseudo-philanthropists furnished food for powder, and indulged their ideas of freedom at their neighbors' expense. The excitement produced caused the Governor to visit Washington and effect agreements by which all recruiting should cease when a county's quota was full, all recruits should be removed from the State, and other similar provisions. A year later, he said to the Legislature: "Had these agreements been carried out, a very different state of feeling would have existed in Kentucky. But, instead of carrying them out, the most offensive and injurious modes were adopted to violate them."

The next step taken by the Government of the United States in the subversion of the government of Kentucky was the destruction of the unalienable right of personal liberty of the citizens, which the State was in duty bound to protect. The Union Governor of the State, whose election was aided by the United States military officers, as above stated, is the witness for the facts. In his message to the Legislature of January, 1865, he says:

"The gravest matter of military outrage has been, and yet is, the arrest, imprisonment, and banishment of loyal citizens without a hearing, and without even a knowledge of the charges against them. There have been a number of this class of arrests, merely for partisan political vengeance, and to force them to pay heavy sums to purchase their liberation. How the spoils so infamously extorted are divided, has not transpired to the public information. For partisan political ends, General John B. Huston was arrested at midnight preceding the election, and hurried off under circumstances of shameful aggravation. He was, however, released in a few days; but that does not atone for the criminality of his malicious arrest and false imprisonment. The battle-scarred veteran, Colonel Frank Wolford, whose name and loyal fame are part of his country's proudest memories, and whose arrest for political vengeance should put a nation's cheek to blush, is yet held in durance vile, without a hearing and without an accusation, so far as he or his friends can ascertain.

"Lieutenant-Governor Jacobs, whose yet unclosed wounds were received in battle for his country, was made a victim to partisan and personal enmity, and hurried without a hearing and without any known accusation through the rebel lines into Virginia. The action in this case is in defiance of Federal and State Constitutions and laws, in defiance of the laws of humanity and liberty, dishonors the cause of our country, and

315

degrades the military rank to the infamous uses of partisan and personal vengeance. Other cases might be mentioned, but these are selected because they are known to the whole country; the acts of these men are part of the glorious history of loyal heroism."

The next step in the progress of the subjugation of the State government was taken by President Lincoln on July 5, 1864, when he issued a proclamation establishing martial law throughout the State, and the suspension of the writ of *habeas corpus*. Civil proceedings were allowed to be continued, "which did not affect the military operations or the constituted authorities of the Government of the United States." Arrests of individuals by military force soon commenced, and a large number of eminent Kentuckians of all professions and pursuits were imprisoned. A group of persons, consisting of judges, magistrates, wealthy merchants, and young women, without having been allowed a hearing, or trial, or any opportunity to vindicate themselves, were banished from the State. In this destruction of the unalienable right of personal liberty, the State government was passive; indeed, it was powerless to resist.

A State election was to be held on the first Monday of August for local officers and a Judge of the High Court of Appeals from one district. Chief-Justice Duvall was one of the two candidates. On July 29th an order was issued by the Major-General, commanding, to the sheriffs of the counties concerned, as follows:

"You will not allow the name of Alvin
Duvall to appear upon the poll-books as a
candidate for office at the coming election."

Another name was substituted. The election of a President of the United States was to be held in November, but the Government of the United States seems to have regarded the vote of the State as unnecessary to secure the reelection of its officials, and refrained from interference. Under these circumstances, the Governor of the State took courage and issued a proclamation to the election officers. It is of no importance except as showing their powers and duties, and how grossly they had neglected them at previous elections. He said:

"As no officer of any rank, from the President down, has any
right or authority to interfere with elections, no order to do so
can legalize the act. If there be sufficient power in the citizens
present, at any place where such interference may be
attempted, to arrest the offenders, and hold them over to
answer to the violated laws, it will be the duty of the sheriff to
make the arrest in such case. He has authority to require the
aid of every citizen, and it should be readily and promptly
given, in defense of a common right—of a blood-bought
franchise. If the force employed to interfere with the election
be too great, at any place of voting, to be arrested, the officers
of election, in such case, should adjourn and not proceed with
the election. If you are unable to hold a free election, your duty
is to hold none at all."

By enlistment, over twenty-two thousand of the most valuable slaves in the State had gone into the service of the United States, and on March 3, 1865, its

Congress passed an act declaring that the wives and children of all such soldiers should be free. But the final moment was near at hand when the annihilation of more than one hundred millions of property and the destruction of one of the most important institutions of the State was to take place by one of those fictions so peculiar to this administration of the Government of the United States. That was the pretended adoption of a constitutional amendment, prohibiting the existence of slavery in the United States. When a whole people suffers itself to be cajoled in this unaccountable manner by its unscrupulous rulers, it argues as little regard for the fundamental law of the Union as for the rights of the States.

The subversion of the State government of Missouri by the Government of the United States was more rapid and more desperate than in the case of Kentucky. As previously stated, the Governor of the State, at the commencement of the difficulties, proposed the most conciliatory terms to the Government of the United States, which were rejected. He then, like a Governor, sensible of his duty to protect the rights of his people and of the sacred obligations of his official oath, issued his proclamation calling into active service fifty thousand of the State militia, "for the purpose of repelling invasion, and for the protection of the lives, liberty, and property of the citizens." He said:

"A series of unprovoked and unparalleled outrages have been inflicted upon the peace and dignity of this Commonwealth and upon the rights and liberties of its people, by wicked and unprincipled men, professing to act under the authority of the Government of the United States; solemn enactments of your Legislature have been nullified; your volunteer soldiers have been taken prisoners; your commerce with your sister States has been suspended; your trade with your own fellow-citizens has been and is subjected to the harassing control of an armed soldiery; peaceful citizens have been imprisoned without warrant of law; unoffending and defenseless men, women, and children have been ruthlessly shot down and murdered; and other unbearable indignities have been heaped upon your State and yourselves."

The plea of the invader was contained in an order issued from Washington to the commanding General in these words:

"The President observes with concern that, notwithstanding the pledge of the State authorities to coöperate in preserving the peace of Missouri, loyal citizens in great numbers continue to be driven from their homes. It is immaterial whether the outrages continue from inactivity or indisposition on the part of the State authorities to prevent them. It is enough that they continue, and it will devolve on you the duty of putting a stop to them summarily by the force under your command, to be aided by such troops as you may require from Kansas, Iowa, and Illinois. . . . The authority of the United States is paramount, and, whenever it is apparent that a movement, whether by order of State authority or not, is hostile, you will not hesitate to put it down."

In this order the only pretext put forward is that of domestic violence. But in that case the Constitution of the United States gives no authority to the United States Government to interfere except on the express conditions of an "application of the Legislature, or of the Executive, when the Legislature can not be convened." There had been no application of the Legislature or of the Executive. On the contrary, the Governor of the State, like a brave man, told the Executive of the United States to keep his hands off, and to keep his military forces without the State, and he pledged himself to preserve its peace and neutrality. But arguments or pledges on the part of the victim have never yet stopped the progress of the remorseless usurper. The subjugation of the State government of Missouri to the will and designs of the Government at Washington had been determined upon, and the sovereignty of the people was to be crushed by troops from the sister States of Kansas, Iowa, and Illinois.

But the bravery of the Governor and the determination of the Legislature caused the Government of the United States to depart from its usually stealthy progress in the invasion of the State government and the sovereignty of the people, and to adopt bolder measures. The Governor was charged with purposes of treason and secession, for his attempt faithfully to discharge the duties of a conscientious Governor to the citizens. Says the commander of the United States forces, in his proclamation:

"The recent proclamation of Governor Jackson, by which he has set at defiance the authorities of the United States and urged you to make war upon them, is but a consummation of his treasonable purposes, long indicated by his acts and expressed opinions, and now made manifest."

These are fine words to come from the satrap of a usurper who invades a State of the Union without lawful permission or authority, with the design to subvert its government and overthrow the sovereignty of its people, and to be applied by him to the only Governor in the Northern States who strove defiantly to protect the unalienable rights and sovereignty of his constituents!

Troops were now poured into the State by the Government of the United States so rapidly as to render the successful opposition of the lawful authorities impossible, and the control of a large portion of the State was soon held by the military forces. The Governor, unable to resist, retired to the southern part of the State. Meantime, the State Convention, which had been called to consider the relations between the Government of the United States and the State of Missouri, and to adopt such measures for vindicating the sovereignty of the State as were necessary, reassembled on the call of its committee. Entirely forgetful of the objects for which the people had called it together, it proceeded to declare the State offices vacant, and to elect a provisional Governor and other officers entirely subservient to the will and behests of the Administration at Washington. The commanding General now declared martial law in the State, and the emancipation of all slaves belonging to persons who had taken an active part with us. This emancipation clause was soon modified by the President as in advance of the times.

The attention of the reader is called to the numerous usurpations and violations of constitutional principles and of laws, by the Government of the

United States and its champions, contained in the few lines of the preceding paragraph, viz.: the invasion with military force, the expulsion of the lawful State authorities, the assumption by the State Convention of unlawful powers, the election and introduction of persons to offices not vacant, the abandonment of all protection of the unalienable rights of the people, the declaration of martial law without any authority for it, and the attempt to emancipate the slaves in violation of every law and constitutional principle.

The severity of the Executive of the United States now began to be felt by the citizens of the State. All disaffected persons were silenced or arrested, prisoners of war were treated as criminals, and every obstacle to complete subjugation to the will of the conqueror sought to be removed. The State government was represented by a provisional Governor; and a State Convention, that adjourned its sessions from year to year, after dallying periodically with the subject of the emancipation of the slaves, finally passed an ordinance for that purpose, to take effect in 1870. This was not immediate emancipation, so the disturbances were kept up in the State until, at a session of the Legislature in February, 1864, a bill was passed for a so-called State Convention to revise the State Constitution, and the election of delegates in November. It is remarkable how much the orders of the commanding General now contained relative to disorderly persons. This was preparatory to the occupation of the polls by the military force, and the exclusion of all opposition voters. The delegates were elected, and the so-called Convention assembled on January 6, 1865. An immediate emancipation ordinance was passed, and the State organization was subjugated to do the will of the usurper and to disregard the will of the sovereign people.

[Footnote 81: Article V, amendment.]
[Footnote 82: Article IV, amendment.]
[Footnote 83: Article VIII, amendment.]
[Footnote 84: Article I, amendment.]
[Footnote 85: Article II, amendment.]

CHAPTER XLIV.

Subjugation of the Northern States.—Humiliating Spectacle of New York.—"Ringing of a Little Bell."—Seizure and Imprisonment of Citizens.—Number seized.—Paper Safeguards of Liberty.—Other Safeguards.—Suspension of the Writ of *Habeas Corpus* absolutely forbidden with One Exception.— How done.—Not able to authorize another.—Abundant Protective Provisions in New York, but all failed.—Case of Pierce Butler.—Arrest of Secretary Cameron.—The President assumes the Responsibility of the Crime.—No Heed given to the Writ of *Habeas Corpus* issued by the Court.—The Governor passive.—Words of Justice Nelson.—Prison overflowing.—How relieved.—Oath required of Applicants for Relief.—Oath declined by some.—Reasons.—Order forbidding the Employment of Counsel by Prisoners.—Victims in almost Every Northern State.—Defeat at the Elections.—Result.—Suit for Damages commenced.—Congress interferes to protect the Guilty.—State Courts subjugated.—How suspend *Habeas Corpus*.—Congress violates the Constitution.—What was New

York?—Writ suspended throughout the United States.-What is
"Loyalty"?—Military Domination.—Correspondence between
General Dix and Governor Seymour.—Seizure of
Newspapers.—Governor orders Arrest of Offenders.—
Interference with the State Election.—Vote of the Soldiers.—
State Agents arrested.—Provost-Marshals appointed in Every
Northern State.—Their Duties.—Sustained by Force.—Trials by
Military Commission.—Trials at Washington.— Assassination
of the President.—Trial of Henry Wirz.—Efforts to implicate
the Author.—Investigation of a Committee of Congress as to
Complicity in the Assassination.—Arrest, Trial, and
Banishment of Clement C. Vallandigham.—Assertions of
Governor Seymour on the Case.

Now follows the humiliating spectacle of the subjugation of the State
government of New York—the "Empire" State, as she calls herself— where, with
all her men and treasures, it might have been supposed that some stanch
defenders of constitutional liberty would have sprung up. On the contrary,
under the pretext of "preserving the Union," her deluded children aided to
destroy the Constitution on which the Union was founded, and put forth all their
strength to exalt the Government of the United States to supremacy. Thus the
States were brought to a condition of subjugation, and their governments
subverted from the protection of the rights for which they were instituted. These
unalienable rights of the people were left without a protector or a shield before
the crushing hand of the usurper; the sovereignty of the people was set aside,
and in its place arose the sovereignty of the Government of the United States.
With the foundation undermined, the superstructure subverted, the ends for
which the Great Republic was organized entirely lost to sight, and the true
balance of the system destroyed, unless the dormant virtue and love for their
inherited rights shall arouse the citizens to a vigorous effort to restore the
republican institutions and powers of the States, the emperors and kings of the
earth have only to await calmly the lapse of time to behold a fulfillment of their
evil prophecies in regard to the "Great Republic" of the world.

To show how the laws were disregarded, and how despotically the personal
liberty of the citizen was invaded, let this example bear witness: The Secretary of
State at Washington, William H. Seward, a favored son of the State of New York,
would "ring a little bell," which brought to him a messenger, to whom was given
a secret order to arrest and confine in Fort Lafayette a person designated. This
order was sent by telegraph to the United States Marshal of the district in which
would be found the person who was to be arrested. The arrest being forcibly
made by the marshal with armed attendants without even the form of a warrant,
the prisoner without the knowledge of any charge against him was conveyed to
Fort Hamilton and turned over to the commandant. An aid with a guard of
soldiers then conveyed him in a boat to Fort Lafayette and delivered him to the
keeper in charge, who gave a receipt for the prisoner. He was then divested of
any weapons, money, valuables, or papers in his possession. His baggage was
opened and searched. A soldier then took him in charge to the designated
quarter, which was a portion of one of the casemates for guns, lighted only from
the port-hole, and occupied by seven or eight other prisoners. All were subjected
to prison fare. Some were citizens of New York, and the others of different

States. This manner of imprisonment was subsequently put under the direction of the Secretary of War, and continued at intervals until the close of the war.

In the brief period between July 1 and October 19, 1861, the Secretary of State, William H, Seward, made such diligent use of his "little bell," that one hundred and seventy-five of the most respectable citizens of the country were consigned to imprisonment in this Fort Lafayette, a strong fortress in the lower part of the harbor of New York. A decent regard for the memory of the friend of Washington, and for the services rendered to the colonies in their struggle for independence, might have led Mr. Seward to select for such base uses some other place than that which bore the honored name of Lafayette.

The American citizen has always, like the ancient Roman, felt that his personal liberty was secure. He supposed himself to be surrounded with numerous paper safeguards, which, together with the love of justice and respect for law, common to his fellow-citizens, would be sufficient for his protection against any usurper. These now proved to be as weak as the paper upon which they were written. What were these supposed safeguards? There was the Constitution of the State of New York, an instrument for the protection and government of the people. It had received the consent of the people of the State who were governed by it, and therefore its powers were "just powers." Its first object was to protect the unalienable rights of its citizens, relative to which it contains various provisions in its Bill of Rights: its declarations respecting personal liberty; its regulations to secure and enforce the great writ of freemen, the *habeas corpus*; the powers granted to the courts which it created; the Legislature; the Executive, in whose hands was placed the richest purse and the strongest sword of the sovereign States to protect the rights of its citizens.

Further safeguards were placed in the Constitution of the United States. These were designed to restrain that Government from any invasion of the citizen's personal liberty. They are as follows:

"The right of the people to be secure in their persons . . . shall not be violated, and no warrant shall issue but upon probable cause, supported by oath, or affirmation, and particularly describing . . . the persons to be seized." [86]

Again:

"No person shall . . . be deprived of life, liberty, or property, without due process of law." [87]

Again:

"No person shall be held to answer for a capital or otherwise infamous crime, unless on a presentment or indictment of a grand jury." [88]

Again:

"In all criminal prosecutions the accused shall enjoy the right to a speedy and public trial, by an impartial jury of the State and district wherein the crime shall have been committed, and to be informed of the nature

321

and cause of the accusation; to be confronted
with the witnesses against him; to have
compulsory process for obtaining witnesses in
his favor, and to have the assistance of
counsel for his defense." [89]
Among the enumerated powers of Congress is the following clause:
"The privilege of the writ of *habeas
corpus* shall not be suspended, unless when
in cases of rebellion or invasion the public
safety may require." [90]

This clause first forbids the suspension of the writ absolutely. A single exception is then made by the words "unless the public safety may require." A condition is attached to this exception which still farther limits it, by the words "in cases of rebellion or invasion." There is still another and far more sweeping limitation attached to this clause. The writ must be suspended by an act of Congress, which can be passed only when Congress is in session. This suspension must be positive and absolute by Congress, not indefinite and dependent on any future contingency. For the acts of Congress are not absolute powers, if between enactment and enforcement they can be set aside by a contingency, unless such contingency was attached in the clause of the grant creating the power. But in these words, of the Constitution there is no contingency expressed. Congress alone by positive enactment can suspend the writ of *habeas corpus*. It can not authorize the President to suspend its force, nor has he any authority under the Constitution to do it. Neither can Congress make an intermittent suspension of the force of the writ; but it must be absolute under the specific condition.

It is evident that the citizen of New York was abundantly provided with the safeguards of personal liberty; yet they all proved to be of no avail to secure and enforce his right in the hour of trial. A few instances will afford an illustration of the facts. Mr. Pierce Butler was suspected of corresponding with persons in the Confederate States. He was arrested in Philadelphia on August 19, 1861, by order of Simon Cameron, then Secretary of War, without process of law and without any assigned cause. His trunks and drawers, wardrobe, and entire apartments were searched, and his private papers taken by the marshal and his four assistants. His office was also examined, and his books and papers taken, and within an hour he was on his way to Fort Lafayette with an armed guard. After five weeks of detention he was liberated. No reason was given for his discharge any more than for his arrest. As Mr. Cameron was about to sail as Minister to Russia, in January ensuing, he was arrested for assault and battery and false imprisonment, at the suit of Mr. Butler. The case was brought to the knowledge of the President of the United States, and on April 18, 1862, the Secretary of State, Seward, replied as follows:

"The communication has been submitted
to the President, and I am directed by him to
say in reply that he avows the proceeding of
Mr. Cameron referred to as one taken by him
when Secretary of War, under the President's
directions, and deemed necessary for the
prompt suppression of the existing rebellion."

The writ of *habeas corpus* was issued by some of the State courts, directing the officer in command at the fort to bring some one or other of the prisoners into court for an investigation of the cause and authority for his detention. But no attention was given to these writs by the officer. Neither did the Governor of the State make any effort to enforce the processes of the courts. He, perhaps, expected that his efforts might be resisted by an overpowering force. But expectations, of whatsoever nature, do not justify or excuse the neglect of a positive duty. It is through such weaknesses that the liberties of mankind have been too often lost.

Thus the Constitution, the laws, the courts, the Executive of the State of New York, were subverted, turned aside from the end for which they were instituted, and all the specific arrangements were of no avail to secure this guaranteed right of its citizens. Probably every one of the prisoners was entirely innocent of any act whatever that was criminal under the laws, either of the State or of the United States.

In opinion they were opposed to the military proceedings of the Government of the United States; and these opinions they had expressed, which liberty is a part of the birthright of freemen. Indeed, Judge Nelson, of the Supreme Court of the United States, in the Circuit of New York, in an opinion delivered about this time, thus expressed himself:

> "Words, oral, written, or printed, however treasonable, seditious, or criminal of themselves, do not constitute an overt act of treason within the definition of the crime. When spoken, written, or printed, in relation to an act or acts which, if committed with a treasonable design, might constitute such overt act, they are admissible as evidence, tending to characterize it and show the intent with which the act was committed."

Finally, the prison in New York Harbor became so full that many prisoners were sent to Fort Warren in the harbor of Boston. At this time the Government of the United States used the Old Capitol at Washington, Fort McHenry of Baltimore, Fort Lafayette at New York, and Fort Warren at Boston, for the confinement of those whom the usurper designated as "state prisoners." Still further to relieve the fullness of the prisons, two men, John A. Dix, of the army, and Edwards Pierrepont, of civil life, were sent to investigate the cases of the prisoners, and release some who were willing to take an "oath of allegiance." Next it was made a condition precedent to an investigation that the said oath should be taken by the prisoner. As an instance, this proposal was made to two persons named Flanders, citizens of the interior of New York. The oath was as follows:

> "I do solemnly swear that I will support, protect, and defend the Constitution and Government of the United States against all enemies, whether domestic or foreign, and that I will bear true faith, allegiance, and loyalty to the same, any ordinance, resolution, or law of any State Convention, or

Legislature, to the contrary notwithstanding; and, farther, that I do this with a full determination, pledge, and purpose, without any mental reservation or evasion whatsoever; and, further, that I will well and faithfully perform all the duties which may be required of me by law."

These persons declined to take the prescribed oath. The reasons which they gave for this refusal furnish painful evidence of the extreme subjugation of the government of the State of New York, and its silent submission to the arbitrary and unconstitutional acts of the Government of the United States, even at the sacrifice of the most sacred rights of freemen. They said:

"We have been guilty of no offense against the laws of our country, but have simply exercised our constitutional rights as free citizens in the open and manly expression of our opinions upon public affairs. We have been placed here without legal charges, or, indeed, any charges whatsoever being made against us, and upon no legal process, but upon an arbitrary and illegal order of the Hon. William H. Seward, Secretary of State of the United States. Every moment of our detention here is a denial of our most sacred rights. We are entitled to and hereby demand an unconditional discharge; and, while we could cheerfully take the oath prescribed by the Constitution of the United States, because we are, always have been, and ever intend to be loyal to that instrument (though at the same time protesting against the right of the Government to impose even such oath upon us as the condition of our discharge), we can not consent to take the oath now required of us, because we hold no office of any kind under the Government of the United States, and it is an oath unknown to and unauthorized by the Constitution, and commits us to the support of the Government though it may be acting in direct conflict with the Constitution, and deprives us of the right of freely discussing, and by peaceful and constitutional methods opposing its measures—a right which is sacred to freedom, and which no American citizen should voluntarily surrender. That such is the interpretation put upon this oath by the Government, and such its intended effect is plainly demonstrated by the fact that it is dictated to this as a condition of our release from an imprisonment inflicted upon us for do other cause than that we have exercised the above-specified constitutional rights."

One important fact which illustrates the flagrant outrage committed on all these prisoners should not be omitted. The Constitution of the United States declares as follows:

"In all criminal prosecutions, the accused shall enjoy the right . . . to have the assistance of counsel for his defense."

On December 3, 1861, the commanding officer at Fort Lafayette came to the prisoners' quarters, and read a document, of which the following is a copy:

"To the political prisoners in Fort Lafayette:
"I am instructed by the Secretary of State
to inform you that the Department of State of
the United States will not recognize any one
as an attorney for political prisoners, and will
look with distrust upon all applications for
release through such channels; and that such
applications will be regarded as additional
reasons for declining to release the prisoners.

"And, further, that if such prisoners wish to make any communication
to the Government, they are at liberty to make it directly to the
State Department.
"SETH C. HAWLEY."

Space will not permit me further to notice the instances of this immense
class of cases. In almost every Northern State the victims of this violence were to
be found. That there was no just cause for these invasions of the rights of the
States, and of the citizens, was demonstrated in the most decisive manner. At
this time (November 4, 1862) the friends of the Administration of the United
States Government were decisively defeated at the elections. On November 22d
ensuing, the War Department issued an order releasing all except prisoners of
war. The order was muffled up in a phraseology suited to hide from the
observation of the people that the result of the elections had stricken home to
the sensibilities of the usurpers. It said:

"*Ordered*—1. That all persons now in
military custody, who have been arrested for
discouraging volunteer enlistments, opposing
the draft,[91] or for otherwise giving aid and
comfort to the enemy, in States where the
draft has been made or the quota of
volunteers and militia has been furnished,
shall be discharged from further military
restraint."

Thus these arrests were for a short period suspended, and then vigorously
renewed.

Many of these persons who had been illegally seized and imprisoned now
commenced suits for damages. This led to another step on the part of the
Government of the United States, by which the judiciary of the State was
entirely subverted and deprived of all jurisdiction in these cases. Congress
passed an act on March 3, 1863, which provided that any order of the President
of the United States, or arrest made under his authority, when pleaded, should
be a defense, in all courts, to any action or prosecution for any search, seizure,
arrest, or imprisonment made, done, or committed, or any acts omitted to be
done, under or by virtue of such order, or under color of any law of Congress.
The act further provided that all actions against officers and others for torts in
arrests might be removed for trial to the next Circuit Court of the United States
held in the district, and said:

"It shall then be the duty of the State court
to accept the surety and proceed no further in
the cause or prosecution, and the bail that

shall have been originally taken shall be
discharged."

It will be noticed that by the terms of this act the case could be removed to
the Circuit Court when the defendant "filed a petition stating the facts verified
by affidavit." Thus the jurisdiction of all the courts of the State of New York was
made to terminate and cease upon the simple word of the defendant
accompanied by an affidavit. But these courts were instituted by the consent of
the governed, for the protection of the personal freedom of the citizen; yet in the
cases brought before them they ordered the removal on the ground that they
involved the question of the constitutionality of an act of Congress, over which
the courts of the United States had a jurisdiction. The absurdity of this plea is
manifest; for it is founded on the presumption that the question, whether, under
authority from the President of the United States, any one, without intervention
of the judicial tribunals, can incarcerate a citizen, is a question which can be
treated as constituting a case arising under the Constitution of the United
States. Any statute authorizing such acts is palpably void, and not entitled to be
a ground for a bearing under an appeal.

The subjugation of the government of the State of New York was made in
another section of the same act of Congress of March 3, 1863. It declares:

"That, during the present rebellion, the
President of the United States, whenever in
his judgment the public safety may require it,
is authorized to suspend the privilege of the
writ of *habeas corpus* in any case throughout
the United States, or any part thereof."

Let us turn to the words of the Constitution of the United States which are
contained in the grant of powers to Congress:

"The privilege of the writ of *habeas
corpus* shall not be suspended, unless when
in cases of rebellion or invasion the public
safety may require it."

It will be seen that two facts are required to exist before the Congress of the
United States can suspend the privilege of this writ. Congress must, therefore,
determine the existence of these facts before it has power constitutionally to act.
If it finds either fact to exist and not the other, it has no power to suspend the
privilege of the writ. There must be rebellion, and the public safety must require
the suspension. When Congress finds these facts to exist, it can enact the
suspension. It is the judgment of Congress alone that can determine that the
public safety requires the suspension. This can not be delegated to the judgment
of any other department of the Government. Therefore, when Congress tells the
President, in the above-mentioned act, that he is authorized to suspend the
privilege of this writ whenever, in his judgment, the public safety may require it,
then that body undertakes to do that for which it has no authority in the
Constitution. The States delegated the power solely to Congress; an act to
transfer the trust to any other depository could rightfully have no force
whatever.

Now, the State of New York, in which this writ was thus suspended by the
Government of the United States, was one of the Northern States and a most
ardent advocate of the Union. It had contributed more men and money to

support the Government of the United States than any other State, and than some whole sections of States. Peace reigned throughout all its borders. Yet, in this quiet and "loyal" State, whose people had given so freely to aid the Government of the United States, a claim was now set up to the right to nullify the rights and immunities of every citizen, by that Government which had already nullified the powers of every court in the State. This was done by the declaration of the President that "the public safety" required the suspension of the privilege of the writ of *habeas corpus.*

The act of Congress was passed on March 3, 1863, and on September 15th the President issued his proclamation, and, referring to the authority claimed to have been granted by the act, he proceeded to say:

"*Whereas,* In the judgment of the President, the public safety does require that the privilege of said writ shall now be suspended throughout the United States, in cases where, by the authority of the President of the United States, military, naval, and civil officers of the United States, or either of them, hold persons under their custody, either as prisoners of war, spies, or aiders or abettors of the enemy, or officers, soldiers, or seamen, enrolled, drafted, or mustered, or enlisted in, or belonging to, the land or naval forces of the United States, or as deserters therefrom, or otherwise amenable to military law, or to the rules or articles of war, or the rules and regulations prescribed for military and naval service by the authority of the President of the United States, or for resisting a draft, or for any other offense against the military or naval service: Therefore I do hereby proclaim and make known that the privilege of the writ of *habeas corpus* is suspended throughout the United States in the several cases before mentioned throughout the duration of said rebellion."

No autocrat ever issued an edict more destructive of the natural right to personal liberty. Not only was the State government of New York deprived of the power to fulfill its obligations to protect and preserve this right of its citizens, but every State government of the Northern States was in like manner subverted. The only distinction known among the citizens was that established by the Government of the United States in answer to the question applied to each one, "Is he loyal or disloyal?" The only test of loyalty was based on submission, and, as usual in such cases, the most abject in spirit were the most loyal to the usurper. Ail those liberties of conduct and action which stamp the true freeman everywhere throughout the world disappeared; and the suppressed voice, the apprehensive look, and the cautious movements were substituted for the free speech, the open brow, and fearless tread which had characterized the American.

Another step in the subjugation of the government of the State of New York was made by the domination over it of the military power of the Government of the United States. This took place in a time of peace in the State, when the courts were all open and the civil administration of affairs was unobstructed. On July 30, 1863, the United States commanding General of that department addressed a letter to Governor Seymour, saying:

"As the draft under the act of Congress of March 3, 1863, for enrolling and calling out the national forces, will probably be resumed in this city (New York) at an early day, I am desirous of knowing whether the military power of the State may be relied on to enforce the execution of the law, in case of forcible resistance to it. I am very anxious there should be perfect harmony of action between the Federal Government and that of the State of New York; and if, under your authority to see the laws faithfully executed, I can feel assured that the act referred to will be enforced, I need not ask the War Department to put at my disposal, for the purpose, troops in the service of the United States."

Governor Seymour replied on August 3d:

"I have this day sent to the President of the United States a communication in relation to the draft in this State. I believe his answer will relieve you and me from the painful questions growing out of an armed enforcement of the conscription law in this patriotic State, which has contributed so largely and freely to the support of the national cause during the existing war."

On August 8th General Dix writes again:

"It is my duty, as commanding officer of the troops in the service of the United States in this department, if called on by the enrolling officers, to aid them in resisting forcible opposition to the execution of the law; and it is from an earnest desire to avoid the necessity of employing for the purpose any of my forces, which have been placed here to garrison the forts and protect the public property, that I wished to see the draft enforced by the military power of the State, in case of armed or organized resistance to it. . . . I designed, if your coöperation could not be relied on, to ask the General Government for a force which should be adequate to insure the execution of the law and to meet any emergency growing out of it."

Meantime Governor Seymour received no answer to his letter to the President. He had asked for a suspension of the draft, on the ground that the enrollments in the city were excessive as compared with other portions of the State, and that due credit was not given for the past. He therefore replied to General Dix, saying:

"As you state in your letter that it is your duty to enforce the act of Congress, and, as you apprehend its provisions may excite popular resistance, it is proposed you should

328

know the position which will be held by the State authorities. Of course, under no circumstances, can they perform duties expressly confided to others, nor can they undertake to relieve others from their proper responsibilities. But there can be no violations of good order, or riotous proceedings, no disturbances of the public peace, which are not infractions of the laws of the State; and those laws will be enforced under all circumstances. I shall take care that all the executive officers of this State perform their duties vigorously and thoroughly, and, if need be, the military power will be called into requisition. As you are an officer of the General Government, and not of the State, it does not become me to make suggestions to you with regard to your action under a law of Congress. You will, of course, be governed by your instructions and your own views of duty."

On August 18th General Dix thus wrote to the Governor:

"Not having received an answer from you, I applied to the Secretary of War on the 14th inst. for a force adequate to the object. The call was promptly responded to, and I shall be ready to meet all opposition to the draft."

The force sent by the Secretary of War, to keep the peace and subjugate the sovereignty of the people, amounted to forty-two regiments and two batteries. There was no occasion for the exertion of their powers, but the wrong to the State of New York was none the less gross.

Again, the subjugation of the government of the State of New York by the domination of the military power was made still more manifest by another act on the part of the Government of the United States. A spurious proclamation, seeming to have been issued by the President, calling for four hundred thousand men, by a fraudulent imposition appeared in two papers of New York City (the "Journal of Commerce" and the "World") on the morning of May 18, 1864. It was immediately contradicted by the authorities at Washington, and orders were issued, under which the offices of these papers were entered by armed men, the property of the owners seized, the premises held by force for several days, and the publications suspended. At the same time the office of the independent telegraph line was occupied by a military force in the name of the Government of the United States. The operators were taken into custody, and the proprietors of the newspapers were ordered to be arrested and imprisoned. But these orders were suspended.

Governor Seymour immediately instructed the District Attorney to proceed against the offenders, saying:

"In the month of July last, when New York was a scene of violence, I gave warning that

329

'the laws of the State must be enforced, its
peace and order maintained, and the property
of its citizens protected at every hazard.' The
laws were enforced at a fearful cost of blood
and life. The declaration I then made was not
intended merely for that occasion, or against
any class of men. It is one of an enduring
character, to be asserted at all times, and
against all conditions of citizens without favor
or distinction. Unless all are made to bow to
the law, it will be respected by none. Unless
all are made secure in their rights of person
and property, none can be protected."

An investigation was made by one of the city judges, and warrants were
issued for the arrest of Major-General Dix and several of his officers. They
voluntarily appeared by counsel on July 6th, and the argument was set down for
the 9th. On that day the counsel for the defense said:

"Since this warrant was issued, the
President of the United States has issued
another order to General Dix, which directs
him that, while this civil war lasts, he 'must
not relieve himself from his command, or be
deprived of his liberty to obey any order of a
military nature which the President of the
United States directs him to execute.'"

The result of the arguments was that the officers were held to await the
action of the grand jury, who, however, took no action on the charges. The guilty
person was arrested in two or three days after the appearance of the
proclamation, and imprisoned in Fort Lafayette; the newspaper and telegraph
offices were restored to the owners, and the publications resumed. But the
government of New York never obtained any indemnification of these losses by
its citizens.

Another subversion of the State government was brought about by the
military interference on the part of the Government of the United States with
the State election. This was in 1864, when President Lincoln and General
McClellan were the candidates for the Presidency of the United States. As usual,
in all these cases, proceedings to work up a pretended necessity for interference
on the part of the United States Government were commenced by the
appearance of a grandiloquent proclamation from the commanding General,
Dix, telling what horrible designs, there was reason to believe, the agents of the
Confederate States in Canada had prepared to be executed on election-day, by
an invasion of voters from Canada to colonize different points. Therefore, to
avert these dreadful dangers and arrest the guilty parties, it was necessary that
provost-marshals, sustained by a military force, should be present with
authority at the polls. At the same time the State Department issued a dispatch,
saying:

"Information has been received from the
British provinces to the effect that there is a
conspiracy on foot to set fire to the principal

cities in the Northern States on the day of the
Presidential election."

Thus was created an apparent necessity for the military force to be very
active on the day of election. Governor Seymour issued a proclamation, saying:

"There is no reason to doubt that the
coming election will be conducted with the
usual quiet and order."

Major-General Butler was sent to take command in the city, and seven
thousand additional men were placed in the forts of the harbor, and
proclamations were issued, threatening, by the United States Government, the
severest punishment upon every person who might attempt improperly to vote
at the election in the State of New York.

The State Legislature, at its previous session, had passed an act to provide for
the vote of the soldiers in the field, to be taken previous to the day of election.
Agents were appointed by the State government, to the localities where the
soldiers were stationed, to receive the votes. The informers of the United States
Government immediately brought charges of fraud against some of these agents,
and they were seized by the military authorities, sent to Washington, cast into
prison, and held to be tried by a military commission. The Governor of New
York immediately appointed Amasa J. Parker and two other most respectable
citizens as commissioners, to proceed to Washington in behalf of the State and
investigate the difficulties. They informed the Governor that several hundred
ballots, which had been seized, were given up, and that they visited the principal
agent of the State of New York in his prison, through the permission of Edwin
M. Stanton, Secretary of War. They reported thus:

"The undersigned availed themselves of
the permit granted them to visit Colonel
North, M. M. Jones, and Levi Cohn. They
found them in the 'Carroll Prison,' in close
confinement. They then learned that Messrs.
North and Cohn had been confined together
in one room, and had not been permitted to
leave it for a moment during the four days
they had been prisoners, even for the
purposes of answering the calls of nature.
They had been supplied with meager and
coarse prison-rations, to be eaten in their
room, where they constantly breathed the foul
atmosphere arising from the standing odor.
They had no vessel out of which to drink
water, except the one furnished them for the
purpose of urination. They had but one chair,
and had slept three of the nights of their
confinement upon a sack of straw upon the
floor. They had not been permitted to see a
newspaper, and were ignorant of the cause of
their arrest. All communication between them
and the outer world had been denied them,
and no friend had been allowed to see them.

The undersigned complained to the acting superintendent, who seemed humanely disposed, but justified his course by the prison rules and the instructions of his superiors."

The commissioners further say:

"From the best investigation the undersigned have been able to make, though there may have been irregularities, they have found no evidence that any frauds, either against any elector or the elective franchise, have been committed by any person connected with the New York agency."

The commissioners then addressed a communication to the Secretary of War. A few extracts from this communication will show how utter was the subversion of the authority of the government of the State of New York. They say:

"They, North, Cohn, and Jones, were not in the military or naval service of the United States, and by no law of which we are aware were they subject to the martial and military laws of the United States, or to the orders of the War Department. . . . The charges, so far as we can learn, are not for the violation of any law of the United States, but relate to acts purporting to have been done under the law of the State of New York concerning elections, and making provisions for soldiers voting in that State; it being claimed that certain irregularities hare intervened which give reason to suspect that frauds and forgeries are intended, and may be consummated. These suspected and anticipated frauds have respect solely to the election laws of the State of New York, and the action of the Government in making the arrest is claimed to be justified upon the ground that, unless thus prevented, frauds will be perpetrated against the ballot-box at the approaching election in the State of New York. We beg leave, in behalf of the State, respectfully to protest against this jurisdiction, assumed as well over the alleged offense as over the persons of the accused, who are citizens of the State, in its employ, and entitled to its protection. The proper business of the State agency is greatly interfered with by the arrest and detention of the agents, and the State is deprived of its proper jurisdiction over its agents and citizens, over offenses against its laws, and over its own ballot-box and the exercise of the elective franchise within its limits."

The demands made by the State of New York through these commissioners were refused. The persons arrested were finally tried before a military commission, clearly without jurisdiction, in violation of their personal rights, and in usurpation of the just powers of the State. They were, however, acquitted and discharged, glad to get off no worse.

The proposed limits will not permit me further to present the details relative to the subjugation of the State government of New York by the Government of the United States. Neither can space be spared to relate the details of the subjugation of the government of each Northern State. In many the events were similar to those in New York; in others they arose under dissimilar circumstances; but, in all, the sovereignty of the people was entirely disregarded, and the operation of the institutions which had been established for the protection of their rights was suspended, or nullified, by a military force of the Government of the United States. Only such events, therefore, can be stated as serve to show how universal and how complete was the work done by the United States Government to secure a recognition of its supremacy, over not only acts but even words, from every citizen. All were its subjects; the "loyal," as some were called, were its friends, and could be trusted; the "disloyal" were its disaffected subjects, and must be watched by spies and informers, and, if necessary, put in prison to secure their passive submission.

A military domination was established in all of the Northern States, under the pretext of securing the arrest of deserters from the army. This was accomplished on September 24, 1862, by the appointment of a Provost-Marshal-General of the War Department at Washington, and in each State one or more special provost-marshals, who were required to report to and receive instructions from the Provost-Marshal-General. It was made the duty of the special marshals—

"To arrest all deserters, whether regulars, volunteers, or militia, and send them to the nearest military commander or military post, where they can be cared for and sent to their respective regiments; to arrest, upon the warrant of the Judge Advocate, all disloyal persons subject to arrest under the orders of the War Department; to inquire into and report treasonable practices, seize stolen or embezzled property of the Government, detect spies of the enemy, and perform such other duties as may be enjoined on them by the War Department."

To enable these marshals to perform their duties efficiently, they were authorized to call on any available military force within their respective districts, or else to employ the assistance of citizens, constables, sheriffs, or police officers, so far as might be necessary. No trial was allowed to any person thus arrested except before a military commission consisting of military officers designated for the purpose; the prosecutor was the Judge Advocate, and the punishments were exemplary, unusual, and too often such as were unknown to the laws. The State governments within whose domains the courts were open, the civil institutions in quiet operation, and the transactions of peaceful life uniform and constant, were powerless to protect their citizens in their unalienable rights of freedom of speech and personal liberty, and the mandates of their courts were treated with contempt. In utter disregard of the principles of civil liberty, a military control was established in every Northern State, the declarations of rights in their Constitutions were violated, their laws nullified, and the authority of their governments subverted by an absolute and direct usurpation on the part of the Government of the United States.

The country was tilled with horror during 1865 by two trials held before a military commission in the city of Washington. The first commenced on May 13th, and ended on June 29th. The specification was—

"That David E. Harold, Edward Spangler, Lewis Payne, John H. Surratt, Michael O'Loughlin, Samuel Arnold, George A. Atzerott, Samuel A. Mudd, and Mary E. Surratt, did on April 15, 1865, combine, confederate, and conspire together to murder President Abraham Lincoln, Vice-President Andrew Johnson, Lieutenant-General U. S. Grant, and Secretary of State William H. Seward."

President Lincoln had been shot, and Secretary Seward was badly wounded with a knife. The others were uninjured.

The sentence of the commission was that David E. Harold, G. A. Atzerott, Lewis Payne, and Mary E. Surratt, be hanged by the proper military authority, under the direction of the Secretary of War, on July 7, 1865. The others were sentenced to imprisonment at hard labor for a term of years or for life. With only one day's delay, the sentences were carried into execution. John H. Surratt escaped before trial. He was sought for by the spies of the War Department half round the world, and after a long time was found serving as a soldier in the corps of Papal Zouaves at Rome. He was brought back to Washington, tried, and acquitted.

The insertion of my name with those of others, honorable gentlemen, as "inciting and encouraging" these acts, served as an exhibition of the malignant spirit with which justice was administered by the authorities in Washington at that time. The case of Mrs. Surratt, at whose house some of these persons had boarded, awakened much sympathy. She was spoken of by her counsel, Reverdy Johnson, of Maryland, as "a devout Christian, ever kind, affectionate, and charitable," which was confirmed by evidence and uncontradicted. On the day of the execution, her daughter, who was quite a devoted and affectionate person, sought to obtain an audience with President Johnson to implore at least a brief suspension of the sentence of her mother. She was obstructed and prevented from seeing the President by ex-Senator Preston King, of New York, and Senator James H. Lane, of Kansas, who were reported to have been at the Executive Mansion to keep guard over President Johnson. Each of these Senators at a later period committed suicide.

The trial of Major Henry Wirz was the next in importance which came before a military commission. In April, 1865, President Johnson issued a proclamation, stating that, from evidence in possession of the "Bureau of Military Justice," it appeared that I, Jefferson Davis, was implicated in the assassination of President Lincoln, and for that reason he offered a reward of one hundred thousand dollars for my capture. That testimony was subsequently found to be entirely false, having been a mere fabrication. The manner in which this was done will be presently stated. Meantime, certain persons of influence and public position at that time, either aware of the fabricated character of this testimony or convinced of its insufficiency to secure my conviction on a trial, sought to find ample material to supply this deficiency, in the great mortality of the soldiers we had captured during the war and imprisoned at Andersonville.[92]

Orders were therefore issued by the authorities of the United States Government to arrest a subaltern officer, Captain Henry Wirz, a foreigner by birth, poor, friendless, and wounded, and held as a prisoner of war. He had been included in the surrender of General J. E. Johnston. On May 7th he was placed in the "Old Capitol" Prison at Washington. The poor man was doomed before he was heard, and the permission to be heard according to law was denied him. Captain Wirz had been in command at the Confederate prison at Andersonville. The first charge alleged against him was that of conspiring with myself, Secretary Seddon, General Howell Cobb, General Winder, and others, to cause the death of thousands of the prisoners through cruelty, etc. The second charge was alleged against himself for murder in violation of the laws and customs of war.

The military commission before which he was tried was convened by an order of President Johnson, of August 19th, directing the officers detailed for that purpose to meet as a special military commission on August 20th, for the trial of such prisoners as might be brought before it. The commission convened, and Wirz was arraigned on the charges above mentioned, and pleaded not guilty. At the suggestion of the Judge Advocate, Joseph Holt, he was remanded to prison and the court adjourned. The so-called trial afterward came on, and lasted for three months, but no evidence whatsoever was produced showing the existence of such a conspiracy as had been charged. Wirz was, however, pronounced guilty, and, in accordance with the sentence of the commission, he was executed on November 10, 1865.

On April 4, 1867, Mr. Louis Schade, of Washington, and the attorney for Wirz on the trial, in compliance with the request of Wirz so to do, as soon as the times should be propitious, published a vindication of his character. The following is an extract from this publication:

"On the night previous to the execution of the prisoner, some parties came to the confessor of Wirz (Rev. Father Boyle) and also to me. One of them informed me that a high Cabinet officer wished to assure Wirz that, if he would implicate Jefferson Davis with the atrocities committed at Andersonville, his sentence should be commuted. He (the messenger, whoever he was) requested me to inform Wirz of this. In presence of Father Boyle, I told him next morning what had happened. The Captain simply and quietly replied: 'Mr. Schade, you know that I have always told you that I do not know anything about Jefferson Davis. He had no connection with me as to what was done at

Andersonville. If I knew anything of him, I would not become a traitor against him or anybody else to save my life.' Thus ended the attempt to suborn Captain Wirz against Jefferson Davis."

The following is an extract from a letter of Captain C. B. Winder to Mrs. Davis, dated Eastern Shore of Virginia, January 9, 1867:

"The door of the room which I occupied while in confinement at the Old Capitol Prison, Washington, was immediately opposite Captain Wirz's door—both of which were occasionally open. About two days before Captain Wirz's execution, I saw three or four men pass into his room, and, upon their coming out, Captain Wirz told me that they had given him assurances that his life would be spared and his liberty given to him if he (Wirz) could give any testimony that would reflect upon Mr. Davis or implicate him directly or indirectly with the condition and treatment of prisoners of war, *as charged* by the United States authorities; that he indignantly spurned these propositions, and assured them that, never having been acquainted with Mr. Davis, either officially, personally, or socially, it was utterly impossible that he should know anything against him, and that the offer of his life, dear as the boon might be, could not purchase him to treason and treachery to the South and his friend."

The following letter is from the Rev. Father F. E. Boyle, of Washington:

"WASHINGTON, D. C., *October 10, 1880.*

"Hon. JEFFERSON DAVIS.

"DEAR SIR: . . . I know that, on the evening before the day of the execution of Major Wirz, a man visited me, on the part of a Cabinet officer, to inform me that Major Wirz would be pardoned if he would implicate Jefferson Davis in the cruelties of Andersonville. No names were given by this messenger, and, upon my refusal to take any action in the matter, he went to Mr. Louis Schade, counsel for Major Wirz, with the same purpose and with a like result.

"When I visited Major Wirz the next morning, he told me that the same proposal had been made to him, and had been rejected

with scorn. The Major was very indignant,
and said that, while he was innocent of the
cruel charges for which he was about to suffer
death, he would not purchase his liberty by
perjury and a crime, such as was made the
condition of his freedom. I attended the
Major to the scaffold, and he died in the peace
of God, and praying for his enemies. I know
he was indeed innocent of all the cruel
charges on which his life was sworn away, and
I was edified by the Christian spirit in which
he submitted to his persecutors. Yours very
truly,

"F. E. BOYLE."

In the other case of the fabrication of evidence by some of the authorities in Washington relative to myself, it will be sufficient here to present what others have said and done. The subject is noticed in these pages only to show the desperate extremities to which the agents of the Government of the United States proceeded in order to compass my ignominious death. Three principal measures were resorted to for the accomplishment of this object: the charge in the case of Wirz, above mentioned; the fabrications in the case now under consideration; and the cruel and inhuman treatment inflicted upon me while a prisoner in Fortress Monroe.

At the session of Congress of 1865-'66, a committee was appointed in the House of Representatives "to inquire into and report upon the alleged complicity of Jefferson Davis with the assassination of the late President Lincoln," or words to that effect. George S. Boutwell was chairman of the committee, and the majority of the members were extreme advocates of the war. The charge emanated from the "Bureau of Military Justice," as it was designated—a similar institution to the "Secret Committee" of the French Revolution. Of this institution Judge-Advocate Joseph Holt was the chief. After an investigation continuing through several months, a majority of the committee made their report to Congress.

"That report not only failed to establish
the charge, but the committee were forced to
confess in it that the witnesses, on whose
testimony Holt had affected to rely, were
wholly untrustworthy. Shortly after this
report was presented to the House, Mr. A. J.
Rogers, of the committee, a very respectable
member from New Jersey, made a minority
report. He asserted that much of the evidence
was altogether suppressed, and that the
witnesses, who had received large sums of
money from Holt for testifying to the
criminality of Mr. Davis, recanted their
evidence before the committee, and
acknowledged that they had perjured
themselves by testifying to a mass of

falsehoods; that they had been tutored to do
so by one S. Conover; and that, from him
down through all the miserable list, the very
names under which these hired informers
were known to the public were as false as the
narratives to which they had sworn." [93]

Much more might be added to show the evil purpose of these men, together
with the correspondence of Holt and his associates, but it would be out of place
if it was put in these pages.

Another case of this kind occurred in the State of Ohio, in April, 1863, in the
arrest, trial, and banishment of Clement L. Vallandigham. On April 13th Major-
General Ambrose E. Burnside, commanding the Department, issued an order,
declaring—

"That, hereafter, all persons found within
our lines who commit acts for the benefit of
the enemies of our country will be tried as
spies or traitors, and, if convicted, will suffer
death." (The different classes of persons were
then named in the order.) "The habit of
declaring sympathies for the enemy will no
longer be tolerated in this department.
Persons committing such offenses will be at
once arrested, with a view to being tried as
above stated, or sent beyond our lines into the
lines of their friends. It must be distinctly
understood that treason, expressed or
implied, will not be tolerated in this
department."

Mr. Vallandigham commented upon this order, on May 1st, at a public
meeting of citizens. Three days afterward a body of soldiers was sent by railroad
from Cincinnati to Dayton, who, with violence, broke into his residence at three
o'clock in the morning, seized, and hurried him to the cars before a rescue could
be made, and departed for Cincinnati, where he was confined in a military
prison. He was brought to trial before a military commission on May 6th. The
specification made against him in the charge was that "he addressed a large
meeting of citizens at Mount Vernon, and did utter sentiments in words, or in
effect, as follows: declaring the present war 'a wicked, cruel, and unnecessary
war'; a war not being waged for the preservation of the Union'; 'a war for the
purpose of crushing out liberty and creating a despotism'; 'a war for the freedom
of the blacks and the enslavement of the whites'; stating that, 'if the
Administration had so wished, the war could have been honorably terminated
months ago'; characterizing the military order 'as a base usurpation of arbitrary
authority'; declaring 'that he was at all times and upon all occasions resolved to
do what he could to defeat the attempts now made to build up a monarchy upon
the ruins of our free government.'" He was adjudged as guilty, and sentenced to
confinement in Fort Warren, Boston Harbor, during the war. This sentence was
changed by President Lincoln to banishment to the Confederate States. This
military usurpation was spoken of by Governor Seymour, of New York, in a
letter written at the time, in these words:

338

"The transaction involved a series of offenses against our most sacred rights. It interfered with the freedom of speech; it violated our rights to be secure in our homes against unreasonable searches and seizures; it pronounced sentence without a trial, save one which was a mockery, which insulted as well as wronged. The perpetrators now seek to impose punishment, not for an offense against law, but for a disregard of an invalid order, put forth in utter violation of the principles of civil liberty. If this proceeding is approved by the Government and sanctioned by the people, it is not merely a step toward revolution, it is revolution; it will not only lead to military despotism, it establishes military despotism. If it is upheld, our liberties are overthrown. The safety of our persons, the security of our property, will hereafter depend upon the arbitrary wills of such military rulers as may be placed over us, while our constitutional guarantees will be broken down. Even now the Governors and the courts of some of the great Western States have sunk into insignificance before the despotic powers claimed and exercised by military men who have been sent into their borders."

A large number of such arrests were made in Ohio, newspapers were suspended, and editors imprisoned. Like scenes were very numerous in Indiana and Illinois. In Pennsylvania arrests were made, newspapers suspended, editors imprisoned, and offices destroyed. In New Hampshire, Vermont, and Wisconsin many similar scenes occurred. The provost-marshal system was used as a weapon of vindictiveness against influential citizens of opposite political views throughout all the Northern States. No one of such persons knew when he was safe. A complaint of his neighbors, supported by affidavit of "disloyal" words spoken or "disloyal" acts approved, received prompt attention from all marshals. Everything was brought into subjection to the will of the Government of the United States and its military officers.

In view of all the facts here presented relative to the Northern States, let the reader answer where the sovereignty *de facto* resided. Most clearly in the Government of the United States. That presided over the ballot-box, held the keys of the prisons, arrested all citizens at its pleasure, suspended or suppressed newspapers, and did whatever it pleased under the declaration that the public welfare required it. But, under the principles of American liberty, the sovereignty is inherent in the people as an unalienable right; and, for the preservation and protection of this and other rights, the State governments were instituted. If, therefore, the people have lost this inherent sovereignty, it is evident that the State governments have failed to afford that protection for which they were instituted. If they have thus failed, it has been in consequence of their subversion and loss of power to fulfill the object for which they were established. This subversion was achieved when the General Government, under the pretext of preserving the Union, made war on its creators the States, thus changing the nature of the Federal Union, which could rightfully be done only by the sovereign, the people of the States, in like manner as it was originally formed. If they should permit their sovereignty to be usurped and themselves to be subjugated, individuals might remain, States could not. Of their wreck a nation might be built, but there could not be a Union, for that implies entities united, and of a State which has lost its sovereignty there may only be written, "*It was.*"

[Footnote 86: Article IV, amendment.]
[Footnote 87: Article V, amendment.]
[Footnote 88: Article V, amendment.]
[Footnote 89: Article VI, amendment.]
[Footnote 90: Article I, section 9.]
[Footnote 91: The first act of Congress providing for an enrollment and draft was passed on March 8, 1363, three and a half months later than this order.]
[Footnote 92: See chapter on exchange of prisoners.]
[Footnote 93: Baltimore "Gazette," September 25, 1866.]

CHAPTER XLV.

Inactivity of the Army of Northern Virginia.—Expeditions of Custer, Kilpatrick, and Dahlgren for the Destruction of Railroads, the Burning of Richmond, and Killing the Officers of the Government.—Repelled by Government Clerks.—Papers on Dahlgren's Body.—Repulse of Butler's Raid from Bermuda Hundred.—Advance of Sheridan repulsed at Richmond.—Stuart resists Sheridan.—Stuart's Death.—Remarks on Grant's Plan of Campaign.—Movement of General Butler.—Drury's Bluff.—Battle there.—Campaign of Grant in Virginia.

Both the Army of Northern Virginia and the army under General Meade remained in a state of comparative inaction during the months of January and February, 1864.

On February 26, 1864, while General Lee's headquarters were at Orange Court-House, two corps of the army of the enemy left their camp for Madison Court-House. The object was, by a formidable feint, to engage the attention of General Lee, and conceal from him their plans for a surprise and, if possible, capture of the city of Richmond. This was to be a concerted movement, in which General Butler, in command of the forces on the Peninsula, was to move up and make a demonstration upon Richmond on the east, while Generals Custer and Kilpatrick and Colonel Dahlgren were to attack it and enter on the west and north.

Two days later another army corps left for Madison Court-House, and other forces subsequently followed. At the same time General Custer, with two ten-inch Parrott guns and fifteen hundred picked men, marched for Charlottesville by the James City road. His purpose was to destroy the Orange and Alexandria Railroad, running by Charlottesville to Gordonsville, where the junction was made of the railroad running north from Lynchburg, with the Central running to Richmond. The capture of the army stores there, the destruction of the tracks running south, west, and east, and cutting the telegraph, would have severed the communication between Lee's army and Richmond by that route. This movement, with the destruction of railroads by General Kilpatrick, and of the Central Railroad and the James River and Kanawha Canal by Colonel Dahlgren, would have isolated that army from its base of supplies.

[Illustration: General Wade Hampton]

Three hours later, on the same day on which General Custer started, General Kilpatrick with five thousand picked cavalry and a light battery of six guns, left Stevensburg, near Culpeper Court-House, for the lower fords of the Rapidan. His object was to make a dash upon Richmond for the purpose of releasing the United States prisoners, and doing whatever injury might be possible. He moved rapidly, destroying railroads and depots, and plundering the country, but found no obstacle except in being closely harassed in his rear by Colonel Bradley T. Johnson with his sixty Marylanders, who, with extraordinary daring, activity, and skill, followed him until he reached the line of the defenses of Richmond. There, while attacked in the rear by Colonel Johnson and his pickets driven in, he was at the same time opposed in front by Colonel W. H. Stevens, who, with a detachment of engineer troops, manned a few sections of light artillery. After an engagement of thirty minutes, Kilpatrick's entire force began to retreat in the direction of the Meadow Bridge on the Central Railroad. At night his camp-fires were discovered by General Wade Hampton, who dismounted one hundred men to act as infantry, and, supported by the cavalry, opened his two-gun battery upon the enemy at short range. He then attacked the camp of Davies's and of a part of two other brigades. The camp was taken, and the whole force of Kilpatrick fled at a gallop, leaving one hundred and five prisoners and more than one hundred horses.

Colonel Dahlgren started with General Kilpatrick, but at Spottsylvania Court-House was dispatched with five hundred men to Frederickhall, a depot of the Central Railroad, where some eighty pieces of our reserve artillery had been parked. His orders were to destroy the artillery, the railroads, and telegraph-lines. Finding the artillery too well guarded, he proceeded to destroy the line of railroad as far as Hanover Junction. Thence he moved toward the James River and Kanawha Canal, which he reached twenty-two miles west of Richmond. Thence his command moved toward the city, pillaging and destroying dwelling-houses, out-buildings, mills, canal-boats, grain, and cattle, and cutting one lock on the canal. The first resistance met was by a battalion of General G. W. C. Lee's force, consisting of about two hundred and twenty of the armory-men, under command of their major, Ford. This small body was driven back until it joined a battalion of the Treasury Department clerks, who, in the absence of their major, Henly, were led by Captain McIlhenney. The officers and men were all clerks of the Treasury Department, and, like those of other departments and many citizens of Richmond, who were either too old or too young to be in the army, were enrolled and organized to defend the capital in the absence of troops. Captain McIlhenney, as soon as he saw the enemy, promptly arranged to attack. This was done with such impetuosity that Dahlgren and his men wore routed, leaving some eighteen killed, twenty to thirty wounded, and as many more prisoners. About a hundred horses, with equipments, a number of small-arms, and one three-inch Napoleon gun were captured. Our loss was one captain and two lieutenants killed, three lieutenants and seven privates wounded—one of the latter mortally. This feat of the Clerks' Battalion commanded the grateful admiration of the people, and the large concourse that attended the funeral of the fallen expressed the public lamentation.

Dahlgren now commenced his retreat. To increase the chances of escape, the force was divided, he leading one party in the direction of King and Queen County. The home guard of the country turned out against the raiders, and, being joined by a detachment from the Forty-second Battalion of Virginia Cavalry and some furloughed cavalry-men of Lee's army, surprised and attacked the retreating column of Dahlgren, killed the leader, and captured nearly one hundred prisoners, with negroes, horses, etc.

On the body of Dahlgren was found an address to his officers and men, another paper giving special orders and instructions, and one giving his itinerary, the whole disclosing the unsoldierly means and purposes of the raid, such as disguising the men in our uniform, carrying supplies of oakum and turpentine to burn Richmond, and, after releasing their prisoners on Belle Isle, to exhort them to destroy the hateful city, while on all was impressed the special injunction that the city must be burned, and "Jeff Davis and Cabinet killed."

The prisoners, having been captured in disguise, were, under the usages of war, liable to be hanged as spies, but their protestations that their service was not voluntary, and the fact that as enlisted men they were subject to orders, and could not be held responsible for the infamous instructions under which they were acting, saved them from the death-penalty they had fully incurred. Photographic copies of the papers found on Dahlgren's body were taken and sent to General Lee, with instructions to communicate them to General Meade, commanding the enemy's forces in his front, with an inquiry as to whether such practices were authorized by his Government, and also to say that, if any question was raised as to the copies, the original paper would be submitted. No such question was then made, and the denial that Dahlgren's conduct had been authorized was accepted.

Many sensational stories, having not even a basis of truth, were put in circulation to exhibit the Confederate authorities as having acted with unwarrantable malignity toward the deceased Colonel Dahlgren. The fact was, that his body was sent to Richmond and decently interred in the Oakwood Cemetery, where other Federal soldiers were buried. The enormity of his offenses was not forgotten, but resentment against him ended with his life. It was also admitted that, however bad his preceding conduct had been, he met his fate gallantly, charging at the head of his men when he found himself inextricably encompassed by his foe.

Custer and Kilpatrick, who were to coöperate with him in the expedition, especially the first-named, manifested a saving degree of "that rascally virtue," as Charles Lee, of Revolutionary memory, called it. After the feeble demonstration upon some parked artillery which has been described, he fancied that he heard the roaring of cars coming with reënforcements, and retreated, burning the bridges behind him—a precaution quite in vain, as there were none there to pursue him.

Kilpatrick, followed as above stated by Colonel Bradley T. Johnson, who hung close upon his rear, finally reached the defenses of Richmond. There, out of respect to the field artillery he encountered, he turned off to cross the Chickahominy, and that night he was routed by the cavalry command of our gallant cavalier General Wade Hampton. Thus ended the combined movement with which Northern papers had regaled their readers by announcing as made "with instructions to sack the rebel capital."

During the first week in May, Major-General B. F. Butler landed at Bermuda Hundred with a considerable force, and moved up so as to cut the telegraph line and reach by a raiding party the railroad at Chester, between Richmond and Petersburg. General Ransom, then in command of the defenses at Richmond and those of Drury's Bluff, with a small force, attacked the advance of General Butler, and after a sharp skirmish compelled him to withdraw.

Meantime, because of the warning which Stuart had sent, General Ransom was summoned to Richmond to resist an impending assault by General Sheridan on the outer works north of the city. Taking the two disposable brigades of Gracie and Fry and a light battery, he hastened forward, arriving at the fortifications on the Mechanicsville Turnpike; just in time to see a battery of artillery, then entirely unsupported, repulse the advance of Sheridan. During the night the clerks and citizens, under General G. W. Custis Lee, had formed a thin line along part of the fortifications on the west side of the city. As the day advanced, Oracle's brigade was thrown in front of the works and pressed forward to feel Sheridan; but it was regarded as worse than useless with two small brigades to engage in an open country many times their number of well-appointed cavalry, Sheridan showed no purpose to attack, but withdrew from before our defenses, and the two brigades returned to the vicinity of Drury's Bluff—the approach on the south side of James River, by forces under General Butler, being then considered the most imminent danger to Richmond.

After the battle of the Wilderness, on May 4th and 5th, as hereafter narrated, General Grant moved his army toward Spottsylvania Court-House, and General Lee made a corresponding movement. At this time Sheridan, with a large force of United States cavalry, passed around and to the rear of our army, so as to place himself on the road to Richmond, which, in the absence of a garrison to defend it, he may have not unreasonably thought might be surprised and captured.

Stuart, our most distinguished cavalry commander—fearless, faithful Stuart—soon knew of Sheridan's movement, perceived its purpose, and, with his usual devotion to his country's welfare, hastily collected such of his troops as were near, and pursued Sheridan. He fell upon Sheridan's rear and flank at Beaver Dam Station, where a pause had been made to destroy the railroad, some cars, and commissary's stores, and drove it before him. The route of the enemy being unmistakably toward Richmond, Stuart, to protect the capital, or at least to delay attack, so as to give time to make preparation for defense, made a *détour* around Sheridan, and by a forced march got in front of him, taking position at a place called Yellow Tavern, about seven or eight miles from Richmond. Here, with the daring and singleness of purpose which characterized his whole career, he decided, notwithstanding the great inequality between his force and that of his foe, to make a stand, and offer persistent resistance to his advance. The respective strength of the two commands, as given by Colonel Heros von Borke, chief of General Stuart's staff, was, Stuart, eleven hundred; Sheridan, eight thousand. While engaged in this desperate service, General Stuart sent couriers to Richmond to give notice of the approach of the enemy, so that the defenses might be manned.

343

Notwithstanding the great disparity of force, the contest was obstinate and protracted, and fickle Fortune cheered our men with several brilliant successes. Stuart, who in many traits resembled the renowned Murat, like him was always a leader when his cavalry charged. On this occasion he is represented when he was wounded to have been quite in advance, to have fired the last load in his pistol, and to have been shot by a fugitive whom he found cowering under a fence, and ordered to surrender. The "heavy battalions" at last prevailed, our line was broken, and our chieftain, though mortally wounded, still kept in his saddle, invoking his men to continue the fight.[94] Our gallant chieftain was brought wounded into Richmond, a noble sacrifice on the altar of duty.

Long accustomed to connect him only with daring exploits and brilliant successes, there was much surprise and deeper sorrow when the news spread through the city. Admired as a soldier, loved as a man, honored as a Christian patriot, to whom duty to his God and his country was a supreme law, the intense anxiety for his safety made us all shrink from realizing his imminent danger. When I saw him in his very last hours, he was so calm, and physically so strong, that I could not believe that he was dying, until the surgeon, after I had left his bedside, told me he was bleeding inwardly, and that the end was near.

Grant's plan of campaign, as now revealed to us, was to continue his movement against Lee's army, and, if, as experience had taught him, he should be unable to defeat it and move directly to his objective point, Richmond, he was to continue his efforts so as to reach the James River below Richmond, and thus to connect with the array under General Butler, moving up on the south side of the James. The topography of the country favored that design. The streams in the country in which he was operating all trended toward the southeast, and his change of position was frequently made under cover of them. Butler, in the mean time, was ordered with the force of his department, about twenty thousand, reënforced by Gilmer's division of ten thousand, to move up to City Point, there intrench, and concentrate all his troops as rapidly as possible. From this base he was expected to operate so as to destroy the railroad connections between Richmond and the South. On the 7th of May he telegraphed that he had "destroyed many miles of railroad, and got a position which, with proper supplies, we can hold out against the whole of Lee's army."

At this time Major-General Robert Ransom, as before mentioned, was in command at Richmond, including Drury's Bluff. His force consisted, for the defense of both places, of the men serving the stationary or heavy artillery, and three brigades of infantry—Hunton's at Chapin's Bluff, and Barton's and Gracie's for field service. To these, in cases of emergency, the clerks and artisans in the departments and manufactories, were organized, to be called out as an auxiliary force when needed for the defense of the capital It was with this field force that Ransom, as has been related, moved upon Butler, and drove him from the railroad, the destruction of which he had so vauntingly announced.

A few days thereafter he again emerged from his cover, but this time changed his objective point, and, diverging from the south bank of the James River, moved toward Petersburg, and reached the railroad at Port Walthal Junction, where he encountered some of General Beauregard's command, which had been ordered from Charleston, and was driven from the railroad and turnpike. The troops ordered from Charleston with General Beauregard had, by May 14th, reached the vicinity of Drury's Bluff. In connection with the works and rifle-pits on the bluff, which were to command the river and prevent the ascent of gunboats, an intrenched line had been constructed on a ridge about a mile south of the bluff, running across the road from Richmond to Petersburg. This ridge was higher than the ground on which the fort was built, and was designed to check an approach of the enemy from the south, as well as to cover the rear of the fort. In the afternoon of the 14th I rode down to visit General Beauregard at his headquarters in the field. Supposing his troops to be on the line of intrenchment, I passed Major Drury's house to go thither, when some one by the roadside called to me and told me that the troops were not on the line of intrenchment, and that General Beauregard was at the house behind me.

My first question on meeting him was to learn why the intrenchments were abandoned. He answered that he thought it better to concentrate his troops. Upon my stating to him that there was nothing then to prevent Butler from turning his position, he said he would desire nothing more, as he would then fall upon him, cut him off from his base, etc.

According to my uniform practice never to do more than to make a suggestion to a general commanding in the field, the subject was pressed no further. We then passed to the consideration of the operations to be undertaken against Butler, who had already advanced from his base at Bermuda Hundred. I offered, for the purpose of attacking Butler, to send Major-General Ransom with the field force he had for the protection of Richmond. In addition to his high military capacity, his minute knowledge of the country in which they were to operate made him specially valuable. He reported to General Beauregard at noon on the 15th, received his orders for the battle which was to occur the next day, and about 10 P.M. was, with a division of four brigades and a battery of light artillery, in position in front of the breastworks. Colonel Dunovant, with a regiment of cavalry not under Ransom's orders, was to guard the space between his left and the river, so as to give him information of any movement in that quarter. General Whiting, with some force, was holding a defensive position at Petersburg. General Beauregard proposed that the main part of it should advance and unite with him in an attack upon Butler wherever he should be found between Drury's and Petersburg. To this I offered distinct objection, because of the hazard during a battle of attempting to make a junction of troops moving from opposite sides of the enemy; and proposed that Whiting's command should move at night by the Chesterfield road, where they would not probably be observed by Butler's advance. This march I supposed they could make so as to arrive at Drury's by or soon after daylight. The next day being Sunday, they could rest, and, all the troops being assigned to their positions, could move to make a concerted attack at daylight on Monday. He spoke of some difficulty in getting a courier who knew the route and could certainly deliver the order to General Whiting. Opportunely, a courier arrived from General Whiting, who had come up the Chesterfield road. He then said the order would have to be drawn with a great deal of care, and that he would prepare it as soon as he could. I arose to take leave, and he courteously walked down the stairs with me, remarking as we went that he was embarrassed for the want of a good cavalry commander. I saw in the yard Colonel Chilton, assistant adjutant and inspector-general, and said, "There is an old cavalry officer who was trained in my old regiment, the First Dragoons, and who I think will answer your requirements," Upon his expressing the pleasure it would give him to have

Colonel Chilton, I told him of General Beauregard's want, and asked him if the service would be agreeable to him. He readily accepted it, and I left, supposing all the preliminaries settled. In the next forenoon Colonel Samuel Melton, of the adjutant and inspector-general's department, called at my residence and delivered a message from General Beauregard to the effect that he had decided to order Whiting to move by the direct road from Petersburg, instead of by the Chesterfield route, and, when I replied that I had stated my objections to General Beauregard to a movement which gave the enemy the advantage of being between our forces, he said General Beauregard had directed him to explain to me that upon a further examination he found his force sufficient; that his operations, therefore, did not depend upon making a junction with Whiting.

On Monday morning I rode down to Drury's, where I found that the enemy had seized our line of intrenchments, it being unoccupied, and that a severe action had occurred, with serious loss to us before he could be dislodged. He had crossed the main road to the west, entering a dense wood, and our troops on the right had moved out and were closely engaged with him. We drove him back, frustrating the attempt to turn the extreme right of our line. The day was wearing away, a part of the force had been withdrawn to the intrenchment, and there was no sign of purpose to make any immediate movement. General Beauregard said he was waiting to hear Whiting's guns, and had been expecting him for some time to approach on the Petersburg road. Soon after this, the foe in a straggling, disorganized manner, commenced crossing the road, moving to the east, which indicated a retreat, or perhaps a purpose to turn our left and attack Fort Drury in rear. He placed a battery in the main road and threw some shells at our intrenchment, probably to cover his retiring troops. General Ransom, in an unpublished report, says that, at the time he received the order of battle, General Beauregard told him, "As you know the region, I have given you the moving part of the army, and you will take the initiative." He further states that at dawn of day he moved to the south of Kingsland Creek, formed two lines with a short interval, and at once advanced to the attack. A dense fog suddenly enveloped him, so as to obscure all distant objects. Moving forward, the skirmishers were quickly engaged, and the fighting was pressed so vigorously that by sunrise he had captured a brigade of infantry, a battery of artillery, and occupied about three quarters of a mile of the enemy's temporary breastworks, which were strengthened by wire interwoven among the trees in their front; this was not effected, however, without considerable loss in killed and wounded, and much confusion, owing to the denseness of the fog. General Ransom's report continues:

"Having no ammunition-wagons and requiring replenishment of infantry cartridges, and knowing that delay would mar the effect of the success gained, I sent instantly to Beauregard, reporting what had happened, and asked that Ransom's brigade might come to me at once, so that I might continue the pressure and make good the advantage already gained."

He then describes the further delay in getting ammunition, and his renewal of the request for Ransom's brigade, which he had organized and formerly commanded, but, instead of which, two small regiments were sent to him, the timely arrival of which, it is to be gratefully remembered, enabled him to repulse an advance of the enemy. It would be neither pleasant nor profitable to dwell on the lost opportunity for a complete victory, or to recount the possible consequences which might have flowed from it. On the next morning, our troops moved down the river road as far as Howlett's, about three or four miles, but saw no enemy. The "back door" of Richmond was closed, and Butler "bottled up."

Soon after the affair at Drury's Bluff, General Beauregard addressed to me a communication, proposing that he should be heavily reinforced from General Lee's army, so as to enable him to crush Butler in his intrenchments, and then, with the main body of his own force, together with a detachment from General Lee's army, that he should join General Lee, overwhelm Grant, and march to Washington. I knew that General Lee was then confronting an army vastly superior to his in numbers, fully equipped, with inexhaustible supplies, and a persistence in attacking of which sufficient evidence had been given. I could not therefore expect that General Lee would consent to the proposition of General Beauregard; but, as a matter of courteous consideration, his letter was forwarded with the usual formed endorsement. General Lee's opinion on the case was shown by the instructions he gave directing General Beauregard to straighten his line so as to reduce the requisite number of men to hold it, and send the balance to join the army north of the James.

[Footnote 94: Address of Major H. B. McClellan before Army of Northern Virginia Association.]

CHAPTER XLVI.

General Grant assumes Command in Virginia.—Positions of the Armies.—Plans of Campaign open to Grant's Choice.—The Rapidan crossed.—Battle of the Wilderness.—Danger of Lee.—The Enemy driven back.—Flank Attack.—Longstreet wounded.—Result of the Contest.—Rapid Flank Movement of Grant.—Another Contest.— Grant's Reënforcements.—Hanover Junction.—The Enemy moves in Direction of Bowling Green.—Crosses the Pamunkey.—Battle at Cold Harbor.—Frightful Slaughter.—The Enemy's Soldiers decline to renew the Assault when ordered.—Loss.—Asks Truce to bury the Dead.—Strength of Respective Armies.—General Pemberton.—The Enemy crosses the James.—Siege of Petersburg begun.

It was in March, 1864, that Major-General Ulysses S. Grant, having been appointed lieutenant-general, assumed command of the armies of the United States. He subsequently proceeded to Culpeper and assumed personal command of the Army of the Potomac, although nominally that army remained under the command of General Meade. Reënforcements were gathered from every military department of the United States and sent to that army.

On May 3d General Lee held the south bank of the Rapidan River, with his right resting near the mouth of Mine Run and his left extending to Liberty Mills, on the road from Gordonsville to the Shenandoah Valley. Ewell's corps was on the right, Hill's on the left, and two divisions of Longstreet's corps, having returned from East Tennessee, were encamped in the rear near Gordonsville.

The army of General Grant had occupied the north bank of the Rapidan, with the main body encamped in Culpeper County and on the Rappahannock River.

While Grant with his immense and increasing army was thus posted, Lee, with a comparatively small force, and to which few reënforcements could be furnished, confronted him on a line stretching from near Somerville Ford to Gordonsville. To Grant was left the choice to move directly on Lee and attempt to defeat his army, the only obstacle to the capture of Richmond, and which his vast means rendered supposable, or to cross the Rapidan above or below Lee's position. The second would fulfill the condition, so imperatively imposed on McClellan, of covering the United States capital; the third would be in the more direct line toward Richmond. Of the three he chose the last, and so felicitated himself on his unopposed passage of the river as to suppose that he had, unobserved, turned the flank of Lee's army, got between it and Richmond, and necessitated the retreat of the Confederates to some point where they might resist his further advance. So little could he comprehend the genius of Lee, that he expected him to be surprised, as appears from his arrangements contemplating only combats with the rear-guard covering the retreat. Lee, dauntless as he was sagacious, seized the opportunity, which the movement of his foe offered, to meet him where his artillery would be least available, where his massive columns would be most embarrassed in their movements, and where Southern individuality and self-reliance would be specially effective. Grant's object was to pass through "the Wilderness" to the roads between Lee and Richmond. Lee resolved to fight him in those pathless woods, where mind might best compete with matter.

Providence held its shield over the just cause, and heroic bands hurled back the heavy battalions shattered and discomfited, as will be now briefly described.

In order to cross the Rapidan, Grant's army moved on May 3d toward Germania Ford, which was ten or twelve miles from our right. He succeeded in seizing the ford and crossing. The direct road from this ford to Richmond passed by Spottsylvania Court-House, and, when Grant had crossed the river, he was nearer than General Lee to Richmond. From Orange Court-House there are two nearly parallel roads running eastwardly to Fredericksburg. The one nearest the river is called the "Stone Turnpike," and the other the "Plank-road." The road from the ford to Spottsylvania Court-House crosses the Old Stone Turnpike at the "Old Wilderness Tavern," and, two or three miles farther on, it crosses the plank-road.

As soon as Grant's movement was known, Lee's troops were put in motion. Swell's corps moved on the Stone Turnpike, and Hill's corps on the plank-road, into which Longstreet's force also came from his camp near Gordonsville. Ewell's corps crossed Mine Run, and encamped at Locust Grove, four miles beyond, on the afternoon of the 4th. On the morning of the 5th it was again in motion, and encountered Grant's troops in heavy force at a short distance from the Old Wilderness Tavern, and Jones's and Battle's brigades were driven back in some confusion. Early's division was ordered up, formed across the pike, and moved forward. It advanced through a dense pine-thicket, and, with other brigades of Rodes's division, drove the enemy back with heavy loss, capturing several hundred prisoners and gaining a commanding position on the right. Meantime, Johnson's division, on the left of the pike, and extending across the road to Germania Ford, was heavily engaged in front, and Hays's brigade was sent to his left to participate in a forward movement. It advanced, encountered a large force, and, not meeting with the expected coöperation, was drawn back. Subsequently, Pegram's brigade took position on Hays's left, and just before night an attack was made on their front, which was repulsed with severe loss to the enemy. During the afternoon there was hot skirmishing along the whole line, and several attempts were made by the foe to regain the position from which he had been driven. At the close of the day, Ewell's corps had captured over a thousand prisoners, besides inflicting on the enemy very severe losses in killed and wounded. Two pieces of artillery had been abandoned and were secured by our troops.

A. P. Hill, on the 4th, with Heth's and Wilcox's divisions of his corps, moved eastwardly along the plank-road. They bivouacked at night near Verdiersville, and resumed their march on the 5th with Heth in advance. About 1 P.M. musketry firing was heard in front; the sound indicated the presence of a large body of infantry. Kirkland's brigade deployed on both sides of the plank-road, and the column proceeded to form in line of battle on its flanks. Hill's advance had followed the plank-road, while Ewell's pursued the Stone turnpike. These parallel movements were at this time from three to four miles apart. The country intervening and round about for several miles is known as the "Wilderness," and, having very little open ground, consists almost wholly of a forest of dense undergrowth of shrubs and small trees. In order to open communication with Ewell, Wilcox's division moved to the left, and effected a junction with Gordon's brigade on Ewell's extreme right. The line of battle thus completed extended from the right of the plank-road through a succession of open fields and dense forest to the left of the Stone turnpike. It presented a line of six miles, and the thicket that lay along the whole front of our army was so impenetrable as to exclude the use of artillery save only at the roads. Heth's skirmishers were driven in about 3 P.M. by a massive column that advanced, firing rapidly. The straggle thus commenced in Hill's front continued for two or three hours unabated. Heth's ranks were greatly reduced, when Wilcox was ordered to his support, but the bloody contest continued until night closed over our force in the position it had originally taken. This stubborn and heroic resistance was made by the divisions of Heth and Wilcox, of Hill's corps, fifteen thousand strong, against the repeated and desperate assaults of five divisions—four divisions of Hancock's and one of Sedgwick's corps, numbering about forty-five thousand men. Our forces completely foiled their adversaries, and inflicted upon them most serious loss.[95] During the day the Ninth Corps of the enemy under General Burnside, had come on the field. The third division of Hill's corps, under General Anderson, and the two divisions of Longstreet's corps, did not reach the scene of conflict until dawn of day on the morning of the 6th. Simultaneously the attack on Hill was renewed with great vigor. In addition to the force he had so successfully resisted on the previous day, a fresh division of the enemy's Fifth Corps had secured position on Hill's flank, and coöperated with the column assaulting in front. After a severe contest, the left of Heth's division and the right of Wilcox's were overpowered before the advance of Longstreet's column reached the ground, and were compelled to return. The repulsed portions of the divisions were in considerable disorder. General Lee now came up, and, fully appreciating the impending crisis, dashed amid the fugitives, calling on the men to rally and follow him.

"The soldiers, seeing General Lee's
manifest purpose to advance with them, and
realizing the great danger in which he then
was, begged him to go to the rear, promising
that they would soon have matters rectified.
The General waved them on with some words
of cheer." [96]

The assault was checked.

Longstreet, having come up with two divisions, deployed them in line of
battle, and gallantly advanced to recover the lost ground. The enemy was driven
back over the ground he had gained by his assault on Hill's line, but reformed in
the position previously held by him. About mid-day an attack on his left flank
and rear was ordered by Longstreet. For this purpose three brigades were
detached, and, moving forward, were joined by General J. R. Davis's brigade,
which had been the extreme right of Hill's line. Making a sufficient *détour* to
avoid observation, and, rushing precipitately to attack the foe in flank and
reverse while he was preparing to resist the movement in his front, he was taken
completely by surprise. The assault resulted in his utter rout, with heavy loss on
that part of his line.

Preparations were now made to follow up the advantages gained by a
forward movement of the whole line under General Longstreet's personal
direction. When advancing at the head of Jenkins's brigade, with that officer and
others, a body of Confederates in the wood on the roadside, supposing the
column to be a hostile force, fired into it, killing General Jenkins, distinguished
alike for civil and military virtue, and severely wounding General Longstreet.
The valuable services of General Longstreet were thus lost to the army at a
critical moment, and this caused the suspension of a movement which promised
the most important results; and time was thus afforded to the enemy to rally,
reënforce, and find shelter behind his intrenchments. Under these
circumstances the commanding General deemed it unadvisable to attack.

On the morning of the 6th the contest was renewed on the left, and a very
heavy attack was made on the front, occupied by Pegram's brigade, but it was
handsomely repulsed, as were several subsequent attacks at the same point. In
the afternoon an attack was made on the enemy's right flank, resting in the
woods, when Gordon's brigade, with Johnson's in the rear and followed by
Pegram's, succeeded in throwing it into great confusion, doubling it up and
forcing it back some distance, capturing two brigadier-generals and several
hundred prisoners. Darkness closed the contest. On the 7th an advance was
made which disclosed the fact that Grant had given up his line of works on his
right. During the day there was some skirmishing, but no serious fighting. The
result of these battles was the infliction of severe loss upon the foe, the gain of
ground, and the capture of prisoners, artillery, and other trophies. The cost to
us, however, was so serious as to enforce, by additional considerations, the
policy of Lee to spare his men as much as was possible.

A rapid flank movement was next made by Grant to secure possession of
Spottsylvania Court-House. General Lee comprehended his purpose, and on the
night of the 7th a division of Longstreet's corps was sent as the advance to that
point. Stuart, then in observation on the flank, and ever ready to work or to fight
as the one or the other should best serve the cause of his country, dismounted

his troopers, and, by felling trees, obstructed the roads so as materially to delay the march of the enemy. The head of the opposing forces arrived almost at the same moment on the 8th; theirs, being a little in advance, drove back our cavalry, but in turn was quickly driven from the strategic point by the arrival of our infantry. On the 9th the two armies, each forming on its advance as a nucleus, swung round and confronted each other in line of battle.

The 10th and 11th passed in comparative quiet. On the morning of the 12th the enemy made a very heavy attack on Ewell's front, and broke the line where it was occupied by Johnson's division. At this time and place the scene occurred of which Mississippians are justly proud. Colonel Tenable, of General Lee's staff, states that, on the receipt of one of the messages from General Rodes for more troops, he was sent by General Lee to bring Harris's Mississippi brigade from the extreme right; that General Lee met the brigade and rode at its head until under fire, when a round shot passed so near to him that the soldiers invoked him to go back; and when he said, "If you will promise me to drive those people from our works, I will go back," the brigade shouted the promise, and Colonel Venable says:

> "As the column of Mississippians came up at a double quick an aide-de-camp came up to General Rodes with a message from Ramseur that he could hold out only a few minutes longer unless assistance was at hand. Your brigade was thrown instantly into the fight, the column being formed into line under a tremendous fire and on very difficult ground. Never did a brigade go into fiercer battle under greater trials; never did a brigade do its duty more nobly." [97]

A portion of the attacking force swept along Johnson's line to Wilcox's left, and was checked by a prompt movement on that flank. Several brigades sent to Ewell's assistance were carried into action under his orders, and they all suffered severely. Subsequently, on the same day, some brigades were thrown to the front, for the purpose of moving to the left and attacking the flank of the column which broke Ewell's line, to relieve the pressure on him, and recover the part of the line which had been lost. These, as they moved, soon encountered the Ninth Corps, under Burnside, advancing to the attack. They captured over three hundred prisoners and three battle-flags, and their attack on the enemy's flank, taking him by surprise, contributed materially to his repulse.

Taylor, in his "Four Years with General Lee," says that Lee, having detected the weakness of "the salient" occupied by the division of General Edward Johnson, of Ewell's corps, directed a second line to be constructed across its base, to which he proposed to move the troops occupying the angle. Suspecting another flank movement by Grant, before these arrangements were quite completed, he ordered most of the artillery at this portion of the lines to be withdrawn so as to be available. Toward dawn on the 12th, Johnson, discovering indications of an impending assault, ordered the immediate return of the artillery, and made other preparations for defense. But the unfortunate withdrawal was so partially and tardily restored, that a spirited assault at daybreak overran that portion of the lines before the artillery was put in position, and captured most of the division, including its brave commander.

The above mentioned attacking column advanced, under cover of a pine-thicket, to within a very short distance of a salient defended by Walker's brigade. A heavy fire of musketry and artillery, from a considerable number of guns on Heth's line, opened with tremendous effect upon the column, and it was driven back with severe loss, leaving its dead in front of our works.[98]

Several days of comparative quiet ensued. During this time the army of General Grant was heavily reënforced from Washington.

"In numerical strength his army so much exceeded that under General Lee that, after covering the entire Confederate front with double lines of battle, he had in reserve a large force with which to extend his flank and compel a corresponding movement on the part of his adversary, in order to keep between him and his coveted prize—the capital of the Confederacy." [99]

On the 18th another assault was made upon our lines, but it produced no impression. On the 20th of May, after twelve days of skirmish and battle at Spottsylvania against a superior force, General Lee's information led him to believe that the enemy was about to attempt another flanking movement, and interpose his army between the Confederate capital and its defenders. To defeat this purpose Longstreet was ordered to move at midnight in the direction of Hanover Junction, and on the following day and night Swell's and Hill's corps marched for the same point.

The Confederate commander, divining that Grant's objective point was the intersection of the two railroads leading to Richmond at a point two miles south of the North Anna River, crossed his army over that stream and took up a line of battle which frustrated the movement.

Grant began his flanking movement on the night of the 20th, marching in two columns, the right, under General Warren, crossing the North Anna at Jericho Ford without opposition. On the 23d the left, under General Hancock, crossing four miles lower down, at the Chesterfield or County Bridge, was obstinately resisted by a small force, and the passage of the river was not made until the 24th. After crossing the North Anna, Grant discovered that his movement was a blunder, and that his army was in a position of much peril.

The Confederate commander established his line of battle on the south side of the river, both wings refused so as to form an obtuse angle, with the apex resting on the river between the two points of the enemy's crossing, Longstreet's and Hill's corps forming the two sides, and Little River and the Hanover marshes the base. Ewell's corps held the apex or center.

The hazard of Grant's position appears not to have been known to him until he attempted to unite his two columns, which were four miles apart, by establishing a connecting line along the river. Foiled in the attempt, he discovered that the Confederate army was interposed between his two wings, which were also separated by the North Anna, and that the one could give no support to the other except by a double crossing of the river. That the Confederate commander did not seize the opportunity to strike his embarrassed foe and avail himself of the advantage which his superior generalship had gained, may have been that, concluding from past observation of Grant's tactics, he felt assured that the "continuous hammering" process was to be repeated without reference to circumstances or position. If Lee acted on this supposition, he was mistaken, as the Federal commander, profiting by the severe lessons of Spottsylvania and the Wilderness, with cautious, noiseless movement, withdrew under cover of the night of the 26th to the north side of the North Anna, and moved eastward down to the Pamunkey River.

At Hanover Junction General Lee was joined by Pickett's division of Longstreet's corps, which had been on detached service in North Carolina, and by a small force under General Breckinridge from southwestern Virginia, twenty-two hundred strong. Hoke's brigade, of Early's division, twelve hundred strong, which had been on detached duty at the Junction, here also rejoined its division. On the 29th the whole of Grant's army was across the Pamunkey, while General Lee's army on the next day was in line of battle with his left at Atlee's Station. By another movement eastward the two armies were brought face to face at Cold Harbor on June 3d. Here fruitless efforts were made by General Grant to pierce or drive back the forces of General Lee. Our troops were protected by temporary earthworks, and while under cover of these were assailed by the enemy:

> "But in vain. The assault was repulsed along the whole line, and the carnage on the Federal side was fearful. I[100] well recall having received a report, after the assault, from General Hoke—whose division reached the army just previous to this battle—to the effect that the ground in his entire front, over which the enemy had charged, was literally covered with their dead and wounded; and that up to that time he had not had a single man killed. No wonder that, when the command was given to renew the assault, the Federal soldiers sullenly and silently declined. 'The order[101] was issued through the officers to their subordinate commanders, and from them descended through the wonted channels; but no man stirred, and the immobile lines pronounced a verdict, silent yet emphatic, against further slaughter. The loss on the Union side in this sanguinary action was over thirteen thousand, while on the part of the Confederates it is doubtful whether it reached that many hundreds.' After some disingenuous proposals, General Grant finally asked a truce to enable him to bury his dead. Soon after this he abandoned his chosen line of operations, and moved his army so as to secure a crossing to the south side of James River. The struggle from the

Wilderness to this point covered a period of
over one month, during which time there had
been an almost daily encounter of arms, and
the Army of Northern Virginia had
placed *hors de combat*, of the army under
General Grant, a number exceeding the entire
numerical strength, at the commencement of
the campaign, of Lee's army, which,
notwithstanding its own heavy losses and the
reinforcements received by the enemy, still
presented an impregnable front to its
opponent."

By the report of the United States Secretary of War (Stanton), Grant had, on
the 1st of May, 1864, two days before he crossed the Rapidan, 120,380 men, and
in the Ninth Army Corps 20,780, or an aggregate with which he marched
against Lee of 141,160. To meet this vast force, Lee had on the Rapidan less than
50,000 men. By the same authority it appears that Grant had a reserve upon
which he could draw of 137,672. Lee had practically no reserve, for he was
compelled to make detachments from his army for the protection of West
Virginia and other points, about equal to all the reënforcements which he
received. In the "Southern Historical Papers," vol. vi, page 144, upon the very
reliable authority of the editor, there appears the following statement:

"Grant says he lost, in the campaign from
the Wilderness to Cold Harbor, 39,000 men;
but Swinton puts his loss at over 60,000, and
a careful examination of the figures will show
that his real loss was nearer 100,000. In other
words, he lost about twice as many men as
Lee had, in order to take a position which he
could have taken at first without firing a gun
or losing a man."

On June 12th the movement was commenced by Grant for crossing the
James River. Pontoon-bridges were laid near Wilcox's Wharf for the passage of
his army. J. C. Pemberton, who, after the fall of Vicksburg, was left without a
command corresponding to his rank of lieutenant-general in the provisional
army, in order that he might not stand idle, nobly resigned that commission,
and asked to be assigned to duty according to his rank in the regular army,
which was that of lieutenant-colonel. Ho was accordingly directed to report to
General Lee for service with the Army of Northern Virginia. Being a skillful
artillerist, he was directed to find a position where he could place a mortar so as
to throw shells on the enemy's bridge when it should be put into use. By a daring
reconnaissance and exact calculation, he determined a point from which the
desired effect might be produced by vertical fire, over a wood. At the proper
moment he opened upon the bridge, and his expectations were verified by the
shells falling on the troops harassingly. This, his first service with the Army of
Northern Virginia, was interrupted by the failure to send promptly a cohering
force to protect the mortar, the position of which was disclosed by its fire. The
injury it inflicted caused the Federal commander to send a detachment which
drove away the gunners and captured the mortar.

On the 14th and 15th of June the crossing of Grant's army was completed. It will be remembered that he had crossed the Rapidan on the 3d of May. It had therefore taken him more than a month to reach the south side of the James. In his campaign he had sacrificed a hecatomb of men, a vast amount of artillery, small-arms, munitions of war, and supplies, to reach a position to which McClellan had already demonstrated there was an easy and inexpensive route. It is true that the Confederate army had suffered severely, and, though the loss was comparatively small to that of its opponents, it could not be repaired, as his might be, from the larger population and his facility for recruiting in Europe. To those who can approve the policy of attrition without reference to the number of lives it might cost, this may seem justifiable, but it can hardly be regarded as generalship, or be offered to military students as an example worthy of imitation. After an unsuccessful attempt, by a surprise, to capture Petersburg, General Grant concentrated his army south of the Appomattox River and commenced the operations to be related hereafter.

[Footnote 95: "Four Years with General Lee."]
[Footnote 96: "Four Years with General Lee."]
[Footnote 97: Letter from Colonel C. S Venable, "Southern Historical Society Papers," vol. viii, p. 106, March, 1880.]
[Footnote 98: "Memoir of the Last Year," etc, by General Early.]
[Footnote 99: "Four Years with General Lee."]
[Footnote 100: Taylor, "Four Years with General Lee."]
[Footnote 101: Swinton, "Army of the Potomac," p. 487.]

CHAPTER XLVII.

Situation in the Shenandoah Valley.—March of General Early.—The Object.—At Lynchburg.—Staunton.—His Force.—Enters Maryland.— Attack at Monocacy.—Approach to Washington.—The Works.— Recrosses the Potomac.—Battle at Kernstown.—Captures.—Outrages of the Enemy.—Statement of General Early.—Retaliation on Chambersburg, Pennsylvania.—Battle near Winchester.—Sheridan's Force routed.—Attack subsequently renewed with New Forces.— Incapacity of our Opponent.—Early falls back.—The Enemy retires.—Early advances.—Report of a Committee of Citizens on Losses by Sheridan's Orders.—Battle at Cedar Creek.—Losses, Subsequent Movements, and Captures.—The Red River Campaign.— Repulse and Retreat of General Banks.—Capture of Fort Pillow.

Before the opening of the campaign of 1864, the lower Shenandoah Valley was held by a force under General Sigel, with which General Grant decided to renew the attempt which had been made by Crook and Averill to destroy the Virginia and Tennessee Railroad west of Lynchburg as a means to his general purpose of isolating Richmond; and a prompt movement of General Morgan had defeated those attempts and driven off the invaders. Sigel, with about fifteen thousand men, commenced his movement up the Valley of the Shenandoah. Major-General Breckinridge, commanding in southwestern Virginia, was notified, on the 4th of May, of the movement of Sigel, and started immediately with two brigades of infantry to Staunton, at which place he arrived on the 9th. The reserves of Augusta County, under Colonel Harmon, were called out, numbering several hundred men, and the cadets of the Military Institute at

Lexington, numbering two hundred, voluntarily joined him. With this force Breckinridge decided to march to meet Sigel. General Imboden, with a cavalry force of several hundred, had been holding, as best he might, the upper Valley, and joined Breckinridge in the neighborhood of New Market, informing him that Sigel then occupied that place. Breckinridge having marched so rapidly from Staunton that it was probable that his advance was unknown to the enemy, he determined to make an immediate attack. His troops were put in motion at one o'clock, and by daylight was in line of battle two miles south of New Market. Sigel seems to have been unconscious of any other obstruction to the capture of Staunton than the small cavalry force under Imboden. At this time Lee was engaged with the vastly superior force of Grant, which had crossed the Rapidan, and Sigel's was a movement to get upon our flank, and thus coöperate with Grant in his attempt to capture Richmond. Breckinridge had an infantry force not much exceeding three thousand. The hazard of an attack was great, but the necessity of the case justified it. Breckinridge's force was only enough to form one line of battle in two ranks, the cadets holding the center between the two brigades. There were no reserves, and Colonel Harmon's command formed the guard for the trains. Skirmish lines were promptly engaged, and soon thereafter the enemy fell back beyond New Market, where Sigel, assuming the defensive, took a strong position, in which to wait for an attack. Our artillery was moved forward, and opened with effect upon the enemy's position; then our infantry advanced, "with the steadiness of troops on dress parade, the precision of the cadets serving well as a color-guide for the brigades on either side to dress by. . . . The Federal line had the advantage of a stone wall which served as a breastwork." [102] Sigel's cavalry attempted to turn our right flank, but was repulsed disastrously, and in a few moments the enemy was in full retreat, crossing the Shenandoah and burning the bridge behind him.

Breckinridge captured five pieces of artillery and over five hundred prisoners, exclusive of the wounded left on the field. Our loss was several hundred killed and wounded. General Lee, after receiving notice of this, ordered Breckinridge to transfer his command as rapidly as possible to Hanover Junction. The battle was fought on the 15th, and the command reached Hanover Junction on the 20th of May.

Before General Breckinridge left the Valley, he issued an order thanking his troops, "particularly the cadets, who, though mere youths, had fought with the steadiness of veterans."

Brigadier-General W. E. Jones had, with a small cavalry force, come from southwestern Virginia to the Valley after Breckinridge's departure, and this, with the command of Imboden, only sufficient for observation, was all that remained in the Valley when the Federal General David Hunter, with a larger force than Sigel's, succeeded the latter. Jones, with his cavalry and a few infantry, encountered this force at Piedmont, was defeated and killed. Upon the receipt of this information, Breckinridge with his command was sent back to the Valley.

On June 13th Major-General Early, with the Second Corps of Lee's army, numbering a little over eight thousand muskets and two battalions of artillery, commenced a march to strike Hunter's force in the rear, and, if possible, destroy it; then to move down the Valley, cross the Potomac, and threaten Washington. On the 17th he reached Lynchburg, and Hunter arrived at the same time.

Preparations were made for the attack of Hunter on the 19th, when he began to retreat, and was pursued with much loss, until he was disposed of by taking the route to the Kanawha River. On the 27th Early's force reached Staunton on its march down the Valley. It now amounted to ten thousand infantry and about two thousand cavalry, having been joined by Breckinridge, and Colonel Bradley T. Johnson, with a battalion of Maryland cavalry. The advance was rapid. Railroad bridges were burned, the track destroyed, and stores captured. The Potomac was crossed on the 5th and 6th of June, and the move was made through the gaps of South Mountain to the north of Maryland Heights, which were occupied by a hostile force. A brigade of cavalry was sent north of Frederick to strike the railroads from Baltimore to Harrisburg and Philadelphia, burn the bridges over the Gunpowder, and to cut the railroad between Washington and Baltimore, and threaten the latter place. The other troops moved forward toward Monocacy Junction, where a considerable body of Federal troops under General Wallace was found posted on the eastern bank of the Monocacy, with an earthwork and two block-houses commanding both bridges. The position was attacked in front and on the flank, and it was carried and the garrison put to flight. Between six and seven hundred unwounded prisoners fell into our hands, and the enemy's loss in killed and wounded was far greater than ours, which was about seven hundred.

An advance was made on the 10th nearly to Knoxville, on the Georgetown Pike. On the next day it was continued to Washington, with the hope of getting into the fortifications before they could be manned. But the heat and the dust impeded the progress greatly. Fort Stevens was approached soon after noon, and appeared to be lightly manned, but, before our force could get into the works, a column of the enemy from Washington filed into them on the right and left, skirmishers were thrown out in front, and an artillery-fire was opened on us from a number of batteries. An examination was now made to determine if it were practicable to carry the defenses by assault. "They were found to be exceedingly strong, and consisted of what appeared to be inclosed forts for heavy artillery, with a tier of lower works in front of each, pierced for an immense number of guns, the whole being connected by curtains with ditches in front, and strengthened by palisades and abatis. The timber had been felled within cannon-range all around and left on the ground, making a formidable obstacle, and every possible approach was raked by artillery." As far as the eye could reach, the works appeared to be of the same impregnable character. The exhaustion of our force, the lightness of its artillery, and the information that two corps of the enemy's forces had just arrived in Washington, in addition to the veteran reserves and hundred-days-men, and the parapets lined with troops, led us to refrain from making an assault, and to retire during the night of the 12th. On the morning of the 14th General Early recrossed the Potomac, bringing off the prisoners captured at Monocacy and everything else in safety, including a large number of beef-cattle and horses. There was some skirmishing in the rear between our cavalry and that which was following us, and on the afternoon of the 14th there was artillery-firing across the river at our cavalry watching the fords. Meantime General Hunter had arrived at Harper's Ferry and united with Sigel, and some skirmishing took place; but General Early determined to concentrate near Strasburg, so as to enable him to put the trains in safety, and mobilize his command to make an attack. On the 22d he moved across Cedar

Creek toward Strasburg, and so posted his force as to cover all the roads from the direction of Winchester. Learning on the next day that a large portion of the column sent after him from Washington was returning, and that the Army of West Virginia, under Crook, including Hunter's and Sigel's forces, with Averill's cavalry, was at Kernstown, he determined to attack at once.

After the enemy's skirmishers had been driven in, it was discovered that his left flank was exposed, and General Breckinridge was ordered to move Echols's division undercover of some ravines on our right and attack that flank. The attacking division struck the enemy's left flank in open ground, doubling it up and throwing his whole line into great confusion. The other divisions then advanced, and his rout became complete. He was pursued by the infantry and artillery beyond Winchester. Our loss was very light; his loss in killed and wounded was severe. The whole defeated force crossed the Potomac, and took refuge at Maryland Heights and Harper's Ferry. The road was strewed with debris of the rapid retreat—twelve caissons and seventy-two wagons having been abandoned, and most of them burned.

On the 26th the Confederate force moved to Martinsburg:

"While at Martinsburg," says General Early in his memoir, "it was ascertained beyond all doubt that Hunter had been again indulging in his favorite mode of warfare, and that, after his return to the Valley, while we were near Washington, among other outrages, the private residences of Mr. Andrew Hunter, a member of the Virginia Senate, Mr. Alexander R. Boteler, an ex-member of the Confederate Congress, as well as of the United States Congress, and Edmund I. Lee, a distant relative of General Lee, all in Jefferson County, with their contents, had been burned by his orders, only time enough being given for the ladies to get out of the houses. A number of towns in the South, as well as private country-houses, had been burned by Federal troops, and the accounts had been heralded forth in some of the Northern papers in terms of exaltation, and gloated over by their readers, while they were received with apathy by others. I now came to the conclusion that we had stood this mode of warfare long enough, and that it was time to open the eyes of the people of the North to its enormity by an example in the way of retaliation. I did not select the cases mentioned as having more merit or greater claims for retaliation than others, but because they had occurred within the limits of the country covered by my command, and were

358

brought more immediately to my attention.[103]

"The town of Chambersburg was selected as the one on which retaliation should be made, and McCausland was ordered to proceed with his brigade and that of Johnson's and a battery of artillery to that place, and demand of the municipal authorities the sum of one hundred thousand dollars in gold, or five hundred thousand dollars in United States currency, as a compensation for the destruction of the houses named and their contents; and in default of payment to lay the town in ashes, in retaliation for the burning of those houses and others in Virginia, as well as for the towns which had been burned in other Southern States. A written demand to that effect was also sent to the municipal authorities, and they were informed what would be the result of a failure or a refusal to comply with it. I desired to give the people of Chambersburg an opportunity of saving their town, by making compensation for part of the injury done, and hoped that the payment of such a sum would have the desired effect, and open the eyes of people of other towns at the North to the necessity of urging upon their Government the adoption of a different policy.

"On July 30th McCausland reached Chambersburg, and made the demand as directed, reading to such of the authorities as presented themselves the paper sent by me. The demand was not complied with, the people stating that they were not afraid of having their town burned, and that a Federal force was approaching. The policy pursued by our army on former occasions had been so lenient that they did not suppose the threat was in earnest at this time, and they hoped for speedy relief. McCausland, however, proceeded to carry out his orders, and the greater part of the town was laid in ashes. He then moved in the direction of Cumberland, but found it defended by a strong force. He then withdrew and crossed the Potomac, near the mouth of the South Branch, capturing the garrison and partly destroying the railroad-bridge. Averill pursued from Chambersburg, and surprised and routed Johnson's brigade, and caused a loss of four pieces of artillery and about three hundred prisoners from the whole command."

Meantime a large force, consisting of the Sixth, Nineteenth, and Crook's corps, of the Federal army, had concentrated at Harper's Ferry under Major-General Sheridan. After various manoeuvres, both armies occupied positions in the neighborhood of Winchester. Early had about eight thousand five hundred infantry fit for duty, nearly three thousand mounted men, three battalions of artillery, and a few pieces of horse-artillery. Sheridan's force, according to the best information, consisted of ten thousand cavalry, thirty-five thousand infantry, and artillery that greatly outnumbered ours both in men and guns.

On the morning of September 19th, the enemy began to advance in heavy force on Ramseur's position, on an elevated plateau between Abraham's Creek and Red Bud Run, about a mile and a half from Winchester, on the Berryville road. Nelson's artillery was posted on Ramseur's line, covering the approaches as far as practicable; and Lomax, with Jackson's cavalry and a part of Johnson's, was on the right, watching the valley of Abraham's Creek and the Front Royal road beyond, while Fitzhugh Lee was on the left, across the Red Bud, with cavalry, watching the interval between Ramseur's left and the Red Bud. These troops held the enemy's main force in check until Gordon's and Rodes's divisions arrived, a little after 10 A.M. Gordon was placed under cover in rear of a piece of woods, behind the interval between Ramseur's line and the Red Bud. Rodes was directed to form on Gordon's right, in rear of another piece of woods. Meanwhile, we discovered very heavy columns, that had been massed under cover between the Red Bud and the Berryville road, moving to attack Ramseur on his left flank, while another force pressed him in front. Rodes and Gordon were immediately hurled upon the flank of the advancing columns. But Evans's brigade, of Gordon's division, on the extreme left of our infantry, was forced back through the woods from behind which it had advanced by a column, which followed to the rear of the woods and within musket-range of seven pieces of Braxton's artillery. Braxton's guns stood their ground and opened with canister. The fire was so well directed that the column staggered, halted, and commenced falling back. Just then Battle's brigade moved forward and swept through the woods, driving the enemy before it, while Evans's brigade was rallied and coöperated. Our advance was resumed, and the enemy's attacking columns, the Sixth and Nineteenth Corps, were thrown into great confusion and fled from the field. General Early exclaims, "It was a grand sight to see this immense body hurled back in utter disorder before my two divisions, numbering very little over five thousand muskets!" This affair occurred about 11 A.M., and a splendid victory had been gained. But the enemy still had a fresh corps which had not been engaged, and there remained his heavy force of cavalry. Our lines were now formed across from Abraham's Creek to Red Bud, and were very attenuated. There was still seen in front a formidable force, and away to the right a division of cavalry massed, with some artillery overlapping us at least a mile. Late in the afternoon, two divisions of the enemy's cavalry drove in the small force that had been watching it on the Martinsburg road, and Crook's corps, which had not been engaged, advanced at the same time on the north side of Red Bud and forced back our brigade of infantry and cavalry. A considerable force of cavalry then swept along the Martinsburg road to the skirts of Winchester, thus getting in the rear of our left flank. This was soon driven back by two of Wharton's brigades, and subsequently another charge of cavalry was also repulsed. But many of the men in the front line, hearing the fire in the rear, and thinking they were flanked and about to be cut off, commenced to fall back. At the same time Crook's corps advanced against our left, and Evans's brigade was thrown into line to meet it, but, after an obstinate resistance, that brigade also retired. The whole front line had now given way, but was rallied and formed behind some old breastworks, and with the aid of artillery the progress of the enemy's infantry was arrested. Their cavalry afterward succeeded in getting around on our left, producing great confusion, for which there was no remedy. We now retired through Winchester, a new line was formed, and the hostile advance checked until nightfall. We then retired to Newton without serious molestation. Our trains, stores, sick, and wounded that could be removed had been sent to Fisher's Hill. This battle, beginning with the skirmishing in Ramseur's front, had lasted from daylight until dark, and, at the close of it, we had been forced back two miles, after having repulsed the first attack with great slaughter, and subsequently contested every inch of ground with unsurpassed obstinacy. We deserved the victory, and would have gained it but for the enemy's immense superiority in cavalry. In his memoir General Early says:

"When I look back to this battle, I can but attribute my escape from utter annihilation to the incapacity of my opponent."

Our loss was severe for the size of our force, but only a fraction of that ascribed to us by the foe, while his was very heavy, and some prisoners fell into our hands.

On the 22d, after two days spent in reconnoitering, the enemy prepared to make an attack upon our position at Fisher's Hill; but, as our force was not strong enough to resist a determined assault, orders were given to retire after dark. Before sunset, however, an advance was made against Ramseur's left by Crook's corps. The movement to put Pegram's brigades into line successively to the left produced some confusion, when the enemy advanced along his entire line, and, after a brief contest, our force retired in disorder. We fell back to a place called Narrow Passage, all the trains being removed in safety. Some skirmishing ensued as we withdrew up the Valley, but without important result.

On October 1st our force was in position between Mount Sidney and North River, and the enemy's had been concentrated around Harrisonburg and on the north bank of the river. On the 5th we were reënforced by General Rosser with six hundred mounted men, and Kershaw's division, numbering twenty-seven hundred muskets, with a battalion of artillery. On the morning of the 6th it was discovered that the foe had retired down the Valley. General Early then moved forward and arrived at New Market with his infantry on the 7th. Rosser pushed forward on the back and middle roads in pursuit of the cavalry, which was engaged in burning houses, mills, barns, and stacks of wheat and hay, and had several skirmishes with it.

A committee, consisting of thirty-six citizens and the same number of magistrates, appointed by the County Court of Rockingham County, for the purpose of making an estimate of the losses of that county by the execution of General Sheridan's orders, made an investigation, and reported as follows:

"Dwelling-houses burned, 30; barns burned, 450; mills burned, 31; fences destroyed (miles), 100; bushels of wheat destroyed, 100,000; bushels of corn destroyed, 50,000; tons of hay destroyed, 6,233; cattle carried off, 1,750; horses carried off, 1,750; sheep carried off, 4,200; hogs carried off, 3,350; factories burned, three; furnaces burned, one. In addition there was an immense amount of farming utensils of every description destroyed, many of them of great value, such as reapers and thrashing-machines; also, household and kitchen furniture, and money, bonds, plate, etc., pillaged."

General Early, having learned that Sheridan was preparing to send a part of his troops to Grant, moved down the Valley again on the 12th, and reached Fisher's Hill. The enemy was found on the north bank of Cedar Creek in strong force. He gave no indication of an intention to move, nor did he evince any purpose of attacking us, though the two positions were in sight of each other. At the same time it became necessary for us to move back for want of provisions and forage, or to attack him in his position with the hope of driving him from it. An attack was determined upon by General Early, and, as he was not strong enough to assault the fortified position in front, he resolved to get around one of the enemy's flanks and attack him by surprise. His plan of attack is thus stated by him:

"I determined to send the three divisions of the Second Corps, to wit, Gordon's, Ramseur's, and Pegram's, under General Gordon, to the enemy's rear, to make the attack at 5 A.M., which would be a little before daybreak on the 19th; to move myself with Kershaw's and Wharton's divisions and all the artillery along the pike through Strasburg, and attack the enemy on the front and left flank, as soon as Gordon should become engaged, and for Bosser to move with his own and Wickham's brigade on the back road across Cedar Creek, and attack the enemy's cavalry simultaneously with Gordon's attack, while Lomax should move by Front Royal, cross the river, and come to the Valley pike, so as to strike the enemy wherever he might be, of which he was to judge by the sound of the firing."

Gordon moved at the appointed time. At 1 A.M. Kershaw and Wharton, accompanied by General Early, advanced. At Strasburg, Kershaw moved to the right on the road to Bowman's Mill, and Wharton moved along the pike to Hupp's Hill, with instructions not to display his forces, but to avoid notice until the attack began, when he was to move forward, support the artillery when it came up, and send a force to get possession of the bridge on the pike over the creek. Kershaw's division got in sight of the enemy at half-past three o'clock. He was directed to cross his division at the proper time over the creek as quietly as possible, and to form it into column of brigades as he did so, and advance in that manner against the left breastwork, extending to the right or left as might be necessary. At half-past four he was ordered forward, and, a very short time after he started, the firing from Bosser on our left and the picket-firing at the ford at which Gordon was crossing were heard. Kershaw crossed the creek without molestation and formed his division as directed, and precisely at five o'clock his leading brigade, with little opposition, swept over the left work, capturing seven guns, which were at once turned on the enemy. At the same time Wharton and the artillery were just arriving at Hupp's Hill, and a very heavy fire of musketry was heard in the rear from Gordon's column. Wharton had advanced his skirmishers to the creek, capturing some prisoners, but the foe still held the works on our left of the pike, commanding that road and the bridge, and opened with his artillery on us. Our artillery was at once brought into action, and opened on the enemy, but he soon evacuated his works, and our men from the other columns rushed into them. Wharton was immediately ordered forward, Kershaw's division had swept along the enemy's works on the right of the pike, which were occupied by Crook's corps, and he and Gordon had united at the pike, and their divisions had pushed across it in pursuit. A delay of an hour at the river had occurred in Gordon's movement, which enabled Sheridan partially to form his lines after the alarm produced by Kershaw's attack; and Gordon's, which was after daylight, was therefore met with greater obstinacy by the enemy than it would otherwise have encountered, and the fighting had been severe. Gordon, however, pushed his advance with such energy, that the Nineteenth and Crook's corps were in complete rout, and their camps, with a number of pieces of artillery and a considerable quantity of small-arms, abandoned. The Sixth Corps, which was on the right, and some distance from the point attacked, had had time to get under arms and take position so as to arrest our progress. A fog which had prevailed soon rose sufficiently for us to see the Sixth Corps' position on a ridge to the west of Middletown, and it was discovered to be a strong one. The enemy had not advanced, but opened on us with artillery, and orders were given to concentrate all our guns on him. In the mean time a force of cavalry was moving along the pike, through the fields to the right of Middletown, thus placing our right and rear in great danger. Wharton was ordered to form his division at once, and take position to hold that cavalry in check. Discovering that the Sixth Corps could not be attacked with advantage on its left flank, because the approach in that direction was through an open flat and across a boggy stream with high banks, Gordon in conjunction with Kershaw was ordered to assail the right flank, while a heavy fire of artillery was opened from our right. In a short time eighteen or twenty guns were concentrated on the enemy, and he was soon in retreat. Ramseur and Pegram advanced at once to the position from which he was driven, and just then his cavalry commenced pressing heavily on the right, and Pegram's division was ordered to move to the north of Middletown and take position across the pike against the cavalry. As soon as

Pegram moved, Kershaw was ordered from the left to supply his place. Bosser had attacked the enemy promptly at the appointed time, but had not been able to surprise him, as he was found on the alert on that flank. There was now one division of cavalry threatening our right flank, and two were on the left near the Back road, held in check by Bosser. His force was so weak he could only watch.

After he had been driven from his second position, the enemy had taken a new one about two miles north of Middletown. An advance by Gordon and Kershaw and Ramseur was ordered, but, after it had been made for some distance, Gordon's skirmishers came back, reporting a line of battle in front, behind breastworks, and an attack was not made.

> "It was now apparent that it would not do," says General Early, "to press my troops farther. They had been up all night and were much jaded. In passing over rough ground to attack the enemy at dawn their own ranks had been much disordered and the men scattered, and it had required time to reform them. Their ranks were much thinned by the absence of the men engaged in plundering the enemy's camps."

It was determined, therefore, to try to hold what had been gained, and orders were given to carry off the captured and abandoned artillery, small-arms, and wagons. A number of bold attempts were made, during the subsequent part of the day, by the enemy's cavalry, to break our line on the right, but they were invariably repulsed. Late in the afternoon, his infantry advanced against Ramseur's, Kershaw's, and Gordon's lines, and the attack on Ramseur's and Kershaw's fronts was handsomely repulsed; but a portion of the assailants had penetrated an interval which was between Evans's brigade on the extreme left and the rest of the line, when that brigade gave way, and Gordon's other brigades soon followed. General Gordon made every possible effort to rally his men and lead them back, but without avail. This affair was soon known with exaggerations along Kershaw's and Ramseur's lines, and their men, fearing to be flanked, began to fall back in disorder, though no force was pressing them. At the same time the enemy's cavalry, observing the disorder in our ranks, made another charge on our right, but was again repulsed. Every effort was made to rally the men, but the mass of them continued to resist all appeals. Ramseur succeeded in retaining with him two or three hundred men of his division, and about the same number was retained by Major Goggin from Conner's brigade; these, aided by several pieces of artillery, held the whole force on our left in check for one hour and a half until Ramseur was shot down, and the ammunition of the artillery was exhausted. While the latter was being replaced by other guns, the force that had continued steady gave way also. Pegram's and Wharton's divisions and Wofford's brigade had remained steadfast on the right, and resisted every effort of the cavalry, but no portion of this force could be moved to the left without leaving the pike open to the cavalry, which would have destroyed all hope at once. Every effort to rally the men in the rear having failed, these troops were ordered to retire. The disorder soon extended to them. The greater part of the infantry was halted at Fisher's Hill, and Rosser, whose command had retired in good order on the Back road, was ordered to that point with his cavalry to cover the retreat, and hold that position until the troops were beyond pursuit. He fell back on the forenoon of the 20th, when the enemy had not advanced to that place. The troops were halted at Newmarket, seven miles from Mount Jackson. Our loss in the battle of Cedar Creek was twenty-three pieces of artillery, some ordnance, and medical wagons and ambulances, about 1,860 killed and wounded, and something over a thousand prisoners; 1,500 prisoners were captured from the enemy and brought off, and his loss in killed and wounded was very heavy. We had in this battle about 8,500 muskets and a little over forty pieces of artillery. Sheridan's cavalry numbered 8,700, and his infantry force was fully as large as at Winchester.

Subsequently General Early confronted Sheridan's whole force north of Cedar Creek for two days, November 11th and 12th, without an attack being made upon him. On November 27th the fortified post at New Creek on the Baltimore and Ohio Railroad was surprised and captured by General Rosser. Two regiments of Federal cavalry with their arms and colors were taken, and eight pieces of artillery and a very large amount of ordnance, quartermaster, and commissary stores fell into our hands. Eight hundred prisoners, four pieces of artillery, and some wagons and horses were brought off. When the campaign closed, the invader held precisely the same position in the Valley which he held before the opening of the campaign in the spring.

In the Red River country of Louisiana, it became certain in February, 1864, that the enemy was about to make an expedition against our forces under General Richard Taylor, not so much to get possession of the country as to obtain the cotton in that region. Their forces were to be commanded by Major-General Banks, and to consist of his command, augmented by a part of Major-General Sherman's army from Vicksburg, and accompanied by a fleet of gunboats under Admiral Porter. With these the force under General Steele, in Arkansas, was to coöperate. Taylor's forces at this time consisted of Harrison's mounted regiment with a four-gun battery, in the north toward Monroe; Mouton's brigade, near Alexandria; Polignac's, at Trinity, on the Washita, fifty-five miles distant; Walker's division, at Marksville and toward Simmsport, with two hundred men detached to assist the gunners at Fort De Russy, which, though still unfinished, contained eight heavy guns and two field-pieces. Three companies of mounted men were watching the Mississippi, and the remainder of a regiment was on the Têche.

On March 12th Admiral Porter, with nineteen gunboats and ten thousand men of Sherman's army, entered the Red River. A detachment on the 14th marched to De Russy and took possession of it. On the 15th the advance of Porter reached Alexandria, and on the 19th General Franklin left the lower Têche with eighteen thousand men to meet him. General Steele, in Arkansas, reported his force at seven thousand men. The force of General Taylor at this time had increased to five thousand and three hundred infantry, five hundred cavalry, and three hundred artillerymen; and Liddel on the north had about the same number of cavalry and a four-gun battery. Some reënforcements were soon received. On March 31st Banks's advance reached Natchitoches, and Taylor moved toward Pleasant Hill, arriving on the next day. On April 4th and 5th. He moved to Mansfield, concentrating his force in that vicinity. There two brigades of Missouri infantry and two of Arkansas, numbering four thousand and four hundred muskets, joined him. On April 7th the enemy were reported from

Pleasant Hill to be advancing in force, but their progress was arrested by a body of our cavalry.

General Taylor then selected his position in which to wait for an attack expected on the next day. It was in the edge of a wood, fronting an open field eight hundred yards in width and twelve hundred in length, through the center of which the road to Pleasant Hill passed. On the opposite side of the field was a fence separating it from the pine-forest, which, open on the higher ground and filled with underwood on the lower, spread over the country. The position was three miles in front of Mansfield, and covered a cross-road leading to the Sabine. On each side of the main Mansfield-Pleasant Hill road at two miles' distance, was a road parallel to it, and these were connected by this Sabine cross-road.

On the 8th General Taylor disposed, on the right of the road to Pleasant Hill, Walker's infantry division of three brigades with two batteries; on the left, Mouton's two brigades and two batteries. As the horsemen came in from the front, they took position, dismounted, on Mouton's left. A regiment of horsemen was posted on each of the parallel roads, and cavalry with a battery held in reserve on the main road. Taylor's force amounted to 5,300 infantry, 3,000 mounted men, and 500 artillerymen; total, 8,800. Banks left Grand Ecore with an estimated force of 25,000.

As the enemy showed no disposition to advance, a forward movement of the whole line was made. On the left our forces crossed the field under a heavy fire and entered the wood, where a bloody contest ensued, which resulted in gradually turning their right, which was forced back with loss of prisoners and guns. On the right little resistance was encountered until the wood was entered. Finding that our force outflanked the opponent's left, the right brigade was kept advanced, and we swept everything before us.

His first line, consisting of all the mounted force and one division of the Thirteenth Corps, was in full flight, leaving prisoners, guns, and wagons in our hands. Two miles to the rear of the first position, the Second Division of the Federal Thirteenth Corps was brought up, but was speedily routed, losing guns and prisoners. The advance was continued. Four miles from the original position, his Nineteenth Army Corps was found drawn up on a ridge overlooking a small stream. Sharp work followed, but, as our force persisted, his fell back at nightfall. Twenty-five hundred prisoners, twenty pieces of artillery, several stands of colors, many thousands of small-arms, and two hundred and fifty wagons, were taken.

On the next morning the enemy was found about a mile in front of Pleasant Hill, which occupies a plateau a mile wide from west to east along the Mansfield road. His lines extended across the plateau from the highest ground on the west, his left, to a wooded height on the right of the Mansfield road. Winding along in front of this position was a dry gully cut by winter rains, bordered by a thick growth of young pines. This was held by his advanced infantry, his main line and guns being on the plateau. The force of General Taylor— Churchill's brigade having joined him now—amounted to twelve thousand five hundred men against eighteen thousand of General Banks, among them the fresh corps of General A. J. Smith. The action commenced about 4.30 P.M. It was the plan of General Taylor, as no offensive movement on the part of the enemy was anticipated, to turn both his flanks and subject him to a concentric fire and overwhelm him. The right was successfully turned, but our force on his left did not proceed far enough to outflank him. An obstinate contest ensued, with much confusion, and failure to execute the plan of battle. Night ended the conflict on our right, and both sides occupied their original positions. General Banks made no attempt to recover the ground from which his right and center had been driven. During the night he retreated, leaving four hundred wounded, and his dead unburied. On the next morning he was pursued twenty miles before his rear was overtaken, and on the road were found stragglers, and burning wagons and stores. Our loss in the two actions of Mansfield and Pleasant Hill was twenty-two hundred. At Pleasant Hill the loss was three guns and four hundred and twenty-six prisoners. The loss of the enemy in killed and wounded was larger than ours. We captured twenty guns and twenty-eight hundred prisoners, not including stragglers. Their campaign was defeated. In the second volume of the "Report of the Committee on the Conduct of the War," page 239, a report of Admiral Porter, dated Grand Ecore, April 14, 1864, says:

"The army here has met with a great defeat, no matter what the generals try to make of it," etc.

On April 21st General Banks retreated from Grand Ecore to Alexandria, harassed by a small cavalry force. A large part of our forces had been taken by General E. K. Smith to follow General Steele. On April 28th Porter's fleet was lying above the falls, then impassable, and Banks's army was in and around Alexandria behind earthworks. On May 13th both escaped from Alexandria, and on May 19th Banks crossed the Atchafalaya, and the campaign closed at the place where it began. Porter was able to extricate his eight ironclads and two wooden gunboats by building a dam with transports, as shown in the adjoining cut. General Banks boasted that the army obtained ten thousand bales of cotton, to which Admiral Porter added five thousand more as collected by the navy. This was the compensation reported for the loss of many lives, much public property, and a total defeat. Even for the booty as well as for the escape of their fleet, they were probably indebted to the unfortunate withdrawal of a large part of Taylor's force, as mentioned above.[104]

On April 12, 1864, an attack was made by two brigades of General N. B. Forrest's force, under Brigadier-General J. R. Chalmers, upon Fort Pillow. This was an earthwork on a bluff on the east side of the Mississippi, at the mouth of Coal Creek. It was garrisoned by four hundred men and six pieces of artillery. General Chalmers promptly gained possession of the outer works and drove the garrison to their main fortifications. The fort was crescent-shaped, the parapet eight feet in height and four feet across the top, surrounded by a ditch six feet deep and twelve feet in width. About this time General Forrest arrived and soon ordered his forces to move up. The brigade of Bell, on the northeast, advanced until it gained a position in which the men were sheltered by the conformation of the ground, which was intersected by a ravine. The other brigade, under McCulloch, carried the intrenchments on the highest part of the ridge, immediately in front of the southeastern face of the fort, and occupied a cluster of cabins on its southern face and about sixty yards from it. The line of investment was now short and complete, within an average distance of one hundred yards. It extended from Coal Creek on the north, which was impassable, to the river-bank south of the fort. In the rear were numerous sharpshooters, well posted on commanding ridges, to pick off the garrison whenever they exposed themselves. At the same time, our forces were so placed that the artillery could not be brought to bear upon them with much effect except by a fatal exposure of the gunners. During all this time a gunboat in the river kept up a continuous fire in all directions, but without effect. General Forrest, confident of his ability to take the fort by assault, which it seemed must be perfectly apparent to the garrison, and desiring to prevent further loss of life, sent a demand for an unconditional surrender, with the assurance that they should be treated as prisoners of war. The answer was written with a pencil on a slip of paper, "Negotiations will not attain the desired object." Meantime, three boats were seen to approach, the foremost of which was apparently loaded with troops, and, as an hour's time had been asked for to communicate with the officers of the gunboat, it seemed to be a pretext to gain time for reënforcements. General Forrest, understanding also that the enemy doubted his presence and had pronounced the demand to be a trick, declared himself, and demanded an answer within twenty minutes whether the commander would fight or surrender. Meanwhile, the foremost boat indicated an intention to land, but a few shots caused her to withdraw to the other side of the river, along which they all passed up. The answer from the fort was a positive refusal to surrender. Three companies on the left were now placed in an old rifle-pit and almost in the rear of the fort, and on the right a portion of Barton's regiment of Bell's brigade was also under the bluff and in the rear of the fort.

On the signal, the works were carried without a halt. As the troops poured into the fortification the enemy retreated toward the river, arms in hand and firing back, and their colors flying, doubtless expecting the gunboats to shell us away from the bluff and protect them until they could be taken off or reënforced. As they descended the bank an enfilading and deadly fire was poured in upon them from right and left by the forces in rear of the fort, of whose presence they were ignorant. To this was now added the destructive fire of the regiments that had stormed the fort. Fortunately some of our men cut down the flag, and the firing ceased. Our loss was twenty killed and sixty wounded. Of the enemy two hundred and twenty-eight were buried that evening and quite a number next day. We captured six pieces of artillery and about three hundred and fifty stand of small-arms. The gunboat escaped up the river.

[Footnote 102: I. Stoddard Johnston, "Southern Historical Society Papers," June, 1879, p. 258, *et seq.*]

[Footnote 103: "I had often seen delicate ladies who had been plundered, insulted, ind rendered desolate by the acts of our most atrocious enemies, and, while they did not call for it, yet in the anguished expressions of their features while narrating their misfortunes, there was a mute appeal to every manly sentiment of my bosom for retribution, which I could no longer withstand. On my passage through the lower Valley into Maryland, a lady had said to me, with tears in her eyes: 'Our lot is a hard one, and we see no peace; but there are a few green spots in our lives, and they are when the Confederate soldiers come along and we can do something far them.' May God defend and bless these noble women of the Valley, who so often ministered to the wounded, sick, and dying Confederate soldiers, and gave their last morsel of bread to the hungry! They bore with heroic courage the privations, sufferings, persecutions, and dangers to which the war, which was constantly waged in their midst, exposed them, and

upon no portion of the Southern people did the disasters, which finally befell our army and country, fall with more crushing effect than on them."]
[Footnote 104: "Destruction and Reconstruction," Taylor, p. 162, *et. seq.*]

CHAPTER XLVIII.

Assignment of General J. E. Johnston to the Command of the Army of Tennessee.—Condition of his Army.—An Offensive Campaign suggested.—Proposed Objects to be accomplished.—General Johnston's Plans.—Advance of Sherman.—The Strength of the Confederate Position.—General Johnston expects General Sherman to give Battle at Dalton.—The Enemy's Flank Movement via Snake Creek Gap to Resaca.—Johnston falls back to Resaca.—Further Retreat to Adairsville.—General Johnston's Reasons.—Retreat to Cassville.— Projected Engagement at Kingston frustrated.—Retreat beyond the Etowah River.—Strong Position at Alatoona abandoned.—Nature of the Country between Marietta and Dallas.—Engagements at New Hope Church.—Army takes Position at Kenesaw.—Senator Hill's Letter.— Death of Lieutenant-General Polk.—Battle at Kenesaw Mountain.— Retreat beyond the Chattahoochee.—Results reviewed.—Popular Demand for Removal of General Johnston.—Reluctance to remove him.— Reasons for Removal.—Assignment of General J. B. Hood to the Command.—He assumes the Offensive.—Battle of Peach-tree Creek.— Death of General W. H. T. Walker.—Sherman's Movement to Jonesboro.—Defeat of Hardee.—Evacuation of Atlanta.—Sherman's Inhuman Order.—Visit to Georgia.—Suggested Operations.—Want of coöperation by the Governor of Georgia.—Conference with Generals Beauregard, Hardee, and Cobb, at Augusta.—Departure from Original Plan.—General Hood's Movement against the Enemy's Communications.— Partial Successes.—Withdrawal of the Army to Gadsden and Movement against Thomas.—Sherman burns Atlanta and begins his March to the Sea.—Vandalism.—Direction of his Advance.—General Wheeler's Opposition.—His Valuable Service.—Sherman reaches Savannah.— General Hardee's Command.—The Defenses of the City.—Assault and Capture of Fort McAlister.—The Results.—Hardee evacuates Savannah.

On December 16, 1863, I directed General J. E. Johnston to transfer the command of the Department of Mississippi and East Louisiana to Lieutenant-General Polk, and repair to Dalton, Georgia, to assume command of the Army of Tennessee, representing at that date an effective total of 43,094. My information led me to believe that the condition of that army, in all that constitutes efficiency, was satisfactory, and that the men were anxious for an opportunity to retrieve the loss of prestige sustained in the disastrous battle of Missionary Ridge. I was also informed that the enemy's forces, then occupying Chattanooga, Bridgeport, and Stevenson, with a detached force at Knoxville, were weaker in numbers than at any time since the battle of Missionary Ridge, and that they were especially deficient in cavalry and in artillery and train-horses. I desired, therefore, that prompt and vigorous measures be taken to enable our troops to commence active operations against the enemy as early as practicable. It was important to guard against the injurious results to the morale of the troops, which always attend a prolonged season of inactivity; but the recovery of the territory in Tennessee and Kentucky, which we had been compelled to abandon, and on the supplies of which the proper subsistence of our armies mainly depended, imperatively demanded an onward movement. I believed that, by a rapid concentration of our troops between the scattered forces of the enemy, without attempting to capture his intrenched positions, we could compel him to accept battle in the open field, and that, should we fail to draw him out of his intrenchments, we could move upon his line of communications. The Federal force at Knoxville depended mainly for support on its connection with that at Chattanooga, and both were wholly dependent on uninterrupted communication with Nashville. Could we, then, by interposing our force, separate these two bodies of the enemy, and cut off his communication from Nashville to Chattanooga by destroying the railroad, both conditions were fulfilled. Of the practicability of this movement I had little doubt; of its expediency, if practicable, there could be none. I impressed repeatedly upon General Johnston by letter, and by officers of my staff and others, sent to him by me for the purpose of putting him in possession of these views, the importance of a prompt aggressive movement by the Army of Tennessee. The following were among the considerations presented to General Johnston, at my request, by Brigadier-General W. N. Pendleton, chief of artillery of the Army of Northern Virginia, on April 16, 1864:

1. To take the enemy at disadvantage while weakened, it is believed, by sending troops to Virginia, and having others still absent on furlough.

2. To break up his plans by anticipating and frustrating his combinations.

3. So to press him in his present position as to prevent his heavier massing in Virginia.

4. To defeat him in battle, and gain great consequent strength in supplies, men, and productive territory.

5. To prevent the waste of the army incident to inactivity.

6. To inspirit the troops and the country by success, and to discourage the enemy.

7. To obviate the necessity of falling back, which might probably occur if our antagonist be allowed to consummate his plans without molestation.

General Johnston cordially approved of an aggressive movement, and informed me of his purpose to make it as soon as reënforcements and supplies, then on the way, should reach him. He did not approve the proposed advance into Tennessee. He believed that the Federal forces in Tennessee were not weaker, but if anything stronger, than at Missionary Ridge; that defeat beyond the Tennessee would probably prove ruinous to us, resulting in the loss of his army, the occupation of Georgia by the enemy, the "piercing of the Confederacy in its vitals," and the loss of all the southwestern territory. He proposed, therefore, to stand on the defensive until strengthened, "to watch, prepare, and strike" as soon as possible. As soon as reënforced, he declared his purpose to advance to Ringgold, attack there, and, if successful, as he expected to be, to strike at Cleveland, cut the railroad, control the river, and thus isolate East Tennessee, and, as a consequence, force his antagonist to give battle on this side of the Tennessee River. Simultaneously with, and in aid of, this movement, General Johnston proposed that a large cavalry force should be sent to Middle Tennessee, in the rear of the enemy. These operations, he thought, would result in forcing the Federal army to evacuate the Tennessee Valley, and make an advance into the heart of the State safely practicable.

The irreparable loss of time in making any forward movement as desired having sufficed for the combinations which rendered an advance across the Tennessee River no longer practicable, I took prompt measures to enable General Johnston to carry out immediately his own proposition to strike first at Ringgold and then at Cleveland, proposing that General Buckner should threaten Knoxville, General Forrest advance into or threaten Middle Tennessee, and General Roddy hold the enemy in northern Alabama, and thus prevent his concentration in our front. This movement, although it held out no such promise as did the plan of advance before the enemy had had time to make his combinations, might have been attended with good results had it been promptly executed. But no such movement was made or even attempted. General Johnston's belief that General Grant would be ready to assume the offensive before he could be prepared to do so, proved too well founded, while his purpose, if the Federal army did not attack, that we should prepare and take the initiative ourselves, was never carried out.[105]

On the morning of May 2, 1864, General Johnston discovered that the enemy, under the command of General Sherman, was advancing against him, and two days subsequently it was reported that he had reached Ringgold (about fifteen miles north of Dalton) in considerable force.

At this date the official returns show that the effective strength of the Army of Tennessee, counting the troops actually in position at Dalton and those in the immediate rear of that place, was about fifty thousand. When to these is added General Polk's command (then *en route*), and the advance of which joined him at Resaca, the effective strength of General Johnston's army was not less than 68,620 men of all arms, excluding from the estimate the thousands of men employed on extra duty, amounting, as General Hood states, to ten thousand when he assumed command of the army.

Army at Dalton, May 1, 1864, according to General
Johnston's estimates[106] . . . . 37,652 infantry.
                      2,812 artillery.
                      2,392 cavalry.
Mercer's brigade, joined May 2d . . . . 2,000 infantry.
Thirty-seventh Mississippi Regiment, *en route* 400 "
Dibrell's and Harrison's brigades in rear,
recruiting their horses . . . . 2,336 cavalry.
Martin's division at Cartersville . . . . 1,700 "
                 ———
             49,292
Polk's command 19,330
             ———
Total effective 68,620

To enable General Johnston to repulse the hostile advance and assume the offensive, no effort was spared on the part of the Government. Almost all the available military strength of the south and west, in men and supplies, was pressed forward and placed at his disposal. The supplies of the commissary, quartermaster, and ordnance departments of his army were represented as ample and suitably located. The troops, encouraged by the large accessions of strength which they saw arriving daily, and which they knew were marching rapidly to their support, were eager to advance, and confident in their power to achieve victory and recover the territory which they had lost. Their position was such as to warrant the confident expectation of successful resistance at least. Long mountain-ranges, penetrated by few and difficult roads and paths, and deep and wide rivers, seemed to render our position one from which we could not be dislodged or turned, while that of the enemy, dependent for his supplies upon a single line of railroad from Nashville to the point where he was operating, was manifestly perilous. The whole country shared the hope which the Government entertained, that a decisive victory would soon be won in the mountains of Georgia, which would free the south and west from invasion, would open to our occupation and the support of our armies the productive territory of Tennessee and Kentucky, and so recruit our army in the West as to render it impracticable for the enemy to accumulate additional forces in Virginia.

On May 6th the Confederate forces were in position in and near Dalton, which point General Johnston believed that General Sherman would attack with his whole force. This belief seems to have been held by General Johnston until the evening of May 12th, when, having previously learned the proximity of the advance of Lieutenant-General Polk's command, and that the rest of his troops were hurrying forward to reënforce him, but discovering that the main body of Sherman's army was moving round his left flank, via Snake-Creek Gap to Resaca, under cover of Rocky-Face Mountain, he withdrew his troops from Dalton and fell back on Resaca, situated on the Western and Atlantic Railroad, eighteen miles south of Dalton on a peninsula formed by the junction of the Oostenaula and Conasauga Rivers. The Confederate position at this place was strengthened by continuous rifle-pits and strong field-works, by which it was protected on the flanks on the above-named rivers, and a line of retreat across the Oostenaula secured. Information, on May 15th, that the right of the Federal army was crossing the Oostenaula near Calhoun (four miles south of Resaca), thus threatening his line of communications, induced General Johnston to fall back from Resaca toward Adairsville, thirteen miles south on the railroad. General Johnston, in accounting for his abandonment of his strong position at Dalton, and of his subsequent position at Resaca, states that he was dislodged from the first position—that in front of Dalton—by General Sherman's movement to his right through Snake-Creek Gap, threatening our line of communication at Resaca; and from the position taken at Resaca to meet that movement, by a similar one on the part of the Federal General toward Calhoun—the second being covered by the river, as the first had been by the mountains.

After abandoning Resaca, General Johnston hoped to find a good position near Calhoun; but, finding none, he fell back to a position about a mile north of Adairsville, where the valley of the Oothcaloga was supposed from the map to be so narrow that his army, formed in line of battle across it, could hold the heights on both flanks. On reaching this point, however, it was found that the valley was so much broader than was supposed, that the army, in line of battle, could not obtain the anticipated advantage of ground. Hence a further retreat to Cassville was ordered, seventeen miles farther south, and a few miles to the east of the railroad. Here, supposing that the Federal army would divide, one column following the railroad through Kingston and the other the direct road to the Etowah Railroad Bridge through Cassville, General Johnston hoped that the opportunity would be offered him to engage and defeat one of the enemy's columns before it could receive aid from the other, and, as the distance between them would be greatest at Kingston, he determined to attack at this point. The coming battle was announced in orders to each regiment of the army.

The battle, for causes which were the subject of dispute, did not take place as General Johnston had originally announced, and, instead of his attacking the divided columns of the enemy, the united Federal army was preparing to attack him. Here our army occupied a position which General Johnston describes as "the best that he saw during the war," but owing, as he represents, to an expressed want of confidence on the part of lieutenant-Generals Hood and Polk in their ability to resist the enemy, the army was again (May 19, 1864) ordered to retreat beyond the Etowah.

General Hood, in his official report, and in a book written by him since the war, takes a very different view of the position in rear of Cassville, and states that he and General Polk explained that their corps were on ground commanded and enfiladed by the batteries of the enemy, therefore wholly unsuited for defense, and, unless it was proposed to attack, that the position should be abandoned. General Shoup, a scientific and gallant soldier, confirms this opinion of the defects of the position, as does Captain Morris, chief-engineer of the Army of Mississippi, and others then on duty there.[107]

The next stand of our army was at Alatoona, in the Etowah Mountains, and south of the river of that name; but the reported extension of the Federal army toward Dallas, threatening Marietta, was deemed to necessitate the evacuation of that strong position. The country between Dallas and Marietta, eighteen miles wide, and lying in a due westerly direction from the latter place, constitutes a natural fortress of exceptional strength. Densely wooded, traversed by ranges of steep hills, seamed at intervals by ravines both deep and rugged, with very few roads, and those ill constructed and almost impassable to wheels, it is difficult to imagine a country better adapted for defense, where the advantages of numerical superiority in an invading army were more thoroughly neutralized, or where, necessarily ignorant of the topography, it was compelled to advance with greater caution.

The engagements at New Hope Church, June 27th and 28th, though severe and marked by many acts of gallantry, did not result in any advantage to our army. Falling back slowly as the enemy advanced to Acworth (June 8th), General Johnston made his next stand in that mountainous country that lies between Acworth and Marietta, remarkable for the three clearly defined eminences: Kenesaw Mountain, to the west of the railroad, and overlooking Marietta; Lost Mountain, half-way between Kenesaw and Dallas, and west of Marietta; and Pine Mountain, about half a mile farther to the north, forming, as it were, the apex of a triangle, of which Kenesaw and Lost Mountains form the base. These heights are connected by ranges of lower heights, intersected by numerous ravines, and thickly wooded. The right of our army rested on the railroad, the line extending four or five miles in a westerly direction, protected by strong earthworks, with abatis on every avenue of approach. While the enemy, feeling his way slowly, was skirmishing on the right of our position, our army, our country, and mankind at large, sustained an irreparable loss on June

13th in the death of that noble Christian and soldier, Lieutenant-General Polk. Having accompanied Generals Johnston and Hardee to the Confederate outpost on Pine Mountain, in order to acquaint himself more thoroughly with the nature of the ground in front of the position held by his corps, he was killed by a shot from a Federal battery six or seven hundred yards distant, which struck him in the chest, passing from left to right. Since the calamitous fall of General Albert Sidney Johnston at Shiloh and of General T. J. Jackson at Chancellorsville, the country sustained no heavier blow than in the death of General Polk.

On June 18th, heavy rains having swollen Nose's Creek on the left of our position so that it became impassable, the Federal army, under cover of this stream, extended its lines several miles beyond Johnston's left flank toward the Chattahoochee, causing a further retrograde movement by a portion of his force. For several days brisk fighting occurred at various points of our line.

The cavalry attack on Wheeler's force on the 20th, the attack upon Hardee's position on the 24th, and the general assault upon the Confederate position on the 27th were firmly met and handsomely repulsed. On the 4th of July, it having been reported by General G. W. Smith, in command of about a thousand militia, and occupying the extreme left of our army, that the enemy's "cavalry was pressing him in such force that he would be compelled to abandon the ground he had been holding and retire before morning to General Shoup's line of redoubts," [108] constructed on the high ground near the Chattahoochee and covering the approaches to the railroad-bridge and Turner's Ferry, General Johnston deemed it necessary to abandon his position at Kenesaw on July 5th and fall back to the line constructed by General Shoup, as the enemy's position covered one of the main roads to Atlanta, and was nearer to that city than the main body of General Johnston's force. On the 9th, Sherman having crossed the Chattahoochee with two corps on the day previous, the Confederate army crossed that river and established itself two miles in its rear.

Thus, from Dalton to Resaca, from Resaca to Adairsville, from Adairsville to Alatoona (involving by the evacuation of Kingston the loss of Rome, with its valuable mills, foundries, and large quantities of military stores), from Alatoona to Kenesaw, from Kenesaw to the Chattahoochee, and then to Atlanta; retreat followed retreat, during seventy-four days of anxious hope and bitter disappointment, until at last the Army of Tennessee fell back within the fortifications of Atlanta. The Federal army soon occupied the arc of a circle extending from the railroad between Atlanta and the Chattahoochee River to some miles south of the Georgia Railroad (from Atlanta to Augusta) in a direction north and northeast of Atlanta. We had suffered a disastrous loss of territory.

Whether the superior numerical strength of the enemy, by enabling him to extend his force beyond the flank of ours, did thereby necessitate the abandonment of every position taken by our army, and whether the enemy, declining to assault any of our intrenched camps, would have ventured to leave it in rear, upon his only line of communication and supply, or whether we might have obtained more advantageous results by a vigorous and determined effort to attack him in detail during some of his many flank movements—are questions upon which there has been a decided conflict of opinion, and upon which it would be for me now neither useful nor pleasant to enter. When it became known that the Army of Tennessee had been successfully driven from one strong position to another, until finally it had reached the earthworks constructed for the exterior defense of Atlanta, the popular disappointment was extreme. The possible fall of the "Gate City," with its important railroad communication, vast stores, factories for the manufacture of all sorts of military supplies, rolling-mill and foundries, was now contemplated for the first time at its full value, and produced intense anxiety far and wide. From many quarters, including such as had most urged his assignment, came delegations, petitions, and letters, urging me to remove General Johnston from the command of the army, and assign that important trust to some officer who would resolutely hold and defend Atlanta. While sharing in the keen sense of disappointment at the failure of the campaign which pervaded the whole country, I was perhaps more apprehensive than others of the disasters likely to result from it, because I was in a position to estimate more accurately their probable extent. On the railroads threatened with destruction, the armies then fighting the main battles of the war in Virginia had for some time to a great degree depended for indispensable supplies, yet I did not respond to the wishes of those who came in hottest haste for the removal of General Johnston; for here again, more fully than many others, I realized how serious it was to change commanders in the presence of the enemy. This clamor for his removal commenced immediately after it became known that the army had fallen back from Dalton, and it gathered volume with each remove toward Atlanta. Still I resisted the steadily increasing pressure which was brought to bear to induce me to revoke his assignment, and only issued the order relieving him from command when I became satisfied that his declared purpose to occupy the works at Atlanta with militia levies and withdraw his army into the open country for freer operations, would inevitably result in the loss of that important point, and where the retreat would cease could not be foretold. If the Army of Tennessee was found to be unable to hold positions of great strength like those at Dalton, Resaca, Etowah, Kenesaw, and on the Chattahoochee, I could not reasonably hope that it would be more successful in the plains below Atlanta, where it would find neither natural nor artificial advantages of position. As soon as the Secretary of War showed me the answer which he had just received in reply to his telegram to General Johnston, requesting positive information as to the General's plans and purposes, I gave my permission to issue the order relieving General Johnston and directing him to turn over to General Hood the command of the Army of Tennessee. I was so fully aware of the danger of changing commanders of an army while actively engaged with the enemy, that I only overcame the objection in view of an emergency, and in the hope that the impending danger of the loss of Atlanta might be averted.

The following extracts are made from a letter of the Hon. Benjamin H. Hill, of Georgia, written at Atlanta, October 12, 1878, and handed to me by the friend to whom it was addressed:

* * * * *

"On Wednesday or Thursday, I think the 28th or 29th of June, 1864, a messenger came to my house, sent, as he said, by General Johnston, Senator Wigfall, of Texas, and Governor Brown, of Georgia.

"The purpose of his mission, as he explained, was to persuade me to write a letter to President Davis urging him to order either Morgan or Forrest with five thousand men into Sherman's rear, etc. . . .

"The result of this interview was a determination on my part to go at once to see General Johnston, and place myself at his service. I reached his headquarters near Marietta, on the line of the Kenesaw, on Friday morning, which was the last day of June or the first day of July. We had a full and free interview, and I placed myself unreservedly at his disposal.

"He explained at length that he could not attack General Sherman's army in their intrenchments, nor could he prevent Sherman from ditching round his (Johnston's) flank and compelling his retreat.

"The only method of arresting Sherman's advance was to send a force into his rear, cut off his supplies, and thus compel Sherman either to give battle on his (Johnston's) terms or retreat. In either case, he thought, he could defeat Sherman, and probably destroy his army.

"I said to him, 'As you do not propose to attack General Sherman in his intrenchments, could you not spare a sufficient number of your present army, under Wheeler or some other, to accomplish this work?'

"He said he could not—that he needed all the force he had in front.

"He then said that General Morgan was at Arlington, Virginia, with five thousand cavalry, and, if the President would so order, this force could be sent into Sherman's rear at once.

"He also said that Stephen D. Lee had sixteen thousand men under him in Mississippi, including the troops under Forrest and Roddy, and that, if Morgan could not be sent, five thousand of those under Forrest could do the work. Either Morgan or Forrest, with five thousand men, could compel Sherman to fight at a disadvantage or retreat, and there was no reason why either should not be sent if the President should give the order. He explained that he (General Johnston) had had a consultation with Senator Wigfall and Governor Brown, the result of which was the messenger to me to secure my coöperation to influence President Davis to make the order. I repelled the idea that any influence with the President was needed, and stated that, if the facts were as General Johnston reported them, the reënforcement would be sent on his request.

[Illustration: J. E. Johnston]

"But the situation was so critical, involving, as I believed and explained at length to General Johnston, the fate of the Confederacy, that I said I would go in person to Richmond and lay all the facts before the President, and I did not doubt he would act promptly.

"I then said to General Johnston: 'How long can you hold Sherman north of the Chattahoochee River? This is important, because I must go to Richmond, and Morgan must go from Virginia or Forrest from Mississippi, and this will take some time, and all must be done before Sherman drives you to Atlanta.' General Johnston did not answer this question with directness, but gave me data which authorized me to conclude that he could hold Sherman north of the Chattahoochee River at least fifty-four days, and perhaps sixty days. I made this calculation with General Johnston's data in his presence, and told him the result, and he assented to it. When this result was stated, General Hood, who was present, said, 'Mr. Hill, when we leave our present line, we will, in my judgment, cross the Chattahoochee River very rapidly.' 'Why, what makes you think that?' said General Johnston, with some interest. 'Because,' answered General Hood, 'this line of the Kenesaw is the strongest line we can get in this country. If we surrender this to Sherman, he can reconnoiter from its summit the whole country between here and Atlanta, and there is no such line of defense in the distance.'

"'I differ with your conclusion,' said General Johnston. 'I admit this is a strong line of defense, but I have two more strong lines between this and the river, from which I can hold Sherman a long time.'

"I was delayed *en route* somewhat, and reached Richmond on Sunday morning week, which I think was the 9th day of July. I went to the hotel, and in a few moments was at the Executive mansion.

"This interview with Mr. Davis I can never forget.

"I laid before him carefully, and in detail, all the facts elicited in the conversation with General Johnston, and explained fully the purpose of my mission. When I had gone through, the President took up the facts, one by one, and fully explained the situation. I remember very distinctly many of the facts, for the manner as well as matter stated by Mr. Davis was impressive. 'Long ago,' said the President, 'I ordered Morgan to make this movement upon Sherman's rear, and suggested that his best plan was to go directly from Abingdon through East Tennessee. But Morgan insisted that, if he were permitted to go through Kentucky and around Nashville, he could greatly recruit his horses and his men by volunteers. I yielded, and allowed him to have his own way. He undertook it, but was defeated, and has retreated back, and is now at Abingdon with only eighteen hundred men, very much demoralized, and badly provided with horses.' He next read a dispatch from General Stephen D. Lee, to the effect that A. J, Smith had left Memphis with fifteen thousand men, intended either as a reënforcement for Sherman or for an attack on Mobile; that, to meet this force, he (Lee) had only seven thousand men, including the commands of Forrest and Roddy. He would like to have reënforcements, but anyhow, with or without reënforcements, 'he should meet Smith, and whip him, too.' 'Ah! there is a man for you,' said Mr. Davis. And he did meet Smith with his inferior force, and whipped him, too. He next read a dispatch from a commander at Mobile (who, I think, was General Maury), to the effect that Canby was marching from New Orleans with twenty thousand men, and A. J. Smith from Memphis with fifteen thousand, intending to make a combined attack on Mobile. To meet this force of thirty-five thousand men he had four thousand, and Lee, with Forrest and Roddy, seven thousand, making eleven thousand in all. He asked for reënforcements.

"After going fully through this matter, and showing how utterly General Johnston was at fault, as to the numbers of troops in the different commands, the President said, 'How long did you understand General Johnston to say he could hold Sherman north of the Chattahoochee River?' From fifty-four to sixty days I said, and repeated the facts on that subject as above stated. Thereupon the President read me a dispatch from General Johnston, announcing that he had crossed or was crossing the Chattahoochee River."

* * * * *

"The next day (Monday), Mr. Seddon, the Secretary of War, called to see me. He asked me to reduce my interview with General Johnston to writing, for the use of the Cabinet, and I did so, and gave it to him. Mr. Seddon said he was anxious for General Johnston's removal, and he was especially anxious because, he said, he was one of those who was responsible for his appointment. He had urged his appointment very earnestly, but it was a great mistake, and he desired to do all he could, even at this late day, to atone for it. The President, he said, was averse to the removal. He made the appointment against his own convictions, but thought it a very hazardous thing to remove him now, and he would not do it, if he could have any assurance that General Johnston would not surrender Atlanta without a battle.

"Other members of the Cabinet, I know, had views similar to those expressed by Mr. Seddon. The question, or rather the situation, was referred to General Lee, but he declined to give any positive advice, and expressed regret that so grave a movement as the removal of General Johnston, under the circumstances existing, should be found to be necessary." [109]

* * * * *

"During all the time, a telegraphic correspondence was kept up with General Johnston—the object being to ascertain if he would make a determined fight to save Atlanta. His answers were thought to be evasive. Finally, the question was put to General Johnston categorically to this effect: 'Will you surrender Atlanta without a fight?' To this the answer was regarded as not only evasive, but as indicating the contemplated contingency of surrendering Atlanta, on the ground that the Governor of the State had not furnished, as expected, sufficient State troops to man the city while the army was giving battle outside. 'This evasive answer to a positive inquiry,' said one of the Cabinet to me, 'brought the President over. He yielded very reluctantly.' I was informed of the result at once, and was also informed that Mr. Davis was the last man in the Cabinet to agree to the order of removal.". . .

General Hood assumed command on the 18th of July. In his report of the operations of the army while under his command, he states that the effective strength of his force on that day was forty-eight thousand seven hundred and fifty men of all arms.

Feeling that the only chance of holding Atlanta consisted in assuming the offensive by forcing the enemy to accept battle, General Hood determined, on the 20th of July, to attack the corps of Generals Thomas and Schofield, who were in the act of crossing Peachtree Creek, hoping to defeat Thomas before he could fortify himself, then to fall on Schofield, and finally to attack McPherson's corps, which had reached Decatur, on the Georgia Railroad, driving the enemy back to the creek and into the narrow space included between that stream and the Chattahoochee River. Owing to an unfortunate misapprehension of the order of battle and the consequent delay in making the attack, the movement failed. On the 21st, finding that McPherson's corps was threatening his communications, General Hood resolved to attack him at or near Decatur, in front and on flank, turn his left, and then, following up the movement from the right to the left with his whole army, force the enemy down Peachtree Creek.

This engagement was the hottest of the campaign, but it failed to accomplish any other favorable result than to check General McPherson's movement upon the communications of our army, while it cost heavily in the loss of many officers and men, foremost among whom was that *preux* chevalier and accomplished soldier, Major-General W. H. T. Walker, of Georgia.

Beyond expeditions by the enemy, for the most part by cavalry, to destroy the lines of railroad by which supplies and reënforcements could reach Atlanta, and successful efforts on our part to frustrate their movements, resulting in the defeat and capture of General Stoneman and his command near Macon, the utter destruction of the enemy's cavalry force engaged by General Wheeler at Newnan, and the defeat of Sherman's design to unite his cavalry at the Macon and Western Railroad, and effectually destroy that essential avenue for the conveyance of stores and ammunition for our army, no movement of special importance took place between July 22d and August 26th, at which latter date it was discovered that Sherman had abandoned his works upon our right, and, leaving a considerable force to hold his intrenched position at the railroad-bridge over the Chattahoochee, was marching his main body to the south and southwest of Atlanta, to use it, as he himself has expressed it, "against the communications of Atlanta, instead of against its intrenchments." On the 30th, it being known that he was moving on Jonesboro, the county town of Clayton County, about twenty miles south of Atlanta, General Hood sent two corps under General Hardee to confront him at that point, in the hope that he could drive him across Flint River, oblige him to abandon his works on the left, and then be able to attack him successfully in flank. The attack at Jonesboro was unsuccessful. General Hardee was obliged, on September 1st, to fall back to Lovejoy's, seven miles south of Jonesboro, on the Macon and Western Railroad. Thus, the main body of the Federal army was between Hardee and Atlanta, and the immediate evacuation of that city became a necessity. There was an additional and cogent reason for that movement. Owing to the obstinately cruel policy which the United States Government had pursued for some time, of refusing on any terms to exchange prisoners of war, upward of thirty thousand prisoners were at Andersonville in southwestern Georgia at this time. To guard against the release and arming of these prisoners, General Hood thought it necessary to place our army between them and the enemy, and abandon the project, which he thought feasible, of moving on Sherman's communications and destroying his depots of supplies at Marietta.

Upon abandoning Atlanta, Hood marched his army in a westerly direction, and formed a junction with the two corps which had been operating at Jonesboro and Lovejoy's under General Hardee.

General Sherman, desisting from any further aggressive movement in the field, returned to Atlanta, which had been formally surrendered by the Mayor on September 2d, with the promise, as reported, on the part of the Federal commander, that non-combatants and private property should be respected. Shortly after his arrival, the commanding General of the Federal forces, forgetful of this promise, and on the pretense that the exigencies of the service required that the place should be used exclusively for military purposes, issued an order directing all civilians living in Atlanta, male and female, to leave the city within five days from the date of the order (September 5th). Since Alva's atrocious cruelties to the noncombatant population of the Low Countries in the sixteenth century, the history of war records no instance of such barbarous cruelty as that which this order designed to perpetrate. It involved the immediate expulsion from their homes and only means of subsistence of thousands of unoffending women and children, whose husbands and fathers were either in the army, in Northern prisons, or had died in battle. In vain did the Mayor and corporate authorities of Atlanta appeal to Sherman to revoke or modify this inhuman order, representing in piteous language "the woe, the horror, and the suffering, not to be described by words," [110] which its execution would inflict on helpless women and infant children. His only reply was:

"I give full credit to your statements of the distress that will be occasioned by it, and yet shall not revoke my order, because my orders are not designed to meet the humanities of the case."

At the time appointed, the women and children were expelled from their houses, and, before they were passed within our lines, complaint was generally made that the Federal officers and men who were sent to guard them had robbed them of the few articles of value they had been permitted to take from their homes. The cowardly dishonesty of its executioners was in perfect harmony with the temper and spirit of the order.

During the month of September the Federal army in and around Atlanta made no movement beyond strengthening its defenses and collecting within it large quantities of military supplies. General Hood, meantime, held his troops in the vicinity of Jonesboro. His reports to the War Department represented the morale of his army as "greatly impaired by the recurrence of retreat," decreasing in numbers day by day, and the surrounding country devoid of natural strength or any advantageous position upon which he could retire. With a view to judge better the situation, and then determine after personal inspection the course which should seem best to pursue, I visited General Hood's headquarters at Palmetto. The crisis was grave. It was not to be expected that General Sherman would remain long inactive. The rapidity with which he was collecting recruits and supplies at Atlanta indicated that he contemplated a movement farther south, making Atlanta a secondary base. To rescue Georgia, save the Gulf States, and retain possession of the lines of communication upon which we depended for the supplies of our armies in the field, an effort to arrest the further progress of the enemy was necessary; and to this end the railroads in his rear must be effectually torn up, the great railroad-bridge over the Tennessee River at Bridgeport destroyed, and the communication between Atlanta, Chattanooga, and Nashville completely cut off. Could this be accomplished, all the fruits of Sherman's successful campaign in Georgia would be blighted, his capture of Atlanta would become a barren victory, and he would probably be compelled to make a retreat toward Tennessee, at every mile of which he might be harassed by our army. Or, should he, relying on Atlanta as a base, push forward through Georgia to the Atlantic coast, our army, having cut his communications north of Atlanta, could fall upon his rear, and, with the advantages of a better knowledge of the country, of the surrounding devoted population, of the auxiliary force to be expected under the circumstances, and our superiority in cavalry, it was not unreasonable to hope that retributive justice might overtake the ruthless invader.

My first object was to fill up the depleted ranks of the army, to bring the absentees and deserters back to the ranks, and induce the Governor and State officials to coöperate heartily and earnestly with the Confederate Government in all measures that might be found necessary to give the proposed movement a reasonable prospect of success.

The avowed objection of the Governor of Georgia to the acts of Congress providing for raising troops by conscription, and his persistent opposition to the authority of the Confederate Executive to appoint the generals and staff officers of the volunteer organizations received from the States to form the provisional army of the Confederacy, caused him frequently to obstruct the Government officials in the discharge of their duty, to withhold the assistance which he might be justly expected to render, and, in the contemplation of his own views of the duties and obligations of the Executive and legislative departments of the General Government, to lose sight of those important objects, the attainment of which an exalted patriotism might have told him depended on the coöperation of the State and Confederate governments. The inordinate exemption from military service as State officials of men between the ages of eighteen and forty-five (it was estimated that the number of exempts in November, 1864 amounted to fifteen thousand) was an abuse which I endeavored in vain to correct. Were the majority of the men thus exempted, and who remained at home "that the army might be fed," really engaged in that important service, the end might be said to justify the means; but, for any less exigent demand, patriotism and humane consideration for the brave men at the front required that the number of these exempts should be reduced to the minimum, if, indeed, the number of those unfit for military duty was not sufficient to perform this service. After a thorough inspection of the Army of Tennessee at Palmetto, after conference with several prominent Georgians, and notably with that pure patriot and distinguished statesman and soldier. General Howell Cobb, whose brain and heart and means and energies were all at the service of his country, I proceeded to Augusta during the first week of October, in order, with Generals Hardee and Cobb and other officers of prominence, to meet and confer with General Beauregard, whom I had just assigned to the command of the Military Division of the West, and to impart to him my views as to the exigencies of the occasion, and how I thought that they might be most advantageously met.

Before this time General Hood had already crossed the Chattahoochee with his entire force, moving against the enemy's line of communication. General Forrest, with a strong force of cavalry, had been ordered to Tennessee to strike the railroad from Nashville to Chattanooga. During my visit to Hood's army, I learned that the morale of it had been partially restored, many absentees had returned to duty, and the waning hope of the people was beginning to revive.

The plan of operations which I had discussed with General Hood while at his headquarters was fully explained to General Beauregard at Augusta, and by him cordially approved. It comprised the occupation of a strong position on the enemy's line of communication by the railroad between Atlanta and Chattanooga, the capture of his depots of supplies and the small garrisons left to guard them. If this, as was probable, should cause Sherman to move to attack as in position, in that case, if the tone of the troops justified it, a battle should be joined; otherwise, he should retreat toward Gadsden, where supplies would be collected, and, should Sherman follow him so far, then there, on the dividing line of the States of Georgia and Alabama, the largest practicable number of militia and home-guards of both States would be assembled as an auxiliary force, and there a final stand should be made for a decisive battle. If victorious, as under the circumstances it was hoped we should be, the enemy could not retreat through the wasted country behind him, and must surrender or disperse. If Sherman should not pursue our retiring army to Gadsden, but return to Atlanta to march toward the seacoast, he was to be pursued, and, by our superiority in cavalry, to be prevented from foraging on the country, which, according to our information as to his supplies on hand at Atlanta, and as to his inadequate means of transportation, would be indispensable for the support of his troops. Should Sherman, contrary to that information, have supplies and transportation sufficient to enable him to march across the country, and he should start toward the seacoast, the militia, the local troops, and others who could be employed, should obstruct the roads and fords in his front by felling trees, and, by burning bridges and other available means, delay his progress until his provisions should be consumed and absolute want should deplete if not disintegrate his army. It was supposed that Augusta, on account of our principal powder-manufactory and some important workshops being located there, would be the first objective point of Sherman, should he march toward the east. General Hood's calculation was that, taking a route north of Sherman, where he would have smaller streams to cross, he could reach Augusta as soon as Sherman.

General Cobb, the local commander in Georgia, in addition to obstructing roads, etc., was, in the last supposed contingency, to assemble at Augusta the invalid soldiers, the militia, and others to defend the place. General George W. Rains, an accomplished soldier and military engineer, was instructed to enlarge and strengthen the defenses of the place, and General G. R. Rains, the author of the system of defense by sub-terra shells, was, on the coming of the enemy, to apply his invention to the threatened approaches of the town. There was another contemplated contingency, viz., that Sherman, emboldened by his recent successes, would move against Hood with such overweening confidence as might offer to the latter the opportunity to strike in detail.

After the full conversation with General Beauregard above noticed, General Hardee was called in and asked to give his opinion on the plan, which I regarded as entitled to great consideration, not only because of his high capacity as a soldier, but also because of his long connection with the Army of Tennessee, and minute knowledge of the country in which it was proposed to operate. He had previously been made fully aware of the plans and purposes discussed between General Hood and myself, and stated to General Beauregard substantially that, while he could not say the plan would succeed, he was confident it was the best which we could adopt, and that, if it failed, none other with our means would succeed. General Beauregard left for General Hood's headquarters, as I supposed, to aid in the execution of the proposed plan, to the success of which the larger command with which he was invested, it was hoped, would contribute.

General Hood moved as was expected upon the enemy's line of communication, and his successes at Big Shanty and Acworth, in capturing those stations and thoroughly destroying the railroad between them, and his partial success at Allatoona, caused Sherman, leaving one corps to garrison

Atlanta, to move out with his main body to restore his communications. Hood further succeeded in destroying the railroad from Resaca to Tunnel Hill, capturing the enemy's posts at Tilton, Dalton, and Mill-Creek Gap; but, not deeming his army in condition to risk a general engagement, withdrew his forces in a southwesterly direction toward Gadsden, which place he reached October 20th, finding there supplies adequate for the wants of his troops. Sherman had turned back toward Atlanta, and Hood, instead of hanging on his rear, not allowing him to repair the damage to the railroad, and otherwise harassing him in his march as much as possible, after conference with General Beauregard, decided to continue his march into Tennessee.[111] His reasons for this change of plan are elaborately and forcibly presented in his book, "Advance and Retreat," published since the war, and in which he emphatically contradicts the attempt which has been made to represent that campaign into Tennessee as one projected by me. The correspondence of General Sherman, published in the same work, shows that Hood was not far wrong in the supposition that Sherman would follow the movement made on his line of communication; the only error being that he could thus draw him beyond the limits of Georgia. After my return to Richmond, a telegram from General Beauregard informed me of the change of programme. My objection to that movement remained, and, though it was too late to regain the space and time which had been lost, I replied promptly on November 30, 1864, as follows:

"General BEAUREGARD, care of Colonel W. M. Browne, *Augusta, Georgia.*

"Yours of 24th received. It is probable that the enemy, if short of supplies, may move directly for the coast. When that is made manifest, you will be able to concentrate your forces upon the one object, and I hope, if you can not defeat his attempt, that you may reduce his army to such condition as to be inefficient for further operations.

"Until Hood reaches the country proper of the enemy, he can scarcely change the plans for Sherman's or Grant's campaigns. They would, I think, regard the occupation of Tennessee and Kentucky as of minor importance.

"JEFFERSON DAVIS."

To the arguments offered to show that our army could not, after it had reached the Tennessee River, have effectually pursued Sherman in his march through southern Georgia, it is only needful to reply that the physical difficulties set forth would not have existed, had our army commenced the pursuit from Gadsden.

To make the movement into Tennessee a success, even so far as to recover that country, it was necessary that it should be executed so promptly as to anticipate the concentration of the enemy's forces, but unforeseen and unavoidable delays occurred, which gave full time for preparation. After having overcome many vexatious detentions, Hood on the 20th of November completed his crossing of the Tennessee River at Gunter's Landing, and moved forward into Tennessee on the route to Nashville, whither Sherman had sent

General Thomas for the protection of his depots and communications against an apprehended attack by cavalry under General Forrest.

Most unwilling to criticise the conduct of that very gallant and faithful soldier who, battle-scarred and mutilated, survived the war, and whose recent death our country has so much deplored, I must say after the event, as I did before it, that I consider this movement into Tennessee ill-advised.

Thomas having been sufficiently reënforced in Tennessee to enable him to hold Hood in check, and Sherman relieved from the necessity of defending himself against an active army, and of protecting a long line of railroad communication with a fortified base in his rear, resolved upon his march to the sea, abandoning Atlanta, after having first utterly destroyed that city by fire. Not a single house was spared, not even a church. Similar acts of vandalism marked the progress of the Federal army at Rome, Kingston, Acworth, Marietta, and every town or village along its route, thus carrying out General Sherman's order "to enforce a devastation more or less relentless" along the line of his march, where he only encountered helpless women and children. The arson of the dwelling-houses of non-combatants and the robbery of their property, extending even to the trinkets worn by women, made the devastation as relentless as savage instincts could suggest.

On November 16th Sherman left his intrenchments around Atlanta, and, dividing his army into two bodies, each from twenty-five to thirty thousand strong, the one followed the Georgia Railroad in the direction of Augusta, and the other took the line of the Macon and Western Railroad to Jonesboro. Avoiding Macon and Augusta, they passed through central Georgia, taking Milledgeville on the way, marching in compact column, and advancing with extreme caution, although only opposed by detachments of Wheeler's cavalry and a few hastily formed regiments of raw militia. Partial efforts were made to obstruct and destroy the roads in the front and on the flanks of the invading army, and patriotic appeals by prominent citizens were made to the people, to remove all provisions from its path, but no formidable opposition was made, except at the railroad-bridge over the Oconee, where Wheeler, with a portion of his command and a few militia, held the enemy in check for two or three days. With his small force, General Wheeler daringly and persistently harassed, and, when practicable, delayed the enemy's advance, attacking and defeating exposed detachments, deterring his foragers from venturing far from the main body, defending all cities and towns along the railroad lines, and affording protection to depots of supplies, arsenals, and other important Government works. The report of his operations from November 14th to December 20th displays a dash, activity, vigilance, and consummate skill, which justly entitle him to a prominent place on the roll of great cavalry leaders. By his indomitable energy, operating on all sides of Sherman's columns, he was enabled to keep the Government and commanders of our troops advised of the enemy's movements, and, by preventing foraging parties from leaving the main body, he saved from spoliation all but a narrow tract of country, and from the torch millions worth of property which would otherwise have been certainly consumed.

It soon became manifest that Savannah was General Sherman's objective point. That city was occupied by General W. J. Hardee with about eighteen thousand men, a considerable portion of which was composed of militia, local troops, reserves, and hastily organized regiments and battalions made up of convalescents from the hospitals and artisans from the Government shops. On the 10th of December the enemy's columns reached the immediate vicinity of Savannah, and on the 12th they occupied a semicircular line extending from the Savannah River to the Savannah and Gulf Railroad. The defenses of the city were strong, the earthworks and other fortifications were flanked by inundated rice-swamps extending across the peninsula formed by the Savannah and Ogeechee Rivers, and the causeways leading through them were well fortified by works mounting heavy guns. With a sufficient force to occupy his long lines of defense, General Hardee could have sustained a protracted siege. The city was amply supplied, and its lines of communication were still open. Although Sherman had reached Savannah, he had not yet opened communication with the Federal fleet. Fort McAllister, situated on the right bank of the Ogeechee, about six miles from Ossabaw Sound, was a serious obstacle in his way, as it was a work of considerable strength, mounting twenty-one heavy guns, a deep and wide ditch extending along its front, with every avenue of approach swept by the guns mounted upon its bastions. The fort was held by a garrison of two hundred and fifty men under the command of experienced officers. The work was attacked on the evening of the 13th, and carried by assault after a short and feeble resistance. In consequence of the loss of this fort, Sherman speedily opened communication with the fleet, and became perfectly secure against any future want of supplies. This also enabled him to obtain heavy ordnance for use against the city. He proceeded immediately to take measures to invest Savannah, and in a few days had succeeded in doing so on every side of the city except that fronting the river. While Hardee's troops had not yielded a single position or lost a foot of ground, with the exception of Fort McAllister, when, on December 20th, he discovered that Sherman had put heavy siege-guns in position near enough to bombard the city, and that the enemy was threatening Union Causeway, which extends across the large swamps that lie between Savannah and Charleston, and offered the only practicable line of retreat, he determined to evacuate the place rather than expose the city and its inhabitants to bombardment. He also thought holding it had ceased to be of any special importance, and that his troops could do more valuable service in the field. Accordingly, on the night of December 20th, having destroyed the navy-yard, the ironclads, and other Government property, and razed the fortifications below the city, he withdrew his army and reached Hardeeville on the evening of the 22d, without hindrance or molestation on the part of the enemy.

[Illustration: General John B. Hood]

Having heretofore stated my objections to the plan of sending Hood's army into Tennessee after the fall of Atlanta, I will now follow it in that campaign, relying for the facts on the official report of General Hood of the 15th of February, 1865. The fidelity and gallantry of that officer and the well-known magnanimity of his character are a sufficient guarantee of the impartiality of his narration.

He reported the arrival of his army at Gadsden on the 20th of October, 1864, where he was joined by General P. G. T. Beauregard, commanding the military department. He writes that, after withdrawing from Atlanta, his hope had been that Sherman in following might offer an opportunity to strike him in detail, but in this he was disappointed. Hood reported that the morale of his army, though improved, was not such as, in the opinion of his corps commanders, would justify a general engagement while the enemy remained united. At Gadsden he found a thorough supply of shoes and other stores, but, after a full and free conference with General Beauregard at Tuscumbia, he decided to cross the Tennessee and move against Thomas, who with his corps had been detached by Sherman and sent into Middle Tennessee. General Beauregard had sent orders to General Forrest to move with his cavalry into Tennessee; the main body of Hood's cavalry had been sent to follow Sherman. As the orders to Forrest were accidentally delayed, and Hood had not cavalry enough to protect his trains, he was compelled to wait for the coming of Forrest, and, to hasten the meeting, moved down the river as far as Florence, where he arrived on the 31st of October. This unfortunate delay gave the enemy time to repair the railroad to Chattanooga, and accumulate supplies at Atlanta for a march thence toward the Atlantic coast. Forrest's cavalry joined on the 21st of November, and the movement began. The enemy's forces at that time were concentrated at Pulaski and at Lawrenceburg. Hood endeavored to place his army between these forces and Nashville, but our cavalry, having driven off the enemy at Lawrenceburg, gave notice of our advance, and on the 23d he evacuated Pulaski and moved rapidly by the turnpike and railroad to Columbia. On the evening of the 27th of November our army took position in front of the works at that place. During the night the town was evacuated, and a strong position was taken on the opposite side of the river, about a mile and a half distant. On the evening of the 28th General Forrest crossed Duck River a few miles above Columbia, and in the morning of the 29th Stewart's and Cheatham's corps followed the cavalry, leaving Lieutenant-General Stephen D. Lee's corps confronting the enemy at Columbia. The cavalry and the two infantry corps moved in light marching order, the object being, by advancing rapidly on roads parallel to the Columbia and Franklin turnpike at or near Spring Hill, to cut off that portion of the foe at Columbia. The movement having been discovered after Hood's forces had got well on the flank of the enemy, he began to retreat along the turnpike toward Spring Hill. About noon of that day the cavalry attacked his trains, but found them too strongly guarded to be captured. The retreat was rapidly conducted along the turnpike, with flankers thrown out to protect the main column. Near Spring Hill Major-General Cheatham, being in the advance, commenced to come in contact with the retreating column about two miles from Spring Hill. He was ordered to attack vigorously, and get possession of the turnpike. This was so feebly executed that he failed to attain the object, and the enemy passed on toward Spring Hill. Though the golden opportunity had passed with daylight, Hood did not abandon the hope of effecting by a night movement the end he sought. Accordingly, Lieutenant-General Stewart was furnished with a guide, and ordered to move his corps beyond Cheatham's, and place it across the road beyond Spring Hill. In the dark and confusion, he did not succeed in getting the position desired. About midnight, ascertaining that the enemy was moving in disorder, with artillery, wagons, and troops intermixed, Hood sent instructions to General Cheatham to advance a heavy line of skirmishers, still further to impede the retreat. This was not accomplished. The enemy continued to move along the road in hurry and confusion nearly all the night. Thus was lost a great opportunity for striking him for which we had labored so long—the greatest this campaign had offered, and one of the greatest during the war. Lieutenant-General S. D. Lee, left in front of the enemy at Columbia, was instructed to press him the moment he abandoned his position at that point. He did not abandon his works until dark, showing that his trains obstructed the road for fifteen miles during the day and a great part of the night. At daylight Hood pursued the enemy so rapidly as to compel him to burn a number of his wagons. On the hills about four miles south of Franklin, he made demonstration as if to give battle, but, when our forces deployed for the attack, he retired to Franklin.

From dispatches captured at Spring Hill, Hood learned that Schofield was instructed by Thomas to hold that position until Franklin could be made secure, and thus knew that it was important to attack Schofield promptly, and concluded that, if he should escape at Franklin, he would gain the fortifications about Nashville. Hood reports that "the nature of the position was such as to render it inexpedient to attempt any other flank movement, and I therefore determined to attack him in front and without delay."

As this was one of the bloodiest battles of the war, and its results materially affected the future, before entering on an account of it, I pause for some general reflections. It is not quite easy to determine what my gallant friend Hood meant by the expression, "the nature of the position." It may have referred to the probability that the enemy, if he attempted a flank movement, would retreat rapidly, as he had done from Columbia, and it is now known that a part of his troops and a large part of his train had already been sent across the Harpeth River. Thomas's dispatch indicated a purpose to hold Franklin; and its relation to Murfreesboro, where a garrison was maintained, would seem to render this a probable part of a plan to maintain communication with Chattanooga. Franklin had to us, as a mere *military* question, no other value than that the road to Nashville led through it. Whether it would have been possible to turn the position so promptly as to strike the enemy's line of retreat is a question which no doubt General Hood considered and decided in the negative, otherwise he would surely have preferred to attack the enemy on the march rather than in his intrenchments, especially as these were so near to the town that Hood was restrained from using his artillery on account of the women and children resident in it. The position itself was favorable for defense; the Harpeth River by a short bend flows on two sides of the town, and the works in front had the center so boldly salient, their flanks resting on the river, as to inclose the town in something like a square, two sides being river and two sides intrenchment. The exterior line of defense had been recently and hastily constructed; the interior line was much stronger. Behind the town there were two bridges, one on the main road leading through it, and the other a pontoon-bridge a short distance above it. Hood had served with distinction under Lee and Jackson, and his tactics were of that school. If he had, by an impetuous attack, crushed Schofield's army, without too great a loss to his own, and Forrest could have executed his orders to capture the trains when Schofield's army was crushed, we should never have heard complaint because Hood attacked at Franklin, and these were the hopes with which he made his assault.

On the 30th of November he formed his line of battle. At 4 P.M. he gave the order to advance; his troops moved gallantly forward, carried the first line, and advanced against the interior works; here the engagement was close and fierce; the combatants occupied the opposite sides of the intrenchments, our men carrying them in some places, many being killed entirely inside the enemy's works. Some of the Tennesseeans, after years of absence, saw again their homes, and strove with desperation to expel the invader from them; the contest continued till near midnight, when the enemy abandoned his works and crossed the river, leaving his dead and wounded behind him, We had won a victory, but it was purchased at fearful cost. General Hood, in his letter of December 11, 1864, written near Nashville, reported his entire loss at about four thousand five hundred, and among them was Major-General Cleburne, Brigadier-Generals Gist, John Adams, Strahl, and Granberry, all well known to fame, and whose loss we could ill afford to bear. Around Cleburne thickly lay the gallant men who, in his desperate assault, followed him with the implicit confidence that in another army was given to Stonewall Jackson; and in the one case, as in the other, a vacancy was created which could never be filled. Hood reported that the number of dead left on the field by the enemy indicated that his loss was equal to or near our own; that those of our men who were captured were inside the enemy's works.

The next morning at daylight, the wounded being cared for and the dead buried, Hood moved forward toward Nashville, about eighteen miles distant, and Forrest with his cavalry closely pursued the enemy. On the 2d of December our army took position in front of Nashville about two miles from the city, Lieutenant-General Lee's corps in the center resting on the Franklin turnpike, Cheatham's on the right, Stewart's on the left, and the cavalry on each flank. Hood then commenced to construct detached works to cover the flanks, should offensive movements be attempted against our flank and rear. The enemy still held Murfreesboro with a garrison of about six thousand, strongly fortified; he also had small forces at Chattanooga and Knoxville. It was supposed that he would soon have to take the offensive to relieve his garrisons at those points, or cause them to be evacuated, in which latter case Hood hoped to capture the forces at Murfreesboro, and thus open communication with Georgia and Virginia; and he thought, if attacked in position, that he could defeat Thomas, gain possession of Nashville with its abundant supplies, and thus get the control of Tennessee. The people of the country, in the mean time, were able and willing to furnish our army with supplies, and we had captured rolling-stock to put the railroad to Pulaski in successful operation.

Hood sent Major-General Forrest with the greater part of his cavalry and a division of infantry against Murfreesboro. The infantry did not fulfill expectation, and it was withdrawn. Mercer's and Palmer's brigades of infantry were sent to replace the division. Nothing of importance occurred until the morning of the 15th, and the enemy, having been reënforced by about fifteen thousand men from the trans-Mississippi, attacked simultaneously both flanks of our line. On our right he was repulsed with heavy loss; but on our left, toward evening, he earned some of the partially completed redoubts. During the night of the 15th our line was shortened and strengthened, the left being thrown back and dispositions made to meet any renewed attack. The corps of Major-General Cheatham was transferred from our right to the left. Early on the 16th of December the enemy made a general attack on our lines, accompanied by a heavy fire of artillery. All his assaults were repulsed with heavy loss until 3.30 P.M., when a portion of our line to the left of the center suddenly gave way. Up to this time no battle ever progressed more favorably— the troops in excellent spirits, waving their colors and bidding defiance to the enemy; but the position he then gained being such as to enfilade us, caused our entire line to give way in a few moments and our troops to retreat in the direction of Franklin, most of them in great confusion. Confidence in the ability to hold the line had caused the artillery-horses to be sent to the rear for safety, and the abandonment of the position was so unexpected and sudden that it was not possible to bring forward the horses to remove the guns which had been placed in position, and fifty-four of them were consequently lost. Our loss in killed and wounded was small. At Brentwood, about four miles from the field of battle, the troops were partially rallied, and Lieutenant-General S. D, Lee took command of the rear-guard and encamped for the night. On leaving the field, Hood sent one of his staff-officers to inform General Forrest of our defeat, and to direct him to rejoin the army with as little delay as possible, but heavy rains had so swollen the creeks that he was unable to effect the junction with his main force until it reached Columbia. During the 17th the enemy's cavalry pressed boldly on the retreating column, the open character of the country being favorable to cavalry operations. Lieutenant-General Lee, commanding the covering force, was severely wounded, but not until after he and the corps he commanded had rendered such service as to receive the special commendation of the General commanding the army.

Hood reports that when he left the field before Nashville he had hoped to be able to remain in Tennessee, on the line of Duck River; but, after arriving at Colombia, he became convinced that the condition of the army made it necessary to recross the Tennessee without delay. On the 21st he resumed his march for Pulaski, leaving Major-General Walthall, with five infantry brigades, and General Forrest, with the main body of his cavalry, at Columbia, to cover the movements of the army. The retreat continued, and on the 25th, 26th, and 27th, the army, including the rear-guard, crossed the Tennessee River at Bainbridge. The enemy had followed the rear-guard with all his cavalry and three corps of infantry to Pulaski, and thence the cavalry continued the pursuit to the Tennessee River. After crossing the river, the army moved by easy marches to Tupelo, Mississippi. General Hood reported his losses in the Tennessee campaign to have been about ten thousand men, including prisoners, and that when he arrived at Tupelo he had 18,500 infantry and artillery, and 2,306 cavalry. I again quote from General Hood's report:

"Here, finding so much dissatisfaction throughout the country, as, in my judgment, greatly to impair, if not destroy, my usefulness, and counteract my exertions, and with no desire but to serve my country, I asked to be relieved, with the hope that another might be assigned to the command who might do more than I could hope to accomplish. Accordingly, I was so relieved on the 23d of January, by authority of the President."

Though, as General Hood states in his book, page 273, I was "averse to his going into Tennessee," he might well assume that I "was not, as General Beauregard and himself, acquainted with the true condition of the army" when they decided on the Tennessee campaign. Of the manner in which he conducted it, Isham G. Harris, the Governor of Tennessee, a man of whose judgment, integrity, and manhood I had the highest opinion, wrote to me, on the 25th of December, 1864:

". . . I have been with General Hood from the beginning of this campaign, and beg to say, disastrous as it has ended, I am not able to see anything that General Hood has done that he should not, or neglected any thing that he should, have done, . . . and regret to say that, if all had performed their parts as well as he, the results would have been very different."

To this I will only add that General Hood was relieved at his reiterated request, made from such creditable motives as are expressed in the extract above, taken from his official report, and that it was in no wise due to a want of confidence in him on my part.

[Footnote 105: It was during this time, i. e.. in March and April, 1864, that Forrest made his extraordinary expedition from north Mississippi across Tennessee to Paducah, Kentucky, and continued his operations against depots of supplies, lines of communication, and troops moving to reënforce Sherman—having, on June 11th, a severe action in Tishemingo with a force estimated at eight or nine thousand, supposed to be on their way to join Sherman. The energy, strategy, and high purposes of Forrest, during all this period, certainly entitle him to higher military rank than that of a partisan, and enroll him in the list of great cavalry commanders. Some of his other expeditions are elsewhere mentioned in these pages.]

[Footnote 106: "Narrative," p. 302.]

[Footnote 107: "Advance and Retreat," by J. B. Hood, pp. 98-116.]

[Footnote 108: Johnston's "Narrative," p. 346.]

[Footnote 109: Mr. Seddon, ex-Secretary of War, in a letter written to me on the 10th of February, 1879, states, in regard to his interview with General Lee, that it was held after the determination had been made "to remove General Johnston from his command at Atlanta," and says of the purpose of the interview with General Lee: "It was designed merely to secure General Lee's estimate of qualifications in the selection of a successor for the command."]

[Footnote 110: Mayor Calhoun's Petition to General Sherman, September 11, 1864.]

[Footnote 111: "Advance and Retreat," by General J. B. Hood; letter of General Beauregard to President Davis, p. 278, *et seq.*]

CHAPTER XLIX.

Exchange of Prisoners.—Signification of the Word "loyal."—Who is the Sovereign?—Words of President Lincoln.—The Issue for which we fought.—Position of the United States Government.—Letters of Marque granted by us.—Officers and Crew First Prisoners of the Enemy.—Convicted as "Pirates."—My Letter to President Lincoln.— How received.—Act of Congress relating to Prisoners.—Exchanges, how made.-Answer of General Grant.—Request of United States Congress.—Result.—Commissioners sent.—Agreement.—Disputed Points.—Exchange arranged.—Order to pillage issued.—General Pope's Order.—Proceedings.—Letter of General Lee relative to Barbarities.—Answer of General Halleck.—Case of Mumford.—Effect of Threatened Retaliation.—Mission of Vice-President Stephens.—A Failure.—Excess of Prisoners.—Paroled Men.—Proposition made by us.—No Answer.—Another Arrangement.—Stopped by General Grant.—

His words, "Put the Matter offensively."—Exchange of Slaves.—
Proposition of Lee to Grant.—Reply of Grant.—Further Reply.—His
Dispatch to General Butler.—Another Proposition made by us.—No
Answer.—Proposition relative to Sick and Wounded.—Some
exchanged.—The Worst Cases asked for to be photographed.—
Proposition as to Medicines.—No Answer.—A Final Effort.—
Deputation of Prisoners sent to Washington.—A Failure.—
Correspondence between Ould and Butler.—Order of Grant.—Report of
Butler.—Responsibility of Grant for Andersonville.—Barbarities of
the United States Government.—Treatment of our Men in Northern
Prisons.—Deaths on Each Side.

Perhaps there was no question in the treatment of which the true character
and intentions of the Government of the United States was so clearly exposed as
in the exchange of prisoners. That we should dare to resort to arms for the
preservation of our rights, and "to secure the blessings of liberty to ourselves
and our posterity," was regarded by our enemies as most improbable. Their
aspirations for dominion and sovereignty, through the Government of the
Union, had become so deep-seated and apparently real as to cause that
Government, at its first step, to assume the haughtiness and imperiousness of
an absolute sovereign. "I appeal to all loyal citizens to favor, facilitate, and aid
this effort," said President Lincoln, in the first proclamation, calling for seventy-
five thousand men. The term "loyal" has no signification except as applied to the
sovereign of an empire or kingdom. In a republic the people are the sovereign,
and the term "loyal" or its opposite can have no signification except in relation
to the true sovereign. To say, therefore, that the agent of the sovereign people,
the representative of the system they have organized to conduct their common
affairs, composed the real sovereign, and that loyalty or disloyalty is of
signification in relation to this sovereign alone, is not only a perversion of
language, but an error, that leads straight to the subversion of all popular
government and the establishment of the monarchical or consolidated form. The
Government of the United States is now the sovereign here, says President
Lincoln in this proclamation, and loyalty consists in the maintenance of that
sovereignty against all its foes. The sovereignty of the people and of the several
and distinct States, in his mind, was only a weakness and enthusiasm of the
fathers. The States and the people thereof had become consolidated into a
national Union. "I appeal," says President Lincoln, "to all loyal citizens to favor,
facilitate, and aid this effort to maintain the honor, the integrity, and the
existence of our national Union."

The Confederate States refused thus "to favor, facilitate, and aid this effort to
maintain the honor, the integrity, and the existence of a national Union." They
not only refused to aid, but they took up arms to defeat the consummation of
such a monstrous usurpation of popular rights and popular sovereignty. It was
evident that, if no efforts for a rescue were made, the time would soon come
when the rights of all the States might be denied, and the hope of mankind in
constitutional freedom be for ever lost. This was the usurpation. This lay at the
foundation of the war. Every subsequent act of the Government was another
step in the same direction, all tending palpably to supremacy for the
Government of the United States, the subjugation of the States, and the
submission of the people.

This was the adversary with whom we had to struggle, and this was the issue for which we fought. That we dared to draw our swords to vindicate the rights and the sovereignty of the people, that we dared to resist and deny all sovereignty as inherently existing in the Government of the United States, was adjudged an infamous crime, and we were denounced as "rebels." It was asserted that those of us "who were captured should be hung as rebels taken in the act." Crushing the corner-stone of the Union, the independence of the States, the Federal Government assumed toward us a position of haughty arrogance, refused to recognize us otherwise than as insurrectionists and "rebels," who resisted and denied its usurped sovereignty, and who were entitled to no amelioration from the punishment of death, except such as might proceed only from the promptings of mercy.

On April 17, 1861, I issued a proclamation in which I offered to grant letters of marque and reprisal to seamen. On April 19th President Lincoln issued a counter-proclamation, declaring that, "if any person, under the pretended authority of said States, or under any other pretense, shall molest a vessel of the United States, or the persons or cargo on board of her, such person shall be held amenable to the laws of the United States for the prevention and punishment of piracy," which was death.

Some small vessels obtained these letters of marque and were captured. Their officers and crew constituted the first prisoners that fell into the hands of the enemy. They were immediately imprisoned, and held for trial as pirates. The trial came on later in the year. A report of it states that "the views of all the judges seemed to center upon the one point, that these men were taken in arms against the Government of the United States, and that, inasmuch as the laws of that Government did not recognize the authority under which the men acted, there was no course but to condemn them."

As soon as the treatment of these prisoners was known in Richmond, before their trial and as early as July 6, 1861, I sent by a special messenger a communication to President Lincoln, in substance as follows:

"Having learned that the schooner Savannah, a private armed vessel in the service and sailing under a commission issued by the authority of the Confederate States of America, had been captured by one of the vessels forming the blockading squadron off Charleston Harbor, I directed a proposition to be made to the commanding officer of the squadron for an exchange of officers and crew of the Savannah for prisoners of war held by this Government, 'according to number and rank.' To this proposition, made on the 19th ultimo, Captain Mercer, the officer in command of the blockading squadron, made answer, on the same day, that 'the prisoners' (referred to) 'are not on board any of the vessels under my command.'

"It now appears, by statements made without contradiction in newspapers published in New York, that the prisoners above mentioned were conveyed to that city, and have been treated not as prisoners of war, but as criminals; that they have been put in irons, confined in jail, brought before courts of justice on charges of piracy and treason; and it is even rumored that they have been convicted of the offenses charged, for no other reason than that they bore arms in defense of the rights of this Government and under the authority of its commission.

"I could not, without grave discourtesy, have made the newspaper statements above referred to the subject of this communication, if the threat of treating as pirates the citizens of this Confederacy, armed for its service on the high-seas, had not been contained in your proclamation of the 19th of April last. That proclamation, however, seems to afford a sufficient justification for considering these published statements as not devoid of probability.

"It is the desire of this Government so to conduct the war now existing as to mitigate its horrors as far as may be possible, and, with this intent, its treatment of the prisoners captured by its forces has been marked by the greatest humanity and leniency consistent with public obligation. Some have been permitted to return home on parole, others to remain at large, under similar conditions, within this Confederacy, and all have been furnished with rations for their subsistence, such as are allowed to our own troops. It is only since the news has been received of the treatment of the prisoners taken on the Savannah, that I have been compelled to withdraw these indulgences, and to hold the prisoners taken by us in strict confinement.

"A just regard to humanity and to the honor of this Government now requires me to state explicitly that, painful as will be the necessity, this Government will deal out to the prisoners held by it the same treatment and the same fate as shall be experienced by those captured on the Savannah; and, if driven to the terrible necessity of retaliation by your execution of any of the officers or crew of the Savannah, that retaliation will be extended so far as shall be requisite to secure the abandonment of a practice unknown to the warfare of civilized man, and so barbarous as to disgrace the nation which shall be guilty of inaugurating it.

"With this view, and because it may not have reached you, I now renew the proposition made to the commander of the blockading squadron, to exchange for the prisoners taken on the Savannah an equal number of those now held by us according to rank."

This communication was taken by Colonel Thomas Taylor, who was permitted to visit Washington, but was refused an audience with President Lincoln. He was obliged to content himself with a verbal reply from General Winfield Scott that the communication had been delivered to President Lincoln, and that he would reply in writing as soon as possible. No answer ever came. We were compelled to select by lot from among the prisoners in our hands a number to whom we proposed to mete out the same fate which might await the crew of the Savannah. These measures of retaliation arrested the cruel and illegal purposes of the enemy.

Meantime, as early as May 21, 1861, the Confederate Congress passed an act which provided that—

"All prisoners of war taken, whether on land or sea, during the pending hostilities with the United States, shall be transferred by the captors from time to time, and as often as convenient, to the Department of War; and it shall be the duty of the Secretary of War, with the approval of the President, to issue such instructions to the quartermaster-general and his subordinates as shall provide for the safe custody and sustenance of prisoners of war, and the rations furnished prisoners of war shall be the same in quantity and quality as those furnished to enlisted men in the army of the Confederacy."

This law of Congress was embodied in the orders issued from the War Department and from the headquarters in the field, and no order was ever issued in conflict with its humane provisions.

Nevertheless, the Government of the United States, forgetful of the conduct of Great Britain toward her revolted colonies, apparently refused all consideration of the question of exchange of prisoners, as if impressed with the idea that it would derogate from the dignity of its position to accept any interchange of courtesy. An exchange was therefore occasionally made by the various commanders of troops under flags of truce, while the Federal Government made the paltry pretense of not knowing it. We released numbers at different points on parole, and the matter was compromised in various ways. Fifty-seven wounded soldiers were unconditionally released at Richmond and sent home. In response, twenty of our soldiers, mostly North Carolinians, were released from Bedloe's Island, New York, and sent to Fortress Monroe, to be discharged on condition of taking the oath, so called, of loyalty to the United States Government. Thirty-seven confined in the military prison at Washington were released on taking the oath. On September 3d an exchange was made between General Pillow and Colonel Wallace, of the United States Army. Whereupon General Polk proposed an exchange to General Grant, who replied, on October 14th:

"I can, of my own accordance, make none. I recognize no 'Southern Confederacy' myself, but will communicate with higher authorities for their views."

An exchange was made on October 23d between General McClernand and General Polk. Subsequently, on November 8th, General Grant offered to surrender to General Polk certain wounded men and invalids unconditionally. To this proposition General Polk replied:

"My own feelings would prompt me to waive again the unimportant affectation of declining to recognize these States as belligerents in the interest of humanity; but my Government requires all prisoners to be placed at the disposal of the Secretary Of War."

On November 1st General Fremont made an agreement with General Price, in Missouri, by which certain persons named were authorized to negotiate for the exchange of any persons who might be taken prisoners of war, upon a plan previously arranged. General Hunter, who succeeded General Fremont, on November 7th, repudiated this agreement. A proposition made in the Confederate Congress to return the prisoners captured by us at first Manassas, without any formality whatever, would doubtless have prevailed but for the difficulty in reference to the crew of the Savannah.

But this determination of the United States Government, not to meet us on the equal footing consistent with the modern usages of war and exchange prisoners, thus far prevented any general arrangement for that object. In consequence, however, of the clamors of the Northern people for the restoration of their friends, both Houses of Congress united in a request to President Lincoln to take immediate steps for a general exchange. Instead of complying with this request, two respectable commissioners were, however, appointed to visit the prisoners we held, relieve their necessities, and provide for their comfort at the expense of the United States. It is impossible to conceive any reason for such conduct, unless it was to exasperate and "fire up the Northern heart," as it was expressed, and thus cause the people to make greater efforts for our devastation. This action on the part of the Government was at a later day known by the expression "waving the bloody shirt."

The commissioners arrived at Norfolk, Virginia, but were not allowed to proceed any farther. A readiness on our part to negotiate for a general exchange was manifested, and agreed to by them. This was subsequently approved at Washington. Shortly afterward, on February 14, 1862, an arrangement was made between General Howell Cobb on our part and General Wool, the commander at Fortress Monroe, by the terms of which the prisoners of war in the hands of each Government were to be exchanged man for man, the officers being assimilated as to rank; our privateersmen were to be exchanged on the footing of prisoners of war; any surplus remaining on either side was to be released; and during the continuance of hostilities prisoners taken on either side should be paroled. The exchange proceeded, and about three hundred in excess had been delivered, when it was discovered that not one of our privateersmen had been released, and that our men taken prisoners at Fort Donelson, instead of being paroled, had been sent into the interior. Some of the hostages we held for our privateersmen had gone forward, but the remainder were retained. Being informed of this state of affairs, I recommended to Congress that all of our men who had been paroled by the United States Government should be released from the obligations of their parole so as to bear arms in our defense, in consequence of this breach of good faith on the part of that Government. It was subsequently said, on behalf of the United States Government, that the detention of our privateersmen had been intended to be only temporary, to make it certain that the hostages were coming forward.

It is further stated that the only unadjusted point between Generals Cobb and Wool was, that the latter was unwilling that each party should agree to pay the expenses of transporting their prisoners to the frontier, and this he promised to refer to his Government. At a second interview, on March 1, 1862, General Wool informed General Cobb that his Government would not consent to pay these expenses, and thereupon General Cobb promptly receded from his demand, and agreed to the terms proposed by the other side. But General Wool, who had said at the beginning of the negotiation, "I am clothed with full power for the purpose of arranging for the exchange of prisoners," was now under the necessity of stating that "his Government had changed his instructions." And thus the negotiations were abruptly broken off, and the matter left where it was before.[112] After these negotiations had begun, the capture of Forts Henry and Donelson had given to the United States a considerable preponderance in the number of prisoners held by them, and they at once returned to their original purpose of an equal treatment.

A suspension of exchange for some months ensued. Finally, a storm of indignation beginning to arise among the Northern people at the conduct of their Government, it was forced to yield its absurd pretensions, and, on July 22, 1862, a cartel for the exchange of prisoners was executed, based on the cartel of 1812 between the United States and Great Britain. In accordance with these terms an exchange commenced, and by the middle of August most of the officers of rank on either side, who had been for any long period in captivity, were released.

On the same day on which the cartel was signed, an order was issued by the Secretary of War, in Washington, under instructions from President Lincoln, empowering the military commanders in Virginia and elsewhere "to seize and use any property, real or personal, which may be necessary or convenient for their several commands for supplies or for other military purposes," and "to keep accounts sufficiently accurate and in detail to show quantities and amounts and from whom it shall come, as a basis upon which compensation can be made in proper cases." This was simply a system of plunder, for no compensation would be made to any person unless he could prove his fidelity to the Government of the United States.

On the next day, Major-General Pope, in command of the United States forces near Washington,[113] issued a general order directing the murder of our peaceful inhabitants as spies, if found quietly tilling the farms in his rear, even outside of his lines; and one of his brigadier-generals seized upon innocent and peaceful inhabitants to be held as hostages, to the end that they might be murdered in cold blood if any of his soldiers were killed by some unknown persons, whom he designated as "bushwhackers." Under this state of facts, I issued a general order, recognizing General Pope and his commissioned officers to be in the position which they had chosen for themselves— that of robbers and murderers, and not that of public enemies, entitled, if captured, to be considered as prisoners of war. Some of the military authorities of the United States seemed to suppose that better success would attend a savage war, in which no quarter was to be given and no age or sex to be spared, than had hitherto been secured by such hostilities as were alone recognized to be lawful by civilized men. We renounced our right of retaliation on the innocent, and continued to treat the soldiers of General Pope's army as prisoners of war, confining our repressive measures to the punishment only of commissioned officers as were willing participants in such crimes. General Pope was soon afterward removed from command.

In August a letter involving similar principles was addressed by General R. E. Lee to the commanding General at Washington, General Halleck, making inquiries as to the truth of the case of William B. Mumford, reported to have been murdered at New Orleans by Major-General Benjamin F. Butler, and of Colonel John Owens, reported to have been murdered in Missouri by order of Major-General Pope. I had also been credibly informed that numerous other officers of the army of the United States within the Confederacy had been guilty of felonies and capital offenses, which are punishable by all laws human and divine. Inquiries were made by letter relative to a few of the best-authenticated cases. It was announced that Major-General Hunter had armed slaves for the murder of their masters, and had thus done all in his power to inaugurate a servile war, which is worse than that of the savage, inasmuch as it super-adds other horrors to the indiscriminate slaughter of all ages, sexes, and conditions.

In a letter, dated Port Royal, South Carolina, June 23, 1862, General Hunter said:

"It is my hope to have organized by the end of next fall, and to be able to present to the Government, from forty-eight to fifty thousand of these hardy and devoted soldiers."

Brigadier-General Phelps was reported to have initiated at New Orleans the example set by General Hunter in South Carolina. Brigadier-General G. N. Fitch was stated in the public journals to have murdered in cold blood two peaceful citizens, because one of his men, when invading our country, was killed by some unknown person while defending his home. General Lee was further directed by me to say that, if a reply was not received in fifteen days, it would be assumed that the alleged facts were true, and were sanctioned by the Government of the United States, and on that Government would rest the responsibility of retaliatory measures. The reply of the commanding General (Halleck) at Washington was in these words:

"As these papers are couched in language insulting to the Government of the United

States, I most respectfully decline to receive them."

On August 20, 1862, I issued an order threatening retaliation for the lives of peaceable citizens reported to have been executed by Brigadier-General Fitch. That report was afterward ascertained to be untrue. On the next day I issued another order, which, after reciting the principal facts, directed that Major-General Hunter and Brigadier-General Phelps should be no longer held and treated as public enemies of the Confederate States, but as outlaws; and that in the event of the capture of either of them, or that of any other commissioned officer employed in drilling, organizing, or instructing slaves, with a view to their armed service in this war, he should not be regarded as a prisoner of war, but held in close confinement for execution as a felon, at such time and place as may be ordered.

In the case of William B. Mumford, a letter was received from General Halleck, dated August 7, 1862, stating sufficient causes for a failure to make an earlier reply to the letter of July 6th; asserting that "no authentic information had been received in relation to the execution of Mumford, but measures will be immediately taken to ascertain the facts of the alleged execution," and promising that General Lee should be duly informed thereof. Subsequently, on November 25, 1862, our agent for the exchange of prisoners, Mr. Robert Ould, under my instructions, addressed the agent of the United States, informing him that the explanation promised on August 7th had not been received; and that, if no answer was sent within fifteen days, it would be considered that an answer was declined. On December 3d our agent, Mr. Ould, was apprised by the agent of the United States that his letter had been forwarded to the Secretary of War at Washington, and no answer was returned, which was regarded as a tacit admission of the charge. Besides, I had received evidence fully establishing the fact that the said Mumford, a citizen of the Confederacy, was actually and publicly executed in cold blood by hanging after the occupation of New Orleans by the forces under General Benjamin F. Butler, when said Mumford was an unresisting and non-combatant captive, and for no offenses even alleged to have been committed by him subsequent to the date of the occupation of the city. It appeared that the silence of the Government of the United States and its maintenance of Butler in high office, under its authority, afforded evidence too conclusive that it sanctioned his conduct, and was determined that he should remain unpunished for these crimes. I therefore pronounced and declared the said Butler a felon, deserving capital punishment, and ordered that he be no longer considered and treated as a public enemy of the Confederate States, but as an outlaw and common enemy of mankind; and that, in the event of his capture, the officer in command should cause him to be immediately executed by hanging.

These measures of retaliation were in conformity with the usages of war, and were adapted to check and punish the cruelties of our adversary.

At length, so many difficulties were raised and so many complaints made in the execution of the cartel, that, for the sake of the unfortunate prisoners, I resolved to seek an adjustment through the authorities at Washington. For this purpose Vice-President Stephens offered his services as a commissioner. The following papers will show the proposition we were prepared to make, and

398

illustrate the disposition with which our humane designs were regarded by the enemy:

"RICHMOND, *July 2, 1863.*

"Hon. ALEXANDER H. STEPHENS, *Richmond, Virginia.*

"SIR: Having accepted your patriotic offer to proceed as a military commissioner under flag of truce to Washington, you will receive herewith your letter of authority to the Commander-in-Chief of the Army and Navy of the United States. The letter is signed by me, as Commander-in-Chief of the Confederate land and naval forces.

"You will perceive from the terms of the letter that it is so worded as to avoid any political difficulties in its reception. Intended exclusively as one of those communications between belligerents which public law recognizes as necessary and proper between hostile forces, care has been taken to give no pretext for refusing to receive it on the ground that it would involve a tacit recognition of the independence of the Confederacy. Your mission is simply one of humanity, and has no political aspect.

"If objection is made to receiving your letter on the ground that it is not addressed to Abraham Lincoln as President, instead of Commander-in-Chief, etc., then you will present the duplicate letter which is addressed to him as President and signed by me as President. To this latter, objection may be made on the ground that I am not recognized to be President of the Confederacy. In this event you will decline any further attempt to confer on the subject of your mission, as such conference is admissible only on the footing of perfect equality.

"My recent interviews with you have put you so fully in possession of my views, that it is scarcely necessary to give you any detailed instructions, even were I at this moment well enough to attempt it. My whole purpose is in one word to place this war on the footing of such as are waged by civilized people in modern times, and to divest it of the savage character which has been impressed on it by our enemies, in spite of all our efforts and protests. War is full enough of unavoidable horrors under all its aspects, to justify and even to demand of any Christian rulers who may be unhappily engaged in carrying it on, to seek to restrict its calamities and to divest it of all unnecessary severities. You will endeavor to establish the cartel for the exchange of prisoners on such a basis as to avoid the constant difficulties and complaints which arise, and to prevent for the future what we deem the unfair conduct of our enemies in evading the delivery of the prisoners who fall into their hands; in retarding it by sending them on circuitous routes, and by detaining them sometimes for months in camps and prisons; and in persisting in taking captives non-combatants.

"Your attention is also called to the unheard-of conduct of Federal officers in driving from their homes entire communities of women and children, as well as of men, whom they find in districts occupied by their troops, for no other reason than because these unfortunates are faithful to the allegiance due to their States, and refuse to take an oath of fidelity to their enemies.

"The putting to death of unarmed prisoners has been a ground of just complaint in more than one instance; and the recent execution of officers of our army in Kentucky, for the sole cause that they were engaged in recruiting service in a State which is claimed as still one of the United States, but is also claimed by us as one of the Confederate States, must be repressed by retaliation if not unconditionally abandoned, because it would justify the like execution in every other State of the Confederacy; and the practice is barbarous, uselessly cruel, and can only lead to the slaughter of prisoners on both sides—a result too horrible to be contemplated without making every effort to avoid it.

"On these and all kindred subjects you will consider your authority full and ample to make such arrangements as will temper the present cruel character of the contest, and full confidence is placed in your judgment, patriotism, and discretion that, while carrying out the objects of your mission, you will take care that the equal rights of the Confederacy be always preserved."

"HEADQUARTERS, RICHMOND, *July 2, 1863.*

"SIR: As Commander-in-Chief of the land and naval forces now waging war against the United States, I have the honor to address this communication to you, as Commander-in-Chief of their land and naval forces.

"Numerous difficulties and disputes have arisen in relation to the execution of the cartel of exchange heretofore agreed on by the belligerents, and the commissioners for the exchange of prisoners have been unable to adjust their differences. Their action on the subject of these differences is delayed and embarrassed by the necessity of referring each subject as it arises to superior authority for decision. I believe that I have just grounds of complaint against the officers and forces under your command for breach of the terms of the cartel, and, being myself ready to execute it at all times in good faith, I am not justified in doubting the existence of the same disposition on your part.

"In addition to this matter, I have to complain of the conduct of your officers and troops in many parts of the country, who violate all the rules of war, by carrying on hostilities, not only against armed foes, but against non-combatants, aged men, women, and children; while others not only seize such property as is required for the use of your forces, but destroy all private property within their reach, even agricultural implements; and openly avow the purpose of seeking to subdue the population of the districts where they are operating, by the starvation that must result from the destruction of standing crops and agricultural tools.

"Still, again, others of your officers in different districts have recently taken the lives of prisoners who fell into their power, and justify their act by asserting a right to treat as spies the military officers and enlisted men under my command, who may penetrate for hostile purposes into States claimed by me to be engaged in the warfare now waged against the United States, and claimed by the latter as having refused to engage in such warfare.

"I have heretofore, on different occasions, been forced to make complaint of these outrages, and to ask from you that you should either avow or disclaim having authorized them, and have failed to obtain such answer as the usages of civilized warfare require to be given in such cases.

"These usages justify, and indeed require, redress by retaliation, as the proper means of repressing such cruelties as are not permitted in warfare between Christian peoples. I have, notwithstanding, refrained from the exercise of such retaliation, because of its obvious tendency to lead to a war of indiscriminate massacre on both sides, which would be a spectacle so shocking to humanity and so disgraceful to the age in which we live and the religion we profess, that I can not contemplate it without a feeling of horror that I am disinclined to doubt you would share.

"With the view, then, of making one last solemn attempt to avert such calamities, and to attest my earnest desire to prevent them, if it be possible, I have selected the bearer of this letter, the Hon. Alexander H. Stephens, as a military commissioner to proceed to your headquarters under flag of truce, there to confer and agree on the subjects above mentioned; and I do hereby authorise the said Alexander H. Stephens to arrange and settle all differences and disputes which may have arisen or may arise in the execution of the cartel for exchange of prisoners of war, heretofore agreed on between our respective land and naval forces; also to agree to any just modification that may be found necessary to prevent further misunderstandings as to the terms of said cartel; and finally to enter into such arrangement or understanding about the mode of carrying on hostilities between the belligerents as shall confine the severities of the war within such limits as are rightfully imposed, not only by modern civilization, but by our common Christianity. I am, very respectfully, your obedient servant,
"JEFFERSON DAVIS,
        "*Commander-in-Chief of the land and naval forces of the Confederate States.*
"To ABRAHAM LINCOLN,
        "*Commander-in-Chief of the land and naval fores of the United States.*"

On July 3, 1863, Mr. Stephens proceeded down the James River under a flag of truce, and when near Newport News his further progress was arrested by the orders of the Admiral of the enemy's fleet. The object of his mission, with a request for permission to go to Washington, was made known to that officer, who, by telegraph, communicated with the Government at Washington. The reply of that Government was:

"The request is inadmissible. The customary agents and channels are adequate for all needful military communications and conference between the United States forces and the insurgents."

This was all the notice ever taken of our humane propositions. We were stigmatized as insurgents, and the door was shut in our faces. Does not this demonstrate an intent to subjugate our States?

From the correspondence of our exchange commissioner, Judge Ould, it appears that, from the date of the cartel on July 22, 1862, until the summer of 1863, we had an excess of prisoners. During the interval deliveries were made as fast as the enemy furnished transportation. Indeed, upon more than one occasion they were urged to send increased means of transportation. It was never alleged that we failed or neglected to make prompt deliveries of prisoners who were not held under charges when they had the excess. On the other hand, the cartel was openly and notoriously violated by the Washington authorities. Officers and men were kept in confinement, sometimes in irons or doomed to cells, without charge or trial. Many officers were kept in confinement even after the notices published by the enemy had declared them to be exchanged.

In the summer of 1863 the authorities at Washington insisted upon exchanges limited to such as were held in confinement on either side. This was resisted as in violation of the cartel. Such a construction not only kept in confinement the excess on either side, but ignored all paroles which were held by the Confederate Government. These were very many, being the paroles of officers and men who had been released on capture. The authorities at Washington at that time held few or no paroles. They had all, or nearly all, been surrendered. We gave prisoners as an equivalent for them. As long as we had the excess of prisoners, matters went on smoothly enough; but, as soon as the posture of affairs in that respect was changed, the cartel could no longer be observed. So long as the United States Government held the paroles of Confederate officers and men, they were respected and made the basis of exchange; but when equivalents were obtained for them, and no more were in hand, they would not recognize the paroles which were held by us. In consequence of the position thus assumed by the Government of the United States, the requirement of the cartel that all prisoners should be delivered within ten days was practically nullified. The deliveries which were afterward made were the results of special agreements.

The wish of the Confederate Government, which it was hoped had been accomplished by the cartel, was the prompt release of all prisoners on both sides, either by exchange or parole. When, in 1864, the cartel was so disregarded by the enemy as to indicate that prisoners would be held long in confinement, Andersonville, in Georgia, was selected for the location of a principal prison. The site was chosen because of its supposed security from raids, together with its salubrity, the abundance of water and timber, and the productive farming country around it. General Howell Cobb, then commanding in Georgia, employed a large number of negro laborers in the construction of a stockade and temporary shelter for the number of prisoners it was expected would be assembled there. The number, however, rapidly increased, and, by the middle of May, gangrene and scurvy made their appearance. General John H. Winder, who had been stationed in Richmond in charge of the police and local guards, as well as the general control of prisoners, went to Andersonville in June, and found disease prevailing to such an extent that, to abate the pestilence, he immediately advised the removal of prisoners to other points. As soon as arrangements could be made, he was instructed to disperse them to Millen and elsewhere, as in his judgment might be best for their health, comfort and safety. In July he made arrangements to procure vegetables, recommended details of men to cultivate gardens, and that hospital accommodations should be constructed outside of the prison; all of which recommendations were approved, and as far as practicable executed. In September General Winder, with the main body of the prisoners, removed first to Millen, Georgia, and then to Florence, South Carolina.

Major Wirz thereafter remained in command at Andersonville, and the testimony of Chief-Surgeon Stevenson, of the hospital at Andersonville, bears testimony to the success with which Wirz improved the post, and the good effect produced upon the health of the prisoners. This unfortunate man—who, under the severe temptation to which he was exposed before his execution, exhibited honor and fidelity strongly in contrast with his tempters and persecutors—it now appears, was the victim of men whom, in his kindness, he paroled to take care of their sick comrades, and who, after having violated their parole, appeared to testify against him.

In like manner has calumny pursued the memory of General John H. Winder, a man too brave to be cruel to anything within his power, too well bred and well born to be influenced by low and sordid motives. I have referred only to a few of the facts illustrative of his kindness to the prisoners after he went to Georgia, and they were in keeping with his conduct toward the prisoners at Richmond. This latter fact, together with his sterling integrity and soldierly character, had caused his selection for the chief control of Confederate prisons.

The Adjutant-General, Samuel Cooper, a man as pure in heart as he was sound in judgment, was the classmate of Winder; their lives had been passed in the array in frequent intercourse; and General Cooper, in a letter of July 9, 1871, wrote that "General Winder, who had the control of the Northern prisoners, was an honest, upright, and humane gentleman, and as such I had known him for many years. He had the reputation, in the Confederacy, of treating the prisoners confided to his general supervision with great kindness and consideration."

In January, 1864, and even earlier, it became manifest that, in consequence of the complication in relation to exchanges, the large mass of prisoners on both sides would remain in captivity for many long and weary months, if not for the duration of the war. In order to alleviate the hardships of confinement on both sides, our commissioner, on January 24, 1863, addressed a communication to General E. A. Hitchcock, United States commissioner of exchange, in which he proposed that all prisoners on each side should be attended by a proper number of their own surgeons, who, under rules to be established, should be permitted to take charge of their health and comfort.

It was also proposed that these surgeons should act as commissaries, with power to receive and distribute such contributions of money, food, clothing, and medicines as might be forwarded for the relief of the prisoners. It was further proposed that these surgeons should be selected by their own Government, and that they should have full liberty at any and all times, through the agents of exchange, to make reports, not only of their own acts, but of any matters relating to the welfare of the prisoners.

To this communication no reply of any kind was ever made.

Again, Commissioner Ould, in a communication published in August, 1868, further says:

"About the last of March, 1864, I had several conferences with General B. F. Butler, then agent of exchange at Fortress Monroe, in relation to the difficulties attending the exchange of prisoners, and we reached what we both thought a tolerably satisfactory basis. The day that I left there General Grant arrived. General Butler says he communicated to him the state of the negotiations, and 'most emphatic verbal directions were received from the Lieutenant-General not to take any step by which another able-bodied man should be exchanged until further orders from him'; and that on April 30, 1864, he received a telegram from General Grant 'to receive all the sick and wounded the Confederate authorities may send you, but send no more in exchange.' Unless my recollection fails me, General Butler also, in an address to his constituents, substantially declared that he was directed, in his management of the question of exchange with the Confederate authorities, to put the matter *offensively, for the purpose of preventing an exchange.*"

The signification of the word "offensively," in the preceding line, relates to the exchange of negro soldiers. The Government of the United States contended that the slaves in their ranks were such no longer; that it was bound to accord to them, when made prisoners, the same protection that it gave all other soldiers. We asserted the slaves to be property, under the Constitution of the United States and that of the Confederate States, and that property recaptured from the enemy in war reverts to its owner, if he can be found, or it may be disposed of by its captor.

On October 1st, when the number of prisoners was large on either side. General Lee addressed a note to General Grant, saying:

"With a view of alleviating the sufferings of our soldiers, I have the honor to propose an exchange of the prisoners of war belonging to the armies operating in Virginia, man for man, or upon the basis established by the cartel."

On the next day General Grant replied:

"I could not of a right accept your proposition further than to exchange those prisoners captured within the last three days, and who have not yet been delivered to the commanding General of prisoners. Among those lost by the armies operating against Richmond were a number of colored troops. Before further negotiations are had upon the subject, I would ask if you propose delivering these men the same as white soldiers."

On the next day General Lee said, in rejoinder:

"In my proposition of the 1st inst., to exchange the prisoners of war belonging to the armies operating in Virginia, I intended to include all captured soldiers of the United States, of whatever nation and color, under my control. Deserters from our service and negroes belonging to our citizens are not considered subjects of exchange, and were not included in my proposition. If there are any such among those stated by you to have been captured around Richmond, they can not be returned."

On October 20th General Grant finally answered, saying;

"I shall always regret the necessity of retaliating for wrong done our soldiers, but regard it my duty to protect all persons received into the army of the United States, regardless of color or nationality; when acknowledged soldiers of the Government are captured, they must be treated as prisoners of war, or such treatment as they receive inflicted upon an equal number of prisoners held by us."

This was "putting the matter offensively, for the purpose of preventing an exchange," as recommended by General Grant for the adoption of General Butler.

But let us return to the progress of negotiations. In a dispatch from General Grant to General Butler, dated City Point, August 18, 1864, the former says:

"On the subject of exchange, however, I differ from General Hitchcock. It is hard on our men held in Southern prisons not to exchange them, but it is humanity to those left in the ranks to fight our battles. Every man released on parole, or otherwise, becomes an active soldier against us at once,

either directly or indirectly. If we commence a
system of exchange, which liberates all
prisoners taken, we will have to fight on until
the whole South is exterminated. If we hold
those caught, they amount to no more than
dead men. At this particular time to release all
rebel prisoners North would insure
Sherman's defeat, and would compromise our
safety here."

We now proposed to the Government of the United States to exchange the
prisoners respectively held, officer for officer and man for man. We had
previously declined this proposal, and insisted on the terms of the cartel, which
required the delivery of the excess on either side on parole. At the same time we
sent a statement of the mortality prevailing among the prisoners at
Andersonville.

As no answer had been received relative to this proposal, a communication
was sent, on August 22, 1864, to Major-General E. A. Hitchcock, United States
commissioner of exchange, containing the same proposal which had been before
delivered to the assistant commissioner, and a request was made for its
acceptance.

No answer was received to either of these letters, and on August 31st the
assistant commissioner stated that he had no communication on the subject
from the United States Government, and that he was not authorized to make an
answer.

This offer, which would have released every soldier of the United States
confined in our prisons, was not even noticed. Indeed, the United States
Government had, at that time, a large excess of prisoners, and the effect of the
proposal, if carried out, would have been to release all the prisoners belonging to
it, while a large number of ours would have remained in prison awaiting the
chances of the capture of their equivalents.

Thus, having ascertained that exchanges could not be made, either on the
basis of the cartel, or officer for officer and man for man, we offered to the
United States Government their sick and wounded without requiring any
equivalents. On these terms, we agreed to deliver from ten to fifteen thousand at
the mouth of the Savannah River; and we further added that, if the number for
which transportation might be sent could not be readily made up from sick and
wounded, the difference should be supplied with well men. Although the offer
was made in the summer, the transportation did not arrive until November. And
as the sick and wounded were at points distant from Georgia, and could not be
brought to Savannah within a reasonable time, five thousand well men were
substituted. In return, some three thousand sick and wounded were delivered to
us at the same place. The original rolls showed that some thirty-five hundred
had started from Northern prisons, and that death had reduced the number
during the passage to about three thousand.

On two occasions we were specially asked to send the very sick and
desperately wounded prisoners, and a particular request was made for men who
were so seriously sick that it was doubtful whether they would survive a removal
a few miles down James River. Accordingly, some of the worst cases, contrary to
the judgment of our surgeons, but in compliance with the piteous appeals of the

sick prisoners, were sent away, and after being delivered they were taken to Annapolis, Maryland, and there photographed as specimen prisoners. The photographs at Annapolis were terrible indeed, but the misery they portrayed was surpassed by some of those we received in exchange at Savannah. Why was there this delay between the summer and November in sending vessels for the transportation of sick and wounded, for whom no equivalents were asked? Were Federal prisoners left to suffer, and afterward photographed "to aid in firing the popular heart of the North"?

In the summer of 1864, in consequence of certain information communicated to our commissioner, Mr. Ould, by the Surgeon-General of the Confederate States, as to the deficiency of medicines. Mr. Ould offered to make purchases of medicines from the United States authorities, to be used exclusively for the relief of the Union prisoners. He offered to pay gold, cotton, or tobacco for them, and even two or three prices if required. At the same time he gave assurances that the medicines would be used exclusively for the treatment of Union prisoners; and moreover agreed, on behalf of the Confederate States, if it were insisted on, that such medicines might be brought into the Confederate lines by the United States surgeons, and dispensed by them. Incredible as it may appear, it is, nevertheless, strictly true that no reply was ever received to this offer.

One final effort was now made to obtain an exchange. This consisted in my sending a delegation from the prisoners at Andersonville to plead their cause before the authorities at Washington. It was of no avail. President Lincoln refused to see them. They were made to understand that the interests of the Government of the United States required that they should return to prison and remain there. They carried back the sad tidings that their Government held out no hope of their release.

> "We have a letter from the wife of the chairman of that delegation (now dead) in which she says that her husband always said that he was more contemptuously treated by Secretary of War Stanton than he ever was at Andersonville." [114]

Another prisoner, Henry M. Brennan, writes:

> "I was at Andersonville when the delegation of prisoners spoken of by Jefferson Davis left there to plead our cause with the authorities at Washington; and nobody can tell, unless it be a shipwrecked and famished mariner, who sees a vessel approaching and then passing on without rendering the required aid, what fond hopes were raised, and how hope sickened into despair, waiting for the answer that never came. In my opinion, and that of a good many others, a good part of the responsibility for the horrors of Andersonville rests with General U. S. Grant, who refused to make a fair exchange of prisoners."

The following extracts are from the official report of Major-General Butler to "the Committee on the Conduct of the War," which was appointed by a joint resolution of Congress, during the war:

"Mr. Ould left on the 31st of March, 1864, with the understanding that I would get authority and information from my Government, by which all disputed points could be adjusted, and would then confer with him further, either meeting him at City Point or elsewhere for that purpose. In the mean time exchanges of sick and wounded, and special exchanges, should go on.

"General Grant visited Fortress Monroe on April 1st, being the first time I had ever met him. To him the state of the negotiations as to exchange[115] was verbally communicated; and most emphatic directions were received from the Lieutenant-General not to take any step by which another able-bodied man should be exchanged, until further orders from him."

General Butler next gives the following from General Mulford, United States assistant agent of exchange, addressed to him:

"GENERAL: The Confederate authorities will exchange prisoners on the basis heretofore proposed by our Government—that is, man for man. This proposition was proposed formally to me after I saw you."

General Butler's report continues as follows:

"Accident prevented my meeting the rebel commissioner, so that nothing was done; but after conversation with General Grant, in reply to the proposition of Mr. Ould to exchange all prisoners of war on either side held, man for man, officer for officer, I wrote an argument showing our right to our colored soldiers. This argument set forth our claims in the most offensive form possible, consistently with ordinary courtesy of language, for the purpose of carrying out the wishes of the Lieutenant-General that no prisoners of war should be exchanged. This paper was published so as to bring a public pressure by the owners of slaves upon the rebel Government, in order to forbid their exchange."

The report continues:

"In case the Confederate authorities took the same view as General Grant, believing that an exchange 'would defeat Sherman and imperil the safety of the Armies of the

Potomac and the James,' and therefore should yield to the argument, and formally notify me that their former slaves captured in our uniform would be exchanged as other soldiers were, and that they were ready to return us all our prisoners at Andersonville and elsewhere in exchange for theirs, then I had determined, with the consent of the Lieutenant-General, as a last resort to prevent exchange, to demand that the outlawry against me should formally be reversed and apologized for, before I would further negotiate the exchange of prisoners. But the argument was enough, and the Confederates never offered to me afterward to exchange the colored soldiers who had been slaves, held in prison by them."

Further on in the report General Butler gives the history of some naval exchanges, in the course of which colored prisoners were delivered, and concludes his observations on that head as follows:

"It will be observed that the rebels had exchanged all the naval colored prisoners, so that the negro question no longer impeded the exchange of prisoners; in fact, if we had demanded the exchange of all, man for man, officer for officer, they would have done it."

The conclusion of the report is as follows:

"I have felt it my duty to give an account with this particular carefulness of my participation in the business of exchange of prisoners, the orders under which I acted, and the negotiations attempted, which comprises a faithful narration of all that was done, so that all may become a matter of history. The great importance of the questions; the fearful responsibility for the many thousands of lives which, by the refusal to exchange, were sacrificed by the most cruel forms of death, from cold, starvation, and pestilence of the prison-pens of Raleigh and Andersonville, being more than all the British soldiers killed in the wars of Napoleon; the anxiety of fathers, brothers, sisters, mothers, wives, to know the exigency which caused this terrible, and perhaps, as it may have seemed to them, useless and unnecessary, destruction of those dear to them, by horrible deaths, each and all have compelled me to this exposition, so that it may be seen that those lives were spent as a part of the system of attack upon the rebellion, devised by the wisdom of the General-in-Chief of the armies, to destroy it by depletion, depending upon our superior numbers to win the victory at last. The loyal mourners will doubtless derive solace from this fact, and appreciate all the more highly the genius which conceived the plan, and the success won at so great a cost."

Sufficient facts have been presented to satisfy every intelligent and candid mind of our entire readiness to surrender, for exchange, all the prisoners in our possession, whenever the Government of the United States would honestly meet us for that purpose. At any hour perfect arrangements could have been made with us for the restoration to it of all its soldiers held as prisoners by us, if its authorities at Washington had consented so to do. On them rests the criminality for the sufferings of these prisoners.

Further, the Government of the United States, in order to effect our subjugation, devastated our fields, destroyed our crops, broke up our railroads, and thus interrupted our means of transportation, and reduced our people, our armies, and consequently their soldiers, who were our prisoners, all alike, to the most straitened condition for food. Our medicines for the sick were exhausted, and, contrary to the usage of civilized nations, they were made, by our enemy, contraband of war. After causing these and other distressing events—of which Atlanta, where the women and children were driven into the fields and their houses burned, and Columbia, with its smoking and plundered ruins, were prominent examples—after every effort to excite our slaves to servile war—this Government of the United States turned to the Northern people, and, charging us with atrocious cruelties to their sons, who were our prisoners, appealed to them again and again to recruit the armies and take vengeance upon us by our abject subjugation or entire extermination. It was the last effort of the usurper to save himself.

But there is another scene to be added to these cruelties. During all this time, Northern prisons were full of our brave and heroic soldiers, of whom there were about sixty thousand. The privations which they suffered, the cruelties inspired by the malignant spirit of the Government, which were inflicted upon them, surpass any records of modern history: yet we have had no occasion to seek out a Wirz for public trial before an illegal court, that we might conceal behind him our own neglect and cruel sacrifice of them. That we might clothe our brave men in the prisons of the United States Government, I made an application for permission to send cotton to Liverpool, and therewith purchase the supplies which were necessary. The request was granted, but only on condition that the cotton should be sent to New York and the supplies bought there. This was done by our agent, General Beale. The suffering of our men in Northern prisons caused the application; that it was granted, refutes the statement that our men were comfortably maintained.

Finally, to the bold allegations of ill-treatment of prisoners on our side, and humane treatment and adequate supplies on that of our opponents, it is only necessary to offer two facts: First, the report of the Secretary of War, E. M. Stanton, made on July 19, 1866, shows that, of all the prisoners in our hands during the war, only 22,576 died; while, of the prisoners in our opponents' hands, 26,246 died. Second, the official report of Surgeon-General Barnes, an officer of the United States Government, states that, in round numbers, the number of Confederate States prisoners in their hands amounted to 220,000, the number of United States prisoners in our hands amounted to 270,000. Thus, out of the 270,000 in our hands, 22,000 died; while of the 220,000 of our soldiers in their hands, 26,000 died. Thus, more than twelve per cent. of the prisoners in our opponents' hands died, and less than nine per cent. of the prisoners in our hands died.

When, in this connection, it is remembered how much our resources were reduced, that our supply of medicines required in summer diseases was exhausted, and that Northern men when first residing at the South must undergo acclimation, and that these conditions in the Northern States were the reverse in each particular—the fact that greater mortality existed in Northern than in Southern prisons can only be accounted for by the kinder treatment received in the latter. To present the case in a sentence—we did the best we could for those whom the fortune of war had placed at our mercy; and the enemy, in the midst of plenty, inflicted cruel, wanton deprivation on our soldiers who fell within his power.

In regard to the failure in the exchange of prisoners, General B. F. Butler has irrefutably fixed the responsibility on the Government at Washington and on General Grant. The obstacles thus thrown in the way were not only persistently interposed, but artfully designed to be insurmountable.

On the other hand, the Confederate Government, through Colonel Ould, its commissioner of exchanges, sought by all practicable means to execute the obligations of the cartel, and otherwise to relieve the suffering of prisoners kept in confinement; through a delegation of the Federal prisoners at Andersonville, it sought to attract the notice of their Government to their sufferings; and, finally, confiding in the chivalry characteristic of soldiers, sought, through General Lee, to make an arrangement with General Grant for the exchange of all the prisoners held in their respective commands, and as many more as General Grant could add in response to all held by the Confederate Government.[116]

[Footnote 112: "Southern Historical Society Papers," March, 1876.]
[Footnote 113: See chapter xxxiv.]
[Footnote 114: Editor of Southern Historical Society Papers.]
[Footnote 115: "The negotiations as to exchange, to which General Butler refers, were the points of agreement between General Butler and myself, under which exchanges of all white and free black soldiers, man for man and officer for officer, were to go on, leaving the question as to slaves to be disposed of by subsequent arrangement."— (Letter of Mr. Ould, June, 1879.)]
[Footnote 116: For full and exact information, compiled from official records and other documents, the reader is referred to "Treatment of Prisoners," by J. William Jones, D. D., and to "The Southern Side: or Andersonville Prison, compiled from Official Documents" by R. Randolph Stevenson, M. D.]

CHAPTER L.
Subjugation the Object of the Government of the United States.—The only Terms of Peace offered to us.—Rejection of all Proposals.—

Efforts of the Enemy.—Appearance of Jacques and Gilmore at Richmond.—Proposals.—Answer.—Commissioners sent to Canada.—The Object.—Proceedings.—Note of President Lincoln.—Permission to visit Richmond granted to Francis P. Blair.—Statement of my Interview with him.—My Letter to him.—Response of President Lincoln.—Three Persons sent by me to an Informal Conference.—Their Report.—Remarks of Judge Campbell.—Oath of President Lincoln.—The Provision of the Constitution and his Proclamation compared.—Reserved Powers spoken of in the Constitution.—What are they, and where do they exist?—Terms of Surrender offered to our Soldiers.

That it was the purpose of the Government of the United States to subjugate the Southern States and the Southern people, under the pretext of a restoration of the Union, is established by the terms and conditions offered to us in all the conferences relative to a settlement of differences. All were comprehended in one word, and that was subjugation. If the purpose had been an honorable and fraternal restoration of the Union as was avowed, methods for the adjustment of difficulties would have been presented and discussed; propositions for reconciliation with concessions and modifications for grievances would have been kindly offered and treated; and a way would have been opened for a mutual and friendly intercourse. How unlike this were all the propositions offered to us, will be seen in the proceedings which took place in the conferences, and in the terms of surrender offered to our soldiers. It should be remembered that mankind compose one uniform order of beings, and thus the language of arbitrary power has the same signification in all ages. When Major Pitcairn marched the British soldiers upon the common, at Lexington, in Massachusetts, on April 19, 1775, and, drawing his sword, rushed upon the little line of Continentals, exclaiming: "Disperse, ye rebels! throw down your arms and disperse!" he expressed the same conditions which were offered to us in all our negotiations with the President of the United States and his generals. Does any one doubt that Major Pitcairn meant subjugation, or that Great Britain meant subjugation? Let them as dispassionately construe the Government of the United States in its declarations to us.

Several efforts were made by us to communicate with the authorities at Washington without success. Commissioners were sent before hostilities were begun, and the Government of the United States refused to receive them, or hear what they had to say. A second time I sent a military officer with a communication addressed by myself to President Lincoln. The letter was received by General Scott, who did not permit the officer to see Mr. Lincoln, but promised that an answer would be sent. No answer was ever received. The third time a gentleman was sent whose position, character, and reputation were such as to insure his reception, if the enemy had not been determined to receive no proposals whatever from our Government. Vice-President Stephens made a patriotic tender of his services, in the hope of being able to promote the cause of humanity; and, although little belief was entertained of his success, I cheerfully yielded to his suggestions, that the experiment should be tried. The enemy refused to let him pass through their lines or to hold any conference with him. He was stopped before he reached Fortress Monroe.

If we would break up our Government, dissolve the Confederacy, disband our armies, emancipate our slaves, take an oath of allegiance, binding ourselves to obedience to it and to disloyalty to our own States, the Government of the United States proposed to pardon us, and not to deprive us of anything more than the property already robbed from us, and such slaves as still remained. In order to render the proposals so insulting as to secure their rejection, the President of the United States joined to them a promise to support with his army one tenth of the people of any State who would attempt to set up a government over the other nine tenths; thus seeking to sow discord among the people of the several States, and to excite them to civil war in furtherance of his ends.

The next movement relating to the accommodation of differences occurred in July, 1864, and consisted in the appearance at Richmond of Colonel James F. Jacques, of the Seventy-eighth Illinois Infantry, and James R. Gilmore, of Massachusetts, soliciting an interview with me. They stated that they had no official character or authority, "but were fully possessed of the views of the United States Government, relative to an adjustment of the differences existing between the North and the South," and did not doubt that a free interchange of views would open the way to official negotiations, etc. They had crossed our lines through a letter of General Grant to Colonel Ould, commissioner for the exchange of prisoners. The Secretary of State, Mr. Benjamin, to whom they were conducted, accompanied them to my office. Colonel Jacques expressed the ardent desire he felt, in common with the men of their army, for a restoration of peace, using such emphatic terms as that the men would go home in double-quick time if they could only see peace restored. Mr. Gilmore addressed me, and in a few minutes conveyed the information that the two gentlemen had come to Richmond impressed with the idea that the Confederate Government would accept a peace on the basis of a reconstruction of the Union, the abolition of slavery, and the grant of an amnesty to the people of the States as repentant criminals. In order to accomplish the abolition of slavery, it was proposed that there should be a general vote of all the people of both federations, in mass, and the majority of the vote thus taken was to determine that as well as all other disputed questions. These were stated to be Mr. Lincoln's views. The impudence of the remarks could only be extenuated because of the ignorance displayed and the profuse avowal of the kindest motives and intentions.

I answered that, as these proposals had been prefaced by the remark that the people of the North were a majority, and that a majority ought to govern, the offer was, in effect, a proposal that the Confederate States should surrender at discretion, admit that they had been wrong from the beginning of the contest, submit to the mercy of their enemies, and avow themselves to be in need of pardon for their crimes; that extermination was preferable to dishonor. I stated that, if they were themselves so unacquainted with the form of their own government as to make such propositions, Mr. Lincoln ought to have known, then giving them his views, that it was out of the power of the Confederate Government to act on the subject of the domestic institutions of the several States, each State having exclusive jurisdiction on that point, still less to commit the decision of such a question to the vote of a foreign people. Having no disposition to discuss questions of state with such persons, especially as they bore no credentials, I terminated the interview, and they withdrew with Mr. Benjamin.

The opening of the spring campaign of 1864 was deemed a favorable conjuncture for the employment of the resources of diplomacy. To approach the Government of the United States directly would have been in vain. Repeated efforts had already demonstrated its inflexible purpose—not to negotiate with the Confederate authorities. Political developments at the North, however, favored the adoption of some action that might influence popular sentiment in the hostile section. The aspect of the peace party was quite encouraging, and it seemed that the real issue to be decided in the Presidential election of that year, was the continuance or cessation of the war. A commission of three persons, eminent in position and intelligence, was accordingly appointed to visit Canada, with a view to negotiation with such persons in the North as might be relied upon to aid the attainment of peace. The commission was designed to facilitate such preliminary conditions as might lead to formal negotiations between the two Governments, and they were expected to make judicious use of any political opportunity that might be presented.

The commissioners—Messrs. Clay, of Alabama; Holcombe, of Virginia; and Thompson, of Mississippi—established themselves at Niagara Falls in July, and on the 12th commenced a correspondence with Horace Greeley, of New York. Through him they sought a safe-conduct to Washington. Mr. Lincoln at first appeared to favor an interview, but finally refused on the ground that the commissioners were not authorized to treat for peace. His final announcement to them was the following:

"EXECUTIVE MANSION, WASHINGTON, D. C, *July 18, 1864.*

"*To whom it may concern:*

"Any proposition which embraces the restoration of peace, the integrity of the whole union, and the abandonment of slavery, and which comes by and with an authority that can control the armies now at war against the United States, will be received and considered by the Executive Government of the United States, and will be met by liberal terms on other substantial and collateral points, and the bearer or bearers thereof shall have safe conduct both ways.

"ABRAHAM LINCOLN."

This movement, like all others which had preceded it, was a failure.

On December 30, 1864, I received a request from Mr. Francis P. Blair, a distinguished citizen of Montgomery County, Maryland, for permission to visit Richmond for certain personal objects, which was conceded to him. On January 12, 1865, he visited me, and the following statement of our interview was immediately afterward prepared:

"RICHMOND, VIRGINIA, *January 12, 1865.*

"*Memorandum of a confidential conversation held this day with F. P. BLAIR, of Montgomery County, Maryland.*

"Mr. Blair stated that, not receiving an answer to his application for permission to visit Richmond, which had been sent from the headquarters of General Grant's army, he returned to Washington and there received the reply which had been made to his application, but by some means had been withheld from him and been forwarded after having been opened; that he had originally obtained permission to visit Richmond from Mr. Lincoln, after stating to him that he (Mr. Blair) had for many years held friendly relations with myself. Mr. Lincoln stopped him, though he afterward gave him permission to visit me. He stated, in explanation of his position, that he, being a man of Southern blood, felt very desirous to see the war between the States terminated, and hoped by an interview with me to be able to effect something to that end; that, after receiving the pass which had been sent to him by my direction, he sought before returning to have a conversation with Mr. Lincoln; had two appointments for that purpose, but on each occasion was disappointed, and, from the circumstances, concluded that Mr. Lincoln avoided the interview, and therefore came not only without credentials but without such instructions from Mr. Lincoln as enabled him to speak for him. His views, therefore, were to be regarded merely as his own, and said they were perhaps merely the dreams of an old man, etc. He said, despairing of being able to see me, he had determined to write to me, and had the rough draft of a letter which he had prepared, and asked permission to read it. Soon after commencing to do so, he said (pleasantly) that he found his style was marked by his old pursuit, and that the paper appeared too much like an editorial. He omitted, therefore, portions of it, reading what he considered the main points of his proposition. He had recognized the difference of our positions as not entitling him to a response from me to the arguments and suggestions which he desired to offer. I therefore allowed him to read without comment on my part. When he had finished, I inquired as to his main proposition, the cessation of hostilities and the union of the military forces for the common purpose of maintaining the 'Monroe doctrine'—how that object was to be reached. He said that both the political parties of the United States asserted the Monroe doctrine as a cardinal point of their creed; that there was a general desire to apply it to the case of Mexico. For that purpose a secret treaty might be made, etc. I called his attention to my past efforts for negotiation, and my inability to see—unless Mr. Lincoln's course in that regard should be changed—how we were to take the first step. He expressed the belief that Mr. Lincoln would now receive commissioners, but subsequently said he could not give any assurance on that point, and proposed to return to Washington to explain his project to Mr. Lincoln, and notify me, if his hope proved well founded, that Mr. Lincoln would now agree to a conference for the purpose of entering into negotiations. He affirmed that Mr. Lincoln did not sympathize with the radical men who desired the devastation and subjugation of the Southern States, but that he was unable to control the extreme party, which now had great power in the Congress, and would at the next session have still more; referred to the existence of two parties in the Cabinet, to the reluctant nomination of Mr. Chase to be Chief-Justice, etc. For himself, he avowed an earnest desire to stop the further effusion of blood, as one every drop of whose blood was Southern. He expressed the hope that the pride, the power, and the honor of the Southern States should suffer no shock; looked to the extension of Southern territory even to the Isthmus of Darien, and hoped, if his views found favor, that his wishes would be realized; reiterated the idea of State sovereignty, with illustrations, and accepted the reference I made to explanation given in the 'Globe,' when he edited it, of the proclamation of General Jackson.

"When his attention was called to the brutal atrocities of their armies, especially the fiendish cruelty shown to helpless women and children, as the cause of a deep-seated hostility on the part of our people, and an insurmountable obstacle to an early restoration of fraternal relations, he admitted the necessity for providing a new channel for the bitter waters, and another bond than that of former memories and interests. This was supposed to be contained in the proposed common effort to maintain the 'Monroe doctrine' on the American Continent. It was evident that he counted on the disintegration of the Confederate States if the war continued, and that in any event he regarded the institution of slavery as doomed to extinction. I thought any remark by me on the first proposition would lead to intimations in connection with public men which I preferred not more distinctly to hear than as manifested in his general remarks; on the latter point, for the reason stated, the inequality of his responsibility and mine, I preferred to have no discussion. The only difficulty which he spoke of as insurmountable was that of existing engagements between European powers and the Confederate States. This point, when referred to a second time as the dreaded obstacle to a secret treaty which would terminate the war, was met by me with a statement that we had now no such complication, were free to act as to us should seem best, and desired to keep state policy and institutions free from foreign control. Throughout the conference Mr. Blair appeared to be animated by a sincere desire to promote a pacific solution of the existing difficulty, but claimed no other power than that of serving as a medium of communication between those who had thus far had no intercourse, and were therefore without the co-intelligence which might secure an adjustment of their controversy. To his hopeful anticipation in regard to the restoration of fraternal relations between the sections, by the means indicated, I replied that a cessation of hostilities was the first step toward the substitution of reason for passion, of sense of justice for a desire to injure, and that, if the people were subsequently engaged together to maintain a principle recognized by both, if together they should bear sacrifices, share dangers, and gather common renown, that new memories would take the place of those now planted by the events of this war, and might, in the course of time, restore the feelings which preexisted. But it was for us to deal with the problems before us, and leave to posterity questions which they might solve, though we could not; that, in the struggle for independence by our colonial fathers, had failure instead of success attended their effort, Great Britain, instead of a commerce which has largely contributed to her prosperity, would have had the heavy expense of numerous garrisons, to hold in subjection a people who deserved to be free and had resolved not to be subject. Our conference ended with no other result than an agreement that he would learn whether Mr. Lincoln would adopt his (Mr. Blair's) project, and send or receive commissioners to negotiate for a peaceful solution of the questions at issue; that he would report to him my readiness to enter upon negotiations, and that I knew of no insurmountable obstacle to such a treaty of peace as would secure greater advantage to both parties than any result which arms could achieve.

"*January 14, 1865.*

"The foregoing memorandum of conversation was this day read to Mr. Blair, and altered in so far as he desired, in any respect, to change the expressions employed.

"JEFFERSON DAVIS."

The following letter was given by me to Mr. Blair:

"RICHMOND, VIRGINIA, *January 12, 1865.*

"F. P. BLAIR, Esq.

"SIR: I have deemed it proper and probably desirable to you to give you in this form the substance of remarks made by me to be repeated by you to President Lincoln, etc., etc.

"I have no disposition to find obstacles in forms, and am willing now, as heretofore, to enter into negotiations for the restoration of peace, am ready to send a commission whenever I have reason to suppose it will be received, or to receive a commission if the United States Government shall choose to send one. That, notwithstanding the rejection of our former offers, I would, if you could promise that a commissioner, minister, or

other agent would be received, appoint one
immediately, and renew the effort to enter
into conference with a view to secure peace to
the two countries.

"Yours, etc., JEFFERSON DAVIS."

"WASHINGTON, *January 18, 1865.*

"F. P. BLAIR, Esq.

"SIR: You having shown me Mr. Davis's
letter to you of the 12th instant, you may say
to him that I have constantly been, am now,
and shall continue ready to receive any agent
whom he or any other influential person now
resisting the national authority may
informally send to me with the view of
securing peace to the people of our one
common country.

"Yours, etc., A. LINCOLN."

When Mr. Blair returned and gave me this letter of Mr. Lincoln of January
18th, it being a response to my note to Mr. Blair of the 12th, he said it had been a
fortunate thing that I gave him that note, as it had created greater confidence in
Mr. Lincoln regarding his efforts at Richmond. Further reflection, he said, had
modified the views he formerly presented to me, and that he wanted to have my
attention for a different mode of procedure.

He had, as he told Mr. Lincoln, held friendly relations with me for many
years; they began as far back as when I was a schoolboy at Lexington, Kentucky,
and he a resident of that place. In later years we had belonged to the same
political party, and our views had generally coincided. There was much,
therefore, to facilitate our conference. He then unfolded to me the
embarrassment of Mr. Lincoln on account of the extreme men in Congress and
elsewhere, who wished to drive him into harsher measures than he was inclined
to adopt; whence it would not be feasible for him to enter into any arrangement
with us by the use of political agencies; that, if anything beneficial could be
effected, it must be done without the intervention of the politicians. He,
therefore, suggested that Generals Lee and Grant might enter into an
arrangement by which hostilities would be suspended, and a way paved for the
restoration of peace. I responded that I would willingly intrust to General Lee
such negotiation as was indicated.

The conference then ended, and, to report to Mr. Lincoln the result of his
visit, Mr. Blair returned to Washington. He subsequently informed me that the
idea of a military convention was not favorably received at Washington, so it
only remained for me to act upon the letter of Mr. Lincoln.

I determined to send, as commissioners or agents for the informal
conference, Messrs. Alexander H. Stephens, R. M. T. Hunter, and John A.
Campbell.

A letter of commission or certificate of appointment for each was prepared
by the Secretary of State in the following form:

"In compliance with the letter of Mr.
Lincoln, of which the foregoing is a copy, you
are hereby requested to proceed to

Washington City for conference with him upon the subject to which it relates," etc.

This draft of a commission was, upon perusal, modified by me so as to read as follows:

"RICHMOND, *January 28, 1865.*

"In conformity with the letter of Mr. Lincoln, of which the foregoing is a copy, you are requested to proceed to Washington City for an informal conference with him upon the issues involved in the existing war, and for the purpose of securing peace to the two countries."

Some objections were made to this commission by the United States officials, because it authorized the commissioners to confer for the purpose "of securing peace to the two countries"; whereas the letter of Mr. Lincoln, which was their passport, spoke of "securing peace to the people of our one common country." But these objections were finally waived.

The letter of Mr. Lincoln expressing a willingness to receive any agent I might send to Washington City, a commission was appointed to go there; but it was not allowed to proceed farther than Hampton Roads, where Mr. Lincoln, accompanied by Mr. Seward, met the commissioners. Seward craftily proposed that the conference should be confidential, and the commissioners regarded this so binding on them as to prevent them from including in their report the discussion which occurred. This enabled Mr. Seward to give his own version of it in a dispatch to the United States Minister to the French Government, which was calculated to create distrust of, if not hostility to, the Confederacy on the part of the power in Europe most effectively favoring our recognition.

Why Mr. Lincoln changed his purpose, and, instead of receiving the commissioners at Washington, met them at Hampton Roads, I can not, of course, explain. Several causes may be conjecturally assigned. The commissioners were well known in Washington, had there held high positions, and, so far as there was any peace party there, might have been expected to have influence with its members; but a more important inquiry is: If Mr. Lincoln previously had determined to hear no proposition for negotiation, and to accept nothing less than an unconditional surrender, why did he propose to receive informally our agent? If there was nothing to discuss, the agent would have been without functions.

I think the views of Mr. Lincoln had changed after he wrote the letter to Mr. Blair of June 18th, and that the change was mainly produced by the report which he made of what he saw and heard at Richmond on the night he staid there. Mr. Blair had many acquaintances among the members of the Confederate Congress; and all those of the class who, of old, fled to the cave of Adullam, "gathered themselves unto him."

Mr. Hunter, in a published article on the peace commission, referring to Mr. Blair's visit to Richmond, says: "He saw many old friends and party associates. Here his representations were not without effect upon his old confederates, who for so long had been in the habit of taking counsel with him on public affairs." He then goes on to describe Mr. Blair as revealing dangers of such overwhelming disaster as turned the thoughts of many Confederates toward peace more seriously than ever before. That Mr. Blair saw and noted this serious inclining of many to thoughts of peace, scarcely admits of a doubt; and, if he believed the Congress to be infected by a cabal undermining the Executive in his efforts successfully to prosecute the war, Mr. Lincoln may be naturally supposed thence to have reached the conclusion that he should accept nothing but an unconditional surrender, and that he should not allow a commission from the Confederacy to visit the United States capital.

The report of the commissioners, dated February 5, 1865, was as follows:

"To the President of the Confederate States:

"SIR: Under your letter of appointment of the 28th ult. We proceeded to seek 'an informal conference' with Abraham Lincoln, President of the United States, upon the subject mentioned in the letter. The conference was granted and took place on the 30th ult., on board of a steamer anchored in Hampton Roads, where we met President Lincoln and the Hon. Mr. Seward, Secretary of State of the United States. It continued for several hours, and was both full and explicit. We learned from them that the message of President Lincoln to the Congress of the United States, in December last, explains clearly and distinctly his sentiments as to the terms, conditions, and method of proceeding by which peace can be secured to the people, and we were not informed that they would be modified or altered to obtain that end. We understood from him that no terms or proposals of any treaty, or agreement looking to an ultimate settlement, would be entertained or made by him with the authorities of the Confederate States, because that would be a recognition of their existence as a separate power, which under no circumstances would be done; and, for a like reason, that no such terms would be entertained by him for the States separately; that no extended truce or armistice (as at present advised) would be granted or allowed without a satisfactory assurance in advance of the complete restoration of the authority of the Constitution and laws of the United States over all places within the States of the Confederacy; that whatever consequences may follow from the reestablishment of that authority must be accepted; but that individuals subject to pains and penalties under the laws of the United States might rely upon a very liberal use of the power confided to him to remit those pains and penalties if peace be restored.

"During the conference, the proposed amendment to the Constitution of the United States adopted by Congress on the 31st ultimo was brought to our notice.

"This amendment provides that neither slavery nor involuntary servitude, except for crime, should exist within the United States, or any place within their jurisdiction, and that Congress should have power to enforce this amendment by appropriate legislation. Very respectfully, etc.,

"ALEXANDER H. STEPHENS,
"R. M. T. HUNTER,
"JOHN A. CAMPBELL."

Thus closed the conference, and all negotiations with the Government of the United States for the establishment of peace. Says Judge Campbell, in his memoranda:

"In conclusion, Mr. Hunter summed up what seemed to be the result of the interview: that there could be no arrangements by treaty between the Confederate States and the United States, or any agreements between them; that there was nothing left for them but unconditional submission."

By reference to the message of President Lincoln of December 6, 1864, which is mentioned in the report, it appears that the terms of peace therein stated were as follows:

"In presenting the abandonment of armed resistance to the national authority on the part of the insurgents, as the only indispensable condition to ending the war on the part of the Government, I retract nothing heretofore said as to slavery. I repeat the declaration made a year ago, that 'while I remain in my present position I shall not attempt to retract or modify the emancipation proclamation, nor shall I return to slavery any person who is free by the terms of that proclamation, or by any act of Congress.'

"If the people should, by whatever mode or means, make it an executive duty to reënslave such persons, another, and not I, must be their instrument to perform it."

On the 4th of March, 1861, President Lincoln appeared on the western portico of the Capitol at Washington, and in the presence of a great multitude of witnesses took the following oath:

"I do solemnly swear that I will faithfully execute the office of President of the United States, and will, to the best of my ability, preserve, protect, and defend the Constitution of the United States." The first section of the fourth article of the Constitution of the United States is in these words:

> "No person held to service or labor in one State, under the laws thereof, escaping into another, shall, in consequence of any law or regulation therein, be discharged from such service or labor, but shall be delivered up on claim of the party to whom such service or labor may be due."

The intelligent reader will observe that the words of this section, "in consequence of any law or regulation therein," embrace a President's emancipation proclamation, as well as any other regulation therein. Thus the Constitution itself nullified Mr. Lincoln's proclamation, and made it of no force whatever. Yet he assumed and maintained, with all the military force he could command, that it set every slave free. Which is the higher authority, Mr. Lincoln and his emancipation proclamation or the Constitution? If the former, then what are constitutions worth for the protection of rights?

Again he says:

> "Nor shall I return to slavery any person who is free by the terms of that proclamation or by an act of Congress."

But the Constitution says he shall return them—

> "but shall be delivered up on claim of the party to whom such service is due."

Who shall decide? Which is sovereign, Mr. Lincoln and his proclamation or the Constitution? The Constitution says:

> "This Constitution, and the laws of the United States which shall be made in pursuance thereof, shall be the supreme law of the land."

Was it thus obeyed by Mr. Lincoln as the supreme law of the land? It was not obeyed, but set aside, subverted, overturned by him. But he said in his oath:

> "I do solemnly swear that I will, to the best of my ability, preserve, protect, and defend the Constitution of the United States."

Did he do it? Is such treatment of the Constitution the manner to preserve, protect, and defend it? Of what value, then, are paper constitutions and oaths binding officers to their preservation, if there is not intelligence enough in the people to discern the violations, and virtue enough to resist the violators?

Again the report says:

> "We understood from him that no terms or proposals of any treaty or agreement looking to an ultimate settlement would be entertained or made by him with the authorities of the Confederate States, because that would be a recognition of their existence as a separate power, which under no circumstances would be done; and, for a like

reason, that no such terms would be
entertained by him for the States separately."
Now the Constitution of the United States says, in Article X:
"The powers not delegated to the United
States by the Constitution, nor prohibited by
it to the States, are reserved to the States
respectively, or to the people."
Within the purview of this article of the Constitution the States are
independent, distinct, and sovereign bodies—that is, in their reserved powers
they are as sovereign, separate, and supreme as the Government of the United
States in its delegated powers. One of these reserved powers is the right of the
people to alter or abolish any form of government, and to institute a new one
such as to them shall seem most likely to effect their safety and happiness; that
power is neither "delegated to the United States by the Constitution nor
prohibited by it to the States." On the contrary, it is guaranteed to the States by
the Constitution itself in these words:
"The powers not delegated to the United
States by the Constitution, nor prohibited by
it to the States, are reserved to the States
respectively, or to the people."
Mark the words, "are reserved to the States respectively, or to the people."
No one will venture to say that a sovereign State, by the mere act of accession to
the Constitution, delegated the power of secession. The assertion would be of no
validity if it were made; for the question is one of fact as to the powers delegated
or not delegated to the United States by the Constitution. It is absurd to ask if
the power of secession in a State is delegated to the United States by the
Constitution, or prohibited by it to the States. No trace of the delegation or
prohibition of this power is to be found in the Constitution. It is, therefore, as
the Constitution says, "reserved to the States respectively, or to the people."
The Convention of the State of New York, which ratified the Constitution of
the United States on July 26, 1788, in its resolution of ratification said:
"We do declare and make known . . . that
the powers of Government may be reassumed
by the people, whensoever it shall become
necessary to their happiness; that every
power, jurisdiction, and right, which is not by
the said Constitution clearly delegated to the
Congress of the United States, or to the
departments of the Government thereof,
remains to the people of the several States, or
to their respective State governments, to
whom they may have granted the same. . . .
Under these impressions, and declaring that
the rights aforesaid can not be abridged or
violated," etc., etc., "we, the said delegates, in
the name and in behalf of the people of the
State of New York, do, by these presents,
assent to and ratify the said Constitution."

With this and other conditions stated in the resolution of ratification, it was accepted and approved by the other States, and New York became a member of the Union. The resolution of Rhode Island asserts the same reservation in regard to the reassumption of powers.

It is unnecessary to examine here whether this reserved power exists in the States respectively or in the people; for, when the Confederate States seceded, it was done by the people, acting through, or in conjunction with, the State, and by that power which is expressly reserved to them in the Constitution of the United States. When Mr. Lincoln, therefore, issued his proclamation calling for seventy-five thousand men to subjugate certain "combinations too powerful to be suppressed by the ordinary course of judicial proceedings," he not only thereby denied the validity of the Constitution, but sought to resist, by military force, the exercise of a power clearly reserved in the Constitution, and reaffirmed in its tenth amendment, to the States respectively or to the people for their exercise. But, in order to justify his flagrant disregard of the Constitution, he contrived the fiction of "combinations," and upon this basis commenced the bloody war of subjugation with all its consequences. Thus, any recognition of the Confederate States, or of either of them, in his negotiations, would have exposed the groundlessness of his fiction. But the Constitution required him to recognize each of them, for they had simply exercised a power which it expressly reserved for their exercise. Thus it is seen who violated the Constitution, and upon whom rests the responsibility of the war.

It has been stated above that the conditions offered to our soldiers whenever they proposed to capitulate, were only those of subjugation. When General Buckner, on February 16, 1862, asked of General Grant to appoint commissioners to agree upon terms of capitulation, he replied:

"No terms, except unconditional and immediate surrender, can be accepted."

When General Lee asked the same question, on April 9, 1865, General Grant replied:

"The terms upon which peace can be had are well understood. By the South laying down their arms, they will hasten that most desirable event, save thousands of human lives and hundreds of millions of property not yet destroyed."

When General Sherman made an agreement with General Johnston for formal disbandment of the army of the latter, it was at once disapproved by the Government of the United States, and Sherman therefore wrote to Johnston:

"I demand the surrender of your army on the same terms as were given to General Lee at Appomattox, on April 9th, purely and simply."

It remains to be stated that the Government which spurned all these proposals for peace, and gave no terms but unconditional and immediate surrender, was instituted and organized for the purposes and objects expressed in the following extract, and for no others:

"We, the people of the United States, in order to form a more perfect union, establish justice, insure domestic tranquillity, provide for the common defense, promote the general

welfare, and secure the blessings of liberty to
ourselves and our posterity, do ordain and
establish this Constitution for the United
States of America."

[Footnote 117: General Hampton's letter to General Sherman, February 27,
1865.]

[Footnote 118: "The Story of the Great March, from the Diary of a Staff
Officer." By Brevet Major George Ward Nichols, Aide-de-Camp to
General Sherman. New York: Harper & Brothers, 1865, pp. 112, *et seq.*]

CHAPTER LI.

General Sherman leaves Savannah.—His March impeded.—Difficulty In
collecting Troops to oppose him.—The Line of the Salkehatchie.—
Route of the Enemy's Advance.—Evacuation of Columbia.—Its
Surrender by the Mayor.—Burning the City.—Sherman responsible.—
Evacuation of Charleston.—The Confederate Forces in North
Carolina.—General Johnston's Estimate.—General Johnston assigned
to the Command.—The Enemy's Advance from Columbia to Fayetteville,
North Carolina.—"Foraging Parties."—Sherman's Threat and
Hampton's Reply.—Description of Federal "Treasure-Seekers" by
Sherman's Aide-de-Camp.—Failure of Johnston's Projected Attack at
Fayetteville.—Affair at Kinston.—Cavalry Exploits.—General
Johnston withdraws to Smithfield.—Encounter at Averysboro.—
Battles of Bentonville.—Union of Sherman's and Schofield's
Forces.—Johnston's Retreat to Raleigh.

After the evacuation of Savannah by General Hardee, it soon became known
that General Sherman was making preparations to march northward through
the Carolinas with the supposed purpose of uniting his forces with those of
General Grant before Richmond. General Hardee, having left detachments at
proper points to defend the approaches to Charleston and Augusta, Georgia,
withdrew the rest of his command to the first-named city. General Wheeler's
cavalry held all the roads northward, and, by felling trees and burning bridges,
obstructed considerably the enemy's advance, which in the early part of January
was still further impeded by the heavy rains which had swollen the rivers and
creeks far beyond their usual width and depth.

The seriously impaired condition of our railroad communications in Georgia
and Alabama, the effect of the winter rains on the already poor and ill-
constructed country roads, the difficulty in collecting and transporting supplies,
to impeded the concentration of our available forces, that Generals Beauregard
and Hardee—the former at Columbia, South Carolina, and the latter at
Charleston—could only retard, not prevent, the onward march of the enemy. At
the outset of his movement the Salkehatchie River presented a very strong line
of defense. Its swollen condition at that time, and the wide, deeply inundated
swamps on both sides, rendered it almost impossible to force or outflank the
position if adequately defended. It might have been better if we had then
abandoned the attempt to hold cities of no strategic importance, and
concentrated their garrisons at this point, where the chances of successful
resistance were greater than at any subsequent period of the campaign. For,
even if our expectation had been disappointed, and had the superior numerical

force of the enemy compelled us to withdraw from this line, the choice of several good positions was open to us, any one of which, by moving upon converging lines, we could reach sooner than was possible to Sherman, whose passage of the river must have been much encumbered and delayed by his trains. Of these defensive positions, Branchville and Orangeburg may be regarded as eligible: had Sherman headed his columns toward Charleston, our forces would have been in position to attack him in front and on the flank. Had his objective point been Augusta, he would have had our army in his rear; and had, as proved to be the case, Columbia been the place at which he aimed, our army would have been able to reach there sooner than he could.

[Illustration: Lieutenant-General William J. Hardee]

General Sherman left Savannah January 22, 1865, and reached Pocotaligo on the 24th. On February 3d he crossed the Salkehatchie with slight resistance at River's and Beaufort bridges, and thence pushed forward to the South Carolina Railroad at Midway, Bamberg, and Graham's. After thoroughly destroying the railroad between these places, which occupied three or four days, he advanced slowly along the line of the railroad, threatening Branchville, the junction of the railroads from Augusta to Columbia and Charleston. For a short time it was doubtful whether he proposed to attack Augusta, Georgia, where it was well known we had our principal powder-mill, many important factories and shops, and large stores of army supplies; but on the 11th it was found that he was moving north to Orangeburg, on the road from Branchville to Columbia, the latter city being the objective point of his march. Early on the morning of the 16th the head of his columns reached the Congaree opposite Columbia. The bridge over that stream had been burned by our retreating troops, but a pontoon bridge, built by the enemy under cover of strong detachments who had crossed higher up at Saluda Factory, enabled the main body to pass the river and enter the city on the morning of the 17th, the Confederate troops having previously evacuated it. On the same day the Mayor formally surrendered the city to Colonel Stone, commanding a brigade of the Fifteenth Corps, and claimed for its citizens the protection which the laws of civilized war always accord to non-combatants. In infamous disregard not only of the established rules of war, but of the common dictates of humanity, the defenseless city was burned to the ground, after the dwelling-houses had been robbed of everything of value, and their helpless inmates subjected to outrage and insult of a character too base to be described.

Hypocrisy is the tribute which vice pays to virtue; therefore General Sherman has endeavored to escape the reproaches for the burning of Columbia by attributing it to General Hampton's order to burn the cotton in the city, that it might not fall into the hands of the enemy. General Hampton has proved circumstantially that General Sherman's statement is untrue, and, though in any controversy to which General Hampton may be a party, no corroborative evidence is necessary to substantiate his assertion of a fact coming within his personal observation, hundreds of unimpeachable witnesses have testified that the burning of Columbia was the deliberate act of the Federal soldiery, and that it was certainly permitted, if not ordered, by the commanding General. The following letter of General Hampton will to those who know him be conclusive:

"WILD WOODS, MISSISSIPPI, *April 21, 1866.*

"To Hon. REVERDY JOHNSON, *United States Senate.*

"SIR: A few days ago I saw in the published proceedings of Congress that a petition from Benjamin Kawles, of Columbia, South Carolina, asking for compensation for the destruction of his house by tho Federal army, in February, 1865, had been presented to the Senate, accompanied by a letter from Major-General Sherman. In this letter General Sherman uses the following language: 'The citizens of Columbia set fire to thousands of bales of cotton rolled out into the streets, and which were burning before we entered Columbia; I, myself, was in the city as early as nine o'clock, and I saw these fires, and knew that efforts were made to extinguish them, but a high and strong wind prevented. I gave no orders for the burning of your city, but, on the contrary, the conflagration resulted from the great imprudence of cutting the cotton bales, whereby the contents were spread to the wind, so that it became an impossibility to arrest the fire. I saw in your Columbia newspaper the printed order of General Wade Hampton, that on the approach of the Yankee army all the cotton should thus be burned, and, from what I saw myself, I have no hesitation in saying that he was the cause of the destruction of your city.'

"This charge, made against me by General Sherman, having been brought before the Senate of the United States, I am naturally most solicitous to vindicate myself before the same tribunal. But my State has no representative in that body. Those who should be her constitutional representatives there are debarred the right of entrance into those halls. There are none who have the right to speak for the South; none to participate in the legislation which governs her; none to impose the taxes she is called upon to pay, and none to vindicate her sons from misrepresentation, injustice, or slander. Under these circumstances, I appeal to you, in the confident hope you will use every effort to see that justice is done in this matter.

"I deny, emphatically, that any cotton was fired in Columbia by my order. I deny that the citizens 'set fire to thousands of bales rolled out into the streets.' I deny that any cotton was on fire when the Federal troops entered the city. I most respectfully ask of Congress to appoint a committee, charged with the duty of ascertaining and reporting all the facts connected with the destruction of Columbia, and thus fixing upon the proper author of that enormous crime the infamy he richly deserves. I am willing to submit the case to any honest tribunal. Before any such I pledge myself to prove that I gave a positive order, by direction of General Beauregard, that no cotton should be fired; that not one bale was on fire when General Sherman's troops took possession of the city; that he promised protection to the city, and that, in spite of his solemn promise, he burned the city to the ground, deliberately, systematically, and atrociously. I, therefore, most earnestly request that Congress may take prompt and efficient measures to investigate this matter fully. Not only is this due to themselves and to the reputation of the United States army, but also to justice and to truth. Trusting that you will pardon me for troubling you, I am, very respectfully, your obedient servant,

"WADE HAMPTON."

Were this the only instance of such barbarity perpetrated by General Sherman's army, his effort to escape the responsibility might be more successful, because more plausible; but when the eulogists of his exploits note exultingly that "wide-spreading columns of smoke rose wherever the army went," when it is incontrovertibly true that the line of his march could be traced by the burning dwelling-houses and by the wail of women and children pitilessly left to die from starvation and exposure in the depth of winter, his plea of "not guilty" in the case of the city of Columbia can not free him from the reprobation which outraged humanity must attach to an act of cruelty which only finds a parallel in the barbarous excesses of Wallenstein's army in the Thirty Years' War, and which, even at that period of the world's civilization, sullied the fame of that otherwise great soldier.

In consequence of General Sherman's movements, it was considered advisable to evacuate Charleston (February 17th), that General Hardee's command might become available for service in the field; and thus that noble city and its fortresses, which the combined military and naval forces of the United States, during an eighteen months' siege, had failed to reduce, and which will stand for ever as imperishable monuments of the skill and fortitude of their defenders, were, on February 21st, without resistance, occupied by the Federal forces under General Q. A. Gillmore.

Fort Sumter, though it now presented the appearance of a ruin, was really better proof against bombardment than when first subjected to fire. The upper tier of masonry, from severe battering, had fallen on the outer wall, and shot and shell served only to solidify and add harder material to the mass. Over its rampart the Confederate flag defiantly floated until the city of Charleston was evacuated.

Every effort that our circumstances permitted was immediately and thenceforward made to collect troops for the defense of North Carolina. General Hood's army, the troops under command of General D. H. Hill at Augusta, General Hardee's force, a few thousand men under General Bragg, and the cavalry commands of Generals Hampton and Wheeler, constituted our entire available strength to oppose Sherman's advance. These were collected as rapidly as our broken communications and the difficulty of gathering and transporting supplies would permit.

After the fall of Columbia, General Beauregard, commanding the military department, retreated toward North Carolina. The Army of Tennessee (Hood's) was moving from the west to make a junction with the troops retiring from South Carolina. The two forces, if united with Hardee's command, then moving in the same direction, would, it was hoped, be able to make effective resistance to Sherman's advance. In any event it was needful that they should be kept in such relation to Lee's army as to make a junction with it practicable. In this state of affairs I was informed that General Beauregard, after his troops had entered North Carolina, had decided to march to the eastern part of that State. This would leave the road to Charlotte open to Sherman's pursuing column, which, interposing, would prevent the troops coming from the west from joining Beauregard, enable him to destroy our force in detail by the joint action of his own army and that of Schofield, commanding the district of Wilmington. The anxiety created by this condition of affairs caused me, after full correspondence with General Lee, to suggest to him to give his views to General Beauregard, and I sent to General Beauregard's headquarters the chief-engineer, General J. F. Gilmer, he being possessed fully of my opinions and wishes. General Beauregard modified his proposed movements so as to keep his forces on the left of the enemy's line of march until the troops coming from Hood's army could make a junction. These were the veteran commands of Stevenson, Cheatham, and Stewart. Lieutenant-General S. D. Lee, though he had not entirely recovered from a wound received in the Tennessee campaign, was at Augusta, Georgia, collecting the fragments of Hood's army to follow the troops previously mentioned. They had not moved together, and the first-named division had reached Beauregard's army in South Carolina.

Though it contained an implied compliment, General Lee was not a little disturbed by occasional applications made to have troops detached from his army to reënforce others. The last instance had been a call from General Beauregard for reënforcements from the Army of Virginia. He had always been attentive, and ready as far as he could, to meet the wants of other commands of our army, but at this time those who knew his condition could not suppose he had any men to spare; yet the fact of thinking so was a compliment to his success in resisting the large army which was assailing his small one. There had always been entire co-intelligence and accord between General Lee and myself, but the Congress about this time thought his power would be increased by giving him the nominal dignity of general-in-chief, under which he resumed, as far as he could, the general charge of armies from which, at his urgent solicitation, I had relieved him after he took command, in the field, of the Army of Northern Virginia.

A few days subsequent to the events in North Carolina to which reference has been made, General Lee proposed to me that General J. E. Johnston should be put in command of the troops in North Carolina. He still had the confidence in that officer which I had once felt, but which his campaigns in Mississippi and Georgia had impaired. With the understanding that General Lee was himself to supervise and control the operations, I assented to the assignment. General Johnston, on the 23d of February, at Charlotte, North Carolina, relieved General Beauregard and assumed command. General Lee's first instructions to General Johnston were to "concentrate all available forces and drive back Sherman." The first part of the instructions was well executed; the last part of it was more desirable than practicable, though the brief recital made herein of the events of the campaign claimed the credit due to a vigorous effort.

General Johnston's force, according to his estimate, when he took command, amounted to about sixteen thousand infantry and artillery, and four thousand cavalry; if to this be added the portion of the Army of Tennessee, about twenty-five hundred men, under command of General Stephen D, Lee, which afterward joined the army at Smithfield, North Carolina, and that of General Bragg's command at Goldsboro, which amounted to about eight thousand, the aggregate would be about thirty thousand five hundred men of all arms.

After leaving Columbia, the course of the Federal army through Winnsboro, across the Catawba at Rocky Mount, Hanging Rock, and Peay's Ferry, and in the direction of Cheraw on the Great Pedee, indicated that it would attempt to cross the Cape Fear River at Fayetteville, North Carolina—a town sixty miles south of Raleigh, and of special importance, as containing an arsenal, several Government shops, and a large portion of the machinery which had been removed from Harper's Ferry—and effect a junction at that point with General Schofield's command, then known to be at Wilmington. Up to this time, while no encounter of any magnitude had taken place, the enemy's progress had been much impeded by the Confederate cavalry, and the robbery of private citizens by gangs of armed banditti, called "foraging parties," was in a large measure prevented. The right of an army to forage as it advances through an enemy's country is not questioned. But the right to forage, to collect food for men and horses, does not mean the right to rob household furniture, plate, trinkets, and every conceivable species of private property, and to burn whatever could not be carried away, together with the dwellings. General Sherman complained that some of these "foragers," who were caught in the commission of the above-named offenses, and had added thereto the greater crime of assaulting women, had been summarily dealt with by some of those whose wives and daughters they had outraged, and whose homes they had made desolate; and he informed General Hampton that in retaliation he had ordered a number of Confederate prisoners of war to be put to death. To arrest this brutality General Hampton promptly informed him that, "for every soldier of mine murdered by you, I shall have executed at once two of yours, giving in all cases preference to any officers who may be in our hands," and adding, with a view to check the inhuman system of burning the houses of those citizens whom they had robbed, that he had ordered his men "to shoot down all of your men who are caught burning houses." [117] This notice and the knowledge that General Hampton would keep his word, produced, it is believed, a very salutary effect, and thereafter the fear of punishment wrought a reform which the dictates of honor and humanity had been powerless to effect.

The historian of Sherman's "Great March," in his illustrated narrative of that expedition, describes both with pen and pencil the manner in which "with untiring zeal the soldiers hunted for concealed treasures. . . . Wherever the army halted," he writes, "almost every inch of ground in the vicinity of the dwellings was poked by ramrods, pierced with sabers, or upturned with spades," searching for "valuable personal effects, plate, jewelry, and other rich goods, as well as articles of food, such as hams, sugar, flour, etc. . . . It was comical," adds the chronicler, "to see a group of these red-bearded, barefooted, ragged veterans punching the unoffending earth in an apparently idiotic but certainly most energetic way. If they 'struck a vein,' a spade was instantly put into requisition, and the coveted wealth was speedily unearthed. Nothing escaped the observation of these sharp-witted soldiers. A woman standing upon the porch of a house, apparently watching their proceedings, instantly became an object of suspicion, and she was watched until some movement betrayed a place of concealment. The fresh earth recently thrown up, a bed of flowers just set out, the slightest indication of a change in appearance or position, all attracted the gaze of these military agriculturists. It was all fair spoil of war, and the search made one of the excitements of the march." [118] The author of the work from which the foregoing is an extract was an aide-de-camp on the staff of General Sherman. The playful manner in which he describes these habitual acts of plunder of "plate, jewelry and other rich goods" from private and undefended dwellings shows that not only was such conduct not forbidden by the military authorities, but that it was permitted and applauded, that it was practiced "wherever the army halted" under the eye of the staff-officers of the General commanding, and was looked upon as one of the pleasurable "excitements of the march." Indeed, so agreeable was the impression made by these scenes of robbery of women's "rich goods" that he has adorned his narrative with a full-page illustration, exhibiting a plantation home surrounded by soldiers engaged, as this staff-officer humorously terms it, in "treasure-seeking," while the lady of the house—its only apparent occupant—stands upon the veranda, with hands uplifted, beseeching them not to steal the watch and chain which they are taking out of a vessel which they have just dug up. That the foreign mercenaries, of which the Federal army was largely composed, should have been guilty of such disgraceful conduct, when free from the observation of their officers, is conceivable; but it is difficult to imagine that, in the nineteenth century, such acts as are described above could be committed habitually, in view of the officer of highest rank in the army of a civilized country, and not merely pass unpunished or unrebuked, but be recorded with conspicuous approval in the pages of a military history.

The advance of the enemy's columns across the Catawba, Lynch's Creek, and the Pedee, at Cheraw, though retarded as much as possible by the vigilant skill of our cavalry under Generals Hampton, Butler, and Wheeler, was steady and continuous. General Johnston's hope that, from the enemy's order of moving by wings, sometimes a day's march from each other, he could find an opportunity to strike one of their columns in the passage of the Cape Fear River, when the other was not in supporting distance, was unhappily disappointed.

On March 6th, near Kinston, General Bragg with a reënforcement of less than two thousand men attacked and routed three divisions of the enemy under Major-General Cox, capturing fifteen hundred prisoners and three field-pieces, and inflicting heavy loss in killed and wounded. This success, though inspiring, was on too small a scale to produce important results. During the march from the Catawba to the Cape Fear several brilliant cavalry affairs took place, in which our troops displayed their wonted energy and dash. Among these the most conspicuous were General Butler's at Mount Elon, where he defeated a detachment sent to tear up the railroad at Florence; General Wheeler's attack and repulse of the left flank of the enemy at Hornesboro, March 4th; a similar exploit by the same officer at Rockingham on the 7th; the attack and defeat by General Hampton of a detachment on the 8th; the surprise and capture of General Kilpatrick's camp by General Hampton on the morning of the 10th, driving the enemy into an adjoining swamp, and taking possession of his artillery and wagon-train, and the complete rout of a large Federal party by General Hampton with an inferior force at Fayetteville on the 11th.

As it was doubtful whether General Sherman's advance from Fayetteville would be directed to Goldsboro or Raleigh, General Johnston took position with a portion of his command at Smithfield, which is nearly equidistant from each of those places, leaving General Hardee to follow the road from Fayetteville to Raleigh, which for several miles is also the direct road from Fayetteville to Smithfield, and posted one division of his cavalry on the Raleigh road, and another on that to Goldsboro. On the 16th of March General Hardee was attacked by two corps of the enemy, a few miles south of Averysboro, a place nearly half-way between Fayetteville and Raleigh. Falling back a few hundred yards to a stronger position, he easily repelled the repeated attacks of these two corps during the day, and, learning in the evening that the enemy's corps were moving to turn his left, he withdrew in the night toward Smithfield.

Early in the morning of the 18th General Johnston obtained definite information that General Sherman was marching on Goldsboro, the right wing of his army being about a day's march distant from the left. General Johnston took immediate steps to attack the head of the left wing on the morning of the 19th, and ordered the troops at Smithfield and General Hardee's command to march at once to Bentonville and take position between that village and the road on which the enemy was advancing. An error as to the relative distance which our troops and those of the enemy would have to move, exaggerating the distance between the roads on which the enemy was advancing and diminishing the distance that our troops would have to march, caused the failure to concentrate our troops in time to attack the enemy's left wing while in column; but, when General Hardee's troops reached Bentonville in the morning, the attack was commenced. The battle lasted through the greater part of the day, resulting in the enemy's being driven from two lines of intrenchments, and his taking shelter in a dense wood, where it was impracticable for our troops to preserve their line of battle or to employ the combined strength of the three arms. On the 20th the two wings of the Federal army, numbering, as estimated by General Johnston, upward of seventy thousand, came together and repeatedly attacked a division of our force (Hoke's) which occupied an intrenched position parallel to the road to Averysboro; but every attack was handsomely repulsed. On the next day (21st) an attempt by the enemy to reach

Bentonville in the rear of our center, and thus cut off our only route of retreat, was gallantly defeated by an impetuous and skillful attack, led by Generals Hardee and Hampton, on the front and both flanks of the enemy's column, by which he was compelled to retreat as rapidly as he had advanced. In this attack. General Hardee's only son, a noble boy, charging gallantly with the Eighth Texas Cavalry, fell mortally wounded. On the night of the 21st our troops were withdrawn across Mill Creek, and in the evening of the 22d bivouacked near Smithfield. On the 23d the forces of General Sherman and those of General Schofield were united at Goldsboro, where they remained inactive for upward of two weeks.

On the 9th of April the Confederate forces took up the line of march to Raleigh, and reached that city early in the afternoon of the same day closely followed by the Federal army.

CHAPTER LII.

Siege of Petersburg.—Violent Assault upon our Position.—A Cavalry Expedition.—Contest near Ream's Station.—The City invested with Earthworks.—Position of the Forces.—The Mine exploded, and an Assault made.—Attacks on our Lines.—Object of the Enemy.—Our Strength.—Assault on Fort Fisher.—Evacuation of Wilmington.— Purpose of Grant's Campaign.—Lee's Conference with the President.—Plans.—Sortie against Fort Steadman.—Movements of Grant farther to Lee's right.—Army retires from Petersburg.—The Capitulation.—Letters of Lee.

After the battle of Cold Harbor, the geography of the country no longer enabled General Grant, by a flank movement to his left, to keep himself covered by a stream, and yet draw nearer to his objective point, Richmond. He had now reached the Chickahominy, and to move down the east bank of that stream would be to depart further from the prize he sought, the capital of the Confederacy. His overland march had cost him the loss of more men than Lee's army contained at the beginning of the campaign. He now, from considerations which may fairly be assumed to have been the result of his many unsuccessful assaults on Lee's army, or from other considerations which I am not in a position to suggest, decided to seek a new base on the James River, and to attempt the capture of our capital by a movement from the south. With this view, on the night of June 12th he commenced a movement by the lower crossings of the Chickahominy toward the James River. General Lee learned of the withdrawal on the next morning, and moved to our pontoon-bridge above Drury's Bluff. While Grant's army was making this march to James River, General Smith, with his division, which had arrived at Bermuda Hundred, was, on the night of the 14th, directed to move against Petersburg, with an additional force of two divisions, it being supposed that this column would be sufficient to effect what General Butler's previous attempts had utterly failed to accomplish, the capture of Petersburg and the destruction of the Southern Railroad. On the morning of the 15th the attack was made, the exterior redoubts and rifle-pits were carried, and the column advanced toward the inner works, but the artillery was used so effectively as to impress the commander of the assailants with the idea that there must be a large supporting force of infantry, and the attack was suspended so as to allow the columns in rear to come up.

Hancock's corps was on the south side of the James River, before the attack on Petersburg commenced, and was ordered to move forward, but not informed that an attack was to be made, nor directed to march to Petersburg until late in the afternoon, when he received orders to move to the aid of General Smith. It being night when the junction was made, it was deemed prudent to wait until morning. Had they known how feeble was the garrison, it is probable that Petersburg would have been captured that night; but with the morning came another change, as marked as that from darkness to light. Lee crossed the James River on the 15th, and by a night march his advance was in the entrenchments of Petersburg before the morning for which the enemy was waiting. The artillery now had other support than the old men and boys of the town.

The Confederates promptly seized the commanding points and rapidly strengthened their lines, so that the morning's reconnaissance indicated to the enemy the propriety of postponing an attack until all his force should arrive.

On the 17th an assault was made with such spirit and force as to gain a part of our line, in which, however, the assailants suffered severely. Lee had now constructed a line in rear of the one first occupied, having such advantages as gave to our army much greater power to resist. On the morning of the 18th Grant ordered a general assault, but finding that the former line had been evacuated, and a new one on more commanding ground had been constructed, the assault was postponed until the afternoon; then attacks were made by heavy columns on various parts of our line, with some partial success, but the final result was failure everywhere, and with extraordinary sacrifice of life.

With his usual persistence, he had made attack after attack, and for the resulting carnage had no gain to compensate. The eagerness manifested leads to the supposition that it was expected to capture the place while Lee with part of his force was guarding against an advance on Richmond by the river road. The four days' experience seems to have convinced Grant of the impolicy of assault, for thereafter he commenced to lay siege to the place. On the 21st a heavy force of the enemy was advanced more to our right, in the vicinity of the Weldon Railroad, which runs southward from Petersburg. But General Lee, observing an interval between the left of the Second and right of the Sixth of the enemy's corps, sent forward a column under General A. P. Hill, which, entering the interval, poured a fire into the flank of one corps on the right and the other on the left, doubling their flank divisions up on their center, and driving them with disorder and with heavy loss. Several entire regiments, a battery, and many standards were captured, when Hill, having checked the advance which was directed against the Weldon Railroad, withdrew with his captures to his former position, bringing with him the guns and nearly three thousand prisoners.

On the same night, a cavalry expedition, consisting of the divisions of Generals Wilson and Kautz, numbering about six thousand men, was sent west to cut the Weldon, Southside, and Danville Railroads, which connected our army with the south and west. This raid resulted in important injury to our communications. The enemy's cavalry tore up large distances of the tracks of all three of the railroads, burning the wood-work and laying waste the country around. But they were pursued and harassed by a small body of cavalry under General W. H. F. Lee, and, on their return near Ream's Station, were met, near Sapponey Church, by a force of fifteen hundred cavalry under General Hampton. That officer at once attacked. The fighting continued fiercely throughout the night, and at dawn the enemy's cavalry retreated in confusion. Near Ream's Station, at which point they attempted to cross the Weldon Railroad, they were met by General Fitzhugh Lee's horsemen and a body of infantry under General Mahone, and the force completed their discomfiture. After a brief attempt to force their way, they broke in disorder, leaving behind them twelve pieces of artillery, and more than a thousand prisoners, and many wagons and ambulances. The railroads were soon repaired, and the enemy's cavalry was for the time rendered unfit for service.

Every attempt made to force General Lee's lines having proved unsuccessful, General Grant determined upon the method of slow approaches, and proceeded to confront the city with a line of earthworks, and, by gradually extending the line to his left, he hoped to reach out toward the Weldon and Southside Railroads. To obtain possession of these roads now became the special object with him, and all his movements had regard to that end. Petersburg is twenty-two miles south of Richmond, and is connected with the south and west by the Weldon and Southside Railroads, the latter of which crosses the Danville Railroad, the main line of communication between Richmond and the Gulf States. With the enemy once holding these roads and those north of the city, Richmond would be isolated, and it would have been necessary for the Confederate army to evacuate eastern Virginia.

It will be seen from what has been written that, though the operations against Petersburg have been ordinarily called a siege, it could not in strictness of language be so denominated, as the communications in the rear, as well as to the north and south, were still open. It was really a conflict between opposing intrenchments.

General Grant had crossed a force into Charles City, on the north bank of the James, and thus menaced Richmond with an assault from that quarter. His line extended thence across the neck of the peninsula of Bermuda Hundred, and east and south of Petersburg, where it gradually stretched westward, approaching nearer and nearer to the railroads bringing the supplies for our army and for Richmond. The line of General Lee conformed to that of General Grant. In addition to the works east and southeast of Richmond, an exterior line of defense had been constructed against the hostile forces at Deep Bottom, and, in addition to a fortification of some strength at Drury's Bluff, obstructions were placed in the river to prevent the ascent of the Federal gunboats. The lines thence continued facing those of the enemy north of the Appomattox, and, crossing that stream, extended around the city of Petersburg, gradually moving westward with the works of the enemy. The struggle that ensued consisted chiefly of attempts to break through our lines. These it is not my purpose to notice *seriatim*; some of them, however, it is thought necessary to mention. While at Petersburg, the assaults of the enemy were met by a resistance sufficient to repel his most vigorous attacks; our force confronting Deep Bottom was known to be so small as to suggest an attempt to capture Richmond by a movement on the north side of the James. On the 26th of July a corps of infantry was sent over to Deep Bottom to move against our pontoon-bridges near to Drury's Bluff, so as to prevent Lee from sending reënforcements to the north side of the James, while Sheridan with his cavalry moved to the north side of Richmond to attack the works which, being poorly garrisoned, it was thought might be taken by assault. Lee, discovering the movement after the enemy had gained some partial success, sent over reënforcements, which drove him back and defeated the expedition. On the night of the 28th the infantry corps (Hancock's) was secretly withdrawn from the north side of the river, to coöperate in the grand assault which Grant was preparing to make upon Lee's intrenchments. The uniform failure, as has been stated, of the assaults upon our lines had caused the conclusion that they could only succeed after a breach had been made in the works. For that purpose a subterranean gallery for a mine was run under one of our forts. General Burnside, who conducted the operation, thus describes the work:

"The main gallery of the mine is five hundred and twenty-two feet in length, the side-galleries about forty feet each. My suggestion is that eight magazines be placed in the lateral galleries, two at each end, say a few feet apart, at right angles to the side-gallery, and two more in each of the side-galleries, similarly placed by pairs, situated equidistant from each other, and the end of the galleries, thus:

[Illustration: Mine Galleries]

"I proposed to put in each of the eight magazines from twelve to fourteen hundred pounds of powder, the magazines to be connected by a trough of powder instead of a fuse."

It appears that it was decided that the charge should be eight thousand pounds instead of the larger amount proposed.[119] Between four and five o'clock on the morning of the 30th of July the mine was exploded, and simultaneously the enemy's batteries commenced firing, when, as previously arranged, the column of attack moved forward to the breach, with instructions to rush through it and seize the crest of a ridge in rear of our fort, so as to interpose a force between our troops and in rear of our batteries. A question had arisen as to whether the assaulting column should consist of white or negro troops; of each, there were brigades in General Burnside's division, which occupied that part of the line nearest to the mine, and therefore seems to have been considered as the command from which the troops to constitute the storming column must be selected. The explosion was destructive to our artillery and its small supporting force immediately above the mine.

An opening, one hundred and fifty feet long, sixty feet wide, and thirty feet deep, suddenly appeared in the place of the earthworks, and the division of the enemy selected for the charge rushed forward to pierce the opening. A Southern writer[120] thus describes what ensued:

"The white division charged, reached the crater, stumbled over the *debris*, were suddenly met by a merciless fire of artillery fusillading them right and left and of infantry fusillade them in front; faltered, hesitated, were badly led, lost heart, gave up the plan of seizing the crest in rear, huddled into the crater man on top of man, company mingled with company; and upon this disordered, unstrung, quivering mass of human beings, white and black—for the black troops had followed—was poured a hurricane of shot, shell, canister, musketry, which made the hideous crater a slaughter-pen, horrible and frightful, beyond the power of words. All order was lost; all idea of charging the crest abandoned. Lee's infantry was seen concentrating for the carnival of death; his artillery was massing to destroy the remnants of the charging divisions; those who deserted the crater, to scramble over the debris and run back, were shot down; then all that was left to the shuddering mass of blacks and whites in the pit was to shrink lower, evade the horrible *mitraille*, and wait for a charge of their friends to rescue them or surrender."

The forces of the enemy finally succeeded in making their way back, with a loss of about four thousand prisoners, and General Lee, whose casualties were small, reestablished his line without interruption. This affair was subsequently investigated by a committee of the Congress of the United States, and their report declared that "the first and great cause of the disaster was the employment of white instead of black troops to make the charge."

Attacks continued to be made on our lines during the months of August and September, but, as in former instances, they were promptly repulsed. On August 18th the enemy seized on a portion of the Weldon Railroad near Petersburg, and on the 25th this success was followed up by an attempt, under General Hancock, to take possession of Reams's Station on the same road, farther south. He was defeated by Heth's division and a portion of Wilcox's, under the direction of General A. P. Hill, and, having lost heavily, was compelled to retreat. These events did not, however, materially affect the general result. The enemy's left gradually reached farther and farther westward, until it had passed the Vaughan, Squirrel Level, and other roads running southwestward from Petersburg, and in October was established on the left bank of Hatcher's Run. The movement was designed to reach the Southside Railroad. A heavy column crossed Hatcher's Run, and made an obstinate attack on our lines, in order to break through to the railroad. This column was met in front and flank by Generals Hampton and W. H. F. Lee, with dismounted sharpshooters. Infantry was hastened forward by General Lee, and the enemy was driven back. This closed for the winter active operations against our lines at Petersburg.

When the campaign opened on the Rapidan, General Lee's effective strength was in round numbers sixty thousand of all arms; that of General Grant at the same time one hundred and forty thousand. In the many battles fought before the close of the campaign. Grant's loss had been a multiple of that sustained by Lee; but the large reënforcements he had received, both before and after he crossed the James River, repaired his losses, and must have increased the numerical disparity between the two armies; yet, notwithstanding the great superiority in the number of his force, the long-projected movement for the reduction of Fort Fisher and the capture of Wilmington was delayed, because of Grant's unwillingness to detach any of his troops for that purpose until after active operations had been suspended before Petersburg.

It was proposed to make a combined land and naval attack— Major-General B. F, Butler to command the land-forces, and Admiral D. D. Porter the fleet. The enemy seems about this time to have conceived a new means of destroying forts; it was, to place a large amount of powder in a ship, and, having anchored off the fort, to explode the powder and so destroy the works and incapacitate the garrison as to enable a storming party to capture them. How near to Fort Fisher it was expected to anchor the ship I do not know, nor have I learned how far it was supposed the open atmosphere could be made to act as a projectile. General Whiting, the brave and highly accomplished soldier, who was in command of the defenses of Wilmington, stated that the powder-ship did not come nearer to Fort Fisher than twelve or fifteen hundred yards. He further stated that he heard the report of the explosion at Wilmington, and sent a telegram to Colonel Lamb, the commanding officer at the fort, to inquire what it meant, and was answered, "Enemy's gunboat blown up." No effect, as might have been anticipated, was produced on the fort.[121] From the same source it is learned that the combined force of this expedition was about six thousand five hundred land-troops and fifty vessels of war of various sizes and classes, several ironclads, and the ship charged with two hundred and thirty-five tons of powder. Some of the troops landed, but after a reconnaissance of the fort, which then had a garrison of about six thousand five hundred men, the troops were reembarked, and thus the expedition ended.

On January 15, 1865, the attempt was renewed with a larger number of troops, amounting, after the arrival of General Schofield, to twenty-odd thousand. Porter's fleet also received additional vessels, making the whole number fifty-eight engaged in the attack. The garrison of Fort Fisher had been increased to about double the number of men there on the 24th of December. The iron-clad vessels of the enemy approached nearer the fort than on a former occasion, and the fire of the fleet was more concentrated and vastly more effective. Many of the guns in the fort were dismounted, and the parapets seriously injured, by the fire. The garrison stood bravely to their guns, and, when the assault was made, fought with such determined courage as to repulse the first column, and obstinately contended with another approaching from the land-side, continuing the fight long after they had got into the fort. Finally, overwhelmed by numbers, and after the fort and its armament had been mainly destroyed by a bombardment—I believe greater than ever before concentrated upon a fort—the remnant of the garrison surrendered. The heroic and highly gifted General Whiting was mortally, and the gallant commander of the fort, Colonel Lamb, was seriously, wounded. They both fell into the hands of the enemy. General Hoke, distinguished by brilliant service on other fields, had been ordered down to support the garrison, and under the directions of General Bragg, commanding the department, had advanced to attack the investing force, but a reconnaissance convinced them both that his command was too weak to effect the object. The other forts, of necessity, fell with the main work, Fisher, and were abandoned. Hoke, with his small force retiring through Wilmington, after destroying the public vessels and property, to prevent them from falling into the hands of the enemy, slowly fell back, fighting at several points, and seeking to find in the separation of the vastly superior army which was following him opportunity to attack a force the number of which should not greatly exceed his own, and finally made a junction with General Johnston, then opposing Sherman's advance through North Carolina.

The fixed purpose of General Grant's campaign of 1864 was the capture of Richmond, the Confederate capital. For this he had assembled the large army with which he crossed the Rapidan and fought the numerous battles between there and the James River. For this he had moved against Petersburg, the capture of which in itself was not an object so important as to have justified the effort made to that end. It was only valuable because it was on the line of communication with the more southern States, and offered another approach to Richmond. In his attack upon Petersburg it will be seen from the events already described that he adopted neither of the two plans which were open to him: the one, the concentration of all his efforts to break the line covering Petersburg; the other, to move his army round it and seize the Weldon and Southside Railroads, so as to cut off the supplies of Lee's army and compel the evacuation of both Petersburg and Richmond. Had there been approximate equality between his army and that of Lee, he could not wisely have ventured upon the latter movement against a soldier so able as his antagonist; but the vast numerical superiority of Grant's army might well have induced him to invite Lee to meet him in the open field. He did, however, neither the one nor the other, but something of both.

In the opening of the campaign of 1865, he continued, as he had done in 1864, to extend his line to the left, seeking, after having gained the Weldon Railroad, to reach still farther to that connecting Petersburg with the Richmond and Danville Railroad. Lee, with a well-deserved confidence in his troops and his usual intrepidity, drew from his lines of defense men enough to enable him for a long time to defeat the enemy in these efforts, by extension to turn his right flank. After Grant's demonstration on the north side of the James by sending over Hancock's corps had been virtually abandoned by its withdrawal, Longstreet's corps, which had been sent to oppose it, remained for a long time on the north side of the James. Finally, General Ewell with a few troops, the Richmond reserves, and a division of the navy under Admiral Semmes, held the river and land defenses on the east side of Richmond.

General A. R. Lawton, who had become the quartermaster-general of the Confederate army, ably supported by Lewis E. Harvie, President of the Richmond and Danville Railroad, increased the carrying capacity of that line so as to compensate for our loss of the use of the Weldon Railroad. At the same time, General St. John, chief of the commissariat, by energetic efforts and the use of the Virginia Canal, kept up the supplies of General Lee's army, so as to secure from him the complimentary acknowledgment, made about a month before the evacuation of Petersburg, that the army there had not been so well supplied for many months.

During the months of February and March, Lee's army was materially reduced by the casualties of battle and the frequency of absence without leave. I will not call these absentees deserters, because they did not leave to join the enemy, and again, because in some instances where the facts were fully developed, they had gone to their necessitous families with intent to return and resume their places in the line of battle. His cavalry force had been also diminished by the absence of General Hampton's division, to which permission had been given to go to their home, South Carolina, to get fresh horses, and also to fill up their ranks. Long, arduous, and distant service had rendered both necessary.

In the early part of March, as well as my memory can fix the date, General Lee held with me a long and free conference. He stated that the circumstances had forced on him the conclusion that the evacuation of Petersburg was but a question of time. He had early and fully appreciated the embarrassment which would result from losing the workshops and foundry at Richmond, which had been our main reliance for the manufacture and repair of arms as well as the preparation of ammunition. The importance of Richmond in this regard was, however, then less than it had been by the facilities which had been created for these purposes at Augusta, Selma, Fayetteville, and some smaller establishments; also by the progress which was being made for a large armory at Macon, Georgia. To my inquiry whether it would not be better to anticipate the necessity by withdrawing at once, he said that his artillery and draught horses were too weak for the roads in their then condition, and that he would have to wait until they became firmer. There naturally followed the consideration of the line of retreat. A considerable time before this General Hood had sent me a paper, presenting his views and conclusion that, if it became necessary for the Army of Northern Virginia to retreat, it should move toward Middle Tennessee. The paper was forwarded to General Lee and returned by him with an unfavorable criticism, and the conclusion that, if we had to retreat, it should be in a southwardly direction toward the country from which we were drawing supplies, and from which a large portion of our forces had been derived. In this conversation the same general view was more specifically stated, and made to apply to the then condition of affairs. The programme was to retire to Danville, at which place supplies should be collected and a junction made with the troops under General J. E. Johnston, the combined force to be hurled upon Sherman in North Carolina, with the hope of defeating him before Grant could come to his relief. Then the more southern States, freed from pressure and encouraged by this success, it was expected, would send large reënforcements to the army, and Grant, drawn far from his base of supplies into the midst of a hostile population, it was hoped, might yet be defeated, and Virginia be delivered from the invader. Efforts were energetically continued, to collect supplies in depots where they would be available, and, in furtherance of the suggestion of General Lee as to the necessary improvement in the condition of his horses, the quartermaster-general was instructed to furnish larger rations of corn to the quartermaster at Petersburg.

Though of unusually calm and well-balanced judgment, General Lee was instinctively averse to retiring from his enemy, and had so often beaten superior numbers that his thoughts were no doubt directed to every possible expedient which might enable him to avoid retreat. It thus fell out that, in a week or two after the conference above noticed, he presented to me the idea of a sortie against the enemy near to the right of his line. This was rendered the more feasible, from the constant extension of Grant's line to the left, and the heavy bodies of troops he was employing to turn our right. The sortie, if entirely successful, so as to capture and hold the works on Grant's right, as well as three forts on the commanding ridge in his rear, would threaten his line of communication with his base, City Point, and might compel him to move his forces around ours to protect it; if only so far successful as to cause the transfer of his troops from his left to his right, it would relieve our right, and delay the impending disaster for the more convenient season for retreat.

Fort Steadman was the point against which the sortie was directed; its distance from our lines was less than two hundred yards, but an abatis covered its front. For this service, requiring equal daring and steadiness, General John B. Gordon, well proved on many battle-fields, was selected. His command was the remnant of Ewell's corps, troops often tried in the fiery ordeal of battle, and always found true as tempered steel. Before daylight, on the morning of the 25th of March, Gordon moved his command silently forward. His pioneers were sent in advance to make openings through the obstructions, and the troops rushed forward, surprised and captured the garrison, then turned the guns upon the adjacent works and soon drove the enemy from them. A detachment was now sent to seize the commanding ground and works in the rear, the batteries of which, firing into the gorges of the forts on the right and left, would soon make a wide opening in Grant's line. The guides to this detachment misled it in the darkness of a foggy dawn far from the point to which it was directed. In the mean time the enemy, recovering from his surprise and the confusion into which he had been extensively thrown, rallied and with overwhelming power concentrated both artillery and infantry upon Gordon's command. The supporting force which was to have followed him, notwithstanding the notice which was given by the victorious cheer of his men when they took Fort Steadman, failed to come forward, and Gordon's brilliant success, like the Dead Sea fruit, was turned to ashes at the moment of possession. It was hopeless, with his small force unsupported, to retain the position he had gained. It only remained as far as practicable to withdraw his command to our line, and this the valiant soldier promptly proceeded to do; some of his men were killed on the retreat, many became prisoners—I believe all, or nearly all, of those who had been detached to seize other works, and had not rejoined the main body.

The following letter from General Gordon furnishes some important details of the attack:

"ATLANTA, GEORGIA, *October 16, 1880.*

"MY DEAR MR. PRESIDENT: The attack upon Fort Steadman was made on the night of the 25th March, or rather before light on the morning of the 26th March, 1865. A conference had been held between General Lee and myself at his headquarters the 10th of March, which resulted in General Lee's decision to transfer my corps from the extreme right of our army to the trenches in and around Petersburg, with the purpose of enabling me to carefully examine the enemy's lines, and report to him my belief as to the practicability of breaking them at any point. Within a week after being transferred to this new position, I decided that Fort Steadman

443

could be taken by a night assault, and that it might be possible to throw into the breach thus made in Grant's lines a sufficient force to disorganize and destroy the left wing of his army before he could recover and concentrate his forces, then lying beyond the James and Appomattox Rivers. Fort Steadman was the point at which the earthworks of General Grant most nearly approached our own. This fort was located upon what was known as Hare's Hill, and was in front of the city of Petersburg, and of the point on our lines known as Colquitt's Salient. The two hostile lines could not have been more than two hundred to two hundred and fifty yards apart at this point; and the pickets were so close together that it was difficult to prevent constant conversation between those of the Confederate and Federal armies. Fort Steadman was upon the main line of General Grant's works, and flanked on either side by a line of earthworks and other forts, which completely commanded every foot of the intervening space between the hostile lines. In rear of Fort Steadman were three other forts, two of which, and perhaps all three, could command Fort Steadman, in case of its capture by our forces. These forts in rear of Steadman were protected by an almost impenetrable abatis, while, in front of Fort Steadman itself, and of the main line of which it was a part, was a line of sharpened fence-rails, with the lower ends buried deeply in the ground, their middle resting upon horizontal poles and wrapped with telegraph-wires, and their upper ends sharpened and elevated to the height of four and a half or five feet. These rails, which formed the obstruction in front of General Grant's lines at Fort Steadman and along the flanking works, were, as I said, wrapped with telegraph-wire where they rested on the horizontal poles, so as to prevent an attacking force from pressing them apart, and buried in the ground too deeply to be pulled up, and, sharpened at the upper end, were too high to be mounted by my men. This obstruction, therefore, had to be cut away with axes before the attacking force could enter the fort or lines.

"General Lee, after considering the plan of assault and battle which I submitted to him, and which I shall presently describe, gave me orders to prepare for the movement, which was regarded by both of us as a desperate one, but which seemed to give more promise of good results than any other hitherto suggested. General Lee placed at my disposal, in addition to my own corps, a portion of A. P, Hill's and a portion of Longstreet's, and a detachment of cavalry—in all, about one half of the army.

"The general plan of the assault and battle was this: To take the fort by a rush across the narrow space that lay between it and Colquitt's Salient, and then surprise and capture, by a stratagem, the commanding forts in the rear, thus opening a way for our troops to pass to the rear, and upon the bank of the left wing of Grant's army, which was to be broken to pieces by a concentration of all the forces at my command moving upon that flank. During the night of the 25th my preparations were made for the movement before daylight. I placed three officers in charge of three separate bodies of men, and directed them, as soon as the lines of Fort Steadman should be carried by the assaulting column, to rush through the gap thus produced to the three rear forts—one of these officers and bodies of men to go to each fort, and to approach them from their rear by the only avenue left open and seize those forts. A guide was placed with each of these officers, who was to conduct him and his troops to the rear of the front, which he was to surprise. A body of the most stalwart of my men was organized to move in advance of all the troops, armed with axes, with which they were to cut down the obstruction of sharpened and wire-fastened rails in front of the enemy's lines.

"Next to these were to come three hundred men, armed with bayonets fixed and empty muskets, who were to mount and enter the fort as the axemen cut away the obstruction of sharpened rails, bayoneting the pickets in front and gunners in the fort if they resisted, or sending them to our rear if they

445

surrendered. Next were to cross the three officers and their detachments, who were to capture the three rear forts. Next, a division of infantry was to cross, moving by the left flank, so as to be in position when halted, and fronted to move without any confusion or delay immediately down General Grant's lines, toward his left, capturing his troops, or forcing them to abandon their works and form under our advancing fire at right angles to his line of works.

"Next was to cross the cavalry, who were to ride to the rear, cut the enemy's telegraph-lines, capture his pontoons, and prevent or delay the crossing of reënforcements from beyond the Appomattox. Next, my whole force was to swell the column of attack. Then, as the front of our lines were cleared of the enemy's troops, our divisions were to change front and join in pressing upon the enemy and driving him farther from the other wing of General Grant's army, and widening the breach. Strips of white cloth were tied around the shoulders of our men, so as to designate them in the darkness.

"Just before daylight, when all was ready, I gave the signal, and the axemen rushed across, followed by the bodies armed with bayonets and empty muskets, who captured and sent to the rear the enemy's pickets. The axemen cut away the sharpened rails so rapidly as scarcely to cause a halt of the troops following, who mounted the enemy's works and seized his guns and gunners in the fort, clearing the way and giving safe passage to detachments and larger bodies which were to follow and which did follow. The fort and most of the lines between the fort and the river were captured with the loss of but one man, so far as I could learn. We captured eleven heavy guns, nine mortars, about seven hundred prisoners, as I now recollect, among whom was the brigadier commanding that portion of the line, General McLaughlin.

"Everything was moving as well as I could have desired, when, one after another, all three of the officers, sent to the rear to capture by stratagem the rear forts, sent messengers to inform me that they had passed successfully through the lines of the enemy's reserves in rear of Fort Steadman, and were certainly beyond the rear forts, but that their guides had been lost or had deserted, and that they could not find the forts.

"Although I heard nothing afterward of these guides, yet I did learn of the fate of the three officers and their commands. Some were shot down after daylight, some were captured, and a few, very few, made their way back to our lines. The failure of that portion of the programme left, of course, these three forts manned by the enemy, and his heavy guns made it impossible to carry out literally the details of the plan. Then a large body of the troops sent by General Lee from General Longstreet's corps were delayed by the breaking down of trains, or by some other cause, and did not arrive at the appointed hour, which caused so great a delay that we did not get in the fort and upon the enemy's flank at as early an hour as was expected, and daylight found us with the plan only half executed. At daylight, all the commanding forts in the rear, which we had failed to capture, opened upon Fort Steadman and that portion of the enemy's lines held by our troops. Reënforcements were rapidly brought up, so that it became too hazardous, as General Lee thought, to go forward or attempt it. So he ordered me back (I may say here that I entirely approved of this decision of General Lee). Up to this hour we had lost but few men, and these had been killed or wounded mainly by artillery. But now the enemy's infantry came up and made several assaults. They were repulsed by our troops in Fort Steadman and in the enemy's works on its flanks. It was in the effort to withdraw the troops that our principal loss occurred. A raking fire was kept up across the intervening space over which we had moved in capturing the fort, I was wounded in recrossing to Colquitt's Salient, and many of our men were killed and wounded in making the same passage back to our works.

"As I said at the outset, this attack was regarded by both General Lee and myself as very hazardous; but it seemed necessary to do more than sit quietly waiting for General Grant to move upon our right, while each day was diminishing our strength by disease and death.

"Let me also add that the movement made at Hare's Hill mast have proved a great success but for the unforeseen and unavoidable miscarriages to which I have referred.

"I am, very respectfully, your obedient servant,

"J. B. GORDON.

"Hon. JEFFERSON DAVIS, *Mississippi*."

Immediately following, and perhaps in consequence of this sortie, an extensive attack was made upon our lines to the left of Fort Steadman, but without any decisive results. On the 27th of March the main part of Grant's forces confronting Richmond were moved over to the lines before Petersburg, and his left was on the same day joined by Sheridan's division of cavalry. It will be remembered that Lee had sent Longstreet to the north side of the James as soon as he discovered that Grant had sent a corps across with the supposed purpose of attacking Richmond from that side. It was intended that Longstreet should return whenever the enemy withdrew his main force from the north side of the James; but it appears that this was so secretly done as to conceal the fact from General Longstreet, and that both Hancock and Ord had joined Grant, to swell his forces by two corps before our troops returned to join Lee. Grant, thus strengthened, made a more determined movement to gain the right of Lee's position; before, however, he was ready to make his assault, Lee marched with a comparatively very small force, took the initiative, and on the 31st struck the enemy's advance, and repulsed him in great confusion, following until confronted by the heavy masses formed in open ground in the rear, when Lee withdrew his men back to their intrenchments.

A strategic position of recognized importance was that known as Five Forks. Lee had stationed there Major-General Pickett with his division, and some additional force. On the next day, the 1st of April, this position was assaulted, and our troops were driven from it in confusion. The unsettled question of time was now solved.

Grant's massive columns, advancing on right, left, and center, compelled our forces to retire to the inner line of defense, so that, on the morning of the 2d, the enemy was in a condition to besiege Petersburg in the true sense of that term. Battery Gregg made an obstinate defense, and, with a garrison of about two hundred and fifty men, held a corps in check for a large part of the day. The arrival of Longstreet's troops, and the strength of the shorter line now held by Lee, enabled him to make several attempts to dislodge his assailant from positions he had gained. In one of these, the distinguished soldier whose gallantry and good conduct it has frequently been my pleasure to notice, Lieutenant-General A. P. Hill, who had so often passed unscathed through storms of shot and shell, yielded up the life he had, in the beginning of the war, consecrated to the Confederate cause; and his comrades, while mourning his loss, have drawn consolation from the fact that he died before our flag was furled in defeat.

Retreat was now a present necessity. All that could be done was to hold the inner lines during the day, and make needful preparations to withdraw at night. In the forenoon of Sunday, the 2d, I received, when in church, a telegram announcing that the army would retire from Petersburg at night, and I went to my office to give needful directions for the evacuation of Richmond, the greatest difficulty of which was the withdrawal of the troops who were on the defenses east of the city, and along the James River.

The event had come before Lee had expected it, and the announcement was received by us in Richmond with sorrow and surprise; for, though it had been foreseen as a coming event which might possibly, though not probably, be averted, and such preparation as was practicable had been made to meet the contingency when it should occur, it was not believed to be so near at hand.

At nightfall our army commenced crossing the Appomattox, and, before dawn, was far on its way toward Amelia Court-House, Lee's purpose being, as previously agreed on in conference with me, to march to Danville, Virginia. By a reference to the map, it will be seen that General Grant, starting from the south side of the Appomattox, had a shorter line to Danville than that which General Lee must necessarily follow, and, if Grant directed his march so as to put his forces between Danville and those of Lee, it was quite possible for him to effect it. This was done, and thus Lee was prevented from carrying out his original purpose, and directed his march toward Lynchburg. The enemy, having first placed himself across the route to Danville, at Jetersville, subsequently took up the line of Lee's retreat. His large force of cavalry, and the exhausted condition of the horses of our small number of that arm, gave the pursuing foe a very great advantage; but, worn and reduced in numbers as Lee's army was, the spirit it had always shown flashed out whenever it was pressed. A division would turn upon a corps and drive it; and General Fitzhugh Lee, the worthy successor of the immortal Stuart, with a brigade of our emaciated cavalry, would drive a division of their pursuers. These scenes were repeatedly enacted during the long march from Petersburg to Appomattox Court-House, and have been so vividly and fully described by others that I will pass to the closing event.

Lee had never contemplated surrender. He had, long before, in language similar to that employed by Washington during the Revolution, expressed to me the belief that in the mountains of Virginia he could carry on the war for twenty years, and, in directing his march toward Lynchburg, it may well be that as an alternative he hoped to reach those mountains, and, with the advantage which the topography would give, yet to baffle the hosts which were following him. On the evening of the 8th General Lee decided, after conference with his corps commanders, that he would advance the next morning beyond Appomattox Court-House, and, if the force reported to be there should prove to be only Sheridan's cavalry, to disperse it and continue the march toward Lynchburg; but, if infantry should be found in large force, the attempt to break through it was not to be made, and the correspondence which General Grant had initiated on the previous day should be reopened by a flag, with propositions for an interview to arrange the terms of capitulation. Gordon, whose corps formed the rear-guard from Petersburg, and who had fought daily for the protection of the trains, had now been transferred to the front. On the next morning, before daylight, Lee sent Colonel Venable, one of his staff, to Gordon, commanding the advance, to learn his opinion as to the chances of a successful attack, to which Gordon replied, "My old corps is reduced to a frazzle, and, unless I am supported by Longstreet heavily, I do not think we can do anything more." When Colonel Venable returned with this answer to General Lee, he said, "Then there is nothing left me but to go and see General Grant."

At that time Longstreet, covering the rear, was threatened by Meade, so that there was no ability to reënforce Gordon, and thus to explain why General Lee then realized that the emergency had arisen for the surrender of his army which, in his note to General Grant of the previous day, he had said he did not believe to exist. Colonel Venable, at early dawn, had left Gordon with about five thousand infantry, and Fitzhugh Lee with about fifteen hundred cavalry, and Colonel Carter's battalion of artillery, forming his line of battle to attack the enemy, which, so far as then known, consisted of Sheridan's cavalry, which had got in front of our retreating column. The assault was made with such vigor and determination as to drive Sheridan for a considerable distance; and, if this had been the only obstacle, the road would have been opened for Lee to resume his march toward Lynchburg. After Gordon had advanced nearly a mile, he was confronted by a large body of infantry, subsequently ascertained to be about eighty thousand. To attack that force was, of course, hopeless, and Gordon commenced falling back, and simultaneously the enemy advanced, but suddenly came to a halt. Lee had sent a flag to Grant, who had consequently ordered a suspension of hostilities.

A leader less resolute, an army less heroically resisting fatigue, constant watching, and starvation, would long since have reached the conclusion that surrender was a necessity. Lee had left Petersburg with not more than twenty thousand infantry, five thousand cavalry, and four thousand artillery. Men and horses all reduced below the standard of efficiency by exposure and insufficient supplies of clothing, food,[122] and forage, only the mutual confidence between the men and their commander could have sustained either under the trials to which they were subjected. It is not a matter of surprise that the army had wasted away to a mere remnant, but rather that it had continued to exist as an organized body still willing to do battle. All the evidence we have proves that the proud, cheerful spirit both of the army and its leader had resisted the extremes of privation and danger, and never sunk until confronted by surrender.

General Grant, in response to a communication under a white flag made by General Lee, as stated above, came to Appomattox, where a suitable room was procured for their conference, and, the two Generals being seated at a small table. General Lee opened the interview thus:

"General, I deem it due to proper candor and frankness to say at the very beginning of this interview that I am not willing even to discuss any terms of surrender inconsistent with the honor of my army, which I am determined to maintain to the last."

General Grant replied:

"I have no idea of proposing dishonorable terms, General, but I would be glad if you would state what you consider honorable terms."

General Lee then briefly stated the terms upon which he would be willing to surrender. Grant expressed himself as satisfied with them, and Lee requested that he would formally reduce the propositions to writing.

To present a full and satisfactory account of the circumstances and terms of the surrender, as well as the events immediately preceding the evacuation of Petersburg, and the retreat thence to Appomattox Court-House, I annex the subjoined letters:

"APPOMATTOX COURT-HOUSE, *April 9, 1865.*

"General R. E. LEE, *commanding Confederate States Army:*

"In accordance with the substance of my letter to you of the 8th inst., I propose to receive the surrender of the Army of Northern Virginia on the following terms, to wit:

"Rolls of all the officers and men to be made in duplicate, one copy to be given to an officer designated by me, the other to be retained by such officers as you may designate.

"The officers to give their individual parole not to take arms against the Government of the United States until properly exchanged, and each company or regimental commander to sign a like parole for the men of their commands.

"The arms, artillery, and public property to be parked and stacked and turned over to the officers appointed by me to receive them.

"This will not embrace the side-arms of the officers, nor their private horses or baggage.

"This done, each officer and man will be allowed to return to their homes, not to be disturbed by the United States authority so long as they observe their parole and the laws in force where they may reside.

"Very respectfully,

"U. S. GRANT, *Lieutenant-General.*"

"HEADQUARTERS ARMY OF NORTHERN VIRGINIA, *April 9, 1865.*

"GENERAL: I have received your letter of this date containing the terms of surrender of the Army of Northern Virginia, as proposed by you. As they are substantially the same as those expressed in your letter of the 8th inst., they are accepted. I will proceed to designate the proper officers to carry the stipulations into effect.

"Very respectfully, your obedient servant,

"R. E. LEE."

"PETERSBURG, VIRGINIA, 3 P.M., *April 2, 1865.*

"His Excellency JEFFERSON DAVIS, *Richmond, Virginia.*

"MR. PRESIDENT: Your letter of the 1st is just received. I have been willing to detach officers to recruit negro troops, and sent in the names of many who are desirous of recruiting companies, battalions, or regiments, to the War Department. After receiving the general orders on that subject establishing recruiting depots in the several States, I supposed that this mode of raising the troops was preferred. I will continue to submit the names of those who offer for the service, and whom I deem competent, to the War Department; but, among the numerous applications which are presented, it is difficult for me to decide who are suitable for the duty. I am glad your Excellency has made an appeal to the Governors of the States, and hope it will have a good effect. I have a great desire to confer with you upon our condition, and would have been to Richmond before this, but, anticipating movements of the enemy which have occurred, I felt unwilling to be absent. I have considered our position very critical; but have hoped that the enemy might expose himself in some way that we might take advantage of, and cripple him. Knowing when Sheridan moved on our right that our cavalry would be unable to resist successfully his advance upon our communications, I detached Pickett's division to support it. At first Pickett succeeded in driving the enemy, who fought stubbornly; and, after being reënforced by the Fifth Corps (United States Army), obliged Pickett to recede to the Five Forks on the Dinwiddie Court-House and Ford's road, where, unfortunately, he was yesterday defeated. To relieve him, I had to again draw out three brigades under General Anderson, which so weakened our front line that the enemy last night and this morning succeeded in penetrating it near the Cox road, separating our troops around the town from those on Hatcher's Run. This has enabled him to extend to the Appomattox, thus inclosing and obliging us to contract our lines to the city. I have directed the troops from the lines on Hatcher's Run, thus severed from us, to fall back toward Amelia Court-House, and I do not see how I can possibly help withdrawing from the city to the north side of the Appomattox to-night. There is no bridge over the Appomattox above this point nearer than Goode's and Bevil's over which the troops above mentioned could cross to the north side, and be made available to us; otherwise I might hold this position for a day or two longer, but would have to evacuate it eventually; and I think it better for us to abandon the whole line on James River to-night, if practicable. I have sent preparatory orders to all the officers, and will be able to tell by night whether or not we can remain here another day; but I think every hour now adds to our difficulties. I regret to be obliged to write such a hurried letter to your Excellency, but I am in the presence of the enemy, endeavoring to resist his advance.

"I am most respectfully and truly yours,

"R. E. LEE, *General.*"

[Footnote 119: Testimony of General Burnside, "Report of Committee on the Conduct of the War," vol. i, pp. 16, 17, 1865.]

[Footnote 120: John Esten Cooke, "Life of General R. E. Lee."]

[Footnote 121: "Report of Committee on the Conduct of the War" 1865, vol. ii, pp. 106, 107.]

[Footnote 122: Falsehood and malignity have combined to invent and circulate a baseless story to the effect that food ordered to Amelia Court-House for Lee's troops, was by the Administration at Richmond diverted from its destination, and the soldiers thus left to needless suffering. A further notice will be taken of this slander in a subsequent chapter, and that it had not one atom of truth in it will be shown by conclusive testimony.]

CHAPTER LIII.

General Lee advises the Evacuation of Richmond.—Withdrawal of the Troops.—The Naval Force.—The Conflagration in Richmond.—Telegram of Lee to the President.—The Evacuation complete.—The Charge of the Removal of Supplies intended for Lee's Army.—The Facts.—Arrangement with General Lee.—Proclamation.—Reports of Scouts.

When, on the morning of the 2d of April, the main line of the defenses of Petersburg was broken, and our forces driven back to the inner and last line, General Lee sent the telegram, to which reference has been already made, and advised that Richmond should be evacuated simultaneously with the withdrawal of his troops that night. This left little time for preparation, especially in the matter of providing transportation for the troops holding the eastern defenses of Richmond. To supply the cavalry, artillery, and army-wagons with horses, had so exhausted the stock of Virginia as to leave the quartermaster's department little ability to supplement the small transportation possessed, or required by troops regarded as a stationary defense. The consequence was, that their withdrawal had to be made under circumstances which involved unusual embarrassments upon the march; but soldiers, sailors, and citizens, constituting the "reserves," vied with each other in the performance of the hard duty to which they were called—a night march over unknown roads, to join a retreating army, pursued by a powerful enemy having large bodies of cavalry. The opposing lines of intrenchment north of the James were so near to each other, that our forces could only withdraw when it was too dark for observation; this required that the movement should be postponed until the moon went down, which was at a late hour of the night.

The circumstances attending the withdrawal of Ewell's corps were such as to make its safety the subject of special solicitude. It was small in comparison to that retiring from Petersburg, had a greater distance to march before a junction could be made with the main body, and most of the men were unused to marching. From reports received long after the event, I am able to give the principal occurrences of their campaign.

General G. W. C. Lee moved his division from Chapin's Bluff across the James River, on the Wilton Bridge; the wagons having been loaded under the preparatory order, were sent up in the afternoon to cross at Richmond, and the division moved on to a short distance beyond Tomahawk Church, where it encamped on the night of the 3d. General Kershaw's division, with dismounted men of Gary's cavalry brigade, crossed at Richmond and moved on to the same encampment. Having ascertained that the Appomattox could not be crossed on the route they were pursuing, the column was turned up to the railroad-bridge at the Mattoax Station, which was prepared for the passage of artillery and troops, and the two divisions, with their trains, crossed on the night of the 4th and encamped on the hills beyond the river. On the next day the column moved on to Amelia Court-House; it was now joined by the Naval Battalion, under Commodore Tucker, and the artillery battalion of Major Frank Smith, which had been withdrawn from Howlett's Bluff; both of these were added to G. W. C. Lee's division. The supply-train not being able to cross the Appomattox River near Meadville, went farther up, and, having effected a crossing, proceeded with safety until about four miles from Amelia Court-House, where it was destroyed by a detachment of the enemy's cavalry on the morning of the 5th, with the baggage of G. W. C. Lee's division and about twenty thousand good rations.

At Amelia Court-House Ewell's corps made a junction with Lee's army, but forced marches with men most of whom were untrained by previous campaign had greatly reduced the number of Ewell's command, and the want of rations now was impairing their efficiency. From that place his corps moved in rear of Anderson's, followed by the train of Lee's army, which was covered in rear by Gordon's corps. The march was much impeded by the wagon-trains, consequently slow, and, from frequent halts, fatiguing. About noon of the 6th, after crossing a small stream within several miles of Sailor's Creek, the enemy's cavalry made an attack at the point where the wagon-train turned off to the right. Skirmishers from Lee's division were thrown out, and soon repelled the attack; but it was thought necessary to retain these troops in that position until the trains had passed. General Gordon, who protected the rear, had frequent combats with the pursuers. As soon as the trains were out of the way, Ewell's troops moved on after Anderson's corps. On crossing Sailor's Creek, General Ewell reports that he met General Fitzhugh Lee, from whom he learned that a large force of cavalry held the road in front of Anderson, and was so strongly posted that he had halted. Lee's and Kershaw's divisions moved on to close upon Anderson; but Gordon having followed the wagon and artillery train, the enemy's cavalry and also infantry appeared in the rear, and commenced an attack upon Kershaw's division. Anderson had proposed to Ewell that, if he would hold the enemy in check who was coming up on the rear, he would attack the cavalry in front, to open our line of march in that direction. Lee's and Kershaw's divisions were therefore formed in line of battle faced to the rear. Anderson made the attack, but failed. Meantime an artillery-fire was opened on Kershaw's and Lee's divisions; they, having no artillery to reply, were subjected to the severe trial of standing under a fire which they could not return. In their praise, it was said they unflinchingly bore the test. Supposing probably that their artillery-fire had demoralized our troops, the enemy's infantry advanced. They were repulsed, and that portion which attacked G. W. C. Lee's artillery brigade was charged by it, and driven back across Sailor's Creek. The enemy had now turned the flank of Kershaw's division and obliged it to retire. Ewell, while seeking some route by which his command might be extricated, was captured, and the enemy closed in on Lee's division, surrounding it on every side. Firing ceased, and the division was captured. A like fate befell the division of Kershaw. A portion of Anderson's corps escaped, but Ewell's was all captured. This corps, when it left Richmond, numbered about six thousand men. At the battle of Sailor's Creek there remained about three thousand. The fatigue of constant marching for days and nights to men unaccustomed to such service might sufficiently explain the diminution; but to this must be added the want of rations for the last two days of their campaign. Twenty-eight hundred were taken prisoners, and about a hundred and fifty killed and wounded. From General Ewell's report, I learn that the force of the enemy engaged at Sailor's Creek amounted to thirty thousand men. In closing his report he says:

"The discipline preserved by General G. W. C. Lee in camp and on the march, and the manner in which he handled his troops in action, fully justified the request I had made for his promotion. General Kershaw, who had only been a few days under my command, behaved with his usual coolness and judgment."

Lest any should suppose, from the remark of General Ewell, that I had been unwilling or reluctant to promote my aide-de-camp. Colonel G. W. C. Lee, it is proper to state that the only obstacle to be overcome was Lee's objection to receiving promotion. With refined delicacy he shrank from the idea of superseding men who had been actively serving in the field, and in one case where the objection did not seem to me to have any application, he so decidedly preferred to remain with me, that I yielded to his wishes; but gave him additional rank to command the local troops for the defense of Richmond. His valuable services in that capacity, on various occasions, sustained my high opinion of him as a soldier, and his conduct on that retreat, and in the battle of "Sailor's Creek," for which he is commended, was only what I anticipated.

Of the forces constituting the defense of Richmond on the 2d of April, it only remains to account for the naval force in the James. After General Ewell had withdrawn his command, Admiral Semmes embarked the crews of his gunboats on some small steamers, set fire to his war-vessels, and proceeded up the river to the landing opposite Richmond. Here he found no land transportation awaiting him, and the last railroad train had left at early dawn. He, however, with the energy and capacity so often elsewhere displayed by him, on finding the railroad station deserted, commenced a search for material which, with his steam engineers, he could make available. He states that a few straggling passenger-cars lay uncoupled along the track, and that there was also a small engine, but no fire, and no fuel to make one. They coupled the cars together, his marine sappers and miners cut up a fence for steam-fuel, and thus he got under way, but the engine proved insufficient to draw the train, and at an up-grade he was brought to a halt immediately after starting. One of his engineers, however, found in the workshops another engine; with the two he was able to proceed, and thus to transport his sailors to Danville, the best mode known to him to execute the order sent to him by the Secretary of the Navy, "You will join General Lee in the field with all your forces." [123] When General Longstreet was withdrawn from the north side of the James, Colonel Shipp, Commandant of the Virginia Institute, with the Battalion of Cadets, youths whose gallantry at the battle of New Market has been heretofore noticed, and such convalescents in Richmond as were able to march, moved down to supply the vacancy created by the transfer of Longstreet's force to Petersburg. General Ewell, in command at Richmond, had for its defense the naval force at Drury's Bluff under Commander Tucker, which was organized as a regiment and armed with muskets. On the north side of the James were General Kershaw's division of Confederate troops and General G. W. C, Lee's division, composed mostly of artillery-men armed as infantry, and the "reserves," or "local troops," coöperating with these was Admiral Semmes's naval force on the James. On the night of the 2d of April these forces were withdrawn, and took up their line of march to join General Lee's army on its retreat.

In obedience to a law of the Congress, General Ewell had made arrangements to burn the tobacco at Richmond whenever the evacuation of the city should render the burning necessary, to prevent the tobacco from falling into the hands of the enemy. Orders were also given to destroy certain property of the Confederate States, exceptions being made as in the case of the arsenal, the burning of which would endanger the city. To prevent the possibility of a general conflagration he had advised with the Mayor and City Council, and the necessary precautions were believed to have been taken. General Ewell's report, December 20, 1865, published in the "Historical Society Papers" (vol. i, p. 101), satisfactorily establishes the fact that the conflagration in Richmond of April 3, 1865, did not result from any act of the public authorities. The burning of the tobacco was only resorted to when the alternative was to burn or allow it to fall into the hands of the enemy, who, there was no doubt, would take it without making compensation to the owners. It was a disagreeable necessity, and therefore every opportunity was allowed to the owners of that and other articles of export to place them, if possible, beyond the danger of being applied to the use of the hostile Government. There is no similitude between the destruction of public property made by us and the like act of the invader in our country. The property we destroyed belonged to the Confederate States only. Armories and ship-yards destroyed by them— those, for instance, at Harper's Ferry and Norfolk—were the property of the States in common, which the Federal Government had emphatically declared it was its bounden duty to preserve, and which was its first plea in justification of the act of sending an armed force against the Southern States.

The conflagration at Richmond occurred on the morning of the 3d of April, after I had left the city, and I therefore have only such knowledge in regard to it as was subsequently acquired from others. Those who would learn specifically the facts and speculations in regard to it are referred to the report of General Ewell, which has been above cited. Suffice it to say, the troops of neither army were considered responsible for that calamity.

On Sunday, the 2d of April, while I was in St. Paul's church. General Lee's telegram, announcing his speedy withdrawal from Petersburg, and the consequent necessity for evacuating Richmond, was handed to me. I quietly rose and left the church. The occurrence probably attracted attention, but the people of Richmond had been too long beleaguered, had known me too often to receive notice of threatened attacks, and the congregation of St. Paul's was too refined, to make a scene at anticipated danger. For all these reasons, the reader will be prepared for the announcement that the sensational stories which have been published about the agitation caused by my leaving the church during service were the creations of fertile imaginations. I went to my office and assembled the heads of departments and bureaus, as far as they could be found on a day when all the offices were closed, and gave the needful instructions for our removal that night, simultaneously with General Lee's withdrawal from Petersburg. The event was not unforeseen, and some preparation had been made for it, though, as it came sooner than was expected, there was yet much to be done. My own papers were disposed as usual for convenient reference in the transaction of current affairs, and as soon as the principal officers had left me the executive papers were arranged for removal. This occupied myself and staff until late in the afternoon. By this time the report that Richmond was to be evacuated had spread through the town, and many who saw me walking toward my residence left their houses to inquire whether the report was true. Upon my admission of the painful fact, qualified, however, by the expression of my hope that we would under better auspices again return, the ladies especially, with generous sympathy and patriotic impulse, responded, "If the success of the cause requires you to give up Richmond, we are content."

The affection and confidence of this noble people in the hour of disaster were more distressing to me than complaint and unjust censure would have been.

In view of the diminishing resources of the country on which the Army of Northern Virginia relied for supplies, I had urged the policy of sending families as far as practicable to the south and west, and had set the example by requiring my own to go. If it was practicable and desirable to hold the south side of the James, then, even for merely material considerations, it was important to hold Richmond, and this could best have been done if there had been none there save those who could aid in its defense. If it was not practicable and desirable to hold the south side of the James, then Richmond would be isolated, and if it could have been defended, its depots, foundries, workshops, and mills could have contributed nothing to the armies outside, and its possession would no longer have been to us of military importance. Ours being a struggle for existence, the indulgence of sentiment would have been misplaced.

Being alone in Richmond, the few arrangements needful for my personal wants were soon made after reaching home. Then, leaving all else in care of the housekeeper, I waited until notified of the time when the train would depart; then, going to the station, started for Danville, whither I supposed General Lee would proceed with his army.

In a previous chapter I promised to expose the fiction which imputed to me the removal of supplies intended for Lee's army at Amelia Court-House, Though manufactured without one fiber of truth, it has been copied into so many books, formed the staple of so many jeremiads, and pointed so many malignant reflections, that I deem it proper for myself and others concerned now to present the evidence which will overthrow this baseless fabric.

General I. M. St. John, Commissary-General of the Confederate Army, was requested by me, after the close of the war, to prepare a report in reply to the widely circulated story that Lee's army had been compelled to evacuate Petersburg, and subsequently to surrender because the Administration had failed to provide food for their support. On the 14th of July, 1873, General St. John addressed to me a report of the operations and condition of the commissariat immediately preceding the surrender of Lee's and Johnston's armies. That report, together with confirmatory statements, will be found in the "Southern Historical Society Papers" for March, 1877. From it and the accompanying documents I propose to make brief extracts.

General St. John says that in February, 1865, when he took charge of the commissary bureau, on account of the military status he

"found that the Army of Northern Virginia was with difficulty supplied day by day with reduced rations. . . . I at once proceeded to organize a system of appeal and of private contribution as auxiliary to the regular operations of the commissary service. With the earnest and very active aid of leading citizens of Virginia and North Carolina, this effort was attended with results exceeding expectation. . . . On or before March 15, 1865, the Commissary-General was able to report to the Secretary of War that, in addition to the daily issue of rations to the Army of Northern Virginia, there lay in depot along the railroad between Greensboro, North Carolina, Lynchburg, Staunton, and Richmond, at least ten days' rations of bread and meat, collected especially for that army, and subject to the requisition of its chief commissary officer; also that considerably over 300,000 rations were held in Richmond as a special reserve. . . . There was collected by April 1, 1865, in depot, subsistence stated in detail as follows:

"At Richmond, Virginia, 300,000 rations bread and meat; at Danville, 500,000 rations bread; at Danville, 1,500,000 rations meat; at Lynchburg, 180,000 rations bread and meat; at Greensboro, North Carolina, and vicinity, 1,500,000 rations bread and meat.

"In addition, there were considerable supplies of tea, coffee, and sugar carefully reserved for hospital issues chiefly. These returns did not include the subsistence collections by the field-trains of the Army of Northern Virginia, under orders from its own headquarters, nor the depot collections at Charlottesville, Staunton, and other points upon the Virginia Central Railroad, to meet requisitions from the Confederates operating in the Valley and western Virginia. South and west of Greensboro, North Carolina, the depot accumulations were reserved first to meet requisitions for the forces operating in the Carolinas, and the surplus for Virginia requisitions. . . ."

The report then refers to a conference between the Secretary of War (Breckinridge) and the General commanding (Lee) with the Quartermaster-General (Lawton) and the Commissary-General (St. John). After a general discussion of the wants of the army in clothing, forage, and subsistence, to an inquiry by General Lee, General St. John replied:

"That a daily delivery by cars and canal-boats, at or near Richmond, of about five hundred tons of commissaries' stores was essential to provide for the Richmond siege reserve and other accumulations desired by the General commanding; that the depot collections were already sufficient to assure the meeting of these requisitions, and, if the then existing military lines could be held, the Commissary-General felt encouraged as to the future of his own immediate department."

The procuring of supplies was only one of the difficulties by which we were beset. The deteriorated condition of the railroads and the deficiency of rolling-stock embarrassed transportation, and there was yet another: the cavalry raids of the enemy frequently broke the railroads and destroyed trains. General Lawton, with great energy and good judgment, under the heavy pressure of the circumstances, improved the railroad transportation. I quote again from the report of General St. John:

"Upon the earliest information of the approaching evacuation, instructions were asked from the War Department and the General commanding for the final disposition of the subsistence reserve in Richmond, then reported by Major Claiborne, post commissary, to exceed in quantity 350,000 rations. The reply, 'Send up the Danville Railroad if Richmond is not safe,' was received from the army headquarters, April 2, 1865, and too late for action, as all railroad transportation had then been taken up, by superior orders, for the archives, bullion, and other Government service, then deemed of prior importance. All that remained to be done was to fill every accessible army-wagon; and this was done, and the trains were hurried southward."

It will be seen from this statement that the reply was only directed to the removal of the subsistence reserve if Richmond was not safe. It can not be supposed that such a reply emanated from General Lee, as he surely never contemplated an attempt to hold Richmond after Petersburg was evacuated. General St. John then adds:

"On March 31st, or possibly the morning of April 1st, a telegram was received at the bureau in Richmond, from the commissary officer of the Army of Northern Virginia, requesting breadstuffs to be sent to Petersburg. Shipment was commenced at once, and was pressed to the extreme limit of transportation permitted by the movement of General Longstreet's corps (then progressing southward). No calls, by letter or requisition, from the General commanding, or from any other source, official or unofficial, had been received either by the Commissary-General or the Assistant Commissary-General; nor (as will be seen by the appended letter of the Secretary of War) was any communication transmitted through the department channels to the bureau of subsistence, for the collection of supplies at Amelia Court-House. Had any such requisition or communication been received at the bureau as late as the morning of April 1st, it could have been met from the Richmond reserve with transportation on south-bound trains, and most assuredly so previous to General Longstreet's movement."

On the morning of the 3d the Commissary-General left Richmond and joined General R. E. Lee at Amelia Springs. There were at that time about eighty thousand rations at Farmville, "there held on trains for immediate use." On the morning of the 6th the Commissary-General asked General Lee whether he should send those rations down the railroad or hold them at Farmville. Not receiving instructions, the rations remained at Farmville, and on the 7th the army passing there took a portion of them. On the morning of the 8th the subsistence trains on the railroad at Pamphlin's Station, twenty miles west of Farmville, were attacked by the enemy's cavalry and captured, or burned to avoid capture. The surrender followed on the subsequent day. The foregoing extracts, I think, prove unquestionably that no orders were received to place supplies for Lee's army at Amelia Court-House; that sufficient supplies were in depot to answer the immediate wants of the army, and that the failure to distribute them to the troops on their retreat was due to the active operations of the enemy on all our lines of communication; hence, when the Commissary-General applied to General Lee for instructions as to where supplies should be placed, he says, "General Lee replied in substance that the military situation did not permit an answer." Lest, however, what has been given should not seem conclusive to others, I add confirmatory testimony. General John C. Breckinridge, in a letter to General I. M. St. John, of date May 16, 1871, wrote:

"A few days before the evacuation of Richmond you reported to me that besides supplies accumulated at different distant points in Virginia and North Carolina, you had ten days' rations accessible by rail to [General Lee] and subject to the orders of his chief commissary. I have no recollection of any communication from General Lee in regard lo the accumulation of rations at Amelia Court-House. . . . The second or third day after the evacuation, I recollect you said to General Lee in my presence that you had a large number of rations (I think eighty thousand) at a convenient point on the railroad, and desired to know where you should place them. The General replied that the military situation made it impossible to answer."

In a letter of the date of September, 1865, Lieutenant-Colonel Thomas G. Williams, assistant commissary-general, wrote to General St. John, and from his letter I make the following extract:

"On the morning of April 2, 1865, the chief commissary of General Lee's army was asked by telegram what should be done with the stores in Richmond. No reply was received until night; he then suggested that, if Richmond was not safe, they might be sent up on the Richmond and Danville Railroad. As the evacuation of Richmond was then actively progressing, it was impracticable to move those supplies. . . . In reply to your question with regard to the establishment of a depot of supplies at Amelia Court-House, I have to say that I had no information of any such requisition or demand upon the bureau."

Major J. H. Claiborne, assistant commissary-general, in a letter to General I. M. St. John, from Richmond, June 3, 1873, wrote:

"No order was received by me, and (with full opportunities of information if it had been given) I had no knowledge of any plan to send supplies to Amelia Court-House. Under such circumstances, with transportation afforded, there could readily have been sent about three hundred thousand rations, with due regard to the demand upon this post."

During the retreat, supplies were found at Pamphlin's Depot, Farmville, Danville, Saulsbury, and Charlotte. Major B. P. Noland, chief commissary for Virginia, wrote to General St. John, April 16, 1874. After saying that he had read with care the report of General St. John, and expressing the opinion that it was entirely correct, of which no one in the Confederacy had better opportunities to judge, he writes:

"I think the plan adopted by your predecessor, Colonel Northrop (which was continued by you), for obtaining for the use of the army the products of the country, was as perfect and worked as effectively as any that could have been devised. . . . I left Richmond at one o'clock of the night Richmond was evacuated, with orders from you to make Lynchburg my headquarters, and be ready to forward supplies from that point to the army. I never heard of any order for the accumulation of supplies at Amelia Springs."

Lewis E. Harvie, a distinguished citizen of Virginia, and who at the close of the war was President of the Richmond and Danville and Piedmont Railroads, wrote to General St. John on January 1, 1876. From his letter I make the following extracts, referring to the condition of affairs in 1865. He writes:

"The difficulties of obtaining supplies were very great, particularly when the roads under my charge were cut, and transportation suspended on them, which was the case on one or two occasions for several weeks. Engines and care, and machinery generally, on these roads were insufficient and inadequate from wear and tear to accomplish the amount of transportation required for the Government. . . . The Richmond and Danville and Piedmont Railroads were kept open, and about that time we added largely to its rolling-stock by procuring engines and cars from the different roads on the route of the Virginia and Tennessee Railroad west. Starvation had stared the Army of Northern Virginia in the face; and the commissary department organized an appeal to the people on the line of the Richmond and Danville Railroad for voluntary contributions of supplies, and a number of gentlemen of influence, character, and position, including the most eminent clergymen of the State, addressed them in several counties, urging them to furnish the supply wanted.

"No one who witnessed can ever forget the results. Contribution was universal, and

supplies of food sufficient to meet the wants
of the army at the time were at once sent to
the depots on the road until they were packed
and groaned under their weight; and I affirm
that at the time of the evacuation of
Richmond, the difficulty of delivering
supplies sufficient for the support of the Army
of Northern Virginia under General Lee was
solved and surmounted, for I know that
abundant supplies were in reach of
transportation on the Richmond and Danville
Railroad, being massed in Danville, Charlotte,
and at other points; and, from the increased
motive power above referred to, they could
have been delivered as fast as they were
required. . . . At the time of the evacuation of
the city, there were ample supplies in it, as
well as on the railroad west of Amelia Court-
House, to have been delivered at the latter
place for the retreating army, if its numbers
had been double what they were. No orders
were ever given to any officers or employee of
the Richmond and Danville Railroad to
transport any supplies to Amelia Court-House
for General Lee's army, nor did I ever bear
that any such orders were sent to the
commissary department on the occasion of
the evacuation of Richmond, until after the
surrender of the army."

Mr. Harvie then recites his interview, held on Saturday, the day before
evacuation, with the Quartermaster-General, the Secretary of War, and myself,
from whom he learned that he might go home for a fortnight, there being no
expectation that Richmond would be evacuated in the mean time. He adds that
the next day he was informed by telegraph of the proposed evacuation, and
returned to Richmond, at which place he conferred with myself and the
Secretary of War about the route to be taken by the wagon supply-train, and that
he had a long conversation with me on the care, during our night-ride to
Danville.

In regard to sending supplies to Amelia Court-House, he writes:
"I have never believed that any orders to
place supplies of food at Amelia Court-House
were received by the commissary department
at the time of the evacuation of the city,
because from Richmond, or from the upper
portions of the railroad, if required, they
could at once have been transported without
any delay or difficulty. Neither the road nor
the telegraph was cut or disturbed until the
day after the evacuation of the city."

It may perhaps be thought that the amount of evidence adduced is greater than necessary to disprove the very improbable assertion that, instead of burden-cars, a passenger train had been loaded with provisions for Lee's army at Amelia Court-House, and that these passenger-cars, without being permitted to unload the freight, had, in reckless disregard of the wants of our worn and hard-pressed defenders, been ordered to proceed immediately to Richmond, thus leaving them to starvation, and the necessity to surrender, in order to enable the executive department to escape; but, as I had no personal knowledge of the matter, it was necessary to quote those whose functions brought them into closer communication with the subject to which the calumny related.

In the night of the 2d, the same on which General Ewell evacuated the defenses of the capital and General Lee withdrew from Petersburg, I left Richmond and reached Danville on the next morning.

Neither the president of the railroad, who was traveling with me, nor I knew that there was anything which required attention at Amelia Court-House or other station on the route. Had General Lee's letter to me, written on the afternoon of the 2d, been received at Richmond, which I think it was not, the fact that he proposed to march to Amelia Court-House would have been known; but it would have been unjust to the officers of the commissary department to doubt that any requisition made or to be made for supplies had received or would receive the most prompt and efficient attention. If, however, I had known that General Lee wanted supplies placed at Amelia Court-House, I would certainly have inquired as to the time of reaching that station, and have asked to have the train stopped so as to enable me to learn whether the supplies were in depot or not. The unfounded calumny, after perhaps having given it more consideration than it was worth, is now dismissed.

Though the occupation of Danville was not expected to be permanent, immediately after arriving there rooms were obtained, and the different departments resumed their routine labors. Nothing could have exceeded the kindness and hospitality of the patriotic citizens. They cordially gave as an "Old Virginia welcome," and with one heart contributed in every practicable manner to cheer and aid us in the work in which we were engaged.

The town was surrounded by an intrenchment as faulty in location as construction. I promptly proceeded to correct the one and improve the other, while energetic efforts were being made to collect supplies of various kinds for General Lee's army.

The design, as previously arranged with General Lee, was that, if he should be compelled to evacuate Petersburg, he would proceed to Danville, make a new defensive line of the Dan and Roanoke Rivers, unite his army with the troops in North Carolina, and make a combined attack upon Sherman; if successful, it was expected that reviving hope would bring reënforcements to the army, and Grant, being then far removed from his base of supplies, and in the midst of a hostile population, it was thought we might return, drive him from the soil of Virginia, and restore to the people a government deriving its authority from their consent. With these hopes and wishes, neither seeking to diminish the magnitude of our disaster nor to excite illusory expectations, I issued, on the 5th, the following proclamation, of which, viewed by the light of subsequent events, it may fairly be said it was over-sanguine:

"The General-in-Chief found it necessary to make such movements of his troops as to uncover the capital. It would be unwise to conceal the moral and material injury to our cause resulting from its occupation by the enemy. It is equally unwise and unworthy of us to allow our energies to falter and our efforts to become relaxed under reverses, however calamitous they may be. For many months the largest and finest army of the Confederacy, under a leader whose presence inspires equal confidence in the troops and the people, has been greatly trammeled by the necessity of keeping constant watch over the approaches to the capital, and has thus been forced to forego more than one opportunity for promising enterprise. It is for us, my countrymen, to show by our bearing under reverses, how wretched has been the self-deception of those who have believed us less able to endure misfortune with fortitude than to encounter danger with courage.

"We have now entered upon a new phase of the struggle. Relieved from the necessity of guarding particular points, our army will be free to move from point to point, to strike the enemy in detail far from his base. Let us but will it, and we are free.

"Animated by that confidence in your spirit and fortitude which never yet failed me, I announce to you, fellow-countrymen, that it is my purpose to maintain your cause with my whole heart and soul; that I will never consent to abandon to the enemy one foot of the soil of any of the States of the Confederacy; that Virginia—noble State, whose ancient renown has been eclipsed by her still more glorious recent history; whose bosom has been bared to receive the main shock of this war; whose sons and daughters have exhibited heroism so sublime as to render her illustrious in all time to come—that Virginia, with the help of the people and by the blessing of Providence, shall be held and defended, and no peace ever be made with the infamous invaders of her territory.

"If, by the stress of numbers, we should be compelled to a temporary withdrawal from her limits or those of any other border State,

465

we will return until the baffled and exhausted
enemy shall abandon in despair his endless
and impossible task of making slaves of a
people resolved to be free.

"Let us, then, not despond, my
countrymen, but, relying on God, meet the foe
with fresh defiance and with unconquered
and unconquerable hearts.

"JEFFERSON DAVIS."

While thus employed, little if any reliable information in regard to the Army
of Northern Virginia was received, until a gallant youth, the son of General
Henry A. Wise, came to Danville, and told me that, learning Lee's army was to
be surrendered, he had during the night mounted his fleet horse, and, escaping
through and from the enemy's cavalry, some of whom pursued him, had come
quite alone to warn me of the approaching event. Other unofficial information
soon followed, and of such circumstantial character as to prove that Lieutenant
Wise's anticipation had been realized.

Our scouts now reported a cavalry force to be moving toward the south
around the west side of Danville, and we removed thence to Greensboro, passing
a railroad-bridge, as was subsequently learned, a very short time before the
enemy's cavalry reached and burned it. I had telegraphed to General Johnston
from Danville the report that Lee had surrendered, and, on arriving at
Greensboro, conditionally requested him to meet me there, where General
Beauregard at the time had his headquarters, my object being to confer with
both of them in regard to our present condition and future operations.

[Footnote 123: "Memoirs of Service Afloat," Admiral Semmes, pp. 811-815.]

CHAPTER LIV

Invitation of General Johnston to a Conference.—Its Object.—Its
Result.—Provisions on the Line of Retreat.—Notice of President
Lincoln's Assassination.—Correspondence between Johnston and
Sherman.—Terms of the Convention.—Approved by the Confederate
Government.—Rejected by the United States Government.—
Instructions to General Johnston.—Disobeyed.—Statements of
General Johnston.—His Surrender.—Movements of the President
South.—His Plans.—Order of General E. E. Smith to his Soldiers.—
Surrender.—Numbers paroled.—The President overtakes his Family.—
His Capture.—Taken to Hampton Roads, and imprisoned in Fortress
Monroe.

The invitation to General Johnston for a conference, noticed in a previous
chapter, was as follows:

"GREENSBORO, NORTH CAROLINA, *April 11 1865—12 M.*

"General J. E. JOHNSTON, *headquarters, via Raleigh:*

"The Secretary of War did not join me at
Danville. Is expected here this afternoon.

"As your situation may render best, I will
go to your headquarters immediately after the
arrival of the Secretary of War, or you can
come here; in the former case our conference

must be without the presence of General Beauregard. I have no official report from General Lee. The Secretary of War may be able to add to information heretofore communicated.

"The important question first to be solved is, At what point shall concentration be made, in view of the present position of the two columns of the enemy, and the routes which they may adopt to engage your forces before a proposed junction with General Walker and others. Your more intimate knowledge of the data for the solution of the problem deters me from making a specific suggestion on that point.

"JEFFERSON DAVIS."

In compliance with this request, General J. E. Johnston came up from Raleigh to Greensboro, and with General Beauregard met me and most of my Cabinet at my quarters in a house occupied by Colonel J. Taylor Wood's family. Though I was fully sensible of the gravity of our position, seriously affected as it was by the evacuation of the capital, the surrender of the Army of Northern Virginia, and the consequent discouragement which these events would produce, I did not think we should despair. We still had effective armies in the field, and a vast extent of rich and productive territory both east and west of the Mississippi, whose citizens had evinced no disposition to surrender. Ample supplies had been collected in the railroad depots, and much still remained to be placed at our disposal when needed by the army in North Carolina.

The failure of several attempts to open negotiations with the Federal Government, and notably the last by commissioners who met President Lincoln at Hampton Roads, convinced me of the hopelessness under existing circumstances to obtain better terms than were then offered, i. e., a surrender at discretion. My motive, therefore, in holding an interview with the senior generals of the army in North Carolina was not to learn their opinion as to what might be done by negotiation with the United States Government, but to derive from them information in regard to the army under their command, and what it was feasible and advisable to do as a military problem.

The members of my Cabinet were already advised as to the object of the meeting, and, when the subject was introduced to the generals in that form, General Johnston was very reserved, and seemed far less than sanguine. His first significant expression was that of a desire to open correspondence with General Sherman, to see if he would agree to a suspension of hostilities, the object being to permit the civil authorities to enter into the needful arrangements to terminate the existing war. Confident that the United States Government would not accept a proposition for such negotiations, I distinctly expressed My conviction on that point, and presented as an objection to such an effort that, so far as it should excite delusive hopes and expectations, its failure would have a demoralizing effect both on the troops and the people. Neither of them had shown any disposition to surrender, or had any reason to suppose t^ their Government contemplated abandoning its trust—the maintenance of t^

467

Constitution, freedom, and independence of the Confederate States. From the inception of the war, the people had generally and at all times expressed their determination to accept no terms of peace that did not recognize their independence; and the indignation manifested when it became known that Mr. Lincoln had offered to our commissioners at Hampton Roads a surrender at discretion as the only alternative to a continuance of the war assured me that no true Confederate was prepared to accept peace on such terms. During the last years of the war the main part of the infantry in the Army of Northern Virginia was composed of men from the farther South. Many of these, before the evacuation of Petersburg and especially about the time of Lee's surrender, had absented themselves to go homeward, and, it was reported, made avowal of their purpose to continue the struggle. I had reason to believe that the spirit of the army in North Carolina was unbroken, for, though surrounded by circumstances well calculated to depress and discourage them, I had learned that they earnestly protested to their officers against the surrender which rumor informed them was then in contemplation. If any shall deem it a weak credulity to confide in such reports, something may be allowed to an intense love for the Confederacy to a thorough conviction that its fall would involve ruin, both material and moral, and to a confidence in the righteousness of our cause, which, if equally felt by my compatriots, would make them do and dare to the last extremity.

But if, taking the gloomiest view, the circumstances were such as to leave no hope of maintaining the independence of the Confederate States—if negotiations for peace must be on the basis of reunion and the acceptance of the war legislation—it seemed to me that certainly better terms for our country could be secured by keeping organized armies in the field than by laying down our arms and trusting to the magnanimity of the victor.

For all these considerations I was not at all hopeful of any success in the attempt to provide for negotiations between the civil authorities of the United States and those of the Confederacy, believing that, even if Sherman should agree to such a proposition, his Government would not ratify it; but, after having distinctly announced my opinion, I yielded to the judgment of my constitutional advisers, of whom only one held my views, and consented to permit General Johnston, as he desired, to hold a conference with General Sherman for the purpose above recited.

Then, turning to what I supposed would soon follow, I invited General Johnston to an expression of his choice of a line of retreat toward the southwest. He declared a preference for a different route from that suggested by me, and, yielding the point, I informed him that I would have depots of supplies for his army placed on the route he had selected. The commissary-general, St. John, executed the order, as shown in his report published in the "Southern Historical Society Papers," vol. viii, pp. 103-107.

Referring to the period which followed the surrender of the Army of Northern Virginia, General I. M. St. John, Commissary-General Confederate States Army, writes:

"The bureau headquarters were continued in North Carolina until the surrender of that military department. During the interval preparations were made for the westward movement of forces as then contemplated. In these arrangements the local depots were generally found so full and supplied so well in hand, from Charlotte southwest, that the commissary-general was able to report to the Secretary of War that the requisitions for which he was notified to prepare could all be met. The details of this service were executed, and very ably, by Major J. H. Claiborne, then, and until the end, assistant commissary-general."

Major Claiborne, in his report, writes:

"Being placed under orders as assistant commissary-general, I forwarded supplies from South Carolina to General J. E. Johnston's army, and also collected supplies at six or seven named points in that State for the supposed retreat of General Johnston's army through the State. This duty, with a full determination at the evacuation of this city [Richmond] to follow the fortunes of our cause, gave me opportunity of ascertaining the resources of the country for my department. The great want was that of transportation, and specially was it felt by all collecting commissaries for a few months before the surrender."

It will thus be seen that my expectations, referred to above, caused adequate provision to be made for the retreat of our army, if that result should become necessary by the failure of the attempt to open negotiations for an honorable peace. I had never contemplated a surrender, except upon such terms as a belligerent might claim, as long as we were able to keep the field, and never expected a Confederate army to surrender while it was able either to fight or to retreat. Lee had only surrendered his army when it was impossible for him to do either one or the other, and had proudly rejected Grant's demand, in the face of overwhelming numbers, until he found himself surrounded and his line of retreat blocked by a force much larger than his own.

After it had been decided that General Johnston should attempt negotiation with General Sherman, he left for his army headquarters; and I, expecting that he would soon take up his line of retreat, which his superiority in cavalry would protect from harassing pursuit, proceeded with my Cabinet and staff toward Charlotte, North Carolina. While on the way, a dispatch was received from General Johnston announcing that General Sherman had agreed to a conference, and asking that the Secretary of War, General J. C. Breckinridge, should return to coöperate in it. The application was complied with, and the Postmaster-General, John H. Reagan, also went at my request. He, however, was not admitted to the conference.

We arrived at Charlotte on April 18, 1865, and I there received, at the moment of dismounting, a telegram from General Breckinridge announcing, on information received from General Sherman, that President Lincoln had been assassinated. An influential citizen of the town, who had come to welcome me, was standing near me, and, after remarking to him in a low voice that I had received sad intelligence, I handed the telegram to him. Some troopers encamped in the vicinity had collected to see me; they called to the gentleman who had the dispatch in his hand to read it, no doubt supposing it to be army news. He complied with their request, and a few, only taking in the fact, but not appreciating the evil it portended, cheered, as was natural at news of the fall of one they considered their most powerful foe. The man, who invented the story of my having read the dispatch with exultation, had free scope for his imagination, as he was not present, and had no chance to know whereof he bore witness, even if there had been any foundation of truth for his fiction.

For an enemy so relentless in the war for our subjugation, we could not be expected to mourn; yet, in view of its political consequences, it could not be regarded otherwise than as a great misfortune to the South. He had power over the Northern people, and was without personal malignity toward the people of the South; his successor was without power in the North, and the embodiment of malignity toward the Southern people, perhaps the more so because he had betrayed and deserted them in the hour of their need. The war had now shrunk into narrow proportions, but the important consideration remained to so conduct it that, if failing to secure our independence, we might obtain a treaty or *quasi*-treaty of peace which would secure to the Southern States their political rights, and to the people thereof immunity from the plunder of their private property.

I found some cavalry at Charlotte, and soon had the satisfaction to increase them to five brigades, They had been on detached service, and were much reduced in numbers. Among the troopers who assembled there was the remnant of the command which had spread terror north of the Ohio, under the command of their dauntless leader, General John Hunt Morgan. Their present chief, worthy to be the successor of that hero, was General Basil Duke. Among the atrocious, cowardly acts of vindictive malice which marked the conduct of the enemy, none did or could surpass the brutality with which the dying and dead body of Morgan was treated. Hate, the offspring of fear, they might feel for the valorous soldier while he lived, but even the ignoble passion, vengeance, might have been expected to stop when life was extinct.

On April 13, 1865, General Johnston wrote to General Sherman as follows:
>"The results of the recent campaign in Virginia have changed the relative military condition of the belligerents. I am therefore induced to address you, in this form, the inquiry whether, to stop the further effusion of blood and the devastation of property, you are willing to make a temporary suspension of active operations; . . . the object being to permit the civil authorities to enter into the needful arrangements to terminate the existing war."

General Sherman replied, on the 14th:

"I am fully empowered to arrange with you
any terms for the suspension of hostilities
between the armies commanded by you and
those commanded by myself, and will be
willing to confer with you to that end," etc.,
etc.[124]

In the same volume, at page 327, General Sherman describes an interview
with Mr. Lincoln, held at City Point on the 27th and 28th of March preceding, in
which he says:

"Mr. Lincoln distinctly authorized me to
assure Governor Vance and the people of
North Carolina that, as soon as the rebel
armies laid down their arms, and resumed
their civil pursuits, they would at once be
guaranteed all their rights as citizens of a
common country; and that, to avoid anarchy,
the State governments then in existence, with
their civil functionaries, would be recognized
by him as the government *de facto* till
Congress could provide others."

In a letter of D. D. Porter, vice-admiral, written in 1866, giving his
recollections of that interview, in the same volume, page 330, is found the
following paragraph:

"The conversation between the President
and General Sherman, about the terms of
surrender to be allowed Joe Johnston,
continued. Sherman energetically insisted
that he could command his own terms, and
that Johnston would have to yield to his
demands; but the President was very decided
about the matter, and insisted that the
surrender of Johnston's army must be
obtained on any terms."

Hence it appears that Sherman was authorized to say that he was fully
empowered to arrange for the suspension of hostilities; and, moreover, that he
was instructed by Mr. Lincoln to give "any terms" to obtain the surrender of
Johnston's army.

In regard to the memorandum or basis of agreement, Sherman states, in the
same volume, page 353, that, while in consultation with General Johnston, a
messenger brought him a parcel of papers from Mr. Reagan, Postmaster-
General; that Johnston and Breckinridge looked over them, and handed one of
them to him, which he found inadmissible, and proceeds:

"Then, recalling the conversation with Mr.
Lincoln at City Point, I sat down at the table
and wrote off the terms which I thought
concisely expressed his views and wishes."

But, while these matters were progressing, Mr. Lincoln had been
assassinated, and a vindictive policy had been substituted for his, which
avowedly was, to procure a speedy surrender of the army upon any terms. His

evident wish was to stop the further shedding of blood; that of his successors, like Sherman's, to extract all which it was possible to obtain. From the memoranda of the interview between Mr. Lincoln and Sherman it is clearly to be inferred that, but for the untimely death of Mr. Lincoln, the agreement between Generals Sherman and Johnston would have been ratified; and the wounds inflicted on civil liberty by the "reconstruction" measures might not have left their shameful scars on the United States.

General Sherman, in his "Memoirs," vol. ii, page 349, referring to a conversation between himself and General Johnston at their first meeting, writes:

> "I told him I could not believe that he or General Lee, or the officers of the Confederate army, could possibly be privy to acts of assassination, but I would not say as much for Jeff Davis, George Saunders, and men of that stripe."

On this I have but two remarks to make: First, that I think there were few officers in the Confederate army who would have permitted such a slanderous imputation to be made by a public enemy against the chief executive of their Government; second, that I could not value the good opinion of the man who, in regard to the burning of Columbia, made a false charge against General Wade Hampton, and, having left it to circulate freely for ten years, then in his published memoirs makes this disgraceful admission:

> "In my official report of this conflagration, I distinctly charged it to General Wade Hampton, and confess I did so pointedly, to shake the faith of his people in him," etc.

> "Memorandum, or basis of agreement, made this 18th day of April, A. D. 1865, near Durham Station, and in the State of North Carolina, by and between General Joseph E. Johnston, commanding the Confederate army, and Major-General W. T. Sherman, commanding the army of the United States in North Carolina, both present:

> "1. The contending armies now in the field to maintain their *status quo*, until notice is given by the commanding General of either one to its opponents, and reasonable time, say forty-eight hours, allowed.

> "2. The Confederate armies now in existence to be disbanded and conducted to the several State capitals, there to deposit their arms and public property in the State Arsenal, and each officer and man to execute and file an agreement to cease from acts of war, and abide the action of both Federal and State authorities. The number of arms and munitions of war to be reported to the chief of ordnance at Washington City, subject to future action of the Congress of the United States, and in the mean time to be used solely

to maintain peace and order within the borders of the States respectively.

"3. The recognition by the Executive of the United States of the several State governments, on their officers and Legislatures taking the oath prescribed by the Constitution of the United States; and, where conflicting State governments have resulted from the war, the legitimacy of all shall be submitted to the Supreme Court of the United States.

"4. The reestablishment of all Federal courts in the several States, with powers as defined by the Constitution and laws of Congress.

"5. The people and inhabitants of all States to be guaranteed, so far as the Executive can, their political rights and franchises, as well as their rights of person and property, as defined by the Constitution of the United States and of the States respectively.

"6. The Executive authority of the Government of the United States not to disturb any of the people by reason of the late war, so long as they live in peace and quiet, abstain from acts of armed hostility, and obey laws in existence at any place of their residence.

"7. In general terms, war to cease, a general amnesty, so far as the Executive power of the United States can command, or on condition of the disbandment of the Confederate armies, the distribution of arms, and resumption of peaceful pursuits by officers and men, as hitherto composing said armies. Not being fully empowered by our respective principals to fulfill these terms, we individually and officially pledge ourselves to promptly obtain necessary authority, and to carry out the above programme.

"W. T. SHERMAN, *Major-General, etc., etc.*
"J. E. JOHNSTON, *General, etc., etc.*"

The reader will not fail to observe that the proposition for a suspension of hostilities to allow the civil authorities to negotiate, was not even entertained; that the agreement was, in fact, a military convention, in which all reference to the civil authorities was excluded, except by the admission that the negotiators respectively had principals from whom they must obtain authority, i. e., ratification of the agreement into which they had entered. There seemed to be a special dread on the part of the United States officials lest they should do something which would be construed as the recognition of the existence of a government which for four years they had been vainly trying to subdue. Now, as on previous occasions, I cared little for the form, and therefore only gave my consideration to the substance of the agreement. In consideration of the disbandment of our armies it provided for the recognition of the several State governments, guaranteed to the people of the States their political rights and franchises, as well as their rights of person and property as defined by the Constitution of the United States and other States respectively; promised not to disturb any of the people by reason of the late war, and generally indicated that the United States Government was to be restricted to the exercise of the powers delegated in the Constitution.

Though this convention, if ratified, would not have all the binding force of a treaty, it secured to our people the political rights and safety from pillage, to obtain which I proposed to continue the war. I, therefore, with the concurrence of my constitutional advisers, addressed General Johnston as follows:

"CHARLOTTE, NORTH CAROLINA, *April 24, 1865.*

"General J. E. JOHNSTON, *Greensboro, North Carolina.*

"The Secretary of War has delivered to me the copy you handed to him of the basis of an agreement between yourself and General Sherman. Your action is approved. You will so inform General Sherman; and, if the like authority be given by the Government of the United States to complete the arrangement, you will proceed on the basis adopted.

"Further instructions will be given after the details of the negotiation and the methods of executing the terms of agreement when notified by you of the readiness on the part of the General commanding United States forces to proceed with the arrangement.

"JEFFERSON DAVIS."

From the terms of this letter it will be seen that I doubted whether the agreement would be ratified by the United States Government. The opinion I entertained in regard to President Johnson and his venomous Secretary of War, Stanton, did not permit me to expect that they would be less vindictive after a surrender of our army had been proposed than when it was regarded as a formidable body defiantly holding its position in the field. Whatever hope others entertained that the existing war was about to be peacefully terminated, was soon dispelled by the rejection of the basis of agreement on the part of the Government of the United States, and a notice from General Sherman of termination of the armistice in forty-eight hours after noon of the 24th of April, 1865.

General Johnston communicated to me the substance of the above information received by him from General Sherman, and asked for instructions. I have neither his telegram nor my reply, but can give it substantially from memory. It was that he should retire with his cavalry, and as many infantry as could be mounted upon draught-horses, and some light artillery, the rest of the infantry to be disbanded, and a place of rendezvous appointed. It was unnecessary to say anything of the route, as that had been previously agreed on, and supplies placed on it for his retreating army. This order was disobeyed, and he sought another interview with Sherman, to renew his attempt to reach an agreement for a termination of hostilities. Meantime, General Hampton, commanding the cavalry of Johnston's army, came to me at Charlotte, told me that he feared the army was to be surrendered, and wished permission to withdraw his part of it and report to me. I gave the permission, extending it to all the cavalry, which was in accordance with the instructions I had sent to General Johnston. He returned immediately, but I have since learned from him that the cavalry had been included in a proposition to surrender, before he reached them.

After the expiration of the armistice, I rode out of Charlotte, attended by the members of my Cabinet (except Attorney-General Davis, who had gone to see his family, residing in that section, and the Secretary of the Treasury, Mr. Trenholm, who was too ill to accompany me), my personal staff, and the cavalry which had been concentrated from different, and some of them distant, fields of detached service. The number was about two thousand, and they represented six brigade organizations; though so much reduced in numbers, they were in a good state of efficiency, and among their officers were some of the best in our service. To the troops of this command, whose gallantly had been displayed on many fields, there is due from me a special acknowledgment for the kind consideration shown to me on the marches from Charlotte, when the dark shadows which gathered round us foretold the coming night. General Hampton, finding his troops had been included in the surrender, endeavored to join me to offer his individual service, and to share my fate whatever it might be. He accidentally failed to meet me.

I must now recur to two extraordinary statements made by General J. E. Johnston in regard to myself while at Charlotte, North Carolina, on pages 408 and 409, Johnston's "Narrative." The first is that at Greensboro, on the 19th of April—

> "Colonel Archer Anderson, adjutant-general of the army, gave me two papers, addressed to me by the President. The first directed me to obtain from Mr. J. N. Hendren, Treasury Agent, thirty-nine thousand dollars in silver, which was in his hands, subject to my order, and to use it as the military chest of the army. The second, received subsequently by Colonel Anderson, directed me to send this money to the President at Charlotte. This order was not obeyed, however. As only the military part of our Government had then any existence, I thought that a fair share of the fund still left should be appropriated to the benefit of the army."

And so, as revealed in his "Narrative," he took the money, and divided it among the troops.

When my attention was called to this statement by one who had read the "Narrative," I wrote to Colonel Anderson, referred to book and page, and inquired what letters from me as there described he had received. He responded:

"I do not remember anything connected with the subject, except that there was a payment of silver coin to the army at Greensboro, and I have no papers which would afford information."

My letter-book contains no such correspondence, but has a letter which renders more than doubtful the assertion that I wrote others such as described. The only letter found in my letter-book on the subject of the funds in charge of Hendren is the following:

"GREENSBORO, NORTH CAROLINA, *April 15, 1865.*

"Mr. HENDREN, *C. S. Treasurer, Greensboro, North Carolina.*

"SIR: You will report to General Beauregard with the treasure in your possession, that he may give to it due protection as a military chest to be moved with his army train. For further instructions you will report to the Secretary of the Treasury.

"JEFFERSON DAVIS.

"Official: F. R. LUBBOCK, *Colonel and A. D. C.*"

From the above it will be seen that, while I exercised authority to assign officers to their posts or places of duty, I assumed no control over the public Treasury; but in that connection referred the subordinate to his chief, the Secretary of the Treasury, by whom alone could warrants be drawn against the public funds. How very improbable, then, it is, that I wrote to have the money in the hands of a treasurer sent to me personally! Yet this is what General Johnston claims to have resisted, when without any lawful authority he distributed the money himself. The second statement is:

"As there was reason to suppose that the Confederate Executive had a large sum in specie in its possession, I urged it earnestly, in writing, to apply a part of it to the payment of the army. This letter was intrusted to Lieutenant-Colonel Mason, who was instructed to wait for an answer. Its receipt was acknowledged by telegraph, and an answer promised. After waiting several days to no purpose. Colonel Mason returned without one."

Not recollecting to have met Colonel Mason at Charlotte, I wrote to him, calling his attention to the statement, and asking what was the fact. Not receiving a reply, I renewed the inquiry, but, though considerable time has elapsed, he has not answered. It is quite possible that I might have met the gentleman without recollecting it, but not at all probable that I should have received such a letter and have forgotten it. Such intrusion of advice as to what should be done with the money in the Treasury, and the speculative opinion as to the amount there, I must suppose would have been very promptly rejected if it had been presented to me. For years there had been irregularity and delay in the payment of the troops, and surely no one regretted it more than myself, or had for years tried more sedulously to correct it; but, expecting the army to continue in the field, it was indispensable to have the means of obtaining the necessary supplies for it.

The Secretary of the Treasury, Mr. Trenholm, was ill before we reached Charlotte, and quite so during our stay there, but he knew there was not a large sum of specie in the Treasury, and with patriotic desire had been using it to supply the troops after Confederate money became unavailable for purchases. He did not contemplate the abandonment of our cause, and it would not have taken him a minute to answer that more than all the money he had would be needed in future military operations.

On the 26th, the day on which the armistice terminated, General Johnston again met General Sherman, who offered the same terms which had been made with General Lee, and he says, "General Johnston, without hesitation, agreed to, and we executed the following," which was the surrender of General Johnston's troops, with the condition of their being paroled and the officers being permitted to retain their side-arms, private horses, and baggage.

It is true that these were the terms accepted by Lee, but the condition of the two armies was very different. Lee's supplies had been cut off, his men were exhausted by fatigue and hunger; he had no reënforcements in view; notwithstanding the immense superiority in numbers and equipments of the enemy pursuing, he had from point to point fought them in rear and on both flanks, and had, the day before his line of retreat was closed, rejected the demand for surrender, and only yielded to it after his starving little army had been surrounded by masses through which he tried to, but could not, cut his way.

Johnston's line of retreat was open, and supplies had been placed upon it. His cavalry was superior to that of the enemy, as had been proved in every conflict between them. Maury and Forrest and Taylor still had armies in the field—not large, but strong enough to have collected around them the men who had left Johnston's army and gone to their homes to escape a surrender, as well as those who under similar circumstances had left Lee. The show of continued resistance, I then believed, as I still do, would have overcome the depression which was spreading like a starless night over the country, and that the exhibition of a determination not to leave our political future at the mercy of an enemy which had for four years been striving to subjugate the States would have led the United States authorities to do, as Mr. Lincoln had indicated—give any terms which might be found necessary speedily to terminate the existing war.

Those who look back upon the period when the States were treated as subject provinces, and the Congress left to legislate at its will— when a war professedly waged to bring the seceding States back to the Union, with all the rights and privileges guaranteed by the Constitution, was followed by the utter disregard of those rights, and the miscalled peace was a state of vindictive hostility—will probably think continued war was not the greatest of evils.

I quote again from the "Memoirs" of Sherman, vol. ii, p. 349. Referring to the first interview, he writes:

"I then told Johnston that he must be
convinced that he could not oppose my army,
and that, since Lee had surrendered, he could
do the same with honor and propriety. He
plainly and repeatedly admitted this, and
added that any further fighting would be
'*murder*'; but he thought that, instead of
surrendering piecemeal, we might arrange
terms that would embrace *all* the Confederate
armies."

Sherman further writes that he told Johnston that the terms given to General
Lee's army were most generous and liberal, which he states Johnston "admitted,
but always recurred to the idea of a universal surrender, embracing his own
army, that of Dick Taylor, in Louisiana and Texas, and of Maury, Forrest, and
others, in Alabama and Georgia." Considering the character of the authority
cited, and the extraordinary proposition to provide for a universal surrender by
a district commander, it may be well supposed to require confirmation. I
therefore quote from General Richard Taylor, "Destruction and
Reconstruction," page 224:

"Intelligence of the Johnston-Sherman convention reached us, and
Canby and I were requested by the officers making it to conform to
its terms until the civil authorities acted."

The advice may have been well enough, but, as there was an established
channel of communication, and an order of responsibility necessary for effective
coöperation in the public service, something more than courtesy required that
the Executive should have been advised if not consulted. I had left Charlotte
with no other sure reliance against any cavalry movement of the enemy than the
force which was with me; that, however, I believed to be sufficient for any
probable exigency, if the reënforcements hoped for should not join us on the
way. We proceeded at easy stages; some of the command thought we went too
slow. After making two halts of about half a day each, we reached the Savannah
River. I crossed early in the morning of the 4th of May, with a company, which
had been detailed as my escort, and rode some miles to a farmhouse, where I
halted to get breakfast and have our horses fed. Here I learned that a regiment
of the enemy were moving upon Washington, Georgia, which was one of our
depots of supplies, and I sent back a courier with a pencil-note addressed to
General Vaughn, or the officer commanding the advance, requesting him to
come on and join me immediately. After waiting a considerable time, I
determined to move on with my escort, trusting that the others would overtake
us, and that, if not, we should arrive in Washington in time to rally the citizens
to its defense. When I reached there, scouts were sent out on the different roads,
and my conclusion was that we had had a false alarm. The Secretary of State,
Mr. Benjamin, being unaccustomed to traveling on horseback, parted from me,
at the house where we stopped to breakfast, to take another mode of conveyance
and a different route from that which I was pursuing, with intent to rejoin me in
the trans-Mississippi Department. At Washington, the Secretary of the Navy,
Mr. Mallory, left me temporarily to attend to the needs of his family. The
Secretary of War, Mr. Breckinridge, had remained with the cavalry at the
crossing of the Savannah River. During the night after my arrival in

Washington, he sent in an application for authority to draw from the treasure, under the protection of the troops, enough to make to them a partial payment. I authorized the acting Secretary of the Treasury to meet the requisition by the use of the silver coin in the train. When the next day passed without the troops coming forward, I sent a note to the Secretary of War, showing the impolicy of my longer delay, having there heard that General Upton had passed within a few miles of the town on his way to Augusta to receive the surrender of the garrison and military material at that place, in conformity with orders issued by General Johnston. This was my first positive information of his surrender. Not receiving an immediate reply to the note addressed to the Secretary of War, General Breckinridge, I spoke to Captain Campbell, of Kentucky, commanding my escort, explained to him the condition of affairs, and telling him that his company was not strong enough to fight, and too large to pass without observation, asked him to inquire if there were ten men who would volunteer to go with me without question wherever I should choose. He brought back for answer that the whole company volunteered on the terms proposed. Gratifying as this manifestation was, I felt it would expose them to unnecessary hazard to accept the offer, and told him, in any manner he might think best, to form a party of ten men. With these. Captain Campbell, Lieutenant Barnwell, of South Carolina, Colonels F. E. Lubbock, John Taylor Wood, and William Preston Johnston, of my personal staff, I left Washington. Secretary Reagan remained for a short time to transfer the treasure in his hands, except a few thousand dollars, and then rejoined me on the road. This transfer of the treasure was made to Mr. Semple, a bonded officer of the navy, and his assistant, Mr. Tidball, with instructions, as soon as it could be safely done, to transport it abroad and deliver it to the commercial house which had acted as the financial agent of the Confederate Government, and was reported to have incurred liabilities on its account.

Mr. Reagan overtook me in a few hours, but I saw no more of General Breckinridge, and learned subsequently that he was following our route, with a view to overtake me, when he heard of my capture, and, turning to the east, reached the Florida coast unmolested. On the way he met J. Taylor Wood, and, in an open boat, they crossed the straits to the West Indies. No report reached me at that time, or until long afterward, in regard to the cavalry command left at the Savannah River; then it was to the effect that paroled men from Johnston's army brought news of its surrender, and that the condition of returning home and remaining unmolested embraced all the men of the department who would give their parole, and that this had exercised a great influence over the troops, inclining them to accept those terms. Had General Johnston obeyed the order sent to him from Charlotte, and moved on the route selected by himself, with all his cavalry, so much of the infantry as could be mounted, and the light artillery, he could not have been successfully pursued by General Sherman. His force, united to that I had assembled at Charlotte, would, it was believed, have been sufficient to vanquish any troops which the enemy had between us and the Mississippi River.

Had the cavalry with which I left Charlotte been associated with a force large enough to inspire hope for the future, instead of being discouraged by the surrender in their rear, it would probably have gone on, and, when united with the forces of Maury, Forrest, and Taylor, in Alabama and Mississippi, have constituted an army large enough to attract stragglers, and revive the drooping spirits of the country. In the worst view of the case it should have been able to cross the trans-Mississippi Department, and there uniting with the armies of E. K. Smith and Magruder to form an army, which in the portion of that country abounding in supplies, and deficient in rivers and railroads, could have continued the war until our enemy, foiled in the purpose of subjugation, should, in accordance with his repeated declaration, have agreed, on the basis of a return to the Union, to acknowledge the Constitutional rights of the States, and by a convention, or *quasi*-treaty, to guarantee security of person and property. To this hope I persistently clung, and, if our independence could not be achieved, so much, at least, I trusted might be gained.

Those who have endured the horrors of "reconstruction," who have, under "carpet-bag rule," borne insult, robbery, and imprisonment without legal warrant, can appreciate the value which would have attached to such limited measure of success.

When I left Washington, Georgia, with the small party which has been enumerated, my object was to go to the south far enough to pass below the points reported to be occupied by Federal troops, and then turn to the west, cross the Chattahoochee, and then go on to meet the forces still supposed to be in the field in Alabama. If, as now seemed probable, there should be no prospect of a successful resistance east of the Mississippi, I intended then to cross to the trans-Mississippi Department, where I believed Generals E. K. Smith and Magruder would continue to uphold our cause. That I was not mistaken in the character of these men, I extract from the order issued by General E. K. Smith to the soldiers of the trans-Mississippi Army on the 21st of April, 1865:

> "Great disasters have overtaken us. The Army of Northern Virginia and our General-in-Chief are prisoners of war. With you rest the hopes of our nation, and upon you depends the fate of our people. . . . Prove to the world that your hearts have not failed in the hour of disaster. . . . Stand by your colors—maintain your discipline. The great resources of this department, its vast extent, the numbers, the discipline, and the efficiency of the army, will secure to our country terms that a proud people can with honor accept."

General Magruder, with like heroic determination, invoked the troops and people of Texas not to despond, and pointed out their ability in the interior of that vast State to carry on the war indefinitely.

General D. H. Maury, after his memorable defense of Mobile, withdrew his forces on the 12th of April, at the last moment, and moved toward Meridian. Commodore Farrand, commanding our navy at Mobile Bay, withdrew his armed vessels and steamers up the Tombigbee River, and planted torpedoes in the Alabama below. Forrest and Maury had about eight thousand men, but these were veterans, tried in many hard engagements, and trained to the highest state of efficiency. Before Maury withdrew from Mobile, news had been received of Lee's surrender. Taylor says the news was soon disseminated through his army, but that the men remained steadfast, and manifested a determination to maintain the honor of our aims to the last. On pages 224 and 225 of his book, he gives an account of the intelligence received of the Johnston-Sherman convention of the 18th of April, and of the meeting between Canby and himself to arrange terms for his army, and an agreement that there should be an armistice; but he says, two days after that meeting, news was received of Johnston's surrender, and the capture of President Davis. The latter was untrue, and he does not say who communicated it, but that he was at the same time notified that the Johnston-Sherman convention had been disavowed by the United States Government, and notice given for the termination of the armistice. Under these circumstances he asked General Canby to meet him again, and on the 8th of May, two days before I was actually captured, but which he supposed had already occurred, he agreed with Canby on terms for the surrender of the land and naval forces in Mississippi and Alabama. These terms were similar to those made between Johnston and Sherman; the mounted men were to retain their horses, being their private property.

On the 26th of May, the chief of staff of General E. Kirby Smith, and the chief of staff of General Canby, at Baton Rouge, arranged similar terms for the surrender of the troops in the trans-Mississippi Department. On May 11th, after the last army east of the Mississippi had surrendered, but before Kirby Smith had entered into terms, the enemy sent an expedition from the Brazos Santiago against a little Confederate encampment some fifteen miles above. The camp was captured and burned, but, in the zeal to secure the fruits of victory, they remained so long collecting the plunder, that General J. E. Slaughter heard of the expedition, moved against it, and drove it back with considerable loss, sustaining very little injury to his command. This was, I believe, the last armed conflict of the war, and, though very small in comparison to its great battles, it deserves notice as having closed the long struggle—as it opened— with a Confederate victory.

The total number of prisoners paroled at Greensboro, North Carolina, as reported by General Schofield, was 36,817; in Georgia and Florida, as reported by General Wilson, 52,543; aggregate surrender under the capitulation of General J. E. Johnston, 89,270.[125] How many of this last number were men who left General Johnston's army to avoid the surrender, or were on detached service from the armies of Virginia and North Carolina, I have no means of ascertaining.

The total number in the Department of Alabama and Mississippi paroled by General Canby, under agreement with General Richard Taylor, of the 8th of May, 1865, as reported, was 42,293,[126] to which may be added of the navy a small force—less than 150. The number surrendered by General E. Kirby Smith, commanding the trans-Mississippi Department, as reported, was 17,686.[127] To this small dimension had General Smith's army been reduced when he accepted the terms to which a reference has already been made. This reduction resulted from various causes, but it is believed was mainly due to the reluctance of a large part of his army to accept a parole, preferring to take whatever hazard belonged to absenting themselves without leave and continuing their character of belligerents. A few, but so far as I know very few, even went to the extent of expatriating themselves, and joined Maximilian in Mexico. Against no one as much as myself did the hostility of our victorious enemy manifest itself, but I was never willing to seek the remedy of exile, and always advised those who consulted me against that resort. The mass of our people could not go; the few who were able to do so were most needed to sustain the others in the hour of a common adversity. The example of Ireland after the Treaty of Limerick, and of Canada after its conquest by Great Britain, were instructive as to the duty of the influential men to remain and share the burden of a common disaster.

With General E. K. Smith's surrender the Confederate flag no longer floated on the land; but one gallant sailor still unfurled it on the Pacific. Captain Waddell, commanding the Confederate cruiser Shenandoah, swept the ocean from Australia nearly to Behring's Straits, making many captures in the Okhobak Sea and Arctic Ocean. In August, 1865, he learned from the captain of a British ship that the Confederacy, as an independent Government, had ceased to exist. With the fall of his Government his right to cruise was of course terminated; he therefore sailed for the coast of England, entered the Mersey, and on November 6, 1865, and in due form, surrendered his vessel to the British Government. She was accepted and subsequently transferred to the United States.

After leaving Washington in the manner and for the purpose heretofore described, I overtook a commissary and quartermaster's train, having public papers of value in charge, and, finding that they had no experienced woodsman with it, I gave them four of the men of my small party, and went on with the rest. On the second or third day after leaving Washington, I heard that a band of marauders, supposed to be stragglers and deserters from both armies, were in pursuit of my family, whom I had not seen since they left Richmond, but of whom I heard, at Washington, that they had gone with my private secretary and seven paroled men, who generously offered their services as an escort, to the Florida coast. Their route was to the east of that I was pursuing, but I immediately changed direction and rode rapidly across the country to overtake them. About nightfall the horses of my escort gave out, but I pressed on with Secretary Reagan and my personal staff. It was a bright moonlight night, and just before day, as the moon was sinking below the tree-tops, I met a party of men in the road, who answered my questions by saying they belonged to an Alabama regiment; that they were coming from a village not far off, on their way homeward. Upon inquiry being made, they told me they had passed an encampment of wagons, with women and children, and asked me if we belonged to that party. Upon being answered in the affirmative, they took their leave.

After a short time I was hailed by a voice which I recognized as that of my private secretary, who informed me that the marauders had been hanging around the camp, and that he and others were on post around it, and were expecting an assault as soon as the moon went down. A silly story had got abroad that it was a treasure-train, and the *auri sacra fames* had probably instigated these marauders, as it subsequently stimulated General J. H. Wilson, to send out a large cavalry force to capture the same train. For the protection of my family I traveled with them two or three days, when, believing that they had passed out of the region of marauders, I determined to leave their encampment at nightfall, to execute my original purpose. My horse and those of my party proper were saddled preparatory to a start, when one of my staff, who had ridden into the neighboring village, returned and told me that he had heard that a marauding party intended to attack the camp that night. This decided me to wait long enough to see whether there was any truth in the rumor, which I

482

supposed would be ascertained in a few hours. My horse remained saddled and my pistols in the holsters, and I lay down, fully dressed, to rest. Nothing occurred to rouse me until just before dawn, when my coachman, a free colored man, who faithfully clung to our fortunes, came and told me there was firing over the branch, just behind our encampment. I stepped out of my wife's tent and saw some horsemen, whom I immediately recognized as cavalry, deploying around the encampment. I turned back and told my wife these were not the expected marauders, but regular troopers. She implored me to leave her at once. I hesitated, from unwillingness to do so, and lost a few precious moments before yielding to her importunity. My horse and arms were near the road on which I expected to leave, and down which the cavalry approached; it was therefore impracticable to reach them. I was compelled to start in the opposite direction. As it was quite dark in the tent, I picked up what was supposed to be my "raglan," a water-proof, light overcoat, without sleeves; it was subsequently found to be my wife's, so very like my own as to be mistaken for it; as I started, my wife thoughtfully threw over my head and shoulders a shawl. I had gone perhaps fifteen or twenty yards when a trooper galloped up and ordered me to halt and surrender, to which I gave a defiant answer, and, dropping the shawl and raglan from my shoulders, advanced toward him; he leveled his carbine at me, but I expected, if he fired, he would miss me, and my intention was in that event to put my hand under his foot, tumble him off on the other side, spring into his saddle, and attempt to escape. My wife, who had been watching, when she saw the soldier aim his carbine at me, ran forward and threw her arms around me. Success depended on instantaneous action, and, recognizing that the opportunity had been lost, I turned back, and, the morning being damp and chilly, passed on to a fire beyond the tent. Our pursuers had taken different roads, and approached our camp from opposite directions; they encountered each other and commenced firing, both supposing they had met our armed escort, and some casualties resulted from their conflict with an imaginary body of Confederate troops. During the confusion, while attention was concentrated upon myself, except by those who were engaged in pillage, one of my aides, Colonel J. Taylor Wood, with Lieutenant Barnwell, walked off unobserved. His daring exploits on the sea had made him, on the part of the Federal Government, an object of special hostility, and rendered it quite proper that he should avail himself of every possible means of escape. Colonel Pritchard went over to their battle-field, and I did not see him for a long time, surely more than an hour after my capture. He subsequently claimed credit, in a conversation with me, for the forbearance shown by his men in not shooting me when I refused to surrender.

Wilson and others have uttered many falsehoods in regard to my capture, which have been exposed in publications by persons there present—by Secretary Reagan, by the members of my personal staff, and by the colored coachman, Jim Jones, which must have been convincing to all who were not given over to believe a lie. For this reason I will postpone, to some other time and more appropriate place, any further notice of the story and its variations, all the spawn of a malignity that shames the civilization of the age. We were, when prisoners, subjected to petty pillage, as described in the publications referred to, and in others; and to annoyances such as military *gentlemen* never commit or permit.

On our way to Macon we received the proclamation of President Andrew Johnson offering a reward for my apprehension as an accomplice in the assassination of the late President A. Lincoln. Some troops by the wayside had the proclamation, which was displayed with vociferous demonstrations of exultation over my capture. When we arrived at Macon I was conducted to the hotel where General Wilson had his quarters. A strong guard was in front of the entrance, and, when I got down to pass in, it opened ranks, facing inward, and presented arms.

A commodious room was assigned to myself and family. After a while the steward of the hotel called and inquired whether I would dine with General Wilson or have dinner served with myself and family in my room. I chose the latter. After dinner I received a message from General Wilson, asking whether he should wait upon me, or whether I would call upon him. I rose and accompanied the messenger to General Wilson's presence. We had met at West Point when he was a cadet, and I a commissioner sent by the Congress to inquire into the affairs of the Academy. After some conversation in regard to former times and our common acquaintance, he referred to the proclamation offering a reward for my capture. Taking it for granted that any significant remark of mine would be reported to his Government, and fearing that I might never have another opportunity to give my opinion to A. Johnson, I told him there was one man in the United States who knew that proclamation to be false. He remarked that my expression indicated a particular person. I answered that I did, and the person was the one who signed it, for he at least knew that I preferred Lincoln to himself. Some other conversation then occurred in regard to the route on which we were to be carried. Having several small children, one of them an infant, I expressed a preference for the easier route by water, supposing then, as seemed to do, that I was to go to Washington City. He manifested a courteous, obliging temper, and, either by the authority with which he was invested or by obtaining it from a higher power, my preference as to the route was accorded. I told him that some of the men with me were on parole, and that they all were riding their own horses—private property—that I would be glad they should be permitted to retain them, and I have a distinct recollection that he promised me it should be done; but I have since learned that they were all deprived of their horses, and some who were on parole, viz., Major Moran, Captain Moody, Lieutenant Hathaway, Midshipman Howell, and Private Messec, who had not violated their obligations of parole, but had been captured because they were found voluntarily traveling with my family to protect them from marauders, were sent with me as prisoners of war, and all incarcerated, in disregard of the protection promised when they surrendered. At Augusta we were put on a steamer, and there met Vice-President Stephens; Hon. C. C. Clay, who had voluntarily surrendered himself upon learning that he was included in the proclamation for the arrest of certain persons charged with complicity in the assassination of Mr. Lincoln; General Wheeler, the distinguished cavalry officer, and his adjutant, General Ralls. My private secretary, Burton N. Harrison, had refused to be left behind, and, though they would not allow him to go in the carriage with me, he was resolved to follow my fortunes, as well from sentiment as the hope of being useful. His fidelity was rewarded by a long and rigorous imprisonment. At Port Royal we were transferred to a sea-going vessel, which, instead of being sent to Washington City, was brought to anchor at Hampton

Roads. One by one all my companions in misfortune were sent away, we knew not whither, leaving on the vessel only Mr. Clay and his wife and myself and family. After some days' detention, Clay and myself were removed to Fortress Monroe, and there incarcerated in separate cells. Not knowing that the Government was at war with women and children, I asked that my family might be permitted to leave the ship and go to Richmond or Washington City, or to some place where they had acquaintances, but this was refused. I then requested that they might be permitted to go abroad on one of the vessels lying at the Roads. This was also denied; finally, I was informed that they must return to Savannah on the vessel by which we came. This was an old transport-ship, hardly seaworthy. My last attempt was to get for them the privilege of stopping at Charleston, where they had many personal friends. This also was refused— why, I did not then know, have not learned since, and am unwilling to make a supposition, as none could satisfactorily account for such an act of inhumanity. My daily experience as a prisoner shed no softer light on the transaction, but only served to intensify my extreme solicitude. Bitter tears have been shed by the gentle, and stern reproaches have been made by the magnanimous, on account of the needless torture to which I was subjected, and the heavy fetters riveted upon me, while in a stone casemate and surrounded by a strong guard; but all these were less excruciating than the mental agony my captors were able to inflict. It was long before I was permitted to hear from my wife and children, and this, and things like this, was the power which education added to savage cruelty; but I do not propose now and here to enter upon the story of my imprisonment, or more than merely to refer to other matters which concerns me personally, as distinct from my connection with the Confederacy.

[Footnote 124: "Memoirs of General W. T. Sherman," vol. ii, pp. 346, 347.]
[Footnote 125: "Memoirs of General W. T. Sherman," vol. ii, p. 370.]
[Footnote 126: "Annual Cyclopaedia," 1865, p. 11.]
[Footnote 127: Ibid.]

CHAPTER LV.

Number of the Enemy's Forces in the War.—Number of the Enemy's Troops from Maryland, Kentucky, Missouri, and Tennessee.—Cruel Conduct of the War.—Statements in 1862.—Statements in 1863.— Emancipation Proclamation.—Statements in 1864.—General Hunter's Proceedings near Lynchburg.—Cruelties in Sherman's March through South Carolina.

On April 25th, at Raleigh, North Carolina, General J. E. Johnston capitulated to General Sherman, as has been stated, and his army was disbanded. On May 4th General B. Taylor capitulated with the last of our forces east.

The number of men brought into the field by the Government of the United States during the war, according to the official returns in the Adjutant-General's office, Washington, was 2,678,967. In addition to these, 86,724 paid a commutation.

The rapidity with which calls for men were made by that Government during the last eighteen mouths of the war, and the number brought into the field, were as follows:

Men furnished

Calls of October 17, 1863, and February 1, 1864, for

485

500,000 men for three years 317,092
Call of March 14, 1864, for 200,000 men for three years 259,515
Militia for one hundred days, April to July, 1864 83,612
Call of July 18, 1864, for 500,000 men . . . . 385,163[128]
Call of December 19, 1864, for 300,000 men 211,752
—————
Total men furnished in eighteen months 1,257,134
The number of men furnished on call of the United States Government, previous to October 17, 1863, was as follows:
Men furnished
Call of April 15, 1861, for 75,000 men for three months 91,816
Call of May 3, 1861, for 500,000 men 700,680
Men furnished in May and June, 1862, for three months . . 15,007
Call of July 2, 1862, for 300,000 men for three years . . 421,465
Call of August 4, 1862, for 300,000 militia for nine months 87,588
Proclamation of June 15, 1863, for militia for six months 16,361
Volunteers and militia at various times, of sixty days to one year 13,760
Volunteers and militia at various times for three years 75,156
—————
Total 1,421,833
The number of men furnished to the armies of the United States by the States of Kentucky, Maryland, Missouri, and Tennessee, was as follows:
States. Men furnished.
Kentucky . . . . 70,760 equal to 70,832 three years' men.
Maryland . . . . 46,638 " 41,275 " " "
Missouri . . . . . . 109,111 " 86,530 " " "
Tennessee . . . . 31,092 " 26,394 " " "
————- ————-
Total 262,601 225,031
The public debt of the Government of the United States on July 1, 1861, and on July 1, 1865 was as follows:
Debt, July 1, 1861 . . . . $90,867,828.68
" July 1, 1865 . . . . 2,682,593,026.53
—————
Increase in four years $2,591,725,197.85
Of the manner in which our adversaries conducted the war I had frequent occasion to remark. Those observations made at the time present a more correct representation of facts than could be given in more recent statements. In a message to Congress on August 15, 1862, I said:

"The perfidy which disregarded rights
secured by compact, the madness which
trampled on obligations made sacred by every
consideration of honor, have been intensified
by the malignancy engendered by defeat.
These passions have changed the character of
the hostilities waged by our enemies, who are
becoming daily less regardful of the usages of

civilized war and the dictates of humanity.
Rapine and wanton destruction of private
property, war upon non-combatants, murder
of captives, bloody threats to avenge the death
of an invading soldiery by the slaughter of
unarmed citizens, orders of banishment
against peaceful farmers engaged in the
cultivation of the soil, are some of the means
used by our ruthless invaders to enforce the
submission of a free people to a foreign sway.
Confiscation bills, of a character so atrocious
as to insure, if executed, the utter ruin of the
entire population of these States, are passed
by their Congress and approved by their
Executive. The moneyed obligations of the
Confederate Government are counterfeited by
citizens of the United States, and publicly
advertised for sale in their cities, with a
notoriety that sufficiently attests the
knowledge of their Government; and the
soldiers of the invading armies are found
supplied with large quantities of these forged
notes as a means of despoiling the country
people by fraud out of such portions of their
property as armed violence may fail to reach.
Two at least of the generals of the United
States are engaged, unchecked by their
Government, in exciting servile insurrection,
and in arming and training slaves for warfare
against their masters, citizens of the
Confederacy."

Again, in January, 1863, I said, with regard to the conduct of the war by our
adversaries:

"It is my painful duty again to inform you
of the renewed examples of every conceivable
atrocity committed by the armed forces of the
United States at different points within the
Confederacy, and which must stamp indelible
infamy, not only on the perpetrators, but on
their superiors, who, having the power to
check these outrages on humanity, numerous
and well authenticated as they have been,
have not yet in a single instance, of which I
am aware, inflicted punishment on the
wrong-doers. Since my last communication to
you, one General McNeil murdered seven
prisoners of war in cold blood, and the
demand for his punishment has remained
unsatisfied. The Government of the United

States, after promising examination and explanation in relation to the charges made against General B. F. Butler, has, by its subsequent silence, after repeated efforts on my part to obtain some answer on the subject, not only admitted his guilt, but sanctioned it by acquiescence.... Recently I have received apparently authentic intelligence of another general by the name of Milroy, who has issued orders in West Virginia for the payment of money to him by the inhabitants, accompanied by the most savage threats of shooting every recusant, besides burning his house, and threatening similar atrocities against any of our citizens who shall fail to betray their country by giving him prompt notice of the approach of any of our forces. And this subject has also been submitted to the superior military authorities of the United States, with but faint hope that they will evince any disapprobation of the act.

"A proclamation, dated on January 1, 1863, signed and issued by the President of the United States, orders and declares all slaves within ten of the States of the Confederacy to be free, except such as are found in certain districts now occupied in part by the armed forces of the enemy. We may well leave it to the instinct of that common humanity, which a beneficent Creator has implanted in the breasts of our fellow-men of all countries, to pass judgment on a measure by which several millions of human beings of an inferior race— peaceful, contented laborers in their sphere—are doomed to extermination, while at the same time they are encouraged to a general assassination of their masters by the insidious recommendation 'to abstain from violence, unless in necessary self-defense.'"

The war, which in its inception was waged for forcing us back into the Union, having failed to accomplish that purpose, passed into a second stage, in which it was attempted to conquer and rule our States as dependent provinces. Defeated in this design, our enemies entered upon another, which could have no other purpose than revenge and plunder of private property. In May, 1864, it was still characterized by the barbarism with which it had been previously conducted. Aged men, helpless women and children appealed in vain to the humanity which should be inspired by their condition, for immunity from arrest, incarceration, or banishment from their homes. Plunder and devastation of the property of non-combatants, destruction of private dwellings, and even of edifices devoted to the worship of God, expeditions organized for the sole purpose of sacking cities, consigning them to the flames, killing the unarmed inhabitants, and inflicting horrible outrages on women and children, were some of the constantly recurring atrocities of the invader.

On June 19, 1864, Major-General Hunter began his retreat from before Lynchburg down the Shenandoah Valley. Lieutenant-General Early, who followed in pursuit, thus describes the destruction he witnessed along the route:

"Houses had been burned, and helpless women and children left without shelter. The country had been stripped of provisions, and many families left without a morsel to eat. Furniture and bedding had been cut to pieces, and old men and women and children robbed of all the clothing they had, except that on their backs. Ladies' trunks had been rifled, and their dresses torn to pieces in mere wantonness. Even the negro girls had lost their little finery. At Lexington he had burned the Military Institute with all its contents, including its library and scientific apparatus. Washington College had been plundered, and the statue of Washington stolen. The residence of ex-Governor Letcher at that place had been burned by orders, and but a few minutes given Mrs. Letcher and her family to leave the house. In the county a most excellent Christian gentleman, a Mr. Creigh, had been hung, because, on a former occasion, he had killed a straggling and marauding Federal soldier while in the act of insulting and outraging the ladies of his family." [129]

A letter dated Charleston, September 14, 1865, written by Rev. Dr. John Bachman, then pastor of the Lutheran Church in that city, presents many facts respecting the devastation and robberies by the enemy in South Carolina. So much as relates to the march of Sherman's army through parts of the State is here presented:

"When Sherman's army came sweeping through Carolina, leaving a broad track of desolation for hundreds of miles, whose steps were accompanied with fire, and sword, and blood, reminding us of the tender mercies of the Duke of Alva, I happened to be at Cash's Depot, six miles from Cheraw. The owner was a widow, Mrs. Ellerbe, seventy-one years of age. Her son, Colonel Cash, was absent. I witnessed the barbarities inflicted on the aged, the widow, and young and delicate

489

females. Officers, high in command, were engaged tearing from the ladies their watches, their ear and wedding rings, the daguerreotypes of those they loved and cherished. A lady of delicacy and refinement, a personal friend, was compelled to strip before them, that they might find concealed watches and other valuables under her dress. A system of torture was practiced toward the weak, unarmed, and defenseless, which, as far as I know and believe, was universal throughout the whole course of that invading army. Before they arrived at a plantation, they inquired the names of the most faithful and trustworthy family servants; these were immediately seized, pistols were presented at their heads; with the most terrific curses, they were threatened to be shot if they did not assist them in finding buried treasures. If this did not succeed, they were tied up and cruelly beaten. Several poor creatures died under the infliction. The last resort was that of hanging, and the officers and men of the triumphant army of General Sherman were engaged in erecting gallows and hanging up these faithful and devoted servants. They were strung up until life was nearly extinct, when they were let down, suffered to rest awhile, then threatened and hung up again. It is not surprising that some should have been left hanging so long that they were taken down dead. Coolly and deliberately these hardened men proceeded on their way, as if they had perpetrated no crime, and as if the God of heaven would not pursue them with his vengeance. But it was not alone the poor blacks (to whom they professed to come as liberators) that were thus subjected to torture and death. Gentlemen of high character, pure and honorable and gray-headed, unconnected with the military, were dragged from their fields or their beds, and subjected to this process of threats, beating, and hanging. Along the whole track of Sherman's army, traces remain of the cruelty and inhumanity practiced on the aged and the defenseless. Some of those who were hung up died under the rope, while their cruel murderers have not only been left unreproached and unhung, but have been hailed as heroes and patriots. The list of those martyrs whom the cupidity of the officers and men of Sherman's army sacrificed to their thirst for gold and silver, is large and most revolting. If the editors of this paper will give their consent to publish it, I will give it in full, attested by the names of the purest and best men and women of our Southern land.

"I, who have been a witness to these acts of barbarity that are revolting to every feeling of humanity and mercy, was doomed to feel in my own person the effects of the avarice, cruelty, and despotism which characterized the men of that army. I was the only male guardian of the refined and delicate females who had fled there for shelter and protection. I soon ascertained the plan that was adopted in this wholesale system of plunder, insult, blasphemy, and brutality. The first party that came was headed by officers, from a colonel to a lieutenant, who acted with seeming politeness, and told me that they only came to secure our firearms, and when these were delivered up nothing in the house should be touched. Out of the house, they said, they were authorized to press forage for their large army. I told them that along the whole line of the march of Sherman's army, from Columbia to Cheraw, it had been ascertained that ladies had been robbed and personally insulted. I asked for a guard to protect the females. They said that there was no necessity for this, as the men dare not act contrary to orders. If any did not treat the ladies with proper respect, I might blow their brains out. 'But,' said I, 'you have taken away our arms, and we are defenseless.' They did not blush much, and made no reply. Shortly after this came the second party, before the first had left. They demanded the keys of the ladies' drawers, took away such articles as they wanted, then locked the drawers and put the keys in their pockets. In the mean time, they gathered up the spoons, knives, forks, towels, table-cloths, etc. As they were carrying them off, I appealed to the officers of the first party; they ordered the men to put back the things; the officer of the second party said he would see them d——d first; and, without further ado,

491

packed them up, and they glanced at each other and smiled. The elegant carriage and all the vehicles on the premises were seized and filled with bacon and other plunder. The smokehouses were emptied of their contents and carried off. Every head of poultry was seized and flung over their mules, and they presented the hideous picture in some of the scenes in 'Forty Thieves.' Every article of harness they did not wish was cut in pieces.

"By this time the first and second parties had left, and a third appeared on the field. They demanded the keys of the drawers, and, on being informed that they had been carried off, coolly and deliberately proceeded to break open the locks, took what they wanted, and when we uttered words of complaint were cursed. Every horse, mule, and carriage, even to the carts, was taken away, and, for hundreds of miles, the last animal that cultivated the widow's corn-field, and the vehicles that once bore them to the house of worship, were carried off or broken into pieces and burned.

"The first party that came promised to leave ten days' provisions, the rest they carried off. An hour afterward, other hordes of marauders from the same army came and demanded the last pound of bacon and the last quart of meal. On Sunday, the negroes were dressed in their best suits. They were kicked, and knocked down and robbed of all their clothing, and they came to us in their shirtsleeves, having lost their hats, clothes, and shoes. Most of our own clothes had been hid in the woods. The negroes who had assisted in removing them were beaten and threatened with death, and compelled to show them where they were concealed. They cut open the trunks, threw my manuscripts and devotional books into a mud-hole, stole the ladies' jewelry, hair ornaments, etc., tore many garments into tatters, or gave the rest to the negro women to bribe them into criminal intercourse. These women afterward returned to us those articles that, after the mutilations, were scarcely worth preserving. The plantation, of one hundred and sixty negroes, was some distance from the house, and to this place successive parties of fifty at a time resorted for three long days and nights, the husbands and fathers being fired at and compelled to fly to the woods.

"Now commenced scenes of licentiousness, brutality, and ravishment that have scarcely had an equal in the ages of heathen barbarity, I conversed with aged men and women, who were witnesses of these infamous acts of Sherman's unbridled soldiery, and several of them, from the cruel treatment they had received, were confined to their beds for weeks afterward. The time will come when the judgment of Heaven will await these libidinous, beastly barbarians. During this time, the fourth party, whom, I was informed by others, we had the most reason to dread, had made their appearance. They came, as they said, in the name of the great General Sherman, who was next to God Almighty. They came to burn and lay in ashes all that was left. They had burned bridges and depots, cotton-gins, mills, barns, and stables. They swore they would make the d—-d rebel women pound their corn with rocks, and eat their raw meal without cooking. They succeeded in thousands of instances. I walked out at night, and the innumerable fires that were burning as far as the eye could reach, in hundreds of places, illuminated the whole heavens, and testified to the vindictive barbarity of the foe. I presume they had orders not to burn occupied houses, but they strove all in their power to compel families to fly from their houses that they might afterward burn them. The neighborhood was filled with refugees who had been compelled to fly from their plantations on the seaboard. As soon as they had fled, the torch was applied, and, for hundreds of miles, those elegant mansions, once the ornament and pride of our inland country, were burned to the ground.

"All manner of expedients were now adopted to make the residents leave their homes for the second time. I heard them saying, 'This is too large a house to be left standing, we must contrive to burn it.' Canisters of powder were placed all around the house, and an expedient resorted to that promised almost certain success. The house was to be burned down by firing the outbuildings. These were so near each other that the firing of the one would lead to the destruction of all. I had already succeeded in having a few bales of cotton rolled out of the building, and hoped, if they had to be burned, the rest would also be rolled out, which could have been done in ten minutes by several hundred men who were looking on, gloating over the prospect of another elegant mansion in South Carolina being left in ashes. The torch was applied, and soon the large storehouse was on fire. This communicated to several other buildings in the vicinity, which, one by one, were burned to the ground. At length the fire reached the smoke-house, where they had already carried off the bacon of two hundred and fifty hogs. This was burned, and the fire was now rapidly approaching the kitchen, which was so near the dwelling-house that, should the former burn, the destruction of the large and noble edifice would be inevitable.

"A captain of the United States service, a native of England, whose name I would like to mention here, if I did not fear to bring down upon him the censure of the abolitionists as a friend to the rebels, mounted the roof, and the wet blankets we sent up to him prevented the now smoking roof from bursting into flames. I called for help to assist us in procuring water from a deep well; a young lieutenant stepped up, condemned the infamous conduct of the burners, and called on his company for aid; a portion of them came cheerfully to our assistance; the wind seemed almost by a miracle to subside; the house was saved, and the trembling females thanked God for their deliverance. All this time, about one hundred mounted men were looking on, refusing to raise a hand to help us; laughing at the idea that no efforts of ours could save the house from the flames.

"My trials, however, were not yet over, I had already suffered much in a pecuniary point of view. I had been collecting a library on natural history during a long life. The most valuable of these books had been presented by various societies in England, France, Germany, Russia, etc., who had honored me with membership, and they or the authors presented me with these works, which had never been for sale, and could not be purchased. My herbarium, the labor of myself and the ladies of my house for many years, was also among these books. I had left them as a legacy to the library of the Newbury College, and concluded to send them at once. They were detained in Columbia, and there the torch was applied, and all were burned. The stealing and burning of books appear to be one of the programmes on which the army acted, I had assisted in laying the foundation and dedicating the Lutheran Church at Columbia, and there, near its walls, had recently been laid the remains of one who was dearer to me than life itself. To set that brick church on fire from below was impossible. The building stood by itself on a square but little built up. One of Sherman's burners was sent up to the roof. He was seen applying the torch to the cupola. The church was burned to the ground, and the grave of my loved one desecrated. The story circulated, that the citizens had set their own city on fire, is utterly untrue, and only reflects dishonor on those who vilely perpetrated it. General Sherman had his army under control. The burning was by his orders, and ceased when he gave the command.

"I was now doomed to experience in person the effects of avarice and barbarous cruelty. The robbers had been informed in the neighborhood that the family which I was protecting had buried one hundred thousand dollars in gold and silver. They first demanded my watch, which I had effectually secured from their grasp. They then asked me where the money had been hid. I told them I knew nothing about it, and did not believe there was a thousand dollars worth in all, and what there was had been carried off by the owner, Colonel Cash. All this was literally true. They then concluded to try an experiment on me which had proved so successful in hundreds of other instances.

Coolly and deliberately they prepared to inflict torture on a defenseless, gray-headed old man. They carried me behind a stable, and once again demanded where the money was buried, or 'I should be sent to hell in five minutes.' They cocked their pistols and held them to my head. I told them to fire away. One of them, a square-built, broad-faced, large-mouthed, clumsy lieutenant, who had the face of a demon, and who did not utter five words without an awful blasphemy, now kicked me in the stomach until I fell breathless and prostrate. As soon as I was able, I rose again. He once more asked me where the silver was. I answered as before, 'I do not know.' With his heavy, elephant foot he now kicked me on my back until I fell again. Once more I arose, and he put the same question to me. I was nearly breathless, but answered as before. Thus was I either kicked or knocked down seven or eight times. I then told him it was perfectly useless for him to continue his threats or his blows. He might shoot me if he chose. I was ready and would not budge an inch, but requested him not to bruise and batter an unarmed, defenseless old man. 'Now,' said he, 'I'll try a new plan. How would you like to have both your arms cut off?' He did not wait for an answer, but, with his heavy sheathed sword, struck me on my left arm, near the shoulder. I heard it crack; it hung powerless by my side, and I supposed it was broken. He then repeated the blow on the other arm. The pain was most excruciating, and it was several days before I could carve my food or take my arm out of a sling, and it was black and blue for weeks. (I refer to Dr. Kollock, of Cheraw.) At that moment the ladies, headed by my daughter, who had only then been made aware of the brutality practiced upon me, rushed from the house, and came flying to my rescue. 'You dare not murder my father,' said my child; 'he has been a minister in the same church for fifty years, and God has always protected, and will protect him.' 'Do you believe in a God, miss?' said one of the brutal wretches; 'I don't believe in a God, a heaven, nor a hell.' 'Carry me,' said I, 'to your

General.' I did not intend to go to General Sherman, who was at Cheraw, from whom, I was informed, no redress could be obtained, but to a general in the neighborhood, said to be a religious man. Our horses and carriages had all been taken away, and I was too much bruised to be able to walk. The other young officers came crowding around me very officiously, telling me that they would represent the case to the General, and that they would have him shot by ten o'clock the next morning. I saw the winks and glances that were interchanged between them. Every one gave a different name to the officers. The brute remained unpunished, as I saw him on the following morning, as insolent and as profane as he had been on the preceding day.

"As yet, no punishment had fallen on the brutal hyena, and I strove to nurse my bruised body and heal my wounds, and forget the insults and injuries of the past. A few weeks after this I was sent for to perform a parochial duty at Mars Bluff, some twenty miles distant. Arriving at Florence in the vicinity, I was met by a crowd of young men connected with the militia. They were excited to the highest pitch of rage, and thirsted for revenge. They believed that among the prisoners that had just arrived on the railroad-car, on their way to Sumter, were the very men who committed such horrible outrages in the neighborhood. Many of their houses had been laid in ashes. They had been robbed of every means of support. Their horses had been seized; their cattle and hogs bayoneted; their mothers and sisters had been insulted, and robbed of their watches, ear and wedding rings. Some of their parents had been murdered in cold blood. The aged pastor, to whose voice they had so often listened, had been kicked and knocked down by repeated blows, and his hoary head had been dragged about in the sand. They entreated me to examine the prisoners and see whether I could identify the men that had inflicted such barbarities on me. I told them I would do so, provided they would remain where they were and not follow me. The prisoners saw me at a distance, held down their guilty heads, and trembled like aspen-

leaves. All cruel men are cowards. One of my
arms was still in a sling. With the other I
raised some of their hats. They all begged for
mercy. I said to them, 'The other day you were
tigers—you are sheep now.' But a hideous
object soon arrested my attention. There sat
my brutal enemy—, the vulgar, swaggering
lieutenant, who had ridden up to the steps of
the house, insulted the ladies, and beaten me
most unmercifully. I approached him slowly,
and, in a whisper asked him: 'Do you know
me, sir?—the old man whose pockets you first
searched, to see whether he might not have a
penknife to defend himself, and then kicked
and knocked him down with your fist and
heavy scabbard?' He presented the picture of
an arrant coward, and in a trembling voice
implored me to have mercy: 'Don't let me be
shot; have pity! Old man, beg for me! I won't
do it again! For God's sake, save me! O God,
help me!' 'Did you not tell my daughter there
was no God? Why call on him now?' 'Oh, I
have changed my mind; I believe in a God
now.' I turned and saw the impatient, flushed,
and indignant crowd approaching. 'What are
they going to do with me?' said he. 'Do you
hear that sound—click, click?' 'Yes,' said he,
'they are cocking their pistols.' 'True,' said I;
'and if I raise a finger you will have a dozen
bullets through your brain.' 'Then I will go to
hell; don't let them kill me. O Lord, have
mercy!' Speak low,' said I, 'and don't open
your lips.' The men advanced. Already one
had pulled me by the coat. 'Show us the men.'
I gave no clew by which the guilty could be
identified. I walked slowly through the car,
sprang into the waiting carriage, and drove
off."

[Footnote 128: Reduced by excess on previous calls.]

[Footnote 129: "Memoir of the Last Year of the War," by Lieutenant-General
Early.]

CHAPTER LVI.

Final Subjugation of the Confederate States.—Result of the
Contest.—A Simple Process of Restoration.—Rejected by the United
States Government.—A Forced Union.—The President's Proclamation
examined.—The Guarantee, not to destroy.—Provisional Governors.—
Their Duties.—Voters.—First Movement made in Virginia.—
Government set up.—Proceedings.—Action of So-called

Legislature.—Constitutional Amendment.—Case of Dr. Watson.—
Civil Rights Bill.—Storm brewing.—Congress refuses to admit
Senators and Representatives to Seats.—Committee on
"Reconstruction."—Freedmen's Bureau.—Report of Committee.—
Fourteenth Amendment to the Constitution.—Extent of Ratification.—
Another Step taken by Congress.—Military Commanders appointed over
Confederate States, with Unlimited Powers.—Reconstruction by the
Bayonet.—Course of Proceedings required.—Two Governments for Each
State.—Major-Generals appointed.—Further Acts of Congress.—
Proceedings commenced by the Major-General at Richmond.—Civil
Governor appointed.—Military Districts and Sub-districts.—
Registration.—So-called State Convention.—So-called
Legislature.—Its Action.—Measures required by Congress for the
Enfranchisement of Negroes adopted by the So-called Legislature.—
Assertion of Senator Garret Davis.—State represented in Congress.

When the Confederate soldiers laid down their arms and went home, all
hostilities against the power of the Government of the United States ceased. The
powers delegated in the compact of 1787 by these States, i. e., by the people
thereof, to a central organization to promote their general welfare, had been
used for their devastation and subjugation. It was conceded, as the result of the
contest, that the United States Government was stronger in resources than the
Confederate Government, and that the Confederate States had not achieved
their independence.

Nothing remained to be done but for the sovereigns, the people of each State,
to assert their authority and restore order. If the principle of the sovereignty of
the people, the cornerstone of all our institutions, had survived and was still in
force, it was necessary only that the people of each State should reconsider their
ordinances of secession, and again recognize the Constitution of the United
States as the supreme law of the land. This simple process would have placed
the Union on its original basis, and have restored that which had ceased to exist,
the Union by consent. Unfortunately, such was not the intention of the
conqueror. The Union of free-wills and brotherly hearts, under a compact
ordained by the people, was not his object. Henceforth there was to be
established a Union of force. Sovereignty was to pass from the people to the
Government of the United States, and to be upheld by those who had furnished
the money and the soldiers for the war.

The first step required, therefore, in the process for the reconstruction of the
new and forced Union, was to prepare those who had been the late champions of
the sovereignty of the people to become suitable subjects under the new
sovereign. Standing defenseless, stripped of their property, and exposed, as it
was asserted, to the penalties of insurrection on the one hand, and that of
treason on the other, the President of the United States, Mr. Andrew Johnson,
who, as Vice-President, became President after the death of Mr. Lincoln, on May
29, 1865, thus addressed them:

"To the end, therefore, that the authority
of the Government of the United States may
be restored, and that peace, order, and
freedom may be reestablished, I, Andrew
Johnson, President of the United States, do

499

proclaim and declare that I hereby grant to all
persons who have directly or indirectly
participated in the existing rebellion, except
as hereinafter excepted, amnesty and pardon,
with restoration of all rights of property,
except as to slaves, and except in cases where
legal proceedings under the laws of the
United States providing for the confiscation of
property of persons engaged in the rebellion
have been instituted; but on the condition,
nevertheless, that every such person shall
take and subscribe the following oath or
affirmation, and thenceforward keep and
maintain said oath inviolate; and which oath
shall be registered for permanent
preservation, and shall be of the tenor and
effect following, to wit:

"I, —— ——, do solemnly swear, or affirm,
in presence of Almighty God, that I will
henceforth faithfully support and defend the
Constitution of the United States and the
Union thereunder, and that I will, in like
manner, abide by and faithfully support all
laws and proclamations which have been
made during the existing rebellion with
reference to the emancipation of slaves, so
help me God."

The permission to take this oath was withheld from large classes of citizens.
It will be seen that there are two stipulations in this oath, the first faithfully to
support the Constitution of the United States and the Union thereunder. This
comprises obedience to the laws made in conformity to the Constitution, and is
all that is requisite in the simple oath of allegiance of an American citizen. The
second stipulation is:

"To abide by and faithfully support all laws
and proclamations which have been made
during the existing rebellion with reference to
the emancipation of slaves."

What need was thereof this second stipulation? Because the laws were not
enacted, nor the proclamation issued under any grant of power in the
Constitution or under its authority. Now, the exercise of a power by
Government, for which it has no constitutional authority, is not only a
usurpation, but it destroys the sanction of all written instruments of
government. Also, what has become of the unalienable right of property, which
all the State governments were created to protect and preserve? Where was the
sovereignty of the people under these proceedings? Yet the Confederate citizen
was required to bind himself by an oath to abide by and faithfully support all
these usurpations; the alternative being to resist the Government, or to aid and
abet a violation of the Constitution.

Meanwhile, each of the late Confederate States was occupied by a military force of the Government of the United States, and military orders were the supreme law; and that Government thereby proceeded to establish a State organization based on the principle of its own sovereignty. In the first place, the President of the United States issued a proclamation in such terms as to be applicable to each of the Confederate States wherever its affairs were in such process of subjugation as to permit the commencement of the proposed organization. This proclamation begins by setting forth four propositions as the basis of his authority: First, the Constitution declares that the United States shall guarantee to every State in the Union a republican form of government, and protect each against invasion and domestic violence. Second, the President is Commander-in-Chief of the Army and Navy, as well as chief civil executive officer, and bound to take care that the laws be faithfully executed. Third, the rebellion, in its revolutionary progress, deprived the people of all civil government. Fourth, it becomes necessary and proper to enforce and carry out the obligations of the United States to the people of the State in securing it in the enjoyment of a republican form of government. Therefore, etc.

These propositions call for a notice as well because of their fallacy as their enormity. The third declares that the so-called rebellion, in its progress, deprived the people of each Confederate State of all civil government. There was a government over each Confederate State, then existing and in full operation. It was, in all its internal relations, the same government which existed when the State was a member of the Union, whereby it was recognized by the Government of the United States and by the other States as a lawful and republican State government. It had been created by the free consent of the people of the State, and they had defended it with their lives and their fortunes. It had been denied by the Government of the United States that any one of the Confederate States was a foreign state or outside the Union by its secession. There was, therefore, neither in law nor in fact, any foundation for the assertion that the so-called rebellion had deprived the people of each Confederate State of all civil government.

Having thus stripped each Confederate State of all civil government, it was asserted that the Constitution declares that the United States shall guarantee to each State a republican form of government. But to guarantee is not to create, to organize, or to bring into existence. This can be done for a State government only by the free and unconstrained action of the whole people of a State. The creation of such a government is beyond the powers of the Government of the United States, as has already been shown. After a republican government has been instituted by the people, the Constitution requires the United States to guarantee its existence, and thereby forbids them or their Government to overthrow it and set up a creature of its own. The duty to guarantee commands the preservation of that which already exists. Such were the governments of the Confederate States before the war and after the war. Thus the power granted in the Constitution to preserve and guarantee State governments was perverted to overthrow and destroy republican governments, and to erect in their places military Governors, Legislatures, and judicial tribunals.

The third proposition is that the President is Commander in-Chief of the Army and Navy and the chief civil executive. His troops already occupied each of these States, and held the people in subjection. His proclamation was therefore merely a military order from the hand of the conqueror. Everything which he can do under such a character partakes of the nature, simply and solely, of martial law. Therefore he proceeds under the fourth proposition, wherein it "becomes necessary and proper to carry out the obligations of the United States to the people" of each Confederate State, "in securing them in the enjoyment of a republican form of government." The American people were now about to witness, on an extensive scale, the tyrannical experiment of instituting republican governments by the processes of martial law. They had declared it to be a self-evident truth that it was "the right of the people to alter or to abolish it [their government], and to institute a new government, laying its foundation on such principles, and organizing its powers in such form, as to them shall seem most likely to effect their safety and happiness." [130] This principle of the sovereignty of the people was now rejected, and the sovereignty of fleets and armies was substituted.

"Now, therefore," says the Commander-in-Chief of the Army and Navy, and the chief civil executive officer of the United States, "in obedience to the high and solemn duties imposed upon me by the Constitution of the United States, and for the purpose of enabling the loyal people of said State (or States) to organize a State government, whereby justice may be established, domestic tranquillity restored, and loyal citizens protected in all their rights of life, liberty, and property, I do hereby appoint —— —— provisional Governor of the State" It will be here noticed that all the proceedings are undertaken for the sake of the "loyal" persons in the State. Who is to decide what persons are "loyal"? He who issues the military order—the President and his agent the provisional Governor; and they naturally will decide those to be loyal who support and obey their orders. The free assent and dissent which are the basis of the validity of every political action under our system, are unknown in this case.

The duty of the provisional Governor is declared in the proclamation to be, "to prescribe such rules and regulations as may be necessary and proper for convening a convention composed of delegates to be chosen by that portion of the people of the State who are 'loyal' to the United States, and no others, for the purpose of altering and amending the Constitution thereof." In the third of the four propositions laid down as the basis of authority for the President's proceedings, above mentioned, it is declared that the so-called rebellion, "deprived the people of the State of all civil government"; but here it is made the first duty of the provisional Governor to procure a convention of "loyal" persons "to alter and amend the Constitution" of the State. Thus it seems that there was a State in existence, and a Constitution in full vigor, notwithstanding the above declaration of the President to the contrary. This was that Constitution of the State which was in force during that long and peaceful period through which the Constitution of the United States was observed, and constitutional laws enacted. Now it was to be altered and amended from what the sovereign people of those days had ordained it to be, at the command, and to conform to the views, of another sovereign. The nature of those alterations and amendments will be stated hereafter.

This convention was to possess the authority to exercise all the powers necessary "to restore the State to its constitutional relations with the Federal Government." It was further provided that no person should vote unless he had taken the amnesty oath mentioned on a previous page, and was a qualified voter previous to the secession of the State. The convention or the subsequent Legislature was to prescribe the qualification of all voters afterward—"a power," says the President, "the people of the several States composing the Federal Union have rightfully exercised from the origin of the Government to the present time." The proclamation then continued: "And I do hereby direct: first, that the military commander of the department and all officers and persons in the military and naval service aid and assist the said provisional government in carrying into effect this proclamation; and they are enjoined to abstain from in any way hindering, impeding, or discouraging 'loyal' people from the organization of a State government as herein authorized." The proclamation closed with instructions to the Secretary of each department of the Government to proceed to put in operation his department within the limits of the State.

The first movement for the restoration of the Confederate States to the Union under subjugation was commenced in Virginia. Richmond was occupied by the forces of the United States Government, and the authority of all State officers elected during the war was annulled. Affairs remained in this position until May 9, 1865, when the President of the United States issued an order declaring all the acts and proceedings of the political, military, and civil organizations in the State which had been in insurrection against the United States to be null and void; and that all persons who should attempt to exercise any authority as under the late State or Confederate officers, should be deemed and taken as in rebellion, etc. At this time Francis H. Pierpont, who had assumed to exercise the office of Governor of Virginia over ten counties around Alexandria, was recognized by the President as the true Governor of the State. He was aided to remove the seat of his government from Alexandria to Richmond, and there maintained by the military force. No hostile opposition, however, was anywhere manifested, while at Alexandria delegates from the ten counties had assembled in convention and assumed to amend the State Constitution, and the little so-called legislative body had undertaken to pass various acts of importance. The so-called Governor, in presenting a summary of them, concluded by saying, "Thus, State sovereignty—the *status* of the African race— the armed resistance to the Government of the United States—are disposed of." An election for a new Legislature and State officers was held on October 12th. All were allowed to vote who had not held office under the State government or the Confederacy during the war, after they had taken the amnesty oath. The so-called Legislature assembled and entered upon the regulation of all the affairs of the State. A general act of vagrancy was passed, whereupon the major-general in command issued an order "that no magistrate, civil officer, or other person shall, in any way or manner, apply, or attempt to apply, the provisions of the said statute to any colored person in this department." At the municipal election in Richmond, the Mayor, Attorney, and Superintendent of the Poor, elected, were persons who had held office under the Confederate States. They were not allowed by the military authority to qualify, and subsequently declined.

In 1865 the Congress of the United States passed an act which provided that the following amendment to the Constitution should be submitted to the Legislatures of the several States for ratification or rejection:
"SECTION 1. Neither slavery nor
involuntary servitude, except as a punishment
for crime, whereof the party shall have been

duly convicted, shall exist within the United States, or any place subject to its jurisdiction.

"SECTION 2. Congress shall have full power to enforce this article by appropriate legislation."

One Dr. James L. Watson was tried for killing a negro in Rockbridge County, and acquitted. Major-General Schofield, in command of the military forces of the department, immediately ordered his arrest and trial by a military commission. On the assembling of the commission a writ of *habeas corpus* was sued out of the Circuit Court of Richmond in behalf of Watson, and served on the General. In his answer, he declined compliance with the writ, saying:

"Dr. Watson is held for trial by military commission, under the authority of the act of Congress of July 16, 1866, which act directs and requires the President, through the commissioner and officers of the Freedmen's Bureau, to exercise military jurisdiction over all cases and questions concerning the free enjoyment of the right to have full and equal benefit of all laws and proceedings concerning personal liberty, personal security, etc., by all citizens, without respect to race or color, or previous condition of slavery, of the States whose constitutional relations to the Government of the United States have been discontinued by the rebellion, and have not been restored."

In the mean time, the United States Attorney-General having examined the case, and reported that, in his opinion, the military commission had not competent jurisdiction, the President thereupon directed that the commission be dissolved and the prisoner discharged without delay.

Meantime Congress had passed an act, known as the Civil Rights Bill, and a case came before the Circuit Court, at Alexandria, in which one of the parties offered to produce negro evidence. The Judge (Thomas) ruled that, inasmuch as the State laws of Virginia forbade the introduction of negro testimony in civil suits to which white men alone were parties, the evidence of the negro was inadmissible; and that Congressional legislation could not impair the right of the States to decide what classes of persons were competent to testify in her courts.

A storm was now brewing which was soon to involve the President and Congress in open conflict. The reader will remember that, during the period in which these proceedings took place in Virginia, similar ones occurred in all the remaining Confederate States. Not only in Virginia, but in several of the other States, some persons had been voted for as members of Congress, but in no case had they been admitted to seats. This was one of the measures taken by Congress to indicate its disapproval of the President's plan for the treatment of the late Confederate States.

The difficulties that now arose between the President and Congress had reference entirely to the affairs of the Confederate States. The plan of the

President left the negroes to the care of the States alone after the establishment of their emancipation. Congress desired them to be made American citizens, secure in all the rights of freemen and voters. The refusal to admit Senators and Representatives to Congress from the Confederate States served to arrest the operation of the President's plans to hold these States in abeyance.

No compromise could be made between the two. Each appealed to the Constitution, forgetful that each had sustained all its ruthless violations during the last four years. Congress, therefore, commenced an independent action, and in its reckless course sought, unsuccessfully, to rid itself of the President by impeachment. Its first act, at the commencement of the session, in December, 1865, was the appointment, by a large majority in each House, of a joint Committee of Fifteen, to which was referred all questions relating to the conditions and manner in which Congress would recognize the late Confederate States as members of the Union. Meantime the credentials of all persons sent as Representatives and Senators from them were laid upon the table in each House, there to remain until the final action of the Committee of Fifteen. This was followed by the passage, in February, 1866, of "an act to establish a bureau for the relief of freedmen, refugees, and abandoned lands." It proposed to establish military jurisdiction over all parts of the United States containing refugees and freedmen. This bill was vetoed by the President, and passed over his veto.

In March an act was passed "to protect all persons in the United States in their civil rights, and furnish the means of their vindication." The first section declared all persons born in the United States, and not subject to any foreign power, excluding Indians not taxed, to be citizens of the United States, and enumerates the rights to be enjoyed by those so declared to be citizens. The second section affords discriminating protection to colored persons in the full enjoyment of all the rights secured to them by the preceding section. This bill was vetoed by the President, and passed over his veto.

On June 8, 1866, a majority and a minority report were made by the Committee of Fifteen. Meanwhile, a report had been made from the same committee, at a previous date, in the form of an amendment to the Constitution, which was debated and amended in each House, and finally passed by the requisite majority in each. Thus was to be secured the political support and votes of the negroes, who were expected to be the controlling citizens of the late Confederate States.

The amendment to the Constitution was now submitted to the Legislatures of all the States, to be valid as a part of the Constitution, when ratified by three fourths, in the following form:

"ARTICLE—, SECTION 1. All persons born or naturalized in the United States, and subject to the jurisdiction thereof, are citizens of the United States, and of the State wherein they reside. No State shall make or enforce any law which shall abridge the privileges or immunities of citizens of the United States; nor shall any State deprive any person of life, liberty, or property, without due process of law, nor deny to any person within its jurisdiction the equal protection of the laws.

"SECTION 2. Representatives shall be apportioned among the several States according to their respective numbers, counting the whole number of persons in each State, excluding Indians not taxed. But, when the right to vote at any election for the choice of electors for President and Vice-President of the United States, Representatives in Congress, the executive and judicial officers of a State, or the members of the Legislature thereof, is denied to any of the male inhabitants of such State, being twenty-one years of age, and citizens of the United States, or in any way abridged, except for participation in rebellion or other crime, the basis of representation therein shall be reduced in the proportion which the number of such male citizens shall bear to the whole number of male citizens twenty-one years of age in such State.

"SECTION 3. No person shall be a Senator or Representative in Congress, or elector of President and Vice-President, or hold any office, civil or military, under the United States, or under any State, who, having previously taken an oath as a member of Congress, or as an officer of the United States, or as a member of any State Legislature, or as an executive or judicial officer of any State, to support the Constitution of the United States, shall have engaged in insurrection or rebellion against the same, or given aid or comfort to the enemies thereof. But Congress may by a vote of two thirds of each House remove such disability.

"SECTION 4. The validity of the public debt of the United States, authorized by law, including debts incurred for payment of pensions and bounties for services in suppressing insurrection or rebellion, shall not be questioned. But the United States shall neither assume nor pay any debt or obligation incurred in aid of insurrection or rebellion against the United States, or any claim for the loss or emancipation of any slave; but all such debts, obligations, and claims shall be held illegal and void.

"SECTION 5. The Congress shall have power to enforce, by appropriate legislation, the provisions of this article."

It may here be stated that the restoration of the late Confederate States to all the rights and privileges of States as co-equal members of the Union, under the plan of President Johnson, received the approval of the executive and judicial branches of the Government soon after the cessation of hostilities. Congress, however, not only withheld its assent, but, during its session in 1866, required as a condition precedent to a recognition of any one of these States, and the admission of its Representatives and Senators to seats, the adoption by its Legislature of the above-mentioned amendment. The question really involved in this amendment was the admission to citizenship and the ballot of the negroes in these States. It was the acknowledged fact that the authority to determine this question resided in the States severally and nowhere else. The amendment itself, in its second section, recognized the authority to grant or withhold the elective franchise as existing in the State governments.

This amendment was submitted to the Legislatures of the States immediately after its adoption by Congress in June, 1866, and by March 30, 1867, it had been ratified by twenty States, including West Virginia, Maryland, Missouri, and Tennessee, and rejected by thirteen, including Delaware and Kentucky, and eleven of the late Confederate States. There were thirty-four States at that time, and thirty had voted. A ratification by three fourths was required to make it valid.

When this amendment was presented for ratification to the Legislature of Virginia at its session commencing December, 1866, it was rejected in the Senate by a unanimous vote, and in the House by a vote of seventy-four to one. Meantime the Freedmen's Bureau was organized and put in operation in the State, but the military occupation continued, and the condition of affairs remained unchanged during the proceedings of Congress to construct its plan for subjugation.

After the vote of the States up to March, 1867, it was manifest that no real advance had been made in the extension of the franchise to the negro population of the States. In this position of affairs Congress, on March 2d, adopted an entirety new system of measures relative to the late Confederate States, The fiction upon which these measures were based is thus expressed in the preamble of the first act:

"*Whereas*, No legal State governments, or adequate protection for life or property, now exists in the rebel States of Virginia, North Carolina, South Carolina, Georgia, Alabama, Mississippi, Louisiana, Florida, Texas, and Arkansas; and, *whereas*, it is necessary that peace and good order should be enforced in said States, until loyal and republican State governments can be legally established: therefore, *be it enacted*," etc.

These States were then divided into five military districts, and it was further provided:

"Until the people of the said rebel States shall by law be admitted to representation to the Congress of the United States, all civil governments that may exist therein shall be deemed provisional only, and shall be in all respects subject to the paramount authority of the United States, at any time to abolish, modify, control, and supersede the same, and in all elections to any office under such provisional governments, all persons shall be entitled to vote under the provisions of the fifth section of this act."

Thus these States, when held by military force as conquered territory, with the sovereignty of the people extinct, were not allowed to claim to possess any rights under the Federal Constitution, or any other than such as might be granted by the will of the conqueror. It was asserted that the right to regulate the elective franchise, recognized as belonging to the States in the Union, could not attach to those out of the Union, and having only provisional political institutions. Congress then proceeded to declare, in the fifth section of the bill, the terms upon which a late Confederate State could become a member of the Union:

"SECTION 5. That, when the people of any one of said rebel States shall have formed a Constitution of government in conformity with the Constitution of the United States in all respects, framed by a convention of delegates elected by the male citizens of said State, twenty-one years old and upward, of whatever race, color, or previous condition, who have been resident in said State for one year previous to the day of such election, except such as may be disfranchised for participation in the rebellion or for felony at common law, and when such Constitution shall provide that the elective franchise shall be enjoyed by all such persons as have the qualifications herein stated for electors of delegates, and when such Constitution shall be ratified by a majority of the persons voting on the question of ratification who are qualified as electors for delegates, and when such Constitution shall have been submitted to Congress for examination and approval, and Congress shall have approved the same, and when said State, by a vote of its Legislature elected under said Constitution, shall have adopted the amendment to the Constitution of the United States, proposed by the Thirty-ninth Congress, and known as

Article XIV, and when said article shall have become a part of the Constitution of the United States, said State shall be declared entitled to representation in Congress, and Senators and Representatives shall be admitted therefrom on their taking the oath prescribed by law, and then and thereafter the preceding sections of this act shall be inoperative in said State," etc.

The bill became a law, notwithstanding the veto of the President.

On March 4th a new Congress commenced its session, and on March 23d a supplement to the preceding act was passed. It ordered a registration to be made of the qualified voters in each military sub-district of the State, an election to be held for the State Convention to draft a Constitution for the State, and for delegates to such convention; and that such Constitution should be submitted to the voters for adoption or rejection, and upon its adoption a State government should be organized, etc. The registration was required to be made of all citizens as defined by the "act to protect all persons in the United States in their civil rights," etc. Many disqualifications of voters, arising from participation in the war, were also expressed. This act also became a law, notwithstanding the objections of the President.

It will be seen that this act contemplated two distinct governments in each of the ten States—the one military and the other civil. Both were provisional, and both were to continue until the new State Constitution was framed, and the State was admitted to representation in Congress. The two were to be carried on together, and the people were made subject to both and obliged to obey both. The law was next put in operation by constituting the districts, as follows: 1. Virginia, commander, Major-General Schofield; 2. North Carolina and South Carolina, commander, Major-General Sickles; 3. Georgia, Florida, and Alabama, commander, Major-General John Pope; 4. Mississippi and Arkansas, commander, Major-General Ord; 5. Louisiana and Texas, commander, Major-General Sheridan.

Previous to adjournment, on July 19, 1867, Congress passed an additional supplement to the act of March 3d and the supplement of March 23d. It declared the intent and meaning of the previous acts to have been: that the civil governments of the ten States were not legal governments, and, if continued, were to be subject in all respects to the military commanders and the paramount authority of Congress. It made the acts of the military commanders subject only to the disapproval of the General of the Army, U. S. Grant, and authorized them to remove any person from office under the State government. It further defined the classes disfranchised, and directed that no district commander should be bound in his action by any opinion of any civil officer of the United States.

The President vetoed the bill, and in his message said:

"Thus, over all these ten States, this military government is now declared to have unlimited authority. It is no longer confined to the preservation of the public peace, the administration of criminal law, the registration of voters, and the superintendence of elections; but, 'in all respects,' is asserted to be paramount to the existing civil governments. It is impossible to conceive any state of society more intolerable than this, and yet it is to this condition that twelve millions of American citizens are reduced by the Congress of the United States. Over every foot of the immense territory occupied by these American citizens, the Constitution of the United States is theoretically in full operation. It binds all the people there, and should protect them; yet they are denied every one of its sacred guarantees. Of what avail will it be to any one of these Southern people, when seized by a file of soldiers, to ask for the cause of arrest, or for the production of the warrant? Of what avail to ask for the privilege of bail when in military custody, which knows no such thing as bail? Of what avail to demand a trial by jury, process for witnesses, a copy of the indictment, the privilege of counsel, or that greater privilege, the writ of *habeas corpus*?"

Congress having thus completed its plan of operations, the crashing wheels of subjugation began to move forward. Let us proceed with the narration of affairs in Virginia.

On the appearance of Major-General Schofield at Richmond, all the proceedings of the so-called civil government, for the organization and restoration of the State to the Union, at once ceased, and he assumed command. A board of army officers was named by the commanding General for the purpose of selecting suitable persons for appointment as registering officers throughout the State. In making the selections, the preference was given, first, to officers of the army and of the Freedmen's Bureau, on duty in the State; second, to persons who had been discharged from the Federal army, after "meritorious" services during the war; third, to "loyal" citizens of the county or city where they were to serve. On April 2d an order appeared from the major-general, suspending all elections, whether State, county, or municipal, "under the provisional government," until after the registration was completed. A lecture on the "Chivalry of the South," advertised to be delivered in Lynchburg, was suppressed by the order of the post commander at that place. A warning was given by the major-general to the editor of the Richmond "Times," which said, "The efforts of your paper to foster enmity, create disorder, and lead to violence, can no longer be tolerated." On the refusal of five magistrates of the Corporation Council of Norfolk to receive the testimony of a negro, they were arrested on a process issued under the Civil Rights Bill, and held to bail to appear before the District Court. All armed organizations in the State were disbanded. Inflammatory meetings of freedmen and those who sought their political alliance were held in different parts of the State.

Military commissioners were appointed over sub-districts for the suppression of disorder and violence, for the protection of all persons in their so-called rights of person and property, and clothed with all the powers of justices of a county or police magistrates of a city. The State was also divided into sub-districts, and commanders appointed over the same. These officers were empowered to exercise a general supervision over the military commissioners, and to furnish them, when necessary, with sufficient military force to enable them to discharge their duties. Further orders relative to the qualification of voters were issued by the major-general, in which it was declared that "all persons who voluntarily joined the rebel army, and all persons in that army, whether volunteers or conscripts, who committed voluntarily any hostile act, were thereby engaged in insurrection or rebellion; and all who voted for the ordinance of secession, gave aid and comfort to the enemy. Also all who voluntarily furnished supplies of food, or clothing, arms, ammunition, horses, or mules, or any other material of war, participated in the rebellion," and were disfranchised. The whole number registered was 116,982 whites and 104,772 blacks. The vote for the Convention was 14,835 whites and 92,507 blacks; against the Convention, 61,249 whites and 638 blacks.

The Convention assembled on December 3d and adjourned on April 17, 1868. The Bill of Eights adopted declared that—

"The State shall ever remain a member of the United States of America, and the people thereof a part of the American nation, and all attempts, from whatever source, and upon whatever pretext, to dissolve said Union, or to sever said Union, are unauthorized, and ought to be resisted with the whole power of the State.

"The Constitution of the United States, and the laws of Congress passed in pursuance thereof, constitute the supreme law of the land, to which paramount allegiance and obedience are due from every citizen, anything in the Constitution, ordinances, or laws of any State to the contrary notwithstanding."

Suffrage was granted to every male citizen twenty-one years of age. All officers of the State were required to take the following oath:

"I, —— ——, do solemnly swear that I will support and maintain the Constitution and laws of the United States and the Constitution and laws of the State of Virginia; and that I recognize and accept the civil and political equality of all men before the law," etc.

In addition, all State, city, and county officers were required to take the test-oath prescribed by Congress on July 2, 1862, as follows:

"I do solemnly swear that I have never borne arms against the United States since I have been a citizen thereof; that I have voluntarily given no aid, countenance, counsel, or encouragement to persons engaged in armed hostility thereto; that I have never sought or accepted, nor attempted to exercise the functions of any office whatever, under any authority, or pretended authority, in hostility to the United States;

that I have not yielded a voluntary support to
any pretended government, authority, power,
or Constitution within the United States,
hostile or inimical thereto; and I do further
swear that, to the best of my knowledge and
ability, I will support and defend the
Constitution of the United States against all
enemies, foreign and domestic; that I will
bear true faith and allegiance to the same;
that I will take this obligation freely, without
any mental reservation or purpose of evasion;
and that I will well and faithfully discharge
the duties of the office on which I am about to
enter."

Major-General Schofield, in an address to the Convention in opposition to
these stringent provisions, said:

"You can not find in some of the counties a
sufficient number of men who are capable of
filling the offices, and who can take the oath
you have prescribed here, I have no hesitation
in saying that I believe it impossible to
inaugurate a government upon that basis."

Meantime the so-called Constitution was adopted by the Convention, and
June 2d fixed for the popular vote upon it. But no appropriation was made for
the expenses of the election, and it was not held. Major-General Stoneman now
succeeded Major-General Schofield.

The utter subjugation of the sovereign people of Virginia was now manifest.
Not a public act of the least importance could they do without the consent of the
military chief who ruled over them, and who was a stranger in their State.
Finding the provisions of this Constitution were so restrictive as to exclude from
the elective franchise nearly all of the most intelligent and best-educated
citizens, on account of their participation in the late war, a movement was
commenced for a modification of these clauses or their entire omission. The
sovereignty of the people was extinct, so no relief could be secured except
through the action of the sovereign sitting in Washington. Congress, therefore,
passed an act authorizing the President (Grant), at such time as he might deem
best, to submit the Constitution to the registered voters of Virginia, and also
submit to a separate vote such provisions of the Constitution as he thought
proper. The act also required the Legislature that should be elected to ratify the
fourteenth and fifteenth amendments to the Constitution of the United States,
as a condition precedent "to the readmission of the State into the Union."

The fifteenth article of amendment to the Constitution was passed by
Congress in February, 1869, and submitted to the Legislatures of the
States. It was as follows:

"SECTION 1. The right of citizens of the United States to vote shall
not be denied or abridged by the United States, or by any State, on
account of race, color, or previous condition of servitude.

"SECTION 2. The Congress shall have power to enforce this article by
appropriate legislation."

On the passage of the amendment by the United States Senate, Senator Garrett Davis, of Kentucky, said:

"Sir, your amendments to the Constitution are all void; they are of no effect. They were proposed by a mutilated Congress; they were proposed by a mutilated House of Representatives and Senate."

The election in Virginia took place on July 6, 1869. The vote on the Constitution was, for it, 206,233; against it, 9,189. For the disfranchising clause, 84,404; against it, 124,361. In favor of the test-oath clause, the votes were, 83,114; against it, 124,106. State officers and a Legislature were chosen.

Meantime the civil or provisional Governor had been removed by the military commander, Major-General Stoneman, and the commander of the first district put in the vacancy. At the same time the President-Judge of the Supreme Court of Appeals was a staff-officer of the General commanding, and assigned to that duty; and another one of the judges of that court was an officer of the Federal army, receiving his appointment from the same source.

On October 5th the Legislature assembled, the State officers-elect having already entered upon their duties. The fourteenth and fifteenth amendments to the United States Constitution were adopted, and Senators elected to Congress. On January 26, 1870, a bill for the admission of the State into the Union, "without further condition," was passed. Her subjugation was now completed. The military commanders were withdrawn, and she was left in the hands of "carpet-baggers."

[Footnote 130: Declaration of Independence.]

CHAPTER LVII.

Final Subjugation of the Confederate States (continued).—Slaves declared free by Military Commanders in North Carolina.—Provisional Governor.—Convention.—Military Commander.—Governor-elect turned out.—His Protest.—Members of Congress admitted.—Proceedings in South Carolina.—Arrest of Judge Aldrich.—Military Reversal of Sentence of the Court.—Post Commanders.—Jurors.—Proceedings in Georgia.—President's Plan.—Plan of Congress enforced.—Other Events.—Proceedings in Florida.—Rival Conventions.—Plan of Congress enforced.—Proceedings in Alabama.—Suspension of Bishop Wilmer by the Military Commander.—Military Authority.—Action of Congress.—Proceedings in Mississippi.—Constitutionality of the Act of Congress before the Supreme Court.—Remarks of Chief-Justice Chase.—Military Arrests.—Removals.—The Chief-Justice of the State resigns.—The So-called Constitution rejected.—Ames appointed Governor.—Proceedings in Louisiana.—Plan of Congress enforced.—Other Measures.—Arkansas.—Texas.—Opinion of the United States Attorney-General on Military Commanders.—Consequences that followed the Measures of Congress.—Increase in State Debts.— Increase in Frauds and Crimes.—Examples.—Investigating Committees of Congress.—The Unalienable Rights of Man.—The Sovereignty of the People and the Supremacy of Law gone.

In the preceding chapter the reader will find a narration of the series of measures, adopted by the Government of the United States, to complete the final subjugation of the State of Virginia. The same series was applied, in the same order, to each of the Confederate States. It is, therefore, unnecessary to repeat the narration of these details in their application to the other States. But there were some concurrent incidents and some flagrant outrages in each one which should be stated, in order to afford a full and comprehensive view of the universal denial of unalienable personal rights, the destruction of civil institutions, the disregard of laws, and the cruel and ignominious treatment, inflicted by the authority of the Government of the United States upon individuals in every part of the Southern country.

In North Carolina, immediately on the cessation of hostilities, the Federal General issued an order, declaring that "all persons heretofore held in the State as slaves are now free, and that it is the duty of the army to maintain the freedom of such persons." Another order was then issued, defining and regulating the relations of the freedmen and whites. President Johnson issued his proclamation on May 29th, appointing a provisional Governor, W. W. Holden, as in the case of Virginia. On August 8th the Governor issued his proclamation for an election of delegates to a State Constitutional Convention on September 12th, and stated who would be permitted to vote, and the manner of election. The election was held, and the so-called Convention assembled on October 2, 1865. Its first act declared the uninterrupted existence of the State in the Union, and that the ordinance of secession was null and void. The next prohibited slavery. The payment of the debt contracted during the war, by any future Legislature, was forbidden. The repeal of the secession ordinance and the prohibition of slavery were ratified by the people. An election for State officers and members of Congress was held in November, and those who had taken the amnesty oath were the voters. The so-called Legislature-elect held a session and ratified the amendment to the United States Constitution prohibiting slavery. On December 23d the Governor-elect (Worth) was inaugurated, and the provisional Governor retired, acknowledging Worth to be the legal and "loyal" Governor. Thus the State was subjugated on the plan of President Johnson.

The affairs of the State were thus conducted until the military acts of Congress went into operation, and on March 23, 1867, Major-General Sickles issued his order assuming command. On April 11th he issued an order for the relief of debtors, by prohibiting imprisonment for debt, and ordering the stay of all proceedings for the collection of debts for twelve months. Writs of execution issuing out of the United States Circuit Court were not allowed to be served by the military commander at Wilmington. The question was taken to the Attorney-General at Washington, and General Sickles appeared in his own defense. It was decided by the acting Attorney-General to be "simply a case of a high misdemeanor, legally contemplated." General Sickles was removed, and Major-General Canby succeeded. The State registration was completed In October, and contained the names of 103,060 whites and 71,657 blacks. The so-called election for a Convention was held in November, and the Convention assembled on February 14, 1868. The Bill of Rights adopted contained similar clauses to the one adopted by the Virginia Convention. The Constitution was ratified, and State officers, members of the Legislature, and representatives to Congress were elected on April 23d. The vote for the Constitution was 93,118; against it, 74,109. The so-called Republicans had a majority of seventy on joint ballot in the Legislature.

The State officers elected under the plan of President Johnson had continued in the peaceful administration of their duties. Therefore, on the day of the inauguration of the newly-elected Governor (Holden) the existing Governor (Worth) made a spirited protest, saying:

"I do not recognize the validity of the late election, under which you and those coöperating with you claim to be invested with the civil government of the State. You have no evidence of your election, save the certificate of a major-general of the United States Army. I regard all of you as, in effect, appointees of the military power of the United States, and not as deriving your powers from the consent of those you claim to govern. Knowing, however, that you are backed by military force here, which I could not resist if I would, I do not deem it necessary to offer a futile opposition, but vacate the office without the ceremony of actual eviction, offering no further opposition than this, my protest. I would submit to actual expulsion in order to bring before the Supreme Court of the United States the question as to the constitutionality of the legislation under which you claim to be the rightful Governor of the State, if the past action of that tribunal furnished any hope of a speedy trial. I surrender the office to you under what I deem military duress, without stopping, as the occasion would well justify, to comment on the singular coincidence that the present State government is surrendered, as without legality, to him whose own official sanction, but three years ago, declared it valid.

"I am, very respectfully,
"JONATHAN WORTH,
"*Governor of North Carolina.*"

The so-called Legislature assembled on the appointed day, and the fourteenth amendment to the Constitution of the United States was at once ratified, and on July 11, 1868, the President announced by proclamation that "North Carolina had complied with the conditions prescribed by Congress for her restoration to an equal place in the Union of States."

In South Carolina, proceedings were commenced on June 20, 1865, when President Johnson issued a proclamation similar to the one in the case of Virginia, and appointed Benjamin F. Perry as provisional Governor of the State. He continued all persons in office on taking the amnesty oath, and all laws in force prior to the secession of the State were maintained except those conflicting with the proclamation; delegates to a so-called State Convention were elected on the first Monday of September, and the Convention assembled on the 13th to amend the State Constitution. The ordinance of secession was repealed and slavery abolished. Blacks were made witnesses in all cases where the rights or property of persons of that class were involved. An election of State officers and a so-called Legislature were held. The latter convened on October 25th. The thirteenth amendment to the Constitution of the United States prohibiting slavery was ratified. On November 29th the provisional Governor retired, and the so-called Governor-elect (Orr) was inaugurated. The work of the Legislature was very complete. The courts were open to all persons, with equal civil rights, without distinction of color, and Major-General Sickles, commander of the Military Department of North Carolina and South Carolina, ordered all civil and criminal cases to be tried before them in which the parties were civilians. Previous to this order, and after the cessation of hostilities, provost-marshals and military courts were detailed for duty all over the State. These officers knew only the law martial, and generally very little of that; and took jurisdiction of all cases both civil and criminal, occasioning great annoyance, expense, and vexation, deciding as their prejudice, caprice, or ignorance suggested. After the completion of the so-called State government, however, the vacancies on the bench were filled, and the courts opened throughout the State.

Still the people were made to feel that the military hand was over all. A case occurred in the court in Charleston, before Judge A. P. Aldrich, in which a white man was indicted for petty larceny, tried, and found guilty. The punishment prescribed by the law of the State for this offense was whipping. To this punishment the offender was sentenced. On the next day an armed soldier came to the court-house inquiring for the Judge, who was absent. To an inquiry of the sheriff as to his business, he replied that he was ordered to require the Judge to report at General Bennet's headquarters, who was the military commander of the district. On the next day another soldier in full uniform came to the lodgings of the Judge with a note from the General requesting the former to report at headquarters.

The reply of the Judge was: "As I have no business with you, I decline to report. If you have business with me, it will give me great pleasure to receive you."

On the next day an adjutant appeared saying: "The General is very much engaged, and asks you to come to his office. I will wait your convenience."

"I see I am under arrest," replied the Judge. "I will go now."

The adjutant, in full uniform, escorted him through the most public parts of the city to headquarters, and, entering the office, announced him. The General was sitting, with his cap on, and writing. After some time, having finished, he looked up and said, "Sit down," adding, "That was a curt note you sent to me yesterday."

"No, sir," answered the Judge, "I intended it to be respectful, but, as I had no business with you, I did not see why I should be required to come to your office."

"Do you dispute the authority of the United States Government?" asked the General, tartly.

"No, sir; I am here in obedience to that authority, but I have always supposed that, as a mere matter of courtesy, when one gentleman has business with another, he calls on him. As a matter of etiquette, I believe a Judge of the Superior Court of a State is equal in rank to a brevet brigadier-general."

"We will not discuss the question of rank," replied the General, "but General Sickles requests you to revoke your sentence of the other day and impose some other penalty."

The Judge replied: "I do not impose the penalty; it is the law, and I have no discretion."

He then explained the law, and said there was no relief except by a pardon of the Governor, or by taking the prisoner out of the custody of the sheriff. A few days after, the prisoner was taken from the custody of the Sheriff and discharged. The proceeding was brought to the knowledge of the so-called Governor, who applied to General Sickles to suspend his order, but the latter declined; whereupon the Judge, then at Columbia, to hold the court of the circuit, declared that he would adjourn the court and not proceed on his circuit; that he would not go through the farce of holding a court when judgments and sentences could be arrested and prevented by military order. He then adjourned the court, and passed an order refusing to hold courts while the military order was in force. General Sickles also issued an order reversing a judgment of the Supreme Court. The President about the same time countermanded a like order of the General in North Carolina, and the Judge resumed his duties.

Under the act of Congress of March 2, 1867, the State was divided into ten military districts, and a post commander appointed for each. All local officers, who were regularly elected by the people, were to be appointed by these commanders. Military orders were issued from time to time containing social regulations, etc. One on the subject of criminal arrests and trials required all sheriffs, marshals, and police officers to report to the Provost-Marshal-General of the district, their names, residence, official station, salary, and the authority by which they were appointed; also to investigate and report all particulars of any crime committed, to the Provost-Marshal-General, setting forth name, residence, and description of the offender with the nature of the offense, and steps taken to secure punishment. Sheriffs were directed to make a full report of the condition of all jails and prisons within their jurisdiction. All civil officers in charge of any jail, prison, or workhouse, were required to make full monthly reports of each inmate under their care. All sheriffs, constables, and police officers were required "to obey and execute the lawful orders of the Provost-Marshal-General, to the same effect as they are required by law to obey and execute writs, warrants, or other process issued by civil magistrates," and any resistance or refusal to execute the same subjected the offender to trial by military commission.

Details of the plan to be followed in making the registration were fully laid down, and the order then contained the following instructions:

"Boards will take notice that, according to section 10 of the act of July 19, 1867, they are not to be bound in their action by any opinion of any civil officer of the United States.

"Boards are instructed that all the provisions of the several acts of Congress cited are to be liberally construed, to the end that all the intents thereof be fully and perfectly carried out.

"It is made the duty of the commanding General to remove from office all persons who are disloyal to the Government of the United States, or who use their official influence in any manner to hinder, delay, prevent, or obstruct the due and perfect administration of the reconstruction acts."

On September 5, 1867, Major-General Canby took command. General Sickles, on announcing his retirement, said:

"The undersigned avails himself of the occasion to acknowledge the fidelity and zeal with which the officers and troops under his command have discharged their duties."

The question of the qualification of jurors now became important. General Canby issued an order on September 13th, which required the jurors to be drawn from the "qualified voters," which included the newly emancipated slaves. The Judges met, and sent a respectful request to the General to change the order to conform to the law of the State. By the jury law, as it then stood, no person was qualified to serve as a juror unless he was a free white man, twenty-one years of age. The Judges were sworn to enforce this law and the Constitution of the State. No notice was taken of the application. At the next court in Edgefield, Judge Aldrich, charging the grand jury, brought to their notice the order, the law and the Constitution, and the oath of office, and then declared "he could not and would not obey the order." On going to open the court a few days after, the adjutant of the post delivered to him a military order suspending him from office. He proceeded and opened the court, read the order and stated the circumstances, and, laying aside his gown, directed the sheriff "to let the court stand adjourned while justice is stifled." [131] The major-general appointed another Judge to the vacancy.

The registration of voters was completed in the middle of October, and amounted to 46,346 whites and 78,982 blacks. The vote on a State Convention was taken on November 19th and 20th, and resulted, for the Convention, 130 whites and 68,876 blacks; against the Convention, 2,801 whites. The delegates were 34 whites and 63 blacks. The Convention assembled on January 14, 1868. The Bill of Rights contained provisions similar to that of Virginia, and the Constitution was made to conform to the will of Congress. The ratification of the Constitution, and the election of State officers and a Legislature, took place on April 14, 15, and 16, 1868. The vote for the Constitution was 70,758; against it, 27,288; not voting, but registered, 35,551. The Legislature, with a majority of forty-eight blacks, assembled on July 6th. The fourteenth constitutional amendment was adopted, and the construction of the State by Congress was completed practically on July 13, 1868.

In Georgia, on the cessation of hostilities, the Governor issued a proclamation calling a session of the Legislature. But the commanding General issued an order declaring the proclamation to be null and void. Another military officer, in a letter to the Governor, stated that he was instructed by the President to say to him, that "the persons who incited the war and carried it on will not be allowed to assemble at the call of their accomplice to act again as the Legislature of the State, and again usurp the authority and franchises. In calling the Legislature together again, without the permission of the President, you have perpetrated a fresh crime; and, if any person presumes to answer or acknowledge your call, he will be immediately arrested." The military authorities of the United States then took the control of affairs until the appointment of James Johnson, on June 17th, by the President, as provisional Governor of the State, by a proclamation similar to the one issued in the case of Virginia. On July

13th he issued a proclamation prescribing the regulations for a State Convention. Provost-marshals had been stationed all over the State to regulate local affairs, and the laws in force previous to 1861 were ordered to be enforced. Delegates were elected on October 4th, and the so-called State Convention assembled on October 25th. The ordinance of secession was repealed. The payment of the war debt was prohibited. The emancipation of the slaves was expressly recognized, and a so-called election for State officers, members of the Legislature and of Congress, was appointed to be held on November 15th. The Legislature assembled on December 4th, and unanimously adopted the thirteenth amendment to the Federal Constitution, prohibiting the existence of slavery. Charles J. Jenkins, Governor-elect, was inaugurated, and on December 19, 1865, the provisional Governor relinquished the conduct of the State affairs to the constituted authorities. The Freedmen's Bureau Act and the Civil Rights Act of Congress were enforced by the military authorities.

The State Legislature again assembled on November 1, 1866. The ratification of the fourteenth amendment to the Constitution of the United States was repassed to a joint committee of each House, which reported a resolution to refuse to ratify the same. In the Senate it was adopted unanimously, and in the House by a vote of 132 to 2. On April 1, 1866, Major-General John Pope assumed command in the third military district, containing Georgia, Florida, and Alabama. An unsuccessful effort was made by the State at this time to bring the question of the constitutionality of the "reconstruction" acts of Congress before the Supreme Court. Governor Jenkins took part in the application to the Supreme Court, and, while at Washington, issued an address to the people of the State, urging them to take no action under the laws. He was called upon to make an explanation on his return by General Pope, as parts of the address were declared in violation of the military order of the latter. But as the so-called Governor had not seen the order, his offense was excused. A mayor and aldermen for Augusta were appointed by General Pope; also the sheriff and deputy for Bartow County, and other officers.

An order was issued that jurors should be selected from the list of qualified voters. Judge Reese, of Ocmulgee District, wrote to General Pope, declaring that, under his oath to sustain the laws, he could not conform to the order. General Pope replied with an attempt to show him that he owed allegiance, first of all, to the authority of the United States, as represented by the military power in the State. The argument was of no avail, and the Judge was prohibited from holding court.

The registration of votes was completed early in September, The number registered was 188,647, and the whites had a majority of about 2,000. The election of delegates to the State Convention took place from October 29th to November 3d. Of the delegates, 133 were whites and 33 blacks. The Convention assembled on December 13th, and soon adjourned to January 8, 1868. Meantime, Major-General Meade had relieved General Pope as military commander. The Convention, before this adjournment, ordered the Comptroller to levy a tax to pay its expenses, and directed the State Treasurer to advance forty thousand dollars for its pay and mileage. The ordinance was sent to the Treasurer, endorsed with instructions from General Pope to pay. The Treasurer refused to advance the money, as he was prohibited by the Constitution to do so, except on the warrant of the Governor. General Meade requested the Governor to issue the warrant. He replied that the Constitution forbade any money to be drawn from the Treasury except on an appropriation, whereupon General Meade removed both officers, and appointed others.

The provisions required by the acts of Congress were adopted in the so-called new Constitution. At the same time, certain provisions were inserted, which were intended to afford relief to the people. The Convention, therefore, by resolution, requested General Meade to require the courts to enforce them "until the State was restored to its regular relations with the United States, and the State organization was in full force." An order was, therefore, issued by the General requiring the courts and officers of the State government to enforce the provisions, in all respects, the same as if they had regularly taken effect. One of the Judges, having refused to comply with this order, was removed by General Meade.

The so-called election on the Constitution, and for State officers, and Legislature, and members of Congress, was held on April 20th and following days. The State Constitution was declared to be ratified; Rufus W. Bullock, the so-called Republican candidate, was declared to be elected Governor by a majority of seven thousand votes. The Legislature assembled on July 4, 1868, with three Senators and twenty-five Representatives who were negroes. The fourteenth amendment to the Federal Constitution was adopted, and all the conditions of Congress were fulfilled; and on July 28, 1868, she was declared to be restored to the Union. Subsequently it appeared that the State Convention had made no provision which could be construed as expressly giving the black man a right to hold office, and all these members were expelled from the Legislature. The matter was taken up by Congress, and the State was not fully recognized as in the Union until 1870.

The proceedings in Florida commenced with the usual proclamation of President Johnson. It was issued on July 13, 1865, and appointed William Marvin provisional Governor of the State. On August 3d he issued a proclamation prescribing such rules and regulations as were deemed necessary for the choice of members of a so-called State Constitutional Convention, and appointed October 10th for the day of election, and October 25th as the day on which the delegates should meet. They "annulled" the secession ordinance, passed an ordinance prohibiting slavery, with a preamble in these words: "*Whereas*, slavery has been destroyed in this State by the Government of the United States; therefore," etc. Another ordinance declared void the liabilities contracted for the war. Freedmen were made competent witnesses in any matter wherein a colored person was concerned. An election of State officers, of the members of the Legislature, and of Representatives in Congress, was ordered to be held on November 29th, and the Legislature were required to meet on December 18th. Governor David S. Walker was inaugurated on December 21st, and on January 18, 1866, the provisional Governor surrendered the conduct of the State to the so-called constitutional authorities. At this session of the Legislature, the Lower House unanimously refused to ratify the fourteenth amendment to the Constitution of the United States. The military rule which has prevailed in local affairs was relaxed on April 27, 1866, and all civilians under military arrest were turned over to the civil authorities for trial.

On April 1, 1867, Major-General Pope assumed command under the act of Congress of March 2d. On June 18th a superintendent of registration was appointed, and the conditions for the registration of voters were prescribed. The result of the registration was 11,148 whites and 15,434 blacks. The election of delegates to the so-called State Constitutional Convention was held on November 14th, 15th and 16th, and on January 20, 1868, the Convention assembled, and contained seventeen blacks as members. A disgraceful quarrel arose in the Convention, and twenty members absented themselves. The twenty-one remaining claimed to be a quorum, and formed a Constitution, and adjourned. The absentees then returned, and, with three or four from the other side, organized and proceeded to form a Constitution. The others appeared and claimed their seats. Great disorder prevailed, but by the intervention of Major-General Meade, and by putting in the chair his sub-commander, some degree of order was restored, and such an arrangement effected that the second Constitution was completed. All the requisite measures under it were adopted, and on June 29th, the surrender of the so-called government of the State by the military power of the United States to the civil authority was made. The political quarrel continued long afterward.

In Alabama the proclamation of President Johnson was issued on June 21, 1865, by which Lewis C. Parsons was appointed provisional Governor and the usual proceedings prescribed. On July 20th the Governor issued a proclamation, which renewed the powers of the persons holding the township offices in the State; called a State Constitutional Convention to assemble on September 10th, and reordained the civil and criminal laws, except those relating to slaves, as they existed previous to 1861, and prescribed other regulations. A peaceful election was held, and the delegates to the so-called Convention assembled and took an oath to support the Constitution of the United States and the Union thereof, and all proclamations relative to the emancipation of slaves. Slavery was prohibited, the war debt declared void, and the secession ordinance repealed. An election for State officers, members of the Legislature, and Representatives in Congress, was ordered on the first Monday of November. The new Constitution was not submitted to a vote of the people on account of the delay it would occasion. Robert M. Patton was elected Governor, and the Legislature assembled on November 20th. The amendment to the Constitution of the United States prohibiting the existence of slavery was ratified, and on December 18, 1865, the provisional Governor surrendered the conduct of the affairs of the State to the Governor-elect.

During the existence of the Confederate Government, the Protestant Episcopal Church South was established, and the prayer for the President of the United States and all in civil authority, in the "Book of Common Prayer," was changed to one for the Confederate authorities. Upon the restoration of the authority of the United States, the prayer for the President was omitted altogether, by the recommendation of Bishop Wilmer; whereupon Major-General Woods issued an order by which the Bishop and all his clergy in the diocese of Alabama "were suspended from their functions and forbidden to preach or perform divine service." The order was subsequently set aside by President Johnson.

At the session of the Legislature in November, 1866, the fourteenth amendment to the United States Constitution was rejected by an overwhelming majority.

On assuming command of the Third Military Division under the act of Congress of March 2, 1867, Major-General Pope assigned Major-General Swayne to the "administration of the military reconstruction bill" in Alabama. On April 8th the order directing the proceedings in the registration of voters was issued. Special instructions were issued, as in all the other States, to boards of registers which declared that clerks and reporters of the Supreme Court and inferior courts, and clerks to ordinary county courts, treasurers, county surveyors, receivers of tax-returns, tax-collectors, tax-receivers, sheriffs, justices of the peace, coroners, mayors, recorders, aldermen, councilmen of any incorporated city or town, who were ex-officers of the Confederacy, and who, previous to the war, occupied these offices and afterward participated in the war, were all disqualified and not entitled to registration. Meantime the municipal officers were removed in several places, and in the city of Mobile the police administration was suspended and the maintenance of public order assumed by the commander of the military force. Finally, the chief officers and councilmen of the city were removed, and others appointed by the district commander.

The registration was completed in August, and amounted to 72,748 whites and 88,243 blacks. The vote on the Convention and for delegates was given on the first three days of October. A hundred delegates were chosen, of whom ninety-six were "radicals"—seventeen of them were blacks. On November 5th the so-called Convention assembled and adopted all the amendments required by the act of Congress. The election for the ratification of the Constitution, for State officers, members of the Legislature, and Representatives in Congress, was held on February 4, 1868. A majority of all the registered vote was required to ratify the Constitution, which was 85,000. The vote cast was 75,000.

On June 20, 1868, Congress passed an act which declared that each of the States of North Carolina, South Carolina, Georgia, Florida, Alabama, and Louisiana, should be admitted to representation when its Legislature had ratified the fourteenth amendment to the Constitution of the United States, and farther, "upon the fundamental condition that the Constitution of neither of said States shall ever be so amended or changed as to deprive any citizen, or class of citizens, of the United States of the right to vote in said State, who are entitled to vote by the Constitution thereof, herein recognized, except as a punishment for crime," etc.

The so-called State Legislature assembled on July 13th, and Articles XIII and XIV as amendments to the Constitution of the United States were ratified. The conduct of the affairs of the State was now transferred by General Meade to the new civil authorities.

Mississippi, immediately after the cessation of hostilities, was occupied by a military force of the United States. Meantime the Governor called an extra session of the Legislature, and made provision for a Constitutional Convention; but these measures were set aside by the proclamation of President Johnson, on June 13th, appointing William L. Sharkey provisional Governor. The system of measures embraced in the plan of the President for the restoration of the Confederate States to the Union was immediately commenced and completed in the election of Benjamin G. Humphreys for Governor, with the other State officers, members of the Legislature, and Representatives in Congress.

The fourteenth amendment of the Constitution was unanimously rejected by the Legislature in January, 1867.

Under the act of Congress of March 2, 1867, Major-General Ord assumed command of the Fourth Military Division, consisting of Mississippi and Arkansas. Governor Humphreys sought immediately to bring the question of the constitutionality of this act before the United States Supreme Court. Arguments were heard upon it by the Court. The motion was to enjoin and restrain President Johnson and Major-General Ord from executing the act and supplements. It was denied, and Chief-Justice Chase, on delivering the opinion, said:

> "If the President refuses obedience, it is
> needless to observe that the Court is without
> power to enforce its process. If, on the other
> hand, the President complies with the order
> of the Court, and refuses to execute the act of
> Congress, is it not clear that a collision may
> occur between the executive and the
> legislative departments of the Government?
> May not the House of Representatives
> impeach the President for such refusal?"

Major-General Ord, immediately after assuming command, proceeded to organize boards for the registration of voters and prescribe their qualifications and disqualifications. The latter were so numerous as to embrace, in all these States, every white who had voluntarily done the most simple act to aid or favor any person engaged in the Confederate service, or had incited, by words, others to render such aid, while the entire class of blacks were not disqualified by such acts, as it was assumed that they were done by compulsion. Thus the aim and end of registration, after this manner, in a State, were to throw the entire political power into the hands of the negroes.

Orders were now issued directing the military to coöperate with the civil officers to break up the crime of horse-stealing, to secure to labor its share of the crops, and to protect debtor and creditor from sacrifices by forced sales; to suspend for a time certain sales under execution; to prohibit interference with the legal tenant; to ascertain if distillers had paid their taxes; to investigate complaints made by citizens of persecution by civil authorities; to notify State and municipal officers of the laws of Congress for the organization of their governments on the basis of suffrage without regard to color; to subordinates of the Freedmen's Bureau to investigate all charges against landholders; to require supervisors, inspectors, and boards of registration to obtain the names of suitable persons, white or black, to act as clerks and judges of elections; to close strictly all bar-rooms and saloons for the day when political meetings were held; to remove the city marshal, three justices of the peace, and four members of the City Council of Vicksburg; to appoint other persons to fill the vacancies, who were required to take the test oath of Congress; to forbid the assembling of bodies of citizens under any pretense; to transfer the papers to a military commission whenever a person who had been in the Federal service was indicted and apprehended an unfair trial; to notify overseers of the poor that any neglect to provide for colored paupers would be regarded as a neglect of duty, etc.

The roistered names amounted to 46,636 whites and 60,167 blacks. The military appointment for delegates to the Convention was such as to give to thirty-two counties, having small colored majorities, seventy of the representatives, and to twenty-nine counties, having small white majorities, thirty representatives. On November 5th the election was held, and the so-called Convention assembled on January 8, 1868. The ordinance of secession was declared null and void; the existence of slavery prohibited; payment of the war debt forbidden; universal suffrage established, excepting only criminals; an election to ratify the Constitution and for the election of State officers, a Legislature, and Representatives in Congress, was ordered to be held on June 22d, and a large number of radical amendments adopted. At the election the Constitution was rejected by a majority of 7,629. The opposition candidate was also elected Governor.

On October 1, 1867, the Chief-Justice of the State, A. H. Handy, sent his resignation to the Governor. He said:

"It is apparent that the character and dignity of the Court can not be maintained, and that its powers must be held and exercised in subordination to the behests of a military commander."

On December 28, 1867, Major-General Ord was succeeded by Major-General McDowell. On June 15th the latter issued an order removing Governor Humphreys and appointing Major-General A. Ames to the vacancy. Governor Humphreys declined to vacate the office, saying that the attempt to remove him was a "usurpation of the civil government of Mississippi, unwarranted by and in violation of the Constitution of the United States." A squadron of soldiers was sent by the military commander of the post, which marched in and took possession of the office. The house of the Governor was then demanded for the new incumbent of the office. As Governor Humphreys refused to vacate it, a file of soldiers came and ejected him.

After the rejection of the so-called new Constitution, its friends applied to Congress, as the sovereign, to throw out the vote of several counties and declare the Constitution to be adopted. This action was recommended on the ground, as they said, that the election had not been fairly conducted, and that violence and intimidation had, in many parts of the State, prevented a full and just vote. The Constitution was defeated, not, as thus alleged, by fraud and intimidation, but distinctly for the reason that it was more vindictive in its spirit than the people, white or black, would tolerate, and more prescriptive in its provisions than the acts of Congress required.

In March, 1869, the provisional Governor of the State, Major-General A. Ames, was made the military commander of the Fourth Military District. At the same time a joint resolution was passed by Congress, which ordered that all persons holding office in Mississippi, who could not take the test-oath prescribed in 1862, should be removed from office. By the aid of this weapon it was expected that General Ames would make the State organization so-called Republican. Meanwhile Congress passed an act which authorized the President to submit the Constitution of the State to another election by the people, with a separate vote on its objectionable section. Preparations for this election were commenced by the issue of an order of the military commander prescribing stringent regulations relative to the requisites of voters for registration. The election was held on November 30 and December 1, 1869, and the Constitution was ratified. The vote against disfranchising citizens for serving under the Confederacy during the war was almost unanimous. The so-called Legislature assembled on January 11, 1870. The fourteenth and fifteenth amendments of the United States Constitution were adopted, and on February 12th an act of Congress was passed by which the State was permitted to be represented in that body.

At the beginning of 1865 Louisiana was under the State government constructed by General Banks, as has been stated in previous pages. It occupied New Orleans, and extended its control to the extremity of the military lines. Within this limit it was treated practically as a restored portion of the Union. The United States military draft was enforced. Much disorder in civil affairs prevailed, and some serious disturbances occurred up to the time when Congress undertook its plan of restoration. There was, in fact, a military rule during all that period. On March 19, 1867, Major-General Sheridan was assigned to the command of the Fifth Military District, embracing Louisiana and Texas, in accordance with the act of Congress of March 2d. By this act the existing State government was "declared to be only provisional, and subject to be abolished, modified, controlled, or superseded." Major-General Sheridan began his proceedings with the removal of certain obnoxious officials who were, in his opinion, dangerous to the peace of the community. The registration of voters was ordered to commence on May 1st. To an application to General Grant, the commander-in-chief, for more definite instructions, by Major-General Sheridan, the former replied on June 28th:

"Enforce your own construction of the
military bill, until ordered to do otherwise."

The Legislature having appropriated four million dollars for the repairs of levees, and appointed a board to discharge the duties, Governor Wells became dissatisfied with their action, and appointed another board. Disputes arising between the two boards, Major-General Sheridan removed both, and appointed a third, and enforced its authority. In April, Major-General Sheridan, writing to General Grant, said:

"I fear I shall be obliged to remove
Governor Wells, of this State, who is
impeding me as much as he can."

General Grant replied:

"I would advise that no removals of
Governors of States be made at present. It is a
question now under consideration whether
the power exists, under the law, to remove,
except by special act of Congress, or by trial
under the sixth section of the act promulgated
in Orders 33 (act of March 2d)."

On June 3d Major-General Sheridan issued an order, removing the so-called Governor, saying that, "having made himself an impediment to the faithful execution of the act of Congress of March 2d, by directly and indirectly impeding the General in command in the faithful execution of the law," etc., Benjamin F. Flanders was appointed to fill the vacancy.

The registration ceased on July 31st, with the names of 44,732 whites and 82,907 blacks. Extensive removals from office were now made— among others, twenty-two members of the City Council of New Orleans, also the city treasurer and city surveyor, a justice of peace, sheriff, etc. On August 17th Major-General Sheridan was relieved, and Major-General Hancock succeeded. "Impediments to reconstruction under the laws of Congress" continued to be removed, and other persons assigned to their places.

The election for delegates to the so-called Convention was held on September 27th and 28th, and that body assembled on November 23d. The measures required by the act of Congress were adopted, and an election for its ratification and for State officers, and a Legislature, was held on April 17th and 18th. The Constitution was ratified, and the State officers and members of the Legislature were elected. Meantime Major-General Hancock was relieved, and succeeded by Major-General Buchanan.

After the election, the registrars of the State proposed to install the newly elected officers under the provisions of an ordinance of the Convention. But they were notified by Major-General Buchanan that it could not be done without permission. To avoid any question as to the persons who should hold the offices of so-called Governor and Lieutenant-Governor after the meeting of the Legislature, the district commander was directed by General Grant to remove the former incumbents by military order and set up the individuals lately elected as their successors. This was done on June 27th, and on the 29th the so-called Legislature assembled in pursuance of a notice from the commanding General. The fourteenth amendment to the United States Constitution was adopted; and, as by the act of Congress of June 25th, Louisiana had been restored to representation in that body, the commanding General on July 13, 1868, transferred the administration of civil affairs to the State officers.

I will not pursue these odious details further. Suffice it to say that Texas and Arkansas, having passed through the same military process as their sister Confederate States, were admitted to representation in Congress, the former in 1870 and the latter in 1868.

It will be seen that the power usurped by Congress was without a limitation, and extended to all the political, civil, and social relations. Many of the military commanders seem to have regarded their authority as equally comprehensive. The Attorney-General of the United States, in his official opinion on these acts of Congress, addressed to the President on June 12, 1867, says:

> "It appears that some of the military commanders have understood this grant of power as all-comprehensive, conferring on them the power to remove the executive and judicial officers of the State, and to appoint other officers in their places; to suspend the legislative power of the State; to take under their control, by officers appointed by themselves, the collection and disbursement of the revenues of the State; to prohibit the execution of the laws of the State by the agency of its appointed officers and agents; to change the existing laws in matters affecting

526

purely civil and private rights; to suspend or enjoin the execution of the judgments and decrees of the established State courts; to interfere in the ordinary administration of justice in the State courts, by prescribing new qualifications for jurors; and to change, upon the ground of expediency, the existing relations of the parties to contracts, giving protection to one party by violating the rights of the other party."———— ·· ···-·· ·· ——— —

Many instances are then related by the Attorney-General to confirm his statements. Some of these are worthy of the attention of the reader, although they may have been mentioned on a preceding page. In one district the so-called Governor of a State was deposed under a threat of military force, and another person, called a Governor, appointed by the military commander to fill the place—thus presenting the strange spectacle of an official intrusted with chief power to execute the laws of a State, whose authority was not recognized by the laws he was called on to execute.

In the same district a Judge was, by military order, ejected from his office, and a private citizen was appointed Judge in his place by military authority, and exercised criminal jurisdiction "over all crimes, misdemeanors, and offenses" committed within the territorial jurisdiction of the court. This military appointee was certainly not authorized, as a member of a military tribunal, to try any one for an offense; and he had just as little authority, as a Judge of a criminal court of the State, to try and punish any offender. This person was sole judge in a criminal court whose jurisdiction extended to the life of the accused. In capital cases he might well change places with the criminal, for, if the latter had unlawfully taken life, so too did the Judge.

In another district, a military order commanded the nominal Governor of the State to forbid the assembling of the Legislature, and thus suspended the proper legislative power of the State. In the same district an order was issued "to relieve the Treasurer of the State from the duties, bond, books, papers, etc.", appertaining to his office, and to put an "assistant quartermaster of the United States Volunteers" in place of the removed Treasurer. The duties of this quartermaster-treasurer were thus summed up: He was to make to the headquarters of the district "the same reports and returns required from the Treasurer, and a monthly statement of the receipts and expenditures; he will pay all warrants for salaries which may be or become due, and legitimate expenditures for the support of the Penitentiary, State Asylum, and the support of the provisional State government; but no scrip or warrants for outstanding debts of other kind than those specified, will be paid without special authority from these Headquarters. He will deposit funds in the same manner as though they were those of the United States." These instances will suffice, although many more might be related.

Illegal, unjust, and vindictive as were these gross usurpations of the Congress of the United States in their immediate results, the consequences which followed were still more disastrous. When the late Confederate States were restored to representation in Congress, a large portion of their white citizens remained disfranchised, and the political power of each was in the hands of the blacks and the remnant of the whites. Nor was the military force withdrawn, but it was placed in convenient localities, under the pretext of maintaining order, but in reality to sustain the new rulers. It must be manifest that the sovereignty of the people was now extinct, and those ruled who had the bayonets on their side. With the disfranchised were the intelligence, the virtue, and the political experience; with the voters were the ignorance, the lawless passions, and soon a body of political adventurers from the Northern States, greedy for power and plunder. These quickly won for themselves the distinctive epithet of "carpet-baggers". The governments under the control of such popular sovereigns demonstrated the vindictiveness rather than wisdom of Congress, and soon brought forth their natural fruits of anarchy, fraud, and crime. One or two examples must suffice in which to exhibit these results.

The debt of the ten Confederate States in 1874 was as follows:

Virginia, funded and unfunded $45,718,119.73
North Carolina 38,921,848.05
South Carolina 9,866,627.35
Florida 1,620,809.27
Georgia . . . . $8,105,500 funded
          8,000,000 fraudulent 16,105,500.00
Alabama $10,452,593.30
          15,051,000.00 railroad endorsement 15,503,593.30
Mississippi 3,558,629.24
Louisiana 23,933,407.90
Texas 4,012,421.00
Arkansas 9,561,000.00
          ————————
          $148,801,955.80

It is not claimed that all this amount of indebtedness had been accumulated since the close of the war. Some of the States had debts previous to the war, but a large proportion of the amount had been contracted by the spendthrift governments instituted by Congress, and very little could be found to offset the expenditure.

Again, in Arkansas, on April 16th, Governor Brooks seized and occupied the State-House with a body of armed men and two cannon. On the same day, Governor Baxter proclaimed martial law, and marched with a body of armed men from St. John's College to the Anthony House, and established his headquarters there. Guards were placed along the principal streets, and the State-House was completely surrounded by a cordon of sentinels. Subsequently, he marched to attack the State-House, but a body of troops belonging to the Government of the United States appeared before it. Two so-called Republican Governors of the State, with their troops, were about to fight for the executive office.

In Louisiana, on January 4, 1875, a body of troops of the Government of the United States, on the order of Governor W. P. Kellogg, marched into the hall of the House of Representatives of the State Legislature, while that body was in session, and forcibly seized and took out five members as not entitled to seats. The General in command (De Trobriand) then proceeded to eject the Clerk, and arrested the proceedings of the House. When expostulated with by the Speaker, he replied: "I am but a soldier. These are my orders." The members then retired.

In Mississippi, on December 7, 1874, a serious conflict occurred in Vicksburg between whites and blacks, which resulted in great loss of life and caused a widely-spread alarm. It grew out of frauds committed by public officers.

Again, during the exciting contest in Arkansas, the Congress of the United States appointed a committee to investigate the affairs in that State, and "whether said State had now a government republican in form, the officers of which are duly elected, and, as now organized, ought to be recognized by the Government of the United States."

On December 24, 1874, the Congress of the United States appointed a committee to proceed to New Orleans, and investigate the state of affairs in Louisiana. This committee reported on January 14, 1875, that "they could not agree upon any recommendation; but, upon the situation in Louisiana, as it appeared before us, we are all agreed."

The same Congress, before its adjournment, appointed a committee to proceed to Mississippi and make an investigation of the state of affairs there. Thus committees were kept quite busy in traveling back and forth to these States, and much of the time of Congress was occupied in discussing their affairs, and in efforts to reconcile the quarreling factions of so-called Republicans in them, to the great detriment of the public interests.

Where now were the unalienable rights of man, and sovereignty of the people, with their safeguards; a Constitution with limited powers, the reserved rights of the States, and the supremacy of law equally over both rulers and ruled? All were gone.

It will be seen that, through all these proceedings, the Government of the United States controlled as the sovereign, and sovereignty of the people was extinct. The measures adopted were those prescribed by the Government of the United States; and, subordinate to these and subject to the conditions of these, such others were permitted as the necessities of the people required. Affairs were not in such disorder when the Constitution of the United States was adopted. The uppermost then had come to be the undermost now, and that which was nothing then had grown to be over all now. Will it always be thus? Was the inherent sovereignty of the people destroyed by shot and shell?

The intelligent reader must perceive that this invasion of the natural and unalienable rights of man, the subjugation of the sovereignty of the people, the monstrous usurpations of powers not granted in the Constitution, the trampling under foot of the reserved rights of the States, the disregard of the supremacy of law, and the assumption of the sovereignty of the Government of the United States as the corner-stone of our future political edifice, is a revolution in our system of Government, deep-seated, reaching to the foundations, and sending the poisonous waters of despotism throughout all the branches fed from this fountain. The Confederate States resisted it from the beginning. They drew their swords for the sovereignty of the people, and they fought for the maintenance of their State governments in all their reserved rights and powers, as the only true and natural guardians of the unalienable rights of their citizens, among which the most sacred is, that only the consent of the governed can give vitality and existence to any civil or political institution.

This overthrow of the rights of freemen and the establishment of such new relations required a complete revolution in the principle of the government of the United States, the subversion of the State governments, the subjugation of people, and the destruction of the fraternal Union. The work has been done. Will it stand? Have the eternal principles of the Declaration of Independence been hid from our sight for ever? Or, will they again come forth, "redeemed, disenthralled, regenerated," and rally the reunited people to shout in thunder-tones for sovereignty of the people and the unalienable rights of man?

It has been shown in previous pages that the State governments were instituted to be the special guardians of these unalienable rights of man; but henceforth they must be the sworn defenders of the Government of the United States, not of the Constitution and laws enacted in pursuance thereof, but of such interpolations and perversions of them as, in cases of necessity, that Government should find it convenient to make. Whenever it pleases, it can set them aside; and, whenever it wills, it can destroy them. Unalienable rights are unknown to this war-begotten theory of the Constitution. The day has come in which mankind behold this Government founding its highest claims to greatness and glory upon deeds done in utter violation of those rights which belonged to its own citizens in every State, North and South. The palladium of the freeman, the Bills of Rights, the limitations of power, the written Constitutions, have all lost their sacred authority, and not a man or a State dare, single-handed, gainsay the will of the agency which, feeling power, has forgotten right. It has put its hand on the ballot-box, and the declaration is made that it is not safe to trust the people to vote, except under the inspection of its authority, after the example set by the Roman emperors. When the cause was lost, what cause was it? Not that of the South only, but the cause of constitutional government, of the supremacy of law, of the natural rights of man.

[Footnote 131: This incident in the conduct of the Judge recalls a like exhibition of judicial purity and independence which occurred in the colonial history of South Carolina, and which I present by extracts from the charge of Judge William Henry Drayton, delivered November, 1774. Referring to the nature of the civil liberties of the Carolina colonists, he said: "This is the distinguishing character: English people can not be taxed, nay, they can not be bound by any law unless by their consent, expressed by themselves or their representatives of their own election. This colony was settled by English subjects; by a people from England herself—a people who brought over with them, who planted in this colony, and who transmitted to posterity the invaluable rights of *Englishmen*—rights which no time, no contract, no climate can diminish. . . . By all the ties which mankind hold most dear and sacred; your reverence to your ancestors; your love to your own interests; your tenderness to your posterity; by the lawful obligations of your oath, I charge you to do your duty; to maintain the laws, the rights, the Constitution of your country, even at the hazard of your lives and fortunes.

"Some county judges style themselves the King's servants, a style which sounds harshly in my ears, inasmuch as the being a servant implies obedience to the orders of the master, and such judges might possibly think that, in the present situation of American affairs, my charge is inconsistent with my duty to the King. But for my part, in my judicial character, I know no master but the law; I am a servant, not to the King, but to the Constitution." . . . In the course of his charge, he quotes a "learned judge" as saying: "Every new tribunal erected for the decision of facts, without the intervention of a jury, is a step toward aristocracy, the most oppressive of absolute governments; and it is therefore a duty which every man owes to his country, his friends, his posterity, and himself, to maintain to the utmost of his power this valuable Constitution in all its rights, to restore it to its ancient dignity, if at all impaired; to amend it wherever it is defective, and, above all, to guard with the most jealous circumspection against the introduction of new and arbitrary methods of trial, which, under a variety of plausible pretenses, may in time perceptibly undermine this best preservative of English liberty."—("American Archives," Fourth Series, vol. i, pp. 959, 960.)]

CONCLUSION.

My first object in this work was to prove, by historical authority, that each of the States, as sovereign parties to the compact of Union, had the reserved power to secede from it whenever it should be found not to answer the ends for which it was established. If this has been done, it follows that the war was, on the part of the United States Government, one of aggression and usurpation, and, on the part of the South, was for the defense of an inherent, unalienable right.

My next purpose was to show, by the gallantry and devotion of the Southern people, in their unequal struggle, how thorough was their conviction of the justice of their cause; that, by their humanity to the wounded and captives, they proved themselves the worthy descendants of chivalric sires, and fit to be free; and that, in every case, as when our army invaded Pennsylvania, by their respect for private rights, their morality and observance of the laws of civilized war, they are entitled to the confidence and regard of mankind.

The want of space has compelled me to omit a notice of many noble deeds, both of heroic men and women. The roll of honor, merely, would fill more than the pages allotted to this work. To others, who can say *cuncta quorum vidi*, I must leave the pleasant task of paying the tribute due to their associate patriots.

In asserting the right of secession, it has not been my wish to incite to its exercise: I recognize the fact that the war showed it to be impracticable, but this did not prove it to be wrong; and, now that it may not be again attempted, and that the Union may promote the general welfare, it is needful that the truth, the whole truth, should be known, so that crimination and recrimination may for ever cease, and then, on the basis of fraternity and faithful regard for the rights of the States, there may be written on the arch of the Union, *Esto perpetua*.

Note.—The publishers are responsible for the orthography of these volumes.

[Illustration: Map of Yorktown & Williamsburg, Virginia]
[Illustration: Map of Operations in Kentucky and Tennessee]
[Illustration: Map of Battle of Gettysburg]

Made in the USA
Middletown, DE
21 October 2023

41176358R00314